THE
METROPOLITAN
TABERNACLE
PULPIT

C. H. SPURGEON

THE
METROPOLITAN TABERNACLE PULPIT

Sermons preached and revised in 1892

VOLUME
38

THE BANNER OF TRUTH TRUST

THE BANNER OF TRUTH TRUST
3 Murrayfield Road, Edinburgh EH12 6EL
P O Box 621, Carlisle, Pennsylvania 17013, USA

*

First published by Passmore and Alabaster 1893
First Banner of Truth Trust Edition 1991
ISBN 0 85151 611 4

*

Reprinted by photolithography and
bound in Great Britain by
The Bath Press, Avon

TO

THE ONE GOD OF HEAVEN AND EARTH,

IN

THE TRINITY OF HIS SACRED PERSONS,

BE ALL HONOUR AND GLORY

WORLD WITHOUT END,

AMEN.

TO THE GLORIOUS FATHER, AS THE COVENANT GOD

OF ISRAEL;

TO THE GRACIOUS SON, THE REDEEMER OF HIS PEOPLE;

TO THE HOLY GHOST, THE AUTHOR OF

SANCTIFICATION;

BE EVERLASTING PRAISE FOR THAT GOSPEL OF THE

FREE GRACE OF GOD

HEREIN PROCLAIMED UNTO MEN.

CONTENTS.

No.		Page

2,237 Gratitude for Deliverance from the Grave 1

"I shall not die, but live, and declare the works of the LORD. The LORD hath chastened me sore: but he hath not given me over unto death."—Psalm cxviii. 17, 18.

2,238 "Thou art now the Blessed of the Lord" 13

"Thou art now the blessed of the LORD."—Genesis xxvi. 29.

2,239 Is God in the Camp? 25

"And the Philistines were afraid, for they said, God is come into the camp. And they said, Woe unto us! for there hath not been such a thing heretofore."—1 Samuel iv. 7.

2 240 A Challenge and a Shield... 37

"Who is he that condemneth? It is Christ that died."—Romans viii. 34.

2,241 A Stanza of Deliverance 49

"He brought them forth also with silver and gold: and there was not one feeble person among their tribes."—Psalm cv. 37.

2,242 God's Will about the Future 61

"Go to now, ye that say, To day or to morrow we will go into such a city, and continue there a year, and buy and sell, and get gain: whereas ye know not what shall be on the morrow. For what is your life? It is even a vapour, that appeareth for a little time, and then vanisheth away. For that ye ought to say, If the Lord will, we shall live, and do this, or that. But now ye rejoice in your boastings: all such rejoicing is evil. Therefore to him that knoweth to do good, and doeth it not, to him it is sin."—James iv. 13—17.

2,243 His own Funeral Sermon 73

"For David, after he had served his own generation by the will of God, fell on sleep."—Acts xiii. 36.

2,244 Members of Christ 85

"For we are members of his body, of his flesh, and of his bones."—Ephesians v. 30.

CONTENTS.

No.		Page
2,245	"Living, Loving, Lasting Union"	97

"For we are members of his body, of his flesh, and of his bones."—Ephesians v. 30.

2,246 "Come from the Four Winds, O Breath!" 109

"Then he said unto me, Prophesy unto the wind, prophesy, son of man, and say to the wind, Thus saith the Lord God; Come from the four winds, O breath, and breathe upon these slain, that they may live."—Ezekiel xxxvii. 9.

2,247 Praise for the Gift of Gifts 121

"Thanks be unto God for his unspeakable gift."—2 Corinthians ix. 15.

2,248 Sad Fasts Changed to Glad Feasts 133

"Thus saith the LORD of hosts; The fast of the fourth month, and the fast of the fifth, and the fast of the seventh, and the fast of the tenth, shall be to the house of Judah joy and gladness, and cheerful feasts; therefore love the truth and peace."—Zechariah viii. 19.

2,249 "Even Now" 145

"Even now."—John xi. 22.

2,250 Words to Rest On 157

"And the people rested themselves upon the words of Hezekiah king of Judah."—2 Chronicles xxxii. 8.

2,251 Our Compassionate High Priest 169

"Who can have compassion on the ignorant, and on them that are out of the way; for that he himself also is compassed with infirmity."—Hebrews v. 2.

2,252 The Unknown Giver and the Misused Gifts 181

"For she did not know that I gave her corn, and wine, and oil, and multiplied her silver and gold, which they prepared for Baal. Therefore will I return, and take away my corn in the time thereof, and my wine in the season thereof, and will recover my wool and my flax."—Hosea ii. 8, 9.

2,253 The Perseverance of Faith 193

"Then Jesus answered and said unto her, O woman, great is thy faith: be it unto thee even as thou wilt. And her daughter was made whole from that very hour."—Matthew xv. 28.

2,254 The Two Guards, Praying and Watching 205

"Nevertheless we made our prayer unto our God, and set a watch against them day and night, because of them."—Nehemiah iv. 9.

CONTENTS.

No.		Page
2,255	God Justified, though Man Believes Not	217

"For what if some did not believe? shall their unbelief make the faith of God without effect? God forbid: yea, let God be true, but every man a liar; as it is written, That thou mightest be justified in thy sayings, and mightest overcome when thou art judged."—Romans iii. 3, 4.

2,256 Daniel's Band 229

"O Daniel, a man greatly beloved."—Daniel x. 11.

2,257 Inexcusable Irreverence and Ingratitude 241

"They are without excuse: because that, when they knew God, they glorified him not as God, neither were thankful."—Romans i. 20, 21.

2,258 Where is the Lord? 253

"Then he remembered the days of old, Moses and his people, saying Where is he that brought them up out of the sea with the shepherd of his flock? where is he that put his holy Spirit within him? That led them by the right hand of Moses with his glorious arm, dividing the water before them, to make himself an everlasting name? That led them through the deep, as an horse in the wilderness, that they should not stumble? As a beast goeth down into the valley, the Spirit of the LORD caused him to rest: so didst thou lead thy people, to make thyself a glorious name."—Isaiah lxiii. 11—14.

2,259 The Simplicity and Sublimity of Salvation 265

"He came unto his own, and his own received him not. But as many as received him, to them gave he power to become the sons of God, even to them that believe on his name: Which were born, not of blood, nor of the will of the flesh, nor of the will of the man, but of God."—John i. 11—13.

2,260 Christ's Hospital 277

"He healeth the broken in heart, and bindeth up their wounds."—Psalm cxlvii. 3.

2,261 One Worker Preparing for Another 289

"Now, behold, in my trouble I have prepared for the house of the LORD an hundred thousand talents of gold, and a thousand thousand talents of silver; and of brass and iron without weight; for it is in abundance: timber also and stone have I prepared; and thou mayest add thereto."—1 Chronicles xxii. 14.

CONTENTS.

No.		Page
2,262	Christ's Curate in Decapolis	301

"And they began to pray him to depart out of their coasts. And when he was come into the ship, he that had been possessed with the devil prayed him that he might be with him. Howbeit Jesus suffered him not, but saith unto him, Go home to thy friends, and tell them how great things the Lord hath done for thee, and hath had compassion on thee."—Mark v. 17—19.

2,263 Christ's Plea for Ignorant Sinners 313

"Then said Jesus, Father, forgive them; for they know not what they do."—Luke xxiii. 34.

2,264 Sowing in the Wind; Reaping under Clouds 325

"He that observeth the wind shall not sow; and he that regardeth the clouds shall not reap."—Ecclesiastes xi. 4.

2,265 Harvest Joy 337

"Thou hast multiplied the nation, and increased the joy; they joy before thee according to the joy in harvest, and as men rejoice when they divide the spoil."—Isaiah ix. 3.

2,266 Blessing for Blessing 349

"Blessed be the God and Father of our Lord Jesus Christ, who hath blessed us with all spiritual blessings in heavenly places in Christ: according as he hath chosen us in him before the foundation of the world, that we should be holy and without blame before him in love."—Ephesians i. 3, 4.

2,267 Life from the Dead 361

"And you hath he quickened, who were dead in trespasses and sins."—Ephesians ii. 1.

2,268 A Question for Communicants 373

"What mean ye by this service?"—Exodus xii. 26.

2,269 Impotence and Omnipotence 385

"And a certain man was there, which had an infirmity thirty and eight years. When Jesus saw him lie, and knew that he had been now a long time in that case, he saith unto him, Wilt thou be made whole? The impotent man answered him, Sir, I have no man, when the water is troubled, to put me into the pool: but while I am coming, another steppeth down before me. Jesus saith unto him, Rise, take up thy bed, and walk. And immediately the man was made whole, and took up his bed, and walked."—John v. 5—9.

CONTENTS.

No.		Page
2,270	Two "I Wills" in Isaiah xli.	397

"I will open rivers in high places, and fountains in the midst of the valleys: I will make the wilderness a pool of water, and the dry land springs of water."—Isaiah xli. 18.

| 2,271 | Alone, yet *Not* Alone | 409 |

"Jesus answered them, Do ye now believe? Behold, the hour cometh, yea, is now come, that ye shall be scattered, every man to his own, and shall leave me alone: and yet I am not alone, because the Father is with me."—John xvi. 31, 32.

| 2,272 | Longing to Find God | 421 |

"Oh that I knew where I might find him!"—Job xxiii. 3.

| 2,273 | Fickle Followers | 433 |

"And it came to pass, that, as they went in the way, a certain man said unto him, Lord, I will follow thee whithersoever thou goest. And Jesus said unto him, Foxes have holes, and birds of the air have nests; but the Son of man hath not where to lay his head. And he said unto another, Follow me. But he said, Lord, suffer me first to go and bury my father. Jesus said unto him, Let the dead bury their dead: but go thou and preach the kingdom of God. And another also said, Lord, I will follow thee; but let me first go bid them farewell, which are at home at my house. And Jesus said unto him, No man, having put his hand to the plough, and looking back, is fit for the kingdom of God."—Luke ix. 57—62.

| 2,274 | God's People Melted and Tried | 445 |

"Therefore thus saith the LORD of hosts, Behold, I will melt them, and try them; for how shall I do for the daughter of my people?"—Jeremiah ix. 7.

| 2,275 | Belief, Baptism, Blessing | 457 |

"And he took them the same hour of the night, and washed their stripes; and was baptized, he and all his, straightway. And when he had brought them into his house, he set meat before them, and rejoiced, believing in God with all his house."—Acts xvi. 33, 34.

| 2,276 | Forgiveness, Freedom, Favour | 469 |

"And this is the manner of the release: Every creditor that lendeth ought unto his neighbour shall release it; he shall not exact it of his neighbour, or of his brother; because it is called the LORD's release."—Deuteronomy xv. 2.

| 2,277 | Sychar's Sinner Saved | 481 |

"Jesus answered and said unto her, If thou knewest the gift of God, and who it is that saith to thee, Give me to drink; thou wouldest have asked of him, and he would have given thee living water."—John iv. 10.

CONTENTS.

No.		Page
2,278	Feeding on the Word	493

"Hearken diligently unto me, and eat ye that which is good, and let your soul delight itself in fatness."—Isaiah lv. 2.

| 2,279 | Joy Hindering Faith | 505 |

"And while they yet believed not for joy, and wondered, he said unto them, Have ye here any meat? And they gave him a piece of a broiled fish, and of an honeycomb. And he took it, and did eat before them. And he said unto them, These are the words which I spake unto you, while I was yet with you, that all things must be fulfilled, which were written in the law of Moses, and in the prophets, and in the psalms, concerning me. Then opened he their understanding, that they might understand the scriptures."—Luke xxiv. 41—45.

| 2,280 | God's Handwriting upon David | 517 |

"All this, said David, the LORD made me understand in writing by his hand upon me, even all the works of this pattern."—1 Chronicles xxviii. 19.

| 2,281 | Our Lord in the Valley of Humiliation | 529 |

"And being found in fashion as a man, he humbled himself, and became obedient unto death, even the death of the cross."—Philippians ii. 8.

| 2,282 | David's Prayer in the Cave | 541 |

"Maschil of David; A Prayer when he was in the cave."—Title of Psalm cxlii.

| 2,283 | Christ's One Sacrifice for Sin | 553 |

"Now once in the end of the world hath he appeared to put away sin by the sacrifice of himself."—Hebrews ix. 26.

| 2,284 | "Clear Shining after Rain" | 565 |

"As the tender grass springing out of the earth by clear shining after rain."—2 Samuel xxiii. 4.

| 2,285 | Paul the Ready | 577 |

"I am ready."—Romans i. 15.

| 2,286 | An Ancient Question Modernized | 589 |

"And the people said unto me, Wilt thou not tell us what these things are to us, that thou doest so?"—Ezekiel xxiv. 19.

No.		Page
2,287	"If there be no Resurrection,——"	601

"Now if Christ be preached that he rose from the dead, how say some among you that there is no resurrection of the dead? But if there be no resurrection of the dead, then is Christ not risen: and if Christ be not risen, then is our preaching vain, and your faith is also vain. Yea, and we are found false witnesses of God; because we have testified of God that he raised up Christ: whom he raised not up, if so be that the dead rise not. For if the dead rise not, then is not Christ raised: and if Christ be not raised, your faith is vain; ye are yet in your sins. Then they also which are fallen asleep in Christ are perished. If in this life only we have hope in Christ, we are of all men most miserable."—1 Corinthians xv. 12—19.

| 2,288 | The Empty Place: A Christmas Day Sermon | 613 |

"David's place was empty."—1 Samuel xx. 25.

EXPOSITIONS OF SCRIPTURE.

	PAGE		PAGE
Leviticus xxv. 1—7, 17—22	478	Matthew xxvi. 26—30	382
Deuteronomy xv. 1—18	478	Mark v. 1—20	310
1 Chronicles xxi. 25—30	298	Luke ix. 37—62	442
,, xxii.	298	,, xxiii. 33—46	322
,, xxviii.	526	,, xxiv. 13—48	514
Nehemiah iv. 1—23	214	John i. 1—34	273
Job xxiii.	430	,, iv. 1—42	490
Psalm xxxii.	574	,, v. 1—23	394
,, lvii.	550	,, xvi. 16—33	418
,, ciii.	622	,, xix. 25—30	322
,, cxlviii.	286	Acts xvi. 9—34	466
Ecclesiastes xi.	334	Romans i. 1—25	250
,, xii.	334	,, iii.	226
Isaiah xli. 1—20	406	1 Corinthians xi. 20—34	382
,, xlix. 13—26	346	,, xv. 1—20	611
,, lv.	502	Ephesians i.	358
,, lxiii.	586	,, ii.	370
,, lxiii., lxiv.	261	Philippians ii. 1—18	538
Jeremiah ix.	454	Hebrews ix. 24—28	563
Ezekiel xxxiii. 1—20; 30—33	598	,, x. 1—18	563
Matthew xv. 21—39	202	1 John iv. 9—21	238

INDEX OF SCRIPTURE TEXTS.

VOLUME XXXVIII.

Chap. & Verse.	Page
GENESIS.	
xxvi. 29	13
EXODUS.	
xii. 26	373
DEUTERONOMY.	
xv. 2	469
1 SAMUEL.	
iv. 7	25
xx. 25	613
2 SAMUEL.	
xxiii. 4	565
1 CHRONICLES.	
xxii. 14	289
xxviii. 19	517
2 CHRONICLES.	
xxxii. 8	157
NEHEMIAH.	
iv. 9	205
JOB.	
xxiii. 3	421
PSALMS.	
cv. 37	49
cxviii. 17, 18	1
cxlii.	541
cxlvii. 3	277
ECCLESIASTES.	
xi. 4	325
ISAIAH.	
ix. 3	337
xli. 18	397
lv. 2	493
lxiii. 11—14	253
JEREMIAH.	
ix. 7	445
EZEKIEL.	
xxiv. 19	589
xxxvii. 9	109
DANIEL.	
x. 11	229

Chap. & Verse.	Page
HOSEA.	
ii. 8, 9	181
ZECHARIAH.	
viii. 19	133
MATTHEW.	
xv. 25	193
MARK.	
v. 17—19	301
LUKE.	
ix. 57—62	433
xxiii. 34	313
xxiv. 41—45	505
JOHN.	
i. 11—13	265
iv. 10	481
v. 5—9	385
xi. 22	145
xvi. 31, 32	409
ACTS.	
xiii. 36	73
xvi. 33, 34	457
ROMANS.	
i. 15	577
i. 20, 21	241
iii. 3, 4	217
viii. 34	37
1 CORINTHIANS.	
xv. 12—19	601
2 CORINTHIANS.	
ix. 15	121
EPHESIANS.	
i. 3, 4	349
ii. 1	361
v. 30	85
v. 30	97
PHILIPPIANS.	
ii. 8	529
HEBREWS.	
v. 2	169
ix. 26	553
JAMES.	
iv. 13—17	61

Metropolitan Tabernacle Pulpit.

GRATITUDE FOR DELIVERANCE FROM THE GRAVE.

A Sermon

Intended for Reading on Lord's-day, January 3rd, 1892,

delivered by

C. H. SPURGEON,

at the metropolitan tabernacle, newington,

In connection with the dedication of the Jubilee House, which commemorated the fiftieth year of a life often threatened by grievous sickness.*

"I shall not die, but live, and declare the works of the Lord. The Lord hath chastened me sore: but he hath not given me over unto death."—Psalm cxviii. 17, 18.

How very differently we view things at different times and in differing states of mind! Faith takes a bright and cheerful view of matters, and speaks very confidently, "I shall not die, but live." When we are slack as to our trust in God, and give way to misgivings and doubts and fears, we sing in the minor key, and say, "I shall die. I shall never live through this trouble. I shall one day fall by the hand of the enemy; and that day is hastening on. Hope is failing me. Bad times are at the door. I shall not live through the crisis." Thus our tongues show the condition of the inner man. We talk according to our frames and feelings, and would make others think that things are as we see them with our jaundiced eyes. Is it not a pity that we give a tongue to our unbelief? Would it not be better to be dumb when we are doubtful? Muzzle that dog of unbelief! Dog did I call him? He is a wolf; or shall I call him hound of hell? His voice is as that of Apollyon: it is full of blasphemy against God. Unbelieving utterances will do no good to yourself, and will do harm to those who listen to your babblings. It would be wise to say, "If I should speak thus, I should offend against the generation of thy children. When I thought to know this, it was too painful for me." Let us be dumb with silence when we cannot speak to the glory of God. But, oh, it is a blessed thing, when faith is in our spirit reigning and powerful, to let it have ample opportunity to proclaim the honours of his name! To give his heart a tongue, is wise in man when his heart itself is wise. The more talk we get from the mouth of

---

* Will the reader kindly note the remarks at the end of this sermon, before he reads the discourse?—C. H. S.

No. 2,237.

faith, the better: her lips drop sweet-smelling myrrh. A silent faith, if there be such a thing, robs others of benedictions; and at the same time it does worse, for it robs God of his glory. When we have a joyous faith in full operation, let us be communicative, and let us openly and boldly say, "I shall not die, but live, and declare the works of the Lord." I would follow my own advice, and crave a patient hearing of you.

You know, perhaps, that this text was inscribed by Martin Luther upon his study wall, where he could always see it when at home. Many Reformers had been done to death—Huss, and others who preceded him, had been burnt at the stake; Luther was cheered by the firm conviction that he was perfectly safe until his work was done. In this full assurance he went bravely to meet his enemies at the Diet of Worms, and, indeed, went courageously wherever duty called him. He felt that God had raised him up to declare the glorious doctrine of justification by faith, and all the other truths of what he believed to be the gospel of God; and therefore no faggots could burn him, and no sword could kill him till that work was done. Thus he bravely wrote out his belief, and set it where many eyes would see it, "I shall not die, but live, and declare the works of the Lord." It was no idle boast; but a calm and true conclusion from his faith in God, and fellowship with him. May you and I, when we are tried, be able, through faith in God, to meet trouble with the like brave thoughts and speeches! We cannot show our courage unless we have difficulties and troubles. A man cannot become a veteran soldier if he never goes to battle. No man can get his sea legs if he lives always on land. Rejoice, therefore, in your tribulations, because they give you opportunities of exhibiting a believing confidence, and thereby glorifying the name of the Most High. But take heed that you have faith, true faith in God; and do not become the puppet of impressions, much less the slave of the judgments of others. To have David's faith, you must be as David. No man may take up with a confidence of his own making: it must be a real work of the Spirit, and growth of grace within, grasping with living tendrils the promise of the living God.

I will read the passage from the psalm over again, and we will then consider it by God's help. "I shall not die, but live, and declare the works of the Lord. The Lord hath chastened me sore: but he hath not given me over unto death."

First, here is *the believer's view of his afflictions.* "The Lord hath chastened me sore." Secondly, here is *the believer's comfort under those afflictions.* "He hath not given me over unto death. I shall not die, but live." And, thirdly, here is *the believer's conduct after his afflictions, and after his deliverance from them*—"I shall not die, but live, and declare the works of the Lord."

I. At the outset, here is THE BELIEVER'S VIEW OF HIS AFFLICTIONS. "The Lord hath chastened me sore."

On the surface of the words we see the good man's clear observation that *his afflictions came from God.* It is true he perceived the secondary hand, for he says, "Thou hast thrust sore at me that I might fall." There was one at work who aimed to make him fall. His afflictions were the work of a cruel enemy. Yes; but that enemy's assaults were being overruled by the Lord, and were made to work for his good; so David, in the present verse, corrects himself by saying, "*The Lord* hath chastened me sore. My enemy struck at me that he might make me fall; but in very truth my gracious God was using him to chasten me that I might *not* fall. The enemy was moved by malice, but God was working by him in love to my soul. The second agent sought my ruin, but the Great First Cause wrought my education and establishment."

It is well to have grace enough to see that tribulation comes from God: he fills the bitter cup as well as the sweet goblet. Troubles do not spring out of the dust, neither doth affliction grow up from the ground, like hemlock from the furrows of the field; but the Lord himself kindles the fiery furnace, and sits as a refiner at the door. Let us not dwell too much upon the part played by the devil, as though he were a power co-ordinate with God. He is a fallen creature, and his very existence depends upon the will and permission of the Most High. His power is borrowed, and can only be used as the infinite omnipotence of God permits. His wickedness is his own, but his existence is not self-derived. Blame the devil, and blame all his servants as much as you will; but still believe in the mysterious but consoling truth that, in the truest sense, the Lord sends trials upon his saints. "Explain that statement," say you. Oh, no; I am not called upon to explain it, but to believe it. A great many things, when they are said to be explained by modern thinkers, are merely explained away, and I have not yet begun to learn that wretched art. Remember how Peter told the Jews that he, whom God by his determinate counsel and foreknowledge decreed to die, even his son Jesus Christ, was nevertheless taken by them with wicked hands, when they had crucified and slain him. The death of Christ was pre-determined in the counsel of God, and yet it was none the less an atrocious crime on the part of ungodly men. The omnipotence and providence of God are to be believed; but man's responsibility is not therefore to be questioned. Our afflictions may come distinctly from man, as the result of persecution or malice; and yet they may come with even greater certainty from the Lord, and may be the needful outcome of his special love to us.

For this reason we may wisely moderate our anger against second causes. If you strike a dog with a stick, he will bite the stick; if he were more intelligent, he would snap at the person using the stick; and, if that intelligence were governed by a spirit of obedience, he would yield to the blow, and learn a lesson from it. Thus, when Shimei reviled David, and Abishai, the son of Zeruiah, said unto the king, "Why should this dead dog curse my lord the king? let me go over, I pray thee, and take off his head;" David meekly replied, "So let him curse, because the Lord hath said unto him, Curse David. Who shall then say, Wherefore hast thou done so?" A sight of God's hand in a trial is the end of rebellion against it in the case of every good man. He says, "It is the Lord: let him do what seemeth him good." We may lie at his feet, and cry, "Shew me wherefore thou contendest with me;" but, if the reason does not appear, we must bow in reverent submission, and say with one of old, "I was dumb,

I opened not my mouth; because thou didst it." Job saw the Lord in his many tribulations, and therefore praised him, saying, "The Lord gave, and the Lord hath taken away; blessed be the name of the Lord." Surely there is nothing better for a man of God than to perceive that his smarts and sorrows come from his Father's hand, for then he will say, "The will of the Lord be done." This is the great point in the believer's view of his afflictions: "*He* maketh sore, and bindeth up: *he* woundeth, and *his* hands make whole."

Next, the believer perceives that *his trials come as a chastening*. "The Lord hath *chastened* me sore." When a child is chastised, two things are clear: first, that there is something wrong in him, or that there is something deficient in him, so that he needs to be corrected or instructed; and, secondly, it shows that his father has a tender care for his benefit, and acts in loving wisdom towards him. This is certainly true if his father is an eminently kind and yet prudent parent. Children do not think that there can be any need for chastening them; but when years have matured their judgment, they will know better. "No chastening for the present seemeth to be joyous;" if it did seem joyous, it would not be chastening. The "need be" is not only that we have manifold trials, but that we be in heaviness through them. In the smart of the sorrow lies the blessing of the chastisement. God chastens us in the purest love, because he sees that there is an absolute necessity for it: "for he doth not afflict willingly nor grieve the children of men." Our fathers, according to the flesh, too often corrected us according to their own pleasure, and yet we gave them reverence; but the Father of our spirits corrects us only of necessity—a necessity to which he is too wise to close his eye. Shall we not, therefore, pay greater reverence to him, and bow before him, and live? When Hezekiah was recovered of his sickness, he wrote, "O Lord, by these things men live, and in all these things is the life of my spirit." I find not that men live by carnal pleasure, nor that the life of the spirit is ever found in the wine-vat or in the oil-press; but I do find that life and health often come to saints through briny tears, through the bruising of the flesh, and the oppression of the spirit. So have I found it, and I bear my willing witness that sickness has brought me health, loss has conferred gain, and I doubt not that one day death will bring me fuller life.

Be wise then, dear child of God, and look upon your present affliction as a chastening. "What son is he whom the father chasteneth not?" "As many as I love, I rebuke and chasten." There is not a more profitable instrument in all God's house than the rod. No honey was sweeter than that which dropped from the end of Jonathan's rod; but that is nothing to the sweetness of the consolation which comes through Jehovah's rod. Our brightest joys are the birth of our bitterest griefs. When the woman has her travail pangs, joy comes to the house because the man-child is born; and sorrow is to us also, full often, the moment of the birth of our graces. A chastened spirit is a gracious spirit; and how shall we obtain it except we are chastened? Like our Lord Jesus, we learn obedience by the things which we suffer. God had one Son without sin, but he never had a son without sorrow, and he never will have while the world stands.

Let us, therefore, bless God for all his dealings, and in a filial spirit confess, "Thou, Lord, hast chastened me."

Consider the psalmist's view of his affliction a little more carefully. *He noted that his trials were sore:* he says, "The Lord hath chastened me sore." Perhaps we are willing to own in general that our trouble is of the Lord; but there is a soreness in it which we do not ascribe to him, but to the malice of the enemy, or some other second cause. The false tongue is so ingenious in slander that it has touched the tenderest part of our character, and has cut us to the quick. Are we to believe that this also is, in some sense, of the Lord? Assuredly we are. If it be not of the Lord, then it is a matter for despair. If this evil comes apart from divine permission, where are we? How can a trial be met which is independent of divine rule, and outside of the sacred zone of providential government? It is hopeful when we find that all our ills lie within the ring-fence of omnipotent overruling. It is one comfort that we see a wall of fire round about us, a circle so complete that even the devil, malicious as he is, cannot break through it, to do more than the Lord allows. The camels are gone, the sheep, the oxen, the servants, all are destroyed: all this is most trying; but still it is true—"The Lord gave, and the Lord hath taken away; blessed be the name of the Lord." But, see, another messenger comes, and cries, "There came a great wind from the wilderness, and smote the four corners of the house, and it fell upon the young men, and they are dead." Might not Job, then, have said, "This is a blow which I cannot bear; for it is evidently from the prince of the power of the air"? No, but even after that, he said, "Blessed be the name of the Lord." When his wife said, "Curse God, and die," he still blessed God, and held his integrity. He told her that she spoke as one of the foolish women speaketh, and then he wisely added, "Shall we receive good at the hand of God, and shall we not receive evil?" "In all this Job sinned not, nor charged God foolishly." May we stand fast in patience as he did, even when our troubles overflow!

It is folly to imagine, as we have sometimes done, that we could bear anything except that which we are called upon to endure. We are like the young man who says that he wants a situation. What can you do? He can do anything. That man you never engage, because you know that he can do nothing. So it is with us. If we say, "I could bear anything but this," we prove our universal impatience. If we had the choice of our crosses, the one we should choose would turn out to be more inconvenient than that which God appoints for us; and yet we will have it that our present cross is unsuitable and specially galling. I would say to any who are of that mind, "If your burden does not fit your shoulder, bear it till it does." Time will reconcile you to the yoke if grace abides with you. It is not for us to choose our affliction; that remains with him who chooses our inheritance for us. Read well this word, "The Lord hath chastened me sore," and see the Lord's hand in the soreness of your trial. Even while the wound is raw, and the smart is fresh, be conscious that the Lord is near.

Yet there is in the verse a "but", for the psalmist *perceives that his trial is limited;* "but he hath not given me over unto death." Certain of the *buts* in Scripture are among the choicest jewels we have. Before us is a " but " which shows that, however deep affliction may be, there is a bottom to its abyss. There is a limit to the force, the sharpness, the duration, and the number of our trials.

"If God appoints the number ten,
They ne'er can be eleven."

Whenever the Lord mixes a potion for his people, he weighs each ingredient, measures the bitters, grain by grain, and allows not even a particle in excess to mingle in the draught. Like a careful dispenser, he will not pour out a drop too little or too much.

" To his church, his joy, and treasure,
Every trial works for good:
They are dealt in weight and measure,
Yet how little understood;
Not in anger,
But from his dear covenant love."

Our Father's anger at our sin will never blaze into wrath against us, though in mercy he will smite our sins. Remember, then, this gracious boundary. " The Lord hath chastened me sore : *but* he hath not given me over unto death." We have never yet experienced a trouble which might not have been worse. One affliction kills another : the wind never blows east and west at the same time. When the Lord smites you with his left hand, he sustains you with his right hand ; as tribulations abound, so do consolations abound through Christ Jesus. The whole band of troubles never comes forth at once. Everything painful is graded and proportioned to the man and his strength, and the object for which it is sent. With the trial the Lord makes the way of escape that we may be able to bear it. Faith can see an end and limit where nature's dim eye sees endless confusion. Where carnal sense—

"Sees every day new straits attend,
And wonders where the scene will end,"

faith looks over the intervening space, and comforts herself with that which is yet to come. Faith sings pleasant songs when she foots it over weary roads.

" The road may be rough, but it cannot be long,
So let's smooth it with hope, and cheer it with song."

The Lord keep your faith alive, my brethren and sisters, and then whatever trials surge around you, you will sit on the Rock of ages, above the waves, and joyfully sing praises unto your divine Deliverer ! Oh, how sweet to say, as I now do, "The Lord hath chastened me sore : *but he hath not given me over unto death*"!

II. This brings me, secondly, to consider THE BELIEVER'S COMFORT UNDER HIS AFFLICTIONS. The believer's comfort under his afflictions is this—" I shall not die, but live."

Occasionally this comes in the form of a presentiment. I do not think that I am superstitious : I fancy that I am pretty clear of that vice ; yet I have had presentiments concerning things to come or not to come ; and, moreover, I have met with so many Christian men who, in the time of trouble, have received singular warnings, or sweet assurances of coming deliverance, that I am bound to believe that the Lord does sometimes whisper to the heart of his children, and assure them in trial that they shall not be crushed, and in sickness that they shall not die. How do you understand the story of John Wycliffe, at Lutterworth, in any other way than this? He had been speaking against the monks, and various abuses of the church. He was the first man known to history that preached the gospel in England during the Popish ages—we know him as the Morning Star of the Reformation. He was a man so great that, if he had possessed a printing-press, we might never have needed a Luther; for he had even clearer light than that great Reformer. He lacked the means of spreading his doctrine, which the art of printing supplied. He did much: he prepared everything to Luther's hand; and Luther was but the proclaimer of Wycliffe's doctrine. Wycliffe was ill—very ill, and the friars came round him, like crows round a dying sheep. They professed to be full of tender pity; but they were right glad that their enemy was going to die. So they said to him, "Do you not repent? Before we can give you the viaticum—the last oiling before you die—would it not be well to retract the hard things which you have said against the zealous friars, and his Holiness of Rome? We are eager to forget the past, and give you the last sacrament in peace." Wycliffe begged an attendant to help him to sit up; and then he cried with all his strength, "I shall not die, but live, to declare the works of the Lord, and to expose the wickedness of the friars." He did not die, either: death himself could not have killed him then; for he had more work to do, and the Lord made him immortal till it was done. How could Wycliffe know that he spoke truly? Certainly he was free from all foolhardy brag; but there was upon his mind a foreshadowing of future work that he had to do, and he felt that he could not die till it was accomplished. Now, do not be making up presentiments about all sorts of things, because I have said that sometimes the Lord grants them to his saints. This would be a mischievous piece of absurdity. I remember a young woman, who lived not far from here, who had a presentiment that she would die. I do not think that there was really much the matter with her; but she refused to eat, and was likely to be starved. I went to see her, and she told me that she had a presentiment that she should die, and therefore she should not waste food by eating it. She spoke to me very solemnly about this presentiment, and I replied, "I believe there may be such things." Yes: she was sure I was on her side! Then I went on to say, I once had a presentiment that I was a donkey, and it turned out true in my case; and now I had much the same presentiment about her. This surprised her, and I asked her friends to bring her food. She said she would not eat it; and then I told her that if she was resolved on suicide, I would mention it at a church-meeting that evening, and put her out of the church, since we could not have suicides in our membership. She could not bear to be put out of the church, and began to eat, and it turned out that my presentiment about her was correct; she had been foolish, and she had the good sense to see that it was so. I felt bound to tell you this story, lest you should fancy that I would support you in sentimental nonsense. While there are so many stupid people in the world, we have need to give cautions where the wise do not need them. Forecasts of good from the Lord may come to those who are sore sick; and when they do, they help them to recover. We are of good courage when an inward confidence enables us to say, "I shall not die, but live, and declare the works of the Lord."

This, however, I only mention by the way. When a believer is in trouble, *he derives great comfort from his reliance upon the compassion of God.* The Lord scourges his sons, but he does not slay them. The believer says, "My Father may make me smart with the blows of a cruel one; but will do me no real harm, nor allow anyone else to injure me. He will not lay upon me more than is right, nor above what I am able to bear. He will stay his hand when he sees that I have no strength left. Moreover, I know that even when he brings me very low, still underneath me are the everlasting arms. If the Lord kill, it is to make alive: if he wound, it is that he may heal. I am sure of that." O believer, never let anything drive you away from this confidence, for it has sure truth for its foundation! The Lord is good, and his mercy endureth for ever. It is not killing, but curing, that God means when he takes the sharp lancet in his hand. The nauseous medicine, which makes the heart sick, works the cure of a worse sickness. "His compassions fail not." He may often put his hand into the bitter box, but he has sweet cordials ready to take the taste away. For a small moment has he forsaken us, but with great mercies will he return to us. You have an effectual comfort if your faith can keep its hold upon the blessed fact of the Lord's fatherly compassion.

Next, faith comforts the tried child of God by assuring him of the forgiveness of his sin, and his *security from punishment.* Please to notice the very distinct difference between chastisement and punishment. I do not say between the meaning of the words, but between the two things which just now I would indicate by those terms. Here is a boy who has committed theft. He is brought before a magistrate that he may be punished. Punitive justice will be executed upon him by imprisonment or by a birch rod. Another boy has also stolen—stolen from his father, and he is brought before his father, not to be punished as a law-breaker, but to be chastised. There is a great difference between the punishment awarded by justice, and the chastisement appointed by love. They may be alike in painfulness, but how different in meaning! The father does not give to the child what he would deserve if it were a punishment according to law, but what he thinks will cure him of wrong-doing by making him feel that sin brings sorrow. The magistrate, although he desires the good of the offender, has mainly to consider the law in its bearings upon the whole mass of the population, and he punishes as a matter of justice that which wrongs the commonwealth; but the parent acts on other principles. "The Lord hath chastened me sore," and in that he has acted a fatherly part; "but he hath not given me over unto death," which would have been my lot if he had dealt with me as a judge. My heart trembles at his sword, and cries, "Enter not into judgment with thy servant, O Lord: for in thy sight shall no man living be justified." The sentence of justice has been fulfilled upon our Lord,

GRATITUDE FOR DELIVERANCE FROM THE GRAVE. 9

and our comfort is that now there is nothing punitive in all our troubles. "He hath not dealt with us after our sins; nor rewarded us according to our iniquities;" nor will he do so, for he has already laid our sin upon Christ, and Christ has vindicated the law by bearing its penalty, so that nothing more in the way of penalty is demanded by the moral government of God. That which we receive from the rod of the Lord bears the blessed aspect of chastening from a father's hand; and this is a gladsome fact, which makes even the sharpest smart to be profitable. "Surely the bitterness of death is past," when, in the case of the believer, even death has ceased to be the penalty of sin, and is changed into a sweet falling asleep upon the bosom of the Well-Beloved, to wake up in his likeness. Every other affliction is changed in the same fashion. Our wasps have become bees: their sting is not the prominent thought, but the honey which they lay up in store. "All things work together for good to them that love God," and chastisement is chief among those "all things." What a well of comforting thought is here!

Furthermore, it is a great blessing to a child of God to feel *a full assurance that he has eternal life in Christ Jesus.* "The Lord hath chastened me sore: but he hath not given me over unto death." Notice the words, "Given me over." It is the most awful thing out of hell to be *given over* by God. I fear that there are some such persons. Does not the psalmist refer to such when he says, "They are not in trouble as other men; neither are they plagued like other men. Their eyes stand out with fatness: they have more than heart could wish"? While God's own people are chastened every morning, and plagued all the day long, the ungodly prosper in the world, and increase in riches. Of his chosen the Lord says, "You only have I known of all the families of the earth: therefore I will punish you for all your iniquities." But those who are not the Lord's are left unchastened, because the Lord hath said of them, "Let them alone, they are given unto idols." They are allowed their transient mirth; let them make the most they can of it, for their end will be desolation.

Unbroken prosperity and undisturbed health may be the signs of being "given over unto death"; and they are such in cases where sin is committed without pangs of conscience, or apprehensions of judgment. Such freedom from fear may be maintained even in death: "There are no bands in their death: but their strength is firm." All goes quietly with them: "Like sheep they are laid in the grave." But "in hell they lift up their eyes, being in torments." To be given over unto death is often followed by callousness, presumption, and bravado; but it is a dreadful doom, the direst sentence from the throne of judgment as to this life. But you, dear child of God, have this comfort, *he* has not given *you* over, he is thinking upon you. By scourging you, he is proving that he has not given you over. Men do not prune the vine they mean to uproot; nor thresh out the weeds which they mean to burn. He who is chastened is not given over unto destruction. Years ago, I was taken very ill, in Marseilles, while attempting to come home to England. As I lay in my bed, it seemed as if the cruel mistral wind was driving through my bones, and breaking them with agony. I ordered a fire to be kindled; but when I saw the man begin to light it with a bundle of little branches, I cried out to him, " Pray let me look at that." I found that he was using the dry prunings of the vine, and the tears were in my eyes as I remembered the words—" Men gather them, and cast them into the fire, and they are burned." Comfort followed, for I thought, " I am not unfeeling, like those dried-up shoots; but I am the bleeding vine, which is sharply cut with the pruning-knife; I feel the keen blade in every part of me." Then could I say, "The Lord hath chastened me sore: but he hath not given me over." What joy lies in this, " He hath not given me over"! As long as the father chastens his boy, he has hope of him; if he ceased to do so altogether, we might fear that he thought him too bad to be reclaimed. Be glad, then, dear child of God, that since the Lord chastens you sore, he has not erased your name from his heart, and his hands, nor yielded you up to your enemy's power.

Another meaning may be found in this text, "I shall not die, but live, and declare the works of the Lord. The Lord hath chastened me sore: but he hath not given me over unto death." *We are comforted by reliance upon God's power for success in our life-work.* The critics said—and I must quote this because this sermon is very much a personal one—the critics said, when the lad commenced his preaching, that it was a nine days' wonder, and would soon come to an end. When the people joined the church in great numbers, they were "a parcel of boys and girls." Many of those " boys and girls" are here to-night, faithful to God unto this hour. Then there came upon us a heavy, heavy stroke—a sore chastening, which those of us who were present never will forget if we live for a century; and we seemed to be made the reproach of all men, through an accident which we could not have foreseen or prevented. But still the testimony for God in this place, by the same voice, has not ceased, nor lost its power. Still the people throng to hear the gospel after these thirty years and more, and still the doctrines of grace are to the front, notwithstanding all opposition. In the darkest hour of my ministry, I might have declared, "I shall not die, but live, and declare the works of the Lord." If you have been set on fire by a divine truth, the world cannot put an extinguisher upon you. That candle which God has lighted, the devils in hell cannot blow out. If you are commissioned of God to do a work, give your whole heart to it, trust in the Lord, and you will not fail. I bear my joyful witness to the power of God to work mightily by the most insignificant of instruments.

"The feeblest saint shall win the day,
Though death and hell obstruct the way."

Once more, though we may die, *we are sustained by the expectation of immortality.* When we gather up our feet in our last bed, we may utter this text in a full and sweet sense, "I shall not die, but live." When Wycliffe died as to his body, the real Wycliffe did not die. Some of his books were carried to Bohemia, and John Huss learned the gospel from them, and began to preach. They burnt John Huss, and Jerome of Prague; but Huss foretold, as he died, that another would arise after him, whom they should not be able to put down;

and in due time he more than lived again in Luther. Is Luther dead? Is Calvin dead to-day? That last man the moderns have tried to bury in a dunghill of misrepresentation; but he lives, and will live, and the truths that he taught will survive all the calumniators that have sought to poison it. Die! Often the death of a man is a kind of new birth to him; when he himself is gone physically, he spiritually survives, and from his grave there shoots up a tree of life whose leaves heal nations. O worker for God, death cannot touch thy sacred mission! Be thou content to die if the truth shall live the better because thou diest. Be thou content to die, because death may be to thee the enlargement of thine influence. Good men die as dies the seed-corn which thereby abideth not alone. When saints are apparently laid in the earth, they quit the earth, and rise and mount to heaven-gate, and enter into immortality. No, when the sepulchre receives this mortal frame, we shall not die, but live. Then shall we come to our true stature and beauty, and put on our royal robes, our glorious Sabbath-dress.

III. So I finish with just two or three words on THE BELIEVER'S CONDUCT AFTER TROUBLE AND DELIVERANCE. "I shall not die, but live, and declare the works of the Lord."

Here is *declaration*. If we had no troubles, we should have all the less to declare. A person who has had no experience of tribulation, what great deliverance has he to speak of? Such persons despise the afflicted, and suspect the character of the choicest of men, for lack of power to understand them. What does that man know about the sea who has only walked the beach? Get with an old sailor, who has been a dozen times round the world, and often wrecked, and he will interest you. So the much-tried Christian has great wonders to declare, and these are chiefly the works of the Lord; for "they that go down to the sea in ships, that do business in great waters; these see the works of the Lord, and his wonders in the deep." Tried Christians see how God sustains in trouble, and how he delivers out of it, and they declare his works openly: they cannot help doing so. They are so interested themselves in what God has done that they grow enthusiastic over it; and if they held their peace, the stones would cry out.

If you read the chapter further down, you will find that they not only give forth a declaration, but they offer *adoration*. They are so charmed with what God has done for them, that they laud and magnify the name of the Lord, saying, "I will praise thee: for thou hast heard me, and art become my salvation." The saints of God, when they are rescued from their sorrows, are sure to sing, "My soul doth magnify the Lord, and my spirit hath rejoiced in God my Saviour."

This done, they make a further *dedication* of themselves to their delivering God. As the psalm puts it, "God is the Lord, which hath shewed us light." It was very dark! It was very, very dark! We could not see our hand, much less the hand of God! We were frozen with fear. We thought that we were as dead men, laid out for burial; when suddenly the Lord's face shone in upon us, and all darkness was gone, and we leaped into joyful security, crying "God is the Lord, which hath shewed us light." We were convinced that it was none other than the true God who had removed the midnight gloom. Doubts, infidelities, agnosticisms—they were impossible. We said, "God is the Lord, which hath shewed us light." In the fourth watch of the night, in the prison where the cold stone shut us in, where the darkness had never known a candle, there a light shone round about us, and an angel smote us on the side, and bade us put on our sandals, and gird ourselves, and follow him. We obeyed the word, and our chains fell off; and when we came to the iron gate which had always been our horror, it opened of its own accord, and we went out into the streets of the city, and we scarcely felt that it could be true, but thought we saw a vision. But when we had considered the thing, and found it was even ourselves, and ourselves set in a large place at perfect liberty, then we said, "Bind the sacrifice with cords, even unto the horns of the altar." God hath showed us light, and we will live to him for ever and for ever. Oh, you tried believers, who have, nevertheless, not been given over unto death, who can say to-night, "I shall not die, but live," present yourselves anew unto your delivering Lord as living sacrifices through Jesus Christ your Lord! Amen.

PORTION OF SCRIPTURE READ BEFORE SERMON—Psalm cxviii.

HYMNS FROM "OUR OWN HYMN BOOK"—708, 73 (Part II.), 710.

This sermon begins a new volume; in fact, it commences Vol. XXXVIII. of *The Metropolitan Tabernacle Pulpit*. I have, myself, selected it, and prepared it for the press, because it is most suitable as my own personal testimony at the present moment. The subject is even more my own this day than it was seven and a half years ago; for I have been in deeper waters, and nearer to the mouth of the grave. With my whole soul I praise delivering grace. To the Lord God, the God of Israel, I consecrate myself anew. For the covenant of grace, for the revelation of infallible truth in the Bible, for the atonement by blood, and the immutable love of the ever-blessed Three-in-One, I am a witness; and more and more would I abide faithful to the gospel of the grace of God. I see each day more reasons for faith, and fewer excuses for doubt. Those who will may ship their anchors, and be drifted about by the current of the age; but I would sing, "My heart is fixed, O God, my heart is fixed: I will sing, and give praise!"

The whole passage, Ps. cxviii. 13-18, is inscribed upon a marble slab on the Jubilee House at the back of the Tabernacle, and I am told that many went to read it while I lay in the greatest peril through sore sickness, and were comforted thereby. When the Lord permits me to return, I must raise yet another memorial to his praise.

C. H. Spurgeon

Metropolitan Tabernacle Pulpit.

"THOU ART NOW THE BLESSED OF THE LORD."

A Sermon

INTENDED FOR READING ON LORD'S-DAY, JANUARY 10TH, 1892,

DELIVERED BY

C. H. SPURGEON,

AT THE METROPOLITAN TABERNACLE, NEWINGTON,

On Lord's-day Evening, May 3rd, 1891.

"Thou art now the blessed of the Lord."—Genesis xxvi. 29.

These words truly describe the position of many whom I address at this time. There are hundreds here upon whom my eye can rest, and to any one of whom I might point with this finger, or rather, to whom I might extend this hand, to give a hearty shake, and say, "Thou art now the blessed of the Lord." I need not say it in the same spirit, nor for the same reason, that the Philistines did. They had behaved basely towards Isaac, and now that he had prospered, they urged him to forget the past. They meant, "This is why we trust that you will deal kindly with us, and overlook our hard usage; for, in spite of all, God has so blessed you that you need not be fretful and pettish, and remember what we have done." I am glad that I am under no necessity to strive to make up a quarrel in this way. These many years we have dwelt in peace, and have enjoyed sweet fellowship together. You have borne with my weakness often, and bestowed upon me a wealth of affection which I am sure I do not deserve. So, though I use the language of Abimelech and his friends, my motive is a very different one. Yet the truth is the same concerning many a one here: "Thou art now the blessed of the Lord."

There is, however, much force in the argument which these Philistines used. If God has richly blessed us, notwithstanding all our faults and failures, surely we should learn to forgive many injuries done to ourselves. If the Lord forgives us our debt of ten thousand talents, we must be willing to forgive our fellow-servant his debt of a hundred pence. Child of God, if you are now the blessed of the Lord, you will often turn a blind eye towards the offences of your fellow-men. You will say, "God has so blessed me, that I can well overlook any wrongs that you have inflicted, any hard words that you have said. I am now the blessed of the Lord; so let bygones be bygones." May you have grace given you to do that now, if any of you have had a little squabble with any other! If there have been any difficulties

No. 2,238.

between any of you, I would hope that, before I really get into my subject, while with my finger I point you out, and say to each one of you, "Thou art now the blessed of the Lord," you will immediately say, "As surely as that is true, I do from my very heart forgive all who have offended me, whether Philistines, or Israelites, or Gentiles. How can I do otherwise who myself have received such grace while so unworthy?"

Remember, that this was spoken by the Philistine king as a reason why he wished to have Isaac for a friend. In your choice of friends, choose those who are the friends of God. If you would have a blessing upon your friendship, select a man whom God has blessed. Look out for one who is a disciple of Christ, and say, "Thou art now the blessed of the Lord; therefore I seek thine acquaintance. Come under my roof; you will bring a blessing with you. Speak to me in the street; your morning word will be a benediction to me." It was the old custom with apostolic men to say, as they entered a house, "Peace be unto this house." We have given up all idea of blessing our fellow-men in that way. But why have we done so? Is it from a want of love, or a want of faith in our own prayer that God would make it even so? For my part, I value a good man's blessing. As I drove up a hill, in the country, some time ago, a poor man and his wife were walking down the hill. I had never seen them before; but the woman pulled her husband by his coat; they both stood and looked at me, and at last she said, quite loudly, "It's him, God bless him!" and although her greeting was not quite grammatical, it evidently came from her heart, and I felt happier for it, as I went on my way. I saw her afterwards, and asked her the reason of her words. "Why," she said, "I have read your sermons for many a year, and I could not help saying, 'God bless him!' when I saw you, for you have been a blessing to me." Thus that humble woman, being blessed of the Lord, became a blessing to me; and we all of us, even the most obscure, who know the grace of God, might daily be like a great benediction in the midst of the people. When you think of your minister, say sometimes, "God bless him!" it will do him good to hear it. Say to your friend, "God bless you!" Say to your children, "God bless you, my dear boy! The Lord bless you, my dear girl!" They will be the better for it, if you yourself are the blessed of the Lord. You, grandsires, lay your hands on the children's heads, and bless them; they will not forget it when they grow up. It may be that you will have done much more for them than you have thought. Concerning his flock the Lord says, "I will make them and the places round about my hill a blessing; and I will cause the shower to come down in his season; there shall be showers of blessing." God's people are blessed that they may bless; therefore, for the sake of others, as well as for your own, seek that my text may be abundantly true of you. Make this your prayer—

> "Lord, I hear of showers of blessing,
> Thou art scattering full and free;
> Showers, the thirsty land refreshing;
> Let some droppings fall on me,
>   Even me."

It was for this reason that the Philistines sought the friendship of Isaac, because they could truly say to him, "Thou art now the blessed of the Lord."

I want not so much to preach from this text as to ask every believer in Christ to feel that it is personally true. Once you were condemned; but, being in Christ Jesus, "there is therefore now no condemnation." "Thou art now the blessed of the Lord." Once you were at enmity against God; but now, being reconciled to God by the death of his Son, you are his friend: "Thou art now the blessed of the Lord." "Ye were sometimes darkness, but now are ye light in the Lord." How great the change for the man or woman to whom we can say "Thou art now the blessed of the Lord"!

There was a day when I was cursed, and there was a day when I loved sin, and opposed God's will; but now I love sin no longer, and I find my highest delight in doing the will of my Father in heaven. My soul, if this be true, "thou art now the blessed of the Lord"; thou art a miracle of mercy; thou art a prodigy of grace; and truly, where sin abounded, grace did much more abound." Sit still in your pews, ye people of God, and roll this sweet morsel under your tongue! Once, because you believed not, the wrath of God was resting upon you, but now you can say, "O Lord! I will praise thee: though thou wast angry with me, thine anger is turned away, and thou comfortedst me." Surely then "Thou art now the blessed of the Lord." Thou art poor, perhaps, in this world's goods; but being an heir of the "inheritance incorruptible, and undefiled, and that fadeth not away, reserved in heaven for you," why, "Thou art now the blessed of the Lord." Or, perchance, you are weak and ill, and scarcely able to be in your place; but, though thy flesh and strength fail, "thou art now the blessed of the Lord," for by his grace, you will triumph over all. With many a fear and many a care oppressed, still "thou art now the blessed of the Lord," and on him thou canst cast thy care, and from him receive deliverance from all thy fears. Whatever thy distresses, this overwhelms them all as with a flood of joy. You can join with one who, though in a very humble station in life, says,—

"O joy! 'tis mine, this life divine,
   Life hid with Christ in God;
Once sin-defiled, now reconciled,
   And washed in Jesus' blood.

"Oft far astray from Christ the Way,
   I went with wilful feet;
From hopeless track, love brought me back,
   With words of welcome sweet."

If thou canst truly sing this sweet song, "Thou art now the blessed of the Lord." Thou art not yet perfect; thou art not yet taken out of the body to be with thy Lord in bliss; thou art not yet risen from the dead to stand before the throne of God in thy body of resurrection glory; but yet thou art now, even now, the blessed of the Lord. Will you let the flavour of this sweet truth be in your mouth, and in your heart, while I seek to open up this subject to you?

I. I would remark upon it, first, that, in the case of Isaac, THIS WAS THE TESTIMONY OF ENEMIES. It was Philistines who said, "Thou art now the blessed of the Lord." There are some of God's people who are so evidently favoured of heaven that even those who despise and oppose them cannot help saying of them, "They are the blessed of the Lord." I wish that we were all such, so distinguished by piety, so marked out by strength of faith and prevalence of prayer, that even our Abimelechs might be forced to say to each one of us, "Thou art now the blessed of the Lord." What caused this heathen king and his companions to use such an expression about Isaac? In seeking the reasons which led them to see the bounty of the Lord in the case of Abraham's son, we may find some signs of the blessing of God upon ourselves and upon our children.

I think, first, that *they saw it in his wonderful prosperity*. We read in the twelfth, thirteenth, and fourteenth verses, "Then Isaac sowed in that land, and received in the same year an hundredfold: and the Lord blessed him. And the man waxed great, and went forward, and grew until he became very great: for he had possession of flocks, and possession of herds, and great store of servants." Prosperity is not always a token of blessing. It may be the proof of the Lord's favour, and it may not be. God sometimes gives most to those on earth who will have nothing in heaven; as if, seeing that he cannot bless them in eternity, he would let them enjoy the poor sweets of time. I have heard it said, that prosperity was the blessing of the old covenant, and adversity the blessing of the new. Nevertheless, it is true that worldly prosperity may be sent, and has been sent, to the children of God, as a token of divine favour. It is not always when we eat the quails that they make us ill; God can send them in such a way that we may enjoy them, and be strengthened by them. He can give riches as well as poverty. That was the Philistines' reason, and it is a Philistine's reason. It is not a very satisfactory one, but it has some force, for the Lord Jesus himself gave the sign of blessing upon the meek, saying, "They shall inherit the earth;" and in the same memorable discourse upon the mount, he uttered the exhortation and promise, "Seek ye first the kingdom of God, and his righteousness; and all these things"—the things which the Gentiles seek after— "shall be added unto you." So we may fairly construe the "mercies of God" as a sign of his blessing.

These Philistines had a further reason for thinking that Isaac was blessed of God; *they felt it by divine impression*. A secret spirit whispered to the king, "Touch not mine anointed, and do my prophets no harm." God has a way of making men feel "how awful goodness is." They may jest and jeer against a Christian, but his life vanquishes them. They cannot help it. They must do homage to the supremacy of grace. The promise is still true, "When a man's ways please the Lord, he maketh even his enemies to be at peace with him." God will impress upon the minds even of unbelievers this fact, that such a man, such a woman, is one whom God has blessed. Do you not know some believers who have such an air of other-worldliness about them, that though they mix freely with the people amongst whom they dwell, men instinctively acknowledge that "they have been with Jesus," and have been blessed by him? I do not care to see pictures of the saints of old with a nimbus of light round their heads, even though they have been painted by the old masters, yet there is a something about one who lives a saintly life, a brightness encircling him, like the symbol of God's presence, which separates him from those around him, and leads us to say to him, "Thou art now the blessed of the Lord."

Further, before the Philistines bore this testimony to Isaac, no doubt *they remarked his gentleness*. I do believe that there is nothing that has such power over ungodly men as meekness of spirit, quietness of behaviour, patience of character, and the continual conquest over an evil temper. If you grow angry when people are angry with you, you will have lost your position; but if you can be patient under persecution, if you can smile when they ridicule you, if you can yield your rights, if you can bear and continue to bear, you are greater than the man who takes a city. Remember the blessing promised to the disciples of Christ who are peacemakers. They are not only the children of God, but "*they shall be called* the children of God." People will say, "If any man is a true Christian, he is one;" they will have no doubt about it. When longsuffering, gentleness, and meekness are in the life, men begin to say to such a one, "Thou art now the blessed of the Lord." As the gentleness of God makes us great, the gentleness of the saints brings to God great glory. Anger hath a temporary sovereignty, that melts in the heat of the sun. Quietness of spirit is king over all the land. If thou canst rule thyself, thou canst rule the world. Isaac conquered by his meekness; for when Abimelech saw that he yielded well after well rather than keep up a quarrel, he said to him, "Thou art now the blessed of the Lord." Some of you do not understand this. "What!" you say, "are we not to stick up for ourselves?" That depends upon whose you are; if you are your own, take care of yourselves; but if you are Christ's, let him take care of you. "But," you say, "if you tread on a worm, it will turn." But surely you will not make a worm your pattern? Nay, but let the meek and lowly Christ be your example, and seek to be a partaker of his Spirit. He prayed even for his murderers, "Father, forgive them," and he ever sought to return good for evil. I pray you to do the same, cultivate a gentle spirit, and even worldlings will say to you, "Thou art now the blessed of the Lord."

Now, while these Philistines saw that God blessed Isaac, *they nevertheless envied him*, as we read in the fourteenth verse. How strange it is that men, who do not care to be blessed of God themselves, envy those who are blessed of him! I heard one say, "It is not just that God should have a chosen people." Sir, do you want to be one of God's people? These blessings which God gives to them, do you want to have them? You may have them, if you will. If you will not have them, I pray you do not quarrel with God because he chooses to give them where he wills. There are two great truths, which from this platform I have proclaimed for many years. The first is, that salvation is free to every man who will have it; the second is, that God gives salvation to a people whom he has chosen; and these truths are not in conflict with one another in the least degree. If you want the blessing of the Lord, have it even now, for my commission as an ambassador of Christ is to beseech men to be reconciled to God; if you do not want it, do not quarrel with God for giving it to his own chosen. It was so with those Philistines—they wanted not Jehovah's blessing, and yet they envied Isaac, who had it.

But while they envied him, *they feared him, and courted his favour.* Do I speak to some young believer who has gone into a house of business, or some Christian woman who has been placed in a family where her religion exposes her to opposition? Let me counsel you to go straight on, taking no notice of the hindrances thrown in your way. You will first be envied; after that you will be feared; and after that you will be sought after, and your company will be desired. If you can only keep as firm as Isaac did, never losing your temper, but always being gentle, and meek, and kind, you will conquer; and you who are to-day despised, will yet come to be honoured, even as Isaac was by the very Abimelech who had, just a little while before, asked him to go away.

A man of God, who was bearing testimony for the faith, on one occasion was pushed into a kennel by a person passing by, who said, as he thrust him in, "There, take that, John Bunyan." He took off his hat, and said, "I will take anything if you give me the name of John Bunyan. I count it such an honour to have that title, that you may do anything you like with me." To be identified with those who have been blessed of the Lord is worth more than all the favours of the world. We are in good company. If men despise you, it matters little when God has blessed you. If they push you into the gutter for being a Christian, take your hat off, and thank them, for it is worth while to bear any scorn, that you may have the honour to be numbered with the followers of Christ. Rest assured that if you will count it a privilege even to be mocked for your faith, those who persecute you to-day, will acknowledge your high position to-morrow. It is a grand thing when any one of us thus gets the testimony of our enemies, "Thou art now the blessed of the Lord."

II. Now, secondly, not only did his enemies thus bear witness to Isaac, saying, "Thou art now the blessed of the Lord;" but THIS WAS ALSO THE TESTIMONY OF THE LORD. It was because he had the witness of God that he was able so to behave as to secure the favourable verdict of the Philistines. Like Enoch before his translation, Isaac "had this testimony, that he pleased God," and was thus meekly able to bear the displeasure of the world. When they hunted him from one well, he digged another, yet all the time he with joy drew "water out of the wells of salvation." He might almost have sat for the picture which Jeremiah drew of the blessed man, centuries afterwards, when he said, "Blessed is the man that trusteth in the Lord, and whose hope the Lord is. For he shall be as a tree planted by the waters, and that spreadeth out her roots by the river, and shall not see when heat cometh, but her leaf shall be green; and shall not be careful in the year of drought, neither shall cease from yielding fruit."

Let us see, then, how Isaac had the testimony of God as to his blessedness.

First, this was the Lord's testimony to him *in promises founded upon the covenant* which he had made with Abraham his father. God said to Isaac, "I will be with thee, and will bless thee." In the third verse of this chapter, the promise is made doubly sure to Isaac when God says, "I will perform the oath which I sware unto Abraham thy father." And in the twenty-fourth verse of the chapter, where the promise is renewed, it is still on the ground of the covenant: "I am with thee, and will bless thee, and multiply thy seed for my servant Abraham's sake." Now, do you know anything of the covenant relationship between God and his people? The bulk of Christians nowadays are wholly ignorant on this subject. The preachers have forgotten it; yet the covenant is the top and bottom of all theology. He that is master of the knowledge of the covenants has the key of true divinity. But the doctrine has gone out of date except with a few old-fashioned people, who are supposed to know no better, but who, in spite of all the taunts of their opponents, cling to the doctrines of grace, and find in them the very marrow and fatness of the truth of God. I love the promises of God because they are covenant promises. God has engaged to keep his word with his people in the person of his dear Son. He has bound himself, by covenant with Christ, and will not, cannot go back from his word; and Christ has fulfilled the conditions of the covenant, and he who hath "brought again from the dead our Lord Jesus, that great Shepherd of the sheep, through the blood of the everlasting covenant," will certainly "make you perfect to do his will, working in you that which is well-pleasing in his sight, through Jesus Christ." The promise is a double promise when it is confirmed in Jesus. Though we are poor and worthless creatures, yet we can say with David, "Although my house be not so with God, yet he hath made with me an everlasting covenant, ordered in all things, and sure." Twice God says by Isaiah, "I have given him for a covenant to the people;" thrice happy are they who receive what God hath given, and who, in Christ, enter into that blessed bond. Beloved, if God has laid the promise home to you by the Spirit, and let you see it as a covenant promise, then God has borne this testimony to you: "Thou art now the blessed of the Lord." Thou art blessed now; thou shalt be blessed all thy life long on earth;

> "And when through Jordan's flood,
> Thy God shall bid thee go,
> His arm shall thee defend,
> And vanquish every foe;
> And in this covenant thou shalt view
> Sufficient strength to bear thee through."

Further, the Lord bore testimony to Isaac *in secret manifestation*. He came to him in the watches of the night, and spake with him face to face. None but those who are the blessed of the Lord have such communion with him. "How is it that thou wilt manifest thyself unto us, and not unto the world?" asked Judas, not Iscariot, at the supper-table, before our Lord's betrayal. Ah, Judas! it is simply because thou art not Iscariot, but a true disciple; else hadst thou never known intimately the presence of Christ. If he manifests himself to us in this choice manner, it is because he has blessed us in a way in which he would not bless the ungodly world. "The secret of the Lord is with them that fear him; and he will shew them his covenant." Do you ever get manifestations of Christ? Is the love of God shed abroad in your heart by the Holy Ghost which is given unto you? Then thou hast a divine attestation that "thou art now the blessed of the Lord."

Isaac also found this testimony, I think, *in divine acceptance of his worship*. We find that "he builded an altar," and then he "pitched his tent." Keep up the altar of God in your home, and keep to the right order—the altar first, and the tent second. When God accepts you there, and makes your family altar to be a place of refreshment and delight to you, you will feel that in thus doing he is giving you the sweet assurance that you are now the blessed of the Lord. It is a pity that there are so many houses nowadays without roofs—I mean, houses of Christian people without family prayer. What are some of you at? If your children turn out ungodly, do you wonder at it, seeing that there is no morning and evening prayer, no reading of the Word of God in your home? In every home where the grace of God is known, there should be an altar, from which should rise the incense of praise, and at which the one sacrifice for sin should be pleaded before God day by day. In the midst of such family piety, which I fear is almost dying out in many quarters, you will get the witness, "Thou art now the blessed of the Lord."

Isaac had another proof that he was blessed of God *in swift chastisement for sin*. He told a lie; he said that Rebekah was his sister, whereas she was his wife. Although that might have seemed to prove that he was not blessed of the Lord, the proof of his blessedness was that he was found out, and became ashamed of it. Worldly people may do wrong, and very likely get off scot-free; but if a Christian man ventures to imitate them, his folly will be found out as surely as he is alive. I notice that if, in business, a Christian man goes off the straight line, he will have an accident in his roguery, and be found out; while other men may do ten times as badly, and never be suspected. Rascals who know not God, and who despise the ordinary morality of honest men, may speculate on the Stock Exchange with other peoples' money, and never be found out; but if you who really love God only do it once, and say, "Well, I feel driven to it," you will be caught out as surely as you live. It is one mark of a child of God, that when he does wrong, he gets a whipping. If I were in the street, and saw strange boys breaking windows, I would say, "Go home, or I will find a policeman for you." But if it were my own boy, I would chastise him myself. I would not meddle with the other boys; but with my own I would. So it is with God; who saith, by the mouth of Amos, to his people, "You only have I known of all the families of the earth: therefore I will punish you for all your iniquities." It is a mark of God's blessing a man, that if the man does wrong, he cannot do it with impunity. Whenever your sins make you smart, thank God; for it is better to smart than it is to sin, and better that the smart should wean you from sin than that something sweet should come in to make you the slave of that sin for ever.

Well, I will not dwell further on this. God testified to Isaac's heart, "Thou art now the blessed of the Lord." May he testify that to each one of you who know his name, and have received his covenant promises! May the words come to you like a benediction from the throne of God, and send you out to testify of his goodness, and to bless him who hath blessed us, saying, "Blessed be the God and Father of our Lord Jesus Christ, who hath blessed us with all spiritual blessings in heavenly places in Christ"!

III. Now, in the third place, I must draw your attention to the fact that, though Isaac was the blessed of the Lord, THIS DID NOT SECURE HIM FROM TRIAL. Already I have approached this part of my subject in speaking of the speedy discovery of his sin; but in addition to this, there were other sorrows not directly resulting from his own conduct, but permitted by God in order that he, who was now blessed, should be still further enriched in character and conduct.

Even before Abimelech saw the source of Isaac's grace, he was "the blessed of the Lord"; yet *he had still to move about*. He was a pilgrim and a stranger, as was his father, and he lived as an alien in the land. He was without any inheritance in the country, and though his flocks and herds increased, he dwelt but in tents, while others reared for themselves stately houses and palaces. But God had prepared some better thing for him, and "he looked for a city which hath foundations, whose Builder and Maker is God." Thus, this trial became a means of blessing to him, as trials always do when sanctified by the Spirit of God. If these words reach any child of God whose nest on earth has been disturbed, whose house has been broken up, I would seek to cheer you by the thought of the "continuing city" which shall soon be your portion. If you have, through Christ, an assurance of an abundant entrance there, though you never have a house of your own on earth, and roam from place to place a stranger, seeming to be very often in the way of other people, yet remember that "thou art now the blessed of the Lord." Daily he doth load thee with benefits, and thou canst even now have thy home in his love.

> "He loves, he knows, he cares,
> Nothing *that* truth can dim;
> He gives the very best to those
> Who leave the choice to him."

In spite of the position of blessedness in which Isaac was placed, *he had enemies to meet*. It is true that, at length, his foes became friends; but the blessing of the Lord did not begin with their friendship; they then discovered and confessed the fact; but Isaac had been "the blessed of the Lord" all along. When Abimelech sent him away, and when "the herdmen of Gerar did strive with Isaac's herdmen," he was not shut out from God's favour. Jehovah never bade him depart, nor took from him his good Spirit. So, tried heart, when foes press around thee, and one thing after another seems to go wrong, do not begin to write bitter things against thyself, as though God had forsaken thee. Remember that it is of the Lord that thou art blessed, and not of men. He will never forsake thee, and his deliverance shall soon make thy heart glad. Even in the midst of the trial, "thou art now the blessed of the Lord," and, like Isaac, after you have drunk of the waters of "contention" and "hatred", you will be brought to Rehoboth, where you shall have "room", yea, even to Beer-sheba, "the well of the oath", or "the seventh well", "the well of satiety", where your enemies shall seek your favour, and glorify your Lord.

Isaac had especially one trial that ate into his very soul; *he had domestic sorrow.* Esau's double marriage with Hittite women was a grief to his father and to his mother; and I mention this because there may be some of God's people who are suffering in the like way. I saw one, some days ago, who said, "I am like the Spartan who carried a fox in his bosom, that ate even to his heart, for I have a thankless, ungrateful child;" and, as he spoke to me, I saw the heart-break of the man. Ah! it may be that some of you are in that condition. If any young man or young woman here is causing that grief to a parent, I pray him or pray her to think of it. You are not heartless, I hope: you have not forgotten your mother's prayers or your father's care of you. Do not kill those who gave you being, or insult and vex those to whom you owe so much. But oh, dear brother or sister, if you have come here broken-hearted about your Esau and all that he is doing, I want to take you by the hand and say, "But still thou art the blessed of the Lord. Let this console thee." What if Abraham has his Ishmael? Yet God blessed him. What if Isaac has his Esau? Yet God blessed him. Bear bravely this trial. Take it to the Lord in prayer. Give God no rest, day or night, till he save thy boy, and bring back thy girl. But still, be not despairing; be not cast down; for it is true of thee—and drink in, I pray thee, this cup of consolation—that "thou art now the blessed of the Lord."

Let me speak two or three earnest words in closing. "Thou art now the blessed of the Lord." "*Now.*" Beloved, do labour to get a hold of a present blessing. If you are indeed saved, do not be always thinking of what you are to enjoy in heaven; but seek to be the blessed of the Lord now. Why not have two heavens, a heaven here and a heaven there? What is the difference between a believer's life here and a believer's life there? Only this: here Christ is with us, and there we are with Christ. If we live up to our privileges, this is the only difference we need to know. Try to be "now the blessed of the Lord." I have heard of a traveller who was followed by a beggar, in Ireland, who very importunately asked for alms. As long as there seemed a chance of getting anything, the old woman kept saying, "May the blessing of God follow your honour all through your life!" but when all hope of a gift vanished, she bitterly added, " and never overtake you." But the blessings which God has for his chosen are not of that slow-footed kind which never catch us up. It is written, "All these blessings shall come on thee, and *overtake thee,* if thou shalt hearken unto the voice of the Lord thy God." I beseech you, then, to lay hold of this overtaking blessing. Let it not pass by unheeded. "Thou art *now* the blessed of the Lord."

Next, be very grateful that you are in this position of grace. You might have been in the drink-shop, you might have been speaking infidelity, you might have been in prison, you might have been in hell. But "thou art now the blessed of the Lord." Wherefore, praise the Lord, whose mercy endureth for ever. If you do not lift up your voice, yet lift up your heart, and bless him for the grace which hath made you to differ from other people.

Again, tell others about it. If "thou art now the blessed of the

Lord," communicate to others the sacred secret that has been the means of bringing such joy to thee. Are we earnest enough about the souls of others? Christian men and women, do you love your fellow-creatures, or do you not? How few there are of us who make it our business to be constantly telling out the sweet story of Jesus and his love! I read, the other day, of a chaplain in the Northern army in the lamentable war in the United States, who, while he lay wounded on the battle-field, heard a man, not far off, utter an oath. Though he himself was so badly wounded that he could not stand, yet he wished to reach the swearer to speak a gospel message to him, and he thought, "I can get to him if I roll over." So, though bleeding profusely himself, he kept rolling over and over, till he got to the side of the poor blasphemer, and on the lone battle-field he preached to him Jesus. Some other men came along, and he said to them, "Can you carry me? I fear that I am dying, but I do not want to be taken off the field. I should like you, if you would, to carry me from one dying man to another, all the night long, that I might tell them of a Saviour." What a splendid deed was this! A bleeding man talking to those who were full of sin about a Saviour's bleeding wounds! Oh, you who have no wound, who can walk, and possess all the faculties to fit you for the service, how often you miss opportunities, and refuse to speak of Jesus! "Thou art now the blessed of the Lord," and at this moment I would have you think that the blessed Lord lays his pierced hand on thee, saying, "Go and tell others what I have done for thee." Never cease to tell the divine tale, as opportunity is given, until thy voice is lost in death; then thy spirit shall begin to utter the story in the loftier sphere.

You are coming to the Lord's table, and I invite you, beloved, to come here with much love. Do not come with doubts and fears, with a cold or lukewarm heart. Remember "Thou art now the blessed of the Lord." Come, eat his flesh, and drink his blood. There, on the table, thou wilt see nothing but the emblems of his flesh and blood; but, if thou believest, Christ will feed thee spiritually upon himself, and as thou dost eat that bread of heaven, and drink that wine of life, thou mayest well hear a voice saying, "Thou art now the blessed of the Lord."

Well do I remember the time when I would have given my eyes to be as a dog under the table, to have eaten only the crumbs which fell, as others feasted, and now for forty-and-one years to-day I have sat as a child at the table, blessed be his name!

As I told our friends this morning, this day is an anniversary of peculiar interest to me. Forty-and-one years ago I went down into the river, and was baptized into the name of the Father, and of the Son, and of the Holy Ghost.

> " Yet have been upheld till now:
> Who could hold me up but thou ? "

May you, each of you, as you come to the table, hear a voice saying in your heart, "Now a believer; now justified; now quickened; now regenerate; now in Christ; now dear to the heart of God. 'Thou art now the blessed of the Lord.' "

Oh, that some who came in here without the blessing would get it before they go! He that believeth in Jesus hath all the blessing which Jesus can give to him; forgiveness for the past; grace for the present; and glory for the future. "Blessed are they that have not seen, and yet have believed," is the word of the Lord to thee, thou doubter. He was made a curse for thee, that he might redeem thee from the curse of the broken law, for it is written, "Cursed is every one that hangeth on a tree." He hung on the tree for guilty man. Believe thou in him, and as thou believest, eternal joys shall come streaming down into thy dry and desolate heart, and it shall be said to thee, "Thou art now the blessed of the Lord." You shall be blessed now, and blessed for evermore! God grant it, for our Lord Jesus Christ's sake! Amen.

PORTION OF SCRIPTURE READ BEFORE SERMON—Genesis xxvi.

HYMNS FROM "OUR OWN HYMN BOOK"—758, 757, 786.

LETTER FROM MR. SPURGEON.

DEAR FRIENDS,—I have received letters from readers who speak of reading *with interest* the notes at the end of the sermons. I feared that these jottings had become monotonous, and therefore I am amazed that they should interest so many. I am not able, like Paganini, to discourse sweet music on a single string; and therefore I impute the *interest* spoken of to the love of the reader rather than to the genius of the writer. We are always interested in the smallest details of the lives of those we greatly love.

This present note may record the fact that, on the last evening of 1891, and in the morning of New Year's Day, 1892, I gave two short addresses to about a dozen friends in this hotel. My silence of more than half a year is ending. The chirping of the first spring birds is heard in my land. It is true that I sat down, and talked my little piece, and that I felt glad when it came to an end; but still it has been done, and he that was almost numbered with the dead is now beginning to speak in the ears of the living.

These two little talks, only of interest to my own friends, will probably be preserved in *The Sword and the Trowel* for February, for Mr. Harrald took them down in shorthand. You will all guess how happy I am, for I have now some signs and tokens of returning strength; and I am praising God with all my heart for such a wonderful restoration.

To friends who have lovingly kept up the funds for the various institutions, I send my heartiest thanks, and to all well-wishers my kindest regards.

Yours to serve till death,

Hôtel Beau Rivage, Menton,   C. H. SPURGEON.
January 2, 1892.

Metropolitan Tabernacle Pulpit.

IS GOD IN THE CAMP?

A Sermon

INTENDED FOR READING ON LORD'S-DAY, JANUARY 17TH, 1892,

DELIVERED BY

C. H. SPURGEON,

AT THE METROPOLITAN TABERNACLE, NEWINGTON,

On Thursday Evening, April 9th, 1891.

"And the Philistines were afraid, for they said, God is come into the camp. And they said, Woe unto us! for there hath not been such a thing heretofore."—1 Samuel iv. 7.

ISRAEL was out of gear with God. The people had forgotten the Most High, and had gone aside to the worship of Baal. They had neglected the things of God; therefore they were given up to their enemies. When Jehovah had brought them out of Egypt, he instructed them how they were to live in the land to which he would bring them, and warned them that if they forsook him they would be chastened. His words were plain: "If ye will not for all this hearken unto me, but walk contrary unto me; then I will walk contrary unto you also in fury; and I, even I, will chastise you seven times for your sins." In fulfilment of this threatening, the Philistines had been divinely permitted to make great havoc of the idolatrous Israelites, and to hold them in cruel slavery.

The only way for them to get out of their trouble was to return to God, who, by his judgments, seemed to say, "Hear ye the rod, and who hath appointed it." The only cure for their hurt was to go back with repentance, and renew their faith and their covenant with God. Then all would have been right. But this is the last thing that men will do. Our minds, by nature, love not spiritual things. We will attend to any outward duty, or to any external rite; but to bring our hearts into subjection to the divine will, to bow our minds to the Most High, and to serve the Lord our God with all our heart, and all our soul, the natural man abhors. Yet nothing less than this will suffice to turn our captivity.

Instead of attempting to get right with God, these Israelites set about devising superstitious means of securing the victory over their foes. In this respect most of us have imitated them. We think of a thousand inventions; but we neglect the one thing needful. I may be addressing some who, at this time, are passing through a sore trial, and

No. 2,239.

who therefore think that they must have forgotten some little thing in connection with the externals of religion, instead of seeing that it matters little what outward observance they may neglect, so long as they do not possess the faith, without which it is impossible to please God. They forget the main matter, which is to enthrone God in the life, and to seek to do his will by faith in Christ Jesus. Get right with God; confess thy sin; believe in Jesus Christ, the appointed Saviour; be reconciled to God by the death of his Son; then all will be right between thee and the Father in heaven. We cannot bring men to this, apart from the Spirit of God.

In this sermon I shall have to show you how often, and in how many ways, men seek other methods of cure than the only one, namely, to take the case to God. They heal their hurt slightly. They cry, "Peace! peace!" where there is no peace, and adopt a thousand devious devices rather than accept the only remedy provided by the Great Physician for sin-sick souls. Instead of seeking to become right with God, these Israelites thought that, if they could get the ark of the covenant, which had been the symbol of Jehovah's presence, and bring it from the tent of Shiloh into the midst of their camp, they would then be certain of victory. So they sent and fetched the ark; and when it came into the camp, they were as enthusiastic as if their banners already waved over a victorious host; they lifted up their voices so loudly, that the earth rang again with their shouts, while the Philistines, hearing their exulting shout, and finding out the reason, were greatly afraid. With fearful hearts, and trembling lips, already counting that all was lost, their enemies turned to one another, and said, "God is come into the camp. Woe unto us! for there hath not been such a thing heretofore."

In considering this subject, we will think, first, of *the great mistake* which both Israel and the Philistines made. In the second place, we will consider *the great truth* of which their mistake was a caricature. God *does* come into the camp when his people go forth to fight in his name; and when he really comes, the tide of battle is turned. When I have spoken on these two things, I shall close, as God shall help me, by speaking upon *the great lessons* which all this will teach us, lessons which lie almost upon the very surface of the narrative.

I. First, then, let us consider THE GREAT MISTAKE which both Israelites and Philistines made. The Israelites, instead of seeking to God himself, went to Shiloh to fetch the ark of the covenant. The ark was the sacred place where God revealed himself in the days when his people truly served him; but it was devoid of power, without the presence of him who dwelt between the cherubim. The Israelites were mistaken, for they shouted long before they were "out of the wood." Before they had won any victory, the sight of the ark made them boastful and confident. The Philistines fell into an error of a different kind, for they were frightened without any real cause. They said, "God is come into the camp;" whereas God had not come at all. It was only the ark with the cherubim upon it; God was not there.

The mistake they made was just this: *they mistook the visible for the invisible.* It has pleased God, even in our holy faith, to give us some external symbols—water, and bread, and wine. They are so simple, that it does seem, at first sight, as if men could never have made them objects of worship, or used them as instruments of a kind of witchcraft. One would have thought that these symbols would only have been like windows of agate and gates of carbuncle, through which men would behold the Saviour, and draw near to him. Instead thereof, some have neither looked through the windows nor passed through the gates, but have ascribed to the gates and the windows that which is only to be found in him who is behind them both. It is sad, indeed, when the symbol takes the place of the Saviour! Man is by nature both an atheist and an idolater. These are two shades of the same thing. We want, if we do worship at all, something that we can see. But a god that can be seen is no god; and so the idolater is first cousin to the atheist. He has a god which is no god, for he cannot be a god if he can be apprehended by human senses. This ark of the covenant, which was but a chest of wood covered with gold, with angelic figures on the lid, was simply a token of the presence of God with his people; and these Israelites transformed it into a sacred object, to be highly reverenced, to be worshipped, and, as it appears, to be trusted in. The elders said, "Let us fetch the ark of the covenant of the Lord out of Shiloh unto us, that, when *it* cometh among us, *it* may save us out of the hand of our enemies." They ascribed to the ark what could only be done by God himself. This is the tendency of us all. Anything which we can see, we pine after. Hence we lean upon an arm of flesh: we trust in man, though it is written plainly enough, "Cursed be the man that trusteth in man, and maketh flesh his arm, and whose heart departeth from the Lord." Yet, still we want some symbol, some token, something before our eyes; and if it can be something artistic, so much the better. We lay hold of something beautiful, that will charm the eye, and produce a kind of sensuous feeling, and straightway we mistake our transient emotion for spiritual worship and true reverence. This is the great mistake that many still make; they think that God has come into the camp merely because some outward religious rite or ceremony has been observed, or because some sacred shrine has been set up among them.

These Israelites fell into another mistake, which is also often made to-day: *they preferred office to character.* In their distress, instead of calling upon God, they sent for Hophni and Phinehas. Why did their hearts turn to them? Simply because they were priests, and the people had come to hold the sacred office in such superstitious reverence that they thought that was everything. But these young men were sinners against the Lord exceedingly; they were not even moral men, much less were they spiritual men. They made the house of God to be abhorred, and dishonoured the Lord before all Israel. Yet, because they happened to hold the office of the priesthood, they were put in the place of God. Dear friends, this is a kind of feeling which many indulge. They think they shall be saved if they have a Levite for their priest. They imagine that the worship of God must be conducted properly, because the man who conducts it is in the apostolic succession, and has been duly ordained. You shall see a man eminent for the holiness of his life, for the disinterestedness of his character, for the fidelity of his preaching, for his power in prayer, for the blessing that rests upon his ministry in the conversion of sinners; but he is counted a mere nobody, because he lacks the superstitious qualification which deluded men think so necessary. Here are Hophni and Phinehas, two of the grossest sinners in all the land of Israel; but then, you see, they are in the line of Aaron, and so they are trusted, and indeed are put in the place of God. Now, God forbid that we should say a word against the house of Aaron, or against any who speak in the name of the Lord, whom God has truly called unto his work! But, beloved, this work is not a mere matter of pedigree; it is a question of the abiding presence of God with a man and in a man. Unless God be with the minister whom you hear, to what purpose do you listen? If the leader of the church be not one who walks with God, where will he lead you? "If the blind lead the blind, both shall fall into the ditch." The blind man may wear a badge on his arm to show that he is a certificated guide; but will you be saved from the ditch simply because he belongs to the order of guides, and has his certificate with him? Be not led away by any such vain notion. Yet this is the error into which many have fallen in all ages of the church.

But these people who faced the Philistines made another mistake: *they confounded enthusiasm with faith.* When they saw the ark, they shouted so that the earth rang again. "These are the kind of people I like," says one, "people that can shout." If that is all you want, why do you not go among the bulls of Bashan, and make your home in the midst of them? They can make more noise than any mortal men can make. These Israelites shouted, but there was nothing in their noise, any more than there is in their modern imitators. Anyone who had passed the camp of Israel, that day, might have said that they had "a bright, cheerful, happy service; just the kind of service the people like, you know: nothing dull about it." Hark! how the glad sound rises! Surely these people must have great faith! No, they had not a scrap of the real article. They were under a mistake all the time; and, shout as they might, they had very little to shout about; for in a short time their carcases strewed the plain. The Philistines put an end to their shouting. Now, beloved, when you are worshipping God, shout if you are filled with holy gladness. If the ejaculation comes from your heart, I would not ask you to restrain it. God forbid that we should judge any man's worship! But do not be so foolish as to suppose that because there is loud noise there must also be faith. Faith is a still water, it floweth deep. True faith in God may express itself with leaping and with shouting; and it is a happy thing when it does: but it can also sit still before the Lord, and that perhaps is a happier thing still. Praise can sit silent on the lip, and yet be heard in heaven. There is a passion of the heart too deep for words. There are feelings that break the backs of words; the mind staggers and trembles beneath the weight of them. Frost of the mouth often comes with thaw of the soul; and when the heart's great deeps are breaking up, it sometimes happens that the mouth is not large enough to let the torrents flow, and so it has to be comparatively silent. Do not, therefore, make the mistake of confounding enthusiasm with faith in judging the externals of worship, else you may fall into a thousand blunders. He may worship God who shouts till the earth rings again, and God may accept him; but he may worship God as truly who sits in silence before the Most High, and says not even a word. It is the spiritual worship which is acceptable to God, not the external in any form or shape. It is the heart that has fellowship with the Lord; and it needs little in the way of expressing itself, neither has God tied it down to this way or to that. It may find its own methods of utterance so long as it is truly " moved by the Holy Ghost."

Another mistake these people made that day was this: *they valued novelty above Scriptural order.* "The Philistines were afraid, for they said, God is come into the camp. And they said, Woe unto us! for there hath not been such a thing heretofore." The Israelites probably made the same mistake, fixing their hope on this new method of fighting the Philistines, which they hoped would bring them victory. We are all so apt to think that the new plan of going to work will be much more effective than those that have become familiar; but it is not so. It is generally a mistake to exchange old lamps for new. "There hath not been such a thing heretofore." There is a glamour about the novelty which misleads us, and we are liable to think the newer is the truer. If there has not been such a thing heretofore, some people will take to it at once for that very reason. "Oh," says the man who is given to change, "that is the thing for me!" But it is probably not the thing for a true-hearted and intelligent Christian, for if "there hath not been such a thing heretofore," it is difficult to explain, if the thing be a good one, why the Holy Ghost, who has been with the people of God since Pentecost, and who came to lead us into all truth, has not led the Church of God to this before. If your new discovery is the mind of God, where has Holy Scripture been all these centuries? Believing in the infallible Word and the abiding Spirit, I rather suspect your novelty; at least, I cannot say that I endorse it until I have tested it by the Word of God. "Oh, but we had such a meeting! There never was the like of it," you say. Probably you ought to pray that there may never be the like of it again, for, after all, the meetings in which hearts become broken before God, and in which men believe in the Lord Jesus Christ, the same Saviour who saved their forefathers, who have entered into glory, are no novelty. Those meetings in which men come and give themselves up to God, where "the great transaction" is done, where they become the Lord's, and he becomes theirs, are very old-fashioned things; they have been heretofore. "We have heard with our ears, O God, our fathers have told us what work thou didst in their days, in the times of old:" and if we could only see the like, we would not ask to be able to say, "There hath not been such a thing heretofore." Philistines may like a thing that has not been heretofore; but we like the thing that has been since the days of Pentecost, the things that come from him who is "the same yesterday, and to-day, and for ever"; the workings of that God who changes not, "with whom is no variableness, neither shadow of turning." Let him work his blessed will; and if he chooses to send a new thing on the earth, we will glorify his name; but because there are new things in the world, we will not ascribe them to him, for they may come from quite another quarter. We remember that "Lo, here is Christ, or there!" was the cry against which our Lord warned his disciples. Concerning such a cry the Saviour said, "Believe it not." To you, dear friends, I would say—Stand fast by your great Leader, the blessed, unchangeable Christ, and by the faith once for all delivered to the saints, or else you will be on the road to a thousand blunders.

The mistake made on that battle-field is a mistake which nowadays is frequently imitated. It assumes many forms. We fall into their error when we *confound ritual and spirituality*. Now, every form of religion has its ritual. The Quaker, who sits still, and does not say a word, has a ritual so far; and he that has a thousand rites and ceremonies has a ritual so much farther. But if I have gone through the general routine of the worship of my church, and then think that I have done something acceptable to God, while yet my heart has not communed with him in humble repentance, or faith, or love, or joy, or consecration, I make a great mistake. You may keep on with your religious performances for seventy years or more; you may never miss what our Scotch friends call "a diet of worship"; you may not neglect a single rubric in the whole ritual; but it is all nothing unless the soul has fellowship with God. Godliness is a spiritual thing; for "God is a Spirit; and they that worship him must worship him in spirit and in truth." So far as our forms of worship help us towards this spiritual communion, they are good, but no farther. "Oh, well!" says one, "I never worship beneath a cathedral roof; I am quite content to meet with a few friends in a barn." Do not suppose, my friend, that the meagreness of your accessories has necessarily secured true worship. If thou hast met God in the barn, it is well; and if thy brother has met God in the cathedral, it is also well; but if neither of you has really come to God in the right spirit, I care but little for thy barn, and I care even less for his cathedral. What does it signify how thou hast garnished thine offering if it be not a living sacrifice, acceptable to God by Jesus Christ? A dead thing must not be brought to the altar of God. Remember that, under the Jewish law, they never offered fish upon the altar, because they could not bring it there alive. Everything brought to God as a sacrifice must be alive. Its blood must be poured out warm at the altar's foot. Oh, that you and I might feel that lifting of the soul to God, and that buoyancy of heart, which true spiritual worship alone can bring to us! May our ritual, whether we have much or little, be our guide to God, and not our chain to hold us back from God!

We fall into the same blunder that the Israelites and Philistines made if we *consider orthodoxy to be salvation*. We have secured much that is worth keeping when we have, intellectually and intelligently, laid hold on that divinely-revealed truth, "the gospel of the grace of God"; but we have not obtained everything even then. O sirs, if it were possible for you to believe every word of Christ's teaching, if it were possible to hold with only an intellectual faith the teaching of the apostles, rejecting all besides, and to hold it with an accuracy so great that in no jot or tittle you had made a mistake, it would profit you nothing; for "except a man be born again, he cannot see the kingdom of God." He may understand these things so as to be a theologian, but he must have them wrought into his soul by the Holy Ghost so as to make him a saint, or else he has not really understood them at all. Unless these are thy meat and thy drink, they are nothing to thee; unless thou findest Christ in them, thou wilt find in them thy ruin, they shall be the "savour of death" unto thee. Remember, it was a beautiful tomb in which the dead Christ was laid; but he left it, and there was nothing there but grave-clothes after he had gone; and, in like manner, the best-constructed system of theology, if it has not Christ in it, and if he who holds it be not himself spiritually alive, is nothing more than a tomb in which are trappings for the dead. It is nothing better than a gilded ark, without the presence of God; and although you may shout, and say, "God is come into the camp," it will not be so.

We fall into the same error if we *regard routine as security*, and think that, because we have often done a thing, and have not suffered for it, therefore it will be always well with us. We are all such creatures of habit that, at length, our repeated actions seem to be natural and right. Because sentence against their evil works is not executed speedily, therefore the heart of the sons of men is fully set in them to do evil. But though Pompeii may slumber long at the foot of Vesuvius, at length it is overwhelmed. It behoves every one of us to try our ways, and specially to call in question things which have become a sort of second nature to us. This is the fault of which Peter gives warning concerning the scoffers of the last days, who will say with regard to the blessed truth of Christ's second advent, "Where is the promise of his coming? for since the fathers fell asleep, all things continue as they were from the beginning of the creation." The apostle says of such that "they willingly are ignorant," and therefore are they wilfully ignorant of the terrible and unalterable doom that awaits them at the coming of their Judge.

Thus, like the Israelites, we may shout as we see the ark of the covenant, although our sins have driven the Lord far from us; or, like the Philistines, we may say, "God is come into the camp," and yet he may not be there at all in the sense in which they meant. Thus I might continue to illustrate my text; but time would fail me, and I have yet to speak upon two other points.

II. Having considered the great mistake these people made, I will draw your attention, in the second place, to THE GREAT TRUTH of which their mistake was a caricature. Though what the Philistines said, and what the Israelites thought, on this occasion, was false, it is often true. God does come to the camp of his people, and his presence is the great power of his church. O brethren, what joy comes to us at such a time! I will briefly sketch the scene that takes place when God comes into the camp.

Then, *the truth of the gospel becomes vital*. The doctrines of grace have then with them the grace of the doctrines. Then is Christ not only to us the Truth, but he is also the Way and the Life. The gospel then becomes a sword with two edges, and it does marvellous execution. The Word of God then shows itself to be both a hammer and a fire, smiting and melting those upon whom its power is proved.

Whoever preaches the gospel, when God has come into the camp, speaks with power. He may have little eloquence, and less learning; but if God is with him, and if his heart is all aglow with divine love, he will speak with power, and the people will say, "Surely, God is in this place, and we know it."

When God comes into the camp, *new life is put into prayer*. Instead of the repetition of holy phrases in a cold, feeble, lifeless fashion, the soul empties itself out before the Lord, like water flowing from a fountain; and men and women cry mightily unto him, laying hold upon the horns of the altar; and they come away with both hands full of heaven's own blessing, for they have prevailed with God by mighty wrestling.

By the presence of God in the camp *fresh energy is thrown into service*. There is a way of serving the Lord in which men do the proper thing while they are fast asleep. I am afraid much of our service for God is done when we are asleep, and that it is accompanied by a kind of celestial snoring, instead of being performed when our spiritual faculties are all alert, and the whole man is wide awake. But when God comes into the camp, how he shakes men up, and awakens the slumberers from their dreams! What a quickening, what a vivifying, the presence of God gives! I remember a picture on the Continent that strangely represents the resurrection. Some of the people, who are pictured as being raised from the dead, have some of their bones coming together; others have their heads covered with flesh, but the rest of their body is a skeleton; and nothing seems complete in this strange, wild conception of a mad artist. But there are hundreds of Christian people who seem to be spiritually in as incomplete a stage as those people were supposed to be. They are, I hope, quickened from the dead, but they are not yet fully alive unto God. Some of them are still dead in their head; their intellect has not yet been sanctified: some of them are dead at their hands; they cannot get them into their pockets, or if they manage so much as that, they cannot get them out again: some are dead at heart, they seem to know things very well with the brain, but not to feel them in the soul. But when the Lord comes to us with power, he makes us alive all over; every part of the man is quickened with a divine energy; then men really work for Jesus, and work successfully, too.

When God comes into the camp, his presence *convinces unbelievers*. Sinners turn to the Lord on the right hand, and on the left, in so marvellous a way that our weak faith is often quite astonished. The last persons in the world that we expected to be converted, come to our services, and there find Christ; and many that have been hearers for years, but seemed harder than the lower millstone, become soft as wax to the divine Word. When God comes into the camp, the Holy Ghost convinces men "of sin, of righteousness, and of judgment", the arrows of conviction fly fast and far, and pierce the hearts of the foemen of the King, and the slain of the Lord are many.

The presence of God, moreover, *comforts mourners*. When God comes into the camp, those who are troubled and tried begin to wipe away the tears of sorrow, and feel strengthened to bear their burdens; or, better still, they cast their care on him who is so manifestly near. Our hearts are also cheered by seeing anxious sinners turn their eyes towards the cross of Christ. Then Jesus reveals his love to them, and they perceive it; they fly into his arms, and find salvation there. Oh, what joyful times we have had of late in talking with many who have yielded themselves to Christ, and taken him to be all their salvation, and all their desire! May God stay in the camp with us till every sinner that comes within our ranks, and many also who are outside, shall come to Jesus, and be saved!

When God is in the camp, his presence *infuses daring into faith.* Feeble men begin to grow vigorous, young men dream dreams, and old men see visions. Many begin to plot and plan something for Jesus which, in their timid days, they would never have thought of attempting. Others reach a height of consecration that seems to verge on imprudence. Alabaster boxes get broken, and the precious ointment is poured out upon the Master's head, even though Judas shakes his money-bag, and cries, "To what purpose is this waste?" Adventurers for God are raised up—men like the Portuguese navigators, who passed the Cape of Storms, and called it ever afterwards the Cape of Good Hope. Men begin to mission the slums, the lodging-houses, the dark streets, and after a while those very places become happy hunting-grounds for other Christian workers. Because God is in the camp, many take up the work which at first only the truly brave believer dared to try.

The fact of God being in the camp cannot be hidden, for in a delightful way it *distils joy into worship.* People do not think sermons dull when God is in the camp; and prayer-meetings are not then called "stupid affairs." The saints enjoy fellowship with one another; and when Christian people meet each other, and God is in the camp, they have many a happy word to exchange concerning their Master. Many such seasons we have enjoyed. It has been with us as with the people mentioned by the prophet Malachi: "Then they that feared the Lord spake often one to another: and the Lord hearkened, and heard it, and a book of remembrance was written before him for them that feared the Lord, and that thought upon his name." They had such holy talk that God himself turned eaves-dropper to listen to what they had to say; he liked it so well that he put it down; and he thought so much of it that he said that he would preserve it; and a book of remembrance was made for them that feared the Lord, and that thought upon his name. May there be many more such books of remembrance in our day!

I cannot tell you what innumerable blessings come to the camp of the spiritual Israel when God is there. I hope that we know a little of this even now; and I am sure we want to know a great deal more of it. It is hard work preaching when God is not in the camp. It must be slavery to teach in the Sunday-school when God is not in the camp. And any of you that are seeking souls must have a heavy drag on your spirits when the Lord is away. We might pray on Sabbath mornings, indeed, every day, and before every duty, "If thy presence go not with me, carry us not up hence;" but if the Lord be in the camp, then the wheels no longer drag heavily, but, like the chariots of Amminadib, we fly before the wind. Everything is done gladly, happily, thankfully, believingly, when "God is come into the camp." May he abide in our midst, and may our eyes be opened to see him!

> "Thrice blest is he to whom is given
> The instinct that can tell
> That God is in the field, when he
> Is most invisible."

III. Now, in closing our meditations upon this passage, let us try to learn THE GREAT LESSONS which this incident teaches us.

The first lesson is that which I have been insisting upon all through: *the necessity of the divine presence.* Dear friends, you acknowledge this. There is not one among us who does not know that the Holy Ghost is needful to effect any work. But I am afraid that it is something which we know so well, that we have put it up on a shelf, and there it lies unheeded. But it must not be so with thee, my brother, nor with me. We must pray in the Holy Ghost, or else we shall not pray at all; and we must preach under the influence of the Holy Ghost, or else we shall chatter like sparrows on the window-sill in the morning, and nothing will come of our chattering. Only the Holy Ghost can make anything we do to be effectual. Therefore never begin any work without the Holy Ghost, and do not dare to go on with the impetus that you have gained, but cry again for the Holy Spirit. The "amen" of the sermon needs to be spoken in the power of the Holy Ghost just as much as the first word of the discourse, and every word between the first and the last. Let all your service for God be in the Spirit, or else it is all good for nothing.

Learn, next, that *we should do all we can to obtain the presence of God in the camp.* If there are any preparations which we can make for his coming, let us set about them at once. You who are out of Christ must not think that there is anything for *you* to do before you receive Christ. All the doing has been done.

> "Jesus did it, did it all,
> Long, long ago."

But I am now addressing the people of God, and if we would have God to come very nigh to us, we must prepare the way of the Lord, and make straight in the desert a highway for our God. What can we do to obtain the presence of God in our midst? My time has so far gone that I can only give you a few hints as to what we ought to do if we want to secure that end.

We must confess our helplessness without God, and honestly mean the confession. The first thing that is required of us is to bemoan the fact that, by and of ourselves, we can do nothing; even as our Lord said to his disciples, "Without me ye can do nothing." The sooner we recognize this truth, the better. Our half-doing is our undoing; but when we cease from self, then we make way for God.

We must, next, have a universal desire for the presence of God with us. I mean by that, that every Christian man and every Christian woman must agonize with God that he would come into the camp; not merely some few of us desiring it, but all of us vehemently crying unto the Lord, "Come, Lord, and tarry not."

We must also be very careful in our lives. God will not come to an unholy church. The sacred Dove will never come to a foul nest. There must be a purging and a cleansing, or else he will not come.

Moreover, there must be a conscientious obedience to his word, a strict adherence to his truth, his doctrine, his precepts, to the whole of Christ's rule and law. He will not prosper us unless we are careful to follow every step that he has taken. God help us to have this conscientious care, this coming out from those who may not be thus careful, according to his word, "Come out from among them, and be ye separate, saith the Lord, and touch not the unclean thing; and I will receive you, and will be a Father unto you, and ye shall be my sons and daughters, saith the Lord Almighty."

If we desire this special sense of God's presence, there must be unbroken union. The Spirit of God does not love fighting. He is a dove, and he will not come where there is constant strife. We must be as one man in our love to one another. It was when the disciples were "with one accord in one place" that the Holy Spirit was given on the day of Pentecost; and thus it is in all our Pentecostal seasons. Often a stone seems to lie at the well's-mouth of our choicest blessings; and it cannot be rolled away "until all the flocks be gathered together."

To crown all, there must be a hearty reliance upon God, and a childlike confidence in him. I would recommend you either to believe in God up to the hilt, or else not to believe at all. Believe this Book of God, every letter of it, or else reject it. There is no logical standing-place between the two. Be satisfied with nothing less than a faith that swims in the deeps of divine revelation; a faith that paddles about the edge of the water is poor faith at the best, it is little better than a dry-land faith, and is not good for much. Oh, I pray you, do believe in God, and his omnipotence!

Such are the conditions of obtaining the blessing of God's abiding presence. If these things be in us and abound, we shall be able to shout without making any mistake about the matter, "God has come into the camp."

When God does come to us, *we should seek by all means to retain his presence.* How can this boon be secured?

First, by humble walking with God. If we grow proud because we are honoured by our King's company, and begin to think that there must be, after all, something in us to attract God to us, and cause his face to shine upon us, we shall not long have the Lord among us. Seek, then, to be lowly in his presence.

Next, let much grateful praise be given to him from loyal hearts. If God is saving sinners, let us give him the glory of it. If he is at work among us, let us not go and talk about what *we* have been doing; but let us tell to men and angels, too, what HE has done. Let us never dare to handle God's jewels as if they were our own.

Moreover, there must be perpetual watchfulness. If God be with us, he may give us a great victory, and yet to-morrow we may be defeated because Achan has hidden the goodly Babylonish garment and the wedge of gold. Unless we are sober and vigilant, we may sadly have to mourn that the Lord has withdrawn his presence from us. There is a fierce light that beats around his throne. "Our God is a consuming fire." "Who among us shall dwell with the devouring fire? who among us shall dwell with everlasting burnings?" The Scriptural answer is, "He that walketh righteously, and speaketh uprightly." May God make us men of such calibre as can endure that heat!

And, lastly, there must be an individual fellowship with God on the part of each one of us. It is hard work for the whole church to walk with God every day and all the day; but if each member will see to it that his own personal life is right, the church, as a whole, need fear nothing. Let each one look after his own life, and see that all is right there; then the life of the church will soon be at flood-tide, and when we go forth to the battle, the Philistines will know of a truth that "God is come into the camp." May God speedily raise us all up to this point of personal consecration!

Dear friends, we are having sinners saved in our midst; pray for them. Some are struggling towards the light; seek to help them. If you meet with any such, love them, and cherish them, as a father does his child. I cannot speak longer. Your hearts must tell you what to do. Go on serving the Lord. May he abide with us in power for evermore! Amen.

PORTION OF SCRIPTURE READ BEFORE SERMON—1 Samuel iv.

HYMNS FROM "OUR OWN HYMN BOOK"—968, 448, 992.

LETTER FROM MR. SPURGEON.

BELOVED FRIENDS,—The one want of the church in these times is indicated by the title of this sermon. The presence of God, in saving power, in the church, will put an end to the present plague of infidelity. Men will not doubt his Word when they feel his Spirit. It will be the only security for the success of missionary effort. If God be with his people, they will soon see crowds converted and added to the church. For a thousand reasons, we need that Jehovah should come into the camp, as aforetime he visited and delivered his people from bondage in Egypt.

Could we not all unite in prayer for this as fervently as all united in prayer for my life? It is a far greater and more necessary subject for intercession, and the Lord will not be slow to hear us. Come to thy church, O Lord, in fulness of power to save! If the Great Advent is not yet, indulge us with outpourings of grace, and times of refreshing!

Oh, that all Christendom would take up this pleading, and continue it until the answer came!

Receive, dear readers, my hearty salutations. Personally, I scarcely make progress during this broken weather; but the doctor says I hold my own, and that is more than he could have expected. Whether I live or die, I would say, in the words of Israel to Joseph, "God shall be with you."

Yours ever heartily,

C. H. SPURGEON.

Menton, Jan. 9, 1892.

Metropolitan Tabernacle Pulpit.

A CHALLENGE AND A SHIELD.

A Sermon

INTENDED FOR READING ON LORD'S-DAY, JANUARY 24TH, 1892,

DELIVERED BY

C. H. SPURGEON,

AT THE METROPOLITAN TABERNACLE, NEWINGTON,

On Lord's-day Evening, August 24th, 1890.

"Who is he that condemneth? It is Christ that died."—Romans viii. 34.

HERE are two very wonderful challenges thrown out by the apostle Paul. First, he boldly defies anyone to charge the chosen of God with sin: "Who shall lay any thing to the charge of God's elect?" and then, even if any charges should be brought against them, he defies all our foes to secure an adverse verdict: "Who is he that condemneth?" This would be a very bold challenge even for a man who had been righteous from his youth up. If there had ever been a man, in the history of the world, who from his infancy had known God, and who had grown up serving him, devoting himself entirely to the cause of the Lord Christ; and if he had kept the commandments without fail, as far as man could judge, it would be a very hazardous thing even for him to say, "Who is he that condemneth?" For human righteousness is only human; being human, it is finite; and, being finite, it falls short somewhere or other. The best of men are but men at the best; to be a man is to be a fallen creature, and being fallen creatures, we cannot of ourselves perfectly please the thrice-holy Jehovah. In many things we all offend.

The man who uttered this challenge, "Who is he that condemneth?" and uttered it under the inspiration of God, did not, however, occupy the position of a sinless man. His early years had been spent in opposition to his Saviour. He had been exceedingly mad against the disciples of Christ, and had persecuted them even unto strange cities. In another place he calls himself the very chief of sinners; and yet it is this man who dares to ask the question, "Who is he that condemneth?" It is a bold, brave challenge; but it never could have been uttered by Paul if it had not been accompanied by that next sentence, "It is Christ that died." First, he flings down the gauntlet, and challenges a battle, crying, "Who is he that condemneth?" And then he holds up a shield so broad that he

No. 2,240.

is completely concealed behind it, and every enemy is defeated in the conflict, because "It is Christ that died." Happy shall you and I be if, though covered with sin, though guilty and unclean, we nevertheless shall have faith to believe in the Christ that died, a faith so trong and confident that we shall dare to stand both now, and at the judgment-seat of Christ, and say, "Who is he that condemneth?" May we have this faith on our dying bed, when the pulse is faint and feeble, and heart and flesh begin to fail! May we still, between the very jaws of death, have solid confidence in God, and dare to ask, in the presence of men and devils, too, "Who is he that condemneth?" being made bold to do so because we have believed in the Christ that died.

Paul has, in this case, only one answer to the question, "Who is he that condemneth?" He meets it by the blessed fact that "It is Christ that died." I recommend that we should, each one of us, have but one hope of salvation. As long as we have half-a-dozen, we have half-a-dozen doubtful ones: but when it comes to only one, and that such a sufficient one as the truth that "It is Christ that died," we have a well-founded hope, in which we may rest with confidence. Such a hope as this is "an anchor of the soul, both sure and stedfast"; and the man who has this anchor on board the barque of his life can never suffer spiritual shipwreck. When the Emperor Charles the Fifth went to war with Francis the First, King of France, he sent a herald to him declaring war in the name of the Emperor of Germany, King of Castille, King of Aragon, King of Naples, King of Sicily, and he went on with many more titles, giving his sovereign all the honours that were his due. When the herald of Francis the First took up the gage of battle, he would not be outdone in the list of honours, so he said, "I take up the challenge in the name of Francis the First, King of France; Francis the First, King of France; Francis the First, King of France; Francis the First, King of France; Francis the First, King of France." He just repeated his master's name and office as many times as the other gentleman had titles. So it is a grand thing, whenever Satan comes and begins to accuse you, just to say, "Christ has died, Christ has died." If any confront you with other confidences, still keep you to this almighty plea, "Christ has died." If one says, "I was christened, and confirmed," answer him by saying, "Christ has died." Should another say, "I was baptized as an adult," let your confidence remain the same: "Christ has died." When another says, "I am a sound, orthodox Presbyterian," you stick to this solid ground, "Christ has died." And if still another says, "I am a red-hot Methodist," answer him in the self-same way: "Christ has died." Whatever may be the confidences of others, and whatever may be your own, put them all away, and keep to this one declaration, "It is Christ that died." There is enough in that one truth to include all that is excellent in the others, and to answer all the accusations that may be brought against you. "Who is he that condemneth? It is Christ that died." I would put the trumpet to my lips while I preach, and sound out this one note, praying that it may be a death-blast to all accusations that can be brought against believers in Christ.

I want you to notice that Paul does not even rest his confidence as to the believers' safety upon the fact that they are able to say, "We have trusted in Christ; we have loved Christ; we have served Christ." He allows nothing to mar the glory of this one blessed fact, "It is Christ that died." If he adds anything at all, it is still something about that same Christ—"yea rather, that is risen again, who is even at the right hand of God, who also maketh intercession for us."

This is a subject upon which I delight to speak; for here is all my hope and confidence. In these words I see, first, *a challenge to all comers*: "Who is he that condemneth?" Secondly, I see here, *a remedy for all sin*. If any take up the gage of battle, and say, "We condemn you," we shall have this for our complete answer to every one, "It is Christ that died." And lastly, I see here, *an answer to every accusation* arising from sin. "Who is he that condemneth? It is Christ that died."

I. Here is A CHALLENGE TO ALL COMERS. By the grace of God, the apostle stands defiantly in the midst of all the believer's foes, and flings down the gauntlet before them all. The encounter to which he challenges them is not to be a mere tilt in a tournament, but a battle for life or death. Who enters the lists against the believer? First comes Satan; then the world; then conscience; and last of all the law of God. Over them all the believer triumphs. "It is Christ that died," becomes both his sword and his shield; and when the dread conflict is over, and even while it is raging, he sings, "Thanks be to God, which giveth us the victory through our Lord Jesus Christ."

The first who takes up the believer's challenge is *Satan*. Some do not believe in the personality of the devil; but I am as sure of it as I am of the personality of his children who deny their own father. Those of us who have passed through any spiritual conflicts know that Satan is a terribly real personage. He attacks us on the right hand and on the left, from beneath and from above. Very dexterously, with infernal malice, he endeavours to condemn the child of God. It is his business to be the accuser of the brethren, and he carries it on with very great vigour. He knows enough of our conduct to be able, truthfully, to bring to our memory much that might condemn us. When this fails, he never sticks at an accusation because it does not happen to be true. Being the father of lies, he will accuse us of things of which we are not guilty, or, when it suits his purpose, he will exaggerate our guilt, and make it appear worse than it is, in order that he may drive us to despair. There is only one way to successfully resist the onset of the arch-enemy; but that one way ensures certain victory. Up with your shield, and say, "Yes, it is all true, or it might have been, for my heart is so evil that it would have led me to any sin; but 'It is Christ that died.'" This will defeat your great adversary.

Suppose Satan should come to anyone who is seeking the Saviour, and say, "You will never find the Lord; you have sinned beyond all limit; you are too far gone for mercy to reach you; you must perish;" it will be your highest wisdom to give him this one reply, "It is Christ that died." That short sentence completely answers to all his accusations. There is no terror to him like the terror of the cross. He gloated over the crucifixion once, and he has been distressed and terrified by it ever since. Tell him that you are a sinner, and that if he should paint your sin in its blackest colours, you would not even then despair, for it would still be true that Christ "is able also to save them to the uttermost that come unto God by him." Christ has died, and there is more than enough virtue in his death to atone for the blackest or most crimson sins ever committed by men. Close beside the bottomless pit of our iniquity stands the cross whereon Christ has made recompense for all our faults; and when we set Christ over against the gulf of our sin, we see that he far transcends it. Sin is great, but Christ is greater. His precious blood takes away every stain of guilt. Take care that you do not answer Satan with any other argument than this: "It is Christ that died." Again and again let this blow, from the sword of the Spirit, descend upon him, "It is Christ that died," and you will soon be acclaimed the victor over your greatest foe. In this way "Resist the devil, and he will flee from you."

When you have overcome Satan, *the world* will come forth to attack you, and to dispute your claim to be numbered amongst the people of God. As long as you go with evil companions, they will applaud you. You will be "a jolly good fellow" while you join them in their folly; but when you give up their ways, their habits, and their society, then they will say that you are melancholy, and no longer fit company for such "hail fellows, well met", and they will turn away from you. If you follow after Christ, and find eternal life, when they hear of it, they will sneer at you, and bring up all your past life against you. They will say, "What! *you* converted? You are as bad as any one of us. What! *you* a saint? Well, certainly, you made no pretension to it six months ago; you were about as black as a man could be." The world will begin to throw in the believer's teeth all his former iniquities, when he sets forth with the cry, "Who is he that condemneth?" Tell the world, once for all, that it may condemn you if it pleases, for it condemned the Lord Jesus long ago, and say that, therefore, you think but little of the condemnation of your fellowmen. Tell the men of the world that it is right that they should condemn you for all your past life, for doubtless you have been what they say you are, you will not dispute that fact; but tell them also that what Paul wrote to the Christians at Corinth is true of you, "Ye are washed, ye are sanctified, ye are justified in the name of the Lord Jesus, and by the Spirit of our God." Tell even them that Christ died. If they say that Christ's death does not repair the injury you have done to your fellow-men, tell them that, as far as you can, you mean to make restitution to them; and wherein you have done the world an ill turn, let them know that your Master has done it more good than you ever did it harm. The influence of his holy religion has made abundant atonement to the world for any wrong that you ever did to it. He has rendered more of good to men than you ever rendered of evil. In all your answers to the accusations of the world, take care that you base your hopes concerning forgiven sin upon the death of Christ. The world will, before long, understand what you mean by saying that Christ has made atonement for your sin; and, perhaps, here and there, a few of those who ridiculed you will be inclined to know more about this matter, and in private may come and ask you how the death of Christ has saved your soul. At any rate, meet the attack of the world as you met the attack of Satan, with this weapon only: "It is Christ that died," and you will be "more than conquerors through him that loved us."

The third foe that will seek to condemn you, and one that you have great cause to fear, is *your own conscience;* but the weapon which has discomfited your other foes will also avail you against this one. Still, this foe is fierce and terrible. Let me feel the worm that never dies rather than the stings of an offended conscience, if indeed this is not itself "the worm that dieth not." Fire such as martyrs felt at the stake were but a plaything compared with the flames of a burning conscience. We read that, when David had cut off Saul's skirt, "It came to pass afterward that David's heart smote him." It is an ugly knock that a man's heart gives when it smites him. There is no getting away from yourself, and when you yourself condemn yourself, then you are condemned indeed. You go to your bed, but your conscience is there, and it will not sleep. You go out to your pleasures, but your conscience goes with you, and spoils your mirth. You would forget your guilt in your daily business, but your conscience calls out at such a rate that there is no hearing anything else. Thunderbolts and tornadoes are nothing in force compared with the charges of a guilty conscience.

What is to be done when a man condemns himself? Can he still be valiant, and maintain his ground, calling out, "Who is he that condemneth?" Yes, blessed be God, even this foe can be overcome by the weapon the believer wields in the power of God, for he can tell conscience, as he told his former opponents, "It is Christ that died." It is a wonderful story—this old, old story, of Jesus and his love to guilty sinners; let me tell it once again. God so loved me that he willed to forgive me; but for the sake of the world which he governs righteously he could not forgive me without an atonement for my sin. It would not have been consistent with his justice for him to pass by my sin. What was to be done? His own dear Son came, and stood in my place, and took my sin upon him. Knowing that my sin deserved death, he willingly died, the Just for the unjust, that he might bring me to God. God is well pleased with the death of Christ as the vindication of his justice, and for Christ's sake he says to me, "I have blotted out as a thick cloud thy transgressions, and as a cloud thy sins: return unto me; for I have redeemed thee." Tell conscience that Christ has died for your sins, according to the Scriptures, and it will be perfectly satisfied: it will not go to sleep, but it will use its voice for other purposes, and it will no longer seek to condemn you.

There is still another foe that answers your challenge, "Who is he that condemneth?" Forth it steps into the arena, and we behold *the law of God.* What shall we say to that? The law of God says, "Thou shalt," and we have not done what it commands. The law of God says, "Thou shalt not," and we have done exactly what we were forbidden to do. Only too true is that confession, "We have left undone those things which we ought to have done, and we have done those things which we ought not to have done, and there is no health in us." The law condemned us in former days, and would again overthrow us if we ventured to meet it unarmed. It must condemn sin, for "the law is holy, and the commandment holy and just and good." But when it has attacked us, and done its worst, there comes in the majesty of divine sovereignty. God is King over all, and able to govern the world according to his own mind, which mind is always infinitely just. He decrees that Christ Jesus, the Well-Beloved, even his own other self, who is one with him, should come into the world, and bear the sin of man, make amends to the injured honour of God, and magnify the law before the eyes of the whole universe. If the guilty sinner dies, the law is honoured; but if God shall assume human flesh, and die for that sinner, the law is even more honoured. When Christ Jesus took away our guilt, and "his own self bare our sins in his own body on the tree," justice was more terribly displayed than when guilty sinners sink to hell. We are only creatures after all, and when we are condemned, we sink down into destruction, and suffer for our sin; but he is the eternal God, and when he takes our nature, and cries, "My God, my God, why hast thou forsaken me?" and bleeds his life away in agony, then is the law of God abundantly honoured. Therefore do we say to that law, "Law, thou hast nothing to do with me; I am 'not under law, but under grace.' My Substitute has kept the law on my behalf. He has borne the penalty which I ought to have borne, and I am clear. I am now dead to the law. I have died in Christ, and my life now is that of a child of God, for I have been lifted to that high estate by my redeeming Lord."

There is now nobody left that I know of, that can condemn us, except the Judge; and if we have escaped our opponents—Satan, the world, conscience, and the law, we need not fear to stand even at God's judgment seat. The Judge is now on our side; and none of us need fear anybody's condemnation if the Judge does not condemn us. You come into court with your case, and the counsel on the other side condemns you. When he sits down, he has done his worst; and his witnesses also condemn you; but if the verdict is in your favour, and the judge says that you leave the court with a stainless character, you do not care about the condemnation of the others. Now, there is but one Judge—the man Christ Jesus. It is he that died for us. He cannot bring us in debt to divine justice; for in his own hands and feet are the nail-prints, which are the receipts of justice in full settlement of all claims against us. He has paid all we owed and he will vindicate his own death, and claim for the travail of his soul its due reward, which is the forgiveness and the salvation of all guilty men who come and put their trust in him. Wherefore, since it is only our Judge who can condemn us, and since he is the very Person who has paid our debt for us, and put our sin away, we dare to repeat again, with additional emphasis, our ringing challenge to all the universe, "Who is he that condemneth?"

> "Who now accuseth them,
> For whom their Ransom died?
> Who now shall those condemn
> Whom God hath justified?
> Captivity is captive led;
> For Jesus liveth, who was dead."

II. In the second place, I see in our text A REMEDY FOR ALL SIN. On this I shall speak very briefly. We stand boldly in front of all our foes, because we know that we are free from the evil which once condemned us : it is all gone. Our confidence is therefore strong, and it is so because Christ's dying has removed all sin from all believers.

"Look," says one, "*there is sin*. It is true that you are a believer, but you have sinned often, for years, in all sorts of ways." Yes, as we look, we must confess that it is true, there is the sin. But *yonder is the Saviour*, and he is called Jesus, "For he shall save his people from their sins." He has come on purpose to put away our sin, and when he died, he made an end of it. The answer, therefore, to the statement, "There is sin," is this, "Christ has died."

Another says, "Yes, but then you have been specially guilty, *there is great sin* against a great God. You have continued in it, and persisted in it." True, we do confess that accusation; but then *there is a great sacrifice*, for he that came to save us, laid down his life for us; and greater sacrifice than this could never be. "Christ hath redeemed us from the curse of the law, being made a curse for us : for it is written, Cursed is every one that hangeth on a tree." This is the grandest message of the gospel, that "Christ died for our sins according to the Scriptures." The apostle Paul puts this "first of all", and every true preacher of the good tidings of salvation will follow his example. We have, indeed, in the death of Christ, a great atonement; an atonement so great, that none can measure its height and depth, its length and breadth. The glory of the Person who died, the anguish and the suffering he endured, the love that moved him to give himself up to death for us, all make us see how great the atonement is. There is great sin; that we know only too well: but we also rejoice in the knowledge that there is a great atonement to cover all our sin, "For it is Christ that died."

"But", interrupts another, "*God must punish sin*. It is not optional with him, it is an inevitable law of the universe. Transgress the law, and punishment will follow." It is even so; but listen : God must punish sin, and *God has punished sin*. He took the great mass of the sins of believers, and piled the whole on Christ; and when he hung upon the cross as his people's Substitute, even his Father hid his face from him. He died, the Prince of glory died the ignominious felon's death, in the room and place and stead of guilty men. God *has* punished sin; and when men say, "God must punish sin," we answer, "Sin has been punished, for Christ has died."

Not only is our sin punished, but *the sin is gone*. If my friend over yonder has paid my debt, it is gone. I owe no man anything after the debt has been paid, whether by myself, or by somebody else; and if Christ took our sin upon himself, and suffered for it, the sins for which he suffered are gone, plunged as in a shoreless sea, drowned in the Redeemer's blood. They are gone, and gone for ever!

"He breaks the power of cancelled sin,
 He sets the prisoners free;
His blood can make the foulest clean,
 His blood availed for me."

And that my sins are gone is further clear, for he rose again from the dead. "It is Christ that died, yea rather, that is risen again." If he had not paid the debt, he would have remained in the prison of the grave: but he rose again. He has discharged the debt; and we have still another assurance that it is all gone, for the apostle goes on to speak of Christ "who is even at the right hand of God." He would not be there if he were a debtor. If Christ owed anything to the justice of God by reason of his suretyship engagements, he would not be at God's right hand: but he owes nothing whatever. Both the sinner and the Surety are now free. The debt is paid, and Christ is at the right hand of God. And as to our weaknesses and infirmities, he is there to plead for his people: "Who also maketh intercession for us." He ever liveth to secure effectually the eternal salvation of every soul for whom he died, even for every one who puts his trust in him. Are you among the number? Oh, if you, my dear hearers, knew the joy and peace that would come to you if you but trusted in the doctrine of substitution, you would not rest until you were able to say, "Christ was in my place, that I might stand in his place: my sins were laid on him, that his righteousness might be girded on me." If you understood how delightful it is to get out of yourself into Christ, and to live because Jesus died, you would not linger, and doubt, and fear, but you would say, "If it be so, I will come to Christ, and I will trust him, that with you I may say, 'The chastisement of our peace was upon him, and with his stripes we are healed.'" This, then, is God's great remedy for sin: "It is Christ that died."

III. Now I want your attention while I try to show that this blessed sentence, "It is Christ that died," is AN ANSWER TO EVERY ACCUSATION which, under any circumstances, may arise from sin. We have seen that Christ's death enables us to conquer our foes, and frees us from our sins. It also delivers us from every fear and doubt. The death of Christ gives us a full salvation. I cannot mention all the accusations which sin makes, but I will mention a great many of them very quickly, and show how the man who believes in Christ, the dying Christ, the risen Christ, the reigning Christ, is able to meet and overcome them.

Sometimes the accusing whisper comes to your ear, "*You have sinned against a great God.* It will be a terrible thing to have to answer to the great and mighty God for having so sinned." I will make no answer to that accusation but this: "It is Christ that died." Christ himself, the great and mighty God is the "Interpreter, one among a thousand", able to stand between me and God. It is true that God is great, but he cannot ask for more than divine righteousness, and in Christ I present that. Nay, his law never asked for more than human righteousness. I give him Christ's righteousness, which is a righteousness divine. The law has, therefore, more than it asked for, and I am thus not afraid of the anger of the great God. It is the mighty God himself who came here to be a Man, and to die in our stead, for is it not written that God hath bought his people with his own blood? We read of "the church of God, which he hath purchased with his own blood." It is a strong expression, but as it is Scriptural, we cannot alter it; and we have no wish to do so. Oh, beloved, if we have a God for our Redeemer, though our sins against

God be very many, and though they be very black and foul, yet Christ's infinite sacrifice meets them all.

> "Love of God, so pure and changeless,
> *Blood of God*, so rich and free,
> Grace of God, so strong and boundless,
> Magnify them all in me,
> Even me."

"*You have robbed God of his glory,*" another voice seems to say. "You know how you used to blaspheme his name." Or, perhaps, you were more polite; you did not curse and swear, but the accusation comes: "You argued against God and his Son, and against his blessed gospel; you have robbed him of his glory." To that I give the same answer, "It is Christ that died." I know that I have robbed God of his glory, but Christ has brought all the glory back again. I see "the glory of God in the face of Jesus Christ." A dying Saviour brings more glory to the love of God, ay, and to the justice of God, than any mortal sinner could have done; more than any perfect man, though he lived throughout eternity, could have done. Thus, that doubt is answered by the same all-powerful argument: "It is Christ that died."

"But *you have sinned wilfully,*" says the upbraiding accuser. "You went after evil with all your heart; you know that you did. As a young man, you were a ringleader in evil. You were not one that was stirred up and led on by others; you led other people. You drank down sin as the greedy ox drinks down water." True, true, I sinned wilfully; but then my Lord Jesus came willingly to stand in my stead. He willingly died for me, the wilful sinner. He had power to lay down his life, and he had power to take it again; of his own free will he went to prison and to death, for his people's sake. So the evil wrought by my free will is met and covered by the sovereign obedience of his free will: "It is Christ that died."

"Ah!" says the accuser "but *you sinned against light and knowledge.* You cannot deny it. When you sinned, you were not like the common people of the street, who know no better. You had a godly father; you had a Christian mother; you were trained in the fear of God. You read your Bible in early youth, and you went astray with a vengeance; for when you sinned, you knew that you were sinning, and yet you transgressed." Yes, I know that it was so; I will not debate about it; I will only say, "It is Christ that died," and Christ, to meet my sin against knowledge brings a sacrifice offered with his own full knowledge of all that it involved.

> "This was compassion like a God,
> That when the Saviour knew
> The price of pardon was his blood,
> His pity ne'er withdrew."

"Jesus, knowing that the Father had given all things into his hands," poured out water, and began to wash his disciples' feet, and then went, with full knowledge of all that was before him, to pour out his blood to wash their souls from guilt. In the midst of his agony on the tree, he still had full understanding concerning his sacrifice: "Knowing that all things were now accomplished," he bowed his head, and died.

Thus my ill knowledge is met by the great and heavenly knowledge with which he went about the work of offering a complete atonement in my place and stead. "It is Christ that died."

"Ay, ay!" says yet another accuser; "but *you have sinned with delight.* You took a pleasure in it. You were not as some who were mere drudges to sin. You drank it down like sweet wine, and you could not have too much of it." Ah! it is so; but then my Lord Christ delighted to come to be my Saviour. In the volume of the Book it is written of him: "I delight to do thy will, O my God! yea, thy law is within my heart." I took pleasure in sin; but, "he, for the joy that was set before him, endured the cross, despising the shame." Therefore, over against my delight in sin, I set his delight in presenting to the Father his perfect righteousness and his all-sufficient substitutionary sacrifice: "It is Christ that died."

I do not seem to want to preach. I want to sit down, and suck all the sweetness out of this blessed truth: "It is Christ that died." Ah! but another bitter taunt comes to me, "*You have sinned in spirit.* You not only sinned with your body, with your eyes, your lips, your hands; but you have sinned in imagination and desire very horribly." Ah, brethren! here we must bow our heads. All manner of evil things we commit in our thoughts; sin runs to riot in our spirit. Well, we confess that too; but then Christ suffered in his spirit. The sufferings of his soul were the very soul of his sufferings. He not only groaned in body, when beaten by the Roman soldiers, and pierced with nails and thorns; but in soul he was overwhelmed by exceeding heaviness, and by the desertion of his God. To atone for the sin of my soul there is the sorrow of his soul; if I poured out my soul in sin, he poured out his soul unto death, and he was numbered with the transgressors. "It is Christ that died."

If the black thought then comes up, "Ah! but *you have aforetime refused Christ.* Many times you put him away. You quenched conscience. You went to the house of God, not to pray, but to laugh. Ay, and when Christ would have pulled you away, you held hard on to your sin! You long rejected Christ." Yes; but I set over against that the fact that he always would have me. He loved me to the death; and albeit that he foresaw and foreknew that I should reject him, yet he would not take "No" for an answer from me; but he resolved that his true grace should conquer me truly, and make me willing in the day of his power.

Still the accuser continues reminding us of our past life: "*you have trusted in others,* and turned away from Christ; you went everywhere before you came to him." Did you ever want to hire a horse in a market-town? You went to some place, and asked the price, and thought it too high; then you went away to half-a-dozen other stable-keepers, and could not do any better, so you came back to the first; but he, displeased with you, very possibly said, "I do not want your custom. You have been to everybody else; you may go to them now." I have known a surly man act in that way; but Christ never turns us away because we only come to him when others fail us. Many have gone round the world to look for a saviour other than the Lord Jesus Christ, and they have only come to him when all others have failed them. It is astonishing where men will go to seek salvation. Some go to Rome, and some to Oxford; some go I know not where. They seek in vain; for there is no Saviour to be found except at Calvary; and after you have made the circuit of the globe, and compassed heaven and hell to find another way of salvation, you will have to come back to Christ. Blessed be his name, he will not refuse you even then, if you will but believe in him! The proof of love to the uttermost is that "It is Christ that died."

But I feel a darkness coming down over my spirit, and in the darkness there is a fiendish voice that says, "But *you have committed unknown sins*, sins that nobody else knows, and there have been sins which you yourself did not know. Hidden in your heart there is a damning spot which your eye has not discovered." Here comes in this blessed word taken out of the Greek litany, "By thine unknown sufferings." It is almost as good as Scripture; for Scripture leads us to think of the sufferings of Christ as an unfathomable deep. Who can tell us what Christ's suffering really was? It goes into the region of things unknown; it goes beyond the knowable; for flesh and blood will never be able to comprehend what Jesus suffered when the great flood of human sin came rushing down upon him, and filled his spirit to the brim. "It is Christ that died." My unknown sins are buried in the unknown deeps of his almighty sacrifice.

Ah! but another thought comes up, "You know that he died; but then *you have slain your Lord*. You had a share in his death. You know that every sinner is guilty of the murder of Christ." I know it, I know it to my shame and confusion; yet do I live by him I slew, I am saved by him I murdered; and I glory in the grace that makes such a miracle of mercy possible."

> "With pleasing grief and mournful joy
> My spirit now is filled,
> That I should such a life destroy,
> Yet live by him I killed."

Whether it was by mine or by any other wicked hands, yet it was by "the determinate counsel and foreknowledge of God" that Jesus died, in the stead of all who believe in him: I believe in him, therefore he has died for me. He died for his murderers, for those that mocked and insulted him; for he commanded his disciples to begin preaching the gospel at Jerusalem, where they crucified him, to preach it even to those who had hounded him to his doom. O dear friends, what comfort lies in this word, "It is Christ that died"!

"Ah!" says the accuser, but *you are still sinful*. What if Christ died for all your past sins? What about your present sinfulness?" Well, about that, I have this to say, "It is Christ that died, yea rather, that is risen again, who is even at the right hand of God, who also maketh intercession for us." I believe that, when Christ died, he took all the sins of all his people, past, present, and to come, and when the whole mass was condensed into one bitter cup, he drank it all up

> "At one tremendous draught of love,"

leaving not so much as a single drop of wormwood or gall for any to drink who put their trust in him. Come, my hearer, if what I say to you be true (and I will answer for its truth at God's great judgment-seat), then I pray you believe in the Lord Jesus Christ; for "he that believeth in him shall not be ashamed, nor confounded, world without end." I am in this boat myself. If it sinks, I am lost; but it will not sink, for the Pilot of the Galilean Lake is on board. Come in with me, let us sail together to glory. I will not say, "Let us sink or swim together," for there is no sinking to a soul that rests in Christ. This is a good seaworthy vessel: "It is Christ that died." God has accepted Christ in the place of his people; and you, accepting Christ to stand in your stead, shall find that your sin is put away, that his righteousness is yours, and that you are "accepted in the Beloved." I have once more preached the gospel to you as plainly and as simply as I can. Whether you will receive it, or not, must rest with yourselves. May God the Holy Spirit lead you to trust in "Christ that died"! God bless you! Amen.

PORTION OF SCRIPTURE READ BEFORE SERMON—Romans viii. 26—39.

HYMNS FROM "OUR OWN HYMN BOOK"—537, 553, 297.

LETTER FROM MR. SPURGEON.

MY DEAR READERS,—Your weekly preacher is still weakly; but though his progress towards strength is slow, it has been steadily maintained during the late trying weather. When we consider how many have died, your chaplain is very grateful to be alive, to be able to send forth his usual discourse from the press, and to be, as he hopes, half an inch nearer to his pulpit. Happy will he count himself when he is able to preach with the living voice.

Would it not be well for all the churches to hold special meetings for prayer concerning the deadly scourge of influenza? The suggestion has, no doubt, been made by others; but I venture to press it upon Christians of all denominations that they may, in turn, urge all their pastors to summon such meetings. Our nation is fast learning to forget God. In too many instances ministers of religion have propagated doubt, and the result is a general hardening of the popular feeling, and a greatly-increased neglect of public worship. It is written, "When thy judgments are in the earth, the inhabitants of the world will learn righteousness." Let us, who believe in inspired Scripture, unite our prayers that it may be even so. With a court and a nation in deepest mourning, it is a time to cry mightily unto the Lord.

I have been able again to revise a sermon without assistance. It is upon Psalm cv. 37; and, if the Lord will, it will be published next week.

Yours, in deep sympathy with all the sick and the bereaved,

C. H. SPURGEON.

Menton, Jan. 17, 1892.

Metropolitan Tabernacle Pulpit.

A STANZA OF DELIVERANCE.

A Sermon

INTENDED FOR READING ON LORD'S-DAY, JANUARY 31ST, 1892,

DELIVERED BY

C. H. SPURGEON,

AT THE METROPOLITAN TABERNACLE, NEWINGTON,

On Thursday Evening, July 31st, 1890.

"He brought them forth also with silver and gold: and there was not one feeble person among their tribes."—Ps. cv. 37.

THIS verse has been making music in my heart for several days, and at times it has even claimed utterance from my tongue. I have caught myself singing a solo, with myself as the only hearer; and this has been the theme, "He brought them forth also with silver and gold: and there was not one feeble person among their tribes." I love texts which sing to me, and make me join in their tune. If this verse should get into your hearts, and set you singing in a similar way, you will be entertaining a very pleasant visitor, and it will brighten a dark day for you.

Egypt may very fairly represent those states of sorrow and sadness, depression and oppression, into which God's people come far too frequently. Specially is the house of bondage a true picture of our condition when we are convinced of sin, but are ignorant of the way to escape from its guilt and power. Then sin, which was once our Goshen of pleasure, becomes the iron furnace of fear. Though we yield to sin when under conviction, yet we are no longer its willing subjects: we feel that we are slaves, and we sigh by reason of sore bondage. Glory be to God, he has now brought us out from that state of slavery, and we can sing of freedom given by his own right hand!

Since then we have been permitted, in the order of God's providence, to live among evil persons who have had power over us, and have used it maliciously. They have hated our God, and, therefore, they have hated us, and shown their dislike of us in many harsh and exacting ways. We find no rest with them; but our soul is among lions. They seem as though they would devour us, or else frighten us from following the road to heaven.

Full often has our gracious God delivered his persecuted people from such a sorrowful condition, and brought them out into a large room, wherein he has made them happy with Christian fellowship, and enabled them to go about holy work without let or hindrance. At such times, when God's people have come out from under the yoke

No. 2,241.

of their oppressors, the Lord has "brought them forth also with silver and gold, and there has not been one feeble person among their tribes."

It is also possible to go down again into Egypt by reason of our own depression of spirit, inward conflict, and despondency. If you are like the preacher, you are by no means a stranger to inward sinkings. Though you do not give up your faith, but are still, like father Jacob, keeping your hold while the sinew is shrinking, yet you are "sore broken in the place of dragons." You feel that you are like that bush in the desert, which burned with fire, and, only through a miracle, was not consumed. When under temptations of the flesh, and memories of old sins, Satan himself comes in with his fiery darts, and you have a hard time of it. He will insinuate dark and dreadful thoughts, and you will be haunted by them, day after day, till you feel like the poor Israelites under the lash of the Egyptian taskmaster. Your covenant God will bring you out of that state of anguish and distress; and when he does so, you will sing, "He brought them forth also with silver and gold : and there was not one feeble person among their tribes."

God forbid we should ever repeat that senseless and wicked trust in man, which once made us go down into Egypt for help! We will not go there for pleasure : what have we to do with drinking the waters of the muddy river? We drink of a better river than the Nile, even of the river of the water of life. But we shall go to the region of weakness and pain to die. Unless the Lord should suddenly come in his glory, we shall close our eyes in death as Jacob and Joseph did. Then when we go into the tomb, which will be a kind of Egypt for our body, we shall only tarry there for a season. We shall slumber for a while, each one in his bed of dust, but the trump of the archangel shall awaken us, and our bodies shall rise again. We shall not, however, come from the grave so poor and feeble as we went in. No, we shall be great gainers by our sojourn in the dark abode. Those who see the saints in the day of resurrection, ascending to their thrones from the Egypt of death, may fitly say, "He brought them forth also with silver and gold : and there was not one feeble person among their tribes."

I am going to try to handle my very delightful subject in the following way :—First, *the deliverances of God's people are always wrought by divine power.* Lay the stress on the first word : " HE brought them forth." Secondly, *their deliverances are attended with enrichment.* "He brought them forth also *with silver and gold.*" And, thirdly, *their deliverances are accompanied by a remarkable degree of strength.* "There was not one feeble person among their tribes." May the Holy Spirit make rare music for you upon this harp of three strings!

I. First, then, when we are led out of the Egypt of our sorrow, OUR DELIVERANCE IS BY DIVINE POWER. When Israel came out of Egypt, it was Jehovah who brought forth her armies. When any man is saved from spiritual bondage, *it is the Lord Jesus who looseth the captive.* Some little time ago, I delivered an address at the Mildmay Park Conference upon "Following Jesus in the dark", and the Lord was pleased to bless that word to a great many who were then under a cloud. For this cause I greatly rejoice, but from this happy result I have also had to suffer many things in the following way: it seems as if persons everywhere, having read that address, must needs write to me an account of their trouble, despondency, and darkness of soul. Having written the doleful narrative, they very naturally ask me endless questions by way of trying to find light for themselves out of my experience and knowledge. I have been delighted to answer those questions as far as I can; but there is a limit to human power. I have lately been like a doctor who has suddenly had a new practice handed over to him, when he was already as busy as ever he could be, both night and day. He finds his door besieged by patients who cannot be dismissed with just a word of hope and a dose of medicine, but require a long time in which to tell their griefs and to receive their comfort. Spiritually, my night-bell is always going; and when I visit a sick soul, it requires long and weary nursing. I know, therefore, from that, as well as from my own experience, that if ever a man is delivered from spiritual bondage of heart, it is not by any easy work, or by a hasty word. Nay, all the power of sympathy and experience will fail with some souls. God alone can take away the iron when it enters into the soul. It is of small use for those afflicted in mind to write to me, or to others, if their distress is spiritual, for God only can deliver them. If they are in the dark, we can strike a match as well as anyone else; but since they need the shining of the sun, that remains with the Lord, who alone creates the light. Oh, that the Sun of righteousness would rise with healing beneath his wings, on every soul that now sits in the midnight of despair! Deliverance from a cruel captivity, like that of Israel in Egypt, must be wrought by the high hand and the outstretched arm of Jehovah alone. When such a liberation is performed, then do we rapturously sing, "HE brought them forth."

But this does not exclude the use of means. The Lord used Moses and Aaron, and Moses used his rod and his tongue. Truly Jehovah brought forth Israel, and neither Moses nor Aaron nor the rod in Moses' hand; but yet the Lord's instruments were employed in the service. If the Lord delivers you, my dear afflicted friends, the work will not be done by the preacher, nor by a consoling book, nor by any other means so as to prevent its being of the Lord alone. The use of instrumentality does not hide divine power, but even makes it the more apparent. The man Moses was not only very meek, but he was also so slow in speech that he needed Aaron's help; yet the Lord used him. Aaron was even inferior to Moses; but the Lord used him. As for the rod, it was probably nothing more than a hazel stick, which had been used by Moses in walking and in keeping sheep; but it pleased the Lord to make of that rod a very remarkable use, so that no sceptre of kings was ever so greatly honoured. The Lord took care to employ means which could not pretend to share the honour with himself. Notwithstanding Moses, Aaron, and the rod, "HE brought them forth," and HE alone.

This work of the Lord *does not exclude the action of the will.* The people of Israel came forth freely from the country which had become their house of bondage. "He brought forth his people with joy, and his chosen with gladness." They set out exultingly, glad to escape from the intolerable oppression of Pharaoh, who was to them a tyrant indeed. God does not violate the human will when he saves men: they are not converted against their will, but their will itself is converted. The Lord has a way of entering the heart, not with a crowbar, like a burglar, but with a master-key, which he gently inserts in the lock, and the bolt flies back, the door opens, and he enters. The Lord brought Israel forth; but they had cried unto the Lord by reason of their sore bondage, and they did not receive the blessing without desiring it, yea, and sighing for it; and when it came, they joyfully accepted it, and willingly trusted themselves with him whom the Lord had made to be their mediator and leader, even Moses. They did not share the honour of their deliverance with God, but still they gave their hearty assent and consent to his salvation. Willing as they were to move, it was still true, "HE brought them forth."

Brethren, he must have brought them forth, for *they could never have come forth by themselves.* If you have read enough of Egyptian history to understand the position and the power of the reigning Pharaoh, you will know how impossible it was for a mob of slaves, like the Israelites, to make any headway against that imperious monarch and his absolute power. If they had clamoured and rebelled, the only possible result would have been the slaughter of many, and the still further enslavement of the rest. There was no hope for the most distinguished Israelite against the tyranny of Pharaoh: he would simply cry, "Get you unto your burdens;" and they could do no less. Pharaoh crushed even his own Egyptians, and much more the strangers. You cannot look upon the pyramids and other vast buildings along the Nile, and remember that all these were built with unpaid labour, with the whip continually at the workman's back, without feeling that a pastoral, unarmed race, long held in servitude, could never have obtained deliverance from the power of the Pharaohs, if the omnipotent Jehovah had not espoused their cause. "HE brought them forth."

Beloved, *we* can never escape from the bondage of sin by our own power. Our past guilt, and the condemnation consequent thereon, have locked us up in a dungeon, whose bars we can never break. The prince of darkness, also, has such power over our evil natures that we cannot overcome him, or escape from under his dominion of ourselves. If we are ever set free from sin and Satan, it will be eternally and infinitely true that the Lord brought us forth out of the house of bondage. "Salvation is of the Lord."

Moreover, *the spirit of the people was too crushed to have dared to come forth,* even if they could have achieved liberty by a brave revolt. Four hundred years of slavery had ground the very spirit out of the men of Israel. They toiled, they toiled, they toiled; and when Moses came and talked to them about freedom, at first they listened, and they hoped; but in a few hours they began to murmur, and to complain of Moses, and to cry, "Let us alone, that we may serve the Egyptians." That abject condition was ours before conversion; we were not easily aroused to seek redemption. I remember hearing the gospel, and getting a little comfort from it, and almost immediately falling back into my former hopelessness; and I said in my soul, "I may as well enjoy the pleasures of sin while I can, for I am doomed to perish for my iniquities." The slavery of sin takes away manliness and courage from the spirit; and when bright hope smiles upon us, we answer her with the sullen silence of despair. Was it not so with you, my brethren, in those gloomy days? Therefore, it must be true, that, if the prisoners of sin have come forth, the Lord himself brought them forth. They had not the spirit of men who could dare to carve out their freedom; they were too enfeebled by their own servile spirit. There may be some before me, at this moment, before whom God has set an open door, and yet they dare not go through it. Christ is put before you; you may have him for the trusting; you may have him at once; but you dare not take him. You are commanded to believe, but you dare not believe what you know to be true. You hear us sing the hymn—

> "Only trust him, only trust him,
> Only trust him now;"

but you dare not trust the Lord Jesus, though this is your only hope of obtaining salvation. Your sin has left you paralyzed with despair. O God, bring forth these prisoners, even now! Though they lie in the inner prison, with their feet fast in the stocks, may it be said on earth and sung in heaven concerning them, "HE brought them forth."

Yet the Lord did bring them forth. Not in part, but as a whole, he redeemed his people. Every one of them was set free. Not only all the human beings, but all their cattle came forth, according to the word of the Lord, "Not a hoof shall be left behind." Christ Jesus, in redeeming his people, will have all or none. All that the Father gave him shall come to him; nor shall the power of sin, and death, and hell, be able to hold in captivity one whom Jesus has effectually redeemed, nor one whom his Father chose. All the covenanted ones shall be his in the day when he makes up his jewels. He has paid too much for them to lose one of them. In the loss of one of them too much would be involved: his word, his covenant, his power, his faithfulness, his honour, would all suffer, should one of his little ones perish. Therefore he makes their deliverance effectual, and in very deed he brings them forth.

This deliverance came when the lamb was slain. Pharaoh held Israel captive during all the plagues, but he could not go beyond a certain point. On that same night when they saw the lamb slain, and roasted with fire, while they sat in their houses protected by the blood sprinkled upon the lintel, and the two side posts of their doors, that selfsame night they quitted Egypt. They went forth under that seal of redemption, the blood-red mark of substitutionary sacrifice. My dear hearer, perhaps this very night you also will go forth into glorious liberty. I know you will, if you will by faith look to Jesus as the Lamb slain for you. Will you now accept him as your own, and trust him to be your redemption? Behold, then, the Lamb of God that taketh away the sin of the world! Take his precious blood, and let it be sprinkled on your door, yea, and upon your own self, that the angel of vengeance may pass you by. Can you come and feed on Christ at once, as the Lamb of God's passover? Do you say that this would be a bold and venturesome faith? Yet be so bold and venturesome. Blessed be the name of the Lord, none were ever rejected who dared to trust Jesus! We will sing about you and others if you have faith in the great sacrifice, and this will be our song, "HE brought them forth."

Israel cannot remain under slavery to Egypt when once the redemption price has been accepted, and the blood has been sprinkled. None know freedom from sin but those who trust the atoning blood. God forbid that I should point you to any way of hope but this one path; for without shedding of blood there is no remission of sin!

I have perhaps said enough on this point; but assuredly I have fallen short, unless I have made you know each one that deliverance from sin is solely by the power of God. "It is not of him that willeth, nor of him that runneth, but of God that sheweth mercy." Unless a supernatural power is put forth in it, any form of deliverance from sin is worth nothing. If you have been born again from below, you will go below; you must be born again from above if you are to go above. There is no true liberty but that wherewith Christ makes you free. "If the Son shall make you free, ye shall be free indeed." Do you know what it is, dear friends, to be brought out of prison by a miracle of grace, by a revelation of the Holy Ghost, by the blood of Jesus shed for many? If so, you will join with all the saints in singing, "As for his people, HE brought them forth."

II. But now we reach a very pleasing part of our theme. We have now to note that OUR DELIVERANCE WAS ATTENDED WITH ENRICHMENT: "He brought them forth also *with silver and gold*." "Oh!" says one, "I remember all about that transaction. That is the silver and gold which they borrowed from the Egyptians with no intention of repaying the loan. I have always thought that was a thievish trick." It was a very unfortunate mistake of our translators when they rendered the original by the word "borrowed", for it is not the correct word. Our Revised Version has it more accurately, "And the children of Israel did according to the word of Moses; and they *asked* of the Egyptians jewels of silver, and jewels of gold, and raiment: and the Lord gave the people favour in the sight of the Egyptians, so that they let them have what they asked." Even if you were forced to read the word "borrowed", it might mean nothing amiss, for all borrowing and nonpayment is not thieving. "Oh!" say you, "that is a new doctrine." Let me state the case. If I borrow upon the security of my property, and leave the property in the hand of the lender, he will not complain if the security is worth more than the loan. These Israelites had lands and houses and other property which they could not carry with them, and now that their sudden removal involved a forced sale, they could say to those who lived near them, "Here is our land, what will you give us upon it?" The people took the immovable property of the Israelites, and if they granted them a loan upon it, they were well aware of what they were doing, and were not defrauded. But we have no need thus to defend Israel. The Great Proprietor of all things bade them ask, and influenced the minds of their neighbours to give. It was just that these poor people, who had been working without fee or reward, and had thereby screened the native Egyptians from much forced labour, should have some remuneration. The people of Egypt were, in part, afraid of them and of their God, and were also, in measure, sympathetic with them under their cruel oppression, and so they forced presents upon the Israelites, hoping to get their blessing before they departed, to save them from further plagues which might visit the land. The natives as good as said, "Take whatever you please of us, for we have all treated you ill. Only leave us alone; for plagues and deaths fall upon us thick and fast so long as Pharaoh detains you here." However, this is not my point. I am dealing with more spiritual things. When God brings his people out of bondage, they come out enriched in the best and most emphatic sense.

This seemed very unlikely. It looks to the afflicted as if they could not be profited by trials such as theirs. If they can only escape by the skin of their teeth, they will feel perfectly satisfied. Depressed spirits cannot lift their thoughts so high as to think of the gold of increased joy, or the silver of enlarged knowledge, or the jewels of holy graces. "I am," said one, "quite prepared to sit down behind the door in heaven, or at the feet of the least of all the saints, so long as I may but get there." In some respects this is a very proper feeling. But this is not God's way of acting: he did not lead forth his people in a poverty-stricken way, but "He brought them forth also with silver and gold." Your Deliverer means to enrich you spiritually when he sets you free from your sorrow and trouble.

It was very far from being the design of their enemies to enrich Israel: Pharaoh had intended to work them down to the last ounce of strength, and keep them in abject poverty; in fact, one chief object of his oppression was to kill down the race, lest they should too greatly multiply. But the Lord turned the curse into a blessing; "The more they afflicted them, the more they multiplied and grew;" and the harder they worked, the healthier they became, so that "there was not one feeble person among their tribes." This was not according to their enemies' will; but the will of the Lord is paramount. Even so it is not the devil's will to drive a man nearer to Christ, but yet his temptations and assaults are often used of the Lord to make the best and most experienced Christians. Satan is the scullion in God's kitchen, and he has to scour the vessels of mercy. Trials and afflictions, which threaten to kill us, are made to sanctify us; and sanctification is the best form of enrichment. How much we owe to sorrow and sickness, crosses and losses! Our bondage ends in our coming forth with much that is better than silver and gold.

Thus do we come forth from conviction of sin. "Now tell me," says one, "what does a man gain by being in a desponding, sorrowful condition, convinced of sin, and full of fears?" By the work of the Holy Spirit he will gain much. He will obtain a clearer knowledge of the evil of sin. This is a rare thing nowadays, when we have so many believers who were never penitent. It is a great thing for a child, who has the habit of stealing apples, to get himself well filled with the sourest of them, and feel the gripes strong within him. He will never touch such fruit any more. It is a great thing for a man, in his early days, to know what a sour apple sin is, and to feel heartache and soul-anguish because of the exceeding bitterness of his evil ways. It is a lasting lesson. As the burnt child dreads the fire, and the scalded dog is afraid even of cold water, so the discipline of conscience, through divine grace, breeds a holy caution, and even a hatred of sin. We have few Puritans because we have few penitents. An awful sense of guilt, an overwhelming conviction of sin, may be the foundation stone of a gloriously holy character.

The tried and tempted man will also see clearly that salvation is all of grace. He feels that, if he ever rises from his despondency, he can never dare to take an atom of the honour of the deliverance to himself; it must be of free grace only. He can do nothing, and he knows it. When a child of God can spell GRACE, and can pronounce it clearly, as with the true Jerusalem accent, he has gained a great deal of spiritual silver and gold. I have heard a brother stutter over that word, "free grace", till it came out very like "free will." As for myself, that Shibboleth I pronounce without faltering, for my free will is that which I daily try to master and bring into complete subjection to the will of God, and to free grace I owe everthing. Blessed is that man, who, by his experience, has been made to know that free grace is the source of every blessing and privilege, and that salvation is all of grace from first to last. By a knowledge of the great gospel principle of grace, men are brought forth also with silver and gold.

Such persons gain by their soul trouble a fund of healthy experience. They have been in the prison, and have had their feet made fast in the stocks. "Well," says one, "I do not want to feel that sort of treatment." No, but suppose you had felt it, the next time you met with a brother who was locked up in the castle of Giant Despair, you would know how to sympathize with him and help him. You who never felt a finger-ache cannot show much sympathy with broken bones. I take it to be a great gain to a man to be able to exhibit sympathy towards sufferers of all kinds, and especially towards spiritual sufferers. If you can enter into the condition of a bondsman, because you have yourself been a bondsman in Egypt, and God has brought you out, then you will be qualified to comfort those that mourn.

Thus, you see, in various ways, the Lord's people are enriched by the sorrows from which they are delivered by God. "HE brought them forth also with silver and gold." Persons who come to Christ suddenly, and find peace immediately, have much to be grateful for; and they may be helpful to others of a similar character; but those who suffer long law-work, and have deep searchings of heart, before they can enter into rest, have equal reasons for thankfulness, since they obtain a fitness for dealing with special cases of distressed conscience. Where this is the result of severe trial, we may well say that the Lord has brought them forth with silver and gold.

Thus do saints come out of persecution. The church is refined by the fires of martyrdom. The heap on the Lord's threshing-floor is more largely made up of real wheat after the winnowing fan has been used upon it. Individual piety is also deeper, stronger, nobler in persecuting times than at other seasons. Eminent saints have usually been produced where the environment was opposed to truth and godliness. To this day the bride of Christ has for her fairest jewels the rubies of martyrdom. Out of each period of fierce persecution the Lord has brought forth his people the better for the fires. "HE brought them forth also with silver and gold."

Thus do believers come out of daily afflictions. They become wealthier in grace, and richer in experience. Have you noticed how real those men are who have known sharp trial? If you want an idle evening of chit-chat, go and talk to the gentleman with a regular income, constant good health, and admiring friends; he will amuse your leisure hour. But if you are sad and sorrowful, and need conversation that will bless you, steer clear of that man's door. Look into the faces of the frivolous, and turn away as a thirsty man from an empty cistern. He that has never had his own cheek wet with tears, cannot wipe my tears away. Where will you go in the day of trouble? Why, to that good old man whose sober experience has not robbed him of cheerfulness, though it has killed his sinful folly. He has been poor, and he knows the inconvenience of straitened means; he has been ill, and can bear with the infirmities of the sick; he has buried his dearest ones, and has compassion for the bereaved. When he begins to talk, the tone of his voice is that of a sympathetic friend. His lips drop fatness of comfort. What a gain is his acquaintance! A man of God, whose life has been full of mental exercises and spiritual conflict, as well as outward tribulation, becomes, through divine grace, a man of large wealth of knowledge, prudence, faith, foresight, and wisdom, and he is to the inexperienced like some great proprietor, by whom multitudes of the poorer class are fed and guided, housed and set to work. Those who have been much tried are in the peerage of the church. A man who has been in the furnace, and has come out of it, is a marked man. I think I should know Shadrach, Meshach, and Abednego even now if I were to meet them. Though the smell of fire had not passed upon them, I feel sure that it left a glow upon their countenances, and a glory upon their persons, which we find nowhere else. They are henceforth called "the three holy children": they were holy before, but now men own it. Do you not think that they were great gainers by the furnace, and is it not true of all the godly whose lives have been made memorable by special tribulation: "HE brought them forth also with silver and gold"?

When you and I reach the shores of heaven, *thus shall we come into glory.* When we come forth out of our graves, it will not be with loss, but with enrichment. We shall leave corruption and the worm behind us, and with them all that earthly grossness which made us groan in these mortal bodies. God will bring us forth also with silver and gold. What golden songs will we sing! What silver notes of gratitude will we pour forth! What jewels of communion with one another, and of communion with our Lord, will adorn our raiment! If we, too, have been men of sorrows and acquainted with grief, how much more fully shall we enter into the joy of our Lord because we entered into his sorrow! We also have suffered for sin, and have done battle for God and for his truth against the enemy. We also have borne reproach, and become aliens to our mother's children; we too have been bruised in the heel, and yet in death have conquered death, even as he did; only by his grace. Hence the joy of fellowship with him through eternity. What news we shall have to tell to angels, and principalities, and powers! The gems of our grateful history will be our trials and deliverances. Coming up from death to eternal life, this will be the sum of it, "HE brought them forth also with silver and gold."

Dear friends, I am anxious to pass on to the third point, for time is flying fast; but I cannot neglect the application of what I have said. I beg those of you who are sad and despondent to notice the truths I have advanced. I want you to believe that your present affliction is for your enrichment. You will come out of this Egypt with much profit of grace. "Let me out," cries one, "only let me out." I pray you, be not impatient. Why rush out naked, when a little patience will be repaid with silver and gold? If I were labouring in Egypt, and heard that it was time for me to start for the land of Canaan, I should be eager to be gone at once; but if I found that I must be hindered for an hour or two, I should certainly utilize the delay by disposing of my lands, and endeavouring to get together treasures which I could carry with me. The delay would not be lost time. Therefore, beloved friend, if you cannot at once obtain comfort, make good use of your affliction. Be always more earnest to profit by your trials than to escape from them. Be more earnest after the heavenly silver and gold than about hurrying away from the scene of conflict and temptation.

III. Thirdly; here is a very wonderful thing. OUR DELIVERANCE IS ACCOMPANIED WITH HEALTH AND STRENGTH : "There was not one feeble person among their tribes." In the thousands of Israel there was not one person who could not march out of the land keeping rank as an efficient soldier. Everyone was fit for the journey through the wilderness. They numbered hard upon two millions, if not more; and it is a very surprising fact that there should not have been one feeble person among their tribes. Mark the word, not only no one sick, but no one "feeble", none with the rheumatism, or other pains which enfeeble walking, or palsies which prevent bearing burdens. This was nothing less than a sanitary miracle, the like of which was never known in the natural order of things.

This fact is typical of the health and strength of the newly saved. The Lord's people, at conversion, are as a rule wonderfully strong in their love to Jesus, and their hatred of sin. In most cases our young converts, when they have truly come to Christ, even if they are a little timid, are vigorous, much in prayer, abounding in zeal, and earnest in speaking out the gospel. Many of them, I believe, would die at the stake readily enough, while they are in their first love. In their earliest days nothing is too hot or too heavy for them, for the sake of Christ Jesus, their Lord. If I want a bit of work to be done which requires dash and self-sacrifice, give me a set of Israelites who have just come out of Egypt, for there is not one feeble person among their tribes. After they have gone some distance into the wilderness, they are apt to forget the right hand of the Lord, and to get fretting and worrying. Very soon many of them are sick, through being bitten by fiery serpents, or smitten with the plague. They begin grumbling and complaining, and run into all sorts of mischief in a short time; but when they first came out, they were so excellent that even the

Lord said, "I remember thee, the love of thine espousals." I have known some of you, after you have been members of the church for a few months, greatly need a very nice cushion to sit upon, and the cosy corner of the pew; whereas once you could stand in the aisle, and not know that you were standing. You have grown wonderfully particular about the singing, and the tunes, and the length of the prayer, and the preacher's attitude, and especially the respect paid to your own dear self. Only very choice service suits you: it would almost insult you if you were put to common work. You were not like that when you were first converted. Do you recollect how the crowd pressed upon you, and yet you were so absorbed in listening to the preacher's voice that you never minded it? What walks you took then to reach the service! I notice, my friend, that when your grace grew short, the miles grew long. When you first joined the church, I said to you, "I fear you live too far off to attend regularly." But you took me up very quickly, and said, "Oh, that is nothing, sir! If I can only get spiritual food, distance is no object." When you get cold in heart, you find it inconvenient to come so far, and you go to a fashionable place of worship, where your musical tastes can be gratified. Yes, when grace declines, fancy rules the mind, and love of ease controls the body, and the soul loses appetite, and grows greedy for empty phrases, and weary of the Word of God. May the Lord grant you grace to be among those of whom it is said, "There was not one feeble person among their tribes"!

Full often it is so with the persecuted. I do not wish that any of you should experience persecution, but I am persuaded it would do some of you good to have a touch of it. A man who has fulfilled an apprenticeship to this hard master, is likely to be a man indeed. If he has endured hardness as a good soldier of Jesus Christ, he will be fit to become an officer in the army, and an instructor of recruits. If I could, by the lifting of my finger, screen every believer from persecution at home and in the workshop, I should hesitate long before I did it, since I am persuaded that the church is never more pure, more holy, more prayerful, or more powerful than when the world is raging against her. The dogs keep off the wolves. The hypocrite declines to enter the church where he will gain nothing but reproach, or worse. When there were stakes at Smithfield, Protestantism meant heroism. When the Lord's covenanting people were meeting among the hills and mosses of Scotland, there were no "moderates" and "modern-thought" men among them. They knew and loved the truth for which they fought, and that truth made them strong.

It would be a glorious day if it were so with all God's people, that there were none feeble. We should, as a church, labour to reach this high standard. We would have the weakest to be as David, and David as the angel of the Lord. We would have our babes become young men, and our young men fathers in Christ. Do we reach this standard at the Tabernacle? Alas! we do not, by a very long way. There are numbers of very feeble persons among our tribes. I will not say a word against them, dear hearts! for I trust they are sincere, though feeble. How greatly I wish that they were more concerned about their own feebleness, for it is a real loss to the cause we have at heart! The feeble hinder the strong. We want all the strength of the host for storming the enemies' ramparts, whereas some of us have to stop behind to nurse the infirm. We should not mind this so much, only these are the same poor creatures that were nursed twenty years ago, and they have made no advance. May the Lord strengthen us all, till we shall all be made fit for the service of Jesus!

Oh, when we meet in the home country, when we once get to glory, what a delight it will be that *there will be no sin or weakness there!* When the Lord has once brought us forth from the world and all its troubles, then all sinful weakness shall be unknown. We shall all be raised in power, and shall be as the angels of God. Are you going there, dear friends? "Yes," says one, "I hope that I am going there; but I am a feeble person." Thank God that you are on the right road, even if you limp. It is better to enter into life halt, and maimed, and feeble, than to run and leap in the way of death. If I can give a lift to anyone who is feeble, I am sure I will. At the same time, I would urge you to cry to the Lord to make you strong, and bid you trust in Christ for the power, which he alone can give, of faith to overcome doubts and fears.

If any of you have not believed unto eternal life, now put your trust in the Lord Jesus. They serve a good Master who trust alone in Jesus, and take up their cross, and follow him. In him is life for the perishing, joy for the sorrowing, rest for the weary, and liberty for the captives. Are you shut up, like a prisoner in a castle? Do but trust in Jesus, and he will batter in the dungeon door, and bring you out. Yea, and he will not give you a penniless liberty, a liberty to perish of want. No, it shall be said of you, and of others like you, "He brought them forth also with silver and gold." Amen, so be it! So be it, even at this moment, good Lord!

PORTION OF SCRIPTURE READ BEFORE SERMON—Psalm cv.

HYMNS FROM "OUR OWN HYMN BOOK"—30, 116, 126.

"THE SWORD AND THE TROWEL." Edited by C. H. SPURGEON.
TABLE OF CONTENTS FOR FEBRUARY, 1892.

Breaking the Long Silence. Addresses by C. H. Spurgeon, at Menton, on the last evening of 1891, and the first morning of 1892.
Lady Hymn-Writers. By W. Y. Fullerton.
A Prayer. By E. A. Tydeman.
Illustrations by the Way. By C. H. Spurgeon.
London Flowers, and those who Sell them. Illustrated.
Gospel Fruit in North Africa. By N. Hardingham Patrick.
The Congo. By G. H. Pike. Illustrated.
"While there's Life there's Hope." By F. E. B.
My Ragged School and its Fortunes. By J. Manton Smith.
Claiming the Promise. By John Burnham.
Christmas Festivities at the Orphanage.

New Portrait of Dr. Pierson, with article on the Metropolitan Tabernacle.
Notices of Books.
Notes. (Portrait and Sketch of Deacon W. Payne. Death of the Duke of Clarence. "The Bible and Modern Criticism." Tabernacle Prayer-meetings. Personal Notes, &c., &c.)
Pastors' College, Metropolitan Tabernacle.
Pastors' College Missionary Association.
Stockwell Orphanage.
Colportage Association.
Society of Evangelists.
Balance-sheets--Pastors' College, Society of Evangelists, and Loan Building and Reserve Fund.

Price 3d. Post free, 4 stamps.

PASSMORE AND ALABASTER, PATERNOSTER BUILDINGS; and all Booksellers.

Metropolitan Tabernacle Pulpit.

GOD'S WILL ABOUT THE FUTURE.*

A Sermon

INTENDED FOR READING ON LORD'S-DAY, FEBRUARY 7TH, 1892,

DELIVERED BY

C. H. SPURGEON,

AT THE METROPOLITAN TABERNACLE, NEWINGTON,

On Thursday Evening, October 16th, 1890.

"Go to now, ye that say, To day or to morrow we will go into such a city, and continue there a year, and buy and sell, and get gain: whereas ye know not what shall be on the morrow. For what is your life? It is even a vapour, that appeareth for a little time, and then vanisheth away. For that ye ought to say, If the Lord will, we shall live, and do this, or that. But now ye rejoice in your boastings: all such rejoicing is evil. Therefore to him that knoweth to do good, and doeth it not, to him it is sin."—James iv. 13—17.

MEN to-day are just the same as when these words were first written. We still find people saying what they are going to do to-day, to-morrow, or in six months' time, at the end of another year, and perhaps still farther. I have no doubt there are persons here who have their own career mapped out before them pretty distinctly, and they feel well-nigh certain that they will realize it all. We are like the men of the past; and this Book, though it has been written so long, might have been written yesterday, so exactly does it describe human nature as it is at the end of this nineteenth century.

The text applies with very peculiar force when our friends and fellow-workers are passing away from us. Sickness and death have been busy in our midst. Perhaps in our abundant service we have been reckoning what this brother would do this week, and what that sister would be doing next week, and so on. Even for God's work we have had our plans, dependent in great measure on the presence of some beloved helpers. They have appeared amongst us in such buoyant health, that we have scarcely thought it possible that they would be struck down all in a moment. Yet so it has often been. The uncertainty of life comes home to us when such things occur, and

---

* It is remarkable that the sermon selected for this week should be so peculiarly suitable for the present trying time. It ought to be read with special solemnity. Oh, that it may be the means of leading many to make the great preparation for the future which only believers in the Lord Jesus Christ have made!

No. 2,242.

we begin to wonder that we have reckoned anything at all safe, or even probable, in such a shifting, changing world as this. With this in full view, I am going to talk about how we ought to behave with regard to the future, and attempt to draw some lessons for our own correction and instruction from the verses before us.

Following the line of the text, and keeping as close to it as we can, we will notice, first, that *counting on the future is folly.* Then we will observe, what is clear enough to us all, that *ignorance of the future is a matter of fact.* In the third place, I shall set before you the main truth of this passage, that *recognition of God in the future is wisdom,* our fourth point shall be, that *boasting of the future is sin;* and our final thought will be, that the *using of the present is a duty.*

I. To begin with, it will need but few words to convince you that COUNTING ON THE FUTURE IS FOLLY. The apostle says, "Go to now!" As if he meant, "you are acting absurdly. See how ridiculous your conduct is." "Go to now, ye that say, To-day or to-morrow we will do such and such a thing." There is almost a touch of sarcasm in the words. The fact of frail, feeble man so proudly ordering his own life and forgetting God, seems to the apostle James so preposterous that he scarcely deems it worth while to argue the point, he only says "Go to now!"

Let us first look at *the form of this folly,* and notice what it was that these people said when they were counting on the future. The text is very full of suggestions upon this matter.

They evidently thought everything was at their own disposal. They said "*We* will go, *we* will continue, *we* will buy, *we* will sell, *we* will get gain." But is it not foolish for a man to feel that he can do as he likes, and that everything will fall out as he desires; that he can both propose and dispose, and has not to ask God's consent at all? He makes up his mind, and he determines to do just what his mind suggests. Is it so, O man, that thy life is self-governed? Is there not, after all, One greater than thyself? Is there not a higher power that can speed thee, or can stop thee? If thou dost not know this, thou hast not yet learned the first letter of the alphabet of wisdom. May God teach thee that everything is not at your disposal; but that the Lord reigneth, the Lord sitteth King for ever and ever!

Notice, that these people, while they thought everything was at their disposal, used everything for worldly objects. What did they say? Did they determine with each other "We will to-day or to-morrow do such and such a thing for the glory of God, and for the extension of his kingdom"? Oh, no, there was not a word about God in it, from beginning to end! Therein they are only too truly the type of the bulk of men to-day. They said, "We will buy; then we will carry our goods to another market at a little distance; we will sell at a profit; and so we will get gain." Their first and their last thoughts were of the earth earthy, and their one idea seemed to be that they might get sufficient to make them feel that they were rich and increased in goods. That was the highest ambition upon their minds. Are there not many who are living just in that way now? They think that they can map out their own life; and the one object of their efforts seems to be to buy and sell, and get gain; or else to obtain honour, or to enjoy pleasure. Their heart rises not into the serene air of heaven; they are still grovelling here below.

All that these men of old spoke of doing was to be done entirely in their own strength. They said, "We will, we will." They had no thought of asking the divine blessing, nor of entreating the help of the Most High. They did not care for that, they were self-contained; they called themselves "self-made men"; and they intended to make money. Who cannot make money who has made himself? Who cannot succeed in business who owes his own character, and his present standing, entirely to his own exertions, and to his own brain? So they were full of self-confidence, and began reckoning for the future without a shadow of doubt as to their own ability. Alas, that men should do even so to-day, that, without seeking counsel of God, they should go forward in proud disdain, or in complete forgetfulness of "the arrow that flieth by day", and "the pestilence that walketh in darkness", until they are suddenly overwhelmed in eternal ruin!

It is evident that to these men everything seemed certain. "We will go into such a city." How did they know they would ever get there? "We will buy and sell, and get gain." Did they regulate the markets? Might there be no fall in prices? Oh, no! they looked upon the future as a dead certainty, and upon themselves as people who were sure to win, whatever might become of others.

They had also the foolish idea that they were immortal. If they had been asked whether men might not die, they would have said, "Yes, of course all men must die some time or other," for all men count all men mortal; but in their hearts they would have made an exception in their own case, if we may judge them by what we were apart from sovereign grace. "All men count all men mortal but themselves." Without any saving clause, they said, "We will continue there a year." How did they know that they would see a single quarter of that year through? But you must not press such men too closely with awkward questions. If you had done so, they would have said, "Do not talk about death; it makes one melancholy."

Having looked at the form of this folly of counting on the future, let us speak a little on *the folly itself*. It is a great folly to build hopes on that which may never come. It is unwise to count your chickens before they are hatched; it is madness to risk everything on the unsubstantial future.

How do we know what will be on the morrow? It has grown into a proverb that we ought to expect the unexpected; for often the very thing happens which we thought would not happen. We are constantly surprised by the events which occur around us. In God's great oratory of providence, there are passages of wondrous eloquence, because of the surprise-power that is in them. They come upon us at unawares, and overwhelm us. How can we reckon upon anything in a world like this, where nothing is certain but uncertainty?

Besides, the folly is seen in the fact of the frailty of our lives, and the brevity of them. "What is your life? It is even a vapour, that appeareth for a little time." That cloud upon the mountain— you see it as you rise in the morning; you have scarcely dressed yourself before all trace of it has gone. Here in our streets, the other night, we came to worship through a thick fog, and found it here even in the house of prayer. But while we worshipped, there came a breath of wind; and on our way home a stranger would not have thought that London had been, but a few hours before, so dark with dirty mist; it had all disappeared. Life is even as a vapour. Sometimes those vapours, especially at the time of sunset, are exceedingly brilliant. They seem to be magnificence itself when the sun paints them with heavenly colours; but in a little while they are all gone, and the whole panorama of the sunset has disappeared. Such is our life. It may sometimes be very bright and glorious; but still it is only like a painted cloud, and very soon the cloud and the colour on it are alike gone. We cannot reckon upon the clouds, their laws are so variable, and their conditions so obscure. Such also is our life.

Why, then, is it, that we are always counting upon what we are going to do? How is it that, instead of living in the eternal future, where we might deal with certainties, we continue to live in the more immediate future, where there can be nothing but uncertainties? Why do we choose to build upon clouds, and pile our palaces on vapour, to see them melt away, as aforetime they have often melted, instead of by faith getting where there is no failure, where God is all in all, and his sure promises make the foundations of eternal mansions? Oh! I would say with my strongest emphasis: Do not reckon upon the future. Young people, I would whisper this in your ears: Do not discount the days to come. Old men, whispering is not enough for you, I would say, with a voice of thunder: Count not on distant years; in the course of nature, your days must be few. Live in the present; live unto God; trust him now, and serve him now; for very soon your life on earth will be over.

We thus see that counting on the future is folly.

II. Secondly, IGNORANCE OF THE FUTURE IS A MATTER OF FACT. Whatever we may say about what we mean to do, we do not know anything about the future. The apostle, by the Spirit, speaks truly when he says, "Ye know not what shall be on the morrow." Whether it will come to us laden with sickness or health, prosperity or adversity, we cannot tell. To-morrow may mark the end of our life; possibly even the end of the age. Our ignorance of the future is certainly a fact.

Only God knows the future. All things are present to him; there is no past and no future to his all-seeing eyes. He dwells in the present tense evermore as the great I AM. He knows what will be on the morrow, and he alone knows. The whole course of the universe lies before him, like an open map. Men do not know what a day may bring forth; but Jehovah knows the end from the beginning. There are two great certainties about things that shall come to pass—one is that God knows, and the other is that we do not know.

As the knowledge of the future is hidden from us, *we ought not to pry into it.* It is perilous, it is wicked, to attempt to lift even a corner of the veil that hides from us the things to come. Search into the things that are revealed in Holy Scripture, and know them, as far as you can; but be not so foolish as to think that any man or woman can tell you what is to happen on the morrow; and do not think so much of your own judgment and foresight as to say, "That is clear; I can predict that." Never prophesy until after the event, and then, of course, you cannot prophesy; therefore never attempt to prophesy at all. You know not what shall be on the morrow, and you ought not to make any unhallowed attempt to obtain the knowledge. Let the doom of King Saul on Mount Gilboa warn you against such a terrible course.

Further, *we are benefited by our ignorance of the future.* It is hidden from us for our good. Suppose a certain man is to be very happy by-and-by. If he knows it, he will be discontented till the happy hour arrives. Suppose another man is to have a great sorrow very soon. It is well that he does not know it, for now he can enjoy the present good. If we could have all our lives written in a book, with everything that was to happen to us recorded therein, and if the hand of Destiny should give us the book, we should be wise not to read it, but to put it by, and say:—

> "My God, I would not long to see
> My fate with curious eyes,
> What gloomy lines are writ for me,
> Or what bright lines arise."

It is sufficient that our heavenly Father knows; and his knowledge may well content us. Knowledge is not wisdom. He is wisest who does not wish to know what God has not revealed. Here, surely, ignorance is bliss: it would be folly to be wise.

Because we do not know what is to be on the morrow, *we should be greatly humbled by our ignorance.* We think we are so wise; do we not? And we make a calculation that we are sure is correct! We arrange that this is going to be done, and the other thing; but God puts forth his little finger, and removes some friend, or changes some circumstance, and all our propositions fall to the ground. It is better for us, when we are low before the throne of God, than when we stand up and plume ourselves because we think we can say, "Oh, I knew it would be so! See how well I reckoned! With what wondrous forethought I provided for it all!" Had God blown upon our plans, they would have come to nought. We know nothing surely. Let that thought humble us greatly.

Seeing that these things are so, *we should remember the brevity, the frailty, and the end of our life.* We cannot be here long. If we live to the extreme age of men, how short our time is! But the most of us will never reach that period wherein we may say one to another, "My lease has run out." How frail is our hold on this world! In a moment we are gone, gone like the moth; you put your finger upon it, and it is crushed. Man is not great; man is less than little. He is as nothing; he is but a dream. Ere he can scarcely say that he is here, we are compelled to say that he is gone.

We are glad that we do not know when our friends are to die; and we feel thankful that we cannot foretell when we shall depart out of this life. What good would it do us? Some who are in bondage through fear of death might be in greater bondage still, while those who are now careless about it would probably feel more content in their carelessness. If they had to live another twenty years, they would say, "At any rate, we may sport away nineteen of them." As for those of us to whom this world is a wilderness, and who count ourselves but pilgrims hurrying through it, we know enough when we know that this is not our rest, because it is polluted, and that the day will soon come when we shall enter the Canaan of our inheritance, and be "for ever with the Lord." Meanwhile, the presence of the Lord makes a heaven even of the wilderness. Since he is with us, we are content to leave the ordering of our lives to his unerring wisdom. We ought, for every reason, to be thankful that we do not know the future; but, at any rate, we can clearly see that to count on it is folly, and that ignorance of it is a matter of fact.

III. Thirdly, RECOGNITION OF GOD WITH REGARD TO THE FUTURE IS TRUE WISDOM. What says our text? "For that ye ought to say, If the Lord will, we shall live, and do this, or that." I do not think that we need always, in every letter and in every handbill, put "If the Lord will"; yet I wish that we oftener used those very words. The fashionable way is to put it in Latin, and even then to abbreviate it, and use only the two consonants, "D.V.", to express it. You know, it is a fine thing when you can put your religion into Latin, and make it very short. Then nobody knows what you mean by it; or, if they do, they can praise your scholarship, and admire your humility. I do not care about those letters "D.V." I rather like what Fuller says when he describes himself as writing in his letter such passages as "God willing", or "God lending me life." He says, "I observe, Lord, that I can scarcely hold my hand from encircling these words in a parenthesis, as if they were not essential to the sentence, but may as well be left out as put in. Whereas, indeed, they are not only of the commission at large, but so of the quorum, that without them all the rest is nothing; wherefore, hereafter, I will write these words freely and fairly, without any enclosure about them. Let critics censure it for bad grammar, I am sure it is good divinity." So he quaintly puts the matter. Still, whether you write, "If the Lord will", or not, always let it be clearly understood; and let it be conspicuous in all your arrangements that you recognize that God is over all, and that you are under his control. When you say, "I will do this or that," always add, in thought if not in word, "If the Lord will." No harm can come to you if you bow to God's sovereign sway.

We should recognize God in the affairs of the future, because, first, *there is a divine will which governs all things.* I believe that nothing happens apart from divine determination and decree; even the little things of life are not overlooked by the all-seeing eye. "The very hairs of your head are all numbered." The station of a rush by the river is as fixed and foreknown as the station of a king, and the chaff from the hand of the winnower is steered as much as the stars in their courses. All things are under regulation, and have an appointed place in God's plan; and nothing happens, after all, but what he permits or ordains. Knowing that, we will not always say, "If the Lord will"; yet we will always feel it. Whatever our purposes may be, there is a higher power which we must ever acknowledge; and there is an omnipotent purpose, before which we must bow in lowliest reverence, saying, "If the Lord will."

But while many of God's purposes are hidden from us, *there is a revealed will which we must not violate.* It is chiefly in reference to this that the Christian should always say, "I will do this or that, provided that, when the time comes, I shall see it to be consistent with the law of God, and with the precepts of the gospel." I say now, "I will do this or that," but certain other things may occur which will render it improper for me to do so. Hence, to be quite in accordance with the Word I so deeply reverence, I must always put in the saving clause, sometimes giving utterance to it, but in every case meaning, whether I put it into words or not, "I will do so and so, if it be right to do it; I will go, or I will stay, if it be the will of God."

In addition to this, *there is a providential will of God which we should always consult.* With this guidance, which comes from the circumstances that surround us, believers are familiar. Sometimes a thing may seem to us to be right enough morally, and yet we may not quite know whether we should do it or not. Or perhaps there are two courses equally right, when judged by the Word of God, and you are uncertain which to follow. The highest wisdom, in such a case, is to wait for God to make the path plain by some act of providence. When you come where two roads meet, in your perplexity pull up, kneel down, and lift your hearts to heaven, asking your Father the way. And whenever we are purposing what we should do—and we ought to make some purposes, for God's people are not to be without forethought or prudence—we should always say, or mean without saying, "All my plans must wait till the Lord sets before me an open door. If God permit, I will do this; but if the Lord will, I will stop, and do nothing. My strength shall be to sit still, unless the Master wishes me to go forward." May I whisper into the ear of some very quick, impetuous, and hasty people, that it would be greatly to their soul's benefit if they knew how to sit still? Many of us seem as if we must always do everything at once, and hence we make no end of muddle for ourselves. There is often a blessed discipline in postponement. It is a grand word, that word "wait"; especially in this particular connection. "Wait on the Lord: be of good courage, and he shall strengthen thine heart: wait, I say, on the Lord." Be patient; sometimes even to be passive in the hand of God will be our strength, and to stand still until the cloudy, fiery pillar moves in front of us, will be our highest wisdom.

There is yet another sense I would give to this expression: *there is a royal will which we would seek to fulfil.* That will is that the Lord's people should be saved, and come to the knowledge of the truth. So, as the servants of the Most High, we go forth to do this or that, "if the Lord will", that is to say, if, by so doing, we can fulfil the great will of God in the salvation of men. I wish that this was the master-motive with all Christians; that we were each willing to say, "I will go and live in such a place if there are souls to be saved there. I will take a house in such a street, if, by living there, I can be of service to my Lord and Master. I will go to China or Africa, or to the ends of the earth, if the Lord will; that is to say, if, by going there, I can be helping to answer that prayer, 'Thy will be done in earth, as it is in heaven.'" Dear Christian friends, do you put yourselves entirely at God's disposal? Are you really his, or have you kept back a bit of yourself from the surrender? If you have retained any portion for yourself, that little reserve that you have made will be the channel by which your life will bleed away. You say, "We are not our own; we are bought with a price:" but do you really mean it? I am afraid that there is a kind of mortgage on some Christians. They have some part they must give, as they fancy, to their own aggrandisement. They are not all for Christ. May the Lord bring us all to his feet in whole-hearted consecration, till we can say, "We will not go to that city unless we can serve God there. We will not buy, and we will not sell, unless we can glorify God by buying and selling; and we will not wish even for the honest gain that comes of trading, unless we can be promoting the will of God by getting it. Our best profit will consist in doing God's will." A man can as much serve God by measuring calico, or by weighing groceries, as he can by preaching the gospel, if he is called to do it, and if he does it in a right spirit. This should always be our one aim, and we should put this ever in the forefront of our life. "I go or I stay, I ascend or I descend, if the Lord will; the Lord's will shall be done in my mortal body whether I live or whether I die."

May this be your resolve, then; let this clause, "if the Lord will", be written across your life, and let us all set ourselves to the recognition of God in the future. It is a grand thing to be able to say, "Wherever I go, and whatever happens to me, I belong to God; and I can say that God will prepare my way as well when I am old and grey-headed as he did when I was a boy. He shall guide me all the way to my everlasting mansion in glory; he was the guide of my youth, he shall be the guide of my old age. I will leave everything to him, all the way from earth to heaven; and I will be content to live only a day at a time; and my happy song shall be—

> "'So for to-morrow and its need
>   I do not pray,
> But keep me, guide me, hold me, Lord,
>   Just for to-day.'"

IV. And now, fourthly, BOASTINGS ABOUT THE FUTURE ARE EVIL. "But now ye rejoice in your boastings: all such rejoicing is evil." I will not say much upon this point, but briefly ask you to notice the various ways in which men boast about the future.

One man says, about a certain matter, "*I will do it, I have made up my mind,*" and he thinks, "You cannot turn me. I am a man who, when he has once put his foot down, is not to be shifted from his place." Then he laughs, and prides himself upon the strength of his will; but his boasting is sheer arrogance. Yet he rejoices in it, and the Word of God is true of such a one: "All such rejoicing is evil."

Another man says, "*I shall do it, the thing is certain;*" and when a difficulty is suggested, he answers "Tut, do not tell me about my proposing and God's disposing; I will propose, and I will also dispose; I do not see any difficulty. I shall carry it out, I tell you. I shall succeed." Then he laughs in his foolish pride, and rejoices in his proud folly.

All such rejoicings are evil. They are foolish; but, what is worse, they are wicked. Do I address myself to any who have no notion about heaven or the world to come, but who feel that they are perfect masters of this world, and, therefore talk in the manner I have indicated, and rejoice as they think how great they are? To such I would earnestly say, "All such rejoicing is evil."

I hear a third man say, "*I can do it. I feel quite competent.*" To him the message is the same, his boasting is evil. Though he thinks to himself, "Whatever comes in my way, I am always ready for it," he is greatly mistaken, and errs grievously. I have often been in the company of a gentleman of this sort, but only for a very little while; for I have generally got away from him as soon as I could. He knows a thing or two. He has got the great secret that so many are seeking in vain. All of you ordinary people, he just snuffs you out. If you had more sense, and could do as he does—well, then, you could be as well off as he is. Poor man! "Nobody needs to be poor," says he. "Nobody needs to be poor. I was poor a little while; but I made up my mind that I would not remain poor. I fought my own way, and I could begin again with a crust, and work myself up." You will notice his frequent use of the capital I, but ah, dear sir, God has thunder-bolts for these great I's! They offend him; they are a smoke in his nostrils. Pride is one of the things which his soul hates. No man ought to speak in such a strain: "All such rejoicing is evil."

But that young man yonder talks in a different tone. He has been planning what he will do when he succeeds; for, of course, he is going to succeed. Well, I hope that he may. He is going to buy, and sell, and get gain; and he says, "*I will do so and so when I am rich.*" He intends then to have his fling, and to enjoy himself; he laughs as he thinks what he will do when his toilsome beginnings are over, and he can have his own way. I would ask him to pause and consider his life in a more serious vein: "All such rejoicing is evil."

There is, of course, a future concerning which you may be certain. There is a future in which you may rejoice. God has prepared for them that serve him a crown of life, and by humble hope you may wear the crown even now. You may, by the thoughts of such amazing bliss, begin to partake of the joy of heaven; and this will do you no harm. On the contrary, it will set your heart at rest concerning your brief stay on earth, for what will it matter to you whether your life is cloudy or bright, short or long, when eternity is secure? But concerning the uncertainties of this fleeting life, if you begin to rejoice, "All such rejoicing is evil."

V. That brings me to my last and most practical point, which is this: THE USING OF THE PRESENT IS OUR DUTY. "Therefore to him that knoweth to do good, and doeth it not, to him it is sin." I take this text with its context. It means that he who knows what he ought to do, and does not do it *at once*, to him it is sin. The text does not refer to men who live in guilty knowledge of duty, and yet neglect it; its message is to men who know the present duty, and who think that they will do it by-and-by.

In the first place, *it is sinful to defer obedience to the gospel.* "He that knoweth to do good, and doeth it not, to him it is sin." Do you say, "I am going to repent"? Your duty is to repent now. "I am going to believe," do you say? The command of Christ is, "Believe now." "After I have believed," says one, "I shall wait a long time before I make any profession. Another says, "I am a believer, and I shall be baptized some day." But as baptism is according to the will of the Lord, you have no more right to postpone it than you have to postpone being honest or sober. All the commands of God to the characters to whom they are given come as a present demand. Obey them now. And if anyone here, knowing that God bids him to believe, refuses to believe, but says that he hopes to trust Christ one of these days, let me read him this: "To him that knoweth to do good, and doeth it not,"—the word is in the present tense,— "to him it is sin."

In the next place, *it is sinful to neglect the common duties of life*, under the idea that we shall do something more by-and-by. You do not obey your parents, young man, and yet you are going to be a minister, are you? A pretty minister you will make! As an apprentice you are very dilatory and neglectful, and your master would be glad to see the back of you; he wishes that he could burn your indentures; and yet you have an idea you are going to be a missionary, I believe? A pretty missionary you would be! There is a mother at home, and her children are neglected while she talks to her neighbours; but when her children are off her hands, she is going to be a true mother in Israel, and look after the souls of others. Such conduct is sin. Mind your children; darn the stockings and attend to your other home duties; and when you have done that, talk about doing something in other places. If present duties are neglected, you cannot make up for the omission by some future piece of quixotic endeavour to do what you were never called to do. If we could all be quiet enough to hear that clock tick, we should hear it say, "Now! now! now! now!" The clock therein resembles the call of God in the daily duties of the hour. "To him that knoweth to do good, and doeth it not, to him it is sin," even though he may dream of how he will, in years to come, make up for his present neglect.

Then, dear friends, *it is sinful to postpone purposes of service.* If you have some grand project and holy purpose, I would ask you not to delay it. My dear friend, Mr. William Olney, whose absence we all mourn to-night,* was a very prompt, energetic man. He was here, he was there, he was everywhere, serving his Lord and Master; and now that he is suddenly stricken down, his life cannot be said to be in any sense unfinished; there is nothing to be done in his business; there is nothing to be done in his relation to this church. There is nothing left undone with regard to anybody. It is all as finished as if he had known that he was going to be struck down. And I believe that that is the way we all ought to live. Mr. Whitefield said that he would not

---

* This sermon was preached at the time that Mr. William Olney, the senior deacon of the Tabernacle church, was lying unconscious, after a paralytic stroke. He fell asleep in Jesus the next morning. On the following Lord's-day evening, the Pastor preached, from Acts xiii. 36, the sermon that will be published next week, "if the Lord will."

go to bed unless he had put even his gloves in their right place. If he should die in the night, he would not like to have anybody asking, "Where did he leave his gloves?" That is the way for a Christian man always to live; have everything in order, even to a pair of gloves. Finish up your work every night; nay, finish up every minute. I have seen Mr. Wesley's Journal, though it is not exactly a "journal"; it does not give an account of what he did in a day, nor even what he did in an hour. He divided his time into portions of twenty minutes each; and I have seen the book in which there is the record of something done for his Lord and Master every twenty minutes of the day. So exactly did he live, that no single half-minute ever seemed to be wasted. I wish that we all lived in that way, so that we looked, not at projects in some distant future that never will be realized, but at something to be done now.

Last Thursday, when I was speaking, I said that some Christian people had never told out the story of the cross to others, and urged them to begin to do so at once. A young friend, sitting in this place, leaned over the front of the pew, and touched a friend sitting there, saying to her, "I would like to speak to you about that." He had never spoken to her before, he did not even know her, and he thus addressed her while the service was proceeding. A member of the church, sitting by her side, who heard what the young man said, was so pleased with his prompt action, that she stayed after the service to sympathize and help, while he explained the way of salvation. The young person, to whom he spoke, came to tell me, last Tuesday, that she had found the Saviour through that well-timed effort. Dear friends, that is the way to serve the Lord. If we were to do things at the moment when they occurred to us, we should do them to purpose. But, oh, how many pretty things you have always meant to do, and have never even attempted! You have strangled the infant projects that have been born in your mind; you have not suffered them to live, and grow up into the manhood of real action. First thoughts are best in the service of God, and the carrying of them out would secure great benefit to others and much fruit for ourselves. "To him that knoweth to do good, and doeth it not, to him it is sin." God help us, if we are saved, to get at this holy business of serving the Lord Christ, which as far exceeds buying, and selling, and getting gain, as the heavens are higher than the earth. Let us do something for Christ at once. You young people that are newly converted, if you do not very soon begin to work for Christ, you will grow up to be idle Christians, scarcely Christians at all; but I believe that to attempt something suited to your ability almost immediately, as God shall direct you, will put you on the line of a useful career. God will bless you, and enable you to do more as the years roll onwards.

I have this last word: "To him that knoweth to do good, and doeth it not, to him it is sin," that is, *it is sinful in proportion to our knowledge.* If there is any brother here, into whose mind God has put something fresh, something good, I pray him to translate it into action at once. "Oh, but nobody has done it before!" Somebody must be first, and why should not you be first if you are sure that it is a good thing, and has come into your heart through God the Holy Ghost? But if you know to do good, and do not do it, it will be sin every minute that you leave it undone. Therefore get at it at once. And you, my sister, who to-night, while sitting here, have been thinking of something you might have done which you have not yet attempted, attempt it at once. Do not let another sun rise, if you can help it, before you have begun the joyful and blessed service. "The time is short." Our opportunities are passing, "For what is your life? It is even a vapour that appeareth for a little time, and then vanisheth away." Be up and doing. Soon we shall be gone. May we never hear the summons to go home while there is anything left undone that we ought to have done for our Lord and Master!

I am conscious of having spoken but very feebly and imperfectly; but, you know, my heart is heavy because of this sore trial which has come upon us through the stroke that has fallen upon our beloved deacon, William Olney; and when the heart is so sad, the brain cannot be very lively. May God bless the word, for Jesus' sake! Amen.

PORTION OF SCRIPTURE READ BEFORE SERMON—James iv.

HYMNS FROM "OUR OWN HYMN BOOK"—90, 39, 211.

When last week's sermon was sent to the printers, MR. SPURGEON was unable to write a letter to go at the end of it, for he was suffering so severely that he could not even dictate a message to his sermon-readers. It was not then anticipated that his illness would take the terrible form it afterwards assumed; but on *Tuesday, January* 26, when the doctor came, he was obliged to report his patient's condition as "serious." Since then, the daily bulletins have carried the sad tidings far and wide; and most of the readers of the sermons probably know, by this time, that their beloved preacher has been suffering from the same malady that so grievously afflicted him during last summer and autumn. His illness, on this occasion, has not developed exactly the same symptoms as before; but at the date of writing this note (Jan. 31), the doctor reports that "*his condition gives cause for the gravest anxiety.*"

It is with profound regret that the Publishers record the death of the beloved Pastor of the Metropolitan Tabernacle. He was called to his rest, at Mentone, on Sunday, January 31st, at 11 p.m.

To all who were privileged to know Mr. SPURGEON, this event has come as a great sorrow; a sorrow which will certainly be shared by every reader of the weekly sermons.

"I heard a voice from heaven saying unto me, Write, Blessed are the dead which die in the Lord from henceforth: Yea, saith the Spirit, that they may rest from their labours; and their works do follow them."—
Rev. xiv. 13.

The weekly Sermon and *The Sword and the Trowel* will be continued as usual, the Publishers having a large quantity of manuscripts and Sermons hitherto unpublished.

Metropolitan Tabernacle Pulpit.

HIS OWN FUNERAL SERMON.*

A Sermon

INTENDED FOR READING ON LORD'S-DAY, FEBRUARY 14TH, 1892,

DELIVERED BY

C. H. SPURGEON,

AT THE METROPOLITAN TABERNACLE, NEWINGTON,

On Lord's-day Evening, October 19th, 1890.

"For David, after he had served his own generation by the will of God, fell on sleep."—Acts xiii. 36.

It is remarkable that David should say, in the sixteenth Psalm, "Thou wilt not leave my soul in hell; neither wilt thou suffer thine Holy One to see corruption," and yet that Paul should say concerning him, when preaching at Antioch, that he "saw corruption." The key to this apparent contradiction is the fact that David did not speak of himself, but of his Lord. Peter, in his memorable sermon on the day of Pentecost, quotes the words of the psalmist, applies them to his risen Redeemer, and distinctly affirms that, in the Psalm, "David speaketh concerning him."

It is worthy of notice that Peter and Paul both use the same argument about this statement of David. These two apostles did not always agree; but however much they might differ about other matters, they were of one mind about the resurrection of Christ. I hope that, whatever differences there may be among the true preachers of the gospel, they will always be one in declaring the resurrection of our Lord. This corner-stone of the gospel must never be displaced or dishonoured. The good news we are commissioned to declare is the same that Paul received and delivered, "that Christ died for our sins according to the Scriptures; and that he was buried, and that he rose again the third day according to the Scriptures." Chief among the Scriptures fulfilled by the resurrection of Christ stands this word, which David, inspired by the Holy Ghost, wrote so long before the

---

* This sermon was preached on the Lord's-day evening after Mr. William Olney "fell on sleep." Long before the beloved preacher was "called home," it was selected for publication this week. Mrs. Spurgeon feels that her dear husband could not have delivered a more suitable discourse for "his own funeral sermon." She has, therefore, given it that title in the hope that many may be blessed by the message which "he, being dead, yet speaketh." Believing that many friends will wish to have this sermon for widespread circulation, the publishers will at once issue it, in book form, price one penny.

No. 2,243.

event: " Thou wilt not leave my soul in hell; neither wilt thou suffer thine Holy One to see corruption." The resurrection of Christ is the top-stone of our faith. Because "he, whom God raised again, saw no corruption," Paul was able to say to his hearers, " Be it known unto you therefore, men and brethren, that through this man is preached unto you the forgiveness of sins: and by him all that believe are justified from all things, from which ye could not be justified by the law of Moses."

The argument of the apostle is this. David could not have meant himself when he said, "Thou wilt not suffer thine Holy One to see corruption;" because David died, and his body was buried, and it did see corruption. He must, therefore, have referred to Christ, who is indeed God's "Holy One." Of him the prophetic word was true, for God did not suffer him "to see corruption." He died, and was laid in the grave, but he rose again on the third day. In that climate there was, while Christ lay in the grave, plenty of time for his body to become corrupt. The spices with which they perfumed the precious body would not have sufficed to keep back corruption; they would have helped to conceal the unpleasant odour which putrefaction brings, but they would not have stopped the process of decay. But Christ rose again, and no corruption had come to his body, for that body was a holy thing; it had no defect, nor taint of sin, as our bodies have. Begotten of the Holy Ghost, it was a pure thing; though born of the Virgin Mary, it was united to the Godhead, and not separated from it even in death; it saw no corruption. There is the apostle's argument, then: David, speaking not of himself, but of someone else, says that the Lord will not suffer him to see corruption; and this he spake by the Spirit of the very Christ whom we preach to you as the Author and Finisher of salvation. He is living and reigning to-day, King of kings and Lord of lords; he that believeth in him, though he were dead, yet shall he live, and live for ever with his risen, reigning Redeemer.

While Paul was speaking in the synagogue at Antioch in Pisidia, he incidentally used the words of our text: " David, after he had served his own generation by the will of God, fell on sleep." That is to be my subject on this occasion; forgetting for the present the main argument, I would only look at this eddy in the current, and draw your attention to the expression which dropped from Paul's lips concerning David. Let us ask, first, *What is it to serve our own generation?* Secondly, *What parts of our generation can we serve?* And, lastly, with tender memories of many who have gone from us, let us ask, *What will happen to us when our service is done?* Even that which happened to David; we shall, like him, "fall on sleep."

I. First, then, WHAT IS IT TO SERVE OUR OWN GENERATION? This is a question which ought to interest us all very deeply. We live in the midst of our own generation, and seeing that we are part of it, we should serve it, that the generation in which our children shall live may be better than our own. Though our citizenship is in heaven, yet, as we live on earth, we should seek to serve our generation while we pass as pilgrims to the better country.

What, then, is it for a man to serve his own generation?

I note, first, that *it is not to be a slave to it.* It is not to drop into the habits, customs, and ideas of the generation in which we live. People talk nowadays about the *Zeitgeist*, a German expression which need frighten nobody; and one of the papers says, "Spurgeon does not know whether there is such a thing." Well, whether he knows anything about the *Zeitgeist* or not, he is not to serve this generation by yielding to any of its notions or ideas which are contrary to the Word of the Lord. The gospel of Jesus Christ is not only for one generation, it is for all generations. It is the faith which needed to be only "once for all delivered to the saints"; it was given stereotyped as it always is to be. It cannot change because it has been given of God, and is therefore perfect; to change it would be to make it imperfect. It cannot change because it has been given of God, and is therefore true; truth changes not. It cannot change because it has been given to answer for ever the same purpose, namely, to save sinners from going down to the pit, and to fit them for going to heaven. That man serves his generation best who is not caught by every new current of opinion, but stands firmly by the truth of God, which is a solid, immovable rock. But to serve our own generation in the sense of being a slave to it, its vassal, and its varlet—let those who care to do so go into such bondage and slavery if they will. Do you know what such a course involves? If any young man here shall begin to preach the doctrine and the thought of the age, within the next ten years, perhaps within the next ten months, he will have to eat his own words, and begin his work all over again. When he has got into the new style, and is beginning to serve the present world, he will within a short time have to contradict himself again, for this age, like every other, is "ever learning, and never able to come to the knowledge of the truth." But if you begin with God's Word, and pray God the Holy Ghost to reveal it to you till you really know it, then, if you are spared to teach for the next fifty years, your testimony at the close will not contradict your testimony at the beginning. You will ripen in experience; you will expand in your apprehension of the truth; you will become more clear in your utterance; but it will be the same truth all along. Is it not a grand thing to build up, from the beginning of life to the end of it, the same gospel? But to set up opinions to knock them down again, as though they were ninepins, is a poor business for any servant of Christ. David did not in that way serve his own generation; he was the master of his age, and not its slave. I would urge every Christian man to rise to his true dignity, and be a blessing to those amongst whom he lives, as David was. Christ "hath made us kings and priests unto God and his Father"; it is not meet that we should cringe before the spirit of the age, or lick the dust whereon "advanced thinkers" have chosen to tread. Beloved, see to this; and learn the distinction between serving your own generation and being a slave to it.

In the next place, in seeking to answer the question, What is it to serve our own generation? I would say, *it is not to fly from it.* If any man says, "The world is so bad, that I will avoid coming into contact with it altogether; even the teaching of Christianity has become so diluted, and is so thoroughly on the Down-grade, that I will have nothing to do with it," he is certainly not serving his own generation. If he shall shut himself up, like a hermit, in his cave, and leave the world to go to ruin as it may, he will not be like David, for he *served* his own generation before he fell asleep. She that goes into a nunnery, and he that enters a monastery, are like soldiers who run away, and hide among the baggage. You must not do anything of the sort. Come forward and fight evil, and triumph over it, whether it be evil of doctrine, evil of practice, or evil of any other kind. Be bold for Christ; bear your witness, and be not ashamed. If you do not take your stand in this way, it can never truly be said of you that you served your generation. Instead of that, the truth will be that you allowed your generation to make a coward of you, or to muzzle you like a dog, and to send you out into the streets neither to bark nor to bite, nor to do anything by which you might prove that there is a soul within you.

If we ask again, What is it to serve our generation? I answer, *it is to perform the common duties of life*, as David did. David was the son of a farmer, a sheep-owner, and he took first of all to the keeping of the sheep. Many young men do not like to do the common work of their own father's business. You do not want to drudge, you say, you want to be a king. Well, there are not many openings in that line of business; and I should not recommend anyone to be eager to enter them if there were. "Seekest thou great things for thyself? seek them not." Before David swayed the sceptre, he grasped the shepherd's crook. He that at home cannot or will not undertake ordinary duties, will not be likely to serve his age. The girl who dreams about the foreign missionary field, but cannot darn her brother's stockings, will not be of service either at home or abroad. Do the commonplace things, the ordinary things that come in your way, and you will begin to serve your generation, as David served his.

But serving our generation means more than this. *It is to be ready for the occasion when it comes.* In the midst of the routine of daily life, we should, by diligence in duty, prepare for whatever may be our future opportunity, waiting patiently until it comes. Look at David's occasion of becoming famous. He never sought it. He did not go up and down among his sheep, sighing, and crying, "Oh, that I could get away from the dull business of looking after these flocks! My brothers have gone to the camp; they will get on as soldiers; but here am I, buried among these rocks, to look after these poor beasts." He was wiser than that; he quietly waited God's time. That is always a wise thing to do. If you are to serve God, wait till he calls you to his work; he knows where to find you when he wants you; you need not advertise yourself to his omniscience. At length the set time came for David. On a certain day, his father bade him go to his brethren, and take them some corn and some loaves, with cheeses for their captain; and he reached the camp just at the time when the giant Goliath was stalking forth, and defying all the armies of Israel to meet him. Now is David's time, and the young man is ready for it. If he had lost that opportunity he might have remained a shepherd all the rest of his days. He tells Saul how he slew both the lion and the bear, and prophesies that the uncircumcised Philistine shall be as one of them, seeing he had defied the armies of the living God. Disdaining Saul's armour, he takes his sling, and his five smooth stones out of the brook, and soon he comes back with the gory head of the giant in his hand. If you want to serve the church and serve the age, beloved friend, be wide awake when the occasion comes. Jump into the saddle when the horse is at your door; and God will bless you if you are on the look-out for opportunities of serving him.

What is it, again, to serve our generation? *It is to maintain true religion.* This David did. He had grave faults in his later life, which we will not extenuate; but he never swerved from his allegiance to Jehovah the true God. No word or action of his ever sanctioned anything like idolatry, or turning aside from the worship of Jehovah, the God of Israel. He bore a noble witness to his Lord. He said, "I will speak of thy testimonies also before kings, and will not be ashamed;" and we may be sure that he was as good as his word, and that when he met with foreign potentates, he vindicated the living God before them. The whole set and current of his life, with the exception of his terrible fall, was to the glory of the God in whom he trusted, and to the praise of that God who had delivered him. We, too, shall truly serve those amongst whom we dwell by maintaining true religion. Had ten righteous men been found in Sodom, it would have been spared, and the world to-day only escapes the righteous judgment of God because of the presence in it of those who fear him, and tremble at his word. The spread of "pure and undefiled religion" is a certain way to serve those around us. To help true religion, David wrote many psalms, which were sung all over the land of Israel. A wonderful collection of poems they are; there is none like them under heaven. Not even a Milton, with all his mighty soarings, can equal David in the height of his adoration of God, and the depth of his experience. That man does no mean service for his time who gives the people new songs which they can sing unto their God. While none can equal the inspired psalms of the Hebrew king, which must ever form the choicest praise-book of the church, other men may, in lesser degree, serve their own generation, by the will of God, in a similar way, and be blessed in the deed.

To serve our own generation is not a single action, done at once, and over for ever; *it is to continue to serve all our life.* Notice well that David served "his own generation"; not only a part of it, but the whole of it. He began to serve God, and he kept on serving God. How many young men have I seen who were going to do wonders! Ah, me! they were as proud of the intention as though they had already done the deed. They took a front seat, and they seemed to think that everybody ought to admire them because of what they were going to do; but they were so pleased with the project that they never carried it out. They thought that they might meet with some mishap if they really attempted to do the thing, and the project was so beautiful that they preserved it under a glass shade, and there it is now. Nothing has been accomplished; nothing has been done, though much has been thought of. This is folly. Some, too, begin well, and they serve their God earnestly for a time, but on a sudden their service stops. One cannot quite tell how it happens, but we never hear of them afterwards. Men, as far as I know them, are wonderfully like horses. You get a horse, and you think, "This is a first-rate animal," and so it is. It goes well for a while, but on a sudden it drops lame, and you have to get another. So it is with church-members. I notice that, every now and then, they get a singular lameness. To very many we have to say, even as Paul said to the Galatians, "Ye did run well; who did hinder you, that ye should not obey the truth?" But David continually served God to the end of his life. May we all, by divine grace, thus serve our whole generation, too!

Yet more is included in this faithful serving of our generation. *It is to prepare for those who are to come after us.* David served his generation to the very end by providing for the next generation. He was not permitted to build the temple; but he stored up a great mass of gold and silver to enable his son Solomon to carry out his noble design, and build a house for God. This is real service; to begin to serve God in early youth; to keep on till old age shall come; and even then to say, "I cannot expect to serve the Lord much longer, but I will prepare the way as far as I can for those who will come after me." Many years ago, Dr. Rippon, the minister of this church, which then worshipped in New Park Street, was wont to prophesy about his successor. When he was very old, after having been pastor for more than sixty years, it is in the memory of some still living that he was accustomed to pray for the minister who should come after him. The old man was looking forward to one who should come and carry on the work after he was obliged to leave it. So must you and I do. We must be looking ahead as far as ever we can, not with unbelieving anxiety or unholy curiosity; but after the fashion in which David prepared abundantly before his death. If we cannot find a successor to enter upon our service when we have to leave it, yet let us do all we can to make his work the easier when he comes to it.

II. In the second place, let us ask a question even more practical than the first: WHAT PARTS OF OUR GENERATION CAN WE SERVE? It is truly written, "None of us liveth to himself:" we either help or hinder those amongst whom we dwell. Let us see to it that we serve our age, and become stepping-stones rather than stumbling-blocks to those by whom we are surrounded. We shall serve our generation best by being definite in our aim. In trying to reach everybody we may help nobody. The wise man tries to serve somebody in particular: where, then, should we make the effort? In answering that question, I divide the generation in which we live into three parts.

First, there is *the part that is setting.* Some are like the sun going down in the west; they will be gone soon. Serve them, dear brethren. You that are in health and vigour, comfort them, strengthen them, and help them all you can. Be a joy to that dear old man, who has been spared to you even beyond the allotted threescore years and ten, and praise God for the grace that has upheld him through his long pilgrimage. Look on his grey hairs as a crown of glory; make his descent to the grave as easy as you can. He once was as young as you are; he once had the vigour that you have. Console him, cheer him, give him the respect that is due to his many years. Do not let him feel that you consider him an old fogey who lingers, superfluous, on the stage; but learn from his experience, imitate his perseverance, and ask God to be with you in your old age, as he is with him.

The second portion of our generation which we can serve is *the part that is shining.* I mean those in middle life, who are like the sun at its zenith. They are working hard, bearing the burden and heat of the day; as yet their bones are full of marrow, and they are strong men ready for service for the Lord. Seek to sustain their hands in every possible way. Help them all you can. As one of those in middle life, I especially ask the help of all my Christian brethren, members of this church, or of any other church, who can aid me by their sympathies and their prayers. Get closer to one another, and fill up the vacant spaces that death's arrows continue to make in our ranks. Suffer nothing to be left undone which may further the work of Christ, or help the people around you who are so quickly passing away. Many of us have been together for nearly forty years, and when, one after another, our dear brethren are taken away, let it be everybody's ambition to try to make up what shall be lacking through their departure. This is what is due to those who are like the shining part of our generation.

Specially, however, I want to speak to you about serving your own generation in *the part that is rising;* the young people who are like the sun in the east, as yet scarcely above the horizon. This part of our generation is specially the care of parents and Sunday-school teachers; but let us not leave it entirely to them. We can, most of us, do something to serve this portion of our generation before we fall asleep. Beloved, I commend to your care and attention the children and young people who abound in our midst. In them lies our hope for the future of God's cause on earth.

In the first place, they are the most reachable. Happily, we can get at the children. The mass of people in London go to no place of worship now; the old habit of attending church or chapel seems to have been given up; but the people will still let the children go to Sunday-school, even if they do it from no better motive than that of getting them out of the way in the afternoon, or in order that the house may be quiet without them. Anyhow, if you open a school anywhere in London, you can quickly get it filled with children. If you cannot do one thing, do another. If you cannot reach the fathers and the mothers, though you should earnestly try to get at them, yet, if you can reach the children, take care that you lose no opportunity of teaching them the things of God. This is the work that lies nearest to you; seek to accomplish it: and "whatsoever thy hand findeth to do, do it with thy might."

Moreover, the children are the most impressible. What can we do with the man who is hardened in sin? The grace of God can reach him, I know; but the children as yet have not known these evil ways; they are horrified when they hear about them. Teach them. While yet the clay is soft, mould it for God. May the Lord himself help you, dear Sunday-school teachers, and others who labour amongst the children, to do your work right well! Nobly are you serving your own generation, and the generation to follow.

The salvation of the children ought to be sought with double diligence, for they will last the longest. If a man of sixty or seventy is converted, he will have only a short time for serving God here; for he will soon be gone. If a child is converted, a long life of usefulness may enrich the church of God. Therefore, look after the children. If you had a gathering of Christian men and women, and were to put the question to them, "How many of you were converted before you were one-and-twenty?" you would be greatly surprised to find that probably five out of six would answer that, in early years, they were led to know the grace of God, and trust in Christ as their Saviour. I tried the experiment one evening with a number of friends who had come together from different places. "How many of you owe your salvation to your father's prayers, your mother's instruction, or your Sunday-school teachers' influence in youth?" I asked; and almost every one out of a company of about five-and-twenty said that it was in early youth that God blessed some instrumentality to their conversion.

Remember, too, that those who are converted when children usually make the best saints. These of whom I have just spoken, who gave the answer that they were converted in their youth, were ministers of the gospel. I do not know whether the same rule is true among ordinary Christians; but among those who have become leaders of men, in nearly every case they yielded to Christ while they were young. Our thoughts at this time cannot but be occupied with our dear friend, William Olney, who has just been taken from us so suddenly, to our unutterable grief. He was as earnest as a youth as he was when he became an old man. Indeed, I never knew a moment when he was not earnest. I never even knew him to be dull or depressed; he seemed to be always joyous and glad. He would almost frighten me sometimes with his jubilation under pain; for when he was in agonies of suffering, and could only sit on the platform for a short time, there was never anything like depression about him. He was just as glad and happy as if he had been in perfect health. I wish that it were so with all of us. Young Christians do become the best Christians. Early piety is usually eminent piety; so seek to catch the children while they are young, and train them for the Lord, then they will be ready to serve their generation in their turn.

We ought to look after the children, again, for they are specially named by Christ. He said, "Feed my sheep;" but he also said, "Feed my lambs." I would almost be inclined to say that the Lord made the same division of the generation as I have done. When he said, the first time, "Feed my sheep," he may have meant the old sheep. When he said, the second time, "Feed my sheep," he may have had specially in mind the middle-aged ones. There is no doubt that when he said, "Feed my lambs," he meant the young people. Christ gave the lambs a place all to themselves: "Feed my lambs." I wish Christians would consider more seriously how the children ought to be looked after by the church. I read, the other day, of a boy who wished to join in membership with the people of God. His father said that he was too young, and kept him back. He was big enough, however, to be sent out to fold the sheep one night. When he came in, his father said, "Jack, have you folded the sheep?" "Yes," he said; "I folded all the *sheep*," laying great stress on the last word. "And did you put the lambs in?" asked his father. "No," he replied, "I left the lambs outside; they were too young to go in." "Oh, boy!" said the father; "you know more than I do, after all; they were the very ones that needed most to be folded. You may go and see the minister about joining the church as soon as you like." If any believers in Christ need specially to be taken into the church, it is those who have come to Jesus in their youth. I pray you, serve your generation by giving the children and young people your most loving attention and care.

Look after the children of this generation, again, for the dangers around them at the present time are almost innumerable. What a time this is for boys! You cannot read the daily papers without being shocked by the accounts of the wrong-doing of mere boys. This is an age which seems to make snares on purpose to entrap them. There are "penny dreadfuls" enough to poison the whole generation; they are full of stories of crime with a false halo about it, so that it is made to seem like heroism. These vile stories are everywhere; perhaps your own boy has one, unknown to you, and is reading it while you are sitting here. Everywhere traps are laid for the feet of our boys. Serve your generation by warning them of their danger, and trying to keep them free from the evils by which they are surrounded. Satan gets the advantage over many a young life by causing even right things to be put to wrong uses; and in all sorts of ways he lays traps for young people. Oh, parents and teachers, do try to give your boys a backbone of moral honesty! Try to show them that they have not come into this world merely to please themselves; that there is something better to be done than that. Do not rest till you have led them to the Saviour, for no boy is safe till he is converted. No girl is safe in the streets of this city till she has a new heart and a right spirit. The times are perilous; yet if we speak a word of warning, we are called sour Puritans. It always makes me laugh when I am called a sour Puritan, because you know there is nobody with a quicker eye for fun, or with a deeper vein of mirth than I have. At the same time, I like to have humour, and anything of cheerfulness and brightness in life, consecrated to God. But when mirth is made a plank on which a man can go into sin and iniquity, then we will saw that plank to pieces. You must be saved from sin, young men; you must be kept from evil, young women, if you are to be truly happy. May God's grace put in your way wise, godly friends, parents, and teachers, who shall serve their generation by leading you into the paths of peace!

III. Now, I have done when I have tried, for just a minute or two, to answer this question: WHAT WILL HAPPEN TO US WHEN OUR SERVICE IS DONE? "David, after he had served his own generation by the will of God, fell on sleep." The day's work is done; the worker is weary; he falls on sleep: what can he do better? It was all "by the will of God." To what part of the sentence do you think that clause belongs? Did David serve his generation by the will of God; or did he fall asleep by the will of God? Both. Guided by the will of God, he did his work on earth; and calmly resigned to the will of God, he prepared to die. Even when passing away, he served his generation by giving Solomon some last charges concerning the kingdom, saying, "I go the way of all the earth; be thou strong, and show thyself a man." Over both his life and his death may be written the words, "By the will of God." Oh, that we may all so live, that even in death we may serve our generation; may it be true of us that "whether we live, we live unto the Lord; and whether we die, we die unto the Lord; whether we live therefore or die, we are the Lord's"! Thus "the will of God" shall be done both in our service and in our sleep.

David is an example of what will befall those who know Christ, at the end of their service. *He did not go to sleep till his work was done.* "David, after he had served his own generation by the will of God, fell on sleep." Do not want to die till you have done your work. When brethren say, "Oh, I wish I could go to heaven! Oh, when shall I get home?" they remind me of a man who, when he begins work on Monday, says, "I wish it was Saturday night." We do not want servants like that, nor does God either. Be willing to live for two hundred and fifty years, if God wills it. Be willing to live till strength fails you, if God wills it; you can still bear your dying testimony to the Lord's faithful and unchanging love. Do not be in a hurry to go home to heaven. Do not want to go to sleep till you also have served your generation well. When David had served his generation, he fell on sleep. We are told that, in the early days of Christianity, when believers were falling asleep in Jesus, their friends did not bid them "good-bye," but "good-night." So we say, in the words of that beautiful hymn—

> "Sleep on, belovèd, sleep, and take thy rest;
> Lay down thy head upon thy Saviour's breast:
> We love thee well; but Jesus loves thee best—
>   Good-night! Good-night! Good-night!
>
> Only 'good-night,' belovèd—not 'farewell!'
> A little while, and all his saints shall dwell
> In hallowed union, indivisible—
>   Good-night!
>
> Until we meet again before his throne,
> Clothed in the spotless robe he gives his own,
> Until we know even as we are known—
>   Good-night!"

But, next, we are told that *when his work was done, he fell on sleep.* Did his soul sleep? By no means. It is not his soul that is spoken of here, for we read that he "saw corruption." Souls do not see corruption. Paul is speaking of David's body. "He fell on sleep, and was laid unto his fathers, and saw corruption." His body fell into its last, long sleep, and saw corruption. If you like to take the words in the wider sense, he was asleep as far as the world was concerned; he had done with it. No sorrow came to him, no earthly joy, no mingling with the strife of tongues, no girding on his harness for the war. "He fell on sleep." He had nothing to do with anything that was done under the sun. And that is the case with our dear friend whom we miss from his place to-day, and it will soon be the case also with you and with me. There is not much here worth stopping for; and when our work is finished, like David, we shall fall on sleep. We shall then be asleep to all the declensions of the age, all the strifes of men, and all else which gives us sorrow of heart.

Does not this word further mean that *his dying was like going to sleep?* It usually is so with God's people. Some die with a considerable measure of pain; but, as a rule, when believers pass away, they just shut their eyes on earth, and open them in heaven. I have had infinitely more pleasure at death-beds than I have had at weddings. I have been to many marriage-feasts, I have gone there at duty's call; but I can confirm what Solomon said, "It is better to go to the house of mourning, than to go to the house of feasting : for that is the end of all men ; and the living will lay it to his heart." I am not aware that I have gained anything at the wedding, but I have gained much at the dying bed, as I have seen the joy and peace and rapture of girls and youths, and men and women, passing away joyfully to be "for ever with the Lord." I have known some of our number here who were too bashful and backward ever to say much for Christ when they were well; but when I went to see them die, there was not a bit of bashfulness about them. They spoke out so boldly that I have said to them, "Why, if you get better, you must preach for me one of these Sundays"; and they have smiled and said that they would never get better. They have known this, and they have rejoiced to think that they were going where they would not need any preacher, but would see their Lord Jesus face to face. How they have brightened up at the mention of his dear name! Some of them have sung then, though I never knew them to sing before; and some of them have told of things which they seemed to see and hear, which eye hath not seen, nor ear heard, till God has revealed them to the departing spirit. You remember such dying beds, do you not? Was it your mother, or your father, who passed away in that glorious style? Perhaps it was a brother beloved, or a sister, or a friend. Well, if we know Christ, it shall be ours by-and-by to sleep in him. You who believe in Christ ought no more to dread death than you dread going to sleep at night. You will, ere you sleep, commit yourself to God, and as you put your head on the pillow, the similitude of death will be upon you, even sleep, which one has called "death's cousin." You will not be afraid of that. Why, then, should any dismay seize you in prospect of that which is but another sleep? Rather sing to yourself :—

> "Since Jesus is mine, I'll not fear undressing,
> But gladly put off these garments of clay ;
> To die in the Lord is a covenant blessing,
> Since Jesus to glory through death led the way."

Let us follow where he leads. Perchance some of us may tarry until he comes again. There will be no death for such; they will but change the service of their generation for the service of the glorified. "Behold, I shew you a mystery ; we shall not all sleep, but we shall all be changed." Then, when the trumpet shall sound, this corruptible shall put on incorruption, those who sleep in Christ shall awake in resurrection splendour, and together we shall serve our Lord day and night in his temple for ever. Meanwhile, serve your own generation by the will of God; and if the Lord tarry, you will fall on sleep, even as David did. May God bless you who believe in Jesus, and save the unsaved who are in our midst, for our Lord Jesus Christ's sake! Amen.

PORTION OF SCRIPTURE READ BEFORE SERMON—Acts xiii. 14—43.

HYMNS FROM "OUR OWN HYMN BOOK"—879, 694, 844.

The note at the end of last week's sermon informed all readers that the long-dreaded blow had at length fallen, and that their much-loved preacher had been called to his heavenly home. His voice will no more be heard on earth; but he will continue to speak for his Lord through the press, and especially by his sermons.

Attention has been already directed to the overruling hand of God in the selection of the sermons to be published at this memorable time. The one for next week will be the third in the series preached in connection with the death of the late Mr. William Olney, the text being Ephesians v. 30; and the following week, the address by MR. SPURGEON, at Mr. William Olney's funeral service in the Tabernacle, will be published. A considerable portion of this address was *revised by Mr. Spurgeon with his own hand*. With it the publishers will give *a portrait of the beloved preacher*, and also a portrait of the late Mr. W. Olney.

The revision of the weekly sermons, and the editorship of *The Sword and the Trowel*, will remain in the hands of those who have carried on the work during MR. SPURGEON'S long illness. He was only able, personally, to revise two sermons throughout the many months that he was laid aside. These will now have a special value in the estimation of his many friends. They are the two entitled, "Gratitude for Deliverance from the Grave" (No. 2,237), and "A Stanza of Deliverance" (No. 2,241).

There is not much that can be recorded here concerning MR. SPURGEON'S last illness, and his falling asleep in Jesus. *The Sword and the Trowel* for March will contain an account of the varying experiences in the sunny land, from the time when he delivered his two New Year addresses until all that remained of him was borne away to the railway-station, *en route* for England, amid tokens of widespread sorrow and sympathy. Amongst other items of interest will be reports of the last two Sabbath evening services conducted by MR. SPURGEON at the Hôtel Beau Rivage; and later numbers of *The Sword and the Trowel* will furnish the readers with descriptions of "Mr. Spurgeon's last drives at Menton", with reproductions of photographs taken under his personal supervision.

Metropolitan Tabernacle Pulpit.

MEMBERS OF CHRIST.

A Sermon

Intended for Reading on Lord's-day, February 21st, 1892,

DELIVERED BY

C. H. SPURGEON,

AT THE METROPOLITAN TABERNACLE, NEWINGTON,

On Thursday Evening, October 23rd, 1890.

"For we are members of his body, of his flesh, and of his bones."—Ephesians v. 30.

Yesterday, when I had the painful task of speaking at the funeral of our dear friend, Mr. William Olney, I took the text which I am going to take again now. I am using it again because I did not then really preach from it at all, but simply reminded you of a favourite expression of his, which I heard from his lips many times in prayer. He very frequently spoke of our being one with Christ in "living, loving, lasting union"—three words which, in addition to being alliterative, are very comprehensive as to the nature of our union with Christ. Those three words, you will remember, were the heads of my discourse,* in the presence of that remarkable gathering which crowded this place to do honour to the memory of our brother, whose highest ambition was always to honour his Lord, whom he so faithfully served.

Paul here speaks only of true believers, men who are quickened by divine grace and made alive unto God. Of them, he says, not by way of romance, nor of poetical exaggeration, but as an undisputed matter of fact, "We are members of his body, of his flesh, and of his bones." That there is a true union between Christ and his people is no fiction or dream of a heated imagination. Sin separated us from God, and in undoing what sin has done, Christ joins us to himself in a union more real than any other in the whole world.

This union is very near, and very dear, and very complete. We are so near to Christ, that we cannot be nearer; for we are one with him. We are so dear to Christ, that we cannot be dearer. Consider

---

* This address will be issued next week, completing the series relating to the late Mr. W. Olney. Many friends may wish to preserve the whole set; they can readily do so, as the four discourses will be included in the February part of *The Metropolitan Tabernacle Pulpit* (Price 5d.; post free, 6d.). The funeral address, to be published next week, will come to many with a peculiarly solemn sacredness just now, for a considerable portion of it was *revised by Mr. Spurgeon with his own hand*. With it the publishers will give *a portrait of the beloved preacher*, and also a portrait of the late Mr. W. Olney.

No. 2,244.

how close and tender is the tie when it is true that Christ loved us, and gave himself for us. It is a union more intimate than any other which exists amongst men; for "Greater love hath no man than this, that a man lay down his life for his friends." We were his enemies when Christ died for us, that he might save us, and make us so one with himself, that from him our life should be drawn, and that in him our life should be hid. It is, then, a very near and dear union which Christ has established between himself and his redeemed; and this union could not be more complete than it is.

It is, also, a most wonderful union. The more you think of it, the more you will be astonished, and stand in sacred awe before such a marvel of grace. Well did Kent say—

> "O sacred union, firm and strong,
> How great the grace, how sweet the song,
> That worms of earth should ever be
> One with Incarnate Deity!"

But so it is. Even the incarnation of Christ is not more wonderful than his living union with his people. It is a thing to be considered often; it is the wonder of the skies; and is chief among those things which "the angels desire to look into." On the surface of this truth you may not see much; but the longer you gaze, and the more the Holy Spirit assists you in your meditation, the more you will see in this wonderful sea of glass mingled with fire. My soul exults in the doctrine that Christ and his people are everlastingly one.

This is a very cheering doctrine. He that understands it has an ocean of music in his soul. He that can really grasp and feed upon it will often sit in the heavenly places with his Lord, and anticipate the day when he shall be with him, and shall be like him. Even now, since we are one with him, there is no distance between us, we are nearer to him than anything else can ever be. The very idea of union makes us forget all distance: indeed, distance is altogether annihilated. Love joins us so closely with Christ, that he becomes more to us than our very selves; and though now we see him not, yet believing, we rejoice with joy unspeakable and full of glory.

In passing, I may say that this doctrine is very practical. It is not merely a piece of sugar for your mouth; it is a light for your path, for "he that saith he abideth in him ought himself also so to walk even as he walked." We must take care that the love that was round about Christ's feet, is always shining on our path. We must go about doing good, following in the steps of our Lord. It would be giving the lie to this doctrine if we lived in sin; for, if we are one with him, then must we be in this world even as he was; and being filled with his Spirit, must seek to reproduce his life before the world.

These thoughts may serve as an introduction to a fuller consideration of this great subject; and I shall begin by saying that, in Holy Scripture, *the union between Christ and his people is set forth under various forms.* Then I will try to show you that *the metaphor in our text is full of meaning;* and, in the third place, I will prove to you that *the doctrine of our union with Christ has its practical lessons.* As we delight our hearts in the glorious truth that "we are members of his body, of his flesh, and of his bones," may we determine to live as those who are thus closely joined to the Lord of life!

I. Our first thought is, that THIS UNION IS SET FORTH UNDER SEVERAL FORMS. The blessed fact is almost beyond our highest thought: what wonder, then, that language fails adequately to describe it! Simile after simile is used. I am only going to mention four of them.

The union between Christ and the believer is described as the union of *the foundation and the stone.* "To whom coming, as unto a living stone, disallowed indeed of men, but chosen of God, and precious, ye also, as lively stones, are built up a spiritual house." We are built on Christ, and built up into him. We lie upon him just as the stone rests on the foundation. Well may we sing—

"All my hope on thee is stayed,
All my help from thee I bring"!

The stone is one with the foundation in its dependence. In the time of our need we press the closer to Christ; the heavier our hearts, the more we bear our weight upon him. It is the heavy stone that clings to the foundation; the light stone, perchance, might be blown away. But we cling at all times, depending wholly upon him, even as the stone rests upon the rock beneath. The stone does not bear up its own weight: it just rests where it is put. So do we rest on Christ. He is the foundation, and we repose on him.

Again, the stone is one with the foundation in its adhesion. In the course of time, the stone becomes more and more knit to it. When first the mortar is placed there, and is wet, you might shake the stone. But, by-and-by, the mortar dries, and the stone seems to bite into the foundation, and holds fast to it. In old Roman walls, you cannot get a stone away; for the cement, which joins the stone to its fellow, is as strong as the stone itself; and, truly, that which joins us to Christ is stronger than we are. We might be broken, but the bond of love, which holds us like a mighty cement to Christ, who is our foundation, can never be broken away. We have actually become one with him, as I have often seen stones in the walls of an old castle become one with each other. You could not get them away; they were part and parcel of the wall, and it would have been necessary to blow the wall to pieces before you could separate the stones from one another. So have we, by God's grace, become one with Christ, experimentally and indissolubly. The course of years has bound us still faster to him.

The stone is one with the foundation, moreover, in its design. The architect, in placing the stone, was following out his plan. He planned the foundation, and thought of every course; and the stone is essential to the wall, even as the foundation is essential to the stone. Thus we are one with Christ in the design of God. Reverently we say it, that God's purpose comprehends not only Christ, but the whole company of his elect; and without his chosen people, the design of Jehovah can never be accomplished. He is building a temple to his praise; but a temple cannot be all foundation. There is a necessity for every stone in the wall; in the divine purpose, there is a necessity that such a one should be a living stone, and such a one should be another living stone. The weakest and the meanest of the Lord's people are as necessary as the noblest and most beautiful, though indeed all are without any praise until they are built into the wall. He that chose Christ, chose all his people; he arranged that they should be built up together, and in him "all the building fitly framed together groweth unto an holy temple in the Lord." Oh, I like to think of each one of us, however insignificant we may appear to be, as being bricks or stones in that great temple of almighty grace! Perhaps some of us may stand where everybody can see us. Others may be embedded in the wall, where nobody can see us; but what does it matter? If we are in the wall at all, it is well. Wherever we are placed, we are joined to Christ; and therefore no one has a pre-eminence over any other, because we are all alike built upon the one foundation, even Jesus Christ our Lord, into whom we daily grow, pressing closer and closer to him in experience, and holding tighter and tighter to him by faith.

The second aspect in which our union with Christ is represented in the Scriptures, is that of *the vine and the branches.* "I am the vine, ye are the branches," is the word of Christ to his disciples. The former simile of the foundation and the stone does not suggest any idea of life. Hence, the apostle, in using it, had to speak of Christ as a living stone, and of us as living stones. It is a somewhat odd figure, and yet it is strictly true; for you and I have no more spiritual life in us than stones, except as a miracle makes us live; and then, though we are living, yet, like stones, we are apparently inert and lifeless, albeit we are really quickened by a supernatural work, and made living stones. But the figure is not congruous.

This second simile, however, conveys to us the idea of life, for a vine is no vine if it is dead, and its branches are no true branches unless they are alive. There is a living union between Christ and his people; and I hope that I can appeal to the experience of many here present who know that there is a living union between them and Christ. Happy is the man who can say, "I live; yet not I, but Christ liveth in me: and the life which I now live in the flesh I live by the faith of the Son of God, who loved me, and gave himself for me"!

The union is even more than a union of life; it is a union of derived life. The branch is in such union with the stem that it receives all its sap from it; it could not live unless the living juices flowed from the stem into it. And such is our life. Christ pours his life-blood into us. Perpetually, as long as he exists, he seems to be oozing out into his people. In fact, when his wounds were open, he bled life into us; and when his heart was burst, he changed our hearts, and gave them life, though they once were hearts of stone. We are so one with Christ, that we at first received our life from him, and we continue to receive it from him every moment.

In consequence of the life of Christ in us, we grow. The growing of the branch is really the growing of the vine. It is because the stem grows that it sends its growth into the branch, and manifests it there. As Christ pours his life-force into us, he makes us grow, to the praise of the glory of his grace.

Fruit-bearing is the ultimate end of our union to Christ. We are one with him that we may bring forth fruit unto his praise. Dear friends, are we really doing this? Are we not satisfied with a nominal union to Christ, even though we bear no fruit to his honour?

We ought to be very distressed when we are barren and unfruitful; remembering that the great Husbandman has a sharp knife, and that it is written, "Every branch in me that beareth not fruit he taketh away." Oh, that none of my hearers may ever be in Christ in that false way, but may we all be in him in a union so true and vital as shall cause us to bear fruit to his praise; for then, though we shall be pruned, we shall never be cut off from the vine!

The third metaphor which the Saviour deigns to give of this union is that of *the husband and the wife.* "For the husband is the head of the wife, even as Christ is the head of the church." Here you have a union, not only of life, but also of love. It is worthy of notice that the two words, "live" and "love", should be so like each other. In spiritual things, the two things are not only similar, they are exactly alike. Love is the life; and life is always first sent, and chiefly sent in the form of love.

With the true husband, his wife is himself. The Scripture saith, "He that loveth his wife loveth himself;" and I believe that Christ considers that, when he loves his church, he loves himself. His care for us is now his care for himself. Since he has taken us to be in eternal wedded union with himself, he regards us as himself, and he cares for us as he cares for himself: "For we are members of his body, of his flesh, and of his bones." No sane man will injure his own flesh. "No man ever yet hated his own flesh; but nourisheth and cherisheth it, even as the Lord the church." So Christ takes care of his people, because he regards them as being bound to himself by those bonds which make them to be as himself. Hence we are kept as the apple of his eye.

Remember that, in every family, the wife is the mother of the children; and so it is in the church of Christ. He would have us all bear unto him a holy spiritual seed. If we abide in him, we shall be able to propagate our faith, and bring others into the church. Every believer should have this object before him as the joy of his life; for thus shall Christ "see his seed, he shall prolong his days, and the pleasure of the Lord shall prosper in his hand."

The wife, too, is the keeper of the house. She takes care of the household concerns of her husband. And so would the Lord Christ have his people care for his interests, and for all that belongs to him; for he has committed these things to us, as the husband commits his treasure to his wife. He has left us in custody of all that he has. In one sense we are the stewards of his household, but in another and a dearer sense, we are united to him by marriage bonds which can never be broken. It is a sweet subject; but I cannot linger upon it. You must let your own thoughts be fragrant with its aroma. However close may be the union of husband and wife, the union between the believer and Christ is closer still. Oh, to realize more and more of it each day!

> "O Jesus! make thyself to me
> A living, bright reality;
> More present to faith's vision keen
> Than any outward object seen.
> More dear, more intimately nigh,
> Than e'en the sweetest earthly tie!"

All human imagery fails to set forth the union between Christ and his people; but the figure in our text is that of *the head and the members*. The apostle says of Christ, that "we are members of his body, of his flesh, and of his bones." Christ is the Head, and we are members of his body. Wonderful union this! In the first metaphor, the foundation and the stone, we had the idea of rest: in the second, the vine and the branches, the idea of life; the union of husband and wife gave us the thought of love; now here we have the suggestion of identity. There are two lives in the husband and the wife, but there is only one life in the head and the body; and in this respect this metaphor brings out the true relation of Christ to his people more clearly than any other.

There is a wonderful union between the head and the members of the body. It is a union of life, and a union of the body which always continues. The husband may have to travel miles away from the wife; but it can never be that the head can travel away from the body. If I were to hear of any man whose head was a foot, or even an inch, away from his body, I should say that he was dead. There must be perpetual union between the head and the members, or else death follows; and the death, mark you, not only of the body, but of the head as well. They are dead when they are divided. How glorious is this thought when we apply it to the Lord and his redeemed people! Their union is everlasting. They would die if separated from him, and even he would cease to be did he lose them; for, somehow or other, they are so joined, that he will not be without them: he cannot be without them, for that were for the Head of the church to be divided from the members of his mystical body. Thus it is that we are able to sing—

"And this I do find, we two are so joined,
He'll not be in glory, and leave me behind."

II. Having thus shown you these four figures—and there are others, but I have not time to speak upon them—I now come to the one before us in the text, and remark that THIS METAPHOR IS FULL OF MEANING: "We are members of his body, of his flesh, and of his bones." There are seven points to which I would ask your attention.

There is here *union of life, union of relationship, and union of service*. See what I mean. Your hand never studies what it can do for the head; but when the head wishes the hand uplifted, immediately up goes the hand; and when the head wishes that the hand should go down, down it goes in an instant. There is no deliberation or discussion about the matter. The head and the members, in a healthy body, are practically one. If you happen to be ill, it may be different. I have sometimes seen, in a person semi-paralyzed, the leg throw itself out without any guidance from the head; I have seen the hand quiver and tremble without the will of the head; and sometimes—how often has it happened to me!—the head has willed that the hand should turn over the pages of a book, and the hand has been unable to do it. When disease gets into the system, straightway the members do not obey the head; but in a healthy body, the head does but will a thing, and at once the hand fulfils it. Did you never notice when you were falling, how, without thought, your hands always tried to save your head? If any person were about to strike you, you would not deliberate; but up would go your arm to protect your head. This law is also true in the spiritual life. All true Christians will do anything to save their Head. He saved us, and now our desire is to save him. We cannot bear that he should be insulted, that his gospel should be despised, or that anything should be done against his sacred dignity. We are so one with our glorious Head, that the moment anyone strikes at him, up goes our hand immediately in his defence. Oh! I trust that you know what this means; if you are ever put to the pain of hearing Christ's gospel falsely preached, or seeing professedly Christian men bringing disgrace upon his dear name, you feel at once that you would rather bear any pain, or any reproach, than that Christ should be injured. The hand is so one with the head, that it endeavours to screen it.

Between the head and the members there is also *union of feeling*. If the head aches, you feel it all over, you are altogether ill; and if your finger aches, your head does not feel well. There is such a sympathy between all parts of the body that, "whether one member suffer, all the members suffer with it; or one member be honoured, all the members rejoice with it. Now, ye are the body of Christ, and members in particular." Christ is our Head, and the Head specially suffers with the members. I do not know whether it is always so clear that one hand suffers with another hand, as it is clear that the head suffers with either hand. So is it in the church. It may not always be clear that all the members sympathize with one another, but it is always clear that Christ sympathizes with each one of his people. There is a quicker way, somehow, from the head to the hand, than there is from one hand to the other; and there is a keener sympathy between Christ and his people than there often is between one of his servants and another. It is written concerning his people that "In all their affliction he was afflicted." In all thy sorrows, child of God, thy heavenly Head feels the pain!

There is, moreover, a *union of mutual necessity* between the members and the head. The head wants the body. Now, I must speak very guardedly here, when I refer the thought to Christ, but still it is true. What would my head be without my body? It would be a ghastly sight. And Christ without his people would be incomplete. A dying Christ, redeeming nobody! A living Christ, with no one to live by his life, would be a grim failure! Christ on Calvary, and souls going down to hell, with none saved by his precious blood! Christ incarnate on the cross, without a single man saved by his incarnation and his death! It would be a fearful sight. The church is said to be Christ's fulness—"The church, which is his body, the fulness of him that filleth all in all." This is a wonderful expression. Now, the fulness of the head is the body; take the body away from the head, what is it? As to the body, what could it be without the head? If your head were gone, you could not have swiftness of foot, or deftness of hand, or strength of heart. No; there remains nothing for the head if it is severed from the body; and nothing for the body if it is separated from the head. There is between them a union of mutual necessity.

There is, farther, between the head and the members a *union of nature.* I will not attempt to describe the chemical composition of human flesh; but it is quite clear that my head is made of the same flesh as my members. There is no difference between the flesh of the one and the flesh of the other. So, though our covenant Head is now in heaven, and his feet are on earth, yet still Christ is so one by nature with his people, that he is very man of very man, as much as he is very God of very God. If you deny his humanity, I do not think that you will long hold his divinity. And if you deny his Deity, you have sadly destroyed the perfection of his humanity; for a perfect man he could not be if he so acted as to make men think that he was God when he was not. To us he is God-Man in one person, whom we love and adore; his nature is the same as our nature, and we are joined to him for ever.

> "Lord, Jesus, are we ONE with thee?
> Oh, height! Oh, depth of love!
> With thee we died upon the tree,
> In thee we live above.
>
> "Oh, teach us, Lord, to know and own
> This wondrous mystery,
> That thou with us art truly ONE,
> And we are ONE with thee!"

Between Christ and his people there is also a *union of possession.* Nothing belongs to my head that does not belong to my hand. Whatever my head can claim as its own, my hand may claim as its own. Whatever belongs to Christ belongs to you, poor believer! Since Christ is rich, can you be poor? Even his Father is your Father, and his heaven is your heaven; for you are so one with him that all the broad possessions of his infinite wealth are given freely to you. He bestows upon you his bounty, not only "to the half of the kingdom", but the whole of it. Joined to him, all that he has is yours.

Between the Lord and his church there is also a *union of present condition.* Christ is very dear to his Father's heart. "This is my beloved Son, in whom I am well pleased," was the word which came from the opened heaven concerning Christ; and as God delights in Christ, so is he also well pleased with you who are in Christ. Yea, he is as pleased with you as he is with Christ; for he sees you in Christ, and Christ in you. God makes no division between you and him to whom he has joined you. "What therefore God hath joined together, let no man put asunder." Certainly God will never separate that which he has united in Christ. Do not put yourself asunder from Christ, even in your thoughts, by supposing that you are not well-beloved of God even as is your covenant Head.

Last of all, there is a *union of future destiny.* Whatever Christ is to be, you are to be a sharer of it all. How can you die while Jesus lives? How can the body die, while the head lives? If we go through the waters, they cannot overflow us until they overflow our head. While a man's head is above water, he cannot be drowned. And Christ up yonder, in the eternities of glory, can never be conquered: neither can those be vanquished who are one with him. For ever and for ever, till the Christ shall die, till the immortal Son of God expires, you who are united to him in the purpose of God, and in the faith which now lays hold of him, shall live and reign. "Because I live, ye shall live also." Is not that a quietus to every fear of destruction? You are so one with him that, when the sun becomes a burnt-out coal, and the moon is turned into a clot of blood, when the stars fall as the leaves of autumn, and heaven and earth shall melt away, going back into the nothingness from which Omnipotence hath called them, you shall live, for he shall live who is your Head. "We believe that we shall also live with him: knowing that Christ being raised from the dead dieth no more; death hath no more dominion over him." Where he goes we shall follow. I have heard it said that, when a thief is able to get his head through the bars of the window, his body can easily follow. I am not sure of that; but I know that where my Lord has gone, his members shall surely be. "I am he that liveth, and was dead; and, behold, I am alive for evermore," is a word that is meant for your consolation. Take it home. "We are members of his body, of his flesh, and of his bones," and, as Doddridge sings—

> "Since Christ and we are one,
> Why should we doubt or fear?
> If he in heaven hath fixed his throne,
> He'll fix his members there."

III. Lastly, and briefly, THIS DOCTRINE HAS ITS PRACTICAL LESSONS, which I will try to set forth plainly, so that those of us who are members of Christ may bring greater joy and glory to our Head than we have brought aforetime.

To begin with, I would say, if we are indeed one with Christ, *we should have no doubt about it.* It used to be a fashion, and I fear it is in some quarters still, to think that mistrust of our own condition, and doubt concerning our own salvation, is a kind of virtue. I have met with good people, who would not say that they were saved; they "hoped" that they were; and I have met with others who were not sure that they were cleansed by the precious blood of Christ; they "trusted" that they were. This state of mind is not a credit either to Christ, or to ourselves. If I told my son something, and he were to say to me, "I hope you will keep your word, father," I should not feel that he treated me as he ought. Surely, to believe Christ up to the hilt is the way to honour him. If we are one with him, we lose the comfort of it if we do not know certainly the fact of our blessed union; we miss much of the confidence that comes of it if we do not clearly apprehend the reality; and we are robbed of much of the joy which it brings, and know little of the meaning of that word "the joy of the Lord is your strength," unless we believe simply like children, and take the word to mean what it says, and are certain about it. This is an age of doubt; but, as for me, I will have none of it; I have doubted enough, and more than enough; I have done with it long ago; and I can say with Paul, "I know whom I have believed, and am persuaded that he is able to keep that which I have committed unto him against that day." Salvation is by faith. Damnation comes by doubt. Doubt is the death of all comfort, the destruction of all force, the enemy of God and man.

If we are one with Christ, *we should go through the world like princes;* we should be like Abraham among his fellows, who claimed no princedom, and wore no crown, yet who could say to the King of Sodom what he had already vowed to God, "I will not take from a thread unto a shoe-latchet, and I will not take anything that is thine, lest thou shouldest say, I have made Abram rich." If you are one with Christ, treat the world in that way. O world, thou canst not bless me! God hath blessed me. Thou canst not curse me! God hath blessed me. Dost thou laugh? Laugh, if it pleaseth thee. Dost thou frown? What signifieth it to me? If God has smiled upon me, thou mayest spurn me. If I am one with Christ, I expect that thou shouldest think but little of me; for thou didst spurn my Head. Should the body of Christ expect better treatment than the Head received?

If we are one with Christ, we shall remember that *to dishonour ourselves is to implicate our Lord.* If I dishonour any part of my body, my head feels the shame of it; and since we are the members of Christ, we should be very careful how we behave, lest we should cause him pain. Men will judge of Christ by his people. If I caught sight of a pair of legs very unsteadily walking along the street, I should be inclined to say that they belonged to a drunken head. If our walk among men is not such "as becometh the gospel", what hard thoughts those around us may have of our Saviour! Of course, we know that any ill estimate of him will be false, for he is all fair, and there is no spot in him; but still his name and his cause will suffer dishonour. Let us not, then, injure or defile ourselves, lest we should bring reproach upon him whom we love!

In the next place, if we are one with him, *to think of him should be very natural.* There are many of us who could say, without any exaggeration, that, though we do not think so much of our Lord as we should, and are not so much with him in contemplation as we desire, yet we have spent more time with him than we have spent with anybody else, more than with wife, or children, or our dearest companions in the church or in the world. And we know him better than we know anybody else. Little as we know compared with what we hope to know, yet his love has become to us now the brightest, the most conspicuous fact in all our history. We know but few things; but we know that we are one with Christ in a union never to be broken. We know him, too, by our intercourse with him. We saw him this morning; we have seen him during the day; we shall see him again to-night. I should not like to go to bed with any other thought upon my mind than this—

> "Sprinkled afresh with pardoning blood,
> I lay me down to rest,
> As in the embraces of my God,
> Or on my Saviour's breast."

If we are one with him, *to live with him should be the most natural thing in our lives.* Have I not heard, however, of some professors who have not had communion with Christ for many a day? I talked once with a brother, who said a great deal about many things; and when he had complained of this and of that, I leant forward to him, and said, "Brother, how long is it since you have had close fellowship with Christ?" He answered, "Oh, there you have got me!" When I asked him, "What do you mean by that?" he answered, "I am afraid that I have not had fellowship with Christ for months." I had suspected that it must have been so, or else his conversation would not have been of the kind it was. What a sad thing it must be for a wife to live in her husband's house, and not speak to him for weeks! But how much worse it is for us to profess to be one with Christ, and yet have no sort of communication with him by the month together! This is something perfectly horrible. God save us all from such a thing! May we think continually of our Lord, and ever live with him, because we are one with him!

Again, being one with Christ, *to serve him should be very natural.* Indeed we exist but to do his will, and to glorify his name. Of what use are my hands and feet unless they move at the impulse of my head? They are but encumbrances unless they are ready to obey the bidding of my mind. If your arms hang helpless, you do not know what to do with them; whichever side you turn, they are in the way. To be paralyzed is most unnatural, yet I fear me there are many of us of but little use to our Master. We hear his word, but do not obey it; he calls for helpers, and we run not at his bidding! Come, come, this will not do. We are members of Christ, and the one purpose of our life should be to serve our Head. God help us all to do it!

I will not continue longer. I leave you to draw the many inferences which naturally spring from our being one with Christ. Our heaven lies in our union with him. Ay, and sometimes when we realize our oneness with Christ, we can hardly think that we should be happier in heaven than we are now! May you all have this enjoyment! Oh, you would think that we raved, if we told you the unspeakable delight, the immeasurable bliss, which communion with Christ has brought into our souls. I desire that all of you should know the same rapture. I never enjoy a thing without wishing everybody to enjoy it; therefore, when I come to this point of being one with Christ, and the delight it brings, I would to God that you all knew it, too! But alas! you do not; some of you do not even desire it. I have been talking something like Dutch to some of you to-night; you have not comprehended my language at all. May the very fact that you have not understood it, or cared about it, lead you to suspect that there is a joy which you have not known, and a life which you have not found; and when you know that it is so, "Seek ye the Lord while he may be found, call ye upon him while he is near." If you seek him with all your heart, you will surely find him; and very soon you also will be brought into "living, loving, lasting union" with Christ.

Remember that the least touch of faith is sufficient to save the soul. That poor woman, who came behind Christ in the throng, only touched the hem of his garment, yet that timid touch brought healing and health to her. Virtue went out of him into her, and she was made whole of her plague. If thou canst only touch the Lord by the finger of thy faith, ay, though it be thy little finger, it shall be well with thee; though thy hand be quivering with the palsy of unbelief, yet, still, if thou hast faith enough to touch him, to come into contact with him, thou hast set the whole machinery of salvation in motion. God give thee to find eternal life even now! Why not? If my dear friend were here, of whom this drapery is a memorial, he would say to me, "Oh, tell them to taste and see that the Lord is good; blessed are all they that trust in him!" You know how fond he was of that verse we sang yesterday—

> "Oh, make but trial of his love;
> Experience will decide
> How blest are they, and only they,
> Who in his truth confide!"

God bless you all, for Christ's sake! Amen.

PORTION OF SCRIPTURE READ BEFORE SERMON—Ephesians v.

HYMNS FROM "OUR OWN HYMN BOOK"—760, 761, 762.

Readers of the Sermons have probably all seen the very full reports, published in the daily and weekly newspapers, of the memorial and funeral services relating to their now glorified preacher. Those who took part in the impressive meetings at the Tabernacle, or gazed upon the almost countless multitude that thronged the road from Newington to Norwood, or formed part of the privileged company that gathered around the grave, must have felt that they were spectators of a scene without parallel in the history of this generation, at least. Comparatively few were able to hear all the tributes of love to the dear departed one, the gospel he so faithfully preached, and the Saviour he so fondly loved. Many will be glad to know, therefore, that a *Memorial Volume* will be issued, as soon as possible, containing a complete report of all the public services of the past week. Full particulars will be announced in due course.

MRS. SPURGEON, and all the members of the bereaved family, as well as the officers and members of the Tabernacle Church, are deeply grateful for the almost innumerable expressions of sympathy which they have received from all parts of the world, and all sections of the Church. They cannot attempt to acknowledge these communications personally; but through various channels they have sought to convey the assurance of their heartfelt gratitude; and MRS. SPURGEON has written a special "Message of Thanks" for the March issue of *The Sword and the Trowel*, which will be a Memorial number, containing all that can be recorded at present concerning its late beloved Editor. MRS. SPURGEON continues to be very graciously upheld under her sore bereavement; but she is not yet strong enough to return home.

Metropolitan Tabernacle Pulpit.

"LIVING, LOVING, LASTING UNION."

ADDRESS

DELIVERED BY

PASTOR C. H. SPURGEON

AT THE FUNERAL OF

MR. WILLIAM OLNEY,

OCTOBER 22*nd*, 1890,

WITH NEW PORTRAITS OF

PASTOR C. H. SPURGEON

AND

MR. WILLIAM OLNEY.

LONDON:
PASSMORE AND ALABASTER, PATERNOSTER BUILDINGS.

PRICE ONE PENNY.

No. 2,245.

"LIVING, LOVING, LASTING UNION."

FUNERAL ADDRESS

Intended for Reading on Lord's-day, February 28th, 1892.

"For we are members of his body, of his flesh, and of his bones."—Ephesians v. 30.

Before the funeral, at Norwood Cemetery, of the late Mr. William Olney, senior deacon of the church at the Metropolitan Tabernacle, a service was held in the Tabernacle. The building was crowded with sympathizing friends, who came to testify the affection they bore to the beloved deacon who had been so suddenly called from their midst. The senior Pastor presided.

The hymn, "They are gathering homeward one by one," was sung, and Pastor James A. Spurgeon offered prayer. The hymn "Why do we mourn departing friends?" followed, and C. H. Spurgeon then read and expounded 1 Corinthians xv. The Rev. Burman Cassin, Rector of St. George's, Southwark, briefly engaged in prayer, and the assembly sang the thirty-fourth Psalm, in the version beginning—

> "Through all the changing scenes of life,
> In trouble and in joy,
> The praises of my God shall still
> My heart and tongue employ."

The hymn commencing, "For ever with the Lord!" was sung, and a concluding prayer was offered by Mr. James Spurgeon.

Pastor C. H. Spurgeon then rose, and said:—As I am in a very unfit condition to speak to you this morning, I shall have to try for once to keep away from my subject; for if I dwell upon it, it will master me, and I shall not be able to speak to you at all. I am trying to suppress my feelings, that I may be able to find words.

I am going to speak about the favourite expression of my brother William Olney, which he frequently used in prayer. I wonder whether you will agree with me as to what it was. As my memory serves me, I have heard him a score of times, at least, use the following sentence when he drew very near to the Lord his God in prayer. He said, "Lord Jesus, we are one with thee. We feel that we have a living, loving, lasting union with thee." I think that you must remember that gem of his. Those three words have stuck by me; and ever since he has gone, I have found myself repeating them to myself involuntarily—"a living, loving, lasting union." He owed everything to that. He consciously enjoyed a living, loving, lasting union with the Lord Jesus Christ; and if you and I have that, we have all that we want for time and for eternity. If we have it not, we have nothing. Take any one of us by himself alone; he is lost, ruined, and undone. Take that same person linked with Christ by a living, loving, lasting union, and he is a saint—saved, sanctified, and sure to be glorified.

I have taken for my text the words which occur in the fifth

chapter of the Epistle to the Ephesians, and the thirtieth verse. Concerning our Lord Jesus, the apostle Paul says, "*We are members of his body, of his flesh, and of his bones.*"

"We", that is, his believing people, "are members of his body, of his flesh, and of his bones." He is our Head, and we are the members of the body, and so we are joined to him by a living, loving, lasting union.

I am not going beyond those three words; they shall be my three points, but at the same time I will keep to my text.

I. BETWEEN THE TRUE BELIEVER AND CHRIST THERE IS A LIVING UNION. There was just that between my brother William Olney and his Lord. A living union! When he joined the church of Christ, he did not offer it the distinguished honour of his name, and then slip away, and give his life to politics, or to business, or to amusement; but when the church had his name on its roll, it received the whole of the man, body, soul and spirit; and this because there was life in him.

His union to Christ was not nominal, but actual. He was not merely covered with the Christian name, but he had the Christian spirit and the Christian life within him. Yes, his union to Christ was a living union; not merely that of reliance, by which the stone leans upon the foundation; though he had that, for never man understood more clearly the doctrine of faith in Christ. Christ was his only trust and confidence, and he came to him as the stones come home to the foundation stone. But it was a living union in his case, for the fruits of life were produced. It was the union of the branch to the stem in that blessed vine which is Christ himself, even as he says, "I am the vine, ye are the branches."

Now what does this living union to Christ mean?

It means, first of all, *Christ's life laying hold of us.* "For as the Father hath life in himself; so hath he given to the Son to have life in himself." He is full of life, and when he takes hold of us, and raises our life into his, there is truly a living union between him and us.

But, further, this living union is *Christ's life in us.* It is given to him, not only to take us in our feebleness; but it is his divine prerogative to impart life to us, and to call dead men, and to make them live. "For as the Father raiseth up the dead, and quickeneth them; even so the Son quickeneth whom he will." This is how we come to have life in connection with him. His life flows into us, as out of the tree into the branches: so that we can truly say, with the apostle, "I live; yet not I, but Christ liveth in me: and the life which I now live in the flesh, I live by the faith of the Son of God, who loved me, and gave himself for me." The living union begins with our Lord's life, and then that life flows into us, and we begin to live also.

It was so with our friend, whom we so sadly miss from our midst to-day. A new life, a life of holiness, a life of service, a life of communion with God, began in him, by oneness with Christ, and it was continued in him by the same means. There was a living union: the life of Christ had begotten life in him, and this was seen continually in the fruit that he bore. I should not know, if I had to describe my departed brother, which word to associate most fully with him, "life" or "love." He was as full of life as ever he could be. He used to amaze us by his energy—I mean not merely physical or even mental energy, but his never-ceasing, overflowing spiritual energy. If any of us were dull, *he* never was; and he would not let us be dull for long. He would often tell us, when we were not well, that he thought we looked amazingly well, and he would try to cheer us up somehow or other, for he himself never seemed to lack for life, or fire, or force. I might almost say that, up to the last moment, he was energetic; he died full of life. He was intense in the very highest degree until struck down; and he was thus intense, not because of mere mental activity, but because of the burning zeal for God that was in his soul, and this zeal was the result of his living union with the Lord Jesus Christ.

Because of this life of Christ which was in him, he bore suffering without flinching. If there was anything that could equal the industry of his work, it was the heroism of his patience. He has often amazed us by his fortitude. We have admired the way in which he has triumphed in Christ in spite of his sufferings; but we have felt that we could scarcely hope to imitate him to the letter. He went as far in the way of bearing pain with patience as he went in the direction of serving God with enthusiasm; and this is saying a very great deal for any man. Therefore I do not say it for the man; but in praise of the grace of God which helped him, whether he was active or passive, still to be buoyant and bright because of the living union which subsisted between him and Christ. A verse of the Psalm we have just sung, which was a great favourite of his, truly describes the resolution of his life :—

> "Of his deliverance I will boast,
> Till all that are distress'd,
> From my example comfort take,
> And charm their griefs to rest."

Christ dwelling in him in fulness could both work and suffer. The fact that Christ lives in the believer is as real as that he once lived on earth in a human body. He came then with a double-handed blessing. He came both to do his Father's will and to bear the burden of the souls of men. He was active in doing good; and when the appointed time came, he as willingly bore the burden of the sins of men, and suffered to the death without complaint. In like manner Christ lived in our dear friend, making him strong both to do and to suffer. God grant also to you and to me to have such a living union to Christ!

Do you know anything of this experience, my dear friends? Many of you do; it is your life to be one with Christ. But to some of you I must be talking an unmeaning jargon. O souls, if the life of Christ is not in you, you are dead while you live, and you will die for ever when you die! Unless you get linked to Christ, you will then be driven from the presence of God, and away from all that makes true life and joy. Lay hold on Christ, and you will " lay hold on eternal life "; for he is " that eternal life which was with the Father, and was manifested unto us," and living contact with him is our only hope either for the present or for the future. If you are vitally joined to Christ, it is well with your soul; but if you are divided from Immanuel, and have no living union to Christ, there is no eternal life for you. "He that believeth on the Son hath everlasting life: and he that believeth not the Son shall not see life; but the wrath of God abideth on him."

> "Living or dying, Lord,
> I ask but to be thine,
> My life in thee, thy life in me,
> Makes heaven for ever mine."

II. The next word to "living", in my dear brother's frequent use, was "loving." BETWEEN THE TRUE BELIEVER AND CHRIST THERE IS A LOVING UNION. And oh, the union of a soul to Christ is made so sweet because it is as loving as it is living! My brother William Olney truly loved. He seemed to have a love to everybody. He never was so pleased as when he was pleasing other people; and he would go a long way, sometimes, to try and please people who would not be pleased, and sometimes people who ought not to be pleased. But still, his great ambition in life was to love others, and to make others love Christ. Love ruled supreme in his actions. His union to Christ was not cold and formal, stiff and narrow; he had a union to Christ that was warm, human, intense, fervent, loving. There was fire in the man, and the fire was the ardent flame of great affection to the Lord Jesus Christ.

I would like to have a talk about this loving union to Christ on some other occasion, when I could trust myself more than I can do now at this very solemn service.* Still, there are a few things that may be said upon this subject even now.

Christ's love to us begins this loving union. Its source is not in ourselves; but in love eternal, love immeasurable, love which caused itself, free-grace love, love to the unworthy, love to enemies, love to those who had no life, no strength, and no hope apart from him. Christ loved us so that he deigned to join himself to us in eternal union. The great Artesian well from which we drink, and which has tapped the divine fountains, is the love of Christ. This is where all our hope, and our joy, and our love begin. "Herein is love, not that we loved God, but that he loved us." In connection with this same truth of union with Christ, and fruitbearing as the result of it, our Lord himself says, "Ye have not chosen me, but I have chosen you." When his love thus made choice of us, he entered into covenant with his Father concerning his people; and before we were born he identified himself with us, so that in the purpose of God from all eternity we were accepted in him. But union with us meant union with our sins; and though the Son of God could never be overcome of evil, or become a sharer in human guilt, yet by the blessed mystery of his unity with his people, he could take their sin upon himself, and bear it in his own body on the tree. Thus, as there is no past or future to the eyes of him before whom all events are spread out in one eternal "now", the Son of God was able to atone for the

---

* On the following evening, Thursday, October 23rd, 1890, Mr. Spurgeon preached on this subject. The discourse, entitled "Members of Christ" (No. 2,244), delivered on that occasion, was published last week.

PASTOR C. H. SPURGEON.

Born at Kelvedon, Essex, June 19th, 1834.

Fell asleep in Jesus at Menton, France, January 31st, 1892.

DEACON WILLIAM OLNEY.

Born, May 10th, 1821.

Went Home, October 17th, 1890.

iniquities of those who, through all the ages, would be truly joined to him. His love that chose us did not shrink back from the awful payment which our debt rendered necessary: it was stronger than death, and mightier than the grave. Many waters could not quench it; many floods could not drown it; nor will it cease to exert its blessed influence over us until it shall bring us home to the mansions above; and not even then, for Christ's love is everlasting. By this loving union Christ brings us safely through all the temptations of life; the ransomed spirits of such as are joined to him are taken to be with Christ the instant they are absent from the body; and at last out of the tomb that same love shall call the body, and on the glad day of resurrection it shall be clearly seen how wonderful is the love which made our Lord so one with us. This, then, is the way in which we came to a loving union with Christ; he began to love us with a love that had no beginning, which has no measure, and which shall know no change nor end, and therefore he united himself to us for ever. Well might Kent praise the name of the Lord for the wonders wrought by such love as this as he sang:—

> "Heirs of God, joint heirs with Jesus,
>   Long ere time its race begun;
> To his name eternal praises!
>   Oh! what wonders love hath done!
>   One with Jesus,
> By eternal union one."

Our love to Christ completes this loving union. We first learn of his love to us, and then as the result of that, we are brought to love him. Ours is a poor little love, not worthy of his acceptance; but, such as it is, we give it all to him; and he will not refuse it, or despise it. Oh, that we all might be joined to Christ in love now! I am sure that my brother, who has gone from us, knew this union more than most of us. When we once got upon this glorious theme in private conversation, or when he touched upon it himself in his own public prayers, how his spirit seemed to burn and glow! He was always at home when speaking of the love of Christ, or of the love of Christ's people to their Lord. He could truly say, as I trust many of us will truly say now,—

> "I give my heart to thee,
>   O Jesus, most desired!
> And heart for heart the gift shall be,
>   For thou my soul hast fired:
> Thou hearts alone would'st move,
>   Thou only hearts dost love:
> I would love thee as thou lov'st me,
>   O Jesus most desired!"

In this loving union, *Christ's love to us and our love to Christ flow in the same channel.* Together they make a stream of love of a glorious kind. We love one another for Christ's sake; we love sinners for Christ's sake. We love the truth as Christ loves the truth. We love the Father in the same manner that Christ loves the Father, though not to the same degree. There is, in fact, but one love in the Head and in all the members. What the Head loves all the body loves.

As one man we go with Christ. Being united to him, his desires and longings become our desires and longings, too; we grow into his likeness, and "are changed into the same image from glory to glory, even as by the Spirit of the Lord."

Do you know anything about loving union to Christ? I feel sure that the great mass of those assembled here both know it and rejoice in it. Oh, to know it more! Oh, that his love were shed abroad more richly in our hearts! Now, by the Holy Ghost that is given to us, may we experience, not only the tiny rivulets of love that some of us have had in past days, but may we get to the torrents of love, may we be swept away by it, till, like a mighty ocean, it covers all our nature, and becomes to us a very heaven begun below!

III. Our third point is that, BETWEEN THE TRUE BELIEVER AND CHRIST THERE IS A LASTING UNION. The whole phrase which our dear departed friend used so frequently was "living, loving, lasting union." O friends, what a sad thing it would be for anyone to have only a temporary union to Christ! If I am speaking to any who were members of this church years ago, but who are not even professors now—if I am addressing some who seemed to be earnest Christians once, but who have gone back from following Christ—I would earnestly remind you that no union with Christ is living and loving unless it is also lasting.

The man who is truly united to Christ does not become an apostate. It is all in vain to seem to put on Christ for a time, and then, after a little while, to put him off again. That is the religion of the hypocrite, or of the mere temporary professor. But not so was it with our dear brother who is sleeping yonder. When he joined the church—I think that it is rather more than fifty-four years ago—he gave himself to the Lord, and he has been kept and sustained and upheld till now. Why, there are some of you who have been members of four or five denominations during that time! You have changed your views with the varying seasons, and have altered oftener than we care to remember, while here was he, keeping steadfast and immovable all the time, remaining ever a member of the same church, and going on steadily with his work. It seems to me that some of you build for a year, and pull down, then build again, and pull down once more. Why, you are not building at all unless your building stands; and you are not truly in union with Christ unless the union is lasting union; and that it will not be unless it is living union! Your profession of Christ will be a lie, and will help to sink you lower than the lowest hell unless you endure to the end. Make sure work with what you do in religion. Do not play at being a Christian. If you are converted, be converted with your whole heart. If you have faith in Christ, have vital faith, or do not pretend to have any. Be real; be true to the core. Be satisfied with nothing short of that union which the Spirit of God works in the hearts of those who, without reserve, yield to his power; else that which you seem to have will not be a lasting thing with you, and at the end you will be utterly cast off.

Now think of the joy of this fact. *Our union with Christ is not only lasting, it is everlasting.* With great boldness we utter the challenge. "Who shall separate us from the love of God which is in Christ Jesus our Lord?" It is true that we hold Christ, and that we will hold him tighter still; but the greater mercy is that he holds us, and he will never let us go. Does he not say concerning his sheep, "I give unto them eternal life; and they shall never perish, neither shall any man pluck them out of my hand"? And will he not be true to his word? You may take Christ from our hand, but you cannot take us from Christ's hand; he holdeth us fast; he is married to us, and he himself declares, "The Lord, the God of Israel, saith that he hateth putting away." He will have no divorce between our soul and himself. This living, loving, lasting union, which we have already found to be such a glorious reality, is to last for ever and ever, blessed be the name of the Lord!

I want you, beloved friends, to draw much comfort from this truth, and then I will have done. *Christ will not lose his members.* My head would not willingly lose a little finger, and Christ our Head will not lose one of us if "we are members of his body, of his flesh, and of his bones." Think you that Christ can be mutilated? Think you that he will lose even the least joint of his least finger? Never shall that be true. The word written of his body of flesh is equally true concerning his mystical body, which is his church. "A bone of him shall not be broken." Not even the smallest and most insignificant believer in Christ shall be lost, else would his body be incomplete. He is a perfect Christ, and you that are members of his body shall never be cut away from him by the wounds of Satan's sword, the surgery of infidelity, or any earthly accident or diabolical temptation. If you are one with him, you will be one with him for ever, for the union between you and your Lord is an eternal union, and to break it would be to disfigure and mutilate the Christ of God.

Furthermore, in that we are one with Christ, *he will raise our bodies.* "We are members of his body, of his flesh, and of his bones;" and, though I do not insist upon it, this verse has to me a kind of ring about it, which would lead us to believe that if we are members of his body, he will take even our bodies to be members of himself. Christ will not leave our brother in the grave. His body will see corruption; but the tomb shall only be like a refining pot, to separate the precious from the vile. When Moses brought Israel out of Egypt, he said, "There shall not an hoof be left behind;" and when that One who is greater than Moses shall bring forth his people from their graves, there shall not a bone or a piece of a bone of his redeemed be left in the region of death. When the angel brought Peter out of prison, he told him to put his shoes on. "Bind on thy sandals," was the angelic direction. He would not leave even an old pair of slippers in the prison when he brought Peter out. The deliverance was to be absolutely complete. Thus, too, when Christ shall bid us put on our garments which he shall prepare for us in the resurrection, no integral part of the man shall be left behind. O grave, thou must give up thy prey! O death, thou must yield up thy spoils! Our bodies are the temples of the Holy Ghost, and therefore they as well as our souls must be set free from the power of the last enemy. "Wherefore comfort one another with these words," whether it be concerning your own death, or the death of this dear friend, on whose coffin we look just now.

Beloved, we are parting with our brother, William Olney, for a while; but *we shall meet again.* We are so one with each other in truth and experience, that we cannot be separated. He was a member of Christ's body, and of his flesh, and of his bones; so am I; and so are you, my fellow-believer. The members of one body must be one. And we shall meet our departed friend again before long. Perhaps before another week, some of us may see his face. I wonder what he has been doing already in that land of light and liberty. Mr. Fullerton writes me, saying that he would not wonder if he spent last Sunday in telling the spirits above how he had spent the Sunday previous, and making them all wonder at what the grace of God had done among poor sinners down here on earth. He could tell the tale of Haddon Hall, and of this Tabernacle, recounting the story of what the Lord has done in saving men and women; and I do not think that angels and the redeemed could be better occupied than in hearing what the Lord has been doing in his new creation here below. Very probably the conjecture is right, for the grace of God reaches us " to the intent that now unto the principalities and powers in heavenly places might be known by the church the manifold wisdom of God." When they hear the story yonder, they will take down their harps, and raise new hallelujahs to God and to the Lamb. Think not that I talk strangely. The angels rejoice over one sinner that repenteth, and they will yet more rejoice when a messenger, newly come from the midst of God's salvation-work, shall tell them of scores that have been brought to the Saviour's feet.

Beloved friends, *eternity is ours;* and a joyous eternity it will be to those who are one with Jesus Christ, in "living, loving, lasting union." We shall ascend to "the realms of the blest" soon. There is a ladder waiting for us to climb; and when we mount it, we shall have no reason to mourn. It is but for a little time that we shall have to keep the night-watches. The watchman of the night doth cry, "The morning cometh." The night of weeping will soon be past. "Until the day break, and the shadows flee away," be of good courage. Patiently hope, "and quietly wait for the salvation of the Lord." He will surely come again; and even the tears of to-day shall be recompensed to you abundantly.

I pray that every blessing may rest upon every mourner this day. Indeed, dear friends, while we mourn with you, we cannot but congratulate you that you have had such a husband, such a father, such a brother, as our friend who is now taken home. I will not say that you have lost him, for that would not be true. God lent him to you for a long time, and now he has taken him back. I think that it is about fifteen years ago, since, in the ordinary course of things, he might have been expected to have died; at least, so it seemed at the time he was so sick; yet with many tears and intercessions we prayed him back, and God has given him something like Hezekiah's extra portion of life. We ought to be very thankful for that. In those fifteen years, how much he has done! How much God has done by him for us all! Wherefore we will not sorrow so as to complain, but we will sorrow only so as to submit. The Lord be with you evermore! Amen.

THE SWORD AND THE TROWEL.

Established and for 27 years Edited by C. H. SPURGEON.

TABLE OF CONTENTS OF SPECIAL MEMORIAL NUMBER, March, 1892.

Mrs. Spurgeon's Message of Thanks to the many Correspondents who have so lovingly shared her sorrow (with Portrait).
C. H. S. on John xvii. 24.
Portrait of C. H. Spurgeon, 1856.
Portrait of C. H. Spurgeon, 1891.
Mrs. Spurgeon's Menton Memorial Texts.
Mr. Spurgeon's Pocket-books (containing entries of peculiarly special interest).
Letter from Rev. John Spurgeon (with Portrait).
Pastor Charles Spurgeon's Loving Tribute to the Memory of his Beloved Father (with Portraits of Charles and Thomas Spurgeon).
A Note from Georgia, U.S.A., from an Orphanage Old Boy.
Pastor J. A. Spurgeon's Personal Thanks, and General Letter to all Helpers of the Institutions (with Portrait).
Another Star in Heaven. By W. Y. Fullerton (with Portrait).
Mr. Spurgeon's Senior Secretary's "Wreath."
The "Armour-bearer's" Last Despatch concerning his Glorified Captain (with views of the Study at "Westwood", and Hôtel Beau Rivage, Menton; and including two short articles written by C. H. S. in January, reports of the last two services conducted by Mr. Spurgeon on January 10 and 17, and a *fac-simile* outline of sermon prepared by him for delivery on January 17).
Re-united in Glory. (Portraits of C. H. S. and his Mother; Deacons W. Higgs, W. Olney, and B. W. Carr; and Professor Rogers.)
Reports of Memorial Services at Menton and the Tabernacle, and of the Funeral at Norwood Cemetery. By various writers.
His Prayer was Answered. Poem, by E. A. Tydeman.
In Memoriam. Poem on close of C. H. S's New Year's address, by K. Russell.
In Memoriam: an Acrostic. By E. Putley.
Reminiscences of the President, by Pastors' College Brethren.
The Head-master, Stockwell Orphanage (with Portrait).
Testimony of two Neighbours: Revs. R. Taylor and J. W. W. Moeran.
Notices of Books, written by C. H. S.
Notes.
Lists of Donations—Pastors' College, Pastors' College Missionary Association, Society of Evangelists, Stockwell Orphanage, Colportage Association.

64 pages. Price 3d.; Post Free, 5d.

PASSMORE & ALABASTER, Paternoster Buildings;
AND ALL BOOKSELLERS.

Metropolitan Tabernacle Pulpit.

"COME FROM THE FOUR WINDS, O BREATH!"

A Sermon

INTENDED FOR READING ON LORD'S-DAY, MARCH 6TH, 1892,

DELIVERED BY

C. H. SPURGEON,

AT THE METROPOLITAN TABERNACLE, NEWINGTON,

On Thursday Evening, May 15th, 1890.

"Then said he unto me, Prophesy unto the wind, prophesy, son of man, and say to the wind, Thus saith the Lord God; Come from the four winds, O breath, and breathe upon these slain, that they may live."—Ezekiel xxxvii. 9.

ACCORDING to some commentators, this vision in the valley of dry bones may refer to three forms of resurrection. Holy Scripture is so marvellously full of meaning, that one interpretation seldom exhausts its message to us. The chapter before us is an excellent example of this fact; and supplies an illustration of several Scriptural truths.

Some think they see here a parable of the resurrection of the dead. Assuredly, Ezekiel's vision pictures what will happen in the day when "the trumpet shall sound, and the dead shall be raised." No matter how dry the bones may be, the bodies of those who sleep in the dust of the earth shall rise again. That which was sown shall spring up from the grave; and, in the case of the children of God, it shall wear a new glory. At the word of Christ it shall come to pass: "For the hour is coming, in the which all that are in the graves shall hear his voice, and shall come forth; they that have done good, unto the resurrection of life; and they that have done evil, unto the resurrection of damnation."

Others see here the resurrection of the almost destroyed host of Israel, which had been divided into two companies, and carried away captive to Babylon. Plague and pestilence and the sword of the Chaldean had gone far to cut off the chosen nation; but God promised to restore his people, thus mingling mercy with judgment, and again setting in the cloud the bow of his everlasting covenant. A partial fulfilment of this promise was given when, for a while, the Lord set up again the tribes of Israel at Jerusalem, and they had a happy rest before the coming of Christ. But Israel's full restoration is yet to be accomplished. The people shall be gathered out of the graves in which, as a nation, they have so long lain buried, and shall be placed in their own land, and then will come to pass the word of Jehovah:

No. 2,246.

"Then shall ye know that I the Lord have spoken it, and performed it, saith the Lord."

There are others who, looking beyond the literal for the spiritual teaching, see, and, I think, rightly see, that here is a picture of the recovery of ungodly men from their spiritual death and corruption— a parable of the way in which sinners are brought up from their hopeless, spiritually dead condition, and made to live by the power of the Holy Ghost. I shall, at any rate, use the text in this sense, for I am not now aiming at the interpretation of prophecy, nor concerned greatly with what is to happen in the future. Neither do I wish to conduct you into the deep things of God; but I am just now thinking of practical uses to which I can put this incident, in order to stir up God's people to deal with the Holy Spirit as he should be dealt with, and to urge the unconverted to seek the Lord, in the hope that some of them, as dead and dry as the bones in the valley of vision, may be made to live by his divine power.

Nothing gave me greater comfort, this week, than when I received a note from one saying that, last Thursday night, while I was preaching from the text "Let your soul delight itself in fatness," she was enabled to lay hold on Christ. I had rather have such tidings than hear the gladdest news of a worldly kind that could be brought to me. Oh, that now also some poor heart may find rest in Christ while we are talking of that divine Spirit who becomes a Comforter to all those to whom he has been first a Quickener! May he come and cause men to live, and then afterwards make them full of gladness! It is his blessed office first to bestow life, and then to give light. Living unto God is the earliest experience of the redeemed, afterwards comes joy in God by the Holy Ghost.

I. Now, first, in using this text, as I have said, for practical purposes, I am going to make this remark upon it: WE ARE NOTHING WITHOUT THE HOLY SPIRIT. I speak, my brethren, now, to you who love the souls of men. I know that there are some among you here who preach and teach with all earnestness, with broken-hearted love; and for the glory of Christ you try to bring men to believe in Jesus. In thus endeavouring to save the souls of lost and ruined men, you are engaged in a noble work. But I dare say that you have often felt, what I also fully realize, that you have not gone far in your holy service before you are brought face to face with the fact that, in itself, the work you propose to do is an utter impossibility. We begin our labour according to the Word of the Lord, and we prophesy. God helping us, we can do that; and, though the burden of the Lord be heavy, yet if we are told to prophesy again, we can, by his grace, do that also. We can prophesy to dry bones, or prophesy to the wind, according to God's commandment. We are not afraid of seeming to be foolish, since we know that, when "the world by wisdom knew not God, it pleased God by the foolishness of preaching to save them that believe." But when we preach the Word, and as the result of our preaching expect men to be saved, and so saved that we may know it, we come all of a sudden upon an iron-bound coast, and can get no further. We find that men are dead; what is wanted is that they shall be quickened; and *we* cannot quicken them. There are a great many things we can do—and God forbid that we should leave one of them undone!—but when we come to the creation of life, we have reached a mysterious region into which we cannot penetrate; we have entered the realm of miracles, where Jehovah reigns supreme. The prerogative to give life or to take it away must remain with the Most High; the wit and wisdom of man are altogether powerless to bestow life upon even the tiniest insect. We know of a surety, doctrinally, and we know it with equal certainty by experience, that we can do nothing towards the quickening of men apart from the Spirit of God. If he does not come, and give life, we may preach till we have not another breath left, but we shall not raise from the tomb of sin even the soul of a little child, or bring a single sinner to the feet of Christ.

How, then, should this fact affect us? Because of our powerlessness, shall we sit still, doing nothing, and caring nothing? Shall we say, "The Spirit of God must do the work, therefore I may fold my arms, and take things easily"? Beloved, we cannot do that. Our heart's desire and prayer for our fellow-men is that they might be saved; and we have sometimes felt that, for their sakes, we could almost be willing to be accursed, if we might bring eternal life to them. We cannot sit still: we do not believe that it was God's intent that any truth should ever lead us into sloth: at any rate, it has not so led us; it has carried us in quite the opposite direction. Let us try to be as practical in this matter as we are in material things. We cannot rule the winds, nor create them. A whole parliament of philosophers could not cause a capful of wind to blow. The sailor knows that he can neither stop the tempest nor raise it. What then? Does he sit still? By no means. He has all kinds of sails of different cuts and forms to enable him to use every ounce of wind that comes; and he knows how to reef or furl them in case the tempest becomes too strong for his barque. Though he cannot control the movement of the wind, he can use what it pleases God to send. The miller cannot divert that great stream of water out of its channel, but he knows how to utilize it; he makes it turn his mill-wheel. Though he cannot resist the law of gravitation, for there seems to be an almost omnipotent force in it, yet he uses that law, and yokes it to his chariot. Thus, though we cannot command that mighty influence which streams from the omnipotent Spirit of God; though we cannot turn it which way we will, for "the wind bloweth where it listeth," yet we can make use of it; and in our inability to save men, we turn to God, and lay hold of his power.

What, then, are we to do? Face to face with spiritual death, conscious of the fact that we cannot remove it, and fully aware that only the Holy Spirit can quicken dead souls, what shall we do? There are certain ways and means by which we can act properly towards this divine Person; certain attitudes of heart which it would be well for us to take up; and certain results which will follow from a clear apprehension of the true state of the case.

First, by this fact, *we must feel deeply humbled, emptied, and cut adrift from self.* Look you, sir, you may study your sermon; you may examine the original of your text; you may critically follow it out in all its bearings; you may go and preach it with great correctness of expression; but you cannot quicken a soul by that sermon. You may go up into your pulpit; you may illustrate, explain, and enforce the truth; with mighty rhetoric you may charm your hearers; you may hold them spellbound; but no eloquence of yours can raise the dead. Demosthenes might stand for a century between the jaws of death; but the monster would not be moved by anything he or all human orators might say. Another voice than ours must be heard; other power than that of thought or suasion must be brought into the work, or it will not be done. You may organize your societies, you may have excellent methods, you may diligently pursue this course and that; but when you have done all, nothing can come of it if the effort stands by itself. Only as the Spirit of God shall bless men by you, shall they receive a blessing through you. Whatever your ability or experience, it is the Spirit of God who must bless your labour. Therefore, never go to this service with a boast upon your lip of what you can do, or with the slightest trace of self-confidence; else will you go in a spirit which will prevent the Holy Ghost from working with or through you.

O brethren, think nothing of us who preach to you! If ever you do, our power will be gone. If you begin to suppose that such and such a minister, having been blessed of God to so many thousands, will necessarily be the means of the conversion of your friend, you are imputing to a son of man what belongs only to the Son of God; and you will assuredly do that pastor or that minister a serious mischief by tolerating in your heart so idolatrous a thought. We are nothing: you are nothing. "Not by might, nor by power, but by my Spirit, saith the Lord of hosts," is a message that should make us lie in the dust, and utterly despair of doing anything in and of ourselves, seeing that all the power is of God alone. It will do us good to be very empty, to be very weak, to be very distrustful of self, and so to go about our Master's work.

Next, because of our absolute need of the Holy Spirit, *we must give ourselves to prayer before our work, in our work, and after our work.* A man who believes that, do what he may, no soul will be quickened apart from the work of the Spirit of God, and who has a longing desire that he may save souls, will not venture to his pulpit without prayer. He will not deliver his message without a thousand groans and cries to God for help in every sentence that he utters; and when the sermon is done, his work will not be done; it will have scarcely begun. His sermons will be but a text for long-continued prayer. He will be crying to God continually, to anoint him with the heavenly oil. His prayer will be "Let the Spirit of God be upon me, that I may preach deliverance to the captives; else men will still remain in the prison-house in spite of all my toil." And you, beloved, as you believe that doctrine, will not allow the preacher to go to his work without your prayers. You will bear him up in your supplications, feeling that your attendances at the house of God will be all vanity, and the coming together of the people will be as nothing, unless God the Holy Ghost is pleased to bless the Word. This thought will drive you to besiege the throne of grace with strong crying and tears that God would quicken the dead sons of men. If any of you are working without prayer, I will not advise you to cease your work; but I will urge you to begin to pray, not merely as a matter of form, but as the very life of your labours. Let the habit of prayer be constant with you, so that you neither begin any service for God, nor carry it on, nor conclude it, without crying to the Lord for his Holy Spirit to make the work effectual by his almighty power.

We have already gathered much instruction from this truth, if we have learnt to lie low before the Lord, and before the mercy seat.

But we must go a little further. Since everything depends upon the Spirit of God, *we must be very careful to be such men as the Spirit of God can use.* We may not judge others; but have you not met with men whom you could not think the Spirit of God would be likely to bless? If a man is self-sufficient, can the Spirit of God to any large degree bless him? If a man is inconsistent in his daily life, if there is no earnestness about him, if you cannot tell where he is in character or creed, if he contradicts one day what he said the day before, if he is vain-glorious and boastful, is it likely that the Spirit of God will bless him? If any of us should become lazy, indolent, or self-indulgent, we cannot expect the Spirit, whose one end is to glorify Christ, to work with us. If we should become proud, domineering, hectoring, how could the gentle Dove abide with us? If we should become despondent, having little or no faith in what we preach, and not expecting the power of the Holy Spirit to be with us, is it likely that God will bless us? Believe me, dear friends, that a vessel fit for the Master's use must be very clean. It need not be of silver or of gold; it may be but a common earthen vessel; but it must be very clean, for our God is a jealous God. He can spy a finger-mark where our eyes could not see it, even with a microscope; and he will not drink out of a vessel which a moment before was at the lips of Satan. He will not use us if we have been used by self, or if we have allowed ourselves to be used by the world. Oh, how clean should we be who expect the Holy Spirit to make use of us! How careful should we be in our private life as well as in our ordinary walk and conversation! This is no small thing. See to it, my brethren and sisters, for much of the promised blessing may depend upon your carefulness.

Next, since we depend wholly upon the Spirit, *we must be most anxious to use the Word, and to keep close to the truth,* in all our work for Christ among men. The Word of God is the Holy Spirit's sword; he will not wield our wooden weapon. He will only use this true Jerusalem blade of God's own fashioning. Let us, then, set high value on the inspired Word; we shall defeat our adversaries by that sword-thrust, "It is written." So spake the Christ; and so he conquered Satan. So also the Holy Spirit speaketh. Be wise, therefore, and let your reliance be, not on your own wisdom, but on the word to which you can add, "Thus saith the Lord." If our preaching is of that kind, the Holy Ghost will always set his seal to it. But if you have thought it out, and it is your own production, go, good sir, to Her Majesty's offices, and get letters patent for your invention; but the Holy Ghost will have nothing to do with it. He cares nothing about your "original mind." Our Lord Jesus laid aside all originality, and spake only the words of his Father, the words which the Holy Ghost brought to him.

He said to his disciples, in that memorable discourse, before he went out to Gethsemane, "The word which ye hear is not mine, but the Father's which sent me." Let us try to imitate him, being willing not to think our own thoughts, or to speak our own words, but those which God shall give to us. I would rather speak five words out of this Book than fifty thousand words of the philosophers. I had rather be a fool with God than be a wise man with the sagest scientist, for "the foolishness of God is wiser than men; and the weakness of God is stronger than men." You cannot work for Christ except by the Spirit of Christ, and you cannot teach for Christ except you teach Christ; your word will have no blessing upon it, unless it be God's Word spoken through your lips to the sons of men. If we want revivals, we must revive our reverence for the Word of God. If we want conversions, we must put more of God's Word into our sermons; even if we paraphrase it into our own words, it must still be his Word upon which we place our reliance, for the only power which will bless men lies in that. It is God's Word that saves souls, not our comment upon it, however correct that comment may be. Let us, then, be scrupulously careful to honour the Holy Spirit by taking the weapon which he has prepared for us, believing in the full inspiration of the sacred Scriptures, and expecting that God will prove their inspiration by their effect upon the minds and hearts of men.

Again, since we are nothing without the Holy Spirit, *we must avoid in our work anything which is not of him*. We want these dead people raised, and we cannot raise them; only the Spirit of God can do that. Now, in our part of the work, for which God condescendingly uses us, let us take care that there is nothing which would grieve the Spirit, or cause him to go away from us. I believe that, in places where the work of conversion goes on largely, God is much more jealous than he is anywhere else. He watches this church; and if he sees, in the officers of the church, or in the workers, something unholy; if he beholds practices tolerated that are not according to his pure mind; and if, when they are noticed, these evils are winked at, and still further indulged, he will withdraw his blessing until we cease to have a controversy with him. Possibly he might give his blessing to a church which was worse than this in many respects, while he might withdraw it from this church, which has already been so highly favoured, if it countenanced anything contrary to his Word. An ordinary subject of her Majesty might say certain things about her for which he would never be brought to book; but a favourite at court must mind how he behaves. So must we be very sensitive in this divine employment in which we come nearest to Christ; we must be careful to co-operate with him in our work of seeking to pluck brands from the burning. We must mind how we do it, for we may, perhaps, be led to adopt ways and methods which may grieve him; and if we persevere in those ways and methods, after we have learned that they are not according to his will, the Spirit of God will leave us, lest he should seem to be setting his seal upon that of which he does not approve. A headlong zeal even for Christ may leap into a ditch. What we think to be very wise may be very unwise; and where we deem that at least a little "policy" may come in, that little policy may taint the whole, and make a nauseous stench which God will not endure. You must have the Spirit of God; you can do nothing without him; therefore do nothing that would cause him to depart from you.

Moreover, *we must be ever ready to obey the Holy Spirit's gentlest monitions;* by which I mean, the monitions which are in God's Word, and also—but putting this in the second place—such inward whispers as he accords to those who dwell near to him. I believe that the Holy Spirit does still speak to his chosen in a very remarkable way. Men of the world might ridicule this truth, and therefore we speak little of it; but the child of God knows that there are at times distinct movements of the Holy Spirit upon his mind leading in such and such ways. Be very tender of these touches of God. Some people do not feel these movements; but perhaps if they, with a more perfect heart, feared the Lord, his secret might be revealed to them. That great ship at sea will not be moved by a ripple; even an ordinary wave will not stir it; it is big and heavy. But that cork, out yonder, goes up and down with every ripple of the water. Should a great wave come, it will be raised to the crest of it, and carried wherever the current compels. Let your spirit be little before God, and easily moved, so that you may recognize every impulse of the Spirit, and obey it at once, whatever it may be. When the Holy Ghost moves thee to give up such and such a thing, yield it instantly, lest you lose his presence; when he impels thee to fulfil such and such a duty, be not disobedient to the heavenly vision; and when on thy knees he seems to direct thee in prayer, go in that direction; or if he suggests to thee to praise God for such and such a favour, give thyself to thanksgiving. Yield thyself wholly to his guidance. You who are workers, do ask for the wisdom of the Spirit carefully and believingly. I do not understand a man going into the pulpit, and praying the Spirit of God to guide him in what he shall say, and then pulling it all out of his pocket in manuscript. It looks to me as if he shut the Spirit of God out of any special operation; at least, all the help he can expect to have from the Spirit at that particular time must be in the manner of his reading, though of course he may have been guided in what he has written. Still, there is but scant room for the Spirit to manifest his power. In the same way, if you make up your mind how you will deal with people, and what you will say, it may often happen that, in the process, if you forgot all you meant to say, it would be the best thing that could happen to you; and if you said exactly what you did not think it would be prudent to say, it would turn out to be the very best thing that you could say; the unaccustomed method might be the thing that the Spirit of God would bless. Keep yourself, therefore, before that valley of dry bones free to do just what the Spirit of God would have you do, that he, through you, may raise the dead.

Once more: since, apart from the Spirit, we are powerless, *we must value greatly every movement of his power.* Notice, in this account of the vision in the valley, how the prophet draws attention to the fact of the shaking and the noise, and the coming of the sinews and the flesh, even before there was any sign of life. I think that, if we want the Spirit of God to bless us, we must be on the watch to notice everything he does. Look out for the first desire, the first fear! Be glad of anything happening to your people that looks as if it were the work of the Holy Spirit; and, if you value him in his earlier works, he is likely to go on to do more and more, till at last he will give the breath, and the slain host shall arise, and become an army for God. Only you cannot expect the Spirit of God to come and work by you if you are half asleep. You cannot expect the Spirit of God to put forth his power if you are in such a condition that, if he saved half your congregation, you would not know it, and if he saved nobody, you would not fret about it. God will not bless you when you are not all awake. The Spirit of God does not work by sleepy men. He loves to have us alive ourselves, and then he will make others alive by us. See to this, dear friends. If we had more time at our disposal, I would speak longer on this part of the subject; but I have said enough now, if God the Holy Spirit blesses it, upon this first great truth that we are nothing without the Holy Spirit.

II. Now, secondly, we may learn, from the action of Ezekiel on this occasion, that WE MAY SO ACT AS TO HAVE THE HOLY SPIRIT. When he first saw the dry bones, there was no wind nor breath; yet, obeying the voice of the Lord in the vision, the breath came, and life followed. How, then, shall we act? I will only give you in brief a few of the conditions to be observed by us.

If we want the Holy Spirit to be surely with us, to give us a blessing, *we must, in the power of the Spirit, realize the scene in which we are to labour.* In this case, the Holy Spirit took the prophet, and carried him out, and set him down in the midst of the valley which was full of bones. This is just a type of what will happen to every man whom the Spirit means to use. Do you want to save the people in the slums? Then, you must go into the slums. Do you want to have sinners broken down under a sense of sin? You must be broken down yourself; at least, you must get near to them in their brokenness of heart; and be able to sympathize with them. I believe that no man will command power over a people whom he does not understand. If you have never been to a certain place, you do not know the road; but if you have been there yourself, and you come upon a person who has lost his way, you are the man to direct him. When you have been through the same perplexities that trouble others, you can say to them, "I have been there myself: I know all about it. By God's blessing I can conduct you out of this maze." Dear friends, we must have greater sympathy with sinners. You cannot pluck the brand out of the burning if you are afraid of being singed yourself; you must be willing to smut your fingers on the bars of the grate if you would do it. If there is a diamond dropped into a ditch, you must thrust your arm up to your elbow in the mud, or else you cannot expect to pick the jewel out of the mire. The Holy Spirit, when he blesses a man, sets him down in the midst of the valley full of bones, and causes him to pass by them round about until he fully comprehends the greatness and the difficulty of the work to be accomplished, even as the peophet said, "Behold, there were very many in the open valley; and, lo, they were very dry."

Next, if the Holy Spirit is to be with us, *we must speak in the power of faith.* If Ezekiel had not had faith, he certainly would not have preached to dry bones; they made a wretched congregation; and he certainly would not have preached to the wind, for it must have been but a fickle listener. Who but a fool would behave in this manner unless faith entered into the action? If preaching is not a supernatural exercise, it is a useless procedure. God the Holy Ghost must be with us, or else we might as well go and stand on the tops of the hills of Scotland, and shout to the east wind. There is nothing in all our eloquence unless we believe in the Holy Spirit making use of the truth which we preach for the quickening of the souls of men. Our prophesying must be an act of faith. We must preach by faith as much as Noah built the ark by faith; and just as the walls of Jericho were brought down by faith, men's hearts are to be broken by faithful preaching, that is, preaching full of faith.

In addition to this, if we desire to have the Spirit of God with us, *we must prophesy according to God's command*. By prophesying, I do not mean foretelling future events; but simply uttering the message which we have received from the Lord, proclaiming it aloud so that all may hear. You will notice how it is twice said, in almost the same words, " So I prophesied as he commanded me." God will bless the prophesying that he commands, and not any other; so we must keep clear of that which is contrary to his Word, and speak the truth that he gives to us to declare. As Jonah, the second time he was told to go to Nineveh, was bidden by the Lord to "preach unto it the preaching that I bid thee," so must we do if we would have our word believed even as his was. Our message is received when it is the Word of God through us. When the Lord describes the blessing that comes upon the earth by the rain and snow from heaven, he saith, "So shall my Word be that goeth forth out of my mouth." Let us see to it that, before the word goes forth out of our mouth, we have received it from the mouth of God. Then we may hope and expect that the people will receive it also from us. The Spirit of God, that is, the breath of God, goes with the Word of God, and with that alone.

Notice, next, that if we would have the Spirit of God with us, *we must break out in vehemency of desire*. The prophet is to prophesy to the bones; but he does not begin in a formal manner by saying, "Only the winds coming can bring breath to these slain persons." No, he breaks out with an interjection, and with his whole soul heaving with a ground-swell of great desire, he cries, "Come from the four winds, O breath, and breathe upon these slain, that they may live!" He has the people before him in his eye, and in his heart; and he appeals, with mighty desire, to the Spirit of God that he would come and make them live. You will generally find, in our service to-day, that the men who yearn over the souls of their fellow-men are those whom the Spirit of God uses. A man of no desire gets what he longs for; and that is nothing at all.

Then, if we would have more of the power of the Spirit of God with us, *we must see only the divine purpose, the divine power, and the divine working*. God will have his Spirit to go forth with those who see his hand. "When I have opened your graves, O my people, and brought you up out of your graves, and shall put my spirit in you, and ye shall live, and I shall place you in your own land: then shall ye know that I the Lord have spoken it, and performed it, saith the Lord." It is not my plan that God is going to work out; it is his own. It is not my purpose that the Holy Spirit is going to carry out; it is the purpose of the eternal Jehovah. It is not my power, or my experience, or my mode of thought, which will bring men from death to life; it is the Holy Spirit who will do it, and he only. We must apprehend this fact, and get to work in this spirit, and then God the Holy Spirit will be with us.

III. Bear with me, if I fill up all my time, or if I should even stray beyond it. I want now to address unconverted persons, or those who are afraid they are still unsaved; and with the text before us, WE WOULD SPEAK HOPEFULLY TO OUR HEARERS.

You who are not yet quickened by the divine life, or are afraid you are not, *we would exhort you to hear the Word of the Lord*. Though you feel that you are as dead as these dry bones, yet if you want to be saved, be frequent in hearing the Word. "Faith cometh by hearing, and hearing by the Word of God." If you wish to find the divine life, thank God that you have that wish, and frequent those houses where Christ is much spoken of, and where the way of eternal life is very plainly set forth. When you mingle with the worshippers, listen with both your ears; try to remember what you hear; and pray all the while that God will bless it to you. "O ye dry bones, hear the Word of the Lord!"

Next, *we would remind you of your absolute need of life from the Spirit of God*. Put it in what shape you like, you cannot be saved except you are born again; and the new birth is not a matter within your own power. "Ye must be born again,"—" from above," as the margin reads, in the third chapter of John's Gospel. All the religion of which you are capable will not save you, do what you will; strive as you may with outward ceremonies, or religious observances, there is no hope for you but in the Holy Ghost. There is something to be done for you which you cannot do for yourself. We will not water down that truth, but give it to you just as it stands in the Scriptures; we want you to feel its power.

But *we would have you note what the Holy Spirit has done for others*. There are some of your friends who have been born again. They were as helpless and hopeless as you are; but they are now saved. You know they are, for you have seen their lives. Take note of them, for what the Holy Spirit can work in one he can work in another. Let the grace of God in others comfort you concerning yourself, especially when you hear of great drunkards, or great swearers, or very vicious persons, who have been transformed into saints. Say to yourself, "If the Holy Spirit could make a saint out of such a sinner as that, surely he can make a saint out of me." As you see the flesh and sinews on others who were once as dry as bare bones, be encouraged to hope that it may be even so with you ere long.

May I go a little further, and say that, *we would have you observe carefully what is done in yourself?* I think I am speaking to some here who have already undergone a remarkable change. You cannot say that you have spiritual life; you are afraid that you have not. Still, you are not what you used to be. You have put away many things from you that were once a pleasure to you, and now you take a delight in many things which you once despised. There is some hope in that, though it may be nothing more than the sinews coming on the bones, and the flesh upon the sinews. Yet I notice that, where the Holy Ghost begins, he does not leave off till he has finished his work. God takes such a delight in his work, that, having begun it, he completes it. Well did Job say, "Thou wilt have a desire to the work of thine hands." Now, what he has done for you already, encourages me, and should encourage you, to hope that he will yet do much more, continuing his gracious work until life eternal is bestowed upon you.

Furthermore, *we would remind you that faith in Jesus is a sign of life*. If in your heart you can trust yourself to Christ, and believe in him that he can save you, you have eternal life already. "He that believeth on the Son hath everlasting life." If thou canst now, though it be for the first time, trust thyself alone on Christ, faith is the surest evidence of the work of the Holy Ghost. Thou "hast passed from death unto life" already. Thou canst not see the Spirit any more than thou canst see the wind; but, if thou hast faith, that is a blessed vane that turns in the way the Spirit of God blows. "Whosoever believeth that Jesus is the Christ, is born of God." If thou believest, this is true of thee, and if thou dost cast thyself wholly upon Christ, remember that it is written, "He that believeth on him is not condemned;" wherefore be of good cheer.

We beg you not to be led aside to the discussion of difficulties. There are a great many difficulties. To tell dry bones to live, is a very unreasonable sort of thing when tried by rules of logic; and for me to tell you, a dead sinner, to believe in Christ, may seem perfectly unjustifiable by the same rule. But I do not need to justify it. If I find it in God's Word, that is quite enough for me; and if the preacher does not feel any difficulty in the matter, why should you? There is a difficulty, but you have nothing to do with it. There are difficulties everywhere. There is a difficulty in explaining how it is that bread sustains your body; and how that bread, sustaining your body, can be the means of prolonging your life. We cannot understand how the material can impinge upon the spiritual; and there are difficulties in almost everything connected with life. If a man will not do anything till he has solved every difficulty, we had better dig his grave. And you will be in hell if you will not go to heaven without having every difficulty solved for you. Leave the difficulties; there will be time enough to settle them when we get to heaven; meanwhile, if life comes through Jesus Christ, let us have it, and have done with nursing our doubts.

Further, *we would have you long for the visitation of God, the Holy Spirit*. Join with us in the prayer, "Come, Holy Spirit, come with all thy power; come from the four winds, O breath!" One wind will not do, it must come from all quarters. Your heart, filled with all sorts of evil, wants breaking; it wants throwing down like the house of Job's son when Job's children were in it, and "there came a great wind from the wilderness, and smote the four corners of the house, and it fell." Oh, for a wind from the four quarters of heaven, to smite the four corners of the house of your sin, and lay it low! "Come from the four winds, O breath!" As the poet sings—

> "Lifeless in the valley,
> Come, O breath, and breathe!
> New-create and rally!
> Come, O breath, and breathe!
> Blowing where thou listest,
> Thou the word assistest,
> Thou death's power resistest,
> Come, O breath, and breathe!"

Be willing to have the Holy Spirit as he wills to come. Let him come as a north wind, cold and cutting, or as a south wind, sweet and melting. Say, "Come, from any of the four winds, O breath! only come." He can come unexpectedly upon you in the pew during these five minutes that remain. You are perhaps thinking about whether you can catch an early train, and get home. May the Holy Spirit lay hold of you before you leave the building, and get you home in real earnest to your God and to your Father! He can come very mightily. There is a great deal about you that would shut him out. But it is hard to keep wind out when it blows in the fulness of its strength. You may fill up the crevices of the door as you please, but still the wind gets in. Thus, too, is it with the Spirit of God: he comes in might; and he can also come very sweetly. Be not afraid of the Holy Spirit. He can charm you to Christ, as well as drive you to Christ. May he enter your heart even now!

We yearn to see all of you thus made to live. I am praying in my very soul that he would come to every one of you. I do not read that Ezekiel saw part of the valley of dry bones live, and the rest remain dry bones; but that they all lived, and stood upon their feet an exceeding great army. I long to see you all blessed at this service. Why should it not be so? Oh, that the Spirit of God would come and touch everyone of us! Many of you are alive already, blessed be his name! Well, you can have more life, for Christ has come not only that you might have life, but that you "might have it more abundantly." Let the blessed Spirit enter in greater fulness, I beseech you. But pray mightily, that every soul here that is dead may now feel the sacred breath, and begin to live. Then I shall not only hear of one, as last Thursday, but news shall be brought of many upon whom the divine Spirit has sweetly come, and led them to Jesus, to be saved now, and to be saved for ever. God grant it! Amen.

PORTION OF SCRIPTURE READ BEFORE SERMON—Ezekiel xxxvii.

HYMNS FROM "OUR OWN HYMN BOOK"—464, 461, 451.

Metropolitan Tabernacle Pulpit.

PRAISE FOR THE GIFT OF GIFTS.

A Sermon

Intended for Reading on Lord's-day, March 13th, 1892,

DELIVERED BY

C. H. SPURGEON,

AT THE METROPOLITAN TABERNACLE, NEWINGTON,

On Lord's-day Evening, July 27th, 1890.

"Thanks be unto God for his unspeakable gift."—2 Corinthians ix. 15.

In the chapter from which my text is taken, Paul is stirring up the Christians at Corinth to be ready with liberal gifts for the poor saints at Jerusalem. He finishes by reminding them of a greater gift than any they could bring, and by this one short word of praise, "Thanks be unto God for his unspeakable gift," he sets all their hearts a-singing. Let men give as liberally as they may, you can always proclaim the value of their gift: you can cast it up, and reckon its worth; but God's gift is unspeakable, unreckonable. You cannot fully estimate the value of what God gives. The gospel is a gospel of giving and forgiving. We may sum it up in those two words; and hence, when the true spirit of it works upon the Christian, he forgives freely, and he also gives freely. The large heart of God breeds large hearts in men, and they who live upon his bounty are led by his Spirit to imitate that bounty, according to their power.

However, I am not going, on the present occasion, to say anything upon the subject of liberality. I must get straight away to the text, hoping that we may really drink in the spirit of it, and out of full hearts use the apostle's language with intenser meaning than ever as we repeat his words: "Thanks be unto God for his unspeakable gift." I shall commence by saying that *salvation is altogether the gift of God*, and as such is to be received by us freely. Then I shall try to show that *this gift is unspeakable*; and, in the third place, that *for this gift thanks should be rendered to God*. Though it is unspeakable, yet we should speak our praise of it. In this way you will see, as of old preachers used to say, the text naturally falls apart.

I. We begin with the thought that SALVATION IS ALTOGETHER THE GIFT OF GOD. Paul said, "Thanks be unto God for his unspeakable gift." Over and over and over again, have we to proclaim that salvation is wholly of grace: not of works nor of wages, but is the gift of God's great bounty to undeserving men. Often as we have preached

No. 2,247.

this truth, we shall have to keep on doing so as long as there are men in the world who are self-righteous, and as long as there are minds in the world so slow to grasp the meaning of the word " grace ", that is, "free favour", and as long as there are memories that find it difficult to retain the idea of salvation being God's free gift.

Let us say, simply and plainly, that salvation must come to us as a gift from God, for salvation comes to us by the Lord Jesus, and *what else could Jesus be?* The essence of salvation is the gift of God's Only-begotten Son to die for us, that we might live through him. I think you will agree with me that it is inconceivable that men should ever have merited that God should give his Only-begotten Son to them. To give Christ to us, in any sense, must have been an act of divine charity; but to give him up to die on yonder cruel and bloody tree, to yield him up as a sacrifice for sin, must be a free favour, passing the limits of thought. It is not supposable that any man could deserve such love. It is plain that if man's sins needed a sacrifice, he did not deserve that a sacrifice should be found for him. The fact of his need proves his demerit and his guiltiness. He deserves to die; he may be rescued by Another dying for him; but he certainly cannot claim that the eternal God should take from his bosom his Only-begotten and Well-beloved Son, and put him to death. The more you look that thought in the face, the more you will reject the idea that, by any possible sorrow, or by any possible labour, or by any possible promise, a man could put himself into the position of deserving to have Christ to die for him. If Christ is to come to save sinners, it must be as a gift, a free gift of God. The argument, to my mind, is conclusive.

Besides that, over and over again, in God's Word, *we are told that salvation is not of works.* Although there are many who cling to the notion of man's works as a ground of salvation, yet as long as this Book stands, and there are eyes to read it, it will bear witness against the idea of human merit, and it will speak out plainly for the doctrine that men are saved by faith, and not by works. Not once only, but often, it is written, "The just shall live by faith;" moreover, we are told, "Therefore it is of faith, that it might be by grace." The very choice of the way of salvation by believing, rather than by works, is made by God on purpose that he might show that grace is a gift. "Now to him that worketh is the reward not reckoned of grace, but of debt: but to him that worketh not, but believeth on him that justifieth the ungodly, his faith is counted for righteousness." Faith is that virtue, that grace, which is chosen to bring us salvation, because it never takes any of the glory to itself. Faith is simply the hand that takes. When the beggar receives alms, he does not bless the hand that takes, but blesses the hand that gives; therefore do we not praise the faith that receiveth, but the God who giveth the unspeakable gift. Faith is the eye that sees. When we see an object, we delight in the object, rather than in the eye that sees it; therefore do we glory, not in our faith, but in the salvation which God bestows. Faith is appointed as the porter to open the gate of salvation, because that gate turns upon the hinges of free grace.

In the next place, be it always remembered, that we cannot be saved by the merit of our own works, because *holy works are themselves a gift*, the work of the grace of God. If thou hast faith, and joy, and hope, who gave them to thee? These did not spring up spontaneously in thy heart. They were sown there by the hand of love. If thou hast lived a godly life for years, if thou hast been a diligent servant of the church and of thy God, in whose strength hast thou done it? Is there not One who works all our works in us? Could you work out your own salvation with fear and trembling if God did not first work in you both to will and to do of his good pleasure? How can that, then, claim a reward, which is, in itself, the gift of God? I think the ground is cut right away from those who would put confidence in human merit, when we show, first of all, that, in Scripture, salvation is clearly said to be "not of works, lest any man should boast"; and, secondly, that even the good works of believers are the fruit of a renewed life; for "we are his workmanship, created in Christ Jesus unto good works, which God hath before ordained that we should walk in them."

> "All that I *was*, my sin, my guilt,
> My death, was all mine own;
> All that I *am*, I owe to thee,
> My gracious God, alone."

Further, if salvation were not a free gift, *how else could a sinner get it?* I will pass over some of you, who fancy that you are the best people in the world. It is sheer fancy, mark you, without any truth in it. But I will say nothing about you. There are, however, some of us, who know that we were not the best people in the world; we who sinned against God, and knew it, and who were broken in pieces under a sense of our guilt. I know, for one, that there would have been no hope of heaven for me, if salvation had not been the free gift of God to those who deserved it not. After ministering among you for nearly thirty-seven years, I stand exactly where I stood when first I came to Christ, a poor sinner and nothing at all, but taking Christ as the free gift of God to me, as I took him at first, when, yet but a lad, I fled to him for salvation. Ask any of the people of God who have been abundant in service, and constant in prayer, whether they deserve aught at the hand of God, and those who have most to be thankful for will tell you that they have nothing that they have not received. Ask these, whom God has honoured to the conversion of many, whether they lay any claim to the grace of God, whether they have any merit, and whether in their hand they dare bring a price, and seek to buy of God his love; they will loathe the very thought. There is no way to heaven for you and me, my friend convinced of sin, unless all the way we are led by grace, and unless salvation is the gift of God.

But, once more: *look at the privileges which come to us through salvation!* I cannot, as I value those privileges, conceive for a minute that they are purchasable, or that they come to us as the result of our desert. They must be a gift; they are so many and so glorious as to be altogether outside the limit of our furthest search, and beyond the height of our utmost reach. We cannot by our efforts compass any salvation of any sort; but if we could, it certainly would not be such a salvation as this. Let us look, then, at our privileges.

Here comes, first, "the forgiveness of sins, according to the riches of his grace." He that believes in Christ has no sin. His sin is blotted out. It has ceased to be. Christ has finished it, and he is unto God as though he had never sinned. Can any sinner deserve that?

> "Here's pardon for transgressions past,
> It matters not how black their cast,
> And oh, my soul, with wonder view,
> For sins to come, here's pardon too!"

Can any sinner bring a price that will purchase such a boon as that? No; such mercy must be a gift.

Next, everyone that believes in Christ is justified, and looked upon by God as being perfectly righteous. The righteousness of Christ is imputed to him, and he is "accepted in the Beloved." By this he becomes not only innocent, that is, pardoned, but he becomes praiseworthy before God. This is justification. Can any guilty man deserve that? Why, he is covered with sin, defiled from head to foot! Can he deserve to be arrayed in the sumptuous robe of the divine righteousness of Christ, and "be made the righteousness of God in him"? It is inconceivable. Such a blessing must be the gift of infinite bounty, or it can never come to man.

Furthermore, beloved, remember that "now are we the sons of God." Can you realize that truth? As others are not, believers are, the sons of God. He is their Father, and the spirit of adoption breathes within their heart. They are children of his family, and come to him as children come to a father, with loving confidence. Think of being made a son of God, a son of him that made the heavens, a son of him who is God over all, blessed for ever. Can any man deserve that? Certainly not; this also must come as a gift.

Sonship leads on to heirship. "If children, then heirs; heirs of God, and joint-heirs with Christ." My brother, if thou art a believer, all things are thine, this world, and worlds to come. Could you ever deserve all that? Could such an inheritance have come to you through any merits of your own? No, it must be a gift. Look at it, and the blaze of its splendour will strike all idea of merit blind.

Further than that, we are now made one with Christ. Oh, tell everywhere this wonder which God hath wrought for his people! It is not to be understood; it is an abyss too deep for a finite mind to sound. Every believer is truly united to Christ: "For we are members of his body, of his flesh, and of his bones." Every believer is married to Christ, and none of them shall ever be separated from him. Seeing, then, that there is such a union between us and Christ, can you suppose that any man can have any claim to such a position apart from the grace of God? By what merit, even of a perfect man, could we deserve to become one with Christ in an endless unity? Such a surpassing privilege is out of the line of purchase. It is, and can only be, the gift of God. Oneness with Christ cannot come to us in any other way.

Listen yet again. In consequence of our union with Christ, God the Holy Spirit dwells in every believer. Our bodies are his temple. God dwelleth in us, and we dwell in God. Can we deserve that?

Even a perfect keeping of the law would not have brought to men the abiding of the Holy Ghost in them. It is a blessing that rises higher than the law could ever reach, even if it had been kept.

Let me say, furthermore, that if you possess a blessed peace, as I trust you do, if you can say—

> "My heart is resting, O my God;
> I will give thanks and sing;
> My heart is at the secret source
> Of every precious thing;"

that divine peace must surely be the gift of God. If there is a great calm within your soul, an entire satisfaction with Christ your Lord, you never deserved that priceless boon. It is the work of his Holy Spirit, and must be his free gift.

And when you come to die, as you may—unless the Lord comes, as he will—the grace that will enable you fearlessly to face the last enemy will not be yours by any right of your own. If you fall asleep, as I have seen many a Christian pass away, with songs of triumph, with the light of heaven shining on your brow, almost in glory while yet you are in your bed, why, you cannot deserve that! Such a death-bed must be the free gift of God's almighty grace. It cannot be earned by merit; indeed, it is just then that every thought of merit melts away, and the soul hides itself in Christ, and triumphs there.

If this does not convince you, look once more. Let a window be opened in heaven. See the long lines of white-robed saints. Hark to their hallelujahs. Behold their endless, measureless delight. Did they deserve to come there? Did they come to their thrones and to their palms of victory by their own merits? Their answer is, "We have washed our robes, and made them white in the blood of the Lamb;" and from them all there comes the harmonious anthem, "*Non nobis, Domine,*"—"Not unto us, O Lord, not unto us; but unto thy name give glory, for thy mercy and for thy truth's sake." From first to last, then, we see that salvation is all the gift of God. And what can be freer than a gift, or more glorious than the gift of God? No prize can approach it in excellence, no merit can be mentioned in the same hour. O my brethren, we are debtors indeed to the mercy of God! We have received much, and there is more to follow; but it is all of grace from first to last. We know but little yet at what a cost these gifts were purchased for us; but we shall know it better by-and-by, as McCheyne so sweetly sings:—

> "When this passing world is done,
> When has sunk yon glaring sun;
> When I stand with Christ in glory,
> Looking o'er life's finished story,
> Then, Lord, shall I fully know—
> Not till then, how much I owe.
>
> " When I stand before the throne,
> Dressed in beauty not my own;
> When I see thee as thou art,
> Love thee with unsinning heart;
> Then, Lord, shall I fully know,
> Not till then, how much I owe."

II. Now I would try to lead your thoughts in another direction as we consider that THIS GIFT IS UNSPEAKABLE. Do not think it means that we cannot speak about this gift. Ah, how many times have I, for one, spoken upon this gift during the last forty years! I have spoken of little else. I heard of one who said, "I suppose Spurgeon is preaching that old story over again." Yes, that is what he is doing; and if he lives another twenty years, and you come here, it will be "the old, old story" still, for there is nothing like it. It is inexhaustible; it is like an Artesian well that springeth up for ever and ever. We can speak about it; yet it is unspeakable. What mean we, then, by saying it is unspeakable? Well, as I have said already, Christ Jesus our Lord is the sum and substance of salvation, and of God's gift. O God, this gift of thine is unspeakable, and it includes all other gifts beside!

"Thou didst not spare thine only Son,
But gav'st him for a world undone,
And freely with that Blessed One—
Thou givest all."

Consider, first, that Christ is unspeakable *in his person*. He is perfect man, and glorious God. No tongue of seraph, or of cherub, can ever describe the full nature of him whose name is "Wonderful, Counsellor, the mighty God, the everlasting Father, the Prince of peace." This is he whom the Father gave "for us men, and for our sakes." He was the Creator of all things, for "without him was not anything made that was made," yet he was "made flesh and dwelt among us." He filleth all things by his omnipresence; yet he came and tabernacled on the earth. This is that Jesus, who was born of Mary, yet who lived before all worlds. He was that Word, who "was in the beginning with God, and the Word was God." He is unspeakable. It is not possible to put into human language the divine mystery of his sacred being, truly man and yet truly God. But how great the wonder of it! Soul, God gave God for thee! Dost thou hear it? To redeem thee, O believing man, God gave himself to be thy Saviour; surely, that is an unspeakable gift.

Christ is unspeakable, next, *in his condescension*. Can any one measure or describe how far Christ stooped, when, from the throne of splendour, he came to the manger to be swaddled and lie where the horned oxen fed. Oh, what a stoop of condescension was that! The Infinite becomes an infant. The Eternal is dandled on a woman's knee. He is there in the carpenter's shop, obedient to his parents; there in the temple sitting among the doctors, hearing them and asking them questions; there in poverty, crying, "The Son of man hath not where to lay his head;" and there, in thirst, asking of a guilty woman a drink of water. It is unspeakable. That he, before whom the hosts of heaven veiled their faces, should come here among men, and among the poorest of the poor—that he who dwelt amidst the glory and bliss of the land of light, should deign to be a Man of sorrows and acquainted with grief, passes human thought! Such a Saviour is a gift unspeakable.

But if unspeakable so far, what shall I say of the fashion of Christ *in his death?* Beloved, I cannot speak adequately of Gethsemane and the bloody sweat, nor of the Judas kiss, nor of the traitorous flight of the disciples. It is unspeakable. That binding, scourging, plucking of the beard, and spitting in the face! Man's tongue cannot utter the horror of it. I cannot tell you truly the weight of the false accusations, the slanders, and the blasphemies that were heaped on him; nor would I wish to picture the old soldier's cloak flung over his bleeding shoulders, and the crown of thorns, the buffeting, the mailed fists, and the shame and sorrow he endured, as he was thrust out to execution. Do you wish to follow him along the streets, where weeping women lifted up their hearts in tender sympathy for the Lord of love about to die? If you do, it must be in silence, for words but feebly tell how much he bore on the way to the cross.

> "Well might the sun in darkness hide,
> And shut his glories in,
> When God, the mighty Maker, died
> For man, the creature's sin."

Oh, it was terrible that HE should be nailed to the gibbet, that HE should hang there to be ridiculed by all the mob of Jerusalem! The abjects flouted him, the meanest thought him meaner than themselves. Even dying thieves upbraided him. His eyes are choked, they become dim with blood. He must die. He says, "It is finished." He bows his head. The glorious Victim has yielded up his life to put away his people's sin. This is God's gift to you, divine, unspeakable, O ye sons of men!

But that is not all. Christ is unspeakable *in his glory.* When we think of his resurrection, of his ascending to heaven, and of his glory at the right hand of God, words languish on our lips; but in everyone of these positions, he is the gift of God to us; and when he shall come with all the glory of the Father, he will still be to his people the *Theo-dora,* the gift of God, the great unspeakable benediction to the sons of men. I wish that the people of Christ had this aspect of the Lord's glory more continually on their hearts, for though he seems to tarry, yet will he come again the second time, as he promised.

> "With that blessed hope before us,
> Let no harp remain unstrung;
> Let the mighty Advent chorus
> Onward roll on every tongue.
> Maranatha,
> Come, Lord Jesus, quickly come!"

To me, one of the most wonderful aspects of this gift is Christ *in his chosen;* all the Father gave him, all for whom he died, these he will glorify with himself, and they shall be with him where he is. Oh, what a sight will that be when we shall see the King in his beauty, and all his saints beautiful in his glory, shining like so many stars around him who is the Sun of them all! Then, indeed, shall we see what an unspeakable gift did God give to men, when, through that gift, he makes his saints all glorious, even as he predestinated them, "to be conformed to the image of his Son, that he might be the First-born among many brethren."

But we do not need to wait until we see his face to know his glory. Brethren, Christ is unspeakable as the gift of God *in the heart here.* "Oh," say you, "I trust I have felt the love of God shed abroad in my heart!" I rejoice with you, but could you speak it? Often, when I have tried to preach the love of Christ, I have not been able to preach it rightly, because I did not feel it as I ought; but oftener still, I have not been able to tell it out because I felt it so much. I would fain preach in that manner always, and feel Christ's love so much that I could speak it but little. Oh, child of God, if you have known much of Christ, you have often had to weep out your joys instead of speaking them, to lay your finger on your mouth, and be silent because you were overpowered by his glory. See how it was with John: "When I saw him, I fell at his feet as dead." Why did you not preach, John? If he were here to-night, he would say, "I could not preach then, the splendour of the Lord made me dumb. I fell at his feet as dead." This is one reason why the gift of God is unspeakable, because, the more you know about it, the less you can say about it. Christ overpowers us; he makes us tongue-tied with his wondrous revelations. When he reveals himself in full, we are like men that are blinded with excess of vision. Like Paul, on the Damascus road, we are forced to confess, "I could not see for the glory of that light." We cannot speak of it fully. All the apostles and prophets and saints of God have been trying to speak out the love of God as manifested in Christ; but yet they have all failed. I say, with great reverence, that the Holy Ghost himself seems to have laboured for expression, and, as he had to use human pens and mortal tongues, even he has never spoken to the full the measure and value of God's unspeakable gift. It is unspeakable to men by God himself. God can give it; but he cannot make us fully understand it. We have need to be like God himself to comprehend the greatness of his gift when he gives us his Son.

Though we make constant effort, it is unspeakable, even *throughout a long life*. Do you ministers, who have been a long time in one place, ever say to yourselves, "We shall run dry for subjects by-and-by"? If you preach Christ, you never will run short. If you have preached ten thousand sermons about Christ, you have not yet left the shore; you are not out in the deep sea yet. Dive, my brother! With splendour of thought, plunge into this great mystery of free grace and dying love; and when you have dived the farthest, you will perceive that you are as far off the bottom as when you first touched the surface. It is an endless theme; it is unspeakable!

> "Oh, could I speak the matchless worth,
> Oh, could I sound the glories forth
>   Which in my Saviour shine!
> I'd soar and touch the heavenly strings,
> And vie with Gabriel while he sings
>   In notes almost divine."

But I can neither speak it nor sing it as I ought; yet would I finish Medley's hymn, and say,—

> "Well, the delightful day will come
> When my dear Lord will bring me home,
>   And I shall see his face;
> Then with my Saviour, Brother, Friend,
> A blest eternity I'll spend,
>   Triumphant in his grace."

But, even then, Christ will be still *in heaven for ever* a gift unspeakable. Perhaps we shall have another talk together, friends, on this subject when we get there. One good woman said to me, "We shall have more time in eternity than we have now;" to which I replied, "I do not know whether there is any time in eternity, the words look like a contradiction." "Oh, but," said she; "I shall get a talk with you, anyhow; I have never had one yet." Well, I dare say we shall commune up there of these blessed things, when we shall know more about them. As we are to be there for ever and ever, we shall need some great subjects with which to keep up the conversation: what vaster theme can we have than this? Addison, in one of his verses, says—

> "But, oh! eternity's too short
> To utter half thy praise,"

and I have heard simpletons say that the couplet was very faulty; "you cannot make eternity short," they say. That shows the difference between a poet and a critic. A critic is a being all teeth, without any heart; and a poet is one who has much heart, and who sometimes finds that human language is not sufficient to express his thoughts. We shall never have done with Christ in heaven. Oh, my Lord, thy presence will make my heaven!

> "Millions of years my wondering eyes,
> Shall o'er thy beauties rove;
> And endless ages I'll adore
> The glories of thy love."

This wondrous gift of God is an utterly inexhaustible, unspeakable subject.

III. Now, lastly, I come to this point, that FOR THIS GIFT THANKS SHOULD BE RENDERED. The text says, "Thanks be unto God for his unspeakable gift." By this the apostle not only meant that he gave thanks for Christ; but he thus calls upon the church, and upon every individual believer, to join him in his praise. Here do I adopt his language, and praise God on my own behalf, calling upon all of you who know the preciousness of Christ, the gift of God, to unite with me in the thanksgiving. Let us as with one heart say it now, "Thanks be unto God for his unspeakable gift."

Some cannot say this, for they never think of the gift of God. You who never think of God, how can you thank God? There must be "think" at the bottom of "thank." Whenever we think, we ought to thank. But some never think, and therefore never thank. Beloved friend, what are you at? That Christ should die; is it nothing to you? That God "gave his Only-begotten Son, that whosoever believeth in him should not perish, but have everlasting life;" is that nothing to you? Let the question drop into your heart. Press it home upon yourself. Will you say that you have no share in this gift? Will you deliberately give up any hope you may have of ever partaking of the grace of God? Are you determined now to say, "I do not care about Christ"? Well, you would hardly like to say that; but why do you practically declare this to be your intention, if you do not want to say it? Oh, that you might now so think of Christ as to trust him at once, and begin to raise this note of praise!

Some, on the other hand, do not thank God because they are always delaying. Have I not hearers here to-night who were here ten years ago, and were rather more hopeful then than they are now? "There is plenty of time," say you; but you do not say this about other matters. I admired the children, the other day, when the teacher said, " Dear children, the weather is unsettled. You can go out next Wednesday; but do you not think that it would be better to stop a month, so that we could go when the weather is more settled?" There was not a child that voted for stopping a month. All the hands were up for going next Wednesday. Now, imitate the children in that. Do not make it seem as if you were in no hurry to be happy; for as he that believeth in Christ hath eternal life, to postpone having it is an unworthy as well as an unwise thing to do. No, you will have it, I hope, at once. There is a man here who is going to be a very rich man when his old aunt dies. You do not wish that she should die, I am sure; but you sometimes wonder why some people are spared to be ninety, do you not? You are very poor now, and you wish that some of this money could come to you at once; you are not for putting that off. Why should you put off heavenly riches and eternal life? I beseech you to believe in Christ now; then you will be filled with thankfulness and joy.

Some cannot say, " Thanks be unto God for his unspeakable gift," for they do not know whether they have it or not. They sometimes think that they have; they oftener fear that they have not. Never tolerate a doubt on this subject, I implore you. Get full assurance. " Lay hold on eternal life." Get a grip of it. Know Christ: trust Christ wholly: and you have God's word for it, " He that heareth my word, and believeth on him that sent me, hath everlasting life, and shall not come into condemnation, but is passed from death unto life." Then you can say, " Thanks be unto God for his unspeakable gift."

Now, dear friends, let me ask you to join me in this exercise. Let us first unitedly *thank God for this gift*. Put out of your mind the idea that you ought to thank Christ, but not thank the Father. It was the Father that gave Christ. Christ did not die to make his Father love us, as some say that we preach. We have always preached the very opposite, and we have quoted that verse of Kent—

> " 'Twas not to make Jehovah's love
> Towards the sinner flame,
> That Jesus, from his throne above,
> A suffering man became.
>
> " 'Twas not the death which he endured,
> Nor all the pangs he bore,
> That God's eternal love procured,
> For God was love before."

He gave his Son because he already loved us. Christ is the exhibition of the Father's love, and the revelation of Christ is made because of " the love of the Spirit." Therefore, " Thanks be unto God "—the Father, the Son, the Holy Ghost—" for his unspeakable gift."

While you saved ones, every one, raise your note of gratitude, be very careful to *thank God only*. Do not be thinking by whose means you were converted, and begin to thank the servant instead of the Lord whom he serves. Let the man who was used as the instrument in God's hand be told, for his comfort, of the blessing God sent you through him; but thank God, and thank only God, that you were led to lay hold on Christ, who is his unspeakable gift.

Moreover, *thank God spontaneously*. Look at the apostle, and imitate him. When he sounded this peal of praise, his mind was occupied at the time about the collection for the poor saints; but, collection or no collection, he will thank God for his unspeakable gift. I like to see thanks to God come up at what might seem to be an untimely moment. When a man does not feel just as happy as he might be, and yet says, "Thank God," it sounds refreshingly real. I like to hear such a bubbling up of praise as in the case of old Father Taylor, of New York, when he broke down in the middle of a sentence. Looking up at the people, he said, "There now! the nominative has lost its verb; but, hallelujah! I am on the way to glory;" and so he went on again. Sometimes we ought to do just like that. Take an opportunity, when there comes a little interval, just to say, "Whether this is in tune or not, I cannot help it: thanks be unto God for his unspeakable gift."

Lastly, as you receive the precious gift, *thank God practically*. Thank God by doing something to prove your thanks. It is a poor gratitude which only effervesces in words, and shirks deeds of kindness. Real thankfulness will not be in word only, but in deed too, and so it will prove that it is in truth.

"Well, what could I do that would please God?" you say. First, I should think you could look for his lost children. That is sure to please him. Go to-night, and see whether you cannot find one of the erring whom you might bring back to the fold. Would you not please a mother, if she had lost her baby, and you set to work to find it? We want to please God. Seek the lost ones, and bring them in.

If you want to please God, next, succour his poor saints. If you know anything of them, help them. Do something for them for Christ's sake. I knew a woman who used always to relieve anybody that came to her door in the dress of a sailor. I do not think that half those who came to her ever had been to sea at all; but, still, if they came to the door as sailors, she used to say, "Ah! my dear boy was a sailor. I have not seen him for years. He is lost somewhere at sea; but for dear Jack's sake, I always help every sailor that comes to my door." It is a right feeling, is it not? I remember, when I first came to London from my country charge, I used to think that, if I came across a dog or a cat that came from Waterbeach, I would like to feed it. So, for love of Christ, love Christ's poor people. Whenever you find them, say, "My Lord was poor, and so are you, and for his dear sake I will help you."

If you want to please God, next, bear with the evil ones. Do not lose your temper; I mean, by that, do not get angry with the unthankful and the evil. Let your anger be lost in praise for the gift unspeakable. Please God by bearing with evil men, as he bears with you. But if you have a very bad temper, I hope that, in another sense, you may lose it, and never find it any more.

And, lastly, if you want to please God, watch, like the Thessalonians, "for his Son from heaven." The Lord Jesus is coming again, in like manner as he departed, and there is no attitude with which God is more delighted in his saved people than with that of watching for the time when "unto them that look for him shall he appear the second time, without sin unto salvation."

Beloved, may God help you thus to magnify his Son; and to him shall be all the praise! Let us again lift up our glad hallelujah: "Thanks be unto God for his unspeakable gift." Amen.

PORTION OF SCRIPTURE READ BEFORE SERMON—2 Corinthians ix.

HYMNS FROM "OUR OWN HYMN BOOK"—534, 236, 428.

Price Sixpence.

THE GREATEST FIGHT IN THE WORLD.

The Pastors' College Conference Address, 1891.

BY C. H. SPURGEON.

Dr. Pierson, preaching at the Tabernacle, on February 25th, 1892, referred to Mr. Spurgeon's last Conference Address in the following glowing terms:—I read with greatest interest that address that he delivered before the Conference, and which is now published under the title of *The Greatest Fight in the World*. I have no hesitation in saying that I think that that address is the greatest single utterance that Mr. Spurgeon ever gave to the world. It is, I suppose, the last one that he prepared with careful and painstaking elaboration before he left this world. If you will read that address, you will find that it is, in the first place, full of the most glorious gospel truths. In the second place, it fairly bristles with Biblical illustrations and figures of speech; and in the third place, which is more wonderful, it runs in the mould of a Scriptural dialect, as though the man were himself first of all saturated with the phraseology of Scripture, and then, when he came to express himself on that critical occasion, his thoughts fell into the form of a Scriptural expression as naturally as water runs in the channel scooped out for it by the brook. That is a marvellous address. I wish it might be published in the cheapest form, and given away to every living soul that can read the English tongue, and translated into every language on earth, that every man who is open to the convictions of truth might read it; and I would to God that the men who have learned the art of preaching a sermon and leaving out the Christ, or of preaching the Christ in the language of the schools, and so shooting their arrows over the heads of the common people, could, from that single address, learn the secret of telling the story of God, not in words which man's wisdom teacheth, but which the Holy Ghost teacheth, expressing spiritual things in spiritual terms! I never had, in all my little experience, a discourse that made a deeper impression on my mind as to the prophetical style of utterance being reproduced in the prophets of the modern pulpit.

LONDON: PASSMORE & ALABASTER, PATERNOSTER BUILDINGS; and all Booksellers.

Metropolitan Tabernacle Pulpit.

SAD FASTS CHANGED TO GLAD FEASTS.

A Sermon

INTENDED FOR READING ON LORD'S-DAY, MARCH 20TH, 1892,

DELIVERED BY

C. H. SPURGEON,

AT THE METROPOLITAN TABERNACLE, NEWINGTON,

On Lord's-day Evening, September 7th, 1890.

"Thus saith the Lord of hosts; The fast of the fourth month, and the fast of the fifth, and the fast of the seventh, and the fast of the tenth, shall be to the house of Judah joy and gladness, and cheerful feasts; therefore love the truth and peace."—Zechariah viii. 19.

MY time for discourse upon this subject will be limited, as we shall gather around the communion-table immediately afterwards. So in the former part of my sermon I shall give you only an outline of what might be said upon the text if we had time to examine it fully. It will be just a crayon sketch without much light and shade. You will be able to think over the subject at your leisure, and fill up the picture for yourselves!

We have, in the chapters we have read, a blessed message of peace to God's people in the day of their trouble. In the land of their captivity the Jews were in great perplexity. Their sad lament is on record: "By the rivers of Babylon, there we sat down, yea, we wept, when we remembered Zion. We hanged our harps upon the willows in the midst thereof." But their trouble led many of them to seek the Lord, and he was found of them. Welcome is such misery which leads to such mercy. In the seventh chapter we are told that, when they sent unto the house of God, to pray before the Lord, and to say, "Should I weep in the fifth month, separating myself, as I have done these so many years? *Then* came the word of the Lord." Jehovah had put their tears into his bottle, and in answer to their sighing sent them a message of hope. That message has in it much that is very practical. It is a letter full of mercy, but it is directed to certain characters. God does not send indiscriminate mercy. If men go on in their sin, he sends them words of judgment; but when they turn from their wickedness, and are renewed by his grace in the spirit of their minds, then it is that words of comfort are spoken to them.

Reviewing the whole message which Zechariah was commissioned to deliver, and which is summed up in our text, there are three things

No. 2,248.

which stand out in clear prominence. The first is, that *God calls for transformations of character* in the people whom he is going to bless. The second is, that *he promises transmutations of condition* to those whose characters are thus changed and beautified. And, lastly, *he ordains transfigurations of ordinances* as the result of the new character and condition. The whole subject is exceedingly suggestive, and well worthy of careful study when you reach your homes.

We must not lose sight of the fact that, primarily, this message is for Israel according to the flesh, and contains a prophecy of their latter-day glory. God hath not cast off his people whom he did foreknow, and there are majestic words here which still await their fulfilment when the set time shall have come. The Lord "will dwell in the midst of Jerusalem", and make the place of his feet glorious in that day. But as "no prophecy of the Scripture is of any private interpretation," so the message to the Jews also bears a message for us. Let us seek to learn its lessons well.

I. My text reminds me—and the chapter before us emphasizes the fact—that, when God means to bless his people, HE CALLS FOR TRANSFORMATIONS OF CHARACTER. The promise of the abiding presence of the Lord God Almighty is ever preceded by the call to separation and holiness. "The words which the Lord had cried by the former prophets" made it very clear that only with the righteous nation would God dwell; and Zechariah delivers a similar message.

Very remarkable will be the transformations of character which God shall work. According to the text, *love of truth* is to be one of the main effects of the change. These people certainly did not set much value on the truth before; they were in love with every lie, with every false god, and with every false prophet. But God would have them taste of his covenant blessings, and be set free from every false way. It is only the truth which can set men free; yet many there are even to-day who delight to be in bondage to error. How is it with you? Do you love the truth, or can you put up with that which is not true, if it is only pleasant? Say, dear heart, are you anxious after truth—truth in your head, truth in your heart, truth on your tongue, truth in your life? If you are false, and love falsehood, you are taken with a sore disease; and unless you are healed of the plague, you can never enter heaven. You must be transformed and made true, and only the Spirit of truth can effect the mighty change.

Another sign must follow: *love of peace*. The text also says: "Therefore love peace." In some men it is a plain proof of conversion when they desire peace. Some are naturally very hot-tempered, and soon boil over. These are the men of great force of character, or else of great shallowness: it is the small pot which is soon hot. Some are malicious; they can take enmity quietly, and keep it in the refrigerator of their cold hearts, even for years. Such love not peace; they are at war with all who have in any degree disappointed or displeased them. When the grace of God takes away an angry, passionate, malicious disposition, it achieves a great wonder. But then grace is itself a great wonder; and unless this change is wrought in you who need it, you shall not see God, for you cannot enter heaven to go into a passion there. Depend upon it, unless you lose your bad temper, you will never be amongst the ranks of the glorified. It must be conquered and removed, if you are to join the happy hosts on high. "They are without fault before the throne of God;" and so must you be if you are to be numbered amongst that company.

Moreover, those whom God blesses have undergone a transformation as to their conduct with each other. *Righteous dealing* is another effect of the change. Notice the ninth verse of the seventh chapter: "Thus speaketh the Lord of hosts, saying, Execute true judgment." This is at all times a necessary admonition, but never more necessary than now, when so many never dream of justice and goodness: in business and in private life many seem to have no care for righteousness. If the thing will pay, they will rob right and left; and they will only be honest because there is an old saw that saith, "Honesty is the best policy." But he that is honest out of policy is the most dishonest man in the world. May God grant us grace to do what is right at all costs! Christian men, when the grace of God reigns in their souls, would rather be the poorest of the poor than get rich by a single act contrary to uprightness. O beloved members of this church, be upright in all your transactions, clear and straight in your dealings; for how shall you call yourselves the children of the righteous God if you make gain by unholy transactions?

Another point of transformation lies in the exercise of *compassion*. This comes out in that same ninth verse of the seventh chapter: "Shew mercy and compassions every man to his brother." A great mark of a changed heart is when we become tender, pitiful, and kind. Some men have very little of the milk of human kindness about them. You may lay a case before them, and they wonder why you should come to them; and when you see how little they do, you yourself wonder why you ever came to them. Many there are whose hearts are locked up in an iron safe, and we cannot find the key! They have hidden the key themselves; there is no getting at their hearts. One such said to a minister who preached a sermon, after which there was to be a collection, "You should preach to our hearts, and then you would get some money." The minister replied, "Yes, I think that is very likely, for that is where you keep your money." The answer was a very good one. That is just where a great many persons carry their treasure; but when the grace of God comes, and renews the miser's heart, he begins to be generous, he has pity upon the poor, and compassion for the fallen: he loves to bless those who are round about him, and to make them happy. It is a mark of wonderful transformation in the character of some men, when their heart begins to go a little outside their own ribs, and they can feel for the sorrows of other men.

Notice, next, in the tenth verse of that same seventh chapter, that another mark of God's people is *consideration for others*: "Oppress not the widow, nor the fatherless, the stranger, nor the poor." How can he be a child of the all-bountiful Father who would make men work for wages that scarcely keep body and soul together? How can he be a son of the God of love, who will defraud the poor woman whose fingers must go stitch, stitch, stitch, half through the night, before she can get enough to give her even relief from her hunger?

God's children will have nothing to do with this kind of thing. Those who take delight in oppressing the poor, and who make their gain thereby, will be themselves pinched with eternal poverty; they are little likely to enter the golden gates of paradise. There is many a child of God who has lived here in the depths of poverty; and when he gets to heaven, away from all the struggle and bitterness, is he to see the man who was his oppressor here below, coming into glory to sit side by side with him? I trow not.

Once more, where there is a work of grace, it leads men to *brotherliness* of character. "And let none of you imagine evil against his brother in your heart," saith the Lord in the tenth verse of this seventh chapter; and the same thing is repeated in the seventeenth verse of the eighth chapter. I should be sure that some women were converted if they left off imagining evil against others in their hearts. For there are some women—and there are some men, too, I am sorry to say—who cannot think of anybody without thinking evil of them. There are such dreadful persons about, and sometimes we come across them to our dismay. They paint the very saints of God black, and there is no getting away from their slander; nay, let a man live the life of an Enoch, yet would some of these people report evil against him. Slander is no sign of a saint; it is the brand of one who is under the dominion of the devil. "For all these are things that I hate, saith the Lord." God save us from them all!

Thus I have given you a brief outline of the transformations of grace. They are great changes because God works them. When men come to him, and yield themselves up to his divine power, he takes away the heart of stone, and gives them a heart of flesh. He turns their nature to the very reverse of what it was before; then they follow after truth and peace, they love righteousness, and learn kindness, through his good Spirit.

II. The second point to which I would draw your attention, with reference to the methods of God with his people, is that HE PROMISES TRANSMUTATIONS OF CONDITION to those men in whom are found the transformations of character. I have already read this eighth chapter through to you; let us go through it again, and pick out just a note or two of the joy and gladness which are here written in full score.

First, *jealousy is turned into communing love.* God represents himself, in the second verse, as being very jealous about his people; because he loved them so much, he was jealous for them with great fury. The people set up false gods in his own city, even in his own temple, and God was angry with them, and would not dwell with them; but when they repented, and he had cleansed them by his mercy, he says, "I am returned unto Zion, and will dwell in the midst of Jerusalem." What a change! God waits not until, by long obedience, his people win him back. He does not say that he will return when they merit his presence. No, the word comes to us full of surprise and power, "I am returned." Instantly on the repentance, God comes back. A jealous God fights against me. I fly to Christ. He is content. He comes and dwells with me, no longer full of fury, but full of tenderness and love. If any of you have had God fighting against you, in holy jealousy chasing out your sin, happy will you be if you yield yourselves to Christ at once; if you do so, God will come quickly, and make your hearts to be his abode. May many get that transmutation at this good hour!

Next, *desolation is turned into population.* On account of sin, Jerusalem became desolate. "I scattered them with a whirlwind," saith the Lord, "among all the nations whom they knew not. Thus the land was desolate after them, that no man passed through nor returned: for they laid the pleasant land desolate." Zion sat like a widow, nobody came up to her solemn feasts; but God returned to her, and he says, in the fourth verse, "There shall yet old men and old women dwell in the streets of Jerusalem, and every man with his staff in his hand for very age. And the streets of the city shall be full of boys and girls playing in the streets thereof." So that when God comes to bless his people, where there was nobody, there seems to be everybody. When churches and congregations sin, God often minishes them, and brings them low; but when they return to their God, the old saints are seen there again, and there are new-born believers in plenty. God can soon change the estate of his people. It is the same with individual souls who have gone away from God, but afterwards repent and return to him. Then the desolation of heart is forgotten in the joy of the multitude of sweet and holy thoughts and interests, that crowd the heart and life. Old experiences revive, and new life and joy are born, where God comes near to us in grace and power. What a wonderful change this is! May we all taste its bliss!

Another change of condition follows: *scattering is turned into gathering.* God goes on to say that, as he scattered his people, so he will bring them together again from the east and from the west. This, as I have already said, has a first reference to scattered Israel, but how true it also is of us! When the Lord leaves us, we are scattered like sheep without a shepherd in a cloudy and dark day; but when we turn to him, his word is sure. "I will bring them, and they shall dwell in the midst of Jerusalem: and they shall be my people, and I will be their God, in truth and in righteousness." May we know, in our new experience, the truth of that promise, "For a small moment have I forsaken thee; but with great mercies will I gather thee," and may it be to us according to his word!

The next change is, that *poverty is turned into plenty.* Whereas they became poor, and were half-starved with famine, God tells them that the city shall be prosperous: "The vine shall give her fruit, and the ground shall give her increase, and the heavens shall give their dew." God often changes men's circumstances when he changes their hearts. When he has been beating and bruising, if men will but yield to him, he turns to them in love and in plenty. May the Lord do this with any of us who have grieved him, and brought his rod upon us! There is no truer word in the Book of God than this, "Seek ye first the kingdom of God and his righteousness, and all these things shall be added unto you." With the covenant blessings of grace, God often bestows the common blessings of this life, even as it is written in the chapter before us, "I will cause the remnant of this people to possess all these things."

Farther on in the chapter we are told of another change: *ill-will is turned into good-will.* Before the Lord graciously visited them, no man loved his neighbour. So we read in the tenth verse. But when God's grace came, and changed their character, then one city went to another, and said, "Let us go speedily to pray before the Lord, and to seek the Lord of hosts: I will go also;" and they went up to the house of God together. Oh, where the grace of God comes, it makes men friends! Enemies they may have been before, but then they go and seek one another out, and they say, "Come, old friend, let us end all this; give me your hand, and let bygones be bygones." There is nothing like love and unity among the people until the grace of God comes and conquers the natural ill-will which else would have had dominion. May such a transmutation take place between any here who may be at variance, and may all bitterness and hatred, if such things exist, be put away!

Did you not notice also, in the reading of this chapter, how these people had been a curse, and how by the presence of God *the curse is turned into a blessing?* "And it shall come to pass, that as ye were a curse among the heathen, O house of Judah, and house of Israel; so will I save you, and ye shall be a blessing: fear not, but let your hands be strong." When a believer dishonours God, one of the worst results of it is, that he becomes a snare to the people round about him. The very heathen look upon him as a curse. Inconsistent professors are the greatest stumblingblocks to the spread of the cause of Christ. But when their character is changed by the abounding grace of God, they become like overflowing springs, sending streams of blessing far and wide.

Moreover, in the day of blessing, their *reproach is turned into honour.* The nation had been despised; nobody would honour a Jew; but, when they honoured God, then God would honour them, and ten men would take hold of the skirts of a man that was a Jew, saying, "We will go with you: for we have heard that God is with you." A man of God would then become more precious than the gold of Ophir. Well, my friends, when we return to God, God very soon has ways of making us honourable, so that we are of value among men. He makes use of us, and men begin to perceive that we are not to be despised if God is with us, and his blessing rests upon us.

Thus have I hurried over these two points, because I want to dwell a little longer on the text itself; it was necessary, however, to introduce it in this way.

III. Now we come to this fact, which always accompanies God's presence. HE ORDAINS TRANSFIGURATIONS OF ORDINANCES. Four fasts, which had been kept by the Jews, were to be turned into feasts, when the character of the men who observed them had changed, and God had dealt graciously with them. Before this, their fasts had been farces, occasions of self-glorification, and all manner of pride. Now, these days were to be festivals of gladness, and times of drawing near to God, rejoicing in his good gift. In like manner, when a man becomes a believer in Christ, and is renewed, this principle operates; many a fast is turned into a feast, and many a sorrow and sadness into joy and gladness.

When the communion-table shall be uncovered, you will see before you, in the emblems of *the death of our Lord*, what might have been the memory of a fast. The Lord of life and glory was nailed to the accursed tree. He died by the act of guilty men. We, by our sins, crucified the Son of God. The memory of Christ would therefore seem to be all funereal. We might have expected that, in remembrance of his death, we should have been called to a long, sad, rigorous fast. Do not many men think so even to-day? See how they observe Good Friday, a sad, sad day to many; yet our Lord has never enjoined our keeping such a day, or bidden us look back upon his death under such a melancholy aspect. Instead of that, having passed out from under the old covenant into the new, and resting in our risen Lord, who once was slain, we commemorate his death by a festival most joyous. It came after the passover, which was a feast of the Jews; but unlike that feast, which was kept with unleavened bread, this feast is brimful of joy and gladness. It is composed of bread and of wine, without a trace of bitter herbs, or anything that suggests sorrow and grief. The bread and the cup most fitly set forth the death of our Lord and Saviour, and the mode of that death, even by the shedding of his blood; but as they stand before us now, they evoke no tears, they suggest no sighs. The memorial of Christ's death is a festival, not a funeral; and we are to come to the table with gladsome hearts, ay, and go away from it with praises, for " after supper they sang a hymn." At both ends it was psalm-singing. The great Hallel of the Jews commenced it, and another psalm, full of joy and gladness out of the hallelujahs of the psalms, finished it. Oh, what hath God wrought! We crucified the Christ of God; but in that crucifixion we have found our ransom. With wicked hands he was slain by us; but his blessed sacrifice hath put all our sin away for ever. Our hymn rightly asks—

> " ' It is finished;' shall we raise
> Songs of sorrow, or of praise?
> Mourn to see the Saviour die,
> Or proclaim his victory?"

But it justly answers—

> " Lamb of God! thy death hath given
> Pardon, peace, and hope of heaven:
> ' It is finish'd;' let us raise
> Songs of thankfulness and praise!"

As the Lord's Supper leads the way in that direction, I may say that every other fast of the Christian has been transfigured in the same manner. *The Sabbath* is to many people a very dreary day; but to many of us it is a fast which has been turned into a feast. I am often amused when I read the accounts that are given by some people of an English Sabbath-day. In all soberness it is set forth what we Puritans do on this the first day of the week. We wake up in the morning, and say to ourselves, "Another dreadfully miserable day come round," and then we go off to our places of worship, where we sit with frightfully long faces, and listen to terribly dismal sermons; we do not sing, or even smile; but we howl out some ugly psalm, and make ourselves as unhappy as ever we can be. When we come home, we draw down the blinds to keep the sun out. We never go into the garden to admire the flowers. Well, you know all the rest of the story. I think we are descendants of the people who killed the cat on Monday because it caught mice on Sunday—at least, so I have heard. But if I had not read all this, I should not have known it. Often, when I see in the paper some description of myself, I say, "Well, people somehow seem to know me better than I know myself; I never thought anything of the kind; it has never entered my head. Yet here it is in black and white." O beloved friends! our idea of the Lord's-day is altogether different from this hideous caricature of it. If I had to describe our Sabbaths, I should say that they are full of brightness, and joy, and delight. I should tell of our singing, with full hearts, of the happy prospect before us in that land—

"Where congregations ne'er break up,
And Sabbaths have no end."

I am sure we should not be likely to wish to go to that heavenly country if our Sabbaths here were as dreary as some say they are. Why, here in this house, we have had our merriest times! Of old, when the prodigal came back, "they began to be merry," and I have never heard that they have left off; at any rate, I do not think that we have. We have rejoiced with the joy of harvest as we have heard of sinners saved, and have known that we are saved ourselves. I grant you that, before we knew the Lord, it did sometimes seem to our young minds rather a dull thing to read the Bible, and hear sermons, and to keep Sabbaths; but now that we have come to Christ, and he has saved us; now that we are his; the first day of the week, which was a fast, has become a feast, and we look with eager delight for the Sundays to come round one after another. In fact, these Lord's-days are the beds of flowers in our gardens. The week-days are only the gravel paths that yield us little but weariness as we walk along them. Happy Sabbath! we hail thy coming with delight, and sing—

"Welcome, sweet day of rest,
That saw the Lord arise;
Welcome to this reviving breast,
And these rejoicing eyes!

"The King himself comes near,
And *feasts* his saints to-day;
Here we may sit, and see him here,
And love, and praise, and pray."

So, you see, this is a second instance in which what might have been a fast is turned into a feast.

There is another thing that is to some of us now a great feast, though formerly it was as full of weariness as a fast. It is *the hearing of the doctrines of grace*. I know some brethren who always sit very uneasily when I begin to preach the doctrines of grace. I am sorry that it is so, and I hope that they will grow wiser. Still, all of us did not always like to hear about God's electing love and absolute sovereignty; about the special redemption of Christ for his people; and about the union to Christ being an everlasting union, never to be broken. There was a time when we did not join very heartily in the lines—

> "Once in Christ, in Christ for ever,
> Nothing from his love can sever."

But, oh, when your heart gets into full fellowship with God, if it is with you as it is with me, you will be glad to get on that string! Is there anything that gives us greater joy than to know our calling and election, and to make it sure; to know that the Father loved us as he loved Christ from before the foundation of the world, and that he loves us with a love that can never end, and can never change, but will continue when the sun burns black as a coal? It was because they heard these grand doctrines that such crowds used to gather in the Desert in France to hear the old Calvinistic preachers. It was the hold these truths of grace had upon the minds and hearts of men that explains how it was that, under the gospel oaks in England, vast numbers used to come to hear plain, and often illiterate men, preach the gospel. They preached a gospel that had something in it; and the people soon discover the real article when it is set before them. There is much that goes for gospel now, and if you could have a mile of it, you would not get an inch of consolation out of it, for there is nothing in it. But when your soul is heavy, and when your heart is sad, there is nothing like the old faith to put cheer and life into you. How often I have read *Elisha Coles on Divine Sovereignty* through and through when I have been ill! When the heart begins to sink, if one gets a grip of the sovereignty of God, and the way of his grace, whereby he saveth the unworthy, and getteth unto himself glory by his faithfulness to his promise, what had been a fast becomes to the child of God a feast of fat things, and royal cheer of a goodly sort.

You will all go with me in the next point. Sometimes *the day of affliction* becomes as a fast which has been turned into a feast. It is a trying thing to lose one's health, and to be near to death; to lose one's wealth, and to wonder how the children will be fed; to have heavy tidings of disaster come to you day after day in doleful succession. But if you can but grasp the promise, and know that "All things work together for good to them that love God;" if you can see a covenant God in it all, then the fast turns into a feast, and you say, "God is going to favour me again. He is only pruning the vine to make it bring forth better grapes. He is going to deal with me again after his own wise, loving, and fatherly way of discipline." You then hear the Lord saying to you—

> "Then trust me, and fear not: thy life is secure;
> My wisdom is perfect, supreme is my power;
> In love I correct thee, thy soul to refine,
> To make thee at length in my likeness to shine."

I have met with some saints who have been happier in their sickness and in their poverty than ever they were in health and in wealth. I remember how one, who had been long afflicted, and had got well, but had lost some of the brightness of the Lord's presence, which he had enjoyed during his sickness, said, "Take me back to my bed again.

Let me be ill again, for I was well when I was ill. I am afraid that I am getting ill now that I am well." It is often worth while being afflicted in order to experience the great lovingkindness of God, which he bestows so abundantly on us in the hour of trouble and perplexity. Yes, God turns our fasts into feasts, and we are glad in the midst of our sorrow; we can praise and bless his name for all that he does.

Once more: the solemn truth of *the coming of the Lord* is a feast to us, though at first it was a fast. With very great delight we believe that the Lord Jesus Christ will shortly come. He is even now in the act of coming. The passage that we read, "Surely, I come quickly," would be better translated, "Surely, I am coming quickly." He is on the road, and will certainly appear, to the joy of his people, and for the emancipation of the world. There are certain writers who say they know when he is coming; do not you be plagued with them; they know no more about it than you do. "Of that day and hour knoweth no man, no, not the angels of heaven, but my Father only;" said the Lord Jesus. Perhaps the Lord may come sooner than any of us expect; before this "diet of worship" shall break up, he may be here. On the other hand, he may not come for a thousand years, or twice ten thousand years. The times and the seasons are with him, and it is not for us to pry behind the curtain. Those of our number who are unsaved may well dread his coming, for he will come to destroy them that obey not the gospel. "Let all the inhabitants of the land tremble: for the day of the Lord cometh, for it is nigh at hand; a day of darkness, and of gloominess, a day of clouds and of thick darkness." That day will be terror, and not light, to you. When he cometh, he shall judge the earth in righteousness, and woe unto his adversaries; for "He shall rule them with a rod of iron; as the vessels of a potter shall they be broken to shivers." You have grave need to keep the fast of the Second Advent, for to you it is *dies iræ*, day of wrath and day of vengeance, day of dread and day of woe. But if you become a believer, and by grace are transformed, as I described in the early part of this discourse, then it shall be a feast to you. Then you will look out for his appearing as the day of your hope, and will gladly say, "Ay, let him come! Come, Lord, nor let thy chariots wait! Come, Lord! Thy church entreats thee to tarry no longer! Come, thou absent love, thou dear unknown, thou fairest of ten thousand! Come to thy church, and make her glad!" To us the thought of the glorious Advent of Christ is no fast; it is a blessed feast. Our songs never rise higher than when we get on this strain. With what fervour we lift up our voices, and sing—

> "Brothers, this Lord Jesus
> Shall return again,
> With his Father's glory,
> With his angel train;
> For all wreaths of empire
> Meet upon his brow,
> And our hearts confess him
> King of glory now"!

Last of all, to come still more closely home, *the approach of death* is to most men a dreadful fast. Not the Mohammedan Ramadan can be more full of piteous grief than some men when they are obliged to think of death. If some of you were put into a room to-morrow, and were compelled to stay there all day, and to think of death, it would certainly be a very gloomy time to you. You *will* die, however; perhaps suddenly, perhaps by slow degrees. There will come a time when people will walk very gently round your bed, when they will wipe the death-sweat from your brow, when they will bow over you to see whether you still breathe, or whether you have gone. Out of the six thousand persons here to-night, there are some, certainly, who will never see New Year's Day. Usually there is some one who does not see even another Sabbath-day. Almost every week we get an intimation that a hearer of the previous week has died before the next Lord's-day.

Who among us will first be gone? Dare you think of it? O beloved, when once you have peace with God, and you know that you are going to behold his face, whom though you have not seen, yet you love, then you can think of death without trembling. I think that there is nothing more delightful to the man who has the full assurance of faith, than to be familiar with the grave, and with the resurrection morning, and with the white robe, and with the harp of gold, and with the palm, and with the endless song. The thought of death is more a feast to us than a fast; for as Watts sings—

> "Jesus can make a dying bed
> Feel soft as downy pillows are,
> While on his breast I lean my head,
> And breathe my life out sweetly there."

"Well, I shall soon be home," says one old saint; and she speaks of it as she used to speak, when a girl, of the holidays coming, and of her going away from school. "I shall soon behold the King in his beauty," says another; he speaks of it as he might have spoken, when a young man, of his marriage-day. Children of God can not only read *Young's Night Thoughts* without feeling any chill at the solemnities there written out; but they can write in their diaries notes of expectation, at the thought of being with Christ, and almost notes of regret that they have not passed away to the glory, but are still lingering here in the land of shadows. "What?" said one, who had been long lying senseless, when he came back again to consciousness, "And am I here still? I had half hoped to have been in my heavenly Father's home and palace above, long before this; and I am still here." Truly, beloved, the fast is turned into a feast, when we reach this experience. We will not hesitate to say, "Come, Lord, take us to thyself." Oh for a sight of the King in his beauty!

> "Father, I long, I faint to see
> The place of thine abode;
> I'd leave thy earthly courts, and flee
> Up to thy seat, my God."

I knew right well a beloved brother in Christ with whom I was very familiar, who stood up one Sabbath morning, and announced just that verse. I thought of him when I repeated it, and I wondered whether it was quite as true to me as it was to him. He gave it out, and said—

> "Father, I long, I faint to see
> The place of thine abode;
> I'd leave thy earthly courts, and flee
> Up to thy seat, my God!"

Then he stopped, there was a silence; and at last, one of the congregation ventured upstairs into the pulpit, and found that the preacher was gone. His prayer was heard. He was gone to the place of God's abode. Oh, happy they who die thus! The Lord grant that we may never pray against a sudden death! We may almost pray for it when once our soul is right with God. I can join John Newton, and instead of dreading the change, say—

> "Rather, my spirit would rejoice,
> And long, and wish, to hear thy voice;
> Glad when it bids me earth resign,
> Secure of heaven, if thou art mine."

But is Christ yours? Has the fast been changed into a feast for you, by faith in the crucified Saviour? God help you to answer that question with a glad, hearty "Yes"! Then may he make all your life "joy and gladness", changing your fearful fasts into "cheerful feasts", until at length all of us, who believe in Christ, and who love his appearing, shall sit down at the marriage-supper of the Lamb! Amen.

PORTIONS OF SCRIPTURE READ BEFORE SERMON—Zechariah vii. and viii.

HYMNS FROM "OUR OWN HYMN BOOK"—181, 30.

Just Published.

THE ONLY AUTHORIZED LIFE OF MR. SPURGEON.

Price 2s. 6d. With over 50 Illustrations.

FROM THE USHER'S DESK TO THE TABERNACLE PULPIT.

THE LIFE AND LABOURS OF

PASTOR C. H. SPURGEON.

BY

REV. R. SHINDLER,

Author of "Northeram Hall," &c., &c.

PASSMORE AND ALABASTER, PATERNOSTER BUILDINGS; and all Booksellers.

Metropolitan Tabernacle Pulpit.

"EVEN NOW."

A Sermon

INTENDED FOR READING ON LORD'S-DAY, MARCH 27TH, 1892,

DELIVERED BY

C. H. SPURGEON,

AT THE METROPOLITAN TABERNACLE, NEWINGTON,

On Lord's-day Evening, February 8th, 1891.

"Even now."—John xi. 22.

I HOPE that there are a great many persons here who are interested in the souls of those around them. We shall certainly never exercise faith concerning those for whose salvation we have no care. I trust, also, that we are diligent in looking after individuals, especially those who are amongst our own family and friends. This was what Martha did; her whole care was for her brother. It is often easier to have faith that Christ can save sinners in general, than to believe that he can come into our own home, and save some particular member of our household. But, oh, the joy when this comes to pass; when we are able to kneel beside some of our loved ones, and rejoice with them in being made alive by the power of the Holy Ghost! We cannot expect to have this privilege, however, unless like Martha we send our prayer to Jesus, and go to meet him, and tell him of our need. In the presence of Christ it seems very natural to trust him even at the worst extremity. It is when we are at our wits' end that he delights to help us. When our hopes seem to be buried, then it is that God can give us a resurrection. When our Isaac is on the altar, then the heavens are opened, and the voice of the Eternal is heard. Art thou giving way to despair concerning thy dear friend? Art thou beginning to doubt thy Saviour, and to complain of his delay? Be sure that Jesus will come at the right time, though he must be the judge of which is the best time for him to appear.

Martha had a fine faith. If we all had as much honest belief in Christ as she had, many a man, who now lies dead in his sins, would, ere long, hear that voice which would call him forth from his tomb, and restore him unto his friends. Martha's faith had to do with a dreadful case. Her brother was dead, and had been buried, but her faith still lived; and in spite of all things which went against her, she believed in Christ, and looked to him for help in her extremity. Her faith went to the very edge of the gulf, and she said, "But I know, that *even now*, whatsoever thou wilt ask of God, God will give it thee."

Still, Martha had not so much faith as she thought she had. But a few hours after she had confessed her confidence in the power of the Lord Jesus, or perhaps it was only a few minutes, she stood at the grave of her brother, and evidently doubted the wisdom of him she professed to trust. She objected to the stone being removed; and, strong in the admitted facts of the case, she urged her reason, and said, "Lord, by this time he stinketh." Well, but, Martha, you said, not very long ago, "I know that even now the Christ can interpose." Yes, she said it, and she believed it in the way in which most of us believe; but when her faith was sharply tried by a matter of fact, she did not appear to have had all the faith she professed. I suspect this also is true of most of us. We often fancy our confidence in Christ is much stronger than it really is. I think I have told you of my old friend, Will Richardson, who said, when he was seventy-five years of age, that it was a very curious thing, that all the winter through, he thought he should like to be a-harvesting, or out in the hay-field, because he felt so strong. He imagined that he could do as much as any of the youngsters. "But," he said, "do you know, Mr. Spurgeon, when the summer comes, I do not get through the hay-making; and when the autumn comes, I find I have not sufficient strength for reaping?" So it often is in spiritual things. When we are not called upon to bear the trouble, we feel wonderfully strong; but when the trial comes, very much of our boasted faith is gone in smoke. Take heed that ye examine well your faith; let it be true and real, for you will need it all.

However, Christ did not take Martha at her worst, but at her best. When our Lord says, "According to your faith be it unto you," he does not mean "According to your faith in its ebb," but "According to your faith in its flood." He reads the thermometer at its highest point, not at its lowest; not even taking the "mean temperature" of our trust. He gives us credit for our quickest pace; not counting our slowest, nor seeking to discover our average speed in this matter of faith. Christ did for Martha all she could have asked or believed; her brother did rise again, and he was restored to her, and to his friends. In thy case, too, O thou trembling, timorous believer, the Lord Jesus will take thee at thy best, and he will do for thee great things, seeing that thou desirest to believe greatly, and that thy prayer is, "Lord, I believe; help thou mine unbelief!"

The point upon which Martha chiefly rested, when she expressed her faith, was the power of Christ in intercession with his Father. "I know," said she, "that, even now, whatsoever thou wilt ask of God, God will give it thee." Since the omnipotence of God could be claimed, she felt no anxiety as to the greatness of the request. "Whatsoever" was asked could easily be gained, if it was only asked by him who never was denied. Beloved in the Lord, our Christ is still alive, and he is still pleading. Can you believe, even now, that whatever he shall ask of God, God will give it him, and give it you for his dear Son's sake? What an anchorage is the intercession of Christ! "He is able also to save them to the uttermost that come unto God by him, seeing he ever liveth to make intercession for them." Here is a grand pillar to rest the weight of our souls upon : "He ever liveth to make intercession for them." Surely, we may have great faith in him who never wearies, and who never fails; who lives, indeed, for no other purpose than to plead for those who trust in his dying love, and in his living power. "Who is he that condemneth? It is Christ that died, yea, rather, that is risen again, who is even at the right hand of God, who also maketh intercession for us." Fall back upon the intercessory power of Christ in every time of need, and you will find comfort that will never fail you.

It is a grand thing to have faith for the present, not bemoaning the past, nor dreaming of some future faith which we hope may yet be ours. The present hour is the only time we really possess. The past is gone beyond recall. If it has been filled with faith in God, we can no more live on that faith now than we can live to-day on the bread we ate last week. If, on the contrary, the past has been marred by our unbelief, that is no reason why this moment should not witness a grand triumph of trust in the faithful Saviour. Let us not excuse our present lack of faith by the thought of some future blessing. No confidence which we may learn to put in Christ, in the days to come, can atone for our present unbelief. If we ever mean to trust him, why should we not do so now, since he is as worthy of our belief now as he ever will be, and since what we miss now we miss beyond recall.

> "The present, the present is all thou hast
> For thy sure possessing,
> Like the patriarch's angel, hold it fast,
> Till it give its blessing."

In this verse, "I know, that even now, whatsoever thou wilt ask of God, God will give it thee," I want to fix your attention only on the two words, "Even now." We have just sung—

> "Pass me not, O tender Saviour,
> Let me love and cling to thee;
> I am longing for thy favour;
> When thou comest, call for me:
> Even me."

Our hymn was, "Even me." The sermon is to be "Even now." If you have been singing "Even me," and so applying the truth to your own case, say also, with an energy of heart that will take no denial, "Even now," and listen with earnest expectation to that gospel which is always in the present tense: "While it is said, To-day if ye will hear his voice, harden not your heart, as in the provocation." Remember, too, that this is not only the preacher's word, for the Holy Ghost saith, "To-day" : "Even now."

I shall use these words, first, in reference *to those who are concerned about the souls of others*, as Martha was about her dead brother. Believe that Christ can save even now. Then I shall speak *to you who are somewhat concerned about your own souls*. You believe, perhaps, that Christ can save. I want you to be persuaded that he can save you even now; that is to say, at this exact hour and minute, going by the clock, while you hear these words, even now, Christ can forgive; even now, Christ can save; even now, Christ can bless.

I. First, CAN WE BELIEVE THIS WITH REFERENCE TO OTHERS? If you are in the same position as Martha, I can bring out several points of likeness which should encourage you to persevere. You, mother, have prayed for your boy; you, father, have pleaded for your girl; you, dear wife, have been much in prayer for your husband; you, beloved teacher, have frequently brought your class before God; and yet there is a bad case now pressing upon your mind, and your heart is heavy about some dear one, whose condition seems hopeless. I want you to believe that now, even now, Christ can grant your prayer, and save that soul; that now, even now, he can give you such a blessing that the past delay shall be more than recompensed to you.

There is one, for instance, in whom we are deeply interested, and we can say that *the case has cost us great sorrow.* So Martha could have said of Lazarus. "Blessed Master", she might have said, "my brother took the fever"—(for I should think it was a fever that he had)—"and I watched him; I brought cold water from the well, and I laved his burning brow; I was by his bedside all night. I never took off my clothes. Nobody knows how my heart was wrung with anguish as I saw the hot beaded drops upon his brow, and tried to moisten his parched tongue and lips. I sorrowed as though I was about to die myself; but in spite of all that, I believe even now that thou canst help me; even now." Alas! there are many griefs in the world like this. A mother says, "Nobody knows what I have suffered through that son of mine. I shall die of a broken heart because of his conduct." "No one can tell," says a father, "what grief that daughter of mine has caused me. I have sometimes wished that she had never been born." There have been many, many such stories told into my ear, in which a beloved one has been the cause of anguish and agony untold to gracious, loving hearts. To those so sorely troubled I now speak. Can you believe that *even now* the living Intercessor is "mighty to save"? It may be that you are at this moment trembling on the verge of the blessing you so long have sought. God give you faith to grasp it "even now"!

With other persons we are met with a fresh difficulty. *The case has already disappointed us.* That is how some of you have found it, is it not? "Yes," you say, "I have prayed long for a dear friend, and I believed, some time ago, that my prayer was heard, and that there was a change for the better; indeed, there was an apparent change; but it came to nothing." You are just like Martha. She kept saying to herself, "Christ will come. Brother is very ill, but Jesus will come before he dies; I know he will. It cannot be that he will stay away much longer; and when he comes, Lazarus will soon be well." Day after day, Mary and she sent their messenger to look toward the Jordan, to see if Jesus was not coming. But he did not come. It must have been a terrible disappointment to both these sisters; enough to stagger the strongest faith they had ever had in the sympathy of Christ. But Martha got the better of it, and she said, "Even now, though disappointed so bitterly, I believe that thou canst do whatsoever thou wilt." Learn from Martha, my discouraged brother. You thought that your friend was converted, but he went back again; you thought that there was a real work of grace upon his heart, but it turned out to be a mere disappointment, and disappeared, like the mist before the sun. But can you not believe over the head of your disappointment, and say, "I believe even now, even now"? Blessed shall your faith be, if it gets so far.

Perhaps further difficulties have met us. We have attempted to help someone, and *the case has proved our own helplessness.* "Ah, yes," says one, "that exactly describes me. I never felt so helpless in my life. I have done all that I can do, and it amounts to nothing. I have been careful in my example. I have been prayerful in my words. I have been very patient and longsuffering. I have tried to induce my beloved one to go and listen to the gospel here and there. I have put holy books in his way, and all the while I have seized opportunities to plead with him, often with tears in my eyes, and I can do nothing! I am dead beat." Yes, that is just where Martha got to; she had done everything, and nothing seemed to be of the least use. None of the medicines she applied seemed to soothe the sufferer. She had gone down the village, perhaps to the house of Simon the leper, who was a friend of hers, and he possibly advised some new remedies; but nothing seemed to make the least difference. Her brother got worse and worse, until she saw that, though she had nursed him back to health the last time he had been ill, she was now utterly powerless. Then he died. Yet, even though things had gone so far as that, she had faith in Christ. In like manner, your case is beyond your skill; but can you not believe that, even now, the end of nature will be the beginning of grace; can you not even now feel that you shall find that word true, "He shall not fail"? Christ never did fail yet, and he never will. When all the doctors give a patient up, the Great Physician can step in and heal. Can you believe concerning your friend "even now"?

But perhaps you are in a worse plight still. *The case has been given up.* I think I hear one kind, gracious soul, whose hope has been crushed, say, "Well, sir, that is just what we have come to about my boy. We held a little family meeting, and said we must get him to go away to Australia, if we can. If he will only go to America, or somewhere abroad, it will be a relief to have him out of our sight. He keeps coming home intoxicated, and gets brought before the magistrates. He is a disgrace to us. He is a shame to the name he bears. We have given him up." Martha had come to this. She had given her brother up, and had actually buried him; yet she believed in the power of Christ. Ah, there are many people that are buried alive! I do not know that such a thing ever happens in the cemetery; but I know it happens in our streets and homes. Many are buried morally, and given up by us before God gives them up. And, somehow, it is often the given-up people that God delights to bless. Can you believe that even now, *even now,* prayer can be heard, that even now the Holy Ghost can change the nature, and that even now Christ can save the soul? Believest thou this? I shall rejoice if thou canst, and thou too shalt rejoice ere long.

But there is still a lower depth. Here is one who is much concerned about an individual, and *the case is loathsome.* "Though we loved him once," he says, "his character has now become such that it is pestilential to the family. He leads others astray. We cannot think of what he has done without the very memory of his life spreading a taint over our conscience, and over our mind." There are persons alive in the world, who are just masses of living putridity. There may be such here. I should be glad if a word I said could reach them. It is a shocking thing that there are men and women, made in the image of God, with talents and ability, with capacity and conscience, who, nevertheless, seem to live for nothing else but to indulge their licentious passions, and to lead others into vices which else they had never known. There must come an awful day of reckoning to such when the Christ of God shall sit upon the throne, and shall weigh before all men the secret doings of libertines, of debauched men, and depraved women. If any of you have such a one related to you, can you believe that even now Christ can raise that one? Yours is just the same sort of case as Martha had. She could have said, "Brother is buried: worse than that, he stinketh." She did not like to say that of dear Lazarus, her own brother, but she could not help saying it. And there are some men, of whom we are compelled to say, no matter how much our love seeks to shield them, that their character stinks. But can you still believe that, even now, there is hope that God can intervene, and that grace can save? Why, my dear friend, you and I know that it is so! I do believe it; we must all believe it. If it comes to a case very near and dear to you, and you begin to be a little bit staggered, recollect what you used to be yourselves—not openly so depraved, perhaps, but inwardly quite the same, and take hope for these foul men and women from the remembrance of what you were: "and such were some of you; but ye are washed." When John Newton used to preach at St. Mary Woolnoth, he always believed in the possibility of the salvation of the worst of his hearers; for he had been himself one of the vilest of the vile. When he was very old, and they said, "Dear Mr. Newton, you are too old to preach; you had better not go into the pulpit now," he said, "What! shall the old African blasphemer, who has been saved by grace, leave off preaching the gospel while there is breath in his body? Never." I think while there is breath in the body of some of us, we must go on telling the gospel; for, if it saved us, it can save the worst of sinners. We are bound to believe that even now Christ can save even the most horrible and the most vile.

> "His blood can make the foulest clean,
> His blood availed for me."

Perhaps there is even a more desperate difficulty still, with reference to someone whom we would fain see living for God. *The case is beyond our reach.* "Yes," that brother quickly answers, "now you have come to my trouble. I do not even know where my boy is; he ran away, and we have not heard from him for years. How can I help him?" Why, believe that "even now" Christ can speak to him, and save him! He can send his grace where we can send our love. The great difficulty which lies like a stone at the door of the sepulchre will not prevent him speaking the life-giving word. He has all forces at his command, and when he says the word, the stone shall be rolled away, and the son that is lost shall be found; the dead shall be made alive again. Though you cannot reach your son, or your daughter, Christ can meet with them. "The Lord's hand is not shortened, that it cannot save; neither his ear heavy, that it cannot hear." Though your prodigal boy or your wandering girl be at the end of the earth, Christ can reach them, and save them. "Have faith in God." "Even now" Christ can aid you.

> "Faith, mighty faith, the promise sees,
> And looks to God alone,
> Laughs at impossibilities,
> And says, 'It shall be done.'"

I know there are some Christian people who have drifted into the terribly wicked state of giving up their relatives as hopeless. There was a brother here, who is now in heaven, a good, earnest Christian man, whose son had treated him very shockingly indeed, and the father, justly indignant, felt it right to give his son up. He had often tried to help him, but the young man was so scandalous a scapegrace that I did not wonder that the old man turned him away. But one night, as I was preaching here, I spoke in something like the same way in which I have spoken now; and the next morning the old man's arm was about his child's neck. He could not help himself; he felt he must go and find his son out, and seek again to reclaim him. It seemed to have been the appointed time for that boy's salvation, for it pleased God that within a few months that son died, and he passed away with a good hope, through grace, that he had been brought to his Saviour's feet by his father's love. If any of you have a very bad son, go after him, seeking, until by the grace of God, you shall find him. And you that have grown hopeless about your relatives, you must try not to give them up. If other people cast them off, you must not, for they are allied to you by the ties of blood. Seek them out. You are the best person in the world to seek them, and the most likely to find them, if you can believe that even now, when the worst has come to the worst, "even now," almighty grace can step in, and save the lost soul.

Oh, that some here may have faith to claim at this moment the salvation of their friends! May desire be wrought into expectancy, and hope become certainty! Like Jacob at Jabbok, may we lay hold of God, saying, "I will not let thee go, except thou bless me." To such faith the Lord will give a quick response. He that will not be denied shall not be denied. My friend, Hudson Taylor, who has done such a wonderful work for China, is an instance of this. Brought up in a godly home, he, as a young man, tried to imitate the lives of his parents, and failing in his own strength to make himself better, he swung to the other extreme, and began to entertain sceptical notions. One day, when his mother was from home, a great yearning after her boy possessed her, and she went up to her room to plead with God that "even now" he would save him. If I remember aright, she said that she would not leave the room until she had the assurance that her boy would be brought to Christ. At length her faith triumphed, and she rose quite certain that all was well, and that "even now" her son was saved. What was he doing at that time? Having half an hour to spare, he wandered into his father's library, and aimlessly took down one book after another to find some short and interesting passage to divert his mind. He could not find what he wanted in any of the books; so, seeing a narrative tract, he took it up with the intention of reading the story, and putting it down when the sermon part of it began. As he read, he came to the words "the finished work of Christ", and almost at the very moment in which his mother, who was miles away, claimed his soul of God, light came into his heart. He saw that it was by the finished work of Christ that he was to be saved; and kneeling in his father's library, he sought and found the life of God. Some days afterwards, when his mother returned, he said to her, "I have some news to tell you." "Oh, I know what it is!" she answered, smiling, "You have given yourself to God." "Who told you?" he asked, in astonishment. "God told me," she said, and together they praised him, who, at the same moment, gave the faith to the mother, and the life to the son, and who has since made him such a blessing to the world. It was the mother's faith, claiming the blessing "even now", that did it. I tell you this remarkable incident that many others may be stirred up to the same immediate and importunate desire for the salvation of their children and relatives. There are some things we must always pray for with submission as to whether it is the will of God to bestow them upon us: but for the salvation of men and women we may ask without a fear. God delights to save and to bless; and when the faith is given to us to expect an immediate answer to such a prayer, thrice happy are we. Seek such faith even now, I beseech you, "even now."

II. But, in the second place, I want to speak very earnestly to any here who are concerned about their own souls. Jesus can save you "even now." CAN WE BELIEVE THIS FOR OURSELVES? Can you expect the Lord, even while you hear these words, to speak to you the word of power, and bring you forth from your sleep of sin?

For some of you, *the time is late, very late; yet it is not too late.* You are getting into years, my friend. I want you to believe that even now Christ can save you. I often notice the number of old people who come to the Tabernacle. I am glad to see the aged saints; but amongst so many elderly people, no doubt, there are some unsaved sinners, whose grey hairs are not a crown of glory, but a fool's cap. But, however old you are, though you are sixty, seventy, eighty, or even ninety years of age, yet "even now" Christ can give you life. Blessed be God for that! But it is not altogether the years that trouble you; it is your sins. As I have already said, if you have gone to the very extremity of sin, you may believe that, after all these years of wandering, the arms of free grace are still open to receive you "even now." There is an old proverb, "It is never too late to mend." It is ever too late for us to mend ourselves, but it is never too late for Christ to mend us. Christ can make us new, and it is never too late for him to do it. If you come to him, and trust him, he will receive you "even now."

By the longsuffering of God, *there is a time left to you,* in which you may turn to him. What a thousand mercies it is that "even now" is a time of mercy to you: it might have been the moment of your everlasting doom! You have been in accidents; you have been within an inch of the grave many times; you have been ill, seriously ill; you have been well-nigh given up for dead; and here you are yet alive, and still an enemy to God! Plucked by his hand from fire and flood, and, mayhap, from battle; delivered from fever and cholera, and still ungrateful, still rebelling, still spending the life that grace has lent you in resisting the love of God! Long years ago you should have believed in Christ, but the text is "even now." Do not begin to say, "I believe that God could have saved me years ago;" there is no faith in that. Do not meet my earnest plea, by saying, "I believe that God can save me under such-and-such conditions." Believe that he can save you now, up in the top gallery there, just as you are. You came in here careless and thoughtless; yet, even now, he can save you. Away yonder, quite a man of the world, free and easy, destitute of all religious inclinations though you may be, he can save you even now. O God, strike many a man down, as thou didst Saul of Tarsus, and change their hearts by thine own supreme love, as thou canst do it, even now, on the very spot where they sit or stand!

But though God waits to be gracious to you, though you have yet time to repent, remember, *it is but a time, therefore seize it.* Your opportunity will not last for ever. I believe that even now God can save; but if you reject Christ, there will come a time when salvation will be impossible. On earth, as long as a man desires to be saved, he may be saved: while there is life there is hope. I believe that, if a man's breath were going from his body, if he could then look to Christ, he would live. But—

> "There are no acts of pardon passed
> In the cold grave, to which we haste;
> But darkness, death, and long despair,
> Reign in eternal silence there."

Do not venture on that last leap without Christ; but even now, ere the clock strikes another time, fly to Jesus. Trust him "even now."

It is a time of hope. Even now, there is still every opportunity and every preparation for the sinner's salvation. "Behold, now is the accepted time; behold, now is the day of salvation." Shall I give you some reasons for believing that "even now" is a time of hope? There are many good arguments which may be brought forward, in order to banish the thought of despair.

First, *the gospel is still preached.* The old-fashioned gospel is not dead yet. There are a great many who would like to muzzle the mouths of God's ministers; but they never will. The old gospel will live when they are dead; and, because it is still preached to you, you may believe and live. What is the old gospel? It is that, seeing you are helpless to save yourself, or bring yourself back to God, Christ came to restore you; that he took those sins of yours, which were enough to sink you to hell, and bore them on the cross, that he might bring you to heaven. If you will but trust him, even now, he will deliver you from the curse of the law; for it is written, "He that believeth on him is not condemned." If you will trust him, even now, he will give you a life of blessedness, which will never end; for again it is written, "He that believeth on the Son hath everlasting life." Because that gospel is preached, there is hope for you. When there is no hope, there will be no presentation of the gospel. God must, by an edict, suspend the preaching of the gospel ere he can suspend the fulfilment of the gospel promise to every soul that believeth. Since there is a gospel, take it; take it now, even now. God help you so to do!

In the second place, I know there is hope now, "even now"; for *the Christ still lives.* He rose from the dead, no more to die, and he is as strong as ever. "I am he that liveth and was dead," he saith, "and behold, I am alive for evermore. Amen." Those words were spoken to the Apostle John, and when he saw him, he said that "His head and his hairs were white like wool, as white as snow;" but when the spouse saw him, she said, "His locks are bushy, and black as a raven." Yet both saw truly; John's vision of the white hair was to show that Christ is the Ancient of Days; but the view of the spouse was to show his everlasting youth, his unceasing strength and power to save. If there is any difference in him, Christ is to-day more mighty to save than he was when Martha saw him. He had not then completed the work of our salvation, but he has perfectly accomplished it now; and therefore there is hope for everyone who trusts in him. My Lord has gone up yonder where a prayer will find him, with the keys of death and hell jingling at his girdle, and with the omnipotence of God in his right hand. If you believe on him, by his "eternal power and Godhead" he will save you, and save you even now, on the spot, before you leave this house.

Moreover, I know that this is a time of hope, in the next place, because *the precious blood still has power.* All salvation is through the blood of the Lamb. Still—

> "There is a fountain filled with blood,
> Drawn from Immanuel's veins;"

and still, "even now,"—

> "Sinners, plunged beneath that flood,
> Lose all their guilty stains."

The endless efficacy of the atoning sacrifice is the reason why you may come and believe in Jesus, "even now." If that blood had diminished in its force, I should not dare to speak as I do; but I can, "even now," say with confidence,—

> "Dear dying Lamb, thy precious blood
> Shall never lose its power,
> Till all the ransomed church of God
> Be saved to sin no more."

How many have already entered into glory by the blood of the Lamb! When a man comes to die, nothing else will do for him but this: our own works are a poor staff for us when we pass through the river. All those who are now in the land of light have but one confidence, and but one song: they stand upon the merit of Jesus Christ, and they praise the Lamb who was slain, by whose blood they have been cleansed and sanctified. There is no other way of salvation but that. "Even now" that blood has virtue to take away your sin. Christ is a sufficient Saviour, because his death has unexhausted power. Believe that he can save you "even now."

Again, I would remind you that "even now" is a time of hope to you, because *the Spirit still can renew.* He is yet at work, regenerating and sanctifying. He came down at Pentecost to dwell with his people, and he has never gone back again. He is still in the church. Sometimes we feel his mighty power more than at other times, but he is always at work. Oh, you that do not know anything about the power of the Holy Ghost, let me tell you that this is the most wonderful phenomenon that can ever be observed! Those of us, who have seen and known his mighty energy, can bear testimony to it. In my retirement, at Menton, during the last few weeks, if you had seen me, you would have found me sitting every morning, at half-past nine o'clock, at my little table, with my Bible, just reading a chapter, and offering prayer, my family prayer with the little group of from forty to fifty friends, who daily gathered for that morning act of worship. There they met, and the Spirit of God was manifestly moving among them, converting, cheering, comforting. It was because of no effort of mine; it was simply the Word, attended by the Spirit of God, binding us together, and binding us all to Christ. And here, in this house, for seven-and-thirty years, have I in all simplicity preached this old-fashioned gospel. I have just kept to that one theme; content to know nothing else amongst men; and where are they that have preached new gospels? They have been like the mist upon the mountain's brow. They came, and they have gone. And so it will always be with those who preach anything else but the Word of God; for nothing will abide but the mount itself, the everlasting truth of the gospel to which the Holy Ghost bears witness. That same Holy Ghost is able to give you a new heart "even now", to make you a new creature in Christ Jesus at this moment. Believest thou this?

Once more. I know that "even now" Christ can save you, and I pray you to believe it, for *the Father is still waiting to receive returning prodigals.* Still, as of old, the door is open, and the best robe hangs in the hall, ready to be put upon the shoulders of the son who comes back from the far country, even though he returns reeking with the odour of the swine-trough. How longingly the Father looks along the road, to see whether at length some of you are turning homeward! Ah! did you but know the joy that awaits those who come, and the feast which would load the welcoming table, you would "even now" say, "I will arise, and go to my Father." You should have returned long ago; but blessed be his love, which "even now" waits to clasp you to his heart!

Last of all, *faith is but the work of a moment.* Believe and live. Thou hast nothing to do; thou needest no preparations: come as thou art, without a single plea, but that he bids thee come. Come now, "even now." If Christ were far away, the time that is left to some of you might be too short to reach him; if there were many things which first of all you had to do, your life might close before they were half done; if faith had to grow strong before it received salvation, you might be in the place of eternal despair before your faith had time to be more than a mere mustard seed. But Christ is not far away; he is in our midst, he is by your side. You have nothing to do before you trust him, he has done all; and however weak your faith, if it but comes in contact with Christ, it will convey to you instant blessing. " Even now " you may be saved for ever; for—

> " The moment a sinner believes,
> And trusts in his crucified God,
> His pardon at once he receives,
> Redemption in full, through his blood."

Surely all these are sufficient reasons why " even now " is a time of hope to you; may it also be a time of blessing! It shall be so if thou wilt but at this instant cast thyself on Christ. He says to thee that, if thou wilt but believe, thou shalt see the glory of God. Martha saw that glory. Thou shalt see it too if thou hast like precious faith.

I long that God would give me some souls to-night, on this first occasion when I have met an evening congregation since my return from the sunny South. I desire earnestly that he would set the bells of heaven ringing because sinners have returned, and heirs of glory have been born into the family of grace. I stirred you up to pray this morning. Pray mightily that this word to-night, simple but pointed, may be blessed to many.

PORTION OF SCRIPTURE READ BEFORE SERMON—John xi.

HYMNS FROM "OUR OWN HYMN BOOK"—95 (Part II.), 607, 612.

The Sword and the Trowel for April will be a SECOND MEMORIAL NUMBER, only second in interest to the March issue, which has had an unprecedented sale. It will contain *an admirable portrait of Mr. Spurgeon, taken at Menton on January* 8th, with various views photographed under his direction; also photographic blocks of his bedroom at the Hôtel Beau Rivage, the funeral *cortège* at Menton station and Norwood Cemetery, the olive-casket under the palm-branches at the Tabernacle, and the scene around the grave. Pastor J. A. Spurgeon has contributed an article on "Under the Rod"; Dr. Pierson has given an address on "Prayer Promises"; Mrs. Spurgeon has written a note concerning her Book Fund, and a letter to the Students of the Pastors' College; "the armour-bearer" has supplied some "Memorial Jottings"; Pastor T. W. Medhurst has sent "the first student's wreath", and other College brethren have furnished interesting Reminiscences of their beloved President. The Magazine will also contain "Son Tom's" loving tribute to his dear father's memory, the *fac-simile* of a page of Mr. Spurgeon's R. T. S. Pocket-book, the Tabernacle Church "In Memoriam" resolution, poems by Pastors Thomas Spurgeon and E. A. Tydeman, and a statement about the Orphanage and the Electric Railway. The "Notes" will also be specially interesting, as they will report the Tabernacle Annual Church-meeting, the meetings of the Emergency Committee and the London Committee of the College Association, the Orphanage Collectors' meeting, and other gatherings of the month. They will also contain a portrait and brief sketch of Mr. Spurgeon's "armour-bearer." Extra pages will again be given; and as it is anticipated that there will be a great demand for the Magazine, friends are recommended to order in good time the extra numbers they are likely to need.

Price 3d., post-free, 4d.

PASSMORE AND ALABASTER, 4, PATERNOSTER BUILDINGS, LONDON; and all Booksellers.

Metropolitan Tabernacle Pulpit.

WORDS TO REST ON.

A Sermon

INTENDED FOR READING ON LORD'S-DAY, APRIL 3RD, 1892,

DELIVERED BY

C. H. SPURGEON,

AT THE METROPOLITAN TABERNACLE, NEWINGTON,

On Thursday Evening, September 18*th*, 1890.

"And the people rested themselves upon the words of Hezekiah king of Judah."—2 Chronicles xxxii. 8.

It is very beautiful, in reading the story of Hezekiah, to see how the people always went with him. God had prepared the nation for a change, and when the hour came the man came with it. Under his father Ahaz, the people had been idolaters, and had forsaken God; but, when Hezekiah became king, he had a zeal for the worship of Jehovah, and on the very threshold of his reign, he began what proved to be a glorious reformation in the land. He seems to have been a man who was attractive to the people, and they took up his line of things at once with enthusiasm. Whether he proposed to break down the idols, to cleanse the temple, or to bring the tithes into the house of God, they made no objection; but, on the contrary, they followed his word with much vigour and earnestness. It is a grand thing when God sends a man who can guide others aright; especially when, in times of apostasy and spiritual declension, a leader is given who becomes a guide back into the old paths. We should feel exceedingly grateful whenever, in any place, God raises up a judge to deliver Israel, and when the people serve God all the days of that judge.

When our text comes in, the people of Judah were in great straits. The Assyrians, who were both cruel and barbarous in their treatment of others, had invaded the land, and had captured all the country, with the exception of Jerusalem. The city of the Great King was yet untrodden by the armies of the alien; but it looked as if it could not hold out very long, and Hezekiah encouraged his men of war by exciting their faith in their God. "Be strong and courageous," he said to them; "be not afraid nor dismayed for the King of Assyria, nor for all the multitude that is with him." With a ring of triumph in his tone, he told them that with Sennacherib was only an arm of flesh; and though it was a powerful one, yet with them was the omnipotence of God, and therefore there was more with them than with the Assyrians. The past glory of his reign, and the evident depth of his

No. 2,250.

own faith, added weight to his words, and the people believed his testimony. In such a time of great difficulty, when people are apt to mutiny, to find fault with their leaders, and to break up into cliques and parties, they still held to their king, and comforted themselves with the assurance he had given them of help in God. They were not distressed because of the invasion, nor did they despair of their cause. They were, of course, conscious of their great danger; but they found peace, even in their extremity, by quoting to themselves, and to one another, the emboldening language of their king. "The people rested themselves upon the words of Hezekiah king of Judah."

It is not always a good thing to rest upon man's words. It may often be a very evil thing; and because some error has been introduced by "such a dear, good man", it has had the deadlier hold upon masses of men. There have been thousands who have found their way to hell resting upon the words of some priest or pretended teacher who taught other than the truth. And yet, with this grain of caution, we cannot but commend these people, who, when they had a God-sent leader, had both the common-sense and the uncommon confidence to banish their fears at his bidding, seeing that his trust was in the name of the Lord. The people were not perfect, nor was their king; but we commend them, in that they did wisely when they "rested themselves upon the words of Hezekiah king of Judah."

I. Our first consideration shall be, THE KIND OF MAN WHOSE WORDS ARE LIKELY TO BE RESTED ON. There are some in whose words you never have much confidence, because they are flippant in their utterance. They do not appear to be sincere, and those who hear them, make nothing of what they say, for they evidently make nothing of it themselves. You cannot rest in the words of a man who contradicts himself, nor rely much upon one who is of one opinion to-day, who will be of another opinion to-morrow, and who before the third day is over, will be seized with some other new notion. There are men whom we all know in whose word nobody is tempted to put any kind of trust whatever. But, thanks be to God, there are in the Christian church still some in whose words men do trust, men who are as transparent as the clearest crystal, and as reliable as the best steel. These are the kind of men I want to describe; and this man who won the confidence of the people of Jerusalem shall serve us as a type thereof, and enable us to discover the kind of man whose words are likely to be rested on.

To begin with, he must be *a great man*. So it was in the case of "Hezekiah king of Judah." If the people cannot trust their king in matters of war, in whom can they trust? But if they see him to be a good sovereign, walking in the fear of God, and doing his utmost for them, how shall they do otherwise than trust their king? Yet in this matter we must take care, for they who trust in the great may find themselves greatly deceived. "Cursed be the man that trusteth in man, and maketh flesh his arm, and whose heart departeth from the Lord." That man is not truly great who leads us away from the greatest of all, even the Lord who ruleth over all. "It is better to trust in the Lord than to put confidence in princes." There is a kind of greatness that is only a cover for littleness. Sometimes a great title has great selfishness, even great sensuality, lying just underneath it.

But Hezekiah was not a little great man; he was truly a king. He was a born monarch; a kingly man. He was a man of royal mind and noble deed; hence the people did not ill, when, having respect to his greatness, they "rested themselves upon the words of Hezekiah king of Judah."

Moreover, the man who will be trusted will be found to be *a good man*. If he be not really so, he will, at least, be thought to be so. Men will put great trust in the words of one whose life agrees with his teaching. If they can detect something inconsistent in his character, the man's power is ended; but if a man is evidently carried away with the one idea of being and doing good, and consumed with the purpose of glorifying God, then his utterances have power. I know a man who is not an orator; he speaks but very plainly; and yet, if I had my choice, I would sooner hear him than almost any man I ever heard, because, when he speaks, I remember the wondrous life of faith in God, which accompanies his words. I will not say who he is, but almost everybody will guess. It is not what he says, but the man who says it, that makes the impression. It is the life behind the words, the holy confidence in God every day exhibited, the calm restful walk with God which everybody can see in his very face, which, to a thoughtful man, makes his feeblest accent more powerful than the most furious declamation of a mere rhetorician. As Dr. Bonar says,—

> "Thou must be true thyself,
> If thou the truth wouldst teach.
> Thy soul must overflow, if thou
> Another's soul wouldst reach:
> It needs the overflow of heart
> To give the lips full speech."

The man in whose words we are likely to find rest must be a good man. Hezekiah, from all we read of him, was evidently such a one. When greatness and goodness are blended, as in his case, there is sure to be a wide influence exerted. When there is eminence of ability as well as eminence of character found in a man, it often follows that what is described in this verse is true, the people rest themselves upon his words, even as they did upon Hezekiah's.

Again, a man whose words are to be rested upon, must be *a courageous man*. Hezekiah had this qualification. He had waited upon God in prayer, and knew that God would deliver him, so he had bidden farewell to fear; he was calm, and therefore bold. When he spoke to the captains of the soldiers, there was no trepidation in his voice or in his manner. He spoke like one who was—

> "Calm 'mid the bewildering cry,
> Confident of victory."

Courage in one man breeds courage in another, and one coward has the contagion of cowardice about him; many will turn tail when one runs. But, if a man stands like a rock, unmoved, he will soon have a body of others behind him who will have borrowed courage from his example. Paul in the storm is an example of this. I suppose he was a little insignificant-looking Jew, yet when the sailors and the soldiers were alarmed at the tempest, he calmly and quietly told them not to be afraid, and they borrowed courage from his faith. He told them that no harm would come to them; that though the ship would be lost, their lives had been given to him in answer to his prayer; and since they had fasted long, he bade them eat, and they did eat. All his orders were carried out as fully as if he had been the centurion in command of the soldiers, or the captain in charge of the ship. Because he was bold he made them brave; he commanded them, because he could command himself. Oh, my brothers and sisters, may you have the courage of your convictions! May you be brave enough to do right, and to speak right, and to stand up for the gospel, whoever rails at it! If you do, you have only to bide your time; and you will be master over meaner men who cannot be trusted. He that will but "hold the fort" when others are giving up their castles, shall by-and-by, God helping him, behold a race of valiant men, who, like himself, shall believe in their Master's coming, and will not quit the field until he appears. God grant to many here to be bold in the way of holiness, in their own circle, in their own families! They may be assured that there will be found some who will rest upon their words, because they see their courage.

Further, a man who is to have his words much rested in, must also be *a hearty man;* indeed, he must be an enthusiast. Of such a spirit was Hezekiah, for we read in the last verse of the previous chapter, "And in every work that he began in the service of the house of God, and in the law, and in the commandments, to seek his God, he did it with all his heart." This is the kind of man whom people will follow. Let them but see that the whole of the man leads them, and not only a bit of him, and they will quickly learn to rely on his word. Put all your heart into what you do, or else put none of it in. There are some people who seem as if they have no heart, or at least their heart is only a kind of valve for the expulsion of blood, and not over vigorous in that direction, I fear. Any other kind of heart you cannot discover. Nobody will follow mere head. There must be heart displayed by the man who would have a hearty following. If you want to lead others aright, lead them by showing that you yourself love the way. Be intense; be emphatic; throw your whole being into it. Be hearty when you are working, when you are praying, when you are singing. In all that you do for God and for your fellow-Christians, let your heart be manifest; and then it is highly probable that it may happen to you, as it did to Hezekiah, that many will rest upon your words.

In the case of such a man, God will add his sanction by granting success: he will be *a prosperous man.* I did not finish the last verse of the previous chapter just now. It reads: "He did it with all his heart, *and prospered.*" He prospered because he did everything with all his heart. God set his seal to that which he did so heartily. A man may be devout and holy, and yet not be outwardly prospered. Such a man may do useful work for the Lord; but the man whom God chooses for a leader, he will also qualify and bless. He will put his mark upon him; and when people see that a man is enabled by God to go from strength to strength, that his enterprises do not end in disaster, but that by the grace of God he leads his followers on from victory to victory, they are sure to rest themselves upon his word.

Let me add, that he who would help others must be *a man who has respect for God's Word*. We may safely rest ourselves upon a man's words when, like Hezekiah, his words are full of God, and when, evidently, he has nothing to say but what God has first said to him. Such a man becomes the medium by which God speaks to your soul. "With him is an arm of flesh; but with us is the Lord our God to help us, and to fight our battles." Even had this been spoken by another, it was a divine truth, and any man might have rested upon it. If any of us must needs be very original, if we must think out our own theology, and go on speculating from day to day, our people will be very foolish if they ever rest themselves upon our fickle, vapid words. But if the minister of Christ is as God's mouth, if he be dependent upon the Spirit of God for teaching; then God will speak through him, and the people will hear. If his one aim be, not to be original, but to repeat God's thoughts as far as he knows them, and to speak the truth revealed as far as he can get a grip of it, such a man will often come to know that the people are resting themselves upon his words; for his words will be not so much his, but God's words through him. May our prayer then be—

"Lord, speak to me, that I may speak
In living echoes of thy tone;
As thou hast sought, so let me seek
Thy erring children, lost and lone."

Here a word of caution is necessary. Since men are permitted to say words upon which other people rest, let us be careful how we speak. There may be some here, who have attained, by years of holy living and deep experience, to a position of great influence—one of you in a Bible-class, another in a village station, several of you, perhaps, in your pulpits. Brothers and sisters, what a very responsible position we occupy when young people and others are resting upon our words! I will not say whether they are altogether right or wrong in doing so; but I know that this is their habit; therefore, what manner of people ought we to be, how choicely we should use language, how determined we ought to be to let all our teachings be Scriptural, and not to mingle the precious with the vile; remembering the promise, "If thou take forth the precious from the vile, thou shalt be as my mouth"! Do not let us even sportively say what may injure others. I have known children take in earnest what others have said in jest. It were often better that some things were not said even in sport; for such flippant utterances have either misled the children, or they have injured the influence of those who have uttered them when they have spoken another time. Since it so happens that many of those around us are of feeble mind, and need a strong mind to guide them, let those who lead be doubly careful of their conversation and conduct. Since those who know their own weakness lean perhaps too much upon their teachers, let their teachers cry to God that they may be helped to teach nothing but what is right. May you and I never lead another even one inch astray! May none of us ever be in communion with that which is not true! May we stand right out from all connection with that which we feel to be contrary to the mind of God! Let us try to live in such a way that, if another were to take us for an example, he might copy us through and through and do himself no harm. I set before you a very high standard, and one which no man will reach except under divine instruction; but since the necessary teaching is freely given to all who seek it, I would urge you to be quick scholars in the school of grace. I fear very few of us have ever reached this excellent standard, but that is no reason why we should not study our lesson with redoubled energy. Remember that Hezekiah must speak aright when the people of Jerusalem rest themselves upon his words. O Hezekiah, be not silent when thou oughtest to speak; speak not when thou oughtest to be silent; and never speak except when the Lord shall open thy lips, that thy mouth may show forth his praise! Since thou hast this responsibility that the people rest upon thy words, be sure to give them words solid enough, and reliable enough to rest upon. As thou hast "wrought that which was good and right and truth before the Lord", speak also true and right and good words to the people: and then it shall be well both with them and with thee.

II. In the second place, let us turn the other way, and look at THE KIND OF PEOPLE WHO REST ON SUCH A MAN'S WORDS. I am not going to praise all these people, nor am I going to blame them. I wish to use discrimination, and judge each case upon its merits. Sometimes it is the best possible thing for a man to rest himself on the words of another; but often such a course is a very foolish one.

Children do so with their parents, and if they have gracious and godly parents, they do well to rest themselves on their father's or on their mother's word. When I was a boy, I never doubted what my father believed. And when I was under the influence of my grandfather, who taught me the Word of God, I was such a little simpleton, that I never set up my judgment against his. I find that very small boys are not now so foolish; I wish they were wise enough to be as foolish as I was! When I grew up, I never suspected a doctrine because my father believed it. No, my leaning went the other way; and if my godly father found peace and comfort in a word, I thought that what was good for him was good for his son. I was foolish enough to lean on the words of my elders in this way, and somehow, though others often think that such a course is folly, I am glad that it was so. I thank God, too, that my sons were as foolish as their father; and that what their father believed had an attraction for them. I hope that they judged for themselves, as I also tried to do, when I came to riper years; but, at the first, it was the words of my parents that led me to Christ. What I knew of the elements of the gospel I received largely, without a question, from them, and I do not think it was an ill bequest. Now, dear parents, mind that your children are able to believe in you. I like children to have fathers and mothers whom they can trust. A young friend has written me a letter, asking me to preach a sermon on, "Fathers, provoke not your children to anger." Well, will you kindly consider that I have preached it? I fear I could not make a long sermon of it; but it is very necessary to tell some of you parents that I suspect you are not quite so considerate as you ought to be. I do not know the man for whom the word is intended, but I wish that he would take the sermon as if I had preached it to him. Now, fathers and mothers, your children do rest themselves upon your words, if you are fathers and mothers worth having. Be careful, then, of what you say. I like that boy who said, " I know that it is true, for mother said it. Whatever mother says is true, and it is true if it is not true, if mother said it." It is a blessed thing when boys and girls can feel such confidence in their parents that they are sure that their word is beyond all question. It is so much easier for them to have faith in God in the days to come, if first they have been able to have faith in their father and mother. Faith of any kind is so tender a plant, that it should be carefully nourished wherever it is found; and as children often, and rightly too, rest themselves upon the words of their parents, it behoves the parents to give them words whereon they may rest safely.

Illiterate people, who cannot read, belong to another class, who must needs rest themselves upon the words of others. They are but grown-up children, if they are persons of no education, though I am glad to think the number of those who cannot even read their Bible for themselves is constantly decreasing. Still, there are many persons who are so taken up with daily toil that they have no opportunity of searching for themselves. Although God has given many of them gracious judgments, so that they seem to know truth from error by a kind of inward instinct, yet, for the most part, much of the teaching that they receive must come to them as the utterance of some man in whose life they believe, and whom they believe to be under a divine influence which makes him speak continually with an endeavour for their good. Whether this is right or not, it is so; and every man who is placed in a position where many such hang upon his words, must therefore learn to speak only as God speaks by him, lest he himself should sin, and lest the hundreds who accept what he says as being true, should also be led astray.

This is also the case with regard to *unconverted persons who have no spiritual discernment,* and who can have none, in their first hearing of the gospel. Very largely, men believe in Christ not only through the Scriptures, but through the testimony of those who already know the Lord. This was implied by our Saviour's words, in that wondrous intercession with his Father. Christ said concerning his disciples, " Neither pray I for these alone; but for them also which shall believe on me through their word." It is part of the economy of grace that the testimony of the saints shall be used of the Spirit to lead people to Christ. We bear witness to forgiveness which we have received; we bear witness to a change of heart which we have experienced; we bear witness to the condescending gentleness of Christ in welcoming the unworthy; we bear witness to the power of prayer; and like the men of Sychar, the people who hear us, first believe our word, and that leads them to Christ. After they have met with him, they may say, with much truth, " Now we believe, not because of thy saying: for we have heard him ourselves, and know that this is indeed the Christ, the Saviour of the world." Still, it will always be true that, at the beginning, it was because of our saying that they believed. It is a large part of our ministry to bear witness to the truth recorded in the

Book of God; and oftentimes the witness himself is believed, and then what he says is believed because of the faith the hearer has in him. Although some are unworthy of such credence, yet so it does happen. Christian men, you are the Bibles of the people. They do not read the Book, but they read you; and, if they see Christ in you truly represented, they will, perchance, come to a knowledge of him. But, if you caricature him, dreadful evil will come of it. I beseech you, be very careful. If the preacher, when he is addressing a mass of people who never read the Word of God, contorts and distorts the truth, what wonder is it if the people miss the salvation of Christ altogether, seeing that they rest upon his word? If he only gives half of the truth, or only one side of it; if he paints one doctrine out of proportion to another; if he misses the love and tenderness of Christ; and even if he omits the justice and stern truthfulness of God, he may so misrepresent God and Christ, and so misinterpret the whole system of grace to the people, that when they rest upon his words they will be resting on a broken reed, and fall to their eternal destruction.

Persons who naturally run in a groove form another class who rest upon the words of men. There are some people of considerable capacity who, nevertheless, partly from a want of elasticity of mind, and partly from excess of common-sense, are very apt to keep to beaten tracks. They are not altogether to be censured, for some of them are the salt of the earth; but they are a trifle monotonous in their method of life. Still, with some this is very natural. They are like tramcars that only get off the line by accident. Well, I think that, if I were a tramcar, I should like to run on the trams after I got used to it. If they lead in the right direction, we might do much worse than travel by tram. There are, however, a number of people who always will live like that. Having attended at such a place of worship, and having been brought up in the midst of a certain set of godly people, they scarcely deviate one jot from the teaching that they have received. Almost by a necessity of their nature they rest on what they hear.

There is one class more I should like to mention, not because I am fond of them, but for the opposite reason; I mean *those who profess always to do their own thinking*, who will not have any creed, and who say that they will not follow anybody. If you will trace them home, they are, in nine cases out of ten, the veriest slaves that ever lived. They are the bond-servants of some heretic or other, who has put it into their heads that, in following him, they become free men. Why, there are thousands of people that laugh at us for believing in the old doctrine of the fall of men, who, nevertheless, rest themselves implicitly upon the words of some infidel philosopher, or else they follow some favourite heretic in broadcloth upon whom they rest their confidence through thick and thin. They speak much of their deep thought, but they never think; they make up for want of brains by talking the jargon supposed to be spoken by highly intellectual people, though, in most cases, it requires a very vivid imagination to make the supposition. These, who thus take for granted the heterodox words of their favourite leaders, though they do not acknowledge them, incur great guilt, and their leaders are doing grievous mischief in uttering the words upon which their followers stay themselves.

Before I leave this point, I would urge you earnestly to be careful both as to the man you hear, and the words of his on which you rest. I beseech any of you who are attendants here, who are resting yourselves upon my words, to cease that habit. If I tell you anything that is not consistent with God's Word, away with my word, and away with me, too. If you hear from me anything which Christ would not have taught, I shall grieve to the last degree if you believe it. But if you fling it away, and ascribe it to the infirmity and fallibility of the preacher, it will be all the better for you. Or if there are some of you here who are resting yourselves upon any other man's words, I exhort you to know thoroughly the man and his communications, and do not, even when you know him, take his words without an appeal " to the law and to the testimony: if they speak not according to this word, it is because there is no light in them." Bring all men's words to the test of God's words. " Beloved, believe not every spirit; but try the spirits, whether they are of God." Blindly follow no man. "But though we, or an angel from heaven, preach any other gospel unto you than that which we have preached unto you" from this blessed Book, "let him be accursed." When a man has a message from God, listen to him earnestly, with an open mind ready to be taught; but never think of making him the master of your spirit. " The people rested themselves upon the words of Hezekiah the king;" and they did well in doing so; for he was a man worthy of their trust. But had he been another kind of a king, or a man of a different character and temperament, they might have ruined themselves by relying upon the words which he spoke to them. Again, therefore, I utter the caution, be careful both as to the man you hear, and the words of his on which you rest.

III. And now I close with my third head, by asking you to consider THE KIND OF WORDS THAT YOU MAY REST ON. We come to speak now, not of the kind of men who speak restful words, nor of the kind of men who find rest in such words when they are spoken; but of the kind of words in which you and I may rest.

You may safely rest on *words which urge you to faith in God.* Are you exhorted to-night to lay your burden of sin down at Jesus' feet? Obey such a word as that without questioning. You may well rest on words which bid you to believe in Christ, and you may, without fear, believe in him who has all grace and wisdom and power to save and to bless you. Through the hearing of such words, may you soon be able to say—

> " I rest my soul on Jesus,
>   This weary soul of mine;
> His right hand me embraces,
>   I on his breast recline.
> I love the name of Jesus,
>   Immanuel, Christ, the Lord;
> Like fragrance on the breezes,
>   His name abroad is poured."

Are you, who are believers, encouraged to roll your care on your great Father, according to that word, " Casting all your care upon him; for he careth for you"? You will do no wrong in obeying to the full every admonition to believe your God, and to believe his Christ. If our preaching tends to create faith, and foster it, it goes the right way; but, whatever clever things may be said, if the tendency is to undermine faith, and if the words you hear increase that tendency, they are mischievous, eternally mischievous, to the souls of men.

You may always rest, in the next place, on *words which are the words of God himself.* If God has said it, it is sure. If those men could rest themselves upon the words of Hezekiah the king, how is it that some of you, who are God's people, cannot rest yourselves upon the words of God our King? You believe his promises, you say, but still you are very restless. You have some of that terrible fever of unbelief on you. Beloved, try to practise the art of resting yourself upon the Word of God. God has promised me such and such a thing. I believe it, therefore I have got it. "No," you say, "the word is not fulfilled yet." Ah, but I have got it notwithstanding! If a friend gives me a cheque for five pounds, though I have never seen his money, I have the five pounds. I do not want to see his money, for I have his five-pound cheque in my pocket; I have his guarantee for the amount; and though I have not received the coin, I believe that I have the five pounds; and so I have. And if thou believest that thou hast the blessing for which thou hast asked, go thy way, and rejoice that thou hast it, for it is thine in the promise, and God's promise is as valuable as God's fulfilment. Rest yourselves, then, beloved, in the words of God. Are you afraid of being too peaceful? Are you afraid of being too happy? Are you afraid of living too blessed a life? Are any of you afraid of having too much of heaven here below? Well, do not give way to such idle fears. The more thou canst rest, the more will God be pleased with thee. "Comfort ye, comfort ye, my people:" saith your God; "speak ye comfortably to Jerusalem;" and if he bids us comfort you, you may be sure that he wants you to be comforted. Be comforted, therefore. Rest yourselves in his word. I have had to praise with 'bated breath those who rested on Hezekiah's words; I have thrown in little bits of necessary caution and interjections of doubt; but, if you desire to rest on God's Word, I need not caution you against trusting the Lord too much. Though you believe God up to the hilt, though you believe God desperately, though you believe God to the utmost, though you believe him infinitely, he will never fail you. Your confidence in him can never exceed that which he deserves. He will warrant it all. "Whosoever believeth on him shall not be ashamed;" and again it is written, "Ye shall not be ashamed nor confounded world without end." You can never be wrong in resting upon the words of God himself. Even in your greatest weakness you may look to him, and say—

> "I am trusting thee for power,
> Thine can never fail,
> Words which thou thyself shalt give me
> Must prevail."

You may always believe, also, in *words which are sealed by the Lord Jesus.* If the mark of his blood is upon any word, thou needest never doubt it. If he has died, how canst thou perish? If he has bidden thee come, how can he cast thee out? If thou dost rest upon his finished work, how canst thou be condemned? Believe, I pray thee, and rest thee on the blood-besprinkled words of this wondrous Book.

> "The clouds may go and come,
> And storms may sweep the sky;
> The blood sealed friendship changes not,
> Thy cross is ever nigh.

> "I change; he changes not,
> The Christ can never die;
> His word, not mine, the resting-place,
> His truth, not mine, the tie."

Believe also, most firmly, and rest yourself most fully on *words which have been blessed to other men.* If others have been saved by a word, that word will suit thee. If God's promise proved true to my father, it will be true to me. There is no private interpretation of God's "great and precious promises." They are not hedged about with a ring-fence. They are as much mine as they were Abraham's or Jacob's— as much mine as they were Peter's or Paul's; and I will have them, too, by faith, and have what those promises include. Beloved, rest yourselves upon the words of God, upon which others have rested, and you shall find them to be as true in your experience as in the experience of those who have gone before.

Last of all, you may surely rest upon *words which breathe a sense of rest into the soul.* I love all the words of God; but there are some that have an aroma of rest around them. Were you ever in such trouble that, when you read the chapter beginning with those sweet words, "Let not your heart be troubled: ye believe in God, believe also in me," you read it in vain? I think I never did. With the tears in my heart as well as in my eyes, I have read that blessed verse, again and again, and I have been comforted. That eighth chapter of the Epistle to the Romans is a wonderful light when you are in the dark; when I read those glorious doctrines, I find golden stepping-stones through the Slough of Despond. And, as for the Psalms, why the man who wrote most of them seemed to be "not one, but all mankind's epitome." He has lived out all our lives, yours, and mine, and millions besides; his psalms breathe peace around us; and, as we accept the truths they reveal, we are enabled to rest upon them.

To all of us the time will come when we shall want rest. Dear young people, however long you may live, unless the Lord descend from heaven in glory, the time will come when you will die. You will want a pillow then; and, oh, may it be said of all of us then, "The people rested themselves upon the words of Jesus"! These promises are the best pillows for dying heads. There is one that will suit you now, and suit you then. "He hath said, I will never leave thee, nor forsake thee." Go, brother, anywhere on earth, and even up to heaven with that in thy hand: "I will never leave thee, nor forsake thee." Or will this other word suit you better, "My grace is sufficient for thee: for my strength is made perfect in weakness"? But I need not go on giving these words to you; you know them well. If you are not familiar with them, I should advise you to get a little book called *Clarke's Precious Promises*, where you will find them all arranged. General Gordon, who was killed at Kharteum, used to carry a copy in his pocket wherever he went, and he and many others have found it to be a great help to them. Get hold of the promises of God, and when you feel downcast, when the wind is in the east, when the liver does not work, or when you have a real heart-ache, when the dear child is dead, when the beloved wife is sick, or when there is trouble in the house from any cause, then get you the words of the Lord; and may it always be said of you: "The people rested themselves on the words of King Jesus, the King of kings, and Lord of lords"!

Oh, that the Holy Spirit might lead some poor soul to rest on these precious words of God even now for the first time; and unto the Lord shall be praise for ever and ever! Amen.

PORTION OF SCRIPTURE READ BEFORE SERMON—2 Chron. xxxii.

HYMNS FROM "OUR OWN HYMN BOOK"—23 (Vers. II.), 759, 614.

"THE SWORD AND THE TROWEL."

Established and for 27 years Edited by C. H. SPURGEON.

TABLE OF CONTENTS FOR APRIL, 1892—SECOND MEMORIAL NUMBER.

Frontispiece—Last Portrait of Mr. Spurgeon.
Mr. Spurgeon's Last Drives at Menton. By J. W. Harrald. (Illustrated).
"Under the Rod." By Pastor James A. Spurgeon.
"Certainly I will be with Thee." By E. B. Bayly.
The Book Fund. By Mrs. Spurgeon.
Dr. Pierson on Prayer Promises.
Exemption from Trial a Probable Loss.
Travelling in Morocco. By T. Gillard Churcher, M.B., M.R.C.S.
"The Son of His Love." (Poetry.) By Thomas Spurgeon.
The First Lord's-day. (Poetry.) By E. A. Tydeman.
Iron Shoes for Rough Roads.
The Orphanage and the Electric Railway.
What is "Heresy Hunting"?
Mr. Spurgeon's Bedroom at Menton.
The "Armour-bearer's" Memorial Jottings. By J. W. Harrald.
The Funeral *Cortège* at Menton Railway-station.
Fac-simile of page in Mr. Spurgeon's R. T. S. Pocket-book.
The Olive-casket under the Palm-branches at the Tabernacle.
The Tabernacle Church's "In Memoriam" Resolution.
The Funeral *Cortège* entering Norwood Cemetery.
Pastor A. G. Brown delivering his Address at the Grave.
Mrs. Spurgeon's Letter to the Students of the Pastors' College.
"Son Tom's" Loving Tribute to his Dear Father's Memory.
The First Student's "Wreath." By T. W. Medhurst. (With portrait.)
Notices of Books.
Notes. (Portrait and Sketch of Mr. Spurgeon's "Armour-bearer." C. H. Spurgeon Memorial Fund. Mr. Spurgeon's Photographs. Sunday-school Missionary Society. Tabernacle Annual Church Meeting. College. Evangelists. Orphanage. Colportage, &c.)
Contributions for Pastors' College, Pastors' College Missionary Association. Stockwell Orphanage, Colportage Association, Society of Evangelists, and "For the General Work of the Lord as most Required."

Price 3d. Post free, 4 stamps.

PASSMORE AND ALABASTER, 4, PATERNOSTER BUILDINGS, LONDON; and all Booksellers.

Metropolitan Tabernacle Pulpit.

OUR COMPASSIONATE HIGH PRIEST.

A Sermon

INTENDED FOR READING ON LORD'S-DAY, APRIL 10TH, 1892,

DELIVERED BY

C. H. SPURGEON,

AT THE METROPOLITAN TABERNACLE, NEWINGTON,

On *Thursday Evening, April 3rd,* 1890.

"Who can have compassion on the ignorant, and on them that are out of the way; for that he himself also is compassed with infirmity."—Hebrews v. 2.

THE high priest looked Godward, and therefore he had need to be holy; for he had to deal with things pertaining to God. But at the same time he looked manward; it was for men that he was ordained, that, through him, they might deal with God; and therefore he had need to be tender. It was necessary that he should be one who could have sympathy with men; else, even if he could succeed Godward, he would fail to be a link between God and man, from want of tenderness and sympathy with those whom he sought to bring nigh to Jehovah.

Hence, the high priest was taken from among men that he might be their fellow, and have a fellow-feeling with them. No angel entered into the holy place; no angel wore the white garments; no angel put on the ephod and the breastplate with the precious stones. It was a man ordained of God, who for his brothers pleaded in the presence of the Shekinah. Many of us, I trust, have a desire within our hearts to come to God; but we need a high priest, in order that we may draw nigh, one who shall be a man as well as God. We may reflect with joy upon the Godhead of our great High Priest. Inasmuch as it is his right, he counts it not robbery to be equal with God; but he communes with the Father as one that was by him, as one brought up with him, who was daily his delight, rejoicing always before him. But we ought also to be very grateful that we can come into touch with our High Priest on his human side, and rejoice that he is truly man. For thus saith the Lord, "I have laid help upon One that is mighty : I have exalted One chosen out of the people;" he is anointed, it is true, with the oil of gladness above his fellows, but still he and they are one, "for which cause he is not ashamed to call them brethren."

Those who came to the high priest of old, were not often of the

No. 2,251.

rough sort. Those who wished to have fellowship with God through the high priest in the tabernacle or the temple, were generally the timid ones of the people. Remember how she who came when Eli was high priest was "a woman of a sorrowful spirit"; and the high priests had to deal with many such. The sons and daughters of affliction were those who mostly sought the divine oracle, and desired to have communion with God; hence the high priest needed not only to be a man, but a man of tender and gentle spirit. It was necessary that he should be one with whom those with broken hearts, and those who were groaning under a sense of sin, would like to speak. They would dread an austere man, and would, probably, in many cases, have kept away from him altogether. Now, the mercy for us is, that our great High Priest is willing to receive the sinful and the suffering, the tried and the tempted; he delights in those that are as bruised reeds and smoking flax; for thus he is able to display his sacred qualifications. He "can have compassion." It is his nature to sympathize with the aching heart; but he cannot be compassionate to those who have no suffering, and no need. The heart of compassion seeks misery, looks for sorrow, and is drawn towards despondency; for there it can exercise its gracious mission to the full.

Often, when we are trying to do good to others, we get more good ourselves. When I was here one day this week, seeing friends who came to join the church, there came among the rest a very diffident, tender-hearted woman, who said many sweet things to me about her Lord, though she did not think that they were any good, I know. She was afraid that I should not have patience with her and her poor talk; but she said one thing which I specially remember: "I have to-day put four things together, from which I have derived a great deal of comfort," she told me. "And what are they, my sister?" I asked. "Well," she said, "they are those four classes—'the unthankful and the evil, the ignorant and those that are out of the way.' Jesus 'is kind unto the unthankful and to the evil', and he 'can have compassion on the ignorant, and on them that are out of the way,' and I think that I can get in through those four descriptions. Though I am a great sinner, I believe that he will be kind to me, and have compassion upon me." I stored that up; for I thought that one of these days I might want it myself; I tell it to you, for if you do not want it now, you may need it one of these days; you may yet have to think that you have been unthankful and evil, ignorant and out of the way, and it will give you comfort to remember that our Lord Jesus is kind to the unthankful and to the evil, and that he "can have compassion on the ignorant, and on them that are out of the way."

On this latter subject, I would speak at this time, wishing to comfort some who are of a sorrowful spirit, and others who may yet have need of such consolation as this topic gives.

Notice in our text, first, *the sort of sinners with whom our High Priest is concerned*, namely, "the ignorant and them that are out of the way"; secondly, *the sort of High Priest with whom sinners have to deal*— One "who can have compassion on the ignorant, and on them that are out of the way"; and, thirdly, *the sort of infirmities in men that may be sanctified to great uses*. "For that he himself also is compassed with infirmity," is said of an earthly high priest; this it was that made him fit to be a high priest; and there are certain infirmities that we might almost glory in, for they enable us to be like priests unto God, and make us helpful to his sorrowing and suffering children.

I. First, then, let us carefully observe THE SORT OF SINNERS FOR WHOM OUR HIGH PRIEST IS CONCERNED. While it is true that he is willing to receive all sorts of sinners, there are many who never come to him, nor submit to his authority. With those who proudly and rashly stand before God on their own merit, he has nothing to do; but with others of a different character he is greatly concerned.

The people who claim Christ's aid are generally *those who have a very low opinion of themselves.* Out of all the tribes of Israel, those that came to the high priest, to ask him to present their sacrifice to God for them, and to speak a word from God to them, were God-fearing people. No doubt hypocrites, occasionally, did come, and some of a proud spirit who trusted in their own offerings; but I should think that, all the year round, the high priest saw some of the humblest and best people in all Israel. Men and women, in sore trouble, would come to him; and these chastened spirits would be choice spirits. Men and women who were conscious of sin, and longing for pardon, would come to the high priest; men and women who had not sinned after the similitude of a public transgression, who nevertheless felt evil darkening their conscience within, would draw near to him; men and women who had lost the light of God's countenance, and who came longing to have it back again, because they could not live without it, would approach the courts of God's house. All these would be welcome visitors at the high priest's door, and would receive his sympathy and compassion. Such are the people whom Christ our great High Priest now delights to bless. The proud and self-satisfied cannot know his love; but the poor and distressed may ever find in him comfort and joy, because of his nature, and by means of his intercession.

As with the high priest of Israel in the olden time, amongst those who come to our High Priest, are *many whose fear and distress arise from ignorance.* Oh, dear friends, if all the ignorant were to come, we should all come; for we are all ignorant; but there are some who fancy it is otherwise with them. They imagine they know all things, and, professing themselves to be wise, they become fools. These know not their need of the great High Priest. Their folly is proved by their light esteem of him. But among those who come to our great High Priest in heaven, there are none but those who are ignorant.

In the first place, there is a *universal ignorance.* Notwithstanding all that great men may say about what they evolve from their own consciousness, I think that the only thing that a man can evolve from his own consciousness is folly and sin; for there is nothing else there. If he goes on evolving, he will evolve greater folly and greater sin, that is all. But when the Lord deals with men, he makes them feel that they know very little. What do we know of sin? The larger proportion of our sins are probably unknown to us. We do them, and scarcely observe that we have committed them. And who knows the evil that lies in any one sin? Who is he that can weigh his iniquities in scales, or his errors in balances? Upon that one dread subject of sin, we are all like babes; we have not begun to learn more than the alphabet of that awful knowledge. Sinful we are, but it is a part of the effect of sin that we do not know the extent of our sinfulness, and we should not know it at all, if it were not for the teachings of the Holy Spirit.

Again, what do we know of ourselves? Does any man truly know himself? "The proper study of mankind is man," says Pope. I am not sure of that; but I am certain that the proper study of mankind is Christ; for in him we not only can learn about man, but much more besides. But how little we know of ourselves, of our natural weakness, of our evil tendencies, of our proneness in this direction, or in that! "Who can understand his errors? Cleanse thou me from secret faults."

What do we know of God the unsearchable? Is not he past finding out? Who can sufficiently tell of his nature, or of his wondrous attributes? Who can speak adequately of his greatness, or of his glory? Who can number up his years, or declare the whole of his lovingkindness? "O the depth of the riches both of the wisdom and knowledge of God! How unsearchable are his judgments, and his ways past finding out!" On this great subject, as well as on the other topics I have mentioned, there is a universal ignorance. As compared with the light of God, we are in the dim twilight. He that seeth best only seeth men as trees walking.

But, in addition to the ignorance that is universal, there is also a *comparative ignorance* on the part of some; and because of this, the compassion of Christ flows forth to them. Those who are ignorant in this way, are the kind of sinners whom he has come to help as a High Priest. He puts them in a class by themselves.

There are, first, the recent converts—young people whose years are few, and who probably think that they know more than they do; but who, if they are wise, will recognize that, even by reason of the fewness of their years, their senses have not been fully exercised to discern between good and evil. You must not ask them questions about the deep things of God. They have to be satisfied with those blessed parts of Scripture where a lamb may wade; they must not meddle with those parts where leviathan has to swim. Many truths are either above them or below them, much experience is too deep for them. In the presence of many of God's ways, they are compelled to say, "Such knowledge is too wonderful for me; it is high, I cannot attain unto it." The Lord Jesus Christ can take little boys and girls to his bosom; and he does so, while they are as yet ignorant of many things. He loves them; he teaches them; he has compassion on them; and he says of them, "Suffer the little children to come unto me, and forbid them not: for of such is the kingdom of God." Christ receives them in spite of their lack of knowledge, and therefore we must treat such very tenderly. "Take heed that ye despise not one of these little ones;" for our great High Priest has compassion upon their ignorance, and he instructs them. "All thy children shall be taught of the Lord, and great shall be the peace of thy children," when they trust in him who sympathizes with them, and who cares for them.

Others there are who are ignorant because of their little opportunity of getting instruction. Are there not many who are so placed that they have little chance even of learning to read? We are thankful that there will be few left of that sort by-and-by. But there are others who, if they could read, have scarcely sufficient time allowed them to read their Bibles, and who, when they have read them, are very like the Ethiopian eunuch, in that they do not comprehend what they have read. If the question were addressed to them, "Understandest thou what thou readest?" they could truly say, "How can I, except some man should guide me?" There are many, all over our land, who are situated in places where they cannot often hear the gospel, and when they do hear it, it is so mixed up and confused, that it is small wonder they cannot make head or tail of it. Constantly do we meet with persons of that kind, whose ignorance is excusable; for they have had no teaching. They have not had opportunities of reading and searching, as most of us have had; upon these our great High Priest has compassion, and often with their slight knowledge they show more of the fruits of the Spirit than some of us produce even with our more abundant light.

Further than that, there are many that are of a very feeble mind. You can only with difficulty get a thought into their brain, and if you try to get in another idea on the top of it, the second one seems to knock the first one out. They never learn much, and they are so constructed that they never will. In our pilgrim band we have a number who are like Mr. Feeblemind; we may try all that we can with him, but we shall never make a hero of him. Others are like Mr. Ready-to-halt, with his crutches; he did dance once, you will remember, when Giant Despair's head was cut off; but still he had to go on his crutches even then, and he never gave them up till he crossed the river; then he left them to anybody that wanted such things, and, I fear me, there are many who want them to-day. We have those in our company who never will be able to give a systematic statement of the doctrines of grace, though they are full of grace. They could never explain how they were saved; but they *are* saved. I daresay the snail could never explain how he got into the ark, but he did get in; and these feeble ones are in Christ, though they cannot fully explain how they came to that blessed position. Some of these good people are not very apt to receive knowledge: they are not "learnable", if I may coin a word to express my meaning. We cannot make them learn. They are willing to be taught, they are teachable; but they are not "learnable." Ah, well, our blessed High Priest can have compassion on the ignorant, and the feeble-minded!

Beside the universal ignorance of which we have spoken, and this comparative ignorance, there is a *sinful ignorance*. We have some who are ignorant, and no excuse is to be made for them; their ignorance is to be condemned; and if these words reach any who are thus guilty, I would beseech them to pray God to pardon their guilt, and cease to sin in this way any longer. I mean those who are ignorant for want of attention. They are so full of business, and have such a great many other things to think of, that they do not value the means of grace. They say that they cannot attend, but we know that where there is a will there is a way. Perhaps they go once on a Sunday, and never more all the week. Now, if I had to eat one meal a week, and only one, I should want it to be a very good one; but I think that I should hardly be in a good condition for the next one the week following. It is a grand thing to get a little bit by the way, by coming on a Thursday night, or a morsel or two on a Monday, at the prayer-meeting. This stays the heart, and keeps the soul in good order.

Some will never be much above the ignorant, because they have not the ambition to learn. They do not set themselves to study the things of God. They do not sufficiently prize the revelation of God. I pray that they may be stirred up to do so. Though they have been guilty of neglectfulness and forgetfulness, they are not to be deprived of the sweetness of this text. Our Lord can have compassion on the ignorant, and on such as are out of the way. Here stands the great company to which his compassion goes out, and its name is written, " *The ignorant.*" I think that we had better all get into this class; indeed, I am sure that we had better join it, and thus obtain our Lord's compassion. I have seen, at a railway-station, gentlemen with first-class tickets walking up and down the platform unable to find a first-class carriage, and if the train was going on they have jumped in the third-class, so as to get to their journey's end. If there is any man here who does not think that he ought to be put down quite among the ignorant, jump in, brother, because you will get to your journey's end in this compartment, and there is no carriage, just now, for any wise person. There is nothing provided in the train that starts from this text, except that which is provided for the ignorant. The Lord help us personally to rejoice that he can have compassion on the ignorant!

Now comes another description of the sort of sinners for whom our High Priest is concerned. There are *many whose fears arise from being out of the way.* The Lord " can have compassion on the ignorant, and on them that are out of the way." I remember that, when I felt myself to be a very great sinner, and verily thought I was more of a sinner than anybody else, these words were very, very much blessed to me. I read them, " and on them that are out of the way "; and I knew that I was an out-of-the-way sinner. I was then, and I am afraid that I am now, somewhat like a lot out of the catalogue, an odd person who must go by himself. Very well; our High Priest can have compassion on those that are odd, on those that are out-of-the-way, on those who do not seem to be in the common run of people, and do not go with the multitude, but who must be dealt with individually, and by themselves. He can have compassion upon such.

But now let us look at the more exact meaning of the text.

To be out of the way is, in the case of all men, *their natural state.* " All we like sheep have gone astray; we have turned every one to his own way." That is where we are all by nature, and our own way is out of *the* way. Therefore, Christ can have compassion upon all of us who come to him; for he has learnt to deal with those who are out of the way, and such, literally, are we all.

In addition to that, men have gone out of the way by *their own personal folly.* We had enough original sin; but we have added to that another kind of originality in evil.

> "Like sheep we went astray,
> And broke the fold of God;
> Each wandering in a different way;
> But all the downward road."

But there are some who wander most foolishly. You wonder why they sin in the particular way that they do. There seems to be no reason for it, no motive for it, no special temptation in that direction, and yet they will do it. They wander out of the way by themselves. Have you done so, dear friend? The Lord can have compassion on those that are out of the way.

Some are out of the way because of *their seduction from the way by others*. False teachers have taught them, and they have taken up with the error brought before them by a stronger mind than their own. In some cases persons of evil life have had a fascination over them. It is wonderful how, in the cases of young men and young women, they frequently seem to be not themselves, but the evil embodiment of another. They are ruled and governed by the will of somebody else, and not by their own. Thus they are led out of the way. They are like sheep that "have been scattered in the cloudy and dark day." Ah, poor friend, it is ill that you should have been the victim of another's temptation! Do not blame your tempter; blame yourself; but, at the same time, remember that Christ has compassion upon those who have been led out of the way. As by the will of another you were beguiled from the true path, so by the love of Another shall you be won back again, even as it has been with many of us.

Many are out of the way because of *their backslidings after grace has come to them*. Our text comprehends backsliders who were once in the way. To such we may say, "Ye did run well, who did hinder you, that ye should not obey the truth?" Something has been an occasion of stumbling to such; and now, though sitting in the house of God, they know that they are not what they once were, nor what they ought now to be, nor what they must be, nor what I hope they will be, even before I shall finish my discourse. "Turn, O backsliding children, saith the Lord; for I am married unto you." Why will ye wander from the only source of good? "Take with you words, and turn to the Lord." "Come now, and let us reason together, saith the Lord: though your sins be as scarlet, they shall be as white as snow; though they be red like crimson, they shall be as wool." The Lord calls you in infinite tenderness; for he can have compassion upon backsliders, and stop them from becoming apostates, bringing them back unto himself, according to his divine purpose.

Others are out of the way because of *their consciousness of special sin*. Is there here anyone conscious of some great sin in years gone by? Is there a crimson spot upon your hand, which you have tried to wash out, but cannot; some act of your life which you would fain undo, and remove? There it is, still there, always there. Does it fret you by night, and weary you by day, to think of that gross iniquity of yours? Ah, it has put you out of the way! Perhaps you did not grasp all the consequences of what you were doing when you did it. Be comforted by this gracious text. Hear your High Priest pray, "Father, forgive them; for they know not what they do." He pleads your ignorance. You "did it ignorantly in unbelief"; and while this does not excuse you, it puts you in the list of those who are both ignorant and out of the way. Come to this compassionate High Priest, and trust your case in his dear hands; they were pierced because of your sin. Trust your iniquity with him; his heart was opened and set abroach because of your transgression. Come, trust in him. He died because of your sin. "He is able also to save them to the uttermost that come unto God by him, seeing he ever liveth to make intercession for them."

Thus I have, very feebly, set forth the sort of sinners for whom Christ is High Priest; those who are ignorant, and those who are out of the way. This message is for almost everybody here, except my friend over there, who knows everything, and never did anything wrong. He does not want any Christ, and I will not bother him with one. "They that are whole have no need of a physician, but they that are sick," saith the Lord Jesus; and he further adds this word, which shuts out you who never did any harm, "I came not to call the righteous, but sinners to repentance." To be so very learned and so very good in your own estimation is no recommendation to Christ, but the reverse. He comes to men who need compassion, and those he teaches to profit, and leads in the way everlasting.

II. Having seen the sort of sinners with whom our High Priest is concerned, let us, in the second place, look at THE SORT OF HIGH PRIEST WITH WHOM SINNERS HAVE TO DEAL.

Now, if I go back to the high priest under the law, the type would be a fine fatherly man, whose very face invited confidence. I should think that all the people were glad when the high priest was very tender and compassionate. Possibly they had occasionally a high priest who was very high and very mighty; one who was very glad when his day's service was over. If sinners wanted to see him, he was not visible; and when he did talk with them, he was not very gentle. Sometimes he may have said to them, "Now you are stupid, you talk nonsense;" and when any of them were very sad, he said, "You ought to know better than to indulge this foolish nervousness of yours." I think that they were not sorry when that high priest was taken from them. But the pattern high priest was a fatherly-looking man, with love in his eyes, a smile on his face, one who had often sorrowed himself, one to whom all the people could go naturally. There are such men still alive. They are like a harbour for ships. Sometimes it brings a very heavy burden upon them, but yet they are happy men to have such a burden to carry. I think that some of those high priests must have seen a great deal of sin, and a great deal of mercy and divine love. When the poor people went up to the temple, one would say, "I must go in and see the high priest. I have such a burden, and he will be able to help me." Another would say, "No, I shall not go in; I do not need now to take up his time myself. Did not you hear him speak? Why, what he said was just the very thing that I wanted. God gave him the very word that my distress required, and so I can go away in peace." But here and there one would say, "Ah! but I must tell him. It does me good to unburden my heart." Now that is the kind of high priest that we should all have wished for had we been living in those days; but our Lord Jesus is something incomparably better than that.

He is One who can bear with ignorance, forgetfulness, and provocation. How do I know it? Because he bore so wonderfully with the ignorance of people when he was here. It was with a very tender accent that he said to one of his disciples, "Have I been so long time with you, and yet hast thou not known me, Philip?" He had told them many, many times the same thing over again, and yet he was not above repeating it, he had such compassion on them. Sometimes he could not say what he would have liked to say, and yet he bore with the poor men who did not know the burden he had on his heart: he only said, "I have yet many things to say unto you, but ye cannot bear them now." And when, after he had taught them, they still forgot, he did not chide them. I never find that he turned one of them away because of their stupidity; he did not even cast off Thomas for his unbelief. He let them still linger about his person, despite their false notions and their forgetfulness. They must often have grieved him through their ignorance, and through getting out of the way, especially when they got into the way of each desiring to be the greatest. But notwithstanding all, our Lord was never like Moses. Of him it is written that the people of Israel "provoked his spirit, so that he spake unadvisedly with his lips"; but never an impatient word came from those lips into which grace was so abundantly poured. There was never such a meek, and gentle, and quiet spirit as our divine Lord and Master possessed. I need not dwell on that, for you all know what compassion he had upon the ignorant sons of men.

Again, *he is One who can feel for grief, because he has felt the same.* When I have explained compassion as implying meekness of disposition, I have not given you the full meaning of the expression. Not only has our Lord compassion on the ignorant by being gentle towards them, but he sympathizes with them by having a fellow-feeling with them. They got out of the way, and into the thorns; they wandered, and fell into a maze; they were lost on the dark mountains, but he was "a man of sorrows, and acquainted with grief." "In all their affliction he was afflicted." Because of that fellow-feeling he is always very tender and pitiful; and if he finds any of his children sorrowing, he has abundant compassion upon them.

Moreover, *he is One who lays himself out tenderly to help such as come to him.* He did so when he was here in body, and he is the same now; all his life was given in tenderness. You never find Christ throwing bread and meat to the hungry crowd as we throw bones to dogs. He made them sit down on the green grass, and then he blessed the food, and gave it to his disciples, and they distributed it in a quiet, orderly way. And the Lord Jesus Christ has a very loving way now of helping his people. So tenderly does he do it, that the doing of it is almost as great a wonder as the thing that is done. He abounds towards us in all wisdom and prudence, and we may each one say, "Thy gentleness hath made me great." Oh, he is a wonderful Saviour! There is none like him for sympathizing with us, and dealing tenderly with us.

Another thing I have to say of him that never can be said of anybody else, is, that *he is One who never repelled a single person.* Not even the most ignorant, the most out of the way, was ever turned back from him. It was always true : " This man receiveth sinners." And for ever this other word is settled in heaven, " Him that cometh to me I will in no wise cast out."

I have not time to go into this matter fully, but all who have read the life of Christ know what a gentle and tender High Priest he was towards men.

> " Now, though he reigns exalted high,
> His love is still as great.
> Well he remembers Calvary,
> Nor let his saints forget."

His heart is on earth, though he has ascended into the heavens. If anyone here groans after him to-night, he will hear that groan ; and if the wish does not come to a vocal sound at all, but if your heart only aches after him, he will feel that ache of your heart, and know what it means; and if you do not know how to pray, the very desire to pray he will interpret. He can have compassion on the ignorant. And if you do not know what you want, but only know that it is something that you must have or die, he will give it to you ; for he will interpret your wordless desires, and what you cannot read yourself, he will read for you. But, oh, you must have him ; you must have him ; you cannot get to God without him ! I pray that you may feel such confidence in his tenderness that you may come and take him as your own High Priest: if you do, he will be yours at the moment of acceptance. He will never refuse the seeker. He will not hide himself from his own flesh. He will never be distant and strange to any penitent sinner. If thou desirest him, it is because he desires thee ; and if thou hast a spark of wish for him, he has a furnace of desire for thee. Come, and welcome. He can have compassion on the ignorant, and on them that are out of the way. God bless these words! I pray that he may do so, to very many.

III. Now, I want to speak to those of you who are the people of God. I can imagine that some of you here are troubled, perhaps ill, and that you cannot get on as you would like in the world. You seem compassed with infirmities. I want to remind you that there may be a blessing even in your weakness; and that this may be the more clearly seen we will look, in the third place, at the SORT OF INFIRMITY WHICH MAY BE SANCTIFIED AND MADE USEFUL.

The high priest of old was compassed with infirmities, and this was part of his qualification. " Yes," says one, " but he was compassed with sinful infirmities ; but our Lord Jesus had no sin." That is quite true, but please remember that this does not make Christ less tender, but more so. Anything that is sinful hardens; and inasmuch as he was without sin, he was without the hardening influence that sin would bring to bear upon a man. He was all the more tender when compassed with infirmities, because sin was excluded from the list. We will not, then, reckon sin in any form as an infirmity likely to be turned to a great use, even though the grace of God abounds over the sin ; but, beloved friends, let me try and speak to some of you who wish to do good, and set forth some of the things which were sore to bear at the time, and yet have been rich in blessing since.

First think of *our struggles in finding mercy.* Years ago you had a hard time of it when you were seeking the Saviour. I had, and I have always been very glad of it ever since. It was a long while before I could perceive the eternal light, and cast myself on Christ. I thank God that it was so, because I have had to deal with hundreds—I might say, thousands—in a similar case; and if I had found Christ, as many dear friends do, very readily and very easily, I could not have guided them; but now I can sit down by the side of them, and say, "What! have you got into the dark? I have been in the dark, too. You are down in the low dungeon, are you? Well, I was in the lowest dungeon of all. I can show you the way to where the jug of water stands, and the bit of brown bread. I know the way, for I have been there." If you have not had a certain experience, you cannot so well help others who have; but if you were compassed with infirmity in your first coming to Christ, you may use that in helping others to come to him.

Again, *our grievous temptations* may be infirmities which shall be largely used in our service. "What a blessing it would be to live without temptations!" says one. I do not believe it would be a blessing at all. I think that, being without temptation is more of a temptation than having a temptation. There is no devil that is equal to no devil, for when there seems to be none, we get so very quiet and so very easy, and think that everything is going on well, when it is not. Be glad if you have been tempted. Remember that temptation is one of the best books in a minister's library. To be tried, to be afflicted, to be downcast, to be tested—all this helps you to deal with others. You cannot be unto others a helper unless you have been compassed with infirmities. Therefore accept the temptations which trouble you so much, as a part of your education to make you useful to others.

Our sickness may turn out to be in the same category. Of course we would like to be always well. I think that health is the greatest blessing that God ever sends us, except sickness, which is far better. I would give anything to be perfectly healthy; but if I had to go over my time again, I could not get on without those sick beds and those bitter pains, and those weary, sleepless nights. Oh, the blessedness that comes to us through smarting, if we are ministers and helpers of others, and teachers of the people! I do not say that too much of it is to be desired, but the Lord knows how much is too much, and he will never afflict us beyond that he will enable us to bear. But just a touch of sickness now and then may help you mightily. I have heard some brethren preach the gospel in a terribly heartless way. It has been the gospel, but it has been as hard as a Brazil nut; little children could never get at the kernel. These brethren had never had any trouble or affliction; and if you have never had any, you may try to be very tender, but it will be like an elephant picking up a pin; you may try to be patient and sympathetic, but you will not be able to manage it. Glory in your infirmities, then, and in your sicknesses, for they shall be made useful in you for the comfort of God's sick people.

Our trials, too, may thus be sanctified. He that has had no troubles, and no trials, what mistakes he makes! He is like the French lady in the time of famine, who said that she had no patience with the poor people starving because of the price of bread. You could always buy a penny bun for a penny, she said; and therefore she thought there need not be any poverty at all. She was one of the rich ones of the earth. I do not suppose that she had ever had a penny bun in her life, or a penny either. Ah, dear friends! you must, if you are ready to help others, be yourself compassed with infirmity.

Our depressions may also tend to our fruitfulness. A heart bowed down with despair is a dreadful thing. "A wounded spirit who can bear?" But if you have never had such an experience, my dear brother, you will not be worth a pin as a preacher. You cannot help others who are depressed unless you have been down in the depths yourself. You cannot lift others out of despondency and depression, unless you yourself have sometimes need to be lifted out of such experiences. You must be compassed with this infirmity, too, at times, in order to have compassion on those in a similar case.

Herein I think that every one of us should try to make use of all his weaknesses. *Our whole nature as feeble men* may be turned to the noblest use if it calls forth our compassion towards others. Thank God that you are not a man of iron. We had the Iron Duke once, who did famous things, but in a different fight from ours. An iron preacher would need to have iron hearers; and then, I am afraid, that there would come a crash before long. No, no; we must have our weakness and infirmity consecrated to God, and laid at his feet. Let us go, in all our weakness and infirmity, and try to help others who are as ignorant and as out of the way as we once were; and, God blessing us, when we are weak, we shall be strong. When we are less than nothing, the all-sufficiency of God will be all the more manifested. Here I must stop, for our time has gone. May the Lord bless the word, both to the sinner and to the saint, for his name's sake! Amen.

PORTIONS OF SCRIPTURE READ BEFORE SERMON—Hebrews iv. 15, 16; v.

HYMNS FROM "OUR OWN HYMN BOOK"—326, 367, 376.

Metropolitan Tabernacle Pulpit.

THE UNKNOWN GIVER AND THE MISUSED GIFTS.

A Sermon

Intended for Reading on Lord's-day, April 17th, 1892,

DELIVERED BY

C. H. SPURGEON,

AT THE METROPOLITAN TABERNACLE, NEWINGTON,

On Thursday Evening, September 25th, 1890.

"For she did not know that I gave her corn, and wine, and oil, and multiplied her silver and gold, which they prepared for Baal. Therefore will I return, and take away my corn in the time thereof, and my wine in the season thereof, and will recover my wool and my flax."—Hosea ii. 8, 9.

In reading any of the records concerning the people of Israel and the people of Judah, one stands amazed at two things, and scarcely knows which to wonder at most. The first thing which causes astonishment is the great sin of the people; and the next thing, which is even more marvellous, is the great patience of God. I scarcely know which of the two things causes me greater surprise, that men should be so guilty, or that God should be so gracious. On every page of Israel's history, the kindness and forbearance of Jehovah are manifested towards the people whom he had betrothed unto himself. Even in the midst of their backsliding and idolatry, he did not forget the covenant which he had made with their fathers. Yet, in spite of all this goodness, the people sinned times without number, and grieved his Spirit again and again; instead of being led to repentance, they sinned yet more and more. Their iniquity, and the forbearance of God, stand like the two mountain summits of the history of the chosen yet wayward people.

Let us just transfer these thoughts to ourselves, and see if we can, with any justice, cast a stone at the people who, in spite of such love, went so far astray. Alas, we are condemned by the comparison! We are in nothing better than they were. Our case is, perhaps, fuller of contradictions and inconsistencies, if that is possible. Is it not wonderful, first of all, that we should have been so guilty, that we should have persevered in sin so many years, that even after we have known God we should be so unfaithful to him, so unfaithful to our own convictions, and to our own conscience? Is not this awful fact amazing? But that God should love us still, that he should follow us with

No. 2,252.

warning and invitation, that his Holy Spirit should strive with us, and continue to strive until he wins the day, and that despite our shortcomings and our transgressions, he should have remained faithful to us, even to this very hour, is more amazing still. O my soul, sink low in deep humiliation because of thy sinfulness! But, rise higher and yet higher in adoration because of the unutterable love, the boundless mercy of God to thee in spite of thine iniquity. Beloved brethren, if it were possible for us only to know adequately these two things, man's sin and God's love, we should have learned more than the greatest scientists of this world ever knew, and we should have attained to more true wisdom than all earth's philosophers ever possessed. There be some that, in their search for knowledge, have almost seemed to walk the heavens in order to thread the stars, and to dive into the depths to arrange the rocks and all their ancient life; but there are two things that none of the wise amongst men have ever yet been able to compass—two things which unaided reason has ever failed to grasp, and ever will—sin and love; sin for its thunder, and love for its music: sin for its hell, and love for its heaven. But we, who have been taught by the grace of God, do know something of sin: may we know increasingly what an evil thing it is! I trust we also know something of divine love; may we be filled with it, even to overflowing!

But, coming now close to our text, I am going to make four observations upon it.

The first will be one that seems self-evident, yet is often forgotten, namely, that *God is the Giver of every good gift.* "I gave her corn, and wine, and oil." In the second place, I will dwell upon the sad fact that *many seem not to know this.* "She did not know that I gave her corn, and wine, and oil." My third observation will be, that *this ignorance leads to perversion of God's gifts*: the gifts of God were profaned by being "prepared for Baal." In the last place, the solemn truth will demand our attention, that *this ill use of God's gifts causes God to withdraw them.* "Therefore will I return, and take away my corn in the time thereof, and my wine in the season thereof, and will recover my wool and my flax." We lose what we are determined to put to improper uses. So, you see that my discourse promises to be a very practical one.

I. The first thought in the text which claims our attention will be, that GOD IS THE GIVER OF EVERY GOOD GIFT. "I gave her corn, and wine, and oil, and multiplied her silver and gold." Whether we know it or not, it is true that "every good gift and every perfect gift is from above, and cometh down from the Father of lights, with whom is no variableness, neither shadow of turning." Do not, then, exult over thy brother if thou art more richly endowed with God's gifts than he is: "For who maketh thee to differ from another? And what hast thou that thou didst not receive?" All things that we possess have been bestowed upon us; for it is as certain that we brought nothing into the world, as that we shall take nothing out of the world. We receive everything from the great Distributor, who openeth his hand, and satisfieth the desire of every living thing. Though used with reference to a higher gift than any of those mentioned in the text, the words of John the Baptist are true concerning all God's gifts, "a man can receive nothing, except it be given him from heaven."

But someone may say, "Corn and wine are here mentioned first of all; surely these are *the fruit of tillage.* Men sow, and reap. Men plant, and gather grapes. How, then, can these things be the gift of God?" Why, the moment we think seriously of this matter, we perceive that no husbandman can command a harvest! No vine-dresser can be sure of fruit, unless he that rules the heavens, and sendeth the dews, the rains, the snow, and the frosts, shall take care both of the budding vine and of the ripening clusters. All that springs from the earth comes by a miracle of God's benevolence. If God withheld his hand, you might plough your land, but you would wait in vain for the harvest; an unfruitful season would not return to you even so much as the seed which you had sown. When famines come upon the nations, because of blighted harvests, then men ought to understand that the corn, and the wine, and the oil are God's gifts; but, alas, many are very slow to learn even that elementary lesson!

Perhaps others say, "Our share of these things comes to us as *the earnings of labour.*" Of course, in some form or other that must be true. Ever since man fell, that word of God to Adam, "In the sweat of thy face shalt thou eat bread," has been the rule of life for his sons. If men do not till the soil, but dwell in cities, they must still work; but in less pleasant ways than the farmer knows. They may have to toil in murky workshops, where they would be glad to catch a breath of the fresh breezes that come over the fields. I know we get our bread by our work; but then, who finds us work? Who gives us strength to do it? Let God but withdraw from us his gracious power, and our hands would hang feebly at our side. You know how true this is. When you have been laid aside upon the bed of sickness, then have you understood that, unless God gave health, the breadwinner could not go forth to his service, and there would be nothing on the table for the wife and the children. It is God that gives us our bread, however hard we work in order to earn it. Still have we need to present the petition that our Lord taught his disciples, "Give us this day our daily bread."

Besides this, the text also mentions *the gain of commerce.* "I multiplied her silver and her gold." Here, also, God's hand is plainly seen. I admit, of course, that men gain their silver and their gold by trading; but will the ship come home again in safety unless God watches over it? Will the men that go into the bowels of the earth, to dig for minerals, come up alive unless still the providence of God preserves them? Is not the benediction of heaven needed in every enterprise to which men can put their hand? "Except the Lord build the house, they labour in vain that build it: except the Lord keep the city, the watchman waketh but in vain." The success of business is based upon a thousand conditions, and surrounded by many risks, as every merchant knows. How easily God can lay his finger upon any human scheme, and bring to nought all our plans! They used to call those who engaged in commerce "merchant venturers", and they were rightly named. There is many a "peradventure" about business-life in these days of cruel competition, even in our home-trade; and it is even more at a venture that a man goes to a far-off land for gain. God must give him success, if he is to get it. In our bills of lading we even now insert a clause, by which the shipowner disclaims responsibility in certain contingencies, amongst which is mentioned " the act of God " ; and when men despatch a vessel, they often pray, and they always ought to pray, " God speed the ship," for God-speed is needed if it is to reach its destination safely.

But some come by their corn, and their wine, and their silver, and their gold, by *the legacies of friends.* In such a case, you may easily trace the gifts to God. If your parents have left you sufficient for your maintenance, who gave you those parents? Who placed them in a position to be so generous to you? Who arranged the place and manner of your birth but the great Lord of providence? If you are living in specially favourable circumstances, and are able to obtain food, and the other necessaries of life, with a good share of its luxuries, which others can only gain by long labour, if at all, ascribe it, I beseech you, to the bountiful providence of the Most High. If you do not give all the glory to the Giver of these gifts, surely you are forgetting your God.

And yet, perhaps, another says, " I have not laboured with my hands, but I am a man of resources. What I possess is *the result of thought.* I have carefully elaborated an invention, and in a few months I have been able to get for myself what others cannot get with a whole life of toil. Surely I may trace my prosperity to my capacious mind." And if you do so, you will be very foolish, unless you also adore the God who gave you your mind. By whose power is it that you have had the wit to gain wealth so speedily? I beseech you be humble in the presence of God, or you may in a few days lose your reason, for it has often happened that men who have had more wit than others have been among the first to lose it. " Great wit to madness is allied." In many a case it has proved to be so. Remember Nebuchadnezzar, king of Babylon, builder of cities, inventor of great things, and yet "he did eat grass as oxen, and his body was wet with the dew of heaven, till his hairs were grown like eagles' feathers and his nails like birds' claws," because he was proud, and exalted himself against God, neither gave glory for his greatness to the Most High.

We therefore settle it in our hearts as true, once for all, that God is the Giver of the corn, and the wine, and the oil, and the silver, and the gold, and whatever temporal blessings we enjoy. If honestly gained, we trace them to his hand; and we would thank him now and always for every good gift that we have received from him.

I need not make a list of spiritual blessings, nor need I remind you that they all come from God. You know how dependent you are upon him for them. By nature you are dead. What spiritual life can you get for yourselves without God? Can the dead make themselves to live? When you have been made alive, you are pardoned; can you pardon yourselves? Whence can forgiveness come but from God? You have more than pardon if you are a child of God, you are possessed of righteousness; how shall you ever have it but as God arrays you in the righteousness of Christ? Joy and peace are our portion, but both come by believing; they are the gift of God.

Holiness, too, and everything else that prepares us for heaven, **and helps us to reach that blessed place, is the gift of God freely bestowed upon unworthy men.** We were unworthy when he began to bless us, and we are unworthy still; yet the hand that at first bestowed the gift upon us, continues to enrich us every day in all bountifulness. Shall we not praise him, lifting high our grateful song?

> "Come thou fount of every blessing,
> Tune my heart to sing thy grace,
> Streams of mercy, never ceasing,
> Call for songs of loudest praise."

We will not withhold our thanks for such abounding goodness.

> "Oh, to grace how great a debtor
> Daily I'm constrained to be!
> Let that grace, now, like a fetter,
> Bind my wandering heart to thee."

So much for the first point.

II. Now, secondly, and we come closer to our text, MANY SEEM NOT TO KNOW THIS. "She did not know that I gave her corn, and wine, and oil, and multiplied her silver and gold." She did not know, and in this lack of knowledge she stands not alone. There are great numbers in the world who do not know this elementary truth, that all good gifts, of any kind whatsoever, come from the hand of God. Why is this?

With some it arises from *natural ignorance*. Myriads of men know not God as yet; and they are to be pitied, if they have not even heard of him. I fear that in London there are many who have never received even the plainest instruction with regard to God and his Christ. It ought not to be so, seeing that so many in earlier years have passed through our Sunday-schools. But all Sunday-school teaching does not teach. There are many Sunday-schools into which a child may go and come out again, and know but little that will abide with him. It is a pity that this should be the case; but facts go to show that I state no more than the plain truth. There are many whom we may meet in the street who could give us no intelligent account of what they owe to God. They scarcely know who he is. They use his name as a part of their profanity, and that is all. Brethren, I charge you, by the living God, that as far as your ability goes, you do not suffer a single person in London to be ignorant of God, and what men owe to him. With all your might, instruct those with whom you come in contact concerning the great Creator, Preserver, and Judge of men, and show them how all our blessings are to be traced to his generous hand. Thus shall be laid a foundation whereon may rest a saving faith in our Lord Jesus Christ.

There are, however, many more who, from *thoughtless ignorance*, do not know that God gave them their providential mercies. Oh, what a thing it is that the bulk of the people by whom we are surrounded should have a thought for everybody but God! Some persons are strictly honest to their fellow-men, but they never think that they owe God anything. Everybody is treated fitly by them except their Creator. They will be ungrateful to nobody except their very best

Friend; and all for want of thought. Is it not ten thousand pities that so many miss heaven from heedlessness, and that so many go down to hell for want of thinking how they may escape from it? "The wicked shall be turned into hell," says the Psalmist, "and all the nations that forget God." What did these do who thus perish? Did they blaspheme? No; they only forgot God. Did they oppose his purposes? No, it is not said so; but they *forgot* God. That is all. He that forgets his king becomes a traitor. The soldier that forgets his captain becomes a deserter. The child that forgets his mother, becomes a prodigal. But the man that forgets his God is worst of all; his sheer thoughtlessness leads him to the abyss of woe.

Some lose sight of God because of their wrong thoughts. They look upon everything that happens as luck. "I was a lucky fellow," says one. "Wonderfully fortunate I have always been," says another; "I have always had good luck." So God is pushed from his throne, and men pay their tribute to an imaginary something, which is really nothing, but which they call "luck." If luck has actually done anything for you, then by all means worship luck, and pay homage to it; but it is not so. Luck, fortune, and chance are the devil's trinity. If things have gone well with you, it has been so because it has pleased the Most High to favour you. I pray that you may not be unmindful of the heavenly blessing, but thank your God, and bless his name.

"Well," says one, "I do not attribute my success to luck. I say I owe it to myself." So you turn from God, and worship yourself, do you? The Egyptians have been counted the most degraded of all the people of this world, in their worship. They worshipped onions, till Juvenal says, "O blessed people, who grow their gods in their own back gardens!" But I do not think they were quite so degraded as the man that worships himself. If I could bring my soul to worship an onion, I could never degrade myself low enough to worship myself. A man who makes himself his own god is mad. When you begin to adore yourself as a self-made man, you have surely come to the very abyss of absurdity and idolatry. "Know ye that the Lord he is God; it is he that hath made us, and not we ourselves. We are his people, and the sheep of his pasture." Let us not then be guilty of the folly of forgetting him to whom we owe our all. "O come, let us worship and bow down; let us kneel before the Lord our Maker." Still, alas, is it true that some, through their thoughtlessness or their corrupt thoughts about God, know not that he gave them their corn and wine and oil.

There are others who forget God from *assumed ignorance;* they know better, but they profess that they are too intelligent to believe in God. Do you not often hear the proud boastings of such men? Oh! it is folly of the most profound kind for any man to think he is too intelligent, or too clever, to believe in God, or to trace anything to him. "These things happen according to the laws of nature," they say. "The arrangements of nature are fixed and invariable." Thus "nature" becomes nothing more than a false god, which they worship. They have elevated a certain something which they call "nature" into the place of God, and they suppose that God is somehow tied by his own laws, and can never do any other than that which he has been accustomed to do; by such reasoning natural law is lifted up, and made higher than the omnipotent God himself. Go you that worship nature, and worship her if you will. I have not generally found much worship in it. I had a neighbour, who said to me, "I do not go and shut myself up in a stifling atmosphere on a Sunday; I stop at home, and worship the god of nature." I said to him, "He is made of wood, is he not?" "What do you mean?" he said in some surprise. "I think," I answered, "that I have heard you at worship, and you seem to me to adore your god by knocking him down." "Ah!" said he, "have you heard me playing skittles on a Sunday?" "Yes," I said; "you are a pretty fellow to tell me that you stop at home, and worship the god of nature. Your worship is all a lie." When you hear men talk about this god of nature, it often means that they only want an opportunity of having more drink, or of amusing themselves, or of otherwise wasting the hours of God's holy day. As for us, I trust that we shall not assume an ignorance which is not ours. We know that God gave us all we have, and unto him shall be the praise.

A great many have no real lack of knowledge at all, if you search their minds. Theirs is a *practical ignorance*. They know not that God gave them these things, in the sense that they do not confess that it is so. They never speak about him as the one who provideth for all their needs; they never praise him for his bounty. They may, perhaps, jerk out a "Thank God," just as a matter of common speech; but there is no thankfulness in their heart. Practically, they live from year to year as if there were no God, and spend their time and their substance as if they were under no obligation whatever to the great Lord of providence. Practically it may be said of them, "They know not that I gave them their corn and their wine and their oil."

A lower depth is reached by those who do not recognise God because of their *wilful ignorance*; who, because of their deeds of darkness, hate the light, and refuse to acknowledge the gifts of God. Our Father in heaven "maketh his sun to rise on the evil and on the good, and sendeth rain upon the just and the unjust." But the unjust do not receive the refreshing showers as from his hand, nor do those who are evil acknowledge that it is God's sun that shines upon their head. They hate God, and are wilfully ignorant, "having the understanding darkened, being alienated from the life of God through the ignorance that is in them, because of the blindness of their heart."

Now, it does seem to be a very grievous thing that men should be indebted to God for everything, and should never praise him; that they should every morning be awakened by the light that he gives, and every evening be helped to sleep by the shades of darkness with which he mercifully closes the day, and curtains the night; and yet that they should never adore his name. Am I not speaking to some here who, through a tolerably long life, have never thought of their God, or whose thoughts concerning him have been but fitful and feeble? I would like to hold you to your seat for a moment, my friend, while I ask you whether you do not feel ashamed that you have never considered the claims of the Most High, or have never thought that he could have any claims, but have supposed that you had just to live to think of yourself and your friends, and perhaps of your fellow-men, but never of your God? His goodness has been practically denied by you. You have lived as if there were no God, or as if he were too far off to operate upon your life. You live as if you had received nothing from his hands. What you have received ought to have secured for him your service. Yet what have you done? Does a man keep a cow without expecting its milk? Would he keep a horse without putting it to work? Would he own a dog if it did not fawn upon him, and come at his call? Yet God has kept you all these years, and has had nothing from you but sheer forgetfulness, or, possibly, something worse than that. What do you say to this? I press the matter upon you, and ask you carefully to review it before your own conscience, and before the Lord, to whom you must one day give account. Seeing that you have received so much from him, you should, at the very least, acknowledge that he is the Giver of all your good things. May God the Holy Spirit make you confess that you have not dealt well with your God, and strive with you until, by his almighty grace, you shall be constrained to change your evil course, and acknowledge the goodness and mercy you have received from him throughout your whole life!

III. In the third place, when men thus fail to recognize and acknowledge God's goodness, THIS IGNORANCE OFTEN LEADS TO THE PERVERSION OF GOD'S GIFTS. See how God puts it with reference to the people of Israel, "I multiplied her silver and gold, which they prepared for Baal." What a depth of infamy it would be to receive the bounty of one king, and to pay homage therewith before the throne of his rival! This was what Israel did, and alas! too many imitate them to-day. The people burned incense to the false god of the heathen on every hill. "She decked herself with her ear-rings and her jewels, and she went after her lovers, and forgat me, saith the Lord." This was a great iniquity. The very gold which God gave them they fashioned into ornaments for their idol, and poured out the wine that came as a gift from heaven, as an offering at Baal's shrine. There was a certain Indian potentate, who deposed his father from the throne, and then desired that father to send him his jewels, that he might wear them at his own coronation. These people desired God's gifts, in order that they might present them to Baal; and, alas! in this impiety they have many followers. How many there are who are using against God all that he has given them! They have prepared it for Baal.

We do this whenever the gifts of God are used *to augment pride*. This is a temptation that besets us all. We have all a tendency to swell and grow great simply because God has given us more than other people; whereas that but makes us the greater debtors. I have heard that, in the days of imprisonment for debt, there were people in prison who used to be quite proud because they owed ten thousand pounds, and who looked down with scorn upon a poor fellow who had come in there only owing a hundred pounds, or perhaps, only a five-pound note. The more they were in debt, the more they thought of themselves. Now, is not that the case with every proud man? Because you have greater ability, or greater wealth, than another, you owe so much the more to God; and yet you are foolish enough to make that, which ought to be a reason for being humble, a reason for being proud. God surely feels that his gifts are being misused when we handle them so as to make ourselves haughty and important. In doing this we forget him who gave us all, even as Hosea in another place saith concerning the people, "According to their pasture, so were they filled; they were filled, and their heart was exalted; therefore have they forgotten me."

Moreover, the gifts of God are perverted when we use them *to justify sin*, setting our necks stiffly in the way of evil, because, though we have wandered from God, the corn and the oil are still continued to us. "These are my rewards that my lovers have given me," said this nation that went after Baal; therefore she thought that her worship of Baal was worthy to be continued. How horrible a thing it is for a man to boast in his sin, because God does not swiftly follow it with judgment, and to continue therein because God does not at once withdraw his common mercies! Those whose hearts are set in them to do evil, because the sentence against the evil work is not executed speedily, shall have sore distress in the day when, at last, the righteous God arises to judgment.

Again, God's gifts are ill-used when, because of the very abundance of them, we begin *to excuse excess*. The drunkard and the glutton pervert what was meant to be a good gift into an occasion of sin and riot. God gives us all good things richly to enjoy; but when, instead of enjoying them, men abuse them, and ruin themselves, body and soul, by misusing the gifts of heaven, it would be small cause for wonder if God was roused to remove the gifts put to such base use. And since so many of those around us do abuse God's gifts in this manner, it behoves us, who desire to glorify God, to use all things with great temperance, and wholly to abstain from some things, lest we should cause our brother to stumble.

Equally bad is it when a man uses the gifts of God's providence so as *to foster selfishness*. His silver and gold are multiplied; he hoards it up and makes a god of it. The poor are at his gates. There let them keep; why should he trouble about them? The church of God needs his aid. Let it need it. It shall have nothing from him. "Soul," says such a man, "thou must lay up much goods for many years." And, when he has effected his purpose, then he talks to his own soul again, poor creature that it is, and says, "Soul, thou hast much goods laid up for many years: take thine ease; eat, drink, and be merry." He has made a god of his goods, and thus he has perverted God's gifts, and used them to God's dishonour. He has given them to Baal.

It grieves one's heart to see gifts of God used *to oppose God*. What would you have thought of David, when Jonathan gave him his sword and bow, if he had taken the sword, and cut off Jonathan's head, or if he had fitted an arrow to the string, and shot Jonathan to the heart? It would have been base ingratitude. But men fight against God with God's own gifts. A woman endowed with beauty, the rare gift of God, uses it to ensnare others into sin. God gives us garments, and there are some who use their very garments for nothing else but pride, and who go through the world with no motive but display. A man has a musical voice given to him, but he sings what God cannot be pleased to hear, and what no man or woman ought to listen to. Another has great intellect, and he gives himself up to pulling the Bible to pieces, and, as far as he can, to destroy much good. Another has a voice clear and loud, and skill in using it, and you hear him stand up to lead others to war against their Maker, and to sin with a high hand against the King of heaven. Oh, the pity is that there should be so much of good in the world, all heaped up to rot— that so many gifts of God should be used by men against him! When those in high authority oppress the righteous, they use their authority against God; and when men in high standing are seen at police courts advocating that which is injurious to morals, they not only degrade themselves, but they make us think that the "nobility" with which they are said to be endowed must be a myth. God keep us all, dear friends, from ever using the gifts of our Maker against our Maker; and we are certainly acting against him when we go contrary to anything that is honest, lovely, and of good repute; and when, in any way, we sanction that which will do our fellow-creatures wrong, and will be injurious to the interests of true righteousness, and the advancement of the kingdom of Christ!

My text is sadly true with reference to many: "She did not know that I gave her corn, and wine, and oil, and multiplied her silver and gold, which they prepared for Baal." They prepared for God's enemies what God himself had given to them, and what he meant to be used only for his own glory.

IV. And now my fourth observation is this: THIS PERVERSION OFTEN MOVES GOD TO WITHDRAW HIS MISUSED GIFTS. "Therefore will I return, and take away my corn in the time thereof, and my wine in the season thereof, and will recover my wool and my flax."

God has given many of you a great many mercies. Remember that, if you become proud of them, if because you have become fat, like Jeshurun, you begin to kick, he can take his gifts away. If you forsake God who made you, and lightly esteem the Rock of your salvation, he will forsake you, and withdraw his bounty.

He can withdraw his gifts *easily*. "Riches certainly make themselves wings; they fly away as an eagle toward heaven." You have seen the crows on a ploughed field, have you not? There they are, blackening the ground. But clap your hands, and they are gone. So have we often seen it with a man's wealth. There has been a little change in the money market, some little turn in commerce, and all his money has taken to itself wings, and flown away. Is it health and strength that you have, or great wit? Ah, sir, a puff of wind may take away life; a little gas may be fatal to health! We know not what dependent creatures we are. God can easily take away the blessings which he gives, therefore let us remember him in the use of them. "Whether, therefore, ye eat or drink, do all to the glory of God."

Moreover, God can take away his gifts *unexpectedly*. In the text, he says, "I will take away my corn in the time thereof," that is, in harvest, "and my wine in the season thereof," that is, just at the time of vintage. When it seemed as if the harvest and vintage were secure, God would send a sudden blight upon both, and they would perish. God can take things away when they almost touch the tips of our fingers, and he can easily deprive us of misused blessings at the very moment when we think we are most sure of them. "There's many a slip 'twixt the cup and the lip;" and there is many an occasion of final disappointment when we think we have succeeded. We are only secure as we trust in the Giver of all good.

God can take away these things *rightfully*. What would you do yourself if you had one whom you fed who was always kicking against you? Would you feed a dog that was always barking at you, and trying to fly at you, and do you mischief? Is it not right that God should take away providential benefits from men when they misuse them, and pervert them to his dishonour? It is of his grace that these things are ours at all; he has but to withdraw that grace, and to deal with us as we deserve, and lo! we are impoverished at once.

If God does take these things away, I would pray that he may take them from you *mercifully*. I was riding one day with a young gentleman, who was leading a very reckless life indeed, but whose father was a very gracious man. I found that the son had taken to horse-racing, and I said, "That is right; go on as fast as you can. Till you have lost every penny you have, you will scarcely be willing to turn to God. Young fellows like you do not often come home, except round by the swine-trough. When you get down to that, then, I trust, you will cry to God for mercy, and say, 'I will arise, and go to my father.'" He was very much astonished at my advice; but I think it was the right thing to say under the circumstances.

How often have I seen something of this sort take place! The Lord has taken away from a man wealth, or he has taken away health, or else the man has fallen into dishonour; the Lord takes away the corn in the time thereof, and the wine in the season thereof, and then it happens, as we have it in the verse before the text, the afflicted one says, "I will go and return to my first husband; for then was it better with me than now." So long as you come to Christ, I do not mind if you come round by "Weeping-Cross." Even if you come with a broken leg, with the loss of an eye, or with consumption making a prey of you, it will be well; if only your souls be saved, and you come home to the great Father, we will be glad. But why do you want to be whipped to Christ? Why not come willingly? Why do you need to have these truths burnt into you as with a hot iron? Why not learn them easily. "Be ye not as the horse, or as the mule, which have no understanding; whose mouth must be held in with bit and bridle." Be not hard-mouthed with God, for he will master you, if he once take you in hand. If he means to bless you, he will conquer you, though he may have to use rough measures with you. By-and-by, when he has broken you in, he will deal with you in all the infinite tenderness of his compassion; and you will acknowledge that even his roughness was all the result of his love to you.

Now, I close by saying that the Lord may take these things away from us *justly*. He sometimes withdraws his bounty without intending mercy. The sufferings of guilty men here are like the first drops of a horrible tempest that will continue for ever and ever. If they will not turn to him when he calls in mercy, but continue to reject his love, then will he begin to speak in thunder, and the first storm of his righteous wrath shall only be the beginning of an endless hurricane.

> "Ye sinners, seek his grace,
> Whose wrath ye cannot bear;
> Fly to the shelter of his cross,
> And find salvation there."

I have tried to speak very earnestly; but if I have failed to speak as tenderly as I would, may the great Master forgive! Oh, that you would acknowledge your indebtedness to God! Oh, that you would cast away your idols! "As though God did beseech you by us: we pray you in Christ's stead, be ye reconciled to God."

God grant that you may be led by the blessed Spirit to yield yourself to him who has given you so much cause to trust him, and to his name shall be eternal honour! Amen, and amen.

PORTION OF SCRIPTURE READ BEFORE SERMON—Hosea ii.

HYMNS FROM "OUR OWN HYMN BOOK"—709, 524, 596.

Will shortly be published. Price 2s. 6d.

FROM THE PULPIT TO THE PALM-BRANCH.

(Being a Sequel to the Sketch of Mr. Spurgeon's Life and Labours entitled, "From the Usher's Desk to the Tabernacle Pulpit.")

A MEMORIAL OF C. H. SPURGEON.

INCLUDING THE OFFICIAL REPORT OF THE SERVICES IN CONNECTION WITH HIS FUNERAL.

PASSMORE AND ALABASTER, 4, PATERNOSTER BUILDINGS, LONDON; and all Booksellers.

Metropolitan Tabernacle Pulpit.

THE PERSEVERANCE OF FAITH.

A Sermon

INTENDED FOR READING ON LORD'S-DAY, APRIL 24TH, 1892,

DELIVERED BY

C. H. SPURGEON,

AT THE METROPOLITAN TABERNACLE, NEWINGTON,

On Thursday Evening, October 30th, 1890.

"Then Jesus answered and said unto her, O woman, great is thy faith: be it unto thee even as thou wilt. And her daughter was made whole from that very hour."—Matthew xv. 28.

I HAVE frequently spoken to you concerning the faith of this Canaanitish woman, of the way in which Christ tried it, and of the manner in which, at length, he honoured it, and granted all that the suppliant sought. The story is so full of meaning, that one might turn it this way, and that way, and the other way, and always see jewels in it. But now I am going to use it with only one end and aim, namely, to encourage those who have faith enough to seek Jesus, but have not yet, to their joy and peace, been quite able to find him.

This woman had come to her last word. I do not see what more she could have said. When Christ had likened her to a dog, she had consented to it, and said, "Truth, Lord: yet the dogs eat of the crumbs which fall from their masters' table." She had come to her last word, and now Christ gives her his best word. It is his way, sometimes, to make us wait till we are completely exhausted, and can say and do no more; then he comes in with the fulness of his divine power, and gives to us what we have importunately sought at his hands. Our extremity is his opportunity.

I. The first remark which I shall make, and enlarge upon, is that FAITH ALONE CAN KEEP A SOUL SEEKING AFTER CHRIST UNDER DISCOURAGEMENT. Other causes may send us a certain distance along the road, but only faith will bring us to the goal of assured rest.

That which made this woman seek the Saviour was, first of all, parental love. She loved her daughter. She longed to have the devil cast out of her, that her daughter might not be so grievously vexed. That started her going, and carried her some way towards the blessing; but she would have stopped short of the boon she desired if she had relied upon natural love alone.

Her earnestness also to a large extent urged her forward. When she desired healing for her daughter, she meant what she said. When

No. 2,253.

she cried, "Have mercy upon me, O Lord, thou Son of David!" it was with a shrill and piteous voice. She could not bear to be refused. Nobody ever came to Christ who pleaded more from the heart than did this poor Canaanite. She was not an idle repeater of forms of prayer. Her prayer leaped, red-hot, from her soul—"Have mercy on me, O Lord, thou Son of David!" But her earnestness alone would not have upheld her under the ordeal through which she was called to pass. It would have given way if she had not had the believing conviction that Christ could heal her daughter, and that he would do so.

Her humility also helped her greatly. Had she been a proud woman, she would have stood upon her dignity when she was called a dog; but humility came to her help, and she did not resent even the harsh word the Lord used, but still pleaded for her poor child. Now, parental love and earnestness and humility are good things, but they are not enough to enable a soul to cling to Christ, and never let him go. Something more is needed.

This Canaanite was a very sensible woman, wise and prudent. She knew how to turn the hard words of Christ into arguments in her own favour. She would not be put back. If he had not answered her, she would have pleaded with him again. When he did answer her, and say that it was not meet to give the children's bread to dogs, she found even in that dry bone some little marrow on which to feed her heart. But wise as she was, and prudent as she was, she would not have held out to the end, and obtained the blessing she desired for her daughter, if it had not been for her faith.

We may be quite sure that the one thing specially noteworthy in this woman's case was her faith, first, because *we have Christ's word for it.* He said unto her, "O woman, great is thy faith!" He did not say, "Great is thy love to thy child;" nor, "Great is thy earnestness;" nor, "Great is thy importunity;" but he put his finger on the power that had urged her forward, and he said, "O woman, great is thy faith!" And not in this case alone did Christ trace the blessing to faith, but in nearly every instance where a suppliant obtained favour from him, faith was the medium of securing the mercy. Faith is mightier than all other available forces.

Besides this, *we know that faith supports the other graces.* If other graces can help a soul to plead with Christ, they all owe their power to faith. If it had not been for the faith which she had to support it, parental love would not have helped this woman much. If it had not been for faith, she would not have been earnest and importunate. Faith supplies the strength of the other graces; and, whatever they do, it is faith that works through them. Faith is the master-power. Faith hangs on to Christ in the dark, it holds to a silent Christ, it holds to a refusing Christ, it holds to a rebuking Christ, and will not let him go. Faith is the great holdfast that hooks a soul on to the Saviour.

Faith is thus powerful because of its effects. *Faith enlightens, enlivens, and strengthens.* It is written of some of old that "They looked unto him, and were lightened." Faith sheds a light upon many things, and lets us see that even if Christ has a frown on his face, he has love in his heart. Faith looks right into the heart of Christ, and helps us to perceive that he cannot mean anything but mercy to a seeking soul. Faith also enlivens, and when the heart begins to faint, faith brings its smelling bottle, and revives it. David said, "I had fainted, unless I had believed." Believing is the cure for fainting, and you must do one of two things, either believe or faint. Faith is thus a great help to one who is seeking Christ, because it both enlightens and enlivens the soul. Faith also strengthens. It makes the lame take the prey. Beloved, it is because faith thus enlightens and enlivens and strengthens, that it is the grace most useful to a soul that is seeking to lay hold upon Christ, and yet cannot get a comfortable look at his blessed face.

Moreover, *faith lays hold on Christ.* It is like the Greek Antisthenes, who went to a philosopher to learn; but he was a dull scholar, and the philosopher bade him go away. The next time the class met, Antisthenes returned, and the philosopher thereupon sent for a man with a club to drive the stupid scholar away; but he was overcome by his scholar; for Antisthenes said, "There is no club that was ever made that is heavy enough to drive me away from you. Here I mean to stay, and learn whatever you can teach me." Oh, may we have a faith like that, a faith that will say to Christ, "I will not go away from thee. There is no threatening in thy Book that can drive me from thee. I can but perish if I stay with thee, and if I go from thee, I must perish; therefore I will abide with thee evermore, and learn all that thou wilt teach me"! Faith is like the Greek in the days of Xerxes, who seized the boat with his right hand. When they chopped off the right hand, he seized it with his left hand; when they cut off the left hand also, he laid hold of the boat with his teeth, and did not let go till they had severed his head from his body. Soul, if thou canst lay hold on Christ with thy right hand, or with thy left hand, it will be well with thee. Cling to Christ, and say to him with that holy boldness that is the result of faith, "I will not let thee go except thou bless me." Faith, then, holds on to Christ.

Further, I would say that *faith does this best without help.* How often we try to assist faith! We want faith to have some works, some prayers, something or other of our own to help it. It is as if somebody were to try and help me to walk by giving me a big chair to carry. I should not walk so well with the burden, as without it. Have you never heard this parable concerning faith? She had to cross a stream, and the current was strong, and there came one to her who said, "O faith, I will help thee! Come with me up the river till we find a place where we can ford it." Faith said, "No; I was bidden to cross the river here." So another came, and said, "I will build a bridge for you, that you may go over the river with ease;" and he laid a few stones, but not much ever came of it. Yet another said, "I will go and find a boat." But there were no boats about; therefore they asked faith to wait till they built a boat for her. What did she do? She took off her vestments, and plunged into the water. "Thank God," said she, "I can swim;" and so she swam across, and reached the other side without boat, without bridge, and without ford. That is what I should like to see every sinner here do— begin to swim. Do not wait for help. Cast yourself into the stream of everlasting love. Believe in Christ Jesus, and have no more confidence in the flesh, with its bridges and its boats. Commit thyself to the stream of eternal grace, and swim across. Faith can enable you to do it. Nothing else can. Take that lesson home to yourselves, you who are seeking the Saviour at this time.

The only thing that will help you to follow after Christ till you find him, is faith. All your groaning and moaning will not help you. All your doubting and your trembling will be of no avail; your feeling that you are too vile to be saved, and that faith would be presumption in such a sinner as you are, will not aid you. But believe that Christ can save you, and trust to his power and love, and he will save you. Come to him as this woman of Canaan came, with her importunate cry, "Have mercy on me, O Lord, thou Son of David," and he will have mercy on you even as he had upon her. Believe, believe, believe! Thou wilt never come into light by doubting and fearing. The way to liberty lies through this one door of faith. Therefore believe and live.

Thus much upon our first remark, that faith alone can keep a soul seeking after Christ under discouragement.

II. Secondly, FAITH IS EXCEEDINGLY DELIGHTFUL TO CHRIST. What he said to this woman began with an exclamation, as if he was struck with something in her that delighted him. He said, "O woman, great is thy faith!" Notice that he spoke of her faith, and of that alone. He knew about her love; he knew about her earnestness; he knew about her humility; but he said nothing at all about them: his one word of commendation was for her faith, "O woman, great is thy faith!" That is what my Lord is looking for now. He comes round and looks at you, who are sitting in these pews, to see whether you have faith in him. There are several thoughts suggested by this, that should encourage you who are seeking Christ.

He can spy out the beginnings of faith. "If thou hast faith as a grain of mustard seed," he will see it, and he will accept it. If thou hast only now begun to believe that Jesus is the Christ, and to trust him, though thy faith be feeble as a babe that cannot stand, but can only cling to its mother's breast, Jesus will see the beginnings of it. He is "the Author" as well as "the Finisher of our faith." Be thou comforted, then, concerning that tiny trust thou hast in him.

Still, *he is greatly pleased when he sees great faith.* When a great sinner says, "I believe that he is a Saviour great enough to save me;" it brings joy to the heart of Christ. When an old sinner says, "I believe that his precious blood can take away the sin of seventy or eighty years;" the Lord's heart is gladdened. Christ loves a great faith. He deserves great faith, and when he gets it he is highly pleased. "O woman," said he, "great is thy faith!"

He is so delighted with faith, that *he passes by other things for it.* If that woman's ears had been hung with rings, and her neck had been decked with pearls, and her hands had been covered with diamonds, he would not have cared about her ornaments and her beauty. He sees something that he prizes more than any of these things; therefore he says to her, "O woman, great is thy faith!" He is charmed with that choice decoration of her heart. By that treasure " The king is held in his galleries." Christ may say of faith, " Thou hast ravished my heart with one of thy eyes." When we can but look straight to Christ, and trust in him, he is charmed and carried away by our faith.

Why does Christ think so much of faith?

One reason is, because *faith glorifies him.* He thinks much of it, because it thinks so much of him. Faith believes him, faith trusts him, faith lives upon him. He is " the chiefest among ten thousand " and the " altogether lovely " to faith. Therefore, because faith highly esteems Christ, Christ highly esteems faith.

Next, he loves faith because it is *God's appointed way* in which we are to receive blessing. God might have appointed ordinances as the vehicle of grace; but, instead thereof, he has made faith to be the medium of salvation. If thou believest, thou shalt be saved. He that by faith lays hold on Christ, has laid hold on eternal life. " He that believeth and is baptized shall be saved." To the awakened sinner our word is still, " Believe on the Lord Jesus Christ, and thou shalt be saved." Since God has put faith into so eminent a place, our Lord Jesus Christ loves to see it; he takes delight in that which pleases his Father.

Another reason why he loves it is, because *faith is the signal which permits the train of mercy to come to us.* Whenever unbelief holds up its arms, the train of almighty grace stands still. Of a certain place it is said, "He did not many mighty works there because of their unbelief." Their doubt blocked the way. But when faith lowers the signal, the great Driver of heaven's express says, " That road is clear," and he delights to see it, and drives right ahead. Oh, if thou canst but let that signal go down, showing that the line is clear of all obstructions, Christ will surely come to thee! He is glad to come wherever he can bring a blessing, and he rejoices when faith reveals to him a clear road.

Besides, *faith has open arms for embracing Christ.* When he comes to our door, and finds it locked, he stands there till his bitter lament is "my head is filled with dew, and my locks with the drops of the night." But when he comes and the door is open, the poor sinner is so taken up with his beauty that he never thinks of shutting him out. " Oh," says the seeking soul, "if the Lord would but come in!" And as surely as Christ finds the door thus open, he comes in, and dwells there; and makes that heart and that house happy with his divine presence. Christ loves faith because faith gives him a hearty welcome; faith receives him; faith embraces him.

Oh, I would to God you would think of this and exercise faith in the Lord Jesus! May you see that nothing delights Christ like a sinner believing in him, that nothing gives him more joy than to have a saint resting completely upon him without doubt or fear!

Thus have we considered two points; first, that the only way to keep a soul seeking Christ under discouragement is by faith; and, secondly, that nothing pleases Christ like believing on his name.

III. The third point is that FAITH WILL, BEFORE LONG, GET A KIND ANSWER FROM THE LORD JESUS. This poor woman, at the first, received no reply to her petition, " Have mercy on me, O Lord, thou

Son of David!" Then, when Christ did speak to her, he gave her what seemed to be a rough answer. But, after a while, these notes of heavenly music sounded in her ear, " O woman, great is thy faith: be it unto thee even as thou wilt!"

Now, someone here probably says, "I have been praying ever so long, and I have received no cheering reply." Well, if thou believest in Jesus, thou shalt have a good reply before long. If thou canst but hold on to Christ, determined to plead with him till he answers thee, he will answer thee kindly ere long. But keep on believing that he can and will give thee what thou needest, and thou shalt not be disappointed. "Oh," says one, "you do not know who I am! I am an outcast." So was this woman. She was a Canaanitish woman, yet she obtained a blessing from Christ; and thou shalt get one, too, if thou dost follow her in her faith. "Oh, but I do not think that I am fit!" Did Christ ever say to you that you were a dog? He did as good as tell this woman that; yet she held on to him by faith, and prevailed. "Oh, but I have prayed in vain for such a long time!" So did she. She prayed, and for a while she received no answer. "Oh, but I feel worse after I have prayed!" So did she; for instead of getting a comfortable answer, she heard Christ say, "It is not meet to take the children's bread, and to cast it to dogs." You cannot be in a worse plight than she was. "But the devil troubles me," you add. The devil also troubled her. She pleaded about her daughter, who was possessed with a devil; and she kept on pleading and believing. She meant to have Christ. I exhort you to come to the same holy determination. Oh, that Almighty grace might help you so to do; for in so doing you will surely get an answer of peace! You will get a comfortable answer before very long, probably much earlier than you have reckoned upon.

Remember that *Christ delays in order to increase your faith.* Your faith will grow by exercise: therefore he tests it that you may use it, and that thus it may become stronger.

Christ delays in order to increase the blessing itself. While we wait, the blessing becomes bigger, and our hands become stronger to hold it when it does come. You may be sure that our blessed Lord will give you a comfortable answer; for do you not know that he has been sustaining you while you have been pleading, and as yet have received no answer? Did you ever notice, when Joseph's brethren went down into Egypt, that he made himself strange to them, and spoke to them roughly, and put them in prison? But in spite of that, there was one thing he did: when they went back to Jacob, he filled their sacks for them. He would not smile upon them, but he would not starve them; and at last, it is said, "Joseph could not refrain himself," and he "made himself known unto his brethren. He was obliged to show his love at last; but even before he did that, he always filled their sacks for them. Christ will deal with you in like manner; while you are waiting, he will not let you die. Oh, in what wonderful ways did the Lord support me when, through weary years, I was seeking his face! I could not say that I had any comfort that I dared to call my own, and yet there flowed into my soul, somehow, a secret power that enabled me still to hope, and still to hold on; for that I now desire to bless his name, and I tell it for the encouragement of any who may be in soul-trouble as I was. Keep on seeking his grace, dear friend. Believe still; for he must give you a comfortable answer one of these days.

Consider well that *it is contrary to his nature to refuse to bless.* He is brimful of love; and if he does put a sinner back for a while, it is only because it is right and kind and wise to do so. But his heart yearns over every seeking sinner. He wants you more than you want him. He longs after you. He desires to bless you. He must do so; it is his nature so to do.

He must give you a comfortable reply before long, again, for *it is contrary to his glory to refuse.* If he allowed a seeking sinner to die, where would his truth be? Has he not said, "Him that cometh to me I will in no wise cast out"? Our friend, Dr. Barnardo, announces that in his refuges no homeless boy will ever be rejected: that no destitute child shall ever be turned away. Suppose somebody could prove—which, of course, they cannot do—that scores of destitute children were turned away, all confidence in him would be destroyed. And if it could be proved that Christ ever cast out a single soul that came to him, it would take away his honour and his glory. We could never believe him any more. Perish the thought of such a thing!

It is contrary to his word to refuse any seeker, and Christ will keep his word. "Come unto me," saith he, "all ye that labour and are heavy laden, and I will give you rest." If Christ does not give you rest when you come to him, what is his promise worth? My friend, Dr. Pierson, sent me, the other day, an imitation of an American banknote, which they call a "greenback" over there, and on one side of it were these words, "My God shall supply all your need, according to his riches in glory by Christ Jesus." A splendid note that! It had our friend's name on the back, "Arthur T. Pierson"; and he said to me, when he sent it, "If the Lord does not pay you, I will, for I have endorsed the note." I shall never have to look my brother Pierson up, and tell him that the note he endorsed is of no value. There it stands, and stands for ever. God will keep his word. I know it; and I want you poor sinners to know it, too. He cannot run back from his own promise. His word is his bond. To every honest man it is so; but to the thrice-holy God his oath and his promise bind him eternally.

Let me add that, if Christ does not give a comfortable answer to you who believingly seek him, *it is contrary to his custom.* Here are many of us who have known our Lord now for forty years, and we can say that his custom is to hear our prayers, and according to our faith, so is it unto us. Come along, thou blackest sinner out of hell! Come, and wash in the fountain filled with blood, and thou shalt be cleansed, as surely as ever Christ died! Come along, thou lowest, meanest, most self-abhorred, most self-condemned of humankind! Come thou, and look to him, and trust in him; and if thou dost not find peace at once, yet be sure that thou shalt have it before long. "The morning cometh." It is not for long that Christ's mercy can be restrained. He must break forth, like Joseph, weeping over his brethren. He must manifest himself to you in love, and tenderness, and kindness. I will be bound for him any day that it shall be so.

IV. Lastly, we come to a very glorious thought, FAITH GETTING CHRIST'S WORD HATH ALL THINGS. Listen to the text again: "Jesus answered and said unto her, O woman, great is thy faith : be it unto thee even as thou wilt. And her daughter was made whole from that very hour."

Christ's word was *a comforting word.* How the look on this woman's face must have altered when Christ talked to her so! When he answered her never a word, she doubtless had a long and sorrowful face, and probably the big tears stood in her eyes; but now that he began to talk in another strain, how happy she felt! The woman was no more sad. So it is even to-day. One word from Christ can comfort you, even if they talk about putting you into an asylum because you are so melancholy. One word from my Master shall be as the balm of Gilead to your wounds. He will bind up your broken heart. He will comfort you, and speak peace to you, as he did to her. It was a comforting word.

It was also *a commending word,* "O woman, great is thy faith!" She had never been praised like that before. I have no doubt that her husband had praised her. What good husband is there who does not praise his wife, even as it is written of the virtuous woman, "Her husband also, and he praiseth her"? but his praise had never been so sweet as this word from the Lord Jesus. I have no doubt that her daughter had called her all the sweet names she could think of; for she loved her child, and it is only natural to believe that her child loved her. But now, when Christ looks her in the face, and says, "O woman, great"—"ah!" she may have thought; "he is going to say, 'Great is thy sin,' or else, 'Great is thy noise.'" What astonishment must have been hers when he said, "Great is thy faith"! He gave her a gold medal for her faith, ay, something even better than that, she was put in the class called "Highly commended." "O woman, great is thy faith!" It was a commending word; and she needed it.

Next, it was *a commanding word.* Notice that, well. Listen to it: "Be it unto thee." He speaks like a king. And if the Lord now speaks his gracious word with power, as I pray that he may, he will say, "Minister, comfort that woman, who puts her trust in me." He will say, "Ordinances, comfort those weary ones. Bread and wine, be sweet to the taste of those poor troubled ones." He will say, "Prayer-meetings, be a joy to those poor tried ones." It is a commanding voice with which the Lord of hosts speaks, when he says, "Comfort ye, comfort ye, my people, saith your God. Speak ye comfortably to Jerusalem, and cry unto her, that her warfare is accomplished, that her iniquity is pardoned."

In addition to being a commanding word, it was *a creating word.* Why, it was the very word that God himself used when he made the light! He said "*Be,* light." He said to the earth, "Be," and it was. He said to the heavens, "Be," and they were. The word is a fiat. In the Latin it is precisely that, a *fiat.* So here, that same mighty voice says, "Be it unto thee. Be it unto thee." O God, send forth a fiat at this moment to some poor weary heart! Create light; create joy; create peace. He can create all of these in your heart now. Oh, that he might do it by the power of his almighty grace! The faith of this poor Canaanite thus obtained for its reward a creative fiat from the lips of Christ.

Further, it was *a complying word.* You see all these adjectives begin with the same letter: it was a comforting word, a commending word, a commanding word, a creating word, and a complying word. "Be it unto thee even as thou wilt—just as you please, whatever you wish for, and in the way you wish to have it." Christ capitulates to a conquering faith. Nothing ever conquered him yet but faith. His love is stronger than death. Death could not conquer Christ, nor could all the powers of hell. But here he surrenders at discretion to a soul that can vanquish him by believing. "Be it unto thee even as thou wilt." Do you want more joy? Do you want full salvation? Do you want perfect rest? Behold, he says to each of you who can and do believe in him, "Be it unto thee even as thou wilt."

Thus, lastly, this word became *a completing word* "her daughter was made whole from that very hour." From that very hour she was well again. Christ finished that work speedily. He was not long about it. It does not take so long to save a soul as it does for a lightning flash to be visible. You pass from death to life in an instant. When lost, ruined, condemned, the man casts himself at Christ's feet, immediately he is saved. It is not the work of hours, or weeks, or years, when you trust to the finished work of Christ. All that required time, Christ has accomplished. All that now has to be done, can be done in a moment. When a man is thirsty, it does not take him long to drink when the water is there. Remember the invitation with which the Scriptures almost conclude, "Let him that is athirst come. And whosoever will, let him take the water of life freely." The water of life is there; take it. When a man is hungry, it does not take him long to eat when the bread is on the table. God can now give you, who came to this Tabernacle afar off from him, grace which shall enable you to be made nigh at once. He can bring you immediately out of the blackness of sin, and make you on the instant whiter than snow. Make David's prayer your own, "Wash me, and I shall be whiter than snow."

Believe my Lord and Master. Oh, why do you not believe him? Artful doubts and reasonings cease! I would now take the hammer and the nails, and fasten my unbelief and fear to Christ's cross. Hang there, ye thieves, and die! You destroy men's souls, ye doubts and reasonings! Come here, simple faith, thou who hast no wisdom! A mere child thou art, but; O simple faith, thou hast the key of the kingdom! Come, and welcome, into my heart. Will all of you not also believe, and trust in Christ, even now? If you do, you shall be saved. "Be it unto thee even as thou wilt." God bless you! Amen.

PORTION OF SCRIPTURE READ BEFORE SERMON—Matthew xv. 21—39.

HYMNS FROM "OUR OWN HYMN BOOK"—560, 599, 550.

Exposition by C. H. Spurgeon.*
MATTHEW XV. 21—39.

JESUS had been in conflict with Scribes and Pharisees. He never liked such discussions, and though he was always victorious in every controversy, it grieved his spirit.

Verse 21. Then Jesus went thence, and departed into the coasts of Tyre and Sidon.

He was glad to get away, and made a journey over the hills to get at as great a distance as possible from these cavillers.

22. *And, behold, a woman of Canaan came.*

A Syro-Phœnician woman, one of the old, condemned race living in Tyre and Sidon.

22. *A woman of Canaan came out of the same coasts, and cried unto him, saying, Have mercy on me, O Lord, thou son of David.*

You remember the son of David, that is Solomon, was well known in Phœnicia; for the men of Tyre and Sidon cut down the cedars for Solomon, and Hiram helped him in the building of the temple. There had always been a remembrance of this lingering among the Sidonians; so this woman called the Saviour the Son of David.

22. *Have mercy on me, O Lord, thou son of David; my daughter is grievously vexed with a devil.*

"Have mercy on me." The mother identifies herself with her child. When we pray for our children, that is the right way to pray. Intercessory prayer never prevails until we bear the object of our prayer upon our heart, and ask for the blessing we desire for them as a favour to ourselves.

23. *But he answered her not a word.*

Answers to prayers may be delayed; but delays are not always denials. Christ's silence must have been a great trial to the poor woman; but our Lord knew with whom he was dealing.

23. *And his disciples came and besought him, saying, Send her away; for she crieth after us.*

Ah, these disciples made a grand mistake! She did not cry after them; she cried after him; but so they understood it: therefore they said, "Get rid of her; she disturbs us; when we are in the street, we can hear her cry. Send her away; for she crieth after us." Ah! poor disciples, she was not so foolish as to cry after you; she was crying after your Master. If any here have come only to hear the preacher, they have made a great mistake; but if you have come for a word from the Master, I pray that you may be gratified.

---

* The sermons available for future use are those preached on Lord's-day and Thursday evenings. These were usually shorter than the morning discourses. The publishers will issue, with the Sermon, the Exposition that preceded it as often as they are able to do so. They believe that readers will value all of these utterances of the beloved preacher who is now with the Lord. They have heard of many sermon-readers who regularly turn to the portions of Scripture expounded by Mr. Spurgeon, and even read the hymns sung at the Tabernacle. Such friends will now have a very full report of the services held there during the late Pastor's ministry.

THE PERSEVERANCE OF FAITH.

24. *But he answered and said, I am not sent but unto the lost sheep of the house of Israel.*

Christ did what he was sent to do; he was the Messiah, the sent One. He would not go beyond his mission, so he says, "I am sent." He was sent as a Preacher and a Teacher, not to the Gentiles, but to Israel. He had a larger commission in reserve, and was yet to be a Saviour to the Gentiles as well as to the Jews; but for the present he was to be a Shepherd to "the lost sheep of the house of Israel."

25. *Then came she and worshipped him, saying, Lord help me.*

A very short prayer; but how much there was in it!

26, 27. *But he answered and said, It is not meet to take the children's bread, and to cast it to dogs. And she said, Truth, Lord: yet the dogs eat of the crumbs which fall from their masters' table.*

It is the faculty of faith to see in the dark. This woman spied out light in what seemed to be a very dark saying. Did Christ call her a dog? Well, dogs have their privileges when they lie under the table. Even if their master does not throw them a crumb, yet they may take that which falls from his hand. If Jesus would but allow any mercy to drop, as it were, accidentally, this woman would be content.

28, 29. *Then Jesus answered and said unto her, O woman, great is thy faith: be it unto thee even as thou wilt. And her daughter was made whole from that very hour. And Jesus departed from thence.*

When he had done his business, he was off. Our Lord was a great itinerant; he was always on the move. He had come all the way to the parts of Tyre and Sidon to help one woman; and when that one woman had been attended to, he goes back again immediately to his old post by the sea of Galilee.

29, 30. *And Jesus departed from thence, and came nigh unto the sea of Galilee; and went up into a mountain, and sat down there. And great multitudes came unto him, having with them those that were lame, blind, dumb, maimed, and many others, and cast them down at Jesus' feet; and he healed them.*

In the prayer-meeting, held by the deacons and elders this morning, before I came in here, one of our friends observed in prayer that there might be many lame, blind, and maimed in the congregation, and he prayed that they might be brought to Jesus. Let us, by faith, bring them to him, and lay them at his feet. Oh, that this word, "He healed them," might be true again to-day!

31. *Insomuch that the multitude wondered, when they saw the dumb to speak, the maimed to be whole, the lame to walk, and the blind to see: and they glorified the God of Israel.*

Oh, for glory to God! There is no glory to God which equals that which comes from blind eyes which have been made to see; and from dumb lips which have been made to speak. The glories of nature and providence are eclipsed by the glories of grace. May we see such things to-day!

32. *Then Jesus called his disciples unto him, and said, I have compassion on the multitude, because they continue with me now three days, and have nothing to eat: and I will not send them away fasting, lest they faint in the way.*

Ah, dear friends, they were willing to put up with inconvenience to hear the gospel in those days! Three days of sermon-hearing! People want sermons wonderfully short now, and the sermons must be marvellously interesting, too, or else the people grow dreadfully tired. If dinner-time came round, the dinner-bell, at any time, in these days, would drown all the attraction of the pulpit. But here were people that attended Christ's ministry for three days, and they had nothing to eat. He had compassion upon them, and said to his disciples, "I will not send them away fasting, lest they faint in the way."

33, 34. *And his disciples say unto him, Whence should we have so much bread in the wilderness, as to fill so great a multitude? And Jesus saith unto them, How many loaves have ye?*

That is the point. It is idle to enquire about how much you want. "How many loaves have ye?"

34, 35. *And they said, Seven, and a few little fishes. And he commanded the multitude to sit down on the ground.*

It was a token of Christ's presence and power that they were willing to sit down on the ground. Think of thousands of people taking their places in an orderly way to feed upon seven cakes and a few little fishes! Without any demur, the crowd arranged itself into banquet order at the command of Jesus.

36, 37. *And he took the seven loaves and the fishes, and gave thanks, and brake them, and gave to his disciples, and the disciples to the multitude. And they did all eat, and were filled: and they took up of the broken meat that was left seven baskets full.*

They were large baskets, too; not like the small food-baskets mentioned when the five thousand were fed. The word used here is the same that is employed to describe the basket in which Saul was let down by the wall of Damascus.

38. *And they that did eat were four thousand men, beside women and children.*

Now, if the women and children bore the same proportion to the men as they generally do in our congregations, there must have been a very large crowd indeed. Why is the number of the women and children not mentioned? Was it because they were so many? or was it because their appetites being smaller than the appetites of men, the men are put down as the great eaters, and the women and children, as it were, thrown into the count? What a mercy it is that the Lord adds to the church daily a vast number of men, women, and children! The Lord send us many more, until we cannot count them!

39. *And he sent away the multitude, and took ship, and came into the coasts of Magdala.*

He had taught the people, and fed them; so now he goes elsewhere to carry similar blessings to others also.

Metropolitan Tabernacle Pulpit.

THE TWO GUARDS, PRAYING AND WATCHING.

A Sermon

INTENDED FOR READING ON LORD'S-DAY, MAY 1ST, 1892,

DELIVERED BY

C. H. SPURGEON,

AT THE METROPOLITAN TABERNACLE, NEWINGTON,

On Thursday Evening, July 24th, 1890.

"Nevertheless we made our prayer unto our God, and set a watch against them day and night, because of them."—Nehemiah iv. 9.

NEHEMIAH, and the Jews with him, were rebuilding the walls of Jerusalem. Sanballat and others were angry with them, and tried to stop the work. They determined to pounce upon the people on a sudden, and slay them, and so to put an end to what they were doing. Our text tells us what Nehemiah and his companions did in this emergency: "Nevertheless we made our prayer unto our God, and set a watch against them day and night, because of them."

These people had not only to build the wall of Jerusalem, but to watch against their enemies at the same time. Their case is ours. We have to work for Christ. I hope that all of us who love him are trying to do what we can to build up his kingdom; but we need also to watch against deadly foes. If they can destroy us, of course they will also destroy our work. They will do both, if they can. The powers of evil are mad against the people of God. If they can in any way injure or annoy us, you may rest assured that they will do so. They will leave no stone unturned, if it can serve their purpose. No arrows will be left in the quivers of hell while there are godly men and women at whom they can be aimed. Satan and his allies will aim at our hearts every poisoned dart they have.

Nehemiah had been warned of the attack that was to be made upon the city. The Jews who lived near these Samaritans had heard their talk of what they meant to do, and they came and told Nehemiah of the plotting of the adversaries. We also have been warned. As our Lord said to Peter, "Simon, Simon, Satan hath desired to have you, that he may sift you as wheat," so has he, in his word, told us that there is a great and terrible evil power which is seeking our destruction. If Satan can do it, he will not only sift us as wheat, but he will cast us into the fire that we may be destroyed. Brethren, "we are not ignorant of his devices." You are not left in a fool's paradise, to dream of security from trial, and to fancy that you are past temptation.

No. 2,254.

It was well for these people, also, that, being in danger, and being aware of the malice of their enemies, they had a noble leader to incite them to the right course to be pursued. Nehemiah was well qualified for his work. He gave the Jews very shrewd, sensible, and yet spiritual advice, and this was a great help to them in their hour of need. Beloved, we have a better Leader than Nehemiah; we have our Lord Jesus Christ himself, and we have his Holy Spirit, who dwells in us, and shall be with us. I beg you to listen to his wise and good advice. I think he will give it to you through our explanation of the text. He will say to you, what Nehemiah, in effect, said to these people, "Watch and pray." Although the adversaries of the Jews conspired together, and came to fight against Jerusalem, and to hinder the work of rebuilding the wall, Nehemiah says, "Nevertheless we made our prayer unto our God, and set a watch against them day and night, because of them."

In the text, I see *two guards;* first, *prayer:* "We made our prayer unto our God." The second guard is *watchfulness:* "We set a watch." When I have spoken on these two subjects, I shall take, as my third topic, *the two guards together.* "We prayed, and we set a watch." We must have them both if we would defeat the enemy.

I. First, then, dear friends, think of THE FIRST GUARD: "We made our prayer unto our God."

Speaking of this prayer, I would hold it up as a pattern for our prayers in a like condition. It was *a prayer that meant business.* Sometimes, when we pray, I am afraid that we are not transacting business at the throne of grace; but Nehemiah was as practical in his prayer as he was in the setting of the watch. Some brethren get up in our prayer-meetings, and say some very good things; but what they really ask for, I am sure I do not know. I have heard prayers of which I have said, when they were over, "Well, if God answers that prayer, I have not the least idea what he will give us." It was a very beautiful prayer, and there was a great deal of explanation of doctrine and experience in it; but I do not think that God wants to have doctrine or experience explained to him. The fault about the prayer was, that there was not anything asked for in it. I like, when brethren are praying, that they should be as business-like as a good carpenter at his work. It is of no use to have a hammer with an ivory handle, unless you aim at the nail you mean to drive in up to the head; and if that is your object, an ordinary hammer will do as well as a fine one, perhaps better. Now, the prayers of Nehemiah and the Jews were petitions for divine protection. They knew what they wanted, and they asked for it definitely. Oh, for more definiteness in prayer! I am afraid our prayers are often clouds, and we get mists for answers. Nehemiah's prayers meant business. I wish we could always pray in this way. When I pray, I like to go to God just as I go to a banker when I have a cheque to be cashed. I walk in, put the cheque down on the counter, the clerk gives me my money, I take it up, and go about my business. I do not know that I ever stopped in a bank five minutes to talk with the clerks; when I have received my change, I go away and attend to other matters. That is how I like to pray; but there is a way of praying that seems like lounging near the mercy-seat, as though one had no particular reason for being found there. Let it not be so with you, brethren. Plead the promise, believe it, receive the blessing God is ready to give, and go about your business. The prayer of Nehemiah and his companions meant business.

In the next place, it was *a prayer that overcame difficulties.* The text begins with a long word, "nevertheless." If we pull it to pieces, we get three words, never the less; when certain things happen, we will pray never the less; on the contrary, we will cry to our God all the more. Sanballat sneered; but we prayed never the less, but all the more because of his sneers. Tobiah uttered a cutting jest; but we prayed never the less, but all the more because of his mocking taunt. If men make a jest of your religion, pray none the less. If they even become cruel and violent to you, pray none the less; never the less, not a word less, not a syllable less, not a desire less, and not any faith less. What are your difficulties, dear friend, in coming to the mercy-seat? What hindrance lies in your way? Let nothing obstruct your approach to the throne of grace. Turn all stumbling-stones into stepping-stones; and come, with holy boldness, and say, notwithstanding all opposition, "never the less, we made our prayer unto our God." Nehemiah's prayer meant business, and overcame difficulties.

Notice, next, that it was *a prayer that came before anything else.* It does not say that Nehemiah set a watch, and then prayed; but "nevertheless we made our prayer unto our God, and set a watch." Prayer must always be the fore horse of the team. Do whatever else is wise, but not till thou hast prayed. Send for the physician if thou art sick; but first pray. Take the medicine if thou hast a belief that it will do thee good; but first pray. Go and talk with the man who has slandered you, if you think you ought to do so; but first pray. "Well, I am going to do so and so," says one, "and I shall pray for a blessing on it afterwards." Do not begin it till you have prayed. Begin, continue, and end everything with prayer; but especially begin with prayer. Some people would never begin what they are going to do if they prayed about it first, for they could not ask God's blessing upon it. Is there anybody here who is going out of this Tabernacle to a place where he should not go? Will he pray first? He knows that he cannot ask a blessing on it; and therefore he ought not to go there. Go nowhere where you cannot go after prayer. This would often be a good guide in your choice of where you should go. Nehemiah first prayed, and then set a watch.

Once more, it was *a prayer that was continued.* If I read the passage aright, "we made our prayer unto our God, and set a watch against them day and night," it means that, as long as they watched, they prayed. They did not pray their prayer, and then leave off, and go away, as naughty boys do when they give runaway knocks at a door. Having begun to pray, they continued praying. So long as there were any enemies about, the prayer and the watching were never parted. They continued still to cry to him who keepeth Israel as long as they set the watchman of the night to warn them of the foe.

When shall we leave off praying, brothers and sisters? Well, they say that we shall do so when we get to heaven. I am not clear about that. I do not believe in the intercession of saints for us; but

I remember that it is written in the book of Revelation, that the souls under the altar cried, "How long, O Lord?" Those souls are waiting for the resurrection, waiting for the coming of Christ, waiting for the triumph of his kingdom; and I cannot conceive of their waiting there without often crying, "O Lord, how long? Remember thy Son, glorify his name, accomplish the number of thine elect." But certainly, as long as we are here, we must pray. One lady, who professed that she had long been perfect, said that her mind was in such complete conformity with the mind of God, that she need not pray any longer. Poor creature! What did she know about the matter? She needed to begin at the first letter of the alphabet of salvation; and pray, "God be merciful to me, a sinner!" When people imagine they need not to pray, the Lord have mercy upon them!

"Long as they live let Christians pray,
For only while they pray they live."

The prayer which Nehemiah offered was, next, *a prayer that was home-made*. There may be some of you who like prayers made for you; and it may be that, if all in the congregation are to join in the supplication, and every voice is to speak, the prayer must be prepared even as the hymn is; but ready-made prayers always seem to me very much like ready-made clothes, they are meant to fit everybody, and it is very seldom that they fit anybody. For real business at the mercy-seat, give me a home-made prayer, a prayer that comes out of the deeps of my heart, not because I invented it, but because God the Holy Spirit put it there, and gave it such living force that I could not help letting it come out. Though your words are broken, and your sentences disconnected; if your desires are earnest, if they are like coals of juniper, burning with a vehement flame, God will not mind how they find expression. If you have no words, perhaps you will pray better without them than with them. There are prayers that break the backs of words; they are too heavy for any human language to carry.

This prayer, then, whatever it may have been as to its words, was one the pleaders made: "We made our prayer unto our God."

It is very important to notice, however, that it was *a prayer that went to the home of prayer*: "We made our prayer unto our God." You have heard of the man who prayed at Boston, "the hub of the universe", and the report in the paper the next morning was, that "The Rev. Dr. So-and-so prayed the finest prayer that was ever addressed to a Boston audience." I am afraid that there are some prayers of that sort, that are prayed to the congregation. That is not the kind of prayer that God loves. Forget that there is anybody present, forget that a human ear is listening to your accents; and let it be said of your prayer, "Nevertheless we made our prayer unto our God."

It is a very commonplace remark to make, that prayer must go to God if it is to be of any avail; but it is very necessary to make it. When prayer does not go to God, what is the good of it? When you come out of your closet, and feel that you have only gone through a form, how much are you benefited? Make your prayer unto your God.

Speak in his ear, knowing that he is there; and come away knowing that he has replied to you, that he has lifted up the light of his countenance upon you. That is the kind of prayer we need for our protection against our enemies both day and night.

Only once more upon this first point. I gather from the words before me that it was *a prayer saturated with faith.* "We made our prayer unto—God"? No, "unto our God." They had taken Jehovah to be their God, and they prayed to him as their God. They had a full assurance that, though he was the God of the whole earth, yet he was specially their God; and so they made their prayer unto the God who had given himself to them, and to whom they belonged by covenant relationship. "We made our prayer unto *our God.*" Those two little words carry a vast weight of meaning. The door of prayer seems to turn on those two golden hinges,—" our God." If you and I are to be delivered from the evil that is in the world, if we are to be kept building the church of God, we must have for our first guard, mighty, believing prayer, such as Nehemiah and his Jewish friends presented unto the Lord.

II. I have now to speak to you about THE SECOND GUARD: "We set a watch against them day and night, because of them."

This setting of the watch was *a work appointed.* "We set a watch." Nehemiah did not say, "Now, some of you fellows, go and watch," leaving the post of watchmen open to any who chose to take it; but they "set a watch." A certain number of men had to go on duty at a certain point, at a certain hour, and to remain for a certain length of time, and to be on guard against the adversary. "We set a watch." Brethren, if we are to watch over ourselves, and we must do so, we must do it with a definite purpose. We must not say, "I must try to be watchful." No, no; you must be watchful; and your watchfulness must be as distinct and definite an act as your prayer. "We set a watch." Some of you have seen the guards changed at the barracks; there is a special time for each company to mount guard. When you go to bed at night, pray the Lord to guard you during the darkness. In the morning, set a watch when you go to your business. Set a watch when you go to the dinner-table; set a watch when you return home. Oh, how soon we may be betrayed into evil unless we set a watch!

It was *a work carefully done;* for Nehemiah says, "We set a watch against them day and night, because of them." Those last three words would be better rendered, "over against them"; that is, wherever there was an enemy, there he set a watch. They are likely to come up this way. Very well, set a watch there. Perhaps they may shift about, and come up this way. Very well, set a watch there. Possibly they may come climbing over the wall in front here. Well, set a watch there. "We set a watch over against them." One brother has a very hot temper. Brother, set a watch there. Another is very much inclined to levity. Brother, set a watch there. Another is very morose at home, critical, picking holes in other people's coats. Brother, set a watch there. One friend has a tendency to pride, another to unbelief. Set a watch wherever the foe is likely to come. "We made our prayer unto our God, and set a watch over against them."

It was *a work continued;* Nehemiah says, "we set a watch against them day and night." What! is there to be somebody sitting up all night? Of course there is. If Sanballat had told them when he meant to attack them, they might have gone to sleep at other times; but as he did not give them that information, they had to set a watch "day and night." The devil will not give you notice when he is going to tempt you; he likes to take men by surprise; therefore, set a watch day and night.

It was *a work quickened by knowledge.* They knew that Sanballat would come if he could, so they set a watch. The more you know of the plague of your own heart, the more you will set a watch against it. The more you know of the temptations that are in the world through lust, the more should you set a watch. The older you are, the more you should watch. "Oh!" says an aged friend, "you should not say that; it is the young people who go wrong." Is it? In the Old Testament or in the New, have you an instance of a young believer who went astray? The Bible tells us of many old men who were tripped up by Satan when they were not watching; so you have need to set a watch even when your hair turns grey, for you will not be out of gunshot of the devil until you have passed through the gate of pearl into the golden streets of the New Jerusalem.

You and I, dear friends, have need to set a watch against the enemies of our holy faith. Some people ask me, "Why do you talk so much about the 'Down-grade'? Let men believe what they like. Go on with your work for God, and pray to him to set them right." I believe in praying and setting a watch. We have to guard with jealous care "the faith once for all delivered to the saints." When you find, as you do find now, professing Christians and professing Christian ministers denying every article of the faith, or putting another meaning upon all the words than they must have been understood to bear, and preaching lies in the name of the Most High, it is time that somebody set a watch against them. A night-watchman's place is not an easy berth; but I am willing to take that post for my blessed Master's sake. Those professed servants of Christ who enter into an unholy alliance with men who deny the faith will have to answer for it at the last great day. As for us, brethren, when our Lord comes, let him find us watching as well as praying.

But, dear friends, to come home to ourselves, we must set a watch against our own personal adversaries. I hope that, in one sense, you have no personal enemies; that you owe nobody a grudge; but that you live in peace and love towards all mankind. But there are Christian people here, who will go to homes where everybody in the house is against them. Many a godly woman goes from the sanctuary to a drunken husband; many children, converted to God, see anything but what they like to see in their homes. What are they to do in such circumstances? Set a watch. Dear woman, how do know but that you shall be the means of saving your unconverted husband? If so, you must set a watch; do not give him a bit of your mind; you will not convert him that way. And you, dear children, who have come to Christ, and joined the church, mind that you are dutiful and obedient, for otherwise you will destroy all hope of bringing your parents to the Saviour. Set a watch, set a watch. "Oh!" say you, "if I do a little wrong, they magnify it." I know they do; therefore, set a watch; be more careful. Set a watch over your temper, set a watch over your tongue, set a watch over your actions. Be patient, be gentle, be loving. May the Spirit of God work all this in you!

But there is another set of enemies, much more dreadful than these adversaries that are without us, the foes within, the evil tendencies of our corrupt nature, against which we must always set a watch. Perhaps you say, "How can I do this?" Well, first, know what they are. People who are beginning the Christian life should seek to know where their weak points are. I should not wonder, dear friend, if your weak point lies where you think that you are strong. Where you think, "Oh, I shall never go wrong there!"—that is the very place where you are likely to fall. Set a watch wherever any weakness has appeared; and if you have, in the past of your Christian life, grieved the Holy Spirit by anything wrong, set a double watch there. Where you tripped once, you may trip again; for you are the same man. Set a watch, also, dear friend, whenever you feel quite secure. Whenever you feel certain that you cannot be tempted in a particular direction, that proves that you are already as proud as Lucifer. Set a watch, set a watch, set a watch. Avoid every occasion of sin. If any course of conduct would lead you into sin, do not go in that direction. I heard a man say, as an excuse for drinking, "You see, if ever I take a glass of beer, I seem to lose myself, and I must have two or three more." Well, then, if that is the case with you, do not take a glass of beer. "But," says one, "if I get into company, I forget myself." Then, do not go into company. Better go to heaven as a hermit, than go to hell with a multitude. Pluck out your right eye, and cut off your right hand, sooner than that these should cause you to fall into sin. Do not go where you are likely to be tempted. "Well," says one, "but my business calls me into the midst of temptation." I grant you that your business may compel you to go where there are ungodly men; for how could some live at all, if they had not to come into contact with the ungodly?—they would have to go out of the world. Well, then, if that is your case, put on the whole armour of God, and do not go without being prepared to fight the good fight of faith. Set a watch, set a watch, set a watch.

Watch against the beginnings of sin. Remember, Satan never begins where he leaves off; he begins with a little sin, and he goes on to a greater one. When he first tempts men, he does not aim at all he hopes to accomplish; but he tries to draw them aside by little and little, and he works up by degrees to the greater sin he wants them to commit. I do not believe that, at the present time, a Christian man can be too precise. We serve a very precise God: "the Lord thy God is a jealous God." Keep out of many things in which professing Christians now indulge themselves. The question is, whether they are Christians at all. If we must not judge them, at any rate, let us judge for ourselves, and settle it, once for all, that we dare not go where they go; indeed, we have no wish to do so.

Watch for what God has to say to you. In your reading of the Bible, if the Holy Spirit applies a text of Scripture to you with special force, regard it as a hint from your heavenly Father that there is a lesson in it for you. I am often surprised at the way in which the morning text will often instruct me through the whole day. Persons who come to hear the Word of God preached, often find that, within two or three days, there is a reason why the preacher delivered that particular sermon, and a reason why they were led to hear it.

Whenever you see a professing Christian going astray from the way of holiness, do not talk about it, and so increase the mischief. "It is an ill bird that fouls its own nest." Instead of speaking of another's fall, set a watch for yourself, and say, "That is where he slipped, and that is where I may stumble if the grace of God does not keep me. Remember our Saviour's words to the three disciples with him in Gethsemane, "Watch and pray, that ye enter not into temptation."

III. I finish by putting THE TWO GUARDS TOGETHER. "We made our prayer unto our God, and set a watch against them."

Dear friends, neither of these two guards is sufficient alone. *Prayer alone* will not avail. To pray and not to watch, is presumption. You pretend to trust in God, and yet you are throwing yourself into danger, as the devil would have had Christ do, when he tempted him to cast himself down from a pinnacle of the temple. If you pray to be kept, then be watchful.

Prayer without watchfulness is hypocrisy. A man prays to be kept from sin, and then goes into temptation; his prayer is evidently a mere piece of mockery; for he does not carry it out in his practice.

Sometimes, however, ignorance may lead to prayer without watching. There are other things which ought not to be omitted. Let me tell you a simple story. There was a little school-girl who did not often know her lessons, and there was another girl, who sat near her, who always said her lessons correctly. Her companion said to her, "Jane, how is it that you always know your lessons?" Jane replied, "I pray to God to help me, and so I know them." The next day, the other little girl stood up, but she did not know her lesson; and afterwards she said to her friend, "I prayed to God about my lesson, but I did not know it any better than I did yesterday." Jane said, "But did you try to learn the lesson?" "No," she said; "I prayed about it, and I thought that was sufficient." Of course she did not know her lesson without learning it. In the same manner, you must watch as well as pray. There must be the daily guard set upon tongue, and thought, and hand; or else prayer will be in vain.

I have known some people run great risks, and yet say that they have prayed to the Lord to preserve them. I have heard, dozens of times, these words, "I made it a matter of prayer," and I have been ready to grow angry with the man who has uttered them. He has done a wrong thing, and he has excused himself because he says that he made it a matter of prayer. A young man married an ungodly young woman, and yet he said that he made it a matter of prayer! A Christian woman married an ungodly man, and when someone blamed her for disobeying the Word of God, she said that she made it a matter of prayer! If you had really sought divine guidance, you would not have dared to do what the Scriptures expressly forbid to a child of God. Prayer without watching is not sufficient to preserve us from evil.

On the other hand, dear friends, *watching without praying* is equally futile. To say, "I will keep myself right," and never pray to God to keep you, is self-confidence, which must lead to evil. If you try to watch, and do not pray, you will go to sleep, and there will be an end to your watching. It is only by praying and watching that you will be able to keep on your guard. Besides, watching grows wearisome without prayer, and we soon give it up, unless we have a sweet interlude of prayer to give us rest, and to help us to continue watching.

I will not keep you longer when I have said this, *put the two together*, "Watch and pray," or, as my text has it, "Pray and watch." One will help the other. Prayer will call out the watchman, prayer will incite him to keep his eyes open, prayer will be the food to sustain him during the night, prayer will be the fire to warm him. On the other hand, watching will help prayer, for watching proves prayer to be true. Watching excites prayer, for every enemy we see will move us to pray more earnestly. Moreover, watching *is* prayer. If there be true watching, the watching itself is prayer. The two blend the one into the other. Beloved friends, I send you away with my text ringing in your ears, "We made our prayer unto our God, and set a watch against them day and night."

But I have not been speaking to all who are here. Some of you do not pray, some of you cannot set a watch. The message for you is, "Ye must be born again." You cannot attempt Christian duties till first you have the Christian life; and the only way to get the Christian life is to have faith in the Lord Jesus Christ. Come to the fountain which he has filled with his precious blood; wash there, and be clean; and then, quickened by his Spirit, set a watch. I am looking to see some souls brought to Christ at this service, for although I have been preaching to God's people, if they will watch for you, and pray for you, there will come a blessing to you through their watching and their praying. The Lord grant that it may come to many of you! "Seek ye the Lord while he may be found, call ye upon him while he is near." May many seek and find the Lord tonight; and may many call upon him in truth! "Whosoever shall call upon the name of the Lord, shall be saved." God grant that it may be so to everybody here, for Jesu's sake! Amen.

PORTION OF SCRIPTURE READ BEFORE SERMON—Nehemiah iv.

HYMNS FROM "OUR OWN HYMN BOOK"—994, 999, 668.

Exposition by C. H. Spurgeon.

NEHEMIAH IV. 1—23.

Verse 1. *But it came to pass, that when Sanballat heard that we builded the wall, he was wroth, and took great indignation, and mocked the Jews.*

It was needful to rebuild the wall of Jerusalem, which had been lying in ruins. They went on pretty briskly, for everybody had a mind to work. There never was a good work yet but what there were some to oppose it, and there never will be till the Lord comes. Sanballat heard what the Jews were doing, and he was very angry. "He was wroth, and took great indignation." He was all on fire with anger that God's work was being continued.

2. *And he spake before his brethren and the army of Samaria, and said, What do these feeble Jews?*

The enemies of God's people generally take to sneering. It is a very easy way of showing opposition.

2. *Will they fortify themselves? will they sacrifice? will they make an end in a day? will they revive the stones out of the heaps of the rubbish which are burned?*

No doubt these questions were thought to be very witty and very sarcastic. The enemies of Christ are generally good hands at this kind of thing. Well, if it amuses them, I do not know that it need hurt us much; for, after all, it is their way of paying homage to God's power.

3. *Now Tobiah the Ammonite was by him.*

Such a man as Sanballat never lacks friends. If there is a bad man anywhere, there is sure to be another close at hand. The devil does not make a fire with one stick. When he has set the first one alight, he can generally find a faggot to put near it. Tobiah the Ammonite, who was tarred with the same brush as Sanballat the Horonite, was by him.

3. *And he said, Even that which they build, if a fox go up, he shall even break down their stone wall.*

Tobiah, you see, was another great wit. If possible, he excelled his leader in sarcasm. Are any of you the objects of ridicule for Christ's sake? Bear it without being much distressed by it. It will break no bones, after all. If your Lord endured such contradiction of sinners against himself, you may very well bear it without being distressed.

4, 5. *Hear, O our God; for we are despised: and turn their reproach upon their own head, and give them for a prey in the land of captivity; and cover not their iniquity, and let not their sin be blotted out from before thee: for they have provoked thee to anger before the builders.*

This was righteous indignation; but Nehemiah is not a perfect model for us. He was not only stern, but he mingled with his severity a measure of bitterness in his prayer that we must not imitate. Sometimes, when we have seen men plotting against God, seeking to ruin the souls of others, and trying to stop us in our endeavour to build up the church of God, we have felt such language as this trembling on our lips. It were better, however, for us to bow the knee, in humble imitation of our Lord upon the cross, and cry, "Father, forgive them, for they know not what they do."

6. *So built we the wall.*

You half expected to read, "So we stopped building the wall, and answered Sanballat and Tobiah." Not a bit of it. They kept to their work, and let these two men scoff as they pleased.

6. *And all the wall was joined together unto the half thereof: for the people had a mind to work.*

They built the wall half as high as they meant it to be ultimately; but they carried it all round, and joined it well together. If we cannot do all we would like to do, let us do what we can; and let us endeavour, as far as possible, to finish off the part that we do, waiting for better times to carry the walls higher.

7. *But it came to pass, that when Sanballat, and Tobiah, and the Arabians, and the Ammonites, and the Ashdodites, heard that the walls of Jerusalem were made up, and that the breaches began to be stopped, then they were very wroth.*

They were "wroth" before; now they were "very wroth." If a work has no opposition from Satan, we may be half afraid it is good for nothing. If you cannot make the devil roar, you have not done him much harm; but the more he roars, the more cause is there for the angels singing the praises of God before the throne.

8. *And conspired all of them together to come and to fight against Jerusalem, and to hinder it.*

It is wonderful how unanimous bad men can be. It has always struck me as a very startling thing, that you have never heard of any division among the devils in hell. There are no sects among the devils; they seem to work together with an awful unanimity of purpose in their wicked design. In this one thing they seem to excel the family of God. Oh, that we were as hearty and united in the service of God as wicked men are in the service of Satan!

9, 10. *Nevertheless we made our prayer unto our God, and set a watch against them day and night, because of them. And Judah said,—*

Judah, you know, was the lion tribe. Christ is "the Lion of the tribe of Judah." But Judah, instead of being lion-hearted, made a noise more like a mouse than a lion, for Judah said,—

10. *The strength of the bearers of burdens is decayed, and there is much rubbish; so that we are not able to build the wall.*

Poor Judah! He ought to have been bolder and braver; but he was not. It is the same to-day; some, who seemed to be pillars, prove very weak in the hour of trial, and by their cowardice discourage the rest.

11. *And our adversaries said, They shall not know, neither see, till we come in the midst among them, and slay them, and cause the work to cease.*

While some were discouraging the people within the city, their enemies, without the walls, were plotting to take them by surprise, and slay them.

12. *And it came to pass, that when the Jews which dwelt by them came, they said unto us ten times, From all places whence ye shall return unto us they will be upon you.*

These Jews ought to have been helping to build the wall; but they did not come up to the help of the Lord's people. Still, they were sufficiently friendly to tell Nehemiah of the plot that was being hatched by his enemies. God knows how, when his enemies are sinking a mine, to undermine them. If secrecy is necessary to the success of evil, somebody speaks out, and tells the story, so that the plot is discovered.

13. *Therefore set I in the lower places behind the wall, and on the higher places, I even set the people after their families with their swords, their spears, and their bows.*

When Nehemiah knew the danger to which the people were exposed, he took measures to guard against it. I like the common-sense of Nehemiah. He kept the families together. "I set the people after their families, with their swords, their spears, and their bows." Beloved friends, I have no greater joy than such as I had last Tuesday, when I received five children of one family, all brought to Christ. May the Lord make our families to be the guards of the church!

14. *And I looked, and rose up, and said unto the nobles, and to the rulers, and to the rest of the people, Be not ye afraid of them.*

Fear may waken us, but it must never be allowed to weaken us. We should put on the armour, and take the sword and spear and bow when there is cause for fear; we should never dream of running away.

14, 15. *Remember the Lord, which is great and terrible, and fight for your brethren, your sons, and your daughters, your wives, and your houses. And it came to pass, when our enemies heard that it was known unto us, and God had brought their counsel to nought, that we returned all of us to the wall, every one unto his work.*

There was no fighting after all. As soon as the enemy knew that their plot was found out, they did not make any assault. One commentator says:—" Some men, if they had been delivered from danger, would have returned every one to the ale-house ; but these men returned every one to his work." They went back to their building, and continued still in the service of the city.

16, 17. *And it came to pass from that time forth, that the half of my servants wrought in the work, and the other half of them held both the spears, the shields, and the bows, and the habergeons ; and the rulers were behind all the house of Judah. They which builded on the wall, and they that bare burdens, with those that laded, every one with one of his hands wrought in the work, and with the other hand held a weapon.*

The sword and the trowel both guarded the city and builded the wall.

18. *For the builders, every one had his sword girded by his side, and so builded. And he that sounded the trumpet was by me.*

What the trumpet was for, we are told directly.

19, 20. *And I said unto the nobles, and to the rulers, and to the rest of the people, The work is great and large, and we are separated upon the wall, one far from another. In what place therefore ye hear the sound of the trumpet, resort ye thither unto us: our God shall fight for us.*

That is a grand sentence. The moment you hear the trumpet, you are to leave your place on the wall, and come to the point where the enemy is attacking us. But Nehemiah does not say, " You shall fight for us," he puts it much better, " Our God shall fight for us." So he will still.

21. *So we laboured in the work : and half of them held the spears from the rising of the morning till the stars appeared.*

They made long days. Christian people do not want merely eight hours a day for Christ. We can sometimes do eighteen hours' work for him in a day; and we wish that we could do twenty-four.

22, 23. *Likewise at the same time said I unto the people, Let every one with his servant lodge within Jerusalem, that in the night they may be a guard to us, and labour on the day. So neither I, nor my brethren, nor my servants, nor the men of the guard which followed me, none of us put off our clothes.*

Nehemiah was a good leader. He did not say, " Go," he said, " Come "; and he bore the brunt of the service. Like Alexander, who went with the Macedonians into the rough places, and did the hard work, so did Nehemiah. He and those with him did not put off their clothes even for sleeping.

23. *Saving that every one put them off for washing.*

Which was necessary ; for cleanliness is next to godliness. The Lord send us more Nehemiahs, and plenty of people to work with them, who can endure hardness as good soldiers of Jesus Christ, and who will also be good builders of the church of God!

Metropolitan Tabernacle Pulpit.

GOD JUSTIFIED, THOUGH MAN BELIEVES NOT.

A Sermon

INTENDED FOR READING ON LORD'S-DAY, MAY 8TH, 1892,

DELIVERED BY

C. H. SPURGEON,

AT THE METROPOLITAN TABERNACLE, NEWINGTON,

On Lord's-day Evening, August 31st, 1890.

"For what if some did not believe? shall their unbelief make the faith of God without effect? God forbid: yea, let God be true, but every man a liar; as it is written, That thou mightest be justified in thy sayings, and mightest overcome when thou art judged."—Romans iii. 3, 4.

THE seed of Israel had great privileges even before the coming of Christ. God had promised by covenant that they should have those privileges; and they did enjoy them. They had a revelation and a light divine, while all the world beside sat in heathen darkness. Yet so many Jews did not believe, that, as a whole, the nation missed the promised blessing. A great multitude of them only saw the outward symbols, and never understood their spiritual meaning. They lived and died without the blessing promised to their fathers. Did this make the covenant of God to be void? Did this make the faithfulness of God to be a matter of question? "No, no," says Paul, "if some did not believe, and so did not gain the blessing, this was their own fault; but the covenant of God stood fast, and did not change because men were untrue." He remained just as true as ever; and he will be able to justify all that he has said, and all that he has done, and he will do so even to the end. When the great drama of human history shall have been played out, the net result will be that the ways of God shall be vindicated notwithstanding all the unbelief of men.

I am going to talk of our text, at this time, first, as giving to us *a sorrowful reminder*: "For what if some did not believe?" It is sad to be reminded that there always have been some who did not believe. Next, here is *a horrible inference*, which some have drawn from this grievous fact, that is, because some did not believe, it has been hinted that their unbelief would make the faith of God or the faithfulness of God without effect; to which, in the third place, the apostle gives *an indignant reply*: "God forbid: yea, let God be true, but every man a liar; as it is written, That thou mightest be justified in thy sayings, and mightest overcome when thou art judged."

No. 2,255.

I. Well now, first, we have here A SORROWFUL REMINDER. There always have been some who have not believed.

When God devised the great plan of salvation by grace; when he gave his own Son to die as the Substitute for guilty men; when he proclaimed that whosoever believed in Jesus Christ should have everlasting life; you would have thought that everybody would have been glad to hear such good news, and that they would all have hastened to believe it. Christ is so suitable to the sinner. Why does not the sinner accept him? The way of salvation is so simple, so suitable to guilty men, it is altogether so glorious, so grand, that if we did not know the depravity of the human heart, we should expect that every sinner would at once believe the gospel, and receive its boons. But, alas, some have not believed!

Now, *this is stated very mildly*. The apostle says, "For what if some did not believe?" He might have said, "What if many did not believe?" But he is talking to his Hebrew friends, and he wishes to woo them; so he states the case as gently as he can. Remember, dear friends, the carcases of all but two who came out of Egypt fell in the wilderness through unbelief. Only Joshua and Caleb entered the promised land; but the apostle does not wish to unduly press his argument, or speak so as to aggravate his hearers; and he therefore puts it, "For what if some did not believe?" Even in his own day he might have said, "The bulk of the Jewish nation has rejected Christ. Wherever I go, they seek my life. They would stone me to death, if they could, because I preach a dying Saviour's love;" but he does not put it so; he only mentions that some did not believe. Yet this is a very appalling thing, even when stated thus mildly. If all here, except one person, were believers in the Lord Jesus Christ, and it was announced that that one unbeliever would be pointed out to the congregation, I am sure we should all feel in a very solemn condition. But, dear friends, there are many more than one here who have not believed on the Son of God, and who, therefore, are not saved. If the unconverted were not so numerous as they are, they would be looked upon with horror, with pity, with tears. As they are so numerous, there is all the greater need for our tears and our compassion.

The terms of Paul's question suggest *a very sweet mitigation of the sorrow*. "What if some did not believe?" Then it is implied that some *did* believe. Glory be to God, there is a numerous "some" who have believed that Jesus is the Christ; and believing in him, have found life through his name! These have entered into a new life, and now bear a new character, "being born again, not of corruptible seed, but of incorruptible, by the Word of God, which liveth and abideth for ever." Beloved, we do thank God that the preaching of the gospel has not been in vain. Up yonder, more numerous than the stars are they that walk in white robes which they have washed in the blood of the Lamb; and down here, despite our mourning, there is a glorious company, who still follow the Lamb, who is to them their only hope.

Looking at the other side of the case, it is true that, *at times, the "some" who did not believe meant the majority*. It must be admitted that, sometimes, unbelievers have preponderated even among the hearers of the precious Word. Read the story of Israel through, in the Books of Kings and Chronicles, and you will be saddened to find how again and again they did not believe. The history of Israel, from the moment they became a nation, is a very painful one. It is full of the mercy of God; but also full of the treachery of the human heart. In the days of the judges, the people served God while a good judge ruled over them; but as soon as he was dead, they went astray after false gods. I almost think that the Christian Church is in the period of the judges now. When the Lord raises up, here one and there another, to preach his Word faithfully, the people seem to take heed to it; but when the faithful preachers are gone, many of their hearers turn aside again. Blessed be God, we expect the coming of the King soon; and when the King comes, and the period of the judges shall have ended, then shall we enter upon a time of rest and peace. It may be that, even among hearers of the gospel, those who do not believe preponderate over those who do believe. My text sounds like a solemn knell, and there is something terribly awful about it, like the deep rumbling of underground thunder.

Now, dear friends, this unbelief has usually been the case throughout all ages *among the great ones of the earth.* In our Saviour's day they said, " Have any of the rulers or of the Pharisees believed on him?" The gospel has usually had a free course among the poor, and among those whom some call "the lower orders", though why they are said to be lower than others, I do not know, unless it is because the heavier and more valuable things generally sink to the bottom. The church of God owes very little to kings and princes and nobles. She owes far more to fishermen and peasants. Jesus said, "I thank thee, O Father, Lord of heaven and earth, because thou hast hid these things from the wise and prudent, and hast revealed them unto babes. Even so, Father: for so it seemed good in thy sight." I suspect that, until the King himself shall come, we shall still find that the common people will gladly hear the gospel; and that, while Christ the Lord will choose for his own some from all ranks and conditions of men, it will still be true that "not many wise men after the flesh, not many mighty, not many noble, are called."

I think we may also say, with deep solemnity, that *some who have not believed have belonged to the religious and to the teaching class.* In the days of our Lord and his apostles, the scribes and Pharisees were the greatest haters of the doctrine of Christ. Those whom you might have supposed, being most familiar with the Scriptures, the scribes, would soonest have recognized the Messiah, were the men who would not acknowledge him. So it was with the priests, even the chief priests, the men who had to do with the sacrifices and with the temple. They rejected Christ, although they were the religious leaders of the people. Do you suppose it is very different now? Alas, my friends, we may be preachers, and yet not preach the gospel of Christ; we may be members of the church, and yet not savingly know the gospel; we may go in and out of the house of God, and seem to take part in its holy service, and yet, all the while, we may be strangers and foreigners in the presence of the Most High. Believers are not always those whom you would suppose to be believers. The Lord often brings to himself, as in the case of the centurion, of whom we read this morning, far-off ones, rough soldiers, who were not thought likely to feel the power of such gentle teaching as the doctrine of the cross; and they bow before the Saviour. But alas! alas! among those who appear to be the children of the kingdom, brought up in the worship of God, there are some, yea, many, who have not believed on Christ; and, saddest of all, even among those who are the teachers of others in the things of God, there are some that have not savingly believed.

Now, dear friends, if we take the whole range of *the nations favoured with the gospel*, we shall have to say, and say it, as it were, in capital letters, "SOME DO NOT BELIEVE," and that "some" is a very large number. The question of the apostle is, "What if some did not believe?" Well, if I had to ask and answer that question, at this time, I would say, "What if some do not believe?" Then they are lost. "He that believeth not is condemned already, because he hath not believed in the name of the only-begotten Son of God." There still remains, to those who hear the gospel, the opportunity to believe; and, believing, they shall find life through the sacred name. Let us pray for them. If some do not believe, let us, who do believe, make them the constant subject of our prayers; and then let us tell them what is to be believed, and bear our witness to the saving power of the gospel. When we have done that, let us scrupulously take care that our life and conduct are consistent with the doctrine that we teach, so that, if some do not believe, they may be won to Christ by the example of those who do believe in him. Oh, that every Christian here would seek to bring another person to Christ! I pray you, beloved, if you have tasted that the Lord is gracious, be not barren nor unfruitful. If you know the great secret, tell it to others. Tell it out; tell it out; we all want stirring up to this blessed work; I am sure we do. I heard of a Christian who always spoke about Christ to, at least, one person every day. I commend the example for your imitation. How many of us could say that we do that? I know there are some here who do ten times as much as that. It has grown to be a habit with them to speak of Christ to every one they meet; but it is not the habit even of all who believe. It takes some Christians a long time to begin to say anything for their Lord. Let us try and labour hard, that, if some people do not believe, we may bring them to the Saviour, that God may have praise from them also.

II. But now I advance a step further, and dwell upon A HORRIBLE INFERENCE drawn from the fact that some did not believe. The inference was, that their unbelief had made the faith of God, or the faithfulness of God, altogether without effect. I will translate what Paul said without dwelling on his words.

Some will say, "If So-and-so and So-and-so do not believe the gospel, then *religion is a failure.*" We have read of a great many things being failures nowadays. A little time ago, it was a question whether marriage was not a failure. I suppose that, by-and-by, eating our dinners will be a failure, breathing will be a failure, everything will be a failure. But now the gospel is said to be a failure. Why? Because certain gentlemen of professed culture and supposed knowledge do not believe it. Well, dear friends, there have been other things that have not been believed in by very important individuals, and yet they have turned out to be true. I am not quite old enough to remember all that was said about the introduction of the steam-engine, though I remember right well going to see a steam-engine and a railway-train as great wonders when I was a boy. Before the trains actually ran, all the old coachmen, and all the farmers that had horses to sell, would not believe for a moment that an engine could be made to go on the rails, and to drag carriages behind it; and in parliament they had to say that they thought they could produce an engine that could go at the speed of eight miles an hour. They dare not say more, because it would be incredible if they did. According to the wise men of the time, everything was to go to the bad, and the engines would blow up the first time they started with a train. But they did not blow up, and everybody now smiles at what those learned gentlemen (for some of them were men of standing and learning) ventured then to say. Look at the gentlemen who now tell us that the gospel is a failure. They are the successors of those who have risen up, one after the other; whose principal object has been to refute all that went before them. They call themselves philosophers; and, as I have often said, the history of philosophy is a history of fools, a history of human folly. Man has gone from one form of philosophy to another, and every time that he has altered his philosophy, he has only made a slight variation in the same things. Philosophy is like a kaleidoscope. The philosopher turns it round, and exclaims that he has a new view of things. So he has; but all that he sees is a few bits of glass, which alter their form at every turn of the toy. If any of you shall live fifty years, you will see that the philosophy of to-day will be a football of contempt for the philosophy of that period. They will speak, amidst roars of laughter, of evolution; and the day will come, when there will not be a child but will look upon it as being the most foolish notion that ever crossed the human mind. I am not a prophet, nor the son of a prophet; but I know what has befallen many of the grand discoveries of the great philosophers of the past; and I expect that the same thing will happen again. I have to say, with Paul, "What if some did not believe?" It is no new thing; for there have always been some who rejected the revelation of God. What then? You and I had better go on believing, and testing for ourselves, and proving the faithfulness of God, and living upon Christ our Lord, even though we see another set of doubters, and another, and yet another *ad infinitum*. The gospel is no failure, as many of us know.

Is the gospel to be disbelieved because some people will not receive it? I trow not, dear friends. As I have already said, many other things have been believed, although some people have not believed them; and the believers have had the best of it, and so they always will. Has the gospel changed your character? Has the gospel renewed you in the spirit of your mind? Does the gospel cheer and comfort you in the day of sorrow? Does it help you to live, and will it help you to die? Then do not give it up, even though some do not believe it.

Again, dear friends, *has God failed to keep his promise to Israel* because some Israelites did not believe? That is the point that Paul aims at, and the answer is, "No." He did bring Israel into the promised land, though all but two that came out of Egypt died in the wilderness. He did give that promised land to Israel, albeit that, through their unbelief, they who came out of Egypt could not enter Canaan. Because of their unbelief, God smote them, and they were destroyed; yet a nation came up again from their ashes, and God kept his covenant with his ancient people; and to-day he is keeping it. The "chosen seed of Israel's race" is "a remnant, weak and small"; but the day is coming when they shall be gathered in, and we shall then rejoice; for then shall be the fulness of the Gentiles, also, when Israel has come to own her Lord and King. God has not cast away his people, whom he did foreknow; nor has he broken his covenant made with Abraham, nor will he while the world standeth, even though many believe not on him.

Will *God fail to keep his promise to anyone who believes on him?* Because some do not believe, will God's promise therefore fail to be kept to those who do believe? I invite you to come and try. When two of John's disciples enquired of Jesus where he dwelt, he said to them, "Come and see." If any person here will try Christ, as I tried him, when yet a youth, as miserable as I could be, and ready to die with despair, if they shall feel in believing such joy as I felt, if they shall experience such a change of character as passed over me when I believed in Christ, they will not tolerate a doubt. What they have known, and felt, and tasted, and handled of the good Word of God, will prove to them that, if some believe not, yet God abideth faithful, he will never deny himself. One said that she believed the Bible because she was acquainted with the Author of it, which is an excellent reason for believing it. You will believe the gospel if you are acquainted with the Saviour who brings that gospel to us. Personal dealings with God in Christ, personal trust in the living Saviour, will put you out of reach of this strange inference that God will be unfaithful because some do not believe in him.

I am going a step further. *Will God be unfaithful to his Son* if some do not believe? I have heard, sometimes, a fear expressed that Christ will lose those for whom he died. I thank God that I have no fear about that. "He shall see of the travail of his soul, and shall be satisfied." I never come to you, and, *in formâ pauperis*, ask you to accept Christ, begging and praying you to take Christ, because otherwise he will be a loser by you. It is you who must beg of him. He giveth grace as a king bestows his favours; nay more, he lovingly condescends to entreat you to come to him. Suppose that you wickedly say, "We will not have Christ to reign over us." If you think that you will rob him of honour, and bring disgrace upon him by your rejection, you make a great mistake. If you will not have him, others will. If you who are so wise will not have Christ, there are plenty, whom you reckon to be fools, who will take him to be their "wisdom, and righteousness, and sanctification, and redemption." If you who are so gay and frivolous will not have my Lord, you will die in your sins; but there are others who will have him. Do not think that you can by any possibility rob him of his glory. "For what if some did not believe?" This word shall yet become true, "The kingdoms of this world are become the kingdoms of our Lord and of his Christ, and he shall reign for ever and ever." If myriads reject him, there will be myriads who will receive him, and in all things he shall have the pre-eminence; and he will return to his Father not defeated, but more than conqueror over all his foes.

To put the question in another shape, "For what if some did not believe?" *Will God alter his revealed truth?* If some do not believe, will God change the gospel to suit them? Will he seek to please their depraved taste? Ought we to change our preaching because of "the spirit of the age"? Never; unless it be to fight "the spirit of the age" more desperately than ever. We ask for no terms between Christ and his enemies except these, unconditional surrender to him. He will bate no jot or tittle of his claims; but he will still come to you, and say, "Submit yourselves; bow down, and own me King and Lord, and take me to be your Saviour. Look unto me, and be ye saved, all the ends of the earth; for I am God, and beside me there is none else." If you wait till there is a revised version of the gospel, you will be lost. If you wait till there is a gospel brought out that will not cost you so much giving up of sin, or so much bowing of your proud necks, you will wait till you find yourselves in hell. Come, I pray you, come even now, and believe the gospel. It cannot be altered to your taste; therefore alter yourself so as to meet its requirements.

Now suppose that these men, who will not believe, should all concert together to proclaim new views in order to upset the gospel. You see, up to the present time, they never have agreed. One wing of Satan's army of doubters always destroys the other. Just now the great scientists say to the modern-thought gentlemen, and say to them very properly, "If there were no serpent, and no Eve, and no Adam, and no flood, and no Noah, and no Abraham, as you tell us now that all this is a myth, then your whole old Book is a lie." I am very much obliged to those who talk thus to the disciples of the higher criticism. They thought that they were going to have all the scientists on their side, to join them in attacking the ancient orthodoxies. There is a split in the enemy's camp; Amalek is fighting Edom, and Edom is contending against Moab.

But suppose that they were all to agree. Well, what would happen then? I thought I saw a vision once, when I was by the seaside. To my closed eyes, there seemed to come down to the beach at Brighton a huge black horse, which went into the water, and began to drink; and I thought I heard a voice that said, "It will drink the sea dry." My great horse grew, and grew, and grew, till it was such a huge creature that I could scarcely measure it; and still it drank, and drank, and drank. All the while the sea did not appear to alter in the least, the water was still there as deep as ever. By-and-by the animal burst, and its remains were washed up on the beach, and there it lay dead, killed by its own folly. That will be the end of this big black horse of infidelity that boasts that it is going to drink up the everlasting gospel.

I remember that Christmas Evans put this truth rather roughly on one occasion. He said, "There was a dog on the hearthrug, and there was a kettle of boiling water on the fire. As the kettle kept puffing out steam and hot water, the dog sat up and growled. The more the kettle kept on puffing, the more the dog growled; and at last he seized the kettle by the throat, and of course the boiling water killed him." Thus will unbelievers do with the gospel. They growl at it to-day; but if they ever join together, and really make an attack upon it, the gospel will be a savour of death unto death to those who oppose it, as it is a savour of life unto life to those who receive it.

Thus have I mentioned this horrible inference.

III. Now I close by speaking very briefly upon AN INDIGNANT REPLY to this horrible inference.

In reply to the question, "Shall their unbelief make the faith of God without effect?" Paul gives *a solemn negative:* "God forbid." All the opponents of the gospel cannot move it by a hair's breadth; they cannot injure a single stone of this divine building. It remains ever the same. Let them do what they may, they cannot alter it.

Then Paul utters *a vehement protestation:* "Yea, let God be true, but every man a liar." Can you picture this great host? Here they come, all the men who ever lived, unnumbered millions! They come marching up; and we stand like the inspecting general at a review, and see them all go by; and as every man passes, he shouts, "The gospel is not true. Christ did not die. There is no salvation for believers in him." The apostle Paul, standing as it were at the saluting-point, and seeing the whole race of mankind go by, says, "God is true, and every one of you is a liar." "Let God be true, but every man a liar." You know the way that we have of counting heads, and if the majority goes in a particular direction, we almost all go that way. If you count the heads, and there is a general consensus of opinion, you are apt to say, "It must be so, for everybody says so." But what everybody says is not therefore true. "Let God be true, but every man a liar." It is a strange, strong expression; but it is none too strong. If God says one thing, and every man in the world says another, God is true, and all men are false. God speaks the truth, and cannot lie. God cannot change; his word, like himself, is immutable. We are to believe God's truth if nobody else believes it. The general consensus of opinion is nothing to a Christian. He believes God's word, and he thinks more of that than of the universal opinion of men.

Paul next uses *a Scriptural argument.* Whenever he gets thoroughly redhot, and wants an overwhelming argument, he always goes to the divine treasury of revelation. He quotes what David had said in the fifty-first Psalm, "That thou mightest be justified in thy sayings, and mightest overcome when thou art judged."

God will be justified in everything that he has said. You may take every line of the Word of God, and rest assured that God will be justified in having directed the sacred penman to write that line.

God shall also be justified when he judges, and when he condemns men. When he pronounces his final sentence upon the ungodly, "Depart from me, ye cursed, into everlasting fire, prepared for the devil and his angels:" he shall be justified even in that dreadful hour.

A very startling expression is used here: "That thou mightest overcome when thou art judged." Think of this enormous evil; here are men actually trying to snatch the balance and the rod from the hand of God; and presuming to judge his judgments, and to sit as if they were the god of God. Suppose that they could be daring enough to do even that, the verdict would be in God's favour. It would be proved that he had neither said anything untrue, nor done anything unjust. We are confident that, although some do not believe God, he will be justified before men and angels, and we shall have nothing to do but to admire and adore him world without end.

Now, I could say much more; but I will not, except just this, I want those who are the Lord's people to be very brave about the things of God. There has been too much of yielding, and apologizing, and compromising. I cannot bear it; it grieves me to see one truth after another surrendered to the enemy. A brother writes to me, saying, "You do not put so much mirth into your preaching as you used to do. When the captain at sea whistles, then all the sailors feel more cheerful." My friend adds, "Whistle a bit." I will do so. This is my way of whistling to cheer my shipmates. I believe in the everlasting God, and in his unchanging truth; and I am persuaded that the gospel will win the day, however long and stern the conflict rages. Therefore, my brethren, be not ashamed of the gospel, nor of Christ your Lord, who died that he might save you eternally. "Watch ye, stand fast in the faith, quit you like men, be strong." Even if it did come to this, that every other man in the world were against the truth of God, stand you to his word, and say, "Let God be true, but every man a liar."

The other word that I have to say is a message to the unsaved. If you are opposed to God, I beseech you give up your opposition at once. This battle cannot end well for you unless you yield yourself to God. He is your Maker and Preserver; every argument we can use ought to convince you that you should be on his side. I pray you remember that, for you to contend with God, is for the gnat to contend with the fire, or the wax to fight with the flame. You must be destroyed if you come into collision with him. Then yield to him at once. "Kiss the Son, lest he be angry, and ye perish from the way, when his wrath is kindled but a little." What is it to kiss the Son? Why, to accept the Lord Christ as your King and Saviour, to ask him to be your peace and your salvation. Ask him now, before that clock ceases its striking. I pray that some may at this moment say, "I will have Christ, and I will be Christ's." The Lord grant it! This great transaction done now, it shall be done for ever; and you and I will meet on the other side of Jordan, in the land of the blessed, and eternally praise him that loved us, and washed us from our sins in his own blood, and made us kings and priests unto God. The Lord be with you, for Jesu's sake! Amen.

PORTION OF SCRIPTURE READ BEFORE SERMON—Romans iii.

HYMNS FROM "OUR OWN HYMN BOOK"—166, 675, 674.

Exposition by C. H. Spurgeon.

ROMANS III.

Verse 1. What advantage then hath the Jew? or what profit is there of circumcision?

If, after all, both Jew and Gentile were under sin, what advantage had the Jew by the covenant under which he lived? Or what was the benefit to him of the circumcision which was his distinctive mark?

2. Much every way: chiefly, because that unto them were committed the oracles of God.

The Jews were God's chronicle-keepers. They had to guard the holy Books, "the oracles of God." They had also to preserve the knowledge of the truth by those divers rites and ceremonies by which God was pleased to reveal himself of old time.

3. For what if some did not believe? shall their unbelief make the faith of God without effect?

Did he not, after all, bless the Jews though among them were unbelievers? Could it be that their unbelief would turn God from his purpose to bless the chosen people? Would their want of faith affect God's faithfulness?

4. God forbid: yea, let God be true, but every man a liar; as it is written, That thou mightest be justified in thy sayings, and mightest overcome when thou are judged.

However faithless men might be, God was still true and faithful. Paul quotes the Septuagint, which thus renders David's words.

5. But if our unrighteousness commend the righteousness of God, what shall we say?

If it so turns out, that even man's sin makes the holiness of God the more illustrious, what shall we say?

5. Is God unrighteous who taketh vengeance? (I speak as a man)

Paul spoke as a mere carnal man might be supposed to speak. If ever we are obliged, for the sake of argument, to ask a question which is almost blasphemous, let us do it very guardedly, and say something to show that we really do not adopt the language as our own, just as Paul says, "I speak as a man." If the very sin of man is made to turn to the glory of God, is God unjust in punishing that sin?

6. God forbid: for then how shall God judge the world?

God will judge the world; and he does judge the world even now. There are judgments against nations already executed, and recorded on the page of history. If God were unjust, how could he judge the world?

7. For if the truth of God hath more abounded through my lie unto his glory; why yet am I also judged as a sinner?

If God has even turned the opposition of evil men to the establishment of his truth, as he has often done; why, then, are men punished for it? These are deep, dark questions, which come out of the proud heart of man, and Paul ventures to answer them.

8. And not rather, (as we be slanderously reported, and as some affirm that we say,) Let us do evil, that good may come? whose damnation is just.

We never said, we never even thought, that we might do evil that good should come; nay, if all the good in the world could come of a single evil action, we have no right to do it. We must never do evil with the hope of advancing God's cause. If God chooses to turn evil into good, as he often does, that is no reason why we should do evil; and it is no justification of sin. The murder of Christ at Calvary has brought the greatest possible benefit to us; yet it was a high crime against God, the greatest of all crimes, when men turned deicides, and slew the Son of God.

9, 10. *What then? are we better than they? No, in no wise: for we have before proved both Jews and Gentiles, that they are all under sin; as it is written.*

Paul had already proved in this Epistle that both Jews and Gentiles were guilty before God. Now he quotes a set of texts, from Israel's own holy Books, to show the universal depravity of men. Notice how he rings the changes on the words "all" and "none."

10—12. *There is none righteous, no, not one: there is none that understandeth, there is none that seeketh after God. They are all gone out of the way, they are together become unprofitable; there is none that doeth good, no, not one.*

This is the character of all unregenerate men. It is a true description of the whole race of mankind, whether Jews or Gentiles. In their natural state, "there is none righteous . . . . there is none that seeketh after God . . . . there is none that doeth good, no, not one."

13. *Their throat is an open sepulchre; with their tongues they have used deceit; the poison of asps is under their lips:*

Paul does not use flattering words, as those preachers do who prate about the dignity of human nature. Man was a noble creature when he was made in the image of God; but sin blotted out all his dignity.

14—19. *Whose mouth is full of cursing and bitterness: their feet are swift to shed blood: destruction and misery are in their ways: and the way of peace have they not known: there is no fear of God before their eyes. Now we know that what things soever the law saith, it saith to them who are under the law:*

The Jews are comprehended here, for they were specially "under the law." The whole chosen seed of Israel, highly privileged as they were, are described in these terrible words that we have been reading, which Paul quoted from their own sacred Books.

19. *That every mouth may be stopped, and all the world may become guilty before God.*

That is the true condition of the whole world, "guilty before God." This is the right attitude for the whole human race, to stand with its finger on its lip, having nothing to say as to why it should not be condemned.

20. *Therefore by the deeds of the law there shall no flesh be justified in his sight: for by the law is the knowledge of sin.*

All that the law does, is to show us how sinful we are. Paul has been quoting from the sacred Scriptures; and truly, they shed a lurid light upon the condition of human nature. This light can show us our sin; but it cannot take it away. The law of the Lord is like a looking-glass. Now, a looking-glass is a capital thing for finding out where the spots are on your face; but you cannot wash in a looking-glass, you cannot get rid of the spots by looking in the glass. The law is intended to show a man how much he needs cleansing; but the law cannot cleanse him. "By the law is the knowledge of sin." The law proves that we are condemned, but it does not bring us our pardon.

21, 22. *But now the righteousness of God without the law is manifested, being witnessed by the law and the prophets; even the righteousness of God which is by faith of Jesus Christ unto all and upon all them that believe:*

We have no righteousness of our own; but God gives us a righteousness through faith in Christ; and he gives that to everyone who believes.

22, 23. *For there is no difference: for all have sinned, and come short of the glory of God;*

There are degrees of guilt; but all men have sinned. There is no difference in that respect, whatever gradations there may be in the sinners.

24. *Being justified freely by his grace through the redemption that is in Christ Jesus:*

Dear hearers, are you all justified, that is, made just, through the redemption that is in Christ Jesus? You are certainly all guilty in the sight of God; have you all been made righteous by faith in the redemption accomplished on the cross by Christ Jesus our Lord? I beg you to consider this question most seriously; and if you must truthfully answer, "No," may God make you tremble, and drive you to your knees in penitence to cry to him for pardon!

25. *Whom God hath set forth to be a propitiation through faith in his blood, to declare his righteousness for the remission of sins that are past, through the forbearance of God;*

God holds back the axe which, were it not for his forbearance, would cut down the barren tree. He still forbears, and he is ready to pardon and blot out all the past if you will but believe in his dear Son.

26, 27. *To declare, I say, at this time his righteousness: that he might be just, and the justifier of him which believeth in Jesus. Where is boasting then?*

Where is it? It is to be found in a great many people. It is common enough; but where ought it to be? Where does it get a footing? It is shut out. There is no room for boasting in the heart that receives Christ. If a man were saved by works, he would have whereof to glory; boasting would not be shut out. But as salvation is all of grace, through faith in Christ, boasting is barred out in the dark, and faith gratefully ascribes all praise to God.

27—31. *It is excluded. By what law? of works? Nay: but by the law of faith. Therefore we conclude that a man is justified by faith without the deeds of the law. Is he the God of the Jews only? is he not also of the Gentiles? Yes, of the Gentiles also: seeing it is one God, which shall justify the circumcision by faith, and uncircumcision through faith. Do we then make void the law through faith? God forbid: yea, we establish the law.*

Whether Jews or Gentiles, there was no salvation for them by the works of the law; the only way in which the circumcised or the uncircumcised could be justified was by faith. This principle does not make void God's law; on the contrary, it establishes it, and sets it on the only right and solid foundation. The gospel of the grace of God is the best vindication of his law.

The Sword and the Trowel, for May, contains the following articles:—Charles Haddon Spurgeon and the Holy of Holies. By Dr. A. T. Pierson. "As thou Wilt." By Pastor J. A. Spurgeon. Our Master's Messages. (Poetry.) By Thomas Spurgeon. De Profundis. (Poetry.) By E. A. Tydeman. Little Miss Bonser. By V. J. Charlesworth. Mr. Spurgeon's Last Drives at Menton. (Illustrated.) By J. W. Harrald. Mr. Spurgeon's R. T. S. Pocket-book. (Eight outlines of sermons made at Menton in December and January.) The Religious Outlook in France. By Pastor G. Samuel. The C. H. Spurgeon Memorial Fund. Pastors' College Brethren's Reminiscences of their glorified President.

PASSMORE AND ALABASTER, 4, PATERNOSTER BUILDINGS, LONDON; and all Booksellers.

A # Metropolitan Tabernacle Pulpit.

DANIEL'S BAND.

A Sermon

INTENDED FOR READING ON LORD'S-DAY, MAY 15TH, 1892,

DELIVERED BY

C. H. SPURGEON,

AT THE METROPOLITAN TABERNACLE, NEWINGTON,

On Lord's-day Evening, August 3rd, 1890.

"O Daniel, a man greatly beloved."—Daniel x. 11.

IT did not do Daniel any harm to know that he was greatly beloved of God; or else he would not have received that information from heaven. Some people are always afraid that, if Christian people obtain full assurance, and receive a sweet sense of divine love, they will grow proud, and be carried away with conceit. Do not you have any such fear for other people, and especially do not be afraid of it for yourselves. I know of no greater blessing that can happen to any man and woman here, than to be assured by the Spirit of God that they are greatly beloved of the Lord. Such knowledge might do some of us, who are Christians, the greatest conceivable good. Daniel was not injured by knowing that he was greatly beloved. It has often been said that Daniel is the John of the Old Testament, and John is the Daniel of the New Testament. Those two men, Daniel and John, were choice saints. They rose to the greatest height of spiritual obedience, and then to the greatest height of spiritual enjoyment.

The knowledge that we are greatly beloved of God, instead of doing us harm, will be a means of blessing in many ways. If you know, my dear brother, of a surety, that you are a man greatly beloved of God, you will become very humble. You will say, "How could God ever love me?

'What was there in me to merit esteem,
Or give the Creator delight?'"

I think a sense of God's love is even more humbling than a sense of our own sin. When the two are blended, they sink the soul very low, not in depression of spirit, but in its estimate of itself.

A sense of God's love will also excite in you great gratitude. "Oh!" you will say, "how can I repay the Lord for such an amazing favour?" You will be conscious that you never can repay him; but you will

No. 2,256.

begin working out all sorts of schemes and plans to try to show how much you value the love of God. You will bring out your alabaster-box from its hiding-place; you will willingly enough break it, and pour the precious ointment upon the dear head of him who has loved you so greatly. I am sure that a certainty of having the love of God shed abroad in the heart by the Holy Ghost, is one of the greatest promoters of holy gratitude; and holy gratitude is the mother of obedience. When we feel how much we owe, then we seek to know the will of God, and take a delight in doing it. Whatsoever he saith unto us, we are glad to do, as a proof that we really are grateful for "love so amazing, so divine."

This will also consecrate us. I believe that, to know certainly that you are greatly beloved of God, will make you feel that you cannot live as others do. You cannot trifle with sin. He who lives in the heart of the king must be faithful to him. If called to stand in God's immediate presence as a courtier and a favourite, you must take care how you behave yourself, and you will do so. "Ye are not your own; for ye are bought with a price: therefore glorify God in your body, and in your spirit, which are God's." In proportion as we are sure of his love, our love to him will burn like coals of juniper, which have a most vehement heat; and everything contrary to the will of God will be consumed in that blessed flame.

A sense of divine love will also strengthen us. What is there that a man cannot do when he is in love even with one of his own race; but when he gets to be in love with God, and knows of a certainty that he is greatly beloved of God, he would cut his way through a lane of devils, he would face an army of angels, and defeat them all; for love is a conquering grace. When faith is side by side with love, it—

"Laughs at impossibilities,
And says, 'It shall be done;'"

and love goes and does it; for there is nothing which the love of God will not enable us to do.

Moreover, this assurance of God's love will make us very courageous. If thou art a man greatly beloved, and thou knowest it, thou wilt be a brave man. Let me never come into collision with the sword of that man whom God greatly loves; he will cut me in halves. The love of God makes a hero of the man on whom it is fixed. He is in the thick of the fray; he defies sin, and death, and hell. He will burn for Christ; he would be ready to burn a thousand times over when once he was assured that he was the object of the peculiar love of God, and like Daniel, could be addressed as "a man greatly beloved."

This will make a man glad. If we are greatly beloved of God, how can we be miserable and discontented? Oh, no! If you are a man greatly beloved, you will trip with light feet over the hills of sorrow. You will be glad in the Lord, even when you have much to depress and discourage you. You will begin the music of heaven even here, for a sense of God's love in the soul sets all the bells of the heart ringing. He is the gladdest man who has the greatest assurance that he is "a man greatly beloved."

I have said all this as a preface, to show you that you need not be afraid of knowing that God loves you. Some seem to think that a state of doubt is a state of discretion. It is a state of folly. Full assurance of the faithfulness and truthfulness of God is nothing but common-sense spiritualized. To believe a lie, is folly; but to believe the truth is wisdom. If thou art a believer in Christ, though the very least and weakest of believers, thou art a man greatly beloved. Believe it, and be not afraid to rejoice in it. It will have no influence over thee but that which is sanctifying and health-giving.

Well, now, to help us to think of Christ's great love to us, I am going to talk a little, first, about *the case of Daniel*, the man greatly beloved; secondly, about *the case of every believer*, for every believer is a man greatly beloved; and thirdly, about *the case of some special saints*, believers who are the elect out of the elect, the choicest of the choice ones of the Most High. Of these it may truly be said that they are men greatly beloved.

I. First, then, let us consider THE CASE OF DANIEL, who was "a man greatly beloved."

Because Daniel was greatly beloved of God, *he was early tried, and enabled to stand*. While he was yet a youth, he was carried into Babylon, and there he refused to eat the king's meat, or to drink the king's wine. He put it to the test whether, if he fed on common pulse, he would not be healthier and better than if he defiled himself with the king's meat. Now, religion does not stand in meat and drink; but, let me say, a good deal of irreligion does, and it may become a very important point with some as to what they eat and what they drink. Daniel was early tested, and because he was a man greatly beloved of God, he stood the test. He would not yield even in a small point to that which was evil. Young man, if God greatly loves you, he will give you an early decision, and very likely he will put you to an early test. If you are greatly loved, you will stand firm, even about so small a thing as what you eat and drink, or something that looks less important than that. You will say, "I cannot sin against God. I must stand fast, even in the smallest matter, in keeping to the law of the Lord my God." If thou art enabled to do that, thou art a man greatly beloved.

Afterwards, Daniel *was greatly envied, but found faultless*. He was surrounded by envious enemies, who could not bear that he should be promoted over them, though he deserved all the honour he received. So they met together, and consulted how they could pull him down. They were obliged to make this confession, "We shall not find any occasion against this Daniel, except we find it against him concerning the law of his God." O dear friend, you are greatly beloved if, when your enemies meet to devise some scheme for your overthrow, they cannot say anything against you except what they base upon your religion. If, when they sift you through and through, their eager, evil eyes cannot detect a fault; and they are obliged to fall back upon abusing you for your godliness, calling it hypocrisy, or some other ugly name, you are a man greatly beloved.

Further, Daniel *was delivered from great peril*. He was cast into the lions' den because he was a man greatly beloved of God. I think I see some shrink back, and I hear them say, "We do not want to go into the lions' den." They are poor creatures, but Daniel was worth putting in the lions' den; there was enough of him to be put there. Some men would be out of place among lions; cats would be more suitable companions for them; indeed, they are such insignificant beings that they would be more at home among mice. Lions' dens would not be at all in their line. They would imitate Solomon's slothful man, and say, "There is a lion without, I shall be slain in the streets." There is not enough manhood in them to bring them into close quarters with the king of beasts. Even among our hearers there are many poor feeble creatures. A clever man preaches false doctrine, and they say, "Very good. Was it not well put?" Another preaches the gospel, and they say, "Very good; very good." Oh, yes! it is all alike good to some of you, you cannot discern between the true and the false; but Daniel could distinguish between good and evil, and therefore he was thrust into the lions' den. It was, however, a den out of which he was delivered. The lions could not eat him, God loved him too well. The Lord preserved Daniel, and he will preserve you, dear friend, if you belong to "Daniel's band." It is one thing to *sing*:—

"Dare to be a Daniel,
Dare to stand alone;"

but it is quite another thing to *be* a Daniel, and dare to stand alone, when you are at the mouth of the lions' den. If you are like Daniel, you will have no cause for fear even then. If your trial should be like going into a den of lions, if you are a man greatly beloved of God, you will come out again. No lion shall destroy you; you are perfectly safe. The love of God is like a wall of fire round about you.

Once more, Daniel was a man greatly beloved, and therefore *he had revelations from God*. Do not open your eyes with wonder, and say, "I wish that I had all the revelations that Daniel had." Listen to what he says: "I Daniel was grieved in my spirit in the midst of my body, and the visions of my head troubled me;" and again: "As for me Daniel, my cogitations much troubled me, and my countenance changed in me; but I kept the matter in my heart." The revelations he received actually made him ill: "I Daniel fainted, and was sick certain days; afterward I rose up, and did the king's business; and I was astonished at the vision, but none understood it." He whom God loves will see things that will astound him; he will see that which will almost kill him; he will see that which will make him faint and sick well nigh unto death. When one said, "You cannot see God and live," another answered, "Then let me see him if I die." So will those who are greatly beloved say, "Let me see visions of God whatever it may cost me. Let me have communion with him even though it should break my heart, and crush me in the dust. Though it should fill me with sorrow, and make me unfit for my daily business, yet manifest thyself to me, my Lord, as thou dost not unto the world!" Even men greatly beloved, when they deal closely with God, have to find out that they are but dust and ashes in his sight. They have to fall down before the presence of his glorious majesty, as the beloved John did when he fell at Christ's feet as dead.

I will make only one more remark upon Daniel's case, and that is this, *he stood in his lot.* Because he was a man greatly beloved, he had this promise with which to close his marvellous book, "Go thou thy way till the end be: for thou shalt rest, and stand in thy lot at the end of the days." He is a man greatly beloved, but he does not understand all that God has revealed; and he is to go his way, and rest quite satisfied that, whether he understood it or not, it would work him no harm; for when the end came, he would have his place and his portion, and he would be with his Lord for ever. The next time you get studying some prophecy of Scripture, which you cannot make out, do not be troubled; but hear the voice of God saying, "Go thy way. Wait awhile. It will all be plain by-and-by. God is with thee. There remains a rest for thee, a crown that no head but thine can wear, a harp that no fingers but thine can play upon, and thou shalt stand in thy lot at the end of the days."

Thus have I briefly described the case of Daniel.

II. In the second place, I am going to speak of THE CASE OF EVERY BELIEVER, who is also greatly beloved of God. I must be very brief, because of the communion service which is to follow.

Every believer has been *called out from others.* My brother, look at the hole of the pit whence thou wast digged. Like Abraham, thou hast been called out from thy family, and from thy father's house. Possibly, you have not a godly relative. Many here are the only ones of their kith and kin that ever knew the Lord, so far as they know of, or can remember. Behold in this the sovereign, electing love of God. Art not thou a man greatly beloved? Even if thou hast come of a godly stock, yet thou hast seen others who seemed to be nearest to the kingdom, and yet have been cast out from it. Admire the grace of God, which has called thee, and thy father, and thy grandfather, and thy brother, and thy wife, and maybe children, too. Oh, be grateful, and bless the name of the Lord! But "who maketh thee to differ from another?" Who but God, the Giver of all grace, has made thee to differ from the ungodly around thee? Therefore, adore him for his matchless mercy, his distinguishing grace.

Remember, too, that if thou hast been called out from a sinful world, and transformed into a child of God, this is the token that thou hast been *chosen from the beginning.* God loved thee long before he began to deal with thee in a way of grace. Ere thou wast born, Christ died for thee; and ere this world was made, God loved thee with an everlasting love.

> "Before the day-star knew its place,
> Or planets ran their round,"

thy name was in his Book; and thine image was on the heart of Christ, whose delights were with the sons of men. Remember his word by the prophet Jeremiah, "I have loved thee with an everlasting love: therefore with lovingkindness have I drawn thee." Feed on that precious truth, inwardly digest it, let it enter into thy very soul. He hath loved me with an everlasting love; then, surely, I may claim the title of "a man greatly beloved."

Remember, too, that in the fulness of time, thou wast *redeemed with the precious blood of Christ.* Thy God took upon himself thy nature, and on the cross he bore thy sins in his own body on the tree. The chastisement of thy peace was upon him, and with his stripes thou art healed. The bloodmark is on thee now; thou art one for whom he died in that special way which secures effectual salvation to thee. He loved his church, and gave himself for it; and this is the song of that church in heaven, "Thou has redeemed us to God by thy blood out of every kindred, and tongue, and people, and nation; and hast made us unto our God kings and priests: and we shall reign on the earth." If thou hast been redeemed by the precious blood of Jesus, verily, I say unto thee, thou art "a man greatly beloved."

Thou hast been also *pardoned, and put among the Lord's children.* Remember thy sin for a moment. Darest thou remember it? Hast thou remembered it? Then forget it, for God has blotted it out. He has cast all thy sins behind his back. The depths have covered them; there is not one of them left. They sank like lead in the mighty waters of oblivion; and they shall never rise to condemn thee. Thou art forgiven. Perhaps thou wast a drunkard, a swearer, disobedient to parents, or unchaste; but whatever thy sin, the blood of Jesus has cleansed thee, and thou art whiter than the snow; and he has covered thee with the robe of his perfect righteousness, and thou art "accepted in the Beloved." Art thou not a man greatly beloved? I remember one who came creeping to the Saviour's feet, it was myself, black as night, condemned in my own conscience, and expecting to be driven to the place where hope could never come. I came to Christ wearing the weeds of mourning; but, in a moment, when I looked to Jesus, he put on me the garments of salvation. He took away my sin, he placed a fair crown upon my head, and set my feet upon a rock, and established my goings. Blessed be his name! If there is a man in the world who can sing,—

> " Oh, 'twas love, 'twas wondrous love,
> The love of God to me!
> It brought my Saviour from above,
> To die on Calvary;"

I am that man; and you can sing it, too, dear friend, cannot you? I mean you who have been forgiven your trespasses for Christ's sake. I feel sure that your heart is speaking now, even if your tongue is silent, and it says, "Indeed, as a pardoned man, I am greatly beloved."

Since the Lord forgave your sin, you have been a praying man, and God has *heard your prayers.* From the horns of the unicorns has he delivered you; out of the depths of the sea have you cried, and he has rescued you, like Jonah. With the psalmist, you can say, "Verily God hath heard me; he hath attended to the voice of my prayer." Are you not greatly beloved? As our friend, Dr. Taylor, said in prayer this morning, we have a mercy-seat to which we can always go. Not only have we gone to it in the past, but we may go to it whenever we need. We have the *entreé* of the King's palace at will. Are we not men greatly beloved?

Beside that, remember that the Lord has *upheld you* until now. In your pilgrim path, how many times your feet have almost gone! How often you have been tempted, ah! worse than that, how often you have yielded to temptation; yet here you are, your character not ruined, your soul not lost, your face toward Jerusalem, and the enemy's foot is not on your neck yet; and it never will be, glory be to the name of the Lord! When I think of all our experiences in the way in which the Lord hath led us, I can truly say of all his people that they are men and women greatly beloved.

Now to-night you are invited to *feast with Christ and his church;* not to come and be dogs under the table, but to sit with him at the royal banquet, with his banner of love waving over you. You are invited to be his companions here, his comrades at this feast. Oh, what a festival is this sacred supper! Haman thought himself honoured when he was invited to his king's banquet; but what shall we say who are bidden to come to this high festival?

> "What food luxurious loads the board,
> When at his table sits the Lord!
> The wine how rich, the bread how sweet,
> When Jesus deigns the guests to meet!"

Only one thing more will I say under this head; but this story is so marvellous, that we may be for ever telling it, and yet it will never all be told. The love of Christ to some of us has been so wonderful, that when we once begin the theme, we seem to forget all about time, and wish there were no fleeting hours to bid us end our story! Eternity itself will not be too long for telling out "the old, old story, of Jesus and his love."

But, what I was going to say is this, *we shall be with him soon.* Some of us sit here heavy at heart; and there are wrinkles on the brow, and there is a weariness in the frame which makes the wheels of life drag heavily. Beloved, it is but the twinkling of an eye, so brief is life, and we shall be with him where he is, and shall behold his glory. Do you ever try to realize the greatness of that love that will take you to be with Christ, to dwell with him, and to share his glory for ever? Can you put the incorruptible crown on your head to-night in fancy; nay, in faith? Can you, even now, begin to wave the palm of victory, and strike the harp of everlasting praise? Do you feel as if you could, even now, join the sacred songsters above, and sing the heavenly hymn, the hallelujah chorus of the ages yet to be? As surely as we are in Christ to-night, we shall be with Christ by-and-by. Oh, men greatly beloved, to have such a future as this before you, ought to make your heaven begun below!

III. Time fails me, so I must speak of THE CASE OF SPECIAL SAINTS, those who are in a peculiar sense men greatly beloved.

There are some men who are, as I said at the beginning of my discourse, elect out of the elect. Remember, that Christ had seventy choice men, his disciples; but then he had twelve choicer men, his apostles; and he had three of these, who were with him when the others were not; and out of these three he had one John, "that disciple whom Jesus loved." His love is so sweet, that, while I would be grateful to be even outside the seventy, so long as I might be among the five hundred brethren who saw him after he rose from the dead, yet I would then have the ambition to get in among the seventy; and not for the honour of it, but for the love it would bring, I would like to be one of the eleven; and for the same reason I would fain be one of the three, and I would, above measure, be thankful if I might be that one whom Jesus loved. Have you not the same holy aspiration?

Well, now, let me tell you that, if you would be among the choicer spirits, greatly beloved of God, you must be *men of spotless character*. Christ loves great sinners; and even saints that fall, and stain their garments, he will not cast away; but you will never enjoy the fulness of Christ's love unless you keep your garments unspotted from the world. You cannot find a fault in Daniel; and if you want to live on earth so as to be in heaven while you are here, and to drink the wine of Christ's love to the bottom of the chalice, even the spiced wine of his pomegranate, you must watch every step, and observe every word; for our Lord is very jealous, and half a word of evil will grieve him. If you would walk in the light as he is in the light, and have constant fellowship with God, I beseech you, be ye perfect, even as your Father which is in heaven is perfect, and follow after unsullied holiness. The pure in heart shall see God. Oh, that you might everyone have this purity! It is those who have not defiled their garments who shall walk with Christ in white.

The next point is, that men who are greatly beloved are *men of decision*. When Daniel had the lions' den in prospect, because of his faithfulness to his God, " he went into his house; and his window being open in his chamber towards Jerusalem, he kneeled upon his knees three times a day, and prayed, and gave thanks before his God, as he did aforetime." There was no compromising in Daniel's case. If you want to be greatly beloved, do not attempt any compromise with sin. Have nothing to do with policy, and craft, and holding with the true and the false at the same time. If God is to use you in his service, you must be like the tribe of Levi, separate from your brethren, and you must ever be ready to stand up bravely for God and for his eternal truth at any cost. It is my earnest desire that we may have in this church many men and women of this kind, who will be, as Mr. Moody puts it, out and out for Christ.

Next, if you would be men greatly beloved of God, beyond all the rest of his people, on whom special shinings of his face shall come, you must be *much in communion with him*. Daniel fasted and prayed, and communed with God with cries and tears; and God came and revealed himself to him. He was greatly beloved, for he lived near to God. He was no far-off follower of his Lord. He dwelt in the full blaze of the Sun of Righteousness.

If a man is to be greatly beloved of God, he must *live above the world*, as Daniel did. Daniel became a prince, a governor, a man of substance and position; but when Belshazzar promised to clothe him with scarlet, and to put a gold chain about his neck, if he could read and interpret the writing on the wall, he said to the king, "Let thy gifts be to thyself, and give thy rewards to another." Daniel did not want them. When he became great in the land, he walked with God as he had done when he was poor. It is a dangerous thing for some people to be made much of in the world; their heads soon get turned, and they begin to think too much of themselves. He who thinks that he is somebody is nobody; and he whose head begins to swim because of his elevation, will soon have it broken because of his tumbling down from his lofty position. Daniel was a man greatly beloved, and God showed his great love to him by setting him in high places, and keeping him there in safety.

Once more, men who are greatly beloved by the Lord *live wholly for God and for God's people.* You see nothing of selfishness about Daniel. He neither seeks to be great nor to be rich. He loves his own people, Israel; he pleads with God for the seed of Abraham. He is patriotic. He loves Jehovah, and he pleads with him for God's own people. Now, if you want to be greatly beloved, give yourselves up to the service of God and his church.

> " Ye that are men, now serve him,
> Against unnumber'd foes;
> Your courage rise with danger,
> And strength to strength oppose."

No man need wish to be born in a time more suitable for heavenly chivalry than this. To stand alone for God in such an evil age as this, is a great honour. I pray that you may be able to avail yourselves of your privileges. How few care to swim against the current! A strong stream is running in opposition to the truth of God. Many say that the Bible is not half inspired. Many are turning away from Christ, refusing to acknowledge his deity, and some blasphemously speak of his precious blood as a thing of the shambles. O sirs! if somebody does not stand out to-day for the cause of God and truth, what is to become of the nominal church and of a guilty world? If you are loyal to Christ, show it now. If you love him, and his infallible Word, prove it now. Then shall you hear him say to you also, "O man greatly beloved, go thou thy way till the end be: for thou shalt rest, and stand in thy lot at the end of the days." God grant it for Jesu's sake! Amen.

PORTION OF SCRIPTURE READ BEFORE SERMON—1 John iv. 9—21.

HYMNS FROM "OUR OWN HYMN BOOK"—810, 808, 735.

Exposition by C. H. Spurgeon.

1 JOHN IV. 9—21.

Verse 9. In this was manifested the love of God toward us, because that God sent his only begotten Son into the world, that we might live through him.

There is love in our creation; there is love in providence; but most of of all there is love in the gift of Christ for our redemption. The apostle here seems to say, "Now I have found the great secret of God's love to us; here is the clearest evidence of divine love that ever was or ever can be manifested toward the sons of men."

10. *Herein is love, not that we loved God, but that he loved us, and sent his Son to be the propitiation for our sins.*

In us there was no love; there was a hatred of God and goodness. The enmity was not on God's side toward us; but on our side toward him. "He loved us, and sent his Son." The gift of Christ, the needful propitiation for our sins, was all of love on God's part. Justice demanded the propitiation, but love supplied it. God could not be just if he pardoned sin without atonement; but the greatness of the love is seen in the fact that it moved the Father to give his Son to an ignominious death, that he might pardon sinners and yet be just.

11. *Beloved, if God so loved us, we ought also to love one another.*

Here we have a fact and an argument. We ought to love. We ought to love after God's fashion; not because men love us, nor because they deserve anything at our hands. We are too apt to look at the worthiness of those whom we help; but our God is gracious to the unthankful and to the evil. He makes his sun to rise and his rain to fall for the unjust as well as for the righteous, therefore we ought to love the unlovely and the unloving. But just as God has a special love for his own people, we who believe in him ought to have a peculiar affection for all who are his.

12. *No man hath seen God at any time.*

We do not need to see him to love him. Love knows how good he is, though she hath not beheld him. Blessed are they who have not seen God, yet who love him with heart, and mind, and soul, and strength.

12. *If we love one another, God dwelleth in us, and his love is perfected in us.*

He is not far to seek. If you love one another, God is in you; he dwells in you, he is your nearest and dearest Friend, the Author of all other love. The grace of love comes from the God of love.

13. *Hereby know we that we dwell in him, and he in us, because he hath given us of his Spirit.*

And his Spirit is the spirit of love. Wherever it comes, it makes man love his fellow-man, and seek his good; and if you have that love in your heart, it came from God, and you dwell in God.

14. *And we have seen*

Yes, there is something that we have seen. John writes for himself and his fellow-apostles, and he says, "No man hath seen God at any time," but—

14. *We have seen and do testify that the Father sent the Son to be the Saviour of the world.*

John saw him live, and saw him die, and saw him when he had risen from the dead, and saw him as he ascended. So he speaks to the matter of eyesight, and bears testimony that, though we have not seen God, we have, in the person of the representative apostles, seen the Son of God who lived and laboured and died for us.

15. *Whosoever shall confess that Jesus is the Son of God, God dwelleth in him, and he in God.*

Let Christ be God to you, and you are saved. If, in very deed, and of a truth, you take him to be the Son of God, and consequently rest your eternal hopes on him, God dwells in you, and you dwell in God.

16. *And we have known and believed the love that God hath to us.*

How far is this true of all of you? How many here can join with the beloved apostle, and say, "We have known and believed the love that God hath to us"? We know it; we have felt it; we are under its power. We know it still, it remains a matter of faith to us; we believe it. We have a double hold of it. "We know," we are not agnostics. "We believe," we are not unbelievers.

16. *God is love; and he that dwelleth in love dwelleth in God, and God in him.*

This is not mere benevolence; there are many benevolent people who still do not dwell in love. They wish well to their fellow-men; but not to all. They are full of indignation at certain men for the wrong that they have done them. John's words teach us that there is a way of living in which you are in accord with God, and with all mankind; you have passed out of the region of enmity into the realm of love. When you have come there, by the grace of God, then God dwells in you, and you dwell in him.

17. *Herein is our love made perfect, that we may have boldness in the day of judgment:*

That is a wonderful expression, "boldness in the day of judgment." According to some, the saints will not be in the day of judgment. Then, what is the use of "boldness in the day of judgment"? As I read my Bible, we shall all be there, and we shall all give an account unto God. I shall be glad to be there, to be judged for the deeds done in my body; not that I hope to be saved by them, but because I shall have a perfect answer to all accusations on account of my sin. "Who is he that condemneth? It is Christ that died, yea rather, that is risen again, who is even at the right hand of God, who also maketh intercession for us." If I am a believer in Christ,—

> "Bold shall I stand in that great day,
> For who aught to my charge shall lay?
> While through thy blood absolved I am
> From sin's tremendous curse and shame."

17. *Because as he is, so are we in this world.*

Happy Christian men, who can say that! If you live among men as Christ lived among men, if you are a saviour to them in your measure, if you love them, if you try to exhibit the lovely traits of character that were in Christ, happy are you.

18. *There is no fear in love;*

When a man loves with a perfect love, he escapes from bondage.

18. *But perfect love casteth out fear: because fear hath torment. He that feareth is not made perfect in love.*

There is a loving, holy fear, which is never cast out. Filial fear grows as love grows. That sacred dread, that solemn awe of God, we must ever cultivate; but we are not afraid of him. Dear heart, God is your best Friend, your choicest love.

"Yea, mine own God is he,"

you can say; and you have no fear of him now. You long to approach him. Though he is a consuming fire, you know that he will only consume what you want to have consumed; and will purify you, and make your gold to shine more brightly because the consumable alloy is gone from it. He will not consume you, but only that which would work for your hurt if it were left within you. Refining fire, go through my heart! Consume as thou wilt! I long to have sin consumed, that I may be like my God. Say you not so, my brethren?

19. *We love him, because he first loved us.*

The reason for our love is found in free grace. God first loved us, and now we must love him; we cannot help it. It sometimes seems too much for a poor sinner to talk about loving God. If an emmet or a snail were to say that it loved a queen, you would think it strange that it should look so high for an object of affection; but there is no distance between an insect and a man compared with the distance between man and God. Yet love doth fling a flying bridge from our manhood up to his Godhead. "We love him, because he first loved us." If he could come down to us, we can go up to him. If his love could come down to such unworthy creatures as we are, then our poor love can find wings with which to mount up to him.

20. *If a man say, I love God,*

Not, "if a man love God," but, if a man *say*, "I love God." It is a blessed thing to be able to say, "I love God," when God himself can bear witness to the truth of our statement; but the apostle says, *If a man say, I love God,—*

20. *And hateth his brother, he is a liar:*

It is very rude of you, John, to call people liars. But it is not John's rough nature that uses such strong language; it is his gentle nature. When a loving disposition turns its face against evil, it turns against it with great vehemence of holy indignation. You can never judge a man's character by his books. Curiously enough, Mr. Romaine, of St. Anne's Church, Blackfriars, wrote the most loving books that could be; yet he was a man of very strong temper indeed. Mr. Toplady wrote some of the sharpest things that were ever said about Arminians; but he was the most loving and gentle young man that ever breathed. So John, full of love and tenderness, hits terribly hard when he comes across a lie. He is so fond of love, that he cannot have it played with, or mocked and mimicked. "If a man say, I love God, and hateth his brother, he is a liar."

20, 21. *For he that loveth not his brother whom he hath seen, how can he love God whom he hath not seen? And this commandment have we from him, That he who loveth God love his brother also.*

This is that "new commandment" which our Lord gave to his apostles, and through them to his whole church, "That ye love one another as I have loved you." John was, in a special sense, "that disciple whom Jesus loved." It was meet, therefore, that he should be the apostle to be inspired by the Holy Spirit to bring "this commandment" to the remembrance of any who had forgotten it, "This commandment have we from him, That he who loveth God love his brother also." God help us so to do, of his great grace! Amen.

The June number of *The Sword and the Trowel* will contain full Reports of the proceedings at the Fifth Annual Conference of the Pastors' College Evangelical Association. The Report of the College for 1891-2, including many interesting reminiscences of the late beloved President, will be in the same number of the Magazine, which will consist of 112 pages. The price will be the same as usual, 3d. Free by post, 5d. Extra copies should be ordered early.

LONDON: PASSMORE & ALABASTER, PATERNOSTER BUILDINGS; and all Booksellers.

Metropolitan Tabernacle Pulpit.

INEXCUSABLE IRREVERENCE AND INGRATITUDE.

A Sermon

INTENDED FOR READING ON LORD'S-DAY, MAY 22ND, 1892,

DELIVERED BY

C. H. SPURGEON,

AT THE METROPOLITAN TABERNACLE, NEWINGTON,

On Lord's-day Evening, July 13th, 1890.

"They are without excuse: because that, when they knew God, they glorified him not as God, neither were thankful."—Romans i. 20, 21.

THIS first chapter of the Epistle to the Romans is a dreadful portion of the Word of God. I should hardly like to read it all through aloud; it is not intended to be so used. Read it at home, and be startled at the awful vices of the Gentile world. Unmentionable crimes were the common pleasures of those wicked ages; but the chapter is also a striking picture of heathenism at the present time. After a missionary had gone into a certain part of Hindostan, and had given away New Testaments, a Hindoo waited upon him, and asked him this question: "Did you not write that first chapter in the Epistle to the Romans after you came here?" "No," replied the missionary, "I did not write it at all; it has been there nearly two thousand years." The Hindoo said, "Well, if it has not been written since you came here, all I can say is, that it might have been so written, for it is a fearfully true description of the sin of India." It is also much more true, even of London, than some of us would like to know. Even here are committed those vices, the very mention of which would make the cheek of modesty to crimson. However, I am not going to talk about Hindoos; they are a long way off. I am not going to speak about the ancient Romans; they lived a couple of thousand years ago. I am going to speak about ourselves, and about some persons here whom my text admirably fits. I fear that I am speaking to some who are "without excuse: because that, when they knew God, they glorified him not as God, neither were thankful."

I. The first charge against those who are mentioned in my text is, WANT OF REVERENCE. "They knew God," but "they glorified him not as God." They knew that there was a God; they never denied his existence; but they had no reverence for his name, they did not render to him the homage to which he is entitled, they did not glorify him as God.

No. 2,257.

Of many this is still true in this form, *they never think of God.* They go from year to year without any practical thought of God. Not only is he not in their words, but he is not in their thoughts. As the Psalmist puts it, "The wicked, through the pride of his countenance, will not seek after God: God is not in all his thoughts." The marginal reading is very expressive: "All his thoughts are, There is no God." Whether there is a God, or not, makes no practical difference to the wicked; they have so little esteem for him that, perhaps, if we could prove that there were no God, they would feel easier in their consciences. There must be something very wrong with you when you would rather that there were no God. "Well," says one, "I do not care much whether there is a God or not; I am an agnostic." Yes, a gentlemen once told me that he was an agnostic. "Oh!" I said, "that is a Greek word, is it not? And the equivalent Latin word is 'Ignoramus.'" Somehow, he did not like it in Latin nearly as well as in Greek. Oh, dear friends, I could not bear to be an "ignoramus" or an "agnostic" about God! I must have a God; I cannot do without him. He is to me as necessary as food to my body, and air to my lungs. The sad thing is, that many, who believe that there is a God, yet glorify him not as God, for they do not even give him a thought. I appeal to some here, whether this is not true. You go from the beginning of the week to the end of it without reflecting upon God at all. You could do as well without God as with him. Is not that the case? And must there not be something very terrible in the condition of your heart when, as a creature, you can do without a thought of your Creator, when he that has nourished you, and brought you up, is nothing to you, one of whom you never think?

These people, further, *have no right conceptions of God.* The true conception of God is that he is all in all. If God is anything, we ought to make him everything; you cannot put God in the second place. He is Almighty, All-wise, All-gracious, knowing everything, being in every place, constantly present, the emanations of his power found in every part of the universe. God is infinitely glorious; and unless we treat him as such, we have not treated him as he ought to be treated. If there be a king, and he is set to open the door or do menial work, he is not honoured as a king should be. Shall the great God be made a lackey to our lusts? Shall we put God aside, and say to him, "When I have a more convenient season, I will send for thee: when I have more money, I will attend to religion," or, "When I can be religious, and not lose anything by it, then I will seek thee"? Dost thou treat God so? Oh, beware, this is high treason against the King of kings! Wrong ideas of God, grovelling thoughts of God, come under the censure of the text, "When they knew God, they glorified him not as God."

Again, dear friends, there are some who think of God a little, but *they never offer him any humble, spiritual worship.* Do not imagine that God can be worshipped by anything which is merely mechanical or external, but which is not from the heart. A strange god must that god be who is pleased with what some men call worship. I have been into many a Romish church, and seen upon the altar paper flowers that would have been a disgrace to a tap-room; and I have said, " Is God pleased with this kind of thing?" Then I have been into a better building, and I have seen crucifixes and altars adorned like a fine lapidary's shop; and I have said to myself, " They might adorn a bride; but God cares not for jewels." Is your conception of God that he desires your gold and your silver, and your brass and your fine linen, and all these adornments? Thou thinkest that he is such an one as thyself. Surely, thou hast poor conceptions of God. When the organ peals out its melodious tones, but the heart is not in the singing, dost thou think that God has ears like those of a man, that can be tickled with sweet sounds? Why hast thou brought him down to thy level? He is spiritual; the music that delights him is the love of a true heart, the prayer of an anxious spirit. He has better music than all your organs and drums can ever bring to him. If he wanted music, he would not have asked thee, for winds and waves make melodies transcendently superior to all that your chief musicians can compose. Does he want candles when his touch makes the mountains to be great altars, smoking with the incense of praise to the God of creation? Oh, brethren, I fear that it has been true of many who externally appeared to be devout, " when they knew God, they glorified him not as God"! Weep over your sin: now have you glorified him as God. Fall on your face, and be nothing before the Most High: now have you glorified him as God. Accept his righteousness; adore his bleeding Son; trust in his infinite compassion. Now have you glorified him as God, for " God is a Spirit, and they that worship him must worship him in spirit and in truth." How far, my dear hearers, have you complied with that requisition?

Further, the people mentioned in my text did not glorify God, *for they did not obediently serve him.* My dear hearer, have *you* served God? Have you looked upon yourself as a servant of God? When you awoke in the morning, did you say, " What does God expect me to do to-day?" When you have summed up the day, have you applied this test, " How far have I endeavoured to serve God to-day?" There are many who are the servants of themselves; and there is no master more tyrannical than unsanctified self. Many are toiling, like slaves at the galleys, for wealth, for honour, for respectability, for something for themselves. But, remember, if the Lord be God, and he made us, we are bound to serve him. How is it that God has kept you alive these forty years, perhaps twice forty, and yet you have never glorified him as God, by rendering him any service whatsoever? This is a very solemn enquiry. I should like everyone whom it concerns to take it home to his own conscience.

There is another charge to be brought against those who glorified not God, although they knew him; that is, *they did not trust him.* The place for man is under the shadow of God's wings. If he made me, I ought to seek him in the hour of trouble. In the time of my need I should apply to his bounty. If I feel unhappy, I should look to him for comfort. My dear hearers, are there not some of you who never did trust God yet? You run to your neighbours as soon as ever you are in difficulties. You trust your old uncle; but you never trust your God. Oh, what a wretched business is this, if God, who is all truth and all love, does not have the confidence of his own creatures! Remember how the Lord spake by the mouth of Jeremiah: "Cursed be the man that trusteth in man, and maketh flesh his arm, and whose heart departeth from the Lord. For he shall be like the heath in the desert, and shall not see when good cometh; but shall inhabit the parched places in the wilderness, in a salt land and not inhabited. Blessed is the man that trusteth in the Lord, and whose hope the Lord is. For he shall be as a tree planted by the waters, and that spreadeth out her roots by the river, and shall not see when heat cometh, but her leaf shall be green; and shall not be careful in the year of drought, neither shall cease from yielding fruit." The people mentioned in the text knew God, but they did not trust him.

In addition to this, *they did not seek to commune with him.* Are there not some here who never tried to speak to God? It never occurred to you, did it? And God has not spoken to you; at least, you have not known whose voice it was when he did speak. It is a very sad business when a boy, who has been at home with his father and mother for years, has never spoken to them. He came down in the morning, and ate his breakfast; he came in, and devoured his dinner; he took his supper with them night by night; but he never spoke to them. Would you have a boy of that kind living with you? You would be obliged to say, "John, you must go; it pains me to send you away, but I cannot bear to have you sitting here in silence. If I speak to you, you never answer me." Some of you cannot remember the time when you spoke to God, or God spoke to you; it is so very long ago, if it ever did occur in your past experience. There is a man somewhere here who did speak to God the other day. He called upon God with a foul and blasphemous oath. When he was telling a lie, he called upon God to witness to it. Ah! yes, you have broken the silence; but it would have been better not to have spoken, than to have uttered those vile blasphemies against the Most High. Your horrible words have entered into the ears of the Lord God of Sabaoth; and, as the Lord liveth, you will have to answer for them to the great Judge of all men, unless you seek his face, and find forgiveness through his Son. Our Saviour said that, for every *idle* word that men shall speak, they shall give account in the day of judgment; how much more shall they be required to answer for every evil, false, slanderous, blasphemous word they have spoken!

But are there not many persons who have never uttered an oath, and are scrupulously careful about speaking the truth, who have never had any spiritual converse with God? Wretched creatures indeed are you; even though you are wealthy and prosperous, you have missed the highest good, the best blessing that man can know.

There are some who, although they know God, do not glorify him, because, while conscious of their enmity against God, *they do not want to be reconciled to him.* There is a way of perfect reconciliation between God and man. Whosoever believeth in Christ Jesus is at once forgiven; he is adopted into the family of God; he drinks of the wine of the love of God; he is saved with an everlasting salvation. There are many who know this in their minds; but it never excites any desire for it in their hearts. No, whether reconciled or unreconciled, does not trouble them. Knowest thou, O man, that the English of it is, "I defy God; I neither want his love, nor fear his hate; I will lift my face before his thunderbolts, and dare him to do his worst"? Oh, fatal defiance of the blessed God! May the Spirit of God work upon thy conscience now, to make thee see the evil of this condition, and turn from it! While I speak, I feel deeply troubled to have to say what I do; but I am only speaking of what many a conscience here must confess to be true. You live, some of you, knowing God, but not glorifying him as God.

II. Now I take from my text the second accusation, which is certainly quite as sad as the other. Those who are mentioned by Paul are accused of WANT OF GRATITUDE. It is said of them that "when they knew God, they glorified him not as God, neither were thankful."

I cannot say anything much worse of a man than that he is not thankful to those who have been his benefactors; and when you say that he is not thankful to God, you have said about the worst thing you can say of him. Now look not merely at the people who lived in Paul's day, but at those who are living now. I will soon prove ingratitude on the part of many. There are many counts in the indictment we have to bring against them in God's High Court of Justice.

First, *God's law is despised.* You young men and women, who are beginning life, if you are intelligent and wise, say, "We wish that we knew what we ought to do for our own preservation and happiness; and we should also like to know what to avoid lest we should do ourselves harm." Well, now, the book of the law of the ten commands is simply the sanitary regulation of the moral world, telling us what would damage us, and what would benefit us. We ought to be very thankful to have such plain directions. "Thou shalt." "Thou shalt not." But see. God has taken the trouble to give us this map of the way, and to direct us in the only right road; yet some have despised the heavenly guide. They have gone directly in the teeth of that law; in fact, it looks as if the very existence of the law has been a provocation to them to break it. Is not this a piece of dreadful ingratitude? Whenever God says, "Thou shalt not," it is because it would be mischievous to us to do it. Sometimes, in London, when the ice in the parks is not strong enough to bear, they put up boards on which is the word "Dangerous." Who but a fool would go where that danger-signal is? The ten commands indicate what is dangerous: nay, what is fatal. Keep clear of all that is forbidden.

Next, *God's day is dishonoured* by those who are not thankful to him. God has, in great mercy, given us a day, one day in seven, wherein to rest, and to think of holy things. There were seven days that God had in the week. He said, "Take six, and use them in your business." No, we must have the seventh as well. It is as if one, upon the road, saw a poor man in distress, and having but seven shillings, the generous person gave the poor man six; but when the wretch had scrambled on his feet, he followed his benefactor to knock him down, and steal the seventh shilling from him. How many do this! The Sabbath is their day for sport, for amusement, for anything but the service of God. They rob God of his day, though it be but one in seven. This is base unthankfulness. May not many here confess that they have been guilty of it? If so, let no more Sabbaths be wasted; but let their sacred hours, and all the week between, be spent in diligent search after God; and then, when you have found him, the Lord's-day will be the brightest gem of all the seven, and you will sing with Dr. Watts,—

> "Welcome, sweet day of rest,
> That saw the Lord arise;
> Welcome to this reviving breast,
> And these rejoicing eyes!"

Moreover, *God's Book is neglected* by these ungrateful beings. He has given us a Book; here is a copy of it. Was there ever such a Book, so full of wisdom, and so full of love? Let a man look at it on bended knee; for he may find heaven between these pages. But, when God has taken the trouble to make this wonderful Book, there are many who do not take the trouble to read it. Ah, me, what ingratitude! A father's love-letter to his son, and his son leaves it unread! Here is a Book, the like of which is not beneath the cope of heaven, and God has exercised even his omniscience to make it a perfect Book, for all ranks and conditions of men, in all periods of the world's history; and yet, such is man's ingratitude, that he turns away from it.

But there is something much worse; *God's Son is refused* by the unthankful. God had but one Son, and such a Son; one with himself, infinite, holy, his delight! He took him from his bosom, and sent him to this earth. The Son took our nature, and became a servant, and then died the death of a felon, the death of the cross, and all to save us, all for the guilty, all for men who were his enemies. I feel guilty myself while I am talking about it, that I do not burst into tears. This must be one of the mysteries that angels cannot comprehend, that after Christ had died, there were found sinners who would not be saved by him. They refused to be washed in the fountain filled with blood; they rejected eternal life, even though it streamed from the five great founts of his wounded body. They chose hell rather than salvation by his blood. They were so in love with their dire enemy, sin, that they would not be reconciled to God even by the death of his Son. Oh, ingratitude, thou hast reached thy utmost limit now, for thou hast trodden under foot the Son of God, and hast counted the blood of the covenant, wherewith he was sanctified, an unholy thing, and hast done despite unto the Spirit of grace! Is not this terrible?

I might stop here; but, for the sake of pricking the consciences of some, I want to say, dear friends, that there are some persons so ungrateful, that *God's deliverances are forgotten*. Some years ago, I spoke with a soldier who rode in the fatal charge at Balaclava; and when he told me so, I took him by the hand; I could not help it, though he was a stranger to me. The tears were in my eyes, and I said, "Sir, I hope that you are God's man after such a deliverance as that." Almost all the saddles emptied, shot and shell flying to the right and left, death mowing down the whole brigade; yet he escaped. But I did not find that he had given his heart to Christ. Over there is a man who has been in half-a-dozen shipwrecks; and if he does not mind, he will be shipwrecked to all eternity! One here has had yellow fever. Ah, sir, there is a worse fever than that on you now! I cannot speak of all the cases here of strange deliverances; but I do not doubt that I address some who have been between the jaws of death. They have looked over the edge of that dread precipice, beneath which is the fathomless abyss. You vowed that, if God would spare your life, you would never be what you were before; and in truth you are not, for you are worse than ever. You are sinning now against light, and in shameful ingratitude. God have mercy upon you!

How often, dear friends, is there ingratitude on the part of unconverted men in the matter of *God's providences ignored!* Why, look at some of you! You never missed a meal in your lives. When you went to the table, there was always something on it. You never had to lose a night's rest for want of a bed. Some of you, from your childhood, have had all that heart could wish. If God has treated you so, while many are crushed with poverty, should he not have some gratitude from you? You had a good mother; you had a tender father; you have gone from one form of relationship to another with increasing comfort. You are spared, and your mother is spared; your wife and children are spared. Indeed, God has made your path very smooth. Some of you are getting on in business, while other men are failing; some of you have every comfort at home, while others have been widowed, and their children have fallen one after the other. Will you never be grateful? Hard, hard heart, wilt thou never break? Will any mercy bend thee? Must there be a storm of wrath to break thee in pieces, like a potter's vessel? Will not love and tenderness melt thee? I do appeal to some here, whose path has been so full of mercies, that they ought to think of God, and turn to him with sincere repentance and faith.

But one says, "I have had good luck." What can be worse than that? Here is unthankfulness to God indeed, when you ascribe his good gifts to "good luck." "Well, you know, but I have been a very hard-working man." I know you have, but who gave you the strength for your work? "I have had a good supply of brains while others have not." Did you make your own brains? Do you not feel that any man who talks about his own wisdom, and his own wit, writes "FOOL" across his forehead in capital letters? We owe everything to God; shall we give God nothing? Shall we have no gratitude to him from whom all our blessings have come? God forgive us if it has been so, and give us grace to alter our past course at once!

Once more, there is another piece of ingratitude of which many are guilty, *God's Spirit is resisted by them.* The Spirit of God comes to them, and gently touches them. Perhaps he has done so to-night while you have been sitting here. You have said, "Do not talk quite so plainly to us. Give us a little comfort, a little breathing space; and do not be quite so hard on us." I hope that it was the Spirit of God rather than the preacher who was dealing with you. At any rate, he has done so a good many times; and you have tried to drive from your heart your best Friend. You have been so ungenerous to him that, when he came to lead you to Christ, you summoned all your strength, and the devil came to help you, and up till now you have resisted the Spirit of God with some degree of success. The Lord have mercy upon you! But how true is my text still, even of many who are found in the house of prayer, "When they knew God, they glorified him not as God, neither were thankful"!

III. Now I finish with my third point, which is, that THIS IRREVERENCE AND INGRATITUDE WERE AGAINST KNOWLEDGE. "When they knew God, they glorified him not as God, neither were thankful."

Will you kindly notice, that, according to my text, *knowledge is of no use if it does not lead to holy practice?* "They knew God." It was no good to them to know God, for "they glorified him not as God." So my theological friend over there, who knows so much that he can split hairs over doctrines, it does not matter what you think, or what you know, unless it leads you to glorify God, and to be thankful. Nay, your knowledge may be a millstone about your neck to sink you down in woe eternal, unless your knowledge is turned to holy practice.

Indeed, *knowledge will increase the responsibility of those who are irreverent and ungrateful.* Paul says, "They are without excuse: because that, when they knew God, they glorified him not as God, neither were thankful." Whatever excuse might be made for those who never heard of God, there was none for these people. My dear hearers, you also are "without excuse." Many of you have had godly parents, you have attended a gospel ministry, your Sunday-school teachers and Christian friends have taught you the way of salvation; you are not ignorant. If you do not glorify God, if you are not thankful to him, it will be more tolerable for the people of Sodom and Gomorrah at the day of judgment than for you, for they never had the privileges that you have despised. Remember how the Saviour upbraided the cities wherein most of his mighty works were done, because they repented not: "Woe unto thee, Chorazin! Woe unto thee, Bethsaida! for if the mighty works, which were done in you, had been done in Tyre and Sidon, they would have repented long ago in sackcloth and ashes." I hardly know which is the greater wonder, that the people who saw Christ's mighty works did not repent, or that those who would have repented if they had seen those works were not permitted to see them.

I wish, dear friends, that you could get out of this state of not glorifying God, and not being thankful. Surely, you only want to have the case stated, and the Spirit of God to speak to your conscience, to cause you to say, "I cannot bear to be in such a dreadful condition with regard to God any longer." May God enable you to repent to-night! Change your mind. That is the meaning of the word "repent." Change your mind, and say, "We will glorify God. There is a Great First Cause. There is a Creator. There must be an omnipotent, all-wise Being. We will worship him. We will say in our hearts, 'This God shall be our God, and we will trust him if he will but accept us.'"

Then remember the years that are past. They involve a great debt, and you cannot pay it; for, if you go on serving God without a flaw till the end of your life, there is the old debt still due; there are the years that are gone, and "God requireth the years that are past." Well, now, hear what he has done. He has given his dear Son to "bear our sins in his own body on the tree"; and, if you will trust Christ, then know of a surety that Christ has put away your sin, and you are forgiven. "Look,"—that is his word—"Look unto me, and be ye saved, all ye ends of the earth." When the brazen serpent was lifted up, all that those who were bitten had to do was to look at the serpent of brass; and everyone that looked, lived. If any man of that crowd had looked at Moses, that would not have healed him. If he had looked at the fiery serpents, and tried to pull them off, that would not have healed him. But he looked to the brazen serpent, and, as his eyes caught the gleam of the brass, the deadly serpent's bites were healed, and the man lived. Look to Jesus. Look now. May God the Holy Spirit lead you to do so!

"I do not feel fit," says one. That is looking to yourself. "I do not feel my need enough," says another. That is trusting to your sense of need. Away with everything that is in you, or about you, and just trust Christ, and you shall immediately be saved. Whoever, in this great congregation, will but look to Jesus, shall be saved upon the spot. However great your iniquities, however stony your heart, however despairing your mind, look, look, look, look. And then, when you look to Christ, your ingratitude will be forgiven, and it will die. You will love him who has loved you, and you shall be saved, and saved for ever.

When we received eighty-two into the church last Lord's-day evening, I could not help breathing an earnest prayer that this might be the beginning of a revival. May it come to-night, and may many in these two galleries, and down below, be carried away by that blessed tide of mighty grace that shall sweep them off their feet, and land them safe on the Rock of ages!

Will you, dear friends, pray for this? I shall feel that even my poor, weak instrumentality will be quite sufficient for the greatest work if I have your prayers at my back. Will you to-night, at the family altar, or at your own bedsides, make it a special subject of prayer that men, who knew God, but glorified him not as God, and were not thankful, may to-night turn to God? If I could get at some of you who are living without Christ, I should like to do what the Roman ambassadors used to do. When they came to a king who was at war with the empire, they said to him, "Will you have peace with Rome, or not?" If he said that he must have time to think it over, the ambassador, with his rod, drew a ring round the man, and said, "You must decide before you cross that line, for, if you do not say 'Peace' before you step out of it, Rome will crush you with her armies." There are no doors to the pews, else I would say, "Shut those doors, and do not let the people out until God decides them." Lord, shut them in! Lord, arrest them: hold them fast, and let them not go till each one of them has said, "I believe; help thou mine unbelief." May God bless you all, for Jesus' sake! Amen.

Exposition by C. H. Spurgeon.
ROMANS I. 1—25.

Verse 1. *Paul, a servant of Jesus Christ, called to be an apostle, separated unto the gospel of God,*

Paul had not seen the Romans when he wrote this epistle. They were strangers to him, and therefore he begins by asserting his apostleship. "called to be an apostle, separated unto the gospel of God." That expression should be true of every Christian minister. We are not apostles; but we are "separated unto the gospel of God." I do not think that we are called to have anything to do with party politics, or social problems, or any such questions; we are set apart for this purpose, "separated unto the gospel of God." There are plenty of people who can attend to those things better than we can. If we mind our own business, or rather, if we mind our Master's business, we who are ministers will have quite enough to do. "Separated unto the gospel of God." There are some brethren who in preaching are as timid as mice; but on a political platform they can roar like lions. Had not they better take to what they like best, and give up the work at which they are not at home? For my part, I believe that I am like Paul when he says that he was "separated unto the gospel of God." I am set apart unto the gospel, cut off from everything else that I may preach the glorious gospel of the blessed God to the perishing sons of men.

2. *(Which he had promised afore by his prophets in the holy scriptures,)*

Notice, brethren, how reverent the apostles were to Holy Scripture. They had no doubt about its inspiration. They quoted the Old Testament, and delighted to make it a kind of basis for the New Testament: "which he had promised afore by his prophets in the Holy Scriptures."

3, 4. *Concerning his Son Jesus Christ our Lord, which was made of the seed of David according to the flesh; and declared to be the Son of God with power, according to the spirit of holiness, by the resurrection from the dead:*

What a glorious Lord we serve! He is God's Son: "Jesus Christ our Lord." In his human nature, he is a Man of royal race: "of the seed of David." He was a man, therefore he died; but he rose again, for he was more than man: "declared to be the Son of God with power."

5, 6. *By whom we have received grace and apostleship, for obedience to the faith among all nations, for his name: among whom are ye also the called of Jesus Christ:*

That is a sweet name for every truly converted man, "called of Jesus Christ." He has called you personally, he has called you effectually, he has called you out of the world, he has called you into fellowship with himself: "the called of Jesus Christ." The Revised Version has it: "called to be Jesus Christ's." Those who are called by Christ, are called to be his.

7, 8. *To all that be in Rome, beloved of God, called to be saints: Grace to you and peace from God our Father, and the Lord Jesus Christ. First, I thank my God through Jesus Christ for you all, that your faith is spoken of throughout the whole world.*

What contrasts we have in the seventh verse! "In Rome, beloved of God." "In Rome, called to be saints." God has beloved ones in the darkest parts of the earth. There is all the more reason for them to be saints because they are surrounded by sinners. They must have had true faith, or they could not have confessed Christ between the jaws of the lion, for they lived in Rome, with Nero hunting after Christians, as if they had been wild beasts, and yet they were not ashamed of the gospel of Christ.

9. *For God is my witness, whom I serve with my spirit in the gospel of his Son, that without ceasing I make mention of you always in my prayers;*

This man, Paul, did a great deal by prayer. I remember a minister, who is now with the Lord, who was thanked by his people for his wonderful sermons; but he said to them, "You never thanked me for my prayers, yet they were the best part of my service for you." When men of God are mighty in prayer, we owe much to them.

10. *Making request, if by any means now at length I might have a prosperous journey by the will of God to come unto you.*

Paul wanted to go to Rome; but I do not suppose that he ever thought that he would go there at the expense of the government, with an imperial guard to take care of him all the way. We pray, and God gives us the answer to our petitions; but often in a way of which we should never have dreamed. Paul goes to Rome as a prisoner for Christ's sake. Now suppose Paul had gone to Rome in any other capacity, he could not have seen Cæsar, he could not have obtained admission into Cæsar's house. The prison of the Palatine was just under the vast palace of the Cæsars; and everybody in the house could come into the guard-room, and have a talk with Paul if they were minded so to do. I suppose that, whatever I might be willing to pay, I could not get to preach in the palace of the Queen, even in this nominally Christian country; but Paul was installed as a royal chaplain over Cæsar's household in the guard-room of the Palatine prison. How wonderfully God works to accomplish his divine purposes!

11, 12. *For I long to see you, that I may impart unto you some spiritual gift, to the end ye may be established; that is, that I may be comforted together with you by the mutual faith both of you and me.*

Paul wanted his faith to establish theirs, and their faith to establish his. Christians grow rich by an exchange of spiritual commodities; and I am afraid some Christians are very poor because they do not engage in this spiritual bartering one with another. You know how it was in the old time, "They that feared the Lord spake often one to another." Shall I tell you how it is now? They that fear not the Lord speak often one against another. That is a very sad difference. Oh, for more Christian communion; for when we blend our "mutual faith", we are "comforted together"; each believer grows stronger as he cheers his brother in the Lord!

13. *Now I would not have you ignorant, brethren, that oftentimes I purposed to come unto you, (but was let hitherto,) that I might have some fruit among you also, even as among other Gentiles.*

Ah! Paul, you could not go when you wished. Cæsar must convoy you. Your Master would have you go to Rome under the protection of the eagles of the empire. God has servants everywhere; he can make Satan himself provide the body-guard for his faithful apostle's journey.

14. *I am debtor both to the Greeks, and to the Barbarians; both to the wise, and to the unwise.*

Paul felt in debt to everybody. The God who saved him, had saved him that he might preach the gospel in every place he could reach. Brethren, if you have received much from God, you are so much the debtor to men; and you are debtors not only to the respectable, but to the disreputable, debtors not only to those who come to a place of worship, but to the dwellers in the slums, "to the Greeks, and to the barbarians; to the wise and to the unwise."

15. *So, as much as in me is, I am ready to preach the gospel to you that are at Rome also. For I am not ashamed of the gospel of Christ:*

Many other people were ashamed of the gospel of Christ. It was too simple; it had not enough of mystery about it; it had not enough of worldly wisdom about it. Paul says, "I am not ashamed of the gospel of Christ," and then he gives his reason for not being ashamed of it,—

16, 17. *For it is the power of God unto salvation to every one that believeth; to the Jew first, and also to the Greek. For therein is the righteousness of God revealed from faith to faith: as it is written, The just shall live by faith.*

The gospel tells us about this living by faith, this believing, this receiving righteousness through believing, and not through working. This is the sweet story of the cross, of which Paul was not ashamed.

18. *For the wrath of God is revealed from heaven against all ungodliness and unrighteousness of men, who hold the truth in unrighteousness;*

Those last words may be read, "Who hold down the truth in unrighteousness." They will not let the truth work upon their hearts; they will not allow it to operate upon their minds; but they try to make it an excuse for their sin. Is there anybody here who is holding down the truth to prevent its entering his heart? I fear there are some such persons, who have come here for years, and the truth has pricked them, troubled them, made them lie awake at night; but they are holding it down, like one who grasps a wild animal by the ears, and holds it down for fear it should bite him. Oh, sirs, when you are afraid of the truth, you may well be afraid of hell! When you and the truth quarrel, you had better end your fighting soon, for you will have the worst of it if you do not yield: "For the wrath of God is revealed from heaven against all ungodliness and unrighteousness of men, who hold down the truth in unrighteousness."

19, 20. *Because that which may be known of God is manifest in them; for God hath shewed it unto them. For the invisible things of him from the creation of the world are clearly seen, being understood by the things that are made, even his eternal power and Godhead; so that they are without excuse:*

Men who never heard the gospel can see God in his works if they open their eyes. There is written upon the face of nature enough to condemn men if they do not turn to God. There is a gospel of the sea, and of the heavens, of the stars, and of the sun; and if men will not read it, they are guilty, for they are wilfully ignorant of what they might know, and ought to know.

21, 22. *Because that, when they knew God, they glorified him not as God, neither were thankful; but became vain in their imaginations, and their foolish heart was darkened. Professing themselves to be wise, they became fools,*

The way to be a fool is to pretend to be wise. A short cut to wisdom is the confession of folly. The near way to folly is the profession of wisdom.

23, 24. *And changed the glory of the uncorruptible God into an image made like to corruptible man, and to birds, and fourfooted beasts, and creeping things. Wherefore God also gave them up to uncleanness through the lusts of their own hearts, to dishonour their own bodies between themselves:*

It is very easy to make a beast of yourself when you have made a beast to be your god, as the Egyptians did, when they worshipped the god that they had made in the form of an ox, or a crocodile, or a cat.

25. *Who changed the truth of God into a lie, and worshipped and served the creature more than the Creator, who is blessed for ever. Amen.*

There are many preachers who have "changed the truth of God into a lie"; and by their exaltation of man, they have worshipped and served the creature more than the Creator, who is blessed for ever." God save all of us from such idolatry as that! Amen.

HYMNS FROM "OUR OWN HYMN BOOK"—545, 527, 606.

Metropolitan Tabernacle Pulpit.

WHERE IS THE LORD?

A Sermon

INTENDED FOR READING ON LORD'S-DAY, MAY 29TH, 1892,

DELIVERED BY

C. H. SPURGEON,

AT THE METROPOLITAN TABERNACLE, NEWINGTON,

On Thursday Evening, September 4th, 1890.

"Then he remembered the days of old, Moses, and his people, saying, Where is he that brought them up out of the sea with the shepherd of his flock? where is he that put his holy Spirit within him? That led them by the right hand of Moses with his glorious arm, dividing the water before them, to make himself an everlasting name? That led them through the deep, as an horse in the wilderness, that they should not stumble? As a beast goeth down into the valley, the Spirit of the Lord caused him to rest: so didst thou lead thy people, to make thyself a glorious name."—Isaiah lxiii. 11—14.

I TOLD you, in the reading, that Israel had a golden age, a time of great familiarity with God, when Jehovah was very near his people in their sufferings, and was afflicted in their affliction, when he helped them in everything they did, and the angel of his presence saved them. But after all that the Lord had done for them, there came a cold period. The people went astray from the one living and true God. They fell into the ritualism of the golden calf. They must have something visible, something that they could see and worship. Even after they were brought into the promised land, and the Lord had wrought great wonders for them, they turned aside to false gods, till they worshipped strange deities, that were no gods; and provoked Jehovah to jealousy. "They rebelled, and vexed his holy Spirit: therefore he was turned to be their enemy, and he fought against them." Not that he ceased to love his chosen, but he must be just, and he could not patronize sin, so he sent their enemies against them, and they were sorely smitten, and brought very low. Then it was that they began to remember the days of old, and to sigh for him whom they had treated so ill, and they said one to another, "Where is he that brought them up out of the sea with the shepherd of his flock? where is he that put his holy Spirit within him? That led them by the right hand of Moses with his glorious arm, dividing the water before them, to make himself an everlasting name? That led them through the deep, as an horse in the wilderness, that they should not stumble? As a beast goeth down into the valley, the

No. 2,258.

Spirit of the Lord caused him to rest: so didst thou lead thy people, to make thyself a glorious name."

I have but a short time, as the communion service is to follow, and therefore I must leave much unsaid that I think your own imaginations will make up to you at home.

But I shall ask you to notice, first, that the text contains *a sacred, loving remembrance*. It dwells very much upon what God did in the old times, when he was familiar with his people, and they walked in the light of his countenance. After that, I shall call your attention to *an object clearly shining* in the text. We get it twice over. In the twelfth verse, we read, "To make himself an everlasting name." In the fourteenth verse, "To make thyself a glorious name." When I have spoken of those two things, I shall dwell more at length upon *an anxious enquiry*, which is put here twice: "Where is he?" In the eleventh verse you get this repeated question, "Where is he? Where is he?"

I. So then, to begin with, we go back to God's dealings with his people, and with us, and we have A SACRED, LOVING REMEMBRANCE. The people remembered what God did to them. What was it?

As it is here described, he first of all *gave them leaders*. "Where is he that brought them up out of the sea with the shepherd of his flock?" Moses and Aaron, and a band of godly men who were with them, were the leaders of the people, through the sea and through the wilderness. Brethren, we are apt to think too little of our leaders. First of all we think too much of them, and afterwards we think too little of them. We seem to swing like a pendulum between these two extremes. Man is reckoned as if he were everything to some, and God becomes nothing to such; but, without unduly exalting man, we can truly say that it really is a great blessing to the church when God raises up men who are qualified to lead his people. Israel did not go out of Egypt as a mob; they were led out by their armies. They did not plunge into the Red Sea as an undisciplined crowd; but Moses stood there with his uplifted rod, and led them on that memorable day. We may well sigh for those glorious days of old, when God gave his people mighty preachers of his Word. There have been epochs in history that were prolific of great leaders of the Christian church. No sooner did Luther give his clarion call, than God seemed to have a bird in every bush; and Calvin, and Farel, and Melancthon, and Zwingle, and so many besides that I will not attempt to make out the list, joined him in his brave protest against the harlot-church of Rome. "The Lord gave the Word: great was the company of those that published it." The church remembers those happy days, with earnest longing for their return. There were giants in those days; mighty men of renown, well fitted by the Lord to lead his people.

We are next told that God *put his Spirit within these shepherds*. They would have been nothing without it. Where is he that put his Holy Spirit within them? A man with God's Holy Spirit within him, can anybody estimate his worth? God says that he will make a man more precious than the gold of Ophir; but, to a man filled with his Spirit, mines of rubies or of diamonds cannot be set in comparison.

When the eleven apostles went forth, on the day of Pentecost, endowed by the Spirit of God, there were forces in the world whose very tramp might make it quiver beneath their feet. God send us once more many of his servants, within whom he has put his Spirit in an eminent and conspicuous manner, and then we shall see bright days indeed! The command to such still is, "Tarry until ye be endued with power from on high."

Then there was, in the next place, as a happy memory for the church, *a great manifestation of the divine power.* "That led them by the right hand of Moses with his glorious arm, dividing the water before them, to make himself an everlasting name." "The right hand of Moses," by itself, was no more than your right hand or mine; but when God's glorious arm worked by the right hand of Moses, the sea divided, and made a way for the hosts of Israel to pass over. As the Psalmist sings, "He divided the sea, and caused them to pass through; and he made the waters to stand as an heap." The right hand of Moses could not have wrought that miracle; but the glorious arm of the Lord did. What we want to-day, brethren, is a manifestation of divine power. Some of us are praying for it day and night. We have expected it. We do expect it. We are longing for it with a hunger and a thirst insatiable. Oh, when will Jehovah pluck his right hand out of his bosom? When will he make bare his arm, as one that goeth to his work with might and main? Pray, O ye servants of God, for leaders filled with the Spirit, and with the power of God working with them, that multitudes may be converted unto Christ, and the sea of sin be dried up in the advance of his kingdom!

Then, there came to God's people *a very marvellous deliverance:* "That led them through the deep, as a horse in the wilderness, that they should not stumble." Understand by the word "wilderness" here, an expansive grassy plain; a place of wild grass and herbs, for so it means. And as a horse is led where it is flat and level, and he does not stumble, so were the hosts of Israel led through the Red Sea. The bottom of a sea may be stony or gravelly, or it may be full of mire and mud. Probably, there will be huge rocks standing up in the middle of the stream. There may be a sudden fall from one stratum of rock to the other; and to come up from the sea on the further bank would be hard work for struggling people carrying burdens, as these Israelites did; for they went out of Egypt harnessed and laden, bearing their kneading-troughs in their clothes upon their shoulders. But God made that rough sea bottom to be as easy travelling for them as when a horse is led across a flowery meadow. Beloved, God has done so with his church in all time. Her seas of difficulty have had no difficulty about them. He has come in all the glory of his power, and smoothed the way for the ransomed to pass over. Has it not been so with you, my brethren?

And, as a blessed ending to their trials, God *brought them into a place of rest:* "As a beast goeth down into the valley, the Spirit of the Lord causeth him to rest: so didst thou lead thy people." In the desert they rested a good deal; but in Canaan they rested altogether. As the cattle come down from the mountains, where they have been picking up their food, when the plains are fat with grass, and they feed to their full, and lie down and rest, so did God deal with his people, bringing them from all the mountains of their trouble into a sweet valley, a land that flowed with milk and honey, where they might rest. This is a memorial, a sketch of the past.

I read it, first, literally as a sketch of Israel's history. I read it, next, as a sketch of the church's history. There have been times with the church as at Pentecost, and the Reformation, when, though she had wandered, God returned to her, and made bare his arm, and raised up shepherds, and put his Spirit upon them, and then led his people straight ahead through every difficulty, and gave them rest. You are most of you acquainted with the history of the period before Luther's day. It did not seem likely then that the gospel would be preached everywhere throughout Northern Europe; but it was so, and God singularly preserved the first Reformers' lives when they were very precious. Zwingle died in battle; but he should not have been fighting, and he might have died a natural death. But Calvin and Luther, and the rest of them, for the most part, remained until their work was done, and they quietly passed away; and the churches, despite long persecution, had comparative rest. It was so here, and it was so across the border in our sister church of Scotland. She cannot forget the covenanting blood, and the putting to death of those who were for the Crown Rights of King Jesus; but, at last, she had her time of rest. Time would fail me to tell you the long list of shepherds that God gave to his covenanting church, the mighty men who, being dead, yet speak to us by their works, and who, while they lived, made the church of God in Scotland to be glorious with the presence of her Lord.

Well now, the same thing has happened also to us as individuals. We have had our cloudy and dark day, but God has appeared for our help. Some of you could tell how God led you through the deep as through a prairie. You went a way that you never knew, a new way, an untrodden path, as though it were the bottom of a sea but newly dry; but the Lord led you as a groom leads a horse, so that you did not stumble, and before long you came up out of the depths unharmed. With Moses and the children of Israel, you sang the praises of him who had triumphed gloriously; and then you began to learn another song, not so martial, but very sweet: "The Lord is my Shepherd; I shall not want. He maketh me to lie down in green pastures: he leadeth me beside the still waters. In conflicts for the God of Israel, and his everlasting truth, some of us have been counted as the mire of the streets; but therein we do rejoice, and will rejoice; for Jehovah liveth, and he will bring up his people again from Bashan. He will bring them up from the depths of the sea, and there shall be rest again in the midst of Israel, if men are but faithful to God, and faithful to his truth.

Thus much upon the sacred memory of the past.

II. But now, in the second place, I want you to notice, AN OBJECT CLEARLY SHINING, like the morning star. I see, through the text, God's great motive in working these wonders for his people. *It was God who did it all;* my text is full of God. He brought them up out of the sea. He put his Holy Spirit within them. He led them with his glorious arm. He led them through the deep. He caused them to rest. He did it all. When the history of the church is written, there will be nothing on the page but God. I know that her sin is recorded; but he hath blotted that out; and at the end, there will remain nothing but what God has done. When your life and mine shall ring out as a psalm amid the harps of glory, it will be only, "Unto him that loved us and laved us, be glory and dominion for ever and ever." "*Non nobis, Domine.*" "Not unto us, O Lord, not unto us, but unto thy name give glory." So will sing all of us who are the Lord's redeemed, when we have come up out of the great tribulation, and have washed our robes, and made them white in the blood of the Lamb.

But then, why had God done all this? Did he do it because of his people's merits, or numbers, or capacities? He tells them, many a time, "Not for your sakes do I this, saith the Lord God, be it known unto you: be ashamed and confounded for your own ways, O house of Israel." God finds in himself the motive for blessing men who have no merits. If God looked for any motive in us, he would find none. He would see in us many reasons why he should condemn us; but only in himself could he discover the motive of his matchless mercy.

God works his great wonders of grace with the high motive of *making known to his creatures his own glory*, manifesting what he is and who he is, that they may worship him. He tells us in the text that he "led them by the right hand of Moses with his glorious arm, dividing the water before them, to make himself an everlasting name." So he has done, for to this day the highest note of praise to God that we know of, is the one that tells of the deliverance of Israel out of Egypt, and when this world is burnt up, the song that will go up to God in heaven will be the song of Moses, the servant of God, and of the Lamb. Still, if we want a figure and a foretaste of the ultimate victories of God over all his people's enemies, we have to go back to the Red Sea, and look at Miriam's twinkling feet, and hear her fingers making the timbrel resound as she cries, "Sing ye to the Lord, for he hath triumphed gloriously; the horse and his rider hath he thrown into the sea." He did it to make to himself an ever-enduring name, and he has succeeded in that object.

Isaiah adds that the Lord led his people, and brought them into their rest, to make himself "a glorious name." God is glorious in the history of Israel. God is glorious in the history of his church. God is glorious in the history of every believer. The life of a true believer is a glorious life. For himself he claims no honour, but by his holy life he brings great glory to God. There is more glory to God in every poor man and woman saved by grace, and in one unknown and obscure person, washed in the Redeemer's blood, than in all the songs of cherubim and seraphim, who know nothing of free grace and dying love. So you see, beloved, the motive of God in all that he did; and I dwell upon it, though briefly, yet with much emphasis, because this is a motive that can never alter. What if the church of to-day be reduced to a very low condition, and the truth seems to be ebbing out from her shores, while a long stretch of the dreary mud of modern invention lies reeking in the nostrils of God;

yet he that wrought such wonders, to make to himself a name, still has the same object in view. He will be glorious. He will have men know that he is God, and beside him there is none else. Thus saith the Lord God, " All flesh shall know that I the Lord am thy Saviour, and thy Redeemer, the Mighty One of Jacob." "The earth shall be full of the knowledge of the Lord, as the waters cover the sea." O brethren, he is a jealous God still; and when the precious blood of Christ is insulted, God hears it, and forgets it not. When the inspiration of this blessed Book is denied, the Holy Ghost hears it and is grieved, and he will yet bestir himself to defend his truth. When we hear the truth that we love, the dearest and most sacred revelations of our God, treated with a triviality that is nothing less than profane, if we are indignant, so is he, and shall not God avenge his own elect, which cry day and night unto him? I tell you that he will avenge them speedily, though he bear long with his adversaries. God's motive is his own glory. He will stand to that, and he will vindicate it yet; and we need have no doubt, nor even the shadow of a fear, about the ultimate result of a collision between God and the adversaries of his truth. Shall not the moth, that dashes at the candle, die in the flame? How shall the creatures of a day stand out against our God, who is a consuming fire? Here, then, is the hope of the people of God, the constant, persistent, invariable motive of God to make himself glorious in the eyes of men.

III. My third point is, AN ANXIOUS ENQUIRY, which I find twice over in my text. Believing in what God has done, and believing that his motive still remains the same, we begin to cry, " Where is he that brought them up out of the sea with the shepherd of his flock? where is he that put his holy Spirit within him?"

This question suggests that *there is some faith left.* "Where is he?" He is somewhere. Then, he lives. Beloved, the Lord God omnipotent still liveth and reigneth. Many usurpers have tried to turn him from his throne; but he still sits upon it, and reigns amongst his ancients gloriously. He was, and is, and is to come, the Almighty; "Jesus Christ, the same yesterday, to-day, and for ever."

He is; but where is he? The question implies that *some were beginning to seek him.* Where is he? Those were brave days when he was here on the moors, or on the hills of Scotland, or at the stakes of Smithfield, or the prisons of Lambeth Palace. Those were glorious days when Christ was here, and his people knew it, and rejoiced in him. Then the virgin daughter of Zion shook her head at the harlot of Rome, and laughed her to scorn; for she lay in the bosom of her King, and rejoiced in his love. O beloved, do we begin to long after him again? I hope that we do. I trust that the cry of many loyal hearts is, "Come back, King Jesus! When thou art away, all things languish. Adown the streets of Mansoul ride again, O Prince Emmanuel! Then shall the city ring with holy song, and every house shall be bedecked with everything that is beautiful and fair. Only come back!" If the King may but have his own again, I shall be well content to sing old Simeon's song, "Lord, now lettest thou thy servant depart in peace, according to thy word!" The church longs for the King's coming. Where is he? Where is he?

It shows now, dear friends, that she has *begun to mourn over his absence.* I like the reduplicated word. "Where is he? Where is he?" Not, "Where is Moses? Where are the leaders? The fathers, where are they?" Let them keep where they are. But where is he that made the fathers? Where is he that sent us Moses and Aaron? Where is he that divided the waters, and led his people safely? Where is he? Oh, it is a question that I put to all your hearts! Oh, if he were here! One hour of his glorious arm; just a day of his almighty working; and what should we not see? We will not ask for tongues of fire, or mighty rushing winds. Let him be here as he may; but if he be only here, the battle is turned at the gate, and the day of his redeemed is come. We sigh for his appearing.

Where is he, then? as the text asks. Well, *he is hidden because of our sins.* The church has been tampering with his truth. She has given into the hands of critics the Word of God, to cut it with the penknife, to rend away this, and tear out that. She has been dallying with the world. She has tried to gain money for her objects by the basest of means. She has played the harlot in what she has done; for there are no amusements too vile or too silly for her. Even her pastors have filled a theatre of late, to sit there and mark with their applause the labours of the play-actors! To this pass have we come at last, to which we never came before—no, not in Rome's darkest hour; and if you, who profess to be God's servants, do not love Christ enough to be indignant about it, the Lord have mercy upon you! The time has surely come when there should go up one great cry unto the Lord Jehovah that he would make bare his arm again; for well may we say, "Where is he? Where is he?"

For your comfort, the next verse to my text tells you where he is. *He is in heaven.* They cannot expel him from his throne. "Yet have I set my King upon my holy hill of Zion." By every possible contrivance, in these modern days, have they tried to drive Christ out of his own church. A Christless, bloodless gospel defiles many a pulpit, and Christ is thus angered; but he is in heaven still. At the right hand of God he sits; and let this be our continual prayer to him, "Look down from heaven, O Lord! Cast an eye upon thy failing, faltering, fickle church. Look down from heaven."

"Where is he?" Well, *he is himself making an enquiry;* for, as some read the whole passage, it is God himself speaking. He remembered the days of old, Moses and his people; and when he hid himself, and would not work in wrath, yet he said to himself, "Where is he that brought them up out of the sea with the shepherd of his flock?" When God himself, who is always a stranger here,—for are we not strangers with him and sojourners, as all our fathers were?—When God himself begins to ask where he is, and to regret those happier days, something will come of it. "Ye that make mention of the Lord—ye that are the Lord's remembrancers—keep not silence, and give him no rest,—take no rest, and give him no rest,—till he establish, and till he make Jerusalem a praise in the earth." "That little cloud", said one of old, when Julian the apostate threatened to extirpate Christianity, "That little cloud will soon be gone." All that I see to-day of darkness, is but a wave of smoke. Behold, the Lord God himself shall chase it away with a strong west wind. He doth but blow with his wind, and the clouds disappear; and what stands before us to-day shall be as nothing.

I thought, as I came here to-night, that the man who drives the tram car gave me a lesson on how I should look upon all future time. He starts, say at Clapham, with his car. If he could have a view of all that was on the road between Clapham and the Elephant and Castle, the carts, waggons, and other traffic that are exactly where he wants to go, and he were to add all those obstacles together, he might be foolish enough to say, "I shall not complete my course to-night;" but, you see, he starts, and if anything is on the rails, it moves off; and if, perhaps, some sluggish, heavily-laden coal waggon is slow to move, he puts his whistle to his mouth, and gives a shrill blast or two, and lo, it is gone! So when the church, serving her God, begins to look far ahead through prophecy, which she never did understand, and never will, she will think that she will never reach her journey's end. But she will; for God has laid the line. We are on the rails, and the rails do not come to an end till the journey's end is reached; and as we go along, we shall find that everything in our way will move before us; and if it does not, we will pray a bit. We will blow our whistle, and the devil himself will have to move, though all his black horses shall be dragging along the brewer's dray, or what else belongs to him. He will have to get off our track, as surely as God lives; for if Jehovah sends us on his errands, we cannot fail. The old Romans picture Jove as hurling thunderbolts. Sometimes God makes his servants thunderbolts, and when he hurls them, they will go crashing through everything until they reach their mark. Wherefore, be not for a moment discouraged; but trust you in God, and be glad without a shadow of fear.

If any here have never trusted in God, never made him their Friend, or been reconciled to him by the death of his Son, I pray them to think of their present condition. Opposed to God! You are standing in the way of an express train. You are urged to get out of the way. You will not! You are going to throw that train off the rails, you say. Poor fool, I could put mine arms about your neck, and forcibly drag you from the iron way; for assuredly, if you remain there, nothing can come of it but your everlasting destruction. Wherefore, flee, flee, I pray you, from the wrath to come. The train of divine judgment comes thundering along the iron road even now. It shakes the earth. Awake! Rise! Flee! God help you to do so! Behold, the Saviour stands with open arms to be your shelter. Fly to him, and trust in him, and live for ever! Amen.

Exposition by C. H. Spurgeon.
ISAIAH LXIII.—LXIV.

Chapter lxiii. Verses 1—6. *Who is this that cometh from Edom, with dyed garments from Bozrah? this that is glorious in his apparel, travelling in the greatness of his strength? I that speak in righteousness, mighty to save. Wherefore art thou red in thine apparel, and thy garments like him that treadeth in the winefat? I have trodden the winepress alone; and of the people there was none with me: for I will tread them in mine anger, and trample them in my fury; and their blood shall be sprinkled upon my garments, and I will stain all my raiment. For the day of vengeance is in mine heart, and the year of my redeemed is come. And I looked, and there was none to help; and I wondered that there was none to uphold: therefore mine own arm brought salvation unto me; and my fury, it upheld me. And I will tread down the people in mine anger, and make them drunk in my fury, and I will bring down their strength to the earth.*

It is a dark and terrible time; no one at God's side, his people discouraged, Edom triumphant. Then comes the one great Hero of the gospel, the Christ of God; and by his own unaided strength he wins for his people a glorious victory. He is as terrible to his foes as he is precious to his friends. He stands before us as the one hope of his ancient church. There is the picture Isaiah was inspired to paint. Now the prophet goes on to say:—

7. *I will mention the lovingkindnesses of the Lord,*

Are you, dear friends, mentioning the lovingkindnesses of the Lord; or are you silent about them? Learn a lesson from the prophet Isaiah. Talk about what God has done for you, and for his people in all time: "I will mention the lovingkindnesses of the Lord." Let this be the resolve of every one of us who has tasted that the Lord is gracious.

> "Awake, my soul, in joyful lays,
> And sing thy great Redeemer's praise:
> He justly claims a song from me,
> His lovingkindness, oh, how free!
>
> "He saw me ruin'd in the fall,
> Yet loved me, notwithstanding all;
> He saved me from my lost estate,
> His lovingkindness, oh, how great!"

7. *And the praises of the Lord, according to all that the Lord hath bestowed on us, and the great goodness toward the house of Israel, which he hath bestowed on them according to his mercies, and according to the multitude of his lovingkindnesses.*

This is a verse full of sweets; but I must not dwell upon it. My object at this time is to read much, and to say little by way of comment; so I cannot stay to pick out the sweetnesses here. There are very many. This passage is a piece of a honeycomb. Read it when you get home; pray over it, suck the honey out of it, and praise the Lord for it.

8. *For he said,*

In the old time, when God called his people out of Egypt, he said this.

8. *Surely they are my people, children that will not lie:*

Or, children that will not act deceitfully; or, that will not deal falsely.

8. *So he was their Saviour.*

He thought well of them. He treated them as though they were trustworthy. He took them into his confidence. He said, "Surely they will not deceive me." This is speaking after the manner of men, of course; for God knows us, and is never deceived in us. We may deceive others; we may even deceive ourselves; but we can never deceive him.

9. *In all their affliction he was afflicted, and the angel of his presence saved them: in his love and in his pity he redeemed them; and he bare them, and carried them all the days of old.*

Happy Israel! These were her golden days, when she was faithful to God, and God communed very closely with her. Then God was very near to his people, so near that he is represented as carrying them in his arms. He could be seen in a bush; he could be seen in a cloud; he could be seen working with a rod; he was so familiar with his people.

10. *But they rebelled, and vexed his holy Spirit: therefore he was turned to be their enemy, and he fought against them.*

This was a great change in dispensation, though there was no change in the heart of God. He deals roughly with his people when they rebel against him. They would not be improved by tenderness, so now they must be scourged by his rod, and come under his displeasure. When men turn from God, he is "turned to be their enemy."

11. *Then he remembered the days of old,*

His people were never out of his mind, even when they wandered away from him. He remembered the love of their espousals, when they went after him into the wilderness. He remembered the days of old, the happier days, when his people walked closely with him. They also remembered these days. It is strange that they should ever have forgotten them.

11—14. *Moses, and his people, saying, Where is he that brought them up out of the sea with the shepherd of his flock? where is he that put his holy Spirit within him? That led them by the right hand of Moses with his glorious arm, dividing the water before them, to make himself an everlasting name? That led them through the deep, as an horse in the wilderness, that they should not stumble? As a beast goeth down into the valley, the Spirit of the Lord caused him to rest: so didst thou lead thy people, to make thyself a glorious name.*

Now comes a prayer suggested by their condition of sorrow and desertion.

15. *Look down from heaven,*

Thou art still there, though we have wandered. Look down upon us from heaven, O Lord!

15, 16. *And behold from the habitation of thy holiness and of thy glory: where is thy zeal and thy strength, the sounding of thy bowels and of thy mercies toward me? are they restrained? Doubtless thou art our father, though Abraham be ignorant of us, and Israel acknowledge us not; thou, O Lord, art our father, our redeemer; thy name is from everlasting.*

That last sentence may be read, "Thy name is, our Redeemer, from everlasting." This is a sweet plea with God: "We have offended thee; but we are still thy children. We have wandered from thee; but we are still thine own, bought with a price. Thy name of 'Redeemer' is not a temporary one; it is from everlasting to everlasting, therefore look on thy poor children again. Leave us not to perish."

17, 18. *O Lord, why hast thou made us to err from thy ways, and hardened our heart from thy fear? Return for thy servants' sake, the tribes of thine inheritance. The people of thy holiness*

Or, "Thy holy people."

18, 19. *Have possessed it but a little while: our adversaries have trodden down thy sanctuary. We are thine: thou never barest rule over them; they were not called by thy name.*

"Thou didst give us the land by an everlasting covenant; but we have had it only a little while. Lo, the enemy has come in, and driven thine Israel away from her heritage! Can it be so always, O Lord?" Happy times seem very short when they are over; and when they are succeeded by dark trials, we say, "The people of thy holiness, thy holy people have possessed it but a little while. Our adversaries have trodden down thy sanctuary. We are now become (for this is the true rendering of the passage) like those over whom thou hast never borne rule, those who were never called by thy name." That is a sad condition for the church of God to be in; and I am afraid that it is getting into that condition now, sinking to a level with the world, leaving its high calling, quitting the path of the separated people, and becoming just like those whom God never knew, and who were never called by his name. It is a pitiful case; and here comes a prayer like the bursting out of a volcano, as though the hearts of gracious men could hold in the agonising cry no longer:—

Chapter lxiv. Verses 1, 2. *Oh that thou wouldest rend the heavens, that thou wouldest come down, that the mountains might flow down at thy presence, as when the melting fire burneth,*

Or, much better, "as when the brushwood burneth"; for if God does but come to his people, they are ready to catch the flame, like the dry heather which is soon ablaze; and his enemies also shall be like brushwood before the fire.

2, 3. *The fire causeth the waters to boil, to make thy name known to thine adversaries, that the nations may tremble at thy presence! When thou didst terrible things which we looked not for, thou camest down, the mountains flowed down at thy presence.*

O Lord, come again! Thou didst come in the past; repeat thy former acts, and let us see what thou canst do for the avenging of thy people.

4. *For since the beginning of the world men have not heard, nor perceived by the ear, neither hath the eye seen, O God, beside thee, what he hath prepared for him that waiteth for him.*

God is ready to help. He has everything in preparation before our needs begin. He has laid in supplies for all our wants. Before our prayers are presented, he has prepared his answers to them; blessed be his name! You remember how Paul uses this passage, "Eye hath not seen, nor ear heard, neither have entered into the heart of man, the things which God hath prepared for them that love him. But God hath revealed them unto us by his Spirit." The spiritual man is a privileged man.

5. *Thou meetest him that rejoiceth and worketh righteousness, those that remember thee in thy ways:*

God does not wait for us to return to him. He meets us. He comes to us the moment that we turn our feet towards his throne. While we are, like the prodigal, a great way off, he sees us, and has compassion upon us, and runs to meet us.

5. *Behold, thou art wroth; for we have sinned: in those is continuance, and we shall be saved.*

In thy faithfulness, in thy love, in thyself, in thy ways of mercy there is continuance. This is our safety. What are we? Here is the answer:—

6. *But we are all as an unclean thing, and all our righteousnesses are as filthy rags; and we all do fade as a leaf; and our iniquities, like the wind, have taken us away.*

It is not a flattering picture that the prophet draws. Even our righteousnesses are like filthy rags, fit only for the fire; what must our unrighteousnesses be like? We, ourselves, are like the sere leaves on the trees; and just as the wind carries away the faded leaves of autumn, so our sins, like a mighty blast, carry us away.

7. *And there is none that calleth upon thy name, that stirreth up himself to take hold of thee:*

That is a wonderful description of prayer. When a man rouses himself from sinful lethargy, and stirs himself up to take hold of God in prayer, he will become an Israel, a prince prevailing with God.

7, 8. *For thou hast hid thy face from us, and hast consumed us, because of our iniquities. But now, O Lord, thou art our father;*

Adoption does not come to an end because of sin. Regeneration or sonship does not die out; it cannot die out. I am my father's son, and so I always shall be; and if I am my heavenly Father's son, I shall never cease to be so. "Now, O Lord, thou art our Father!" This truth must not be perverted into an argument for sinning; it ought rather to keep us from sinning, lest we should grieve such wondrous love.

8—12. *We are the clay, and thou our potter; and we all are the work of thy hand. Be not wroth very sore, O Lord, neither remember iniquity for ever: behold, see, we beseech thee, we are all thy people. Thy holy cities are a wilderness, Zion is a wilderness, Jerusalem a desolation. Our holy and our beautiful house, where our fathers praised thee, is burned up with fire: and all our pleasant things are laid waste. Wilt thou refrain thyself for these things, O Lord? wilt thou hold thy peace, and afflict us very sore?*

The prophet touches the minor key, and weeps and wails for the sorrows of his people; but he does not neglect to pray. In the next chapter God breaks out, and says, "I am sought of them that asked not for me; I am found of them that sought me not." How much more quickly is he found of them who do seek him! Verily, God does hear prayer; and he will hear prayer; let us not cease to pray to him, as we look round on the sad state of the professing church at this time, and with Isaiah let us cry, "Wilt thou refrain thyself for these things, O Lord? Wilt thou hold thy peace, and afflict us very sore?"

HYMNS FROM "OUR OWN HYMN BOOK"—107 (Song I), 953, 954.

THE SWORD AND THE TROWEL.

CONTENTS OF SPECIAL CONFERENCE NUMBER, JUNE, 1892.

Mr. Spurgeon's First Institution. By Principal D. Gracey.
Christ's Likenesses. Conference Address by Pastor J. A. Spurgeon.
"The Tongue of the Learned." Paper read by Pastor A. Bax, Islington.
Power for Aggressive Service. Paper read by Pastor T. J. Longhurst, Cheltenham.
Addresses delivered at the Conference Service in memory of the late beloved President, by Pastors J. A. and C. Spurgeon, and Dr. Pierson.
Descriptive Reports of the whole of the proceedings at the Fifth Annual Conference of the Pastors' College Evangelical Association. By various Members of the Association.
Editorial Notes.
Lists of Contributions.
Annual Report of the Pastors' College, with Reminiscences of the late President, by many College brethren.

112 pages. Price 3d. Post-free, 5d.

LONDON: PASSMORE & ALABASTER, PATERNOSTER BUILDINGS; and all Booksellers.

Metropolitan Tabernacle Pulpit.

THE SIMPLICITY AND SUBLIMITY OF SALVATION.

A Sermon

INTENDED FOR READING ON LORD'S-DAY, JUNE 5TH, 1892,

DELIVERED BY

C. H. SPURGEON,

AT THE METROPOLITAN TABERNACLE, NEWINGTON,

On Thursday Evening, March 6th, 1890.

"He came unto his own, and his own received him not. But as many as received him, to them gave he power to become the sons of God, even to them that believe on his name: Which were born, not of blood, nor of the will of the flesh, nor of the will of man, but of God."—John i. 11—13.

EVERYTHING here is simple; everything is sublime. Here is that simple gospel, by which the most ignorant may be saved. Here are profundities, in which the best-instructed may find themselves beyond their depth. Here are those everlasting hills of divine truth which man cannot climb; yet here is that plain path in which the wayfaring man, though a fool, need not err, nor lose his way. I always feel that I have no time to spare for critical and captious persons. If they will not believe, neither shall they be established. They must take the consequences of their unbelief. But I can spare all day and all night for an anxious enquirer, for one who is blinded by the very blaze of the heavenly light that shines upon him, and who seems to lose his way by reason of the very plainness of the road that lies before him. In this most simple text are some of the deep things of God, and there are souls here that are puzzled by what are simplicities to some of us; and my one aim shall be, so to handle this text as to help and encourage and cheer some who would fain touch the hem of the Master's garment, but cannot for the press of many difficulties and grave questions which rise before their minds.

Let us go to the text at once, and notice, first, *a matter which is very simple:* "As many as received him . . . . even to them that believe on his name"; secondly, *a matter which is very delightful:* "to them gave he power to become the sons of God"; and thirdly, *a matter which is very mysterious:* "Which were born, not of blood, nor of the will of the flesh, nor of the will of man, but of God."

I. Here is, first, A MATTER WHICH IS VERY SIMPLE; receiving Christ, and believing on his name. Oh, that many here may be able to say,

No. 2,259.

"Yes, I understand that simple matter. That is the way in which I found eternal life"!

The simple matter of which John here speaks is receiving Christ, or, in other words, believing on his name.

Receiving Christ is *a distinctive act*. "He came unto his own, and his own received him not." The very people you would have thought would have eagerly welcomed Christ did not do so; but here and there a man stood apart from the rest, or a woman came out from her surroundings, and each of these said, "I receive Christ as the Messiah." You will never go to heaven in a crowd. The crowd goes down the broad road to destruction; but the way which leadeth to life eternal is a narrow way; "and few there be that find it." They that go to heaven must come out one by one, and say to him that sits at the wicket-gate, "Set my name down, sir, as a pilgrim to the celestial city." They who would enter into life must fight as well as run, for it is an uphill fight all the way, and few there be that fight it out to the end, and win the crown of the victors.

Those who received Christ were different from those who did not receive him; they were as different as white is from black, or light from darkness. They took a distinct step, separated themselves from others, and came out and received him whom others would not receive. Have you taken such a step, dear friend? Can you say, "Yes, let others do as they will, as for me, Christ is all my salvation, and all my desire; and at all hazards I am quite content to be counted singular, and to stand alone; I have lifted my hand to heaven, and I cannot draw back. Whatever others may do, I say, 'Christ for me'"?

As it was a distinctive act, so it was *a personal one:* "To as many as received him." They had to receive Christ each one by his own act and deed. "Even to them that believe on his name." Believing is the distinct act of a person. I cannot believe for you any more than you can believe for me; that is clearly impossible. There can be no such thing as sponsorship in receiving Christ or in faith. If you are an unbeliever, your father and your mother may be the most eminent saints, but their faith does not overlap and cover your unbelief. You must believe for yourself. I have had even to remind some that the Holy Ghost himself cannot believe for them. He works faith in you; but you have to believe. The faith must be your own distinct mental act. Faith is the gift of God; but God does not believe for us; how could he? It is for you distinctly to believe. Come, dear hearer, have you been trying to put up with a national faith? A national faith is a mere sham. Or have you tried to think that you possess the family faith? "Oh, we are all Christians, you know!" Yes, we are all hypocrites; that is what that comes to. Unless each one is a Christian for himself, he is a Christian only in name, and that is to be a hypocrite. Oh, that we might have the certainty that we have each one laid our sins on Jesus, the spotless Lamb of God! God grant that, if we have never done so before, we may do so this very moment!

Mark, next, that, as it was a distinctive and personal act, so *it related to a Person*. I find that the text runs thus, "He came unto his own, and his own received him not. But as many as received him, to them gave he power to become the sons of God, even to them that believe on his name." That religion which leaves out the person of Christ, has left out the essential point. Thou art not saved by believing a doctrine, though it is well for thee to believe it if it be true. Thou art not saved by practising an ordinance, though thou shouldst practise it if thou art one of those to whom it belongs. Thou art not saved by any belief except this, believing on Christ's name, and receiving him. "I take in a body of divinity," says one. Do you? There is no body of divinity that I know of but Christ, who is divinity embodied. Beware of resting on a system of theology. Thou must rest on him who is the true Theology, the Word of God; on Christ, the Son of God in human flesh, living, bleeding, dying, risen, ascended, soon to come; thou must lean on him; for the promise is only to as many as receive him.

This reception of Christ *consisted in faith in him:* "As many as received him . . . . even to them that believe on his name." He was a stranger, and they took him in. He was food, and they took him in, and fed on him. He was living water, and they received him, drank him up, took him into themselves. He was light, and they received the light. He was life, and they received the life, and they lived by what they received. It is a beautiful description of faith, the act of receiving. As the empty cup receives from the flowing fountain, so do we receive Christ into our emptiness. We, being poor, and naked, and miserable, come to him, and we receive riches, and clothing, and happiness in him. Salvation comes by receiving Christ. I know what you have been trying to do; you have been trying to give Christ something. Let me caution you against a very common expression. I hear converts continually told to give their hearts to Jesus. It is quite correct, and I hope that they will do so; but your first concern must be, not what you give to Jesus, but what Jesus gives to you. You must take him from himself as his gift to you, then will you truly give your heart to him. The first act, and, indeed, the underlying act all the way along, is to receive, to imbibe, to take in Christ, and that is called believing on his name. Note that "name." It is not believing a fanciful christ; for there are many christs nowadays, as many christs as there are books, nearly; for every writer seems to make a christ of his own; but the christ that men make up will not save you. The only Christ who can save you is the Christ of God, that Christ who, in the synagogue at Nazareth, found the place where it was written, "The Spirit of the Lord is upon me, because he hath anointed me to preach the gospel to the poor; he hath sent me to heal the brokenhearted, to preach deliverance to the captives, and recovering of sight to the blind, to set at liberty them that are bruised, to preach the acceptable year of the Lord."

You are to believe on *the Christ as he is revealed in the Scriptures.* You are to take him as you find him here; not as Renan, or Strauss, or anybody else, pictures him; but as you find him here. As God reveals him, you are to believe on his name: "the Wonderful, Counsellor, the Mighty God, the Everlasting Father, the Prince of Peace"; Emmanuel, God with us; Jesus, saving from sin; Christ, anointed of the Father. You are to believe on his name, not on the Christ of Rome, nor the Christ of Canterbury, but the Christ of Jerusalem, the Christ of the eternal glory; no christ of a dreamy prophecy, with which some are defaming the true prophetic spirit of the Word, no christ of idealism, no man-made christ; but the eternal God, incarnate in human flesh, as he is here pictured by Psalmist, Prophet, Evangelist, Apostle, very God of very God, yet truly man, in your stead suffering, bearing the sin of men in his own body on the tree. It is believing in this Christ that will effectually save your soul. To believe is to trust. Prove that you believe in Christ by risking everything upon him.

> "Upon a life I did not live,
> Upon a death I did not die,
> I risk my whole eternity."

On him who lived for me, and died for me, and rose again for me, and has gone into heaven for me; on him I throw the whole weight of past, present, and future, and every interest that belongs to my soul, for time and for eternity.

This is a very simple matter, and I have noticed a great many sneers at this simple faith, and a great many depreciatory remarks concerning it; but, let me tell you, there is nothing like it under heaven. Possessing this faith will prove you to be a son of God; nothing short of it ever will. "To as many as received him, to them gave he power to become the sons of God;" and he has given that power to nobody else. This will prove you to be absolved, forgiven. "There is, therefore, now no condemnation to them which are in Christ Jesus;" but if thou hast no faith in Christ Jesus, the wrath of God abideth on thee. Because thou hast not believed on the Son of God, thou art condemned already. One grain of this faith is worth more than a diamond the size of the world; yea, though thou shouldst thread such jewels together, as many as the stars of heaven for number, they would be worth nothing compared with the smallest atom of faith in Jesus Christ, the eternal Son of God.

But whence comes this wonderful power of faith? Not from the faith, but from him on whom it leans. What power Christ has! The power of his manhood suffering, the power of his Godhead bowing on the cross, the power of the God-man, the Mediator, surrendering himself as the great sacrifice for sin; why, he who toucheth this, hath touched the springs of omnipotence! He who comes, by faith, into contact with Christ, has come into contact with boundless love, and power, and mercy, and grace. I marvel not at anything that faith brings when it deals with Christ. Thou hast a little key, a little rusty key, and thou sayest, "By the use of this key I can get all the gold that I want." Yes, but where is the box to which you go for the gold? When you show me, and I see that it is a great chamber filled full of gold and silver, I can understand how your little key can enrich you when it opens the door into such a treasury. If faith be the key which unlocks the fulness of God, "for it pleased the Father that in him should all fulness dwell," then I can understand why faith brings such boundless blessings to him who hath it. Salvation is a very simple business. God help us to look at it simply, and practically, and to receive Christ, and believe on his name!

II. Now, secondly, here is A MATTER WHICH IS VERY DELIGHTFUL: "To them gave he power to become the sons of God."

If I had a week in which to preach from this text, I think that I should be able to get through the first head; but at this time I can only throw out just a few hints. Look at the great and delightful blessing which comes to us by our faith in Christ. We give Christ our faith, and he gives us power to become sons of God, the authority, liberty, privilege, right,—something more than mere strength or force—to be sons of God.

When we believe in Jesus, he indicates to us *the Great Father's willingness to let us be his sons.* We who were prodigals, far away from him, perceive that, when we receive Christ, the Father, who gave us Christ, is willing to take us to be his sons. He would not have yielded up his Only-begotten if he had not willed to take us into his family.

When we believe in Jesus, *he bestows on us the status of sons.* We were slaves before; now we are sons. We were strangers, aliens, enemies; any and every word that means an evil thing might have been applied to us; but when we laid hold on Christ, we were regarded as the sons of God. As a man in Rome, when he was adopted by some great citizen, and publicly acknowledged in the forum as being henceforth that man's son, was really regarded as such, so, as soon as we believe in Jesus, we get the status of sons. "Beloved, now are we the sons of God."

Then Christ does something more for us. *He gives us grace to feel our sonship.* As we sang just now,—

"My faith shall 'Abba, Father,' cry,
And thou the kindred own."

God owns us as his children, and we own him as our Father; and henceforth, "Our Father, which art in heaven," is no meaningless expression, but it comes welling up from the depths of our heart.

Having given us grace to feel sonship, *Christ gives us the nature of our Father.* He gives us "power to become the sons of God." We get more and more like God in righteousness and true holiness. By his divine Spirit, shed abroad in our hearts, we become more and more the children of our Father who is in heaven, who doeth good to the undeserving and the unthankful, and whose heart overflows with love even to those who love not him.

When this nature of sons shall be fully developed, *Christ will bestow his glory upon us.* We shall be in heaven, not in the rear rank, as servants, but nearest to the eternal throne. Unto the angels he has never said, "Ye are my sons"; but he has called us sons, poor creatures of the dust, who believe in Jesus; and we shall have all the honour, and joy, and privilege, and delight that belong to princes of the blood royal of heaven, members of the imperial house of God, in that day when the King shall manifest himself in his own palace.

Some of us could draw parallels, about being made sons, from our own lives. You were once a very tiny child; but you were a son then as much as you are now. So is it with you who have only just begun to believe in Christ; he has given you authority and right to become the sons of God. Very early in our life, our father went down to the registrar's office, and wrote our name in the roll as his sons. We do not recollect that, it is so long ago; but he did it, and he also wrote our names in the family Bible, even as our Father who is in heaven has enrolled our names in the Lamb's Book of Life. You recollect that, as a child, you did not go in the kitchen, to dine with the servants; but you took your seat at the table. It was a very little chair in which you first sat at the table; but as you grew bigger, you always went to the table, because you were a son. The servants in the house were much bigger than you, and they could do a great many things that you could not do, and your father paid them wages. He never paid you any; they were not his sons, but you were. If they had put on your clothes, they would not have been his sons. You had privileges that they had not. I remember that, in the parish where my home was, on a certain day in the year, the church-bell rang, and everybody went to receive a penny roll. Every child had one, and I recollect having mine. I claimed it as a privilege, because I was my father's son. I think there were six of us, who all had a roll; every child in the parish had one. So there are a number of privileges that come to us very early in our Christian life, and we mean to have them, first, because our Lord Jesus Christ has given us the right to have them; and, next, because, if we do not take what he bought for us, it will be robbing him, and wasting his substance. As he has paid for it all, and has given us the right to have it, let us take it.

You were put to school because you were a son. You did not like it; I daresay that you would rather have stopped at home at play. And you had a touch of the rod, sometimes, because you were a son. That was one of your privileges: "for what son is he whom the father chasteneth not?" One day you were in the street with other boys, doing wrong, and your father came along, and punished you. He did not touch your companions, for they were not his sons. You smile at those little things, and you did not at the time count your punishments as privileges; but they were. When the chastening of the Lord comes, call it a privilege, for that is what it is. There is no greater mercy that I know of on earth than good health except it be sickness; and that has often been a greater mercy to me than health.

It is a good thing to be without a trouble; but it is a better thing to have a trouble, and to know how to get grace enough to bear it. I am not so much afraid of the devil when he roars, as I am when he pretends to go to sleep. I think that, oftentimes, a roaring devil keeps us awake; and the troubles of this life stir us up to go to God in prayer, and that which looks to us ill turns to our good. "We know that all things work together for good to them that love God, to them who are the called according to his purpose."

III. Now I come to my last point, that is, A MATTER WHICH IS MYSTERIOUS. We are not only given the status of children, and the privilege of being called sons, but this mysterious matter is one of heavenly birth: "Which were born, not of blood, nor of the will of the flesh, nor of the will of man, but of God."

This new birth is *absolutely needful*. If we are ever to be numbered amongst God's children, we must be born again, born from above. We were born in sin, born children of wrath, even as others; to be God's children, it is absolutely necessary that we should be born again.

The change wrought thereby is *wonderfully radical*. It is not a mere outside washing, nor any touching up and repairing. It is a total renovation. Born again? I cannot express to you all that the change means, it is so deep, so thorough, so complete.

It is also *intensely mysterious*. What must it be to be born again? "I cannot understand it," says one. Nicodemus was a teacher in Israel, and he did not understand it. Does anybody understand it? Does anybody understand his first birth? What know we of it? And this second birth; some of us have passed through it, and know that we have, and remember well the pangs of that birth, yet we cannot describe the movements of the Spirit of God, by which we were formed anew, and made new creatures in Christ Jesus, according to that word from him who sits on the throne, "Behold, I make all things new!" It is a great mystery.

Certainly it is *entirely superhuman*. We cannot contribute to it. Man cannot make himself to be born again. His first birth is not of himself, and his second birth is not one jot more so. It is a work of the Holy Ghost, a work of God. It is a new creation; it is a quickening; it is a miracle from beginning to end.

Here is the point to which I call your special attention, it is *assuredly ours*. Many of us here have been born again. We know that we have, and herein lies the evidence of it, "As many as received him, to them gave he power to become the sons of God, even to them that believe on his name, which were born, not of blood, nor of the will of the flesh, nor of the will of man, but of God." If thou believest on Christ's name, thou art born of God. If thou hast received Christ into thy soul, thou hast obtained that birth that comes not of blood, nor of the will of parents, nor of the will of man, but of God. Thou hast passed from death unto life.

Let no man sit down here, and cover his face, and say, "There is no hope for me. I cannot understand about this new birth." If thou wilt take Christ, to have and to hold, henceforth and for ever, as thy sole trust and confidence, thou hast received that which no line of ancestors could ever give thee; for it is "not of blood." Thou dost possess that which no will of father and mother could ever give thee; for it is "not of the will of the flesh." Thou hast that which thine own will could not bring thee; for it is "not of the will of man." Thou hast that which only the Giver of life can bestow; for it is "of God." Thou art born again; for thou hast received Christ, and believed on his name. I do not urge you to look within, to try and see whether this new birth is there. Instead of looking within thyself, look thou to him who hangs on yonder cross, dying the Just for the unjust, to bring us to God. Fix thou thine eyes on him, and believe in him; and when thou seest in thyself much that is evil, look away to him; and when doubts prevail, look to him; and when thy conscience tells thee of thy past sins, look to him.

I have to go through this story almost every day of the year, and sometimes half a dozen times in a day. If there is a desponding soul anywhere within twenty miles, it will find me out, no matter whether I am at home, or at Mentone, or in any other part of the world. It will come from any distance, broken down, despairing, half insane sometimes; and I have no medicine to prescribe except "Christ, Christ, Christ; Jesus Christ and him crucified. Look away from yourselves, and trust in him." I go over and over and over with this, and never get one jot further, because I find that this medicine cures all soul sicknesses, while human quackery cures none. Christ alone is the one remedy for sin-sick souls. Receive him; believe on his name. We keep hammering at this. I can sympathize with Luther when he said, "I have preached justification by faith so often, and I feel sometimes that you are so slow to receive it, that I could almost take the Bible, and bang it about your heads." I am afraid that the truth would not have entered their hearts if he had done so. This is what we aim at, to get this one thought into a man, "Thou art lost, and therefore such an one as Christ came to save."

One said to me just lately, "Oh, sir, I am the biggest sinner that ever lived!" I replied, "Jesus Christ came into the world to save sinners." "But I have not any strength." "While we were yet without strength, in due time Christ died." "Oh! but," he said, "I have been utterly ungodly." "Christ died for the ungodly." "But I am lost." "Yes," I said, "This is a faithful saying, and worthy of all acceptation, that Christ Jesus came into the world to save sinners." "The Son of man has come to save that which was lost." I said to this man, "You have the brush in your hand, and at every stroke it looks as if you were quoting Scripture. You seem to be making yourself out to be the very man that Christ came to save. If you were to make yourself out to be good and excellent, I should give you this word—Jesus did not come to call the righteous, but sinners to repentance. He did not die for the good, but for the bad. He gave himself for our sins; he never gave himself for our righteousness. He is a Saviour. He has not come yet as a Rewarder of the righteous; that will be in his Second Advent. Now he comes as a great Forgiver of the guilty, and the only Saviour of the lost. Wilt thou come to him in that way?" "Oh! but," my friend said, "I have not anything to bring to Christ." "No," I said, "I know that you have not; but Christ has everything." "Sir," he said, "you do not know me, else you would not talk to me like this;" and I said, "No, and you do not know yourself, and you are worse than you think you are, though you think that you are bad enough in all conscience; but be you as bad as you may, Jesus Christ came on purpose to uplift from the dunghill those whom he sets among princes by his free, rich, sovereign grace."

Oh, come and believe in him, poor sinner! I feel that, if I had all your souls, I would believe in Christ for their salvation; I would trust him to save a million souls if I had them, for he is mighty to save. There can be no limit to his power to forgive. There can be no limit to the merit of his precious blood. There can be no boundary to the efficacy of his plea before the throne. Only trust him, and you must be saved. May his gracious Spirit lead you to do so now, for Christ's sake! Amen.

Exposition by C. H. Spurgeon.
JOHN I. 1—34.

May the Holy Spirit, who inspired these words, inspire us through them as we read them!

Verse 1. *In the beginning was the Word,*

The divine Logos, whom we know as the Christ of God. "In the beginning was the Word." The first words of this Gospel remind us of the first words of the Old Testament: "In the beginning God created the heaven and the earth." Even then "the Word" was; he existed before all time, even from everlasting.

1. *And the Word was with God, and the Word was God.*

I know not how the Deity of Christ can be more plainly declared than in his eternal duration. He is from the beginning. In his glory he was "with God." In his nature he "was God."

2. *The same was in the beginning with God.*

As we have been singing—

"Ere sin was born, or Satan fell;"

ere there was a creature that could fall, "the same was in the beginning with God."

3. *All things were made by him; and without him was not any thing made that was made.*

He that hung upon the cross was the Maker of all worlds. He that became an infant, for our sake, was the Infinite. How low he stooped! How high he must have been that he could stoop so low!

4. *In him was life;*

Essentially, Eternally.

4, 5. *And the life was the light of men. And the light shineth in darkness; and the darkness comprehended it not.*

It never has done so; it never will. You may sometimes call the darkness, the ignorance of men, or the sin of men. If you like, you may call it the wisdom of men, and the righteousness of men, for that is only another form of the same darkness. "The light shineth in darkness; and the darkness comprehended it not."

6. *There was a man sent from God, whose name was John.*

How very different is the style of this verse from those that precede it! How grand, how sublime, are the Evangelist's words when he speaks of Jesus! How truly human he becomes, how he dips his pen in ordinary ink, when he writes: "There was a man sent from God, whose name was John." Yet that was a noble testimony to the herald of Christ. John the Baptist was "a man sent from God."

7. *The same came for a witness, to bear witness of the Light, that all men through him might believe.*

Dear friends, if you and I know our real destiny, and are the servants of God, we are sent that men might, through us, believe in Jesus. John was a special witness; but we ought all to be witnesses to complete the chain of testimony. Every Christian man should reckon that he is sent from God to bear witness to the great Light, that, through him, men might believe.

8, 9. *He was not that Light, but was sent to bear witness of that Light. That was the true Light, which lighteth every man that cometh into the world.*

There was no light from John, except what he reflected from his Lord. All the light comes from Jesus. Every man who comes into the world with any light borrows his light from Christ. There is no other light ; there can be no other. He is " the Light of the world."

10. *He was in the world, and the world was made by him, and the world knew him not.*

This is a sad verse. He was a stranger in his own house. He was unknown amidst his own handiwork. Men whom he had made, made nothing of him. "The world knew him not ; " did not recognize him.

11. *He came unto his own, and his own received him not.*

That favoured circle, the Jewish nation, where revelation had been given, even there, there was no place for him. He must be despised and rejected even by his own nation.

12, 13. *But as many as received him, to them gave he power to become the sons of God, even to them that believe on his name: which were born, not of blood, nor of the will of the flesh, nor of the will of man, but of God.*

To receive Christ, a man must be born of God. It is the simplest thing in all the world, one would think, to open the door of the heart, and let him in ; but no man lets Christ into his heart till first God has made him to be born again, born from above.

14. *And the Word was made flesh, and dwelt among us, (and we beheld his glory, the glory as of the only begotten of the Father,) full of grace and truth.*

They who saw Christ on earth were highly privileged ; but it is a spiritual sight of him alone that is to be desired, and we can have that even now. How full of grace, how full of truth, he is to all those who are privileged to behold him !

15, 16. *John bare witness of him, and cried, saying, This was he of whom I spake, He that cometh after me is preferred before me: for he was before me. And of his fulness have all we received, and grace for grace.*

I wish that we could all say that. Even out of this company, many can say it ; and linking our hands with those who have gone before us, and those who are still with us in the faith, we say unitedly, "Of his fulness have all we received," and we hope to receive from it again to-night, for it is still his fulness. There is never a trace of declining in him. It was fulness when the first sinner came to him ; it is fulness still; it will be fulness to the very end. "And grace for grace." We get grace to reach out to another grace, each grace becoming a stepping-stone to something higher. I do not believe in our rising on the " stepping-stones of our dead selves." They are poor stones ; they all lead downwards. The stepping-stones of the living Christ lead upwards ; grace for grace, grace upon grace, till grace is crowned with glory.

17. *For the law was given by Moses, but grace and truth came by Jesus Christ.*

We know that the law came by Moses. The law has often burdened us, crushed us, convinced us, condemned us. Let us be equally clear that grace and truth come by this divine channel, "Jesus Christ."

18. *No man hath seen God at any time; the only begotten Son, which is in the bosom of the Father, he hath declared him.*

We do not want to see God apart from Christ. I am perfectly satisfied to see the Eternal Light through his own chosen medium, Christ Jesus. Apart from that medium, the light might blind my eyes. "No man hath seen God at any time." Who can look on the sun ? What mind can look on God ? But Christ does not hide the Father ; he manifests him. "The only-begotten Son, which is in the bosom of the Father, he hath declared him."

19—23. *And this is the record of John, when the Jews sent priests and*

Levites from Jerusalem to ask him, Who art thou? And he confessed, and denied not; but confessed, I am not the Christ. And they asked him, What then? Art thou Elias? And he saith, I am not. Art thou that prophet? And he answered, No. Then said they unto him, Who art thou? that we may give an answer to them that sent us. What sayest thou of thyself? He said, I am the voice

Not "I am the Word," but "I am the voice." Christ is the essential Word; we are but the voice to make that Word sound across the desert of human life.

23. *Of one crying in the wilderness, Make straight the way of the Lord, as said the prophet Esaias.*

You see, even as a voice, John was not original. That straining after originality, of which we see so much to-day, finds no warrant among the true servants of God. Even though John is only a voice, yet he is a voice that quotes the Scriptures: "Make straight the way of the Lord, as said the prophet Esaias." The more of Scripture we can voice, the better. Our words, what are they? They are but air. His Word, what is it? It is "grace and truth." May we continually be lending a voice to the great Words of God that have gone before!

24—27. *And they which were sent were of the Pharisees. And they asked him, and said unto him, Why baptizest thou then, if thou be not that Christ, nor Elias, neither that prophet? John answered them, saying, I baptize with water: but there standeth one among you, whom ye know not; he it is, who coming after me is preferred before me, whose shoe's latchet I am not worthy to unloose.*

Ah! dear friends, although it was a lowly expression that John used, you and I often feel that we want something that goes lower even than that. What are we worthy to do for Christ? Yet there are times when, if there is a shoe-latchet to be unloosed, we are too proud to stoop to do it. When there is something to be done that will bring no honour to us, we are too high and mighty to do it. O child of God, if you have ever been in that condition, be greatly ashamed of yourself! John was first in his day, the morning-star of the Light of the gospel, yet even he felt that he was not worthy to do the least thing for Christ. Where shall you and I put ourselves? Paul said that he was "less than the least of all saints." He ran away with a title that might have been very appropriate for us. Well, we must let him have it, I suppose; and we must try to find another like it; or if we cannot find suitable words, God help us to have the humble feeling, which is better still!

28, 29. *These things were done in Bethabara beyond Jordan, where John was baptizing. The next day John seeth Jesus coming unto him, and saith, Behold the Lamb of God, which taketh away the sin of the world.*

John preached a sacrificial Saviour, a sin-bearing Saviour, a sin-atoning Saviour. You and I have nothing else to preach. Let each of us say—

"'Tis all my business here below
To cry, Behold the Lamb!"

30, 31. *This is he of whom I said, After me cometh a man which is preferred before me: for he was before me. And I knew him not:*

Although John knew the Saviour personally, he did not know him officially. He had a token given to him by God, by which he was to know the Messiah; and he did not officially know him till he had that token fulfilled.

31—33. *But that he should be made manifest to Israel, therefore am I come baptizing with water. And John bare record, saying, I saw the Spirit descending from heaven like a dove, and it abode upon him. And I knew him not: but he that sent me to baptize with water, the same said unto me, Upon whom thou shalt see the Spirit descending, and remaining on him, the same is he which baptizeth with the Holy Ghost.*

John would not know of his own judgment. No doubt he was morally certain that Jesus was the Christ. He had been brought up with him; he knew his mother, he had heard of his wondrous birth; John and Jesus must have been often together; but he was not to use his own judgment in this case, but to wait for the sign from heaven; and until he witnessed it, he did not say a word about it. When he saw the Holy Ghost descend upon him, then he knew that it was even he.

34. *And I saw, and bare record that this is the Son of God.*

Hear ye, then, the witness of John. The Christ, who came from Nazareth to be baptized of him in Jordan, he on whom the Holy Ghost descended like a dove, "this is the Son of God." This is the sin-bearing Lamb. Oh, that you and I might fulfil John's expectation, for he spoke that we might believe. He, being dead, yet speaketh. May we believe his witness, and be assured that "this is the Son of God"!

HYMNS FROM "OUR OWN HYMN BOOK"—249, 549, 728.

Now Ready. Uniform with
FROM THE USHER'S DESK TO THE TABERNACLE PULPIT.

Price 2s. 6d. Bound in Cloth, with appropriate design.
Bevelled Boards, Silvered Edges, 3s. 6d.

FROM THE PULPIT TO THE PALM-BRANCH,
A MEMORIAL OF C. H. SPURGEON.

CONTENTS:
FIVE MEMORIAL SERMONS BY DR. A. T. PIERSON.

Descriptive accounts of Mr. Spurgeon's long illness, and partial recovery; his last month at Menton, including verbatim reports of the last two addresses given by him, and the last two articles he wrote; with full particulars of the Memorial and Funeral Services at Menton, Newington, and Norwood; and lists of Churches, Societies, &c., from which expressions of sympathy were received.

Addresses by Revs. Joseph Angus, D.D.; A. T. Pierson, D.D.; Alexander McLaren, D.D.; Canon Fleming, B.D.; Canon Palmer, M.A.; J. Monro Gibson, D.D.; Herber Evans, D.D., T. B. Stephenson, D.D.; A. G. Brown; W. Y. Fullerton; J. Manton Smith; J. W. Harrald; and F. B. Meyer, B.A.; Sir Arthur Blackwood, K.C.B.; Colonel Griffin; Messrs. George Williams, Ira D. Sankey, T. H. Olney, W. Olney, S. R. Pearce, and J. T. Dunn.

List of Illustrations.—Portrait of Mr. C. H. Spurgeon, taken at Menton, January 8th, 1892; Mr. C. H. Spurgeon and Mr. J. C. Houchin at Stambourne; Hôtel Beau Rivage, Menton; Mr. Harrald, Mr. Spurgeon's "armour-bearer"; New Portrait of Mrs. Spurgeon; Mr. Spurgeon's "cosy corner", where he wrote his *Commentary on Matthew*; Mr. Spurgeon's Bedroom after his removal; View of Menton; Funeral Cortège at Menton Station; Pastor James A. Spurgeon; Dr. A. T. Pierson; The Olive-casket in the Tabernacle; The Funeral Cortège entering Norwood Cemetery; Pastor A. G. Brown delivering his address at the grave.

LONDON: PASSMORE AND ALABASTER, PATERNOSTER BUILDINGS, and all Booksellers.

Metropolitan Tabernacle Pulpit.

CHRIST'S HOSPITAL.

A Sermon

INTENDED FOR READING ON LORD'S-DAY, JUNE 12TH, 1892,

DELIVERED BY

C. H. SPURGEON,

AT THE METROPOLITAN TABERNACLE, NEWINGTON,

On Lord's-day Evening, March 9th, 1890.

"He healeth the broken in heart, and bindeth up their wounds."—Psalm cxlvii. 3.

OFTEN as we have read this Psalm, we can never fail to be struck with the connection in which this verse stands, especially its connection with the verse that follows. Read the two together: "He healeth the broken in heart, and bindeth up their wounds. He telleth the number of the stars; he calleth them all by their names." What condescension and grandeur! What pity and omnipotence! He who leads out yonder ponderous orbs in almost immeasurable orbits, nevertheless, is the Surgeon of men's souls, and stoops over broken hearts, and with his own tender fingers closes up the gaping wound, and binds it with the liniment of love. Think of it; and if I should not speak as well as I could desire upon the wonderful theme of his condescension, yet help me by your thoughts to do reverence to the Maker of the stars, who is, at the same time, the Physician for broken hearts and wounded spirits.

I am equally interested in the connection of my text with the verse that goes before it: "The Lord doth build up Jerusalem: he gathereth together the outcasts of Israel." The church of God is never so well built up as when it is built up with men of broken hearts. I have prayed to God in secret many a time, of late, that he would be pleased to gather out from among us a people who should have a deep experience, who should know the guilt of sin, who should be broken and ground to powder under a sense of their own inability and unworthiness; for I am persuaded that, without a deep experience of sin, there is seldom much belief in the doctrines of grace, and not much enthusiasm in praising the Saviour's name. The church needs to be built up with men who have been pulled down. Unless we know in our hearts our need of a Saviour, we shall never be worth much in preaching him. That preacher who has never been converted, what can he say about it? And he who has never been in the dungeon,

No. 2,260.

who has never been in the abyss, who has never felt as if he were cast out from the sight of God, how can he comfort the many who are outcasts, and who are bound with the fetters of despair? May the Lord break many hearts, and then bind them up, that with them he may build up the church, and inhabit it!

But now, leaving the connection, I come to the text itself, and I desire to speak of it so that everyone here who is troubled may derive comfort from it, God the Holy Ghost speaking through it. Consider, first, *the patients and their sickness:* "He healeth the broken in heart." Then, consider, *the Physician and his medicine,* and for a while turn your eyes to him who does this healing work. Then, I shall want you to consider, *the testimonial to the great Physician* which we have in this verse : " He healeth the broken in heart, and bindeth up their wounds." Lastly, and most practically, we will consider, *what we ought to do* towards him who healeth the broken in heart.

I. First, then, consider THE PATIENTS AND THEIR SICKNESS. They are broken in heart. I have heard of many who have died of a broken heart; but here are some who live with a broken heart, and who live all the better for having had their hearts broken; they live another and a higher life than they lived before that blessed stroke broke their hearts in pieces.

There are many sorts of broken hearts, and Christ is good at healing them all. I am not going to lower and narrow the application of my text. The patients of the great Physician are *those whose hearts are broken through sorrow.* Hearts are broken through disappointment. Hearts are broken by bereavement. Hearts are broken in ten thousand ways, for this is a heart-breaking world; and Christ is good at healing all manner of heart-breaks. I would encourage every person here, even though his heart-break may not be of a spiritual kind, to make an application to him who healeth the broken in heart. The text does not say "the spiritually broken in heart", therefore I will not insert an adverb where there is none in the passage. Come hither, ye that are burdened, all ye that labour and are heavy laden ; come hither, all ye that sorrow, be your sorrow what it may; come hither, all ye whose hearts are broken, be the heart-break what it may, for he healeth the broken in heart.

Still, there is a special brokenness of heart to which Christ gives the very earliest and tenderest attention. He heals *those whose hearts are broken for sin.* Christ heals the heart that is broken because of its sin ; so that it grieves, laments, regrets, and bemoans itself, saying, " Woe is me that I have done this exceeding great evil, and brought ruin upon myself! Woe is me that I have dishonoured God, that I have cast myself away from his presence, that I have made myself liable to his everlasting wrath, and that even now his wrath abideth upon me ! " If there is a man here whose heart is broken about his past life, he is the man to whom my text refers. Are you heart-broken because you have wasted forty, fifty, sixty years ? Are you heart-broken at the remembrance that you have cursed the God who has blessed you, that you have denied the existence of him without whom you never would have been in existence yourself, that you have lived to train your family without godliness, without any respect to the Most High God at all? Has the Lord brought this home to you? Has he made you feel what a hideous thing it is to be blind to Christ, to refuse his love, to reject his blood, to live an enemy to your best Friend? Have you felt this? O my friend, I cannot reach across the gallery to give you my hand; but will you think that I am doing it, for I wish to do it? If there is a heart here broken on account of sin, I thank God for it, and praise the Lord that there is such a text as this: "He healeth the broken in heart."

Christ also heals *hearts that are broken from sin*. When you and sin have quarrelled, never let the quarrel be made up again. You and sin were friends at one time; but now you hate sin, and you would be wholly rid of it if you could. You wish never to sin. You are anxious to be clear of the most darling sin that you ever indulged in, and you desire to be made pure as God is pure. Your heart is broken away from its old moorings. That which you once loved you now hate. That which you once hated you now at least desire to love. It is well. I am glad that you are here, for to you is the text sent, "He healeth the broken in heart."

If there is a broken-hearted person anywhere about, many people despise him. "Oh," they say, "he is melancholy, he is mad, he is out of his mind through religion!" Yes, men despise the broken in heart, but such, O God, thou wilt not despise! The Lord looks after such, and heals them.

Those who do not despise them, at any rate avoid them. I know some few friends who have long been of a broken heart; and when I feel rather dull, I must confess that I do not always go their way, for they are apt to make me feel more depressed. Yet would I not get out of their way if I felt that I could help them. Still, it is the nature of men to seek the cheerful and the happy, and to avoid the broken-hearted. God does not do so; he heals the broken in heart. He goes where they are, and he reveals himself to them as the Comforter and the Healer.

In a great many cases people despair of the broken-hearted ones. "It is no use," says one, "I have tried to comfort her, but I cannot do it." "I have wasted a great many words," says another, "on such and such a friend, and I cannot help him. I despair of his ever getting out of the dark." Not so is it with God; he healeth the broken in heart. He despairs of none. He shows the greatness of his power, and the wonders of his wisdom, by fetching men and women out of the lowest dungeon, wherein despair has shut them.

As for the broken-hearted ones themselves, they do not think that they ever can be converted. Some of them are sure that they never can; they wish that they were dead, though I do not see what they would gain by that. Others of them wish that they had never been born, though that is a useless wish now. Some are ready to rush after any new thing to try to find a little comfort; while others, getting worse and worse, are sitting down in sullen despair. I wish that I knew who these were; I should like to come round, and say just to them, "Come, brother; there must be no doubting and no despair to-night, for my text is gloriously complete, and is meant for you. 'He healeth the broken in heart, and bindeth up their wounds.'" Notice that fifth verse, "Great is our Lord, and of great power; his understanding is infinite." Consequently, he can heal the broken in heart. God is glorious at a dead lift. When a soul cannot stir, or help itself, God delights to come in with his omnipotence, and lift the great load, and set the burdened one free.

It takes great wisdom to comfort a broken heart. If any of you have ever tried it, I am sure that you have not found it an easy task. I have given much of my life to this work; and I always come away from a desponding one with a consciousness of my own inability to comfort the heart-broken and cast-down. Only God can do it. Blessed be his name that he has arranged that one Person of the Sacred Trinity should undertake this office of Comforter, for no man could ever perform its duties. We might as well hope to be the Saviour as to be the Comforter of the heart-broken. Efficiently and completely to save or to comfort must be a work divine. That is why the Holy Spirit has undertaken to be the Comforter; and Christ, through the Divine Spirit, healeth the broken in heart, and bindeth up their wounds with infinite power and unfailing skill.

II. Now, secondly, we are going to consider THE PHYSICIAN AND HIS MEDICINE: "He healeth the broken in heart, and bindeth up their wounds." Who is this that healeth the broken in heart?

I answer, that *Jesus was anointed of God* for this work. He said, "The Spirit of the Lord is upon me, because he hath anointed me to preach the gospel to the poor; he hath sent me to heal the broken-hearted." Was the Holy Spirit given to Christ in vain? That cannot be. He was given for a purpose which must be answered, and that purpose is the healing of the broken-hearted. By the very anointing of Christ by the Holy Spirit, you may be sure that our Physician will heal the broken in heart.

Further, Jesus was *sent of God* on purpose to do this work: "He hath sent me to heal the broken-hearted." If Christ does not heal the broken-hearted, he will not fulfil the mission for which he came from heaven. If the broken-hearted are not cheered by his glorious life and the blessings that flow out of his death, then he will have come to earth for nothing. This is the very errand on which the Lord of glory left the bosom of the Father to be veiled in human clay, that he might heal the broken in heart; and he will do it.

Our Lord was also *educated* for this work. He was not only anointed and sent; but he was trained for it. "How?" say you. Why, he had a broken heart himself; and there is no education for the office of comforter like being placed where you yourself have need of comfort, so that you may be able to comfort others with the comfort wherewith you yourself have been comforted of God. Is your heart broken? Christ's heart was broken. He said, "Reproach hath broken my heart; and I am full of heaviness." He went as low as you have ever been, and deeper than you can ever go. "My God, my God, why hast thou forsaken me?" was his bitter cry. If that be your agonized utterance, he can interpret it by his own suffering. He can measure your grief by his grief. Broken hearts, there is no healing for you except through him who had a broken heart himself. Ye disconsolate, come to him! He can make your heart happy and joyous, by the very fact of his own sorrow, and the brokenness of his own heart. "In all our afflictions he was afflicted." He was "tempted in all points like as we are", "a man of sorrows and acquainted with grief." For a broken heart, there is no physician like him.

Once more, I can strongly recommend my Lord Jesus Christ as the Healer of broken hearts, because he is so *experienced* in the work. Some people are afraid that the doctor will try experiments upon them; but our Physician will only do for us what he has done many times before. It is no matter of experiment with him; it is a matter of experience. If you knock to-night at my great Doctor's door, you will, perhaps, say to him, "Here is the strangest patient, my Lord, that ever came to thee." He will smile as he looks at you, and he will think, "I have saved hundreds like you." Here comes one who says, "That first man's case was nothing compared with mine; I am about the worst sinner who ever lived." And the Lord Jesus Christ will say, "Yes, I saved the worst man that ever lived long ago, and I keep on saving such as he. I delight to do it." But here comes one who has a curious odd way of broken-heartedness. He is an out-of-the-way fretter. Yes, but my Lord is able to "have compassion on the ignorant, and on them that are out of the way." He can lay hold of this out-of-the-way one; for he has always been saving out-of-the-way sinners. My Lord has been healing broken hearts well nigh nineteen hundred years. Can you find a brass-plate anywhere in London telling of a physician of that age? He has been at the work longer than that; for it is not far off six thousand years since he went into this business, and he has been healing the broken in heart ever since that time.

I will tell you one thing about him that I have on good authority, that is, he never lost a case yet. There never was one who came to him with a broken heart, but he healed him. He never said to one, "You are too bad for me to heal;" but he did say, "Him that cometh to me, I will in no wise cast out." My dear hearer, he will not cast you out. You say, "You do not know me, Mr. Spurgeon." No, I do not; and you have come here to-night, and you hardly know why you are here; only you are very low and very sad. The Lord Jesus Christ loves just such as you are, you poor, desponding, doubting, desolate, disconsolate one. Daughters of sorrow, sons of grief, look ye here! Jesus Christ has gone on healing broken hearts for thousands of years, and he is well up in the business. He understands it by experience, as well as by education. He is "mighty to save." Consider him; consider him; and the Lord grant you grace to come and trust him even now!

Thus I have talked to you about the Physician for broken hearts; shall I tell you what his chief medicine is? It is his own flesh and blood. There is no cure like it. When a sinner is bleeding with sin, Jesus pours his own blood into the wound; and when that wound is slow in healing, he binds his own sacrifice about it. Healing for broken hearts comes by the atonement, atonement by substitution, Christ suffering in our stead. He suffered for every one who believeth in him, and he that believeth in him is not condemned, and never can be condemned, for the condemnation due to him was laid upon Christ.

He is clear before the bar of justice as well as before the throne of mercy. I remember when the Lord put that precious ointment upon my wounded spirit. Nothing ever healed me until I understood that he died in my place and stead, died that I might not die; and now, to-day, my heart would bleed itself to death were it not that I believe that he "his own self bare our sins in his own body on the tree." "With his stripes we are healed," and with no medicine but this atoning sacrifice. A wonderful heal-all is this, when the Holy Ghost applies it with his own divine power, and lets life and love come streaming into the heart that was ready to bleed to death.

III. My time flies too quickly; so, thirdly, I want you to consider THE TESTIMONIAL TO THE GREAT PHYSICIAN which is emblazoned in my text. It is God the Holy Ghost who, by the mouth of his servant David, bears testimony to this congregation to-night that the Lord Jesus heals the broken in heart, and binds up their wounds. If I said it, you need no more believe it than I need believe it if you said it. One man's word is as good as another's if we be truthful men; but this statement is found in an inspired Psalm. I believe it; I dare not doubt it, for I have proved its truth.

I understand my text to mean this: *he does it effectually*. As I said last Thursday night, if there is a person cast down or desponding within twenty miles, he is pretty sure to find me out. I laugh sometimes, and say, "Birds of a feather flock together;" but they come to talk to me about their despondency, and sometimes they leave me half desponding in the attempt to get them out of their sadness. I have had some very sad cases just lately, and I am afraid that, when they went out of my room, they could not say of me, "He healeth the broken in heart." I am sure that they could say, "He tried his best. He brought out all the choicest arguments he could think of to comfort me." And they have felt very grateful. They have come back sometimes to thank God that they have been a little bit encouraged; but some of them are frequent visitors; I have been trying to cheer them up by the month together. But, when my Master undertakes the work, "He *healeth* the broken in heart," he not only tries to do it, he does it. He touches the secret sources of the sorrow, and takes the spring of the grief away. We try our best; but we cannot do it. You know it is very hard to deal with the heart. The human heart needs more than human skill to cure it. When a person dies, and the doctors do not know the complaint of which he died, they say, "It was heart disease." They did not understand his malady; that is what that means. There is only one Physician who can heal the heart; but, glory be to his blessed name, "He healeth the broken in heart," he does it effectually.

As I read my text, I understand it to mean, *he does it constantly*. "He healeth the broken in heart." Not merely, "He did heal them years ago"; but, he is doing it now. "He *healeth* the broken in heart, and *bindeth up* their wounds." What, at this minute? Ten minutes to eight? Yes, he is doing this work now. "He healeth the broken in heart," and when the service is over, and the congregation is gone, what will Jesus be doing then? Oh, he will still be healing the broken in heart! Suppose this year 1890 should run out, and the Lord does not come to judgment, what will he be doing then? He will still be healing the broken in heart. He has not used up his ointments. He has not exhausted his patience. He has not in the least degree diminished his power. He still healeth. "Oh, dear!" said one, "if I had come to Christ a year ago, it would have been well with me." If you come to Christ to-night, it will be well with you, for "he healeth the broken in heart." "I fear that I have sinned away my day of grace," says one. "He healeth the broken in heart." I do not know who was the inventor of that idea of "sinning away the day of grace." If you are willing to have Christ, you may have him. If you are as old as Methuselah—and I do not suppose you are older than he was—if you want Christ, you may have him. As long as you are out of hell, Christ is able to save you. He is going on with his old work. Because you are just past fifty, you say the die is cast; because you are past eighty, you say, "I am too old to be saved now." Nonsense! He *healeth*, he *healeth*, he is still doing it, "he healeth the broken in heart."

I go further than that, and say that *he does it invariably*. I have shown you that he does it effectually and constantly; but he does it invariably. There never was a broken heart brought to him that he did not heal. Do not some broken-hearted patients go out at the back door, as my Master's failures? No, not one. There never was one yet that he could not heal. Doctors are obliged, sometimes, in our hospitals to give up some persons, and say that they will never recover. Certain symptoms have proved that they are incurable. But, despairing one, in the divine hospital, of which Christ is the Physician, there never was a patient of his who was turned out as incurable. He is able to save to the uttermost. Do you know how far that is—"to the uttermost"? There is no going beyond "the uttermost", because the uttermost goes beyond everything else, to make it the uttermost. "He is able also to save them to the uttermost that come unto God by him." Where are you, friend "Uttermost"? Are you here to-night? "Ah!" you say, "I wonder that I am not in hell." Well, so do I; but you are not, and you never will be, if you cast yourself on Christ. Rest in the full atonement that he has made; for he healeth always, without any failure, "he healeth the broken in heart, and bindeth up their wounds."

As I read these words, it seems to me that *he glories in doing it*. He said to the Psalmist, by the Holy Spirit, "Write a Psalm in which you shall begin with Hallelujah, and finish with Hallelujah, and set in the middle of the Psalm this as one of the things for which I delight to be praised, that I heal the broken in heart." None of the gods of the heathen were ever praised for this. Did you ever read a song to Jupiter, or to Mercury, or to Venus, or to any of them, in which they were praised for binding up the broken in heart? Jehovah, the God of Israel, the God of Abraham, Isaac, and Jacob, the God and Father of our Lord and Saviour Jesus Christ, is the only God who makes it his boast that he binds up the broken in heart. Come, you big, black sinner; come, you desperado; come, you that have gone beyond all measurement in sin; you can glorify God more than anybody else by believing that he can save even you! He can save you, and put you among the children. He delights to save those that seemed farthest from him.

IV. This is my last point: consider WHAT WE OUGHT TO DO.

If there is such a Physician as this, and we have broken hearts, it goes without saying that, first of all, *we ought to resort to him.* When people are told that they have an incurable disease, a malady that will soon bring them to their grave, they are much distressed; but if, somewhere or other, they hear that the disease may be cured after all, they say, "Where? Where?" Well, perhaps it is thousands of miles away; but they are willing to go, if they can. Or the medicine may be very unpleasant or very expensive; but if they find that they can be cured, they say, "I will have it." If anyone came to their door, and said, "Here it is, it will heal you; and you can have it for nothing, and as much as ever you want of it;" there would be no difficulty in getting rid of any quantity of the medicine, so long as we found people sick. Now, if you have a broken heart to-night, you will be glad to have Christ. I had a broken heart once, and I went to him and he healed it; healed it in a moment, and made me sing for joy! Young men and women, I was about fifteen or sixteen when he healed me; I wish that you would go to him now, while you are yet young. The age of his patients does not matter. Are you younger than fifteen? Boys and girls may have broken hearts; and old men and old women may have broken hearts; but they may come to Jesus, and be healed. Let them come to him to-night, and seek to be healed.

When you are about to go to Christ, possibly you ask, "How shall I go to him?" Go by prayer. One said to me, the other day, "I wish that you would write me a prayer, sir." I said, "No, I cannot do that, go and tell the Lord what you want." He replied, "Sometimes I feel such a great want that I do not know what it is I do want, and I try to pray, but I cannot. I wish that somebody would tell me what to say." "Why!" I said, "the Lord has told you what to say. This is what he has said: 'Take with you words, and turn to the Lord: say unto him, Take away all iniquity, and receive us graciously.'" Go to Christ in prayer with such words as those, or any others that you can get. If you cannot get any words, tears are just as good, and rather better; and groans and sighs and secret desires will be acceptable with God.

But add faith to them. *Trust the Physician.* You know that no ointment will heal you if you do not put it on the wound. Oftentimes, when there is a wound, you want something with which to strap the ointment on. Faith straps on the heavenly heal-all. Go to the Lord with your broken heart, and believe that he can heal you. Believe that he alone can heal you; trust him to do it. Fall at his feet, and say, "If I perish, I will perish here. I believe that the Son of God can save me, and I will be saved by him; but I will never look anywhere else for salvation. 'Lord, I believe; help thou mine unbelief!'" If you have come as far as that, you are very near the light; the great Physician will heal your broken heart before very long Trust him to do it now.

When you have trusted in him, and your heart is healed, and you are happy, *tell others about him.* I do not like my Lord to have any tongue-tied children. I do not mean that I want you all to preach. When a whole church takes to preaching, it is as if the whole body were a mouth, and that would be a vacuum. I want you to tell others, in some way or other, what the Lord has done for you; and be earnest in endeavouring to bring others to the great Physician. You all recollect, therefore I need not tell you again, the story that we had about the doctor at one of our hospitals, a year or two ago. He healed a dog's broken leg, and the grateful animal brought other dogs to have their broken legs healed. That was a good dog; some of you are not half as good as that dog. You believe that Christ is blessing you, yet you never try to bring others to him to be saved. That must not be the case any longer. We must excel that dog in our love for our species; and it must be our intense desire that, if Christ has healed us, he should heal our wife, our child, our friend, our neighbour; and we should never rest till others are brought to him.

Then, when others are brought to Christ, or even if they will not be brought to him, be sure to *praise him.* If your broken heart has been healed, and you are saved, and your sins forgiven, praise him. We do not sing half enough. I do not mean in our congregations; but when we are at home. We pray every day. Do we sing every day? I think that we should. Matthew Henry used to say, about family prayer, "They that pray do well; they that read and pray do better; they that read and pray and sing do best of all." I think that Matthew Henry was right. "Well, I have no voice," says one. Have you not? Then you never grumble at your wife; you never find fault with your food; you are not one of those that make the household unhappy by your evil speeches. "Oh, I do not mean that!" No, I thought you did not mean that. Well, praise the Lord with the same voice that you have used for complaining. "But I could not lead a tune," says one. Nobody said you were to do so. You can at least sing as I do. My singing is of a very peculiar character. I find that I cannot confine myself to one tune; in the course of a verse I use half-a-dozen tunes; but the Lord, to whom I sing, never finds any fault with me. He never blames me, because I do not keep to this tune or that. I cannot help it. My voice runs away with me, and my heart too; but I keep on humming something or other by way of praising God's name. I would like you to do the same. I used to know an old Methodist; and the first thing in the morning, when he got up, he began singing a bit of a Methodist hymn; and if I met the old man during the day, he was always singing. I have seen him in his little workshop, with his lapstone on his knee, and he was always singing, and beating time with his hammer. When I said to him once, "Why do you always sing, dear brother?" he replied, "Because I always have something to sing about." That is a good reason for singing. If our broken hearts have been healed, we have something to sing about in time and throughout eternity. Let us begin to do so to the praise of the glory of his grace, who "healeth the broken in heart, and bindeth up their wounds." God bless all the broken hearts that are in this congregation to-night, for Jesus' sake! Amen.

Exposition by C. H. Spurgeon.

PSALM CXLVII.

This is one of the Hallelujah Psalms; it begins and ends with "Praise ye the LORD." May our hearts be in tune, that we may praise the Lord while we read these words of praise!

Verse 1. *Praise ye the LORD:*

It is not enough for the Psalmist to do it himself. He wants help in it, so he says, "Praise *ye* the LORD." Wake up, my brethren; bestir yourselves, my sisters; come, all of you, and unite in this holy exercise! "Praise ye the LORD."

1. *For it is good to sing praises unto our God; for it is pleasant; and praise is comely.*

When a thing is good, pleasant, and comely, you have certainly three excellent reasons for attending to it. It is not everything that is good that is pleasant; nor everything that is pleasant that is good; but here you have a happy combination of goodness, pleasantness, and comeliness. It will do you good to praise God. God counts it good, and you will find it a pleasant exercise. That which is the occupation of heaven must be happy employment. "It is good to sing praises unto our God," "it is pleasant," and certainly nothing is more "comely" and beautiful, and more in accordance with the right order of things, than for creatures to praise their Creator, and the children of God to praise their Father in heaven.

2. *The LORD doth build up Jerusalem:*

Praise his name for that. You love his church; be glad that he builds it up. Praise him who quarries every stone, and puts it upon the one foundation that is laid, even Jesus.

2. *He gathereth together the outcasts of Israel.*

Praise him for that. If you were once an outcast, and he has gathered you, give him your special personal song of thanksgiving.

3. *He healeth the broken in heart, and bindeth up their wounds.*

Praise him for that, ye who have had broken hearts! If he has healed you, surely you should give him great praise.

4. *He telleth the number of the stars; he calleth them all by their names.*

He who heals broken hearts counts the stars, and calls them by their names, as men call their servants, and send them on their way. Praise his name. Can you look up at the starry sky at night without praising him who made the stars, and leads out their host?

5. *Great is our Lord, and of great power: his understanding is infinite.*

Praise him, then; praise his greatness, his almightiness, his infinite wisdom. Can you do otherwise? Oh, may God reveal himself so much to your heart that you shall be constrained to pay him willing adoration!

6. *The LORD lifteth up the meek:*

What a lifting up it is for them, out of the very dust where they have been trodden down by the proud and the powerful! The Lord lifts them up. Praise him for that.

6. *He casteth the wicked down to the ground.*

Thus he puts an end to their tyranny, and delivers those who were ground beneath their cruel power. Praise ye his name for this also. Excuse me that I continue to say to you, "Praise ye the Lord," for, often as I say it, you will not praise him too much; and we need to have our hearts stirred up to this duty of praising God, which is so much neglected. After all, it is the praise of God that is the ultimatum of our religion. Prayer does but sow; praise is the harvest. Praying is the end of preaching, and praising is the end of praying. May we bring to God much of the very essence of true religion, and that will be the inward praise of the heart!

7. *Sing unto the LORD with thanksgiving; sing praise upon the harp unto our God:*

"Unto *our* God." How that possessive pronoun puts a world of endearment into the majestic word "God"! "This God is our God." Come, my hearer, can you call God your God? Is he indeed yours? If so, "Sing unto the LORD with thanksgiving; sing praise upon the harp unto our God."

8. *Who covereth the heaven with clouds, who prepareth rain for the earth, who maketh grass to grow upon the mountains.*

They did not talk about the "laws of nature" in those days. They ascribed everything to God; let us do the same. It is a poor science that pushes God farther away from us, instead of bringing him nearer to us. HE covers the heaven with clouds, HE prepares the rain for the earth, HE makes the grass to grow upon the mountains.

9. *He giveth to the beast his food, and to the young ravens which cry.*

Our God cares for birds and beasts. He is as great in little things as in great things. Praise ye his name. The gods of the heathen could not have these things said of them; but our God takes pleasure in providing for the beasts of the field and the birds of the air. The commissariat of the universe is in his hand: "Thou openest thine hand, and satisfiest the desire of every living thing."

10, 11. *He delighteth not in the strength of the horse: he taketh not pleasure in the legs of a man. The LORD taketh pleasure in them that fear him, in those that hope in his mercy.*

Kings of the olden times rejoiced in the thews and sinews of their soldiers and their horses; but God has no delight in mere physical strength. He takes pleasure in spiritual things, even in the weakness which makes us fear him, even that weakness which has not grown into the strength of faith, and yet hopes in his mercy. "The Lord taketh pleasure in them that fear him, in those that hope in his mercy."

12. *Praise the LORD, O Jerusalem; praise thy God, O Zion.*

Let whole cities join together to praise God. Shall we live to see the day when all London shall praise him? Shall we ever, as we go down these streets, with their multitudes of inhabitants, see the people standing in the doorways, and asking, "What must we do to be saved?" Shall we ever see every house with anxious enquirers in it, saying, "Tell us, tell us, how we can be reconciled to God"? Pray that it may be so. In Cromwell's day, if you went down Cheapside at a certain hour of the morning, you would find every blind drawn down; for the inmates were all at family prayer. There is no street like that in London now. In those glorious Puritan times, there was domestic worship everywhere, and the people seemed brought to Christ's feet. Alas, it was but in appearance in many cases; and they soon turned back to their own devices! Imitating the Psalmist, let us say, "Praise the Lord, O London; praise thy God, O England!"

13. *For he hath strengthened the bars of thy gates; he hath blessed thy children within thee.*

As a nation, we have been greatly prospered, defended, and supplied; and the church of God has been made to stand fast against her enemies, and her children have been blessed.

14, 15. *He maketh peace in thy borders, and filleth thee with the finest of the wheat. He sendeth forth his commandment upon earth: his word runneth very swiftly.*

Oriental monarchs were very earnest to have good post arrangements. They sent their decrees upon swift dromedaries. They can never be compared with the swiftness of the purpose of God's decree. "His word runneth very swiftly." Oh, that the day would come when, over all the earth, God's writ should run, and God's written Word should be reverenced, believed, and obeyed!

16. *He giveth snow like wool:*

Men say, "*it*" snows; but what "*it*" is it that snows? The Psalmist rightly says of the Lord, "HE giveth snow." They say that, according to the condition of the atmosphere, snow is produced; but the believer says, "He giveth snow like wool." It is not only like wool for whiteness; but it is like it for the warmth which it gives.

16. *He scattereth the hoar frost like ashes.*

The simile is not to be easily explained; but it will often have suggested itself to you who, in the early morning, have seen the hoar frost scattered abroad.

17. *He casteth forth his ice like morsels: who can stand before his cold?*

None can stand before his heat; but when he withdraws the fire, and takes away the heat, the cold is equally destructive. It burns up as fast as fire would. "Who can stand before his cold?" If God be gone, if the Spirit of God be taken away from the church, or from any of you, who can stand before his cold? The deprivation is as terrible as if it were a positive infliction. "Who can stand before his cold?"

18. *He sendeth out his word, and melteth them: he causeth his wind to blow, and the waters flow.*

The frozen waters were hard as iron; the south wind toucheth them, and they flow again. What can God not do? The great God of nature is our God. Let us praise him. Oh, may our hearts be in a right key to-night to make music before him!

19. *He sheweth his word unto Jacob, his statutes and his judgments unto Israel.*

This is something greater than all his wonders in nature. The God of nature is the God of revelation. He hath not hidden his truth away from men. He hath come out of the eternal secrecies, and he hath showed his word, especially his Incarnate Word, unto his people. Let his name be praised.

20. *He hath not dealt so with any nation:*

Or, with any other nation. He revealed his statutes and his judgments to Israel; and since their day, the spiritual Israel has been privileged in like manner: "He hath not dealt so with any nation."

20. *And as for his judgments, they have not known them.*

Even to-day there are large tracts of country where God is not known. If we know him, let us praise him.

20. *Praise ye the LORD.*

Hallelujah! The Psalm ends upon its key-note: "Praise ye the LORD." So may all our lives end! Amen.

HYMNS FROM "OUR OWN HYMN BOOK"—386, 537, 587.

Metropolitan Tabernacle Pulpit.

ONE WORKER PREPARING FOR ANOTHER.

A Sermon

INTENDED FOR READING ON LORD'S-DAY, JUNE 19TH, 1892,*

DELIVERED BY

C. H. SPURGEON,

AT THE METROPOLITAN TABERNACLE, NEWINGTON,

On *Thursday Evening, August 14th*, 1890.

"Now, behold, in my trouble I have prepared for the house of the LORD an hundred thousand talents of gold, and a thousand thousand talents of silver; and of brass and iron without weight; for it is in abundance: timber also and stone have I prepared; and thou mayest add thereto."—1 Chronicles xxii. 14.

THE building of the temple is an admirable type of the building of the Church of God. I am afraid that there are some present with us at this time who have never helped to build the spiritual temple for Christ. They are not, themselves, living stones. They are no part of God's spiritual house; and they have never helped to bring their cedar, or iron, or gold to the great Builder of the Church. In fact, there may be some here who have rather helped to pull it down, some who have delighted to throw away the stones, and who have tried to hide from the divine Builder the precious material which he intends to use in the sacred edifice. Judge your own hearts; and if you cannot say that you are a living stone, if you have not helped to build up the Church of Christ, may you repent of your sin, and may the grace of God convert you! But if you are workers for the Lord, if your hearts are right with God, I think that I shall be able to say

---

* This sermon is intended for reading on *the first anniversary of the beloved preacher's birthday since his death.* While he was with us, he always looked for special contributions for the Stockwell Orphanage at this season. He did not seek birthday presents for himself; but he desired that all friends, who wished to show their love to him, would do so by helping to maintain his fatherless family of 500 children. We trust that no one will allow this useful institution to suffer because *his* voice can no longer plead for it; but that, through this sermon, each reader will hear him saying, "Dear friend, the Orphanage still needs thy loving and generous assistance; thou hast often helped it by thy gifts in the past, *and thou mayest add thereto;* or if thou hast not hitherto given to it, others have, *and thou mayest add thereto.*"

Contributions will be gratefully received by the Treasurer, Spurgeons' Orphan Home, Stockwell Orphanage, Clapham Road, London. Collecting-cards and boxes may be obtained of the Secretary. The *Annual Festival* will be held on *Wednesday afternoon and evening, June 22nd.* All friends are invited to be present.

No. 2,261.

some things that will encourage you to work on, even if you should not for a time see any immediate results from your work.

There were many who helped to build the temple: David gathering the materials; Solomon, the master mason, by whose name the temple would afterwards be called; the princes helping him in the great work; strangers, foreigners, and aliens, who dwelt throughout Israel and Judah; these all took their share, and even the Tyrians and Zidonians had a part in the work. Now, we have here many ministers of God and students, Davids and Solomons; but I pray that many, who are strangers as yet, may be enlisted in this holy service by our great Lord and King, and that some, who are farthest off from Christ, Tyrians and Zidonians, who have gone far away from God, may be enabled, by divine grace, to contribute their share to this glorious work of building a house for the living God, a house not made of gold, and silver, and stone, and timber, but a spiritual house for the indwelling of the Holy Spirit.

I. In considering our text, let us notice, first, that DAVID HAD ZEALOUSLY DONE HIS PART, although he might not build the temple. There are many servants of God whose names are little known, who, nevertheless, are doing a work that is essential to the building up of the Church of God. I have known many such, who have never lived to realize any great success; their names have never been written upon any great temples that have been built; but, nevertheless, they have worthily done their part, even as David did.

You see, then, first, that *David had gathered the materials.* Many a man collects people together, and yet he has not the fashioning of them. He is the founder of a Christian congregation; but he does not live to see many conversions. He gets together the raw material upon which another shall work. He ploughs and he sows; but it wants another man to come and water the seed, and perhaps another to gather in the harvest. Still, the sower did his work, and deserves to be remembered for what he did. David did his part of the work, in getting together the materials for the temple.

Besides which, *he fashioned some of the materials.* He had the stones cut from the quarry, and many of them shaped to take their places, by-and-by, in silence in the temple, when it should be reared without sound of hammer or axe. So there are teachers and preachers who help to form the characters of their scholars and hearers, by working away upon their minds and hearts. They will never build up a great church; but still they are knocking the rough edges off the stones. They are preparing and fashioning them; and by-and-by the builder will come and make good use of them.

David had prepared the way for Solomon's temple. It was by his fighting that the time of peace came, in which the temple could be erected. Though he is called a man of blood, yet it was needful that the foes of Israel should be overthrown. There could be no peace till her adversaries had been crushed; and David did that. You do not hear much about the men who prepare the way for others. Somebody else comes along, and apparently does all the work; and his name is widely known and honoured; but God remembers the heralds, the pioneers, the men who prepare the way, the men who, by casting out devils, routing grievous errors, and working needful reforms, prepare the way for the triumphal progress of the gospel.

Moreover, *David found the site for the temple.* He discovered it; he purchased it; and he handed it over to Solomon. We do not always remember the men who prepare the sites for the Lord's temples. Luther is rightly remembered; but there were Reformers before Luther. There were hundreds of men and women who burned for Christ, or who perished in prison, or who were put to cruel deaths for the gospel. Luther comes when the occasion has been made for him, and when a site has been cleared for him upon which to build the temple of God. But God remembers all those pre-Reformation heroes. It may be your lot, dear friend, to clear the site, and to make the occasion for others; and you may die before you see even a corner-stone of your own work laid; for it will be yours when it is finished, and God will remember what you have done.

Further, *it was David who received the plans from God.* The Lord wrote upon his heart what he would have done. He told him, even to the weight of the candlesticks and lamps, everything that was to be arranged. Solomon, wise as he was, did not plan the temple. He had to borrow the designs from his father, who received them direct from God. Many a man is far-seeing; he gets the plan of the gospel into his heart, he sees a way in which great things can be done, and yet he is scarcely permitted to put his own hand to the work. Another will come by-and-by, and will carry out the plan that the first one received; but we must not forget the first man, who went into the secret place of the Most High, and learned in the place of thunder what God would have his people do.

David did one thing more; before he died, *he gave a solemn charge to others;* he charged Solomon, and the princes, and all the people, to carry out the work of building the temple. I revere the man who, in his old age, when there is weight in every syllable that he utters, concludes his life by urging others to carry on the work of Christ. It is something to gather about your last bed young men who have years of usefulness before them, and to lay upon their conscience and their heart the duty of preaching Christ crucified, and winning the souls of men for the Lord.

So you see that David had done his part toward the building of the temple. I should like to ask every believer here, *Have you done your part?* You are a child of God; God has loved you, and chosen you; you have been redeemed with precious blood. You know better than to think of working in order to save yourself; you are saved; but have you diligently done all that you can do for your Lord and Master? It was well said, in the prayer-meeting before this service, that there were several thousand members of this church who could not preach, and there were some who did preach of whom the same thing might be said, for it was poor preaching, after all; and our brother said in his prayer, "Lord, help us who cannot preach, to pray for the man who does!" Have you, dear friend, who cannot preach, made a point of praying for the pastor of the church to which you belong? It is a great sin on the part of church-members if they do not daily sustain their pastor by their prayers.

Then there is much else that you can do for Christ, in your family, in your business, and in the neighbourhood where you live. Could you go to bed to-night, and there close your eyes for the last time, feeling, "I have finished the work which God gave me to do. I have done all that I could for the winning of souls"? I am afraid that I address some who have a talent wrapped in a napkin, hidden away in the earth. My dear man, go home, and dig it up, before it gets altogether covered with rust, to bear witness against you. Take it up, and put it out to heavenly interest, that your Lord may have what he is entitled to receive. O Christian men and women, there must be very much unused energy in the Church of God! We have a great dynamo that is never used. Oh, that each one would do his own part, even as David did his!

We shall soon be gone; our day lasts not very long. "The night cometh when no man can work." Shall it be said of you, or of me, that we wasted our daylight; and then, when the evening shadows came, we were uneasy and unhappy, and though saved by divine grace, we died with sad expressions of regret for wasted opportunities? It is not very long ago that I sat by the bedside of one who was wealthy, I might say very wealthy. I prayed with him. I had hoped to have found him rejoicing in the Lord, for I knew that he was a child of God; but he was a child of God with a little malformation about the fingers. He could never open his hand as he ought to have done. As I sat by his side, he said, "Pray God, with all your might, that I may live three months, that I may have an opportunity of using my wealth in the cause of Christ." He did not live much more than three hours after he said that. Oh, that he had woke up a little sooner to do for the Master's Church and cause what he ought to have done! Then he would not have had that regret to trouble him in his last hours. He knew the value of the precious blood, and he was resting in it; and I had great joy in knowing that all his hope and all his trust were in his Lord, and he was saved; but it was with a great deal of regret and trembling. I would spare any of you who have wealth such trouble on your dying bed.

If there is a young man here, who has the ability to preach the gospel, or to be doing something for Christ, and he is doing nothing, I am sure that it will be a pain to him one of these days. When conscience is thoroughly aroused, and his heart is getting nearer to God than it has been, he will bitterly regret that he did not avail himself of every occasion to talk of Christ, and seek to bring souls to him. I should like these practical thoughts to go round these galleries, and through this area, till some men and women shall say, "We have not done our part, as David did; but by God's grace we will do so, and he shall have all the praise."

That is my first head, then, David had zealously done his part.

II. But, secondly, there is this remarkable fact in the text, DAVID HAD DONE HIS PART IN TROUBLE. Read it: "Now, behold, in my trouble I have prepared for the house of the Lord an hundred thousand talents of gold;" and so on. In the margin of your Bibles, you will find the words, "in my poverty." It is strange that David should talk about poverty when his gifts amounted to many millions of pounds.

David thought little of what he had prepared. He calls it poverty, I think, because it is the way of the saints to count anything that they do for God to be very little. The most generous men in the world think the least of what they give to God's cause. David, with his millions that he gives, says, " In my poverty I have prepared for the house of the Lord." As he looked at the gold and silver, he said to himself, " What is all this to God?" And the brass and the iron, that could not be reckoned, it was so much and so costly; he thought it was all nothing to Jehovah, who fills heaven and earth, whose grandeur and glory are altogether unspeakable. If you have done the most that you can for God, you will sit down, and weep that you cannot do ten times as much. You that do little for the Lord will be like a hen with one chick; you will think a great deal of it. But if you have a great number of works, and you are doing much for Christ, you will wish that you could do a hundred times as much. Your song will be,—

" Oh, for a thousand tongues to sing
My great Redeemer's praise!"

Oh, to be multiplied a thousand-fold, that we might, anywhere and everywhere, serve Jesus with heart, and mind, and soul, and strength! So David here considers that what he did was very little.

Yet, *it was a proof of his sincerity.* That he should be saving all this wealth, and preparing for the house of his God in the time of trouble, was a proof of great sincerity. Some Christians want to have all sunshiny weather, and the birds must sing all day and all night to please them. If they receive a rebuke, or somebody seems a little cold to them, they will do no more. I have seen many, who called themselves Christians, who were like a silly child at play, who says, when something offends him, "'I won't play any more." They run away at the first rough word that they hear. But David, in the day of his trouble, when his heart was ready to break, still went on with his great work of providing for the house of God. Some who have attended this house of prayer have been absent, and when we have enquired the reason, they have said that they had become so poor that they did not like to come. Oh, dear friends, we would like to see you, however poor you are! Why, if you are in trouble, you should come all the more; for where could you go to find comfort better than to the house of God? Never, I pray you, stay away on account of poverty. David said that he had prepared for the house of his God in the time of his trouble; and that proved his sincerity. One said to me, " Ever since I have been a Christian, everything has seemed to go wrong with me." Suppose that everything should be taken away from you, should you not be grateful that you have an eternal treasure in heaven, and that these losses, which might have broken your heart if you had not known the Saviour, are now sent in heavenly discipline to you, and are working for your good? It shows that a man is right with God when he can walk with Christ in the mire and in the slough. God does not want you to wear silver slippers, and to walk on a well-mown, well-rolled grassy lawn, all the way to heaven.

David prepared for the house of the Lord in his trouble; and I have no doubt that *it was a solace to his sorrow*. To have something to do for Jesus, and to go right on with it, is one of the best ways to get over a bereavement, or any heavy mental depression. If you can pursue some great object, you will not feel that you are living for nothing. You will not sit down in despair; for, whatever your trouble may be, you will still have this to live for, " I want to help in building the Church of God, and I will do my part in it whatever happens to me. Come poverty or wealth, come sickness or health, come life or death, as long as there is breath in my body, I will go on with the work that God has given me to do." Do I speak to any who are in great trouble? If you are a Christian, the best advice that I can give you is this, get to work for Christ, and you will forget your trouble. If you are not a Christian, I advise you to trust the Saviour at once, for he is the only solace of spiritual sorrow.

Again, *it was an incentive to service* when David, in his trouble, prepared for the house of the Lord. There were many things in trouble that would tend to damp his ardour, and make him feel as if he could not hold out any longer; but he said to himself, " I must go on with this work for God. His temple must be 'exceeding magnifical', and my son Solomon must build it, so I must go on gathering the materials." So he just roused himself afresh, and went on with his work with new earnestness, whenever his trouble would otherwise have depressed him.

It must also have given an elevation to David's whole life. To have a noble purpose, and to pursue that purpose with all your might, prevents your being like " dumb driven cattle", and lifts you out of the mist and fog of the valley, and sets your feet upon the hill-top, where you can commune with God. I would suggest to our younger friends that they should begin their Christian life with a high purpose, and that they should never forget that purpose; and if trouble should come, they should say, " Let it come; my face is set, like a flint, to do this work to which my Lord has called me, and I will pursue it with all my might." It may seem as if there were no spiritual help in such advice as this; but, believe me, there is. If God shall give you grace to go on with your life-work, he will thereby give you grace to overcome your life-trouble.

Ye who would be like your Master, ask not to have a smooth path, and great success. Remember what a life of sorrow he lived. He was grief's close acquaintance. Yet although he saw but a small Church rising before his bodily eye, he knew that he was doing the work that God had given him to do, and he went on with it through agony and bloody sweat, through shame and spitting. He was not more in earnest when he rode in state through the streets of Jerusalem than he was when he hung on the cross of Calvary. He was resolved to do his work; and in trouble he did it, and he amassed treasure beyond all conception for the building of his Church. Riches of grace and wonders of glory he gathered together by his suffering and his death. If you would be like your Lord, you must be able to say with David, " Behold, in my trouble, I have prepared for the house of the Lord." God give his troubled ones to enter into fellowship with the Lord Jesus Christ in this respect!

III. I am glad that I have come to my third point, for my strength well-nigh fails me. What I have to say here is this: DAVID'S WORK FITS ON TO THE WORK OF ANOTHER. That should be a great joy to some of you who do not see much coming of what you are doing. Your work is going to fit on to somebody else's work.

This is *the order of God's providence* in his Church. It does not often happen that he gives a whole piece of work to one man; but he seems to say to him, "You go and do so much; then I will send somebody else to do the rest." How this ought to cheer some of you up, the thought that your work may be no failure, though in itself it may seem to be so, because it fits on to the work of somebody else who is coming after you, and so it will be very far from a failure! You have sometimes seen a man take a contract to put in the foundations of a house, and to carry it up to a certain height. He has done that; he will not be the builder of that house; that will be the work of the next contractor, who carries up the walls, and puts on the roof, and so forth. Yes, but he who did the foundation-work did a great deal, and he is as much the builder of the house as the man who carries up the walls. So, if you go to a country town or village, and you preach the gospel to a few poor folk, you may never have seemed very successful; but you have been preparing the way for somebody else who is coming after you.

I am told that my venerable predecessor, Dr. Rippon, used often, in his pulpit, to pray for somebody, of whom he knew nothing, who would follow him in the ministry of the church, and greatly increase it. He seemed to have in his mind's eye some young man, who, in after years, would greatly enlarge the number of the flock, and he often prayed for him. He died, and passed away to heaven, about the time that I was born. Older members of the church have told me that they have read the answer to Dr. Rippon's prayers in the blessing that has been given to us these many years. If you keep your eyes open, you will see the same thing happen again. You will notice how one shall do his work, which shall be necessary to some larger work that somebody else will do after him. This is God's way, so that the second man, the Solomon coming after David, may do his work all the better because of what his father has done before him. Solomon had not to spend years in collecting the materials for the temple; he might not have got through the building if he had had that task. His good old father had done all that for him; and all that he had to do was to spend the money that David had gathered, work up the gold, and silver, and brass, and iron, bring in the big stones, and put them in their places, and build the house for God. I daresay that Solomon often thought gratefully of his father David, and what he had done; and you and I, if God blesses us, ought always to think with thanksgiving of the Davids who went before us. If you have success in your class, my sister, remember that there was an excellent Christian woman who had the class before you. You come, young man, into the Sunday-school, and you think that you must be somebody very great because you have had several conversions in your class. How about the brother who had to give up the class through ill-health? You took his place: who knows which of you will have the honour at the last great day?

I was about to say, Who cares? for we do not live for honour, we live to serve God; and if I can serve God best by digging out the cellar, and you can serve God best by throwing out that ornamental bay window, my brother, you go on with your bay window, and I will go on with my cellar, for what matters it what we do so long as the house is built, and God is glorified thereby? It is the way of God in providence to set one man to do part of a work which pieces on to that of another man.

But *this is a terrible blow at self.* Self says, "I like to begin something of my own, and I like to carry it out; I do not want any interference from other people." A friend proposed, the other day, to give you a little help in your service. You looked at him as if he had been a thief. You do not want any help; you are quite up to the mark; you are like a waggon and four horses, and a dog under the waggon as well! There is everything about you that is wanted; you need no help from anybody; you can do all things almost without the help of God! I am very sorry for you if that is your opinion. If you get into God's service, he may say to you, "You shall never begin anything; but shall always come in as the second man;" or, "You shall never finish anything; you shall always be getting ready for somebody else." It is well to have an ambition not to build upon another man's foundation; but do not carry that idea too far. If there is a good foundation laid by another man, and you can finish the structure, be thankful that he has done his part, and rejoice that you are permitted to carry on his work. It is God's way of striking a blow at our personal pride by allowing one man's work to fit on to another's.

I believe that *it is good for the work to have a change of workers.* I am glad that David did not live any longer; for he could not have built the temple. David must die. He has had a good time of service. He has gathered all the materials for the temple. Solomon comes, with young blood and youthful vigour, and carries on the work. Sometimes, the best thing that some of us old folk can do is to go home, and go to heaven, and let some younger man come, and do our work. I know that there are great lamentations about the death of Dr. So-and-So, and Mr. So-and-So; but why? Do you not think that, after all, God can find as good men as those that he has found already? He made those good men, and he is not short of power; he can make others just as good as they have been. I was present at a funeral, where I heard a prayer that rather shocked me. Some brother had said that God could raise up another minister equal to the one that was in the coffin; but prayer was offered by another man, who said that this preacher had been eyes to his blindness, feet to his lameness, and I do not know what beside; and then he said, "Thy poor unworthy dust does not think that thou ever canst or wilt raise up another man like him." So he had not an omnipotent God; but you and I have, and with an omnipotent God it is for the good of the work that David should go to his rest, and that Solomon should come in, and carry on the work.

Certainly, *this creates unity in the Church of God.* If we all had a work of our own, and were shut up to do it, we should not know one another; but now I cannot do my work without your help, my dear friends; and, in some respects, you cannot do your work without my help. We are members one of another, and one helps the other. I hope that I shall never have to do without you. God bless you for all your efficient help! In many Christian works you will have to do without me, one of these days; but that will not matter. There will be somebody who will carry on the work of the Lord; and so long as the work goes on, what matter who does it? God buries the workman, but the devil himself cannot bury the work. The work is everlasting, though the workmen die. We pass away, as star by star grows dim; but the eternal light is never-fading. God shall have the victory. His Son shall come in his glory. His Spirit shall be poured out among the people; and though it be neither this man, nor that, nor the other, God will find the man to the world's end who will carry on his cause, and give to him the glory.

This leaves a place for those who come after. One thing David said to Solomon I like very much, "Thou mayest add thereto." I have quoted that sometimes when the collection has been rather small. I have said to each of our friends who were counting the money, "Thou mayest add thereto." It is not at all a bad text for a collection-sermon; but it may also be used in many other ways.

Here are certain preachers of the gospel. Cannot I put my hand on some young man's shoulder, and say to him, "Thou mayest add thereto; thou hast a good voice; thou hast an active brain; begin to speak for God; there are numbers of godly men in the gospel ministry; if thou art called of God, thou mayest add thereto"? We have a good Sunday-school, though some of you have never seen it. We have a number of loving, earnest teachers; "thou mayest add thereto." Go thou, and teach likewise; or engage in some other work for which the Lord has qualified you.

I wonder whether there is an unconverted man here this evening, or an unconverted woman, whom God has ordained to bless, and to whom he will speak to-night, some stranger whom he will bring in by his almighty grace, some servant of the devil who shall to-night be made a servant of Christ. My Master has a large number of servants; "thou mayest add thereto." If thou wilt yield thyself to Christ, thou mayest come, and help God's people. We want recruits; we are always wanting them. May God lead some, who have been on the side of sin and self, to come out, and say, " Set my name down amongst God's people. By the grace of God, I am going to be on Christ's side, and help to build his temple." Come along, my brother; come along, my sister; we are glad of your help. The work is not all done yet; you are not too late to fight the Lord's battles, nor to win the crown of the victors. The Lord has a large army of the soldiers of the cross; and "thou mayest add thereto." God save thee! Christ bless thee! The Spirit inspire thee! May it be so with very many, for Christ's sake! Amen.

Exposition by C. H. Spurgeon.
1 CHRONICLES XXI. 25—30; XXII.

David was commanded to go to Ornan, or Araunah, the Jebusite, to rear an altar unto the Lord in his threshingfloor. There had been a terrible plague in Jerusalem, in consequence of David's great sin in numbering the people; and they were falling in thousands by the sword of the angel of vengeance. David went up to the threshingfloor of Ornan on Mount Moriah. Ornan was willing to give it to him, but he determined to buy it. We read in the twenty-fifth verse:—

Verses 25—28. *So David gave to Ornan for the place six hundred shekels of gold by weight. And David built there an altar unto the LORD, and offered burnt offerings and peace offerings, and called upon the LORD; and he answered him from heaven by fire upon the altar of burnt offering. And the LORD commanded the angel; and he put up his sword again into the sheath thereof. At that time when David saw that the LORD had answered him in the threshingfloor of Ornan the Jebusite, then he sacrificed there.*

There was the place for the temple, where the angel sheathed his sword. Christ Jesus, in his great atonement, is the corner-stone of the temple where divine justice sheathes its sword. There let the house of God be built. Every true Church of God is founded on the glorious doctrine of the atoning sacrifice. It was a threshingfloor, too; and God has built his Church on a threshingfloor. Depend upon it, the flail will always be going in every true Church, to fetch out the wheat from the chaff. We must have tribulation if we are in the Church of God. The threshingfloor will always be needed until we are taken up to the heavenly garner above.

29, 30. xxii. 1. *For the tabernacle of the LORD, which Moses made in the wilderness, and the altar of the burnt offering, were at that season in the high place at Gibeon. But David could not go before it to enquire of God: for he was afraid because of the sword of the angel of the LORD. Then David said, This is the house of the LORD God, and this is the altar of the burnt offering for Israel.*

Now he knew where the temple was to be built; of a certainty he had discovered that long-predestined site of which God said, "Here will I dwell." This was the very hill whereon Abraham offered up his son Isaac; a hill, therefore, most sacred by covenant to the living God. He delighted to remember the believing obedience of his servant Abraham, and there he would have his temple built.

2. *And David commanded to gather together the strangers that were in the land of Israel; and he set masons to hew wrought stones to build the house of God.*

Observe here a very gracious eye to us who are Gentiles. The temple was built on the threshingfloor of a Jebusite; Ornan was not of the seed of Israel, but one of the accursed Jebusites. It was his land that must be bought for the temple; and now David would employ the strangers who lived in the midst of Israel, but were not of the chosen race, to quarry the stones for the house of God. There was a place for Gentiles in the heart of God, and they had a share in the building of his temple.

3, 4. *And David prepared iron in abundance for the nails for the doors of the gates, and for the joinings; and brass in abundance without weight; also cedar trees in abundance: for the Zidonians and they of Tyre brought much cedar wood to David.*

Here are the Gentiles again, the Zidonians and the men of Tyre; those that went down to the sea in ships, that had no part nor lot with Israel. They were to bring the cedar wood to David. What an opening of doors of hope there was for poor castaway Gentiles in that fact!

5. *And David said, Solomon my son is young and tender, and the house that is to be builded for the LORD must be exceeding magnifical, of fame and of glory throughout all countries: I will therefore now make preparation for it.*

This was beautiful and thoughtful on David's part. It might be too great a strain upon the young man to collect the materials for the temple as well as to build it; therefore David will take his part, and prepare the materials for the house of the Lord. If we cannot do one thing, let us do another; but, somehow, let us help in building the Church of God. The Church to-day seems but a poor thing; but it is to be "exceeding magnifical." The glory of the world is to be the Church of God; and the glory of the Church of God is the Christ of God. Let us do as much as we can to build a spiritual house for our Lord's indwelling.

5—7. *So David prepared abundantly before his death. Then he called for Solomon his son, and charged him to build an house for the LORD God of Israel. And David said to Solomon, My son, as for me, it was in my mind to build an house unto the name of the LORD my God:*

And it was well that it was in his mind. God often takes the will for the deed. If you have a large-hearted purpose in your mind, cherish it, and do your best to carry it out: but if for some reason you should never be permitted to carry out your own ideal, it shall be equally acceptable to God, for it was in your heart.

8. *But the word of the LORD came to me, saying, Thou hast shed blood abundantly, and hast made great wars: thou shalt not build an house unto my name, because thou hast shed much blood upon the earth in my sight.*

In very much of that fighting David had been faultless; for he fought the battles of the people of God. Still, there are some things that men are called to do, for which they are not to be condemned; but they disqualify them for higher work. It was so in David's case; he had been a soldier, and he might help to build the temple by collecting the materials for it, but he must not build it.

9. *Behold, a son shall be born to thee, who shall be a man of rest;*

God's Church is to be a place of rest. God's temple was to be built by "a man of rest."

9. *And I will give him rest from all his enemies round about: for his name shall be Solomon, and I will give peace and quietness unto Israel in his days.*

Then the house of the Lord would be built; no stain of blood would be upon it. The only blood therein should be that of the holy sacrifices, symbolical of the great Sacrifice of Christ.

10, 11. *He shall build an house for my name; and he shall be my son, and I will be his father; and I will establish the throne of his kingdom over Israel for ever. Now, my son, the LORD be with thee; and prosper thou, and build the house of the LORD thy God, as he hath said of thee.*

May such a blessing come upon every young man here! May the Lord be with thee, my son! May the Lord prosper thee, and may he make thee a builder of his house in years to come!

12. *Only the LORD give thee wisdom and understanding, and give thee charge concerning Israel, that thou mayest keep the law of the LORD thy God.*

How much wisdom will be wanted by the young brethren present who hope to be builders of the house of God! When the Lord says to you, "Ask what I shall give you," ask for divine wisdom, ask to be taught of him, and ask that you may have grace to do his will in all things.

13. *Then shalt thou prosper, if thou takest heed to fulfil the statutes and judgments which the LORD charged Moses with concerning Israel: be strong, and of good courage; dread not, nor be dismayed.*

It is a great thing for a Christian to keep his courage up; and especially for a builder of the Church of God to be always brave, and with a stout heart to do God's will, come what may.

14. *Now, behold, in my trouble I have prepared for the house of the LORD an hundred thousand talents of gold, and a thousand thousand talents of silver; and of brass and iron without weight; for it is in abundance: timber also and stone have I prepared; and thou mayest add thereto.*

We are unable to tell exactly the amount of precious metal prepared by David; we have to take into account the value of gold and silver in his day; it was probably not so great as it is now. We know this much; it was an enormous sum which David had gathered for the building of the house of God.

15. *Moreover there are workmen with thee in abundance,*

We must have the workmen; they are more precious than the gold. They cannot be put down at any sum of silver: "there are workmen with thee in abundance."

15. *Hewers and workers of stone and timber, and all manner of cunning men for every manner of work.*

God will find for his Church enough men, and the right sort of men, as long as he has a Church to be built; but he would have us pray him to send forth labourers. We forget that prayer, and hence we have to lament that there are so few faithful servants of God. Cry to the Lord about the lack of labourers; he can soon supply as many as are needed.

16. *Of the gold, the silver, and the brass, and the iron, there is no number. Arise therefore, and be doing, and the LORD be with thee.*

A very nice text for stirring up idle church-members, who are well content with being spiritually fed, but who are doing nothing for the Lord: "Arise therefore, and be doing, and the LORD be with thee!"

17, 18. *David also commanded all the princes of Israel to help Solomon his son, saying, Is not the LORD your God with you?*

What a good reason for working! What an admirable reason for giving! What an excellent reason for helping with the work! "Is not the LORD your God with you?"

18. *And hath he not given you rest on every side?*

If he gives you rest, you are to take no rest, but to get to his work. He is the best workman for God who enjoys perfect rest. It is always a pity to go out to preach or teach unless you have perfect rest towards God. When your own heart is quiet, and your spirit is still, then you can work for God with good hope of success.

18. *For he hath given the inhabitants of the land into mine hand; and the land is subdued before the LORD, and before his people.*

The fighting is over; now go ahead with your building.

19. *Now set your heart and your soul to seek the LORD your God;*

Do not go to build a house for God, and think that is all that is required. You want spiritual communion with God; and you will not do even the common work of sawing and planing and building aright unless you seek God, and are in fellowship with him.

19. *Arise therefore, and build ye the sanctuary of the LORD God, to bring the ark of the covenant of the LORD, and the holy vessels of God, into the house that is to be built to the name of the LORD.*

May God teach us some lessons by this reading! Amen.

HYMNS FROM "OUR OWN HYMN BOOK"—423, 681, 695.

Metropolitan Tabernacle Pulpit.

CHRIST'S CURATE IN DECAPOLIS.

A Sermon

Intended for Reading on Lord's-day, June 26th, 1892,

DELIVERED BY

C. H. SPURGEON,

AT THE METROPOLITAN TABERNACLE, NEWINGTON,

On Lord's-day Evening, April 27th, 1890.

"And they began to pray him to depart out of their coasts. And when he was come into the ship, he that had been possessed with the devil prayed him that he might be with him. Howbeit Jesus suffered him not, but saith unto him, Go home to thy friends, and tell them how great things the Lord hath done for thee, and hath had compassion on thee."—Mark v. 17—19.

That is a striking name for a man, "he that had been possessed with the devil." It would stick to him as long as he lived, and it would be a standing sermon wherever he went. He would be asked to tell the story of what he used to be, and how the change came about. What a story for any man to tell! It would not be possible for us to describe his life while he was a demoniac—the midnight scenes among the tombs, the cutting of himself with stones, the howling, the frightening away of all the travellers that went near him, the binding with chains, the snapping of the manacles, the breaking of the fetters, and a great many details that he alone could enter into when he told the story among his own familiar friends. With what pathos would he tell how Jesus came that way, and how the evil spirit forced him to confront him! He would say, "That was the best thing that could have happened to me, to be brought to the Master of that desperate legion of demons, which had encamped within my nature, and made my soul to be its barracks." He would tell how, in a moment, out went the whole legion at the word of Christ.

There are some people who could tell a story very like this man's, a story of slavery to Satan, and deliverance by the power of Christ. If you can tell such a story, do not keep it to yourself. If Jesus has done great things for thee, be ever ready to speak of it, till all men shall know what Christ can do. I think that great sinners who have been saved are specially called upon to publish the good news, the gospel of the grace of God. If you have been valiant against the truth, be valiant for the truth. If you were not lukewarm when you served Satan, be not lukewarm now that you have come to serve

No. 2,262.

Christ. There are some of us here who might bear the name of "the man that was born blind", or "the leper that was healed", or "the woman that was a sinner"; and I hope that we shall all be willing to take any name or any title that will glorify Christ. I do not find that this man ever prosecuted Mark for libel because he wrote of him as "he that had been possessed with the devil." Oh, no! He owned that he was possessed with the devil once; and he glorified God that he had been delivered by the Lord Jesus.

I. I am going to make a few observations upon the passage I have chosen for a text; and the first observation is this, SEE HOW MEN'S DESIRES DIFFER. We find in the seventeenth verse that, "they began to pray him to depart out of their coasts." In the eighteenth verse, "he that had been possessed with the devil prayed him that he might be with him." The people wanted Christ to go away from them; the man whom he had cured wanted to go wherever he might go. To which class do you belong, my dear friend?

I hope you do not belong to the first class, the class of *the many who pray Jesus to depart from them*. Why did they want him to go?

I think it was, first, because they loved to be quiet, and to dwell at ease. It was a great calamity that had happened; the swine had run into the sea. They did not want any more such calamities, and evidently the Person who had come among them possessed extraordinary power. Had he not healed the demoniac? Well, they did not want him; they did not want anything extraordinary. They were easy-going men, who would like to go on the even tenor of their way, so they asked him to be good enough to go away. There are some people of that kind still living. They say, "We do not want a revival here; we are too respectable. We do not want any stirring preaching here; we are very comfortable. Do not break up our peace." Such men, when they think that God is at work in any place, are half inclined to go elsewhere. They want to be quiet; their motto is, "Anything for a quiet life." "Leave us alone, let us go on our old way," is the cry of these foolish people, as it was the cry of the Israelites, when they said to Moses, "Let us alone, that we may serve the Egyptians."

Possibly these people wanted the Saviour gone because they had an eye to business. That keeping of swine was a bad business. As Jews, they had no business with it. They may have said they did not eat them themselves, they only kept them for other people to eat; and now they had lost the whole herd. I wonder what all those swine would have brought to their owners. As they began calculating how much they had lost, they resolved that the Saviour must go out of their coasts before they lost anything more. I do not wonder that, when men sell intoxicating liquors, for instance, or when they follow any trade in which they cannot make money except by injuring their fellow-men, they do not want Christ to come that way. Perhaps some of you would not like him to see you pay those poor women for making shirts. I am afraid, if Jesus Christ were to come round, and go into some people's business houses, the husband would say to his wife, "Fetch down that book where I enter the wages, and hide it away; I should not like him to see that."

Oh, dear friend, if there be any such reason why you do not want Christ to come your way, I pray that his Holy Spirit may convince you that you do need him to come your way. He who has the most objection to Christ is the man who most wants Christ. Be you sure of this, if you do not desire to be converted, if you do not wish to be born again, you are the person above all others needing to be converted, and to be born again. Is it not a most unwise decision when, for the sake of swine, we are willing to part with Christ? "For what shall it profit a man, if he gain the whole world, and lose his own soul?" He will get a corner in the newspaper, saying that he died worth so many thousands of pounds; and that will not be true, for he was never worth a penny himself. Who would give a penny for him now he is dead? He will cost money to get rid of him, but he cannot take it with him. He was not worth anything; he used his money for selfish purposes; and never used it for the glory of God. Oh, the poverty of an ungodly rich man!

I do not wonder that these people, taken up with themselves, and with the world, prayed Christ "to depart out of their coasts." May he not, even though you may not care to hear him, stop somewhere on the shore? No; when men get excited against religion, they go to great lengths in trying to drive it away from their midst. Many a poor man has lost his cottage, where he had a few prayer-meetings, because his landlord not only did not want Christ himself, but, like the dog in the manger, would not let others have him who did want him. Are any of you in that condition?

I hope that I have some here who are of another kind, like *this poor man, who prayed him that he might be with him.* Why did he want to be with Jesus? I think he wanted to be his attendant to show his gratitude. If he might but wait on Christ, loose the latchets of his shoes, and wash his feet, or prepare his meals, he would feel himself the happiest man on earth. He would love to be doing something for the One who had cast a legion of devils out of him.

Next, he wished not only to be an attendant to show his gratitude, but a disciple that he might learn more of him. What he did know of Christ was so precious, he had personally had such an experience of his gracious power, that he wanted to be always learning something from every word of those dear lips, and every action of those blessed hands. He prayed him that he might be with him as a disciple who wished to be taught by him.

He wanted also to be with him as a comrade, for now that Christ must go, exiled from Decapolis, he seemed to feel that there was no reason why he should remain there himself. "Lord, if thou must leave these Gadarenes, let me leave the Gadarenes, too! Dost thou go, O Shepherd? Then let me go with thee. Must thou cross the sea, and get thee gone, I know not where? I will go with thee to prison and to death." He felt so linked with Christ that he prayed him that he might be with him.

I think that there was this reason, also, one of fear, at the back of his prayer. Perhaps one of that legion of devils might come back again, and if he could keep with Christ, then Christ would turn the devil out again. I should not wonder but that he felt a trembling about him, as if he could not bear to be out of the sight of the great Physician, who had healed him of so grievous an ill. I would say to all here, that we are never safe except we are with Christ. If you are tempted to go where you could not have Christ with you, do not go. Did you ever hear the story of the devil running away with a young man who was at the theatre? It is said that John Newton sent after Satan, and said, "That young man is a member of my church." "Well," replied the devil, "I do not care where he is a member; I found him on my premises, and I have a right to him;" and the preacher could not give any answer to that. If you go on the devil's premises, and he takes you off, I cannot say anything against it. Go nowhere where you cannot take Christ with you. Be like this man, who longs to go wherever Christ goes.

II. Now, secondly, SEE HOW CHRIST'S DEALINGS DIFFER, and how extraordinary they are. Here is an evil prayer: "Depart out of our coasts." He grants it. Here is a pious prayer: "Lord, let me be with thee." "Howbeit Jesus suffered him not." Is that his way, to grant the prayer of his enemies, and refuse the petition of his friends? Yes, it is so sometimes.

In the first case, *when they prayed him to depart, he went.* Oh, dear friends, if Christ ever comes near you, and you get a little touched in your conscience, and feel a throb of something like spiritual life, do not pray him to go away; for if he does go, if he should leave you to yourself, and never come again, your doom is sealed! Your only hope lies in his presence; and if you pray against your one hope, you are a suicide, you are guilty of murdering your own soul.

Jesus went away from these people because it was useless to stop. If they wanted him to go, what good could he do to them? If he spoke, they would not listen. If they heard his message, they would not heed it. When men's minds are set against Christ, what else is to be done but to leave them?

He could spend his time better somewhere else. If you will not have my Lord, somebody else will. If you sit there in your pride, and say, "I want not the Saviour," there is a poor soul in the gallery longing for him, and crying, "Oh that I might find him to be my Saviour!" Christ knew that, if the Gadarenes refused him, the people on the other side of the lake would welcome him on his return.

By going away, he even saved them from yet greater sin. If he had not gone, they might have tried to plunge him into the lake. When men begin to pray Christ to depart out of their coasts, they are bad enough for anything. There might have followed violence to his blessed person, so he took himself away from them. Is it not an awful thing that, if the gospel ministry does not save you, it is helping to damn you? We are a savour to God, always sweet; but in some men we are a savour of death unto death, while in others we are a savour of life unto life. O my hearers, if you will not come to Christ, the seat you occupy is misappropriated! There might be another person sitting there, to whom the gospel might be very precious; and our opportunities for preaching it are none too many. We do not like to waste our strength on stony ground, on hard bits of rock that repel the seed. Rock, rock, rock, wilt thou never break; must we continue to sow thee, though no harvest comes from thee? God change thee, rock; and make thee good soil, that yet the truth may grow upon thee! The evil prayer, then, was answered.

The good prayer was not answered. Why was that? The chief reason was, because the man could be useful at home. He could glorify God better by going among the Gadarenes, and among his own family, and telling what God had done for him, than he could by any attention he could pay to Christ. It is remarkable that Christ took nobody to be his body-servant, or personal attendant, during his earthly ministry. He came not to be ministered unto, but to minister. He did not desire this man to be with him to make him comfortable; he bade him go back to his family, and make known the **power of** Jesus Christ, and seek to win them for God.

Perhaps, too, his prayer was not answered, lest his fear should have been thereby sanctioned. If he did fear, and I feel morally certain that he did, that the devils would return, then, of course, he longed to be with Christ. But Christ takes that fear from him, and as good as says to him, "You do not need to be near me; I have so healed you that you will never be sick again." A patient might say to his doctor, "I have been so very ill, and through your skill have been restored to health, I should like to be near you, so that, if there should be any recurrence of my malady, I might come to you at once." If the doctor should reply, "You may go to Switzerland, or to Australia, if you like;" it would be the best evidence that the doctor had no fears about him, and it ought to put a quietus to his doubts.

You see, then, how Christ's dealings differ with different men. Have I not known some continue in sin, and yet prosper in business, heaping up wealth, and having all that heart could wish? Have I not known others repent, and turn to God, and from that very day they have had more trouble than they ever had before, and their way has been strangely rough? Yes, I have seen them, too; and I have not envied the easy ways of the wicked, neither have I felt that there was anything very wonderful about the rough ways of the righteous; for, after all, it is not the way that is the all-important matter, it is the end of the way; and if I could travel smoothly to perdition, I would not choose to do so; and if the way to eternal life is rough, I take it with all its roughness. At the foot of the Hill Difficulty, Bunyan makes his pilgrim sing—

> "The hill, though high, I covet to ascend,
> The difficulty will not me offend;
> For I perceive the way to life lies here."

III. My third point is this: SEE HOW GOOD A THING IT IS TO BE WITH JESUS. This man entreated of the Lord that he might be with him.

If you have been saved recently, I expect you have a longing in your heart to be with Christ always. I will tell you what shape that longing is likely to take. You were so happy, so joyful, and it was such a blessed meeting, that you said to yourself, "I am sorry it is over; I should like this meeting to have been kept on all night, and the next day, and never to end." Yes, you were of the mind of Peter, when he wanted to build three tabernacles on the holy mount, and to stop there the rest of his days; but you cannot do it; it is no use wishing for it. You must go home to that drinking husband or that scolding wife, to that ungodly father or that unkind mother. You cannot stop in that meeting always.

Perhaps you have another idea of what it is to be with Christ. You are so happy when you can get alone, and read your Bible, and meditate, and pray, and you say, "Lord, I wish I could always do this; I should like to be always upstairs in this room, searching the Scriptures, and having communion with God." Yes, yes, yes; but you cannot do it. There are the children's socks to be mended, there are buttons to be put on the husband's shirts, there are all sorts of odds and ends to be done, and you must not neglect any one of them. Whatever household duties come upon you, attend to them. You wish that you had not to go to the city to-morrow. Would it not be sweet to have an all-night prayer-meeting, and then to have an all-day searching of the Scriptures? No doubt it would; but the Lord has not so arranged it. You have to go to business, so just put on your week-day clothes, and think yourself none the less happy because you have to show your religion in your daily life.

"Ah, well!" says one, and this I very often hear, "I think that I should always be with Christ if I could get right out of business, and give myself up to the service of the Lord." Especially do you think that it would be so if you were a minister. Well, I have nothing to say against the ministry of the gospel. If the Lord calls you to it, obey the call, and be thankful that he has counted you faithful, putting you into the ministry; but if you suppose that you will be nearer to Christ simply by entering the ministry, you are very much mistaken. I daresay that I had about as many of other people's troubles brought to me this morning, after I had done preaching, as would last most men a month. We have to bear with everybody's trouble, and everybody's doubt, and everybody's need of comfort and counsel. You will find yourself cumbered with much serving, even in the service of the Lord; and it is very easy to lose the Master in the Master's work. We want much grace lest this insidious temptation should overcome us even in our ministry. You can walk with Christ, and keep a draper's shop. You can walk with Christ, and sell groceries. You can walk with Christ, and be a working-man, a dock-labourer. You can walk with Christ, and be a chimney-sweep. I do not hesitate to say that, by the grace of God, you can walk with Christ as well in one occupation as another, if it is a rightful one. It might be quite a mistake if you were to give up your business, under the notion that you would be more with Christ if you became a city missionary, or a Bible-woman, or a colporteur, or a captain in the Salvation Army, or whatever other form of holy service you might desire. Keep on with your business. If you can black shoes well, do that. If you can preach sermons badly, do not do that.

"Ah!" says one, "I know how I would like to be with Christ." Yes, yes, I know; you would like to be in heaven. Oh, yes; and it is a laudable desire, to wish to be with Christ, for it is far better than being here! But, mind you, it may be a selfish desire, and it may be a sinful desire, if it be pushed too far. A holy man of God was once asked by a fellow-servant of Christ, "Brother So-and-so, do you not want to go home?" He said, "What?" "Do you not want to go home?" He said, "I will answer you by another question. If you had a man working for you, and on Wednesday he said, 'I wish that it was Saturday,' would you keep him on?" The other thought that he would need a large stock of patience to do so. Why, you know what a fellow is who is always looking for Saturday night, do you not? You will be glad to see the back of him before Saturday comes, for he will be no good for work. Have I a right to be wanting to go to heaven if I can do any good to you here? Is it not more of a heaven to be outside of heaven than inside, if you can be doing more for God outside than in? Long to go when the Lord wills; but if to remain in the flesh be more for the good of the church and the world, and more for the glory of God, waive your desire, and be not vexed with your Master when, after having prayed that you may be with him, it has to be written of you as it was of this man, "Howbeit Jesus suffered him not."

Still, it is a very delightful thing to be with Jesus.

IV. But now, in the fourth place, SEE THAT THERE MAY BE SOMETHING EVEN BETTER THAN THIS. In the sense which I have mentioned, there is something better even than being with Christ.

What is better than being with Christ? Why, to be working for Christ! Jesus said to this man, "Go home to thy friends, and tell them how great things the Lord hath done for thee, and hath had compassion on thee."

This is *more honourable*. It is very delightful to sit at Jesus' feet; but if the most honourable post on the field of battle is the place of danger; if the most honourable thing in the State is to have royal service allotted to you; then the most honourable thing for a Christian is not to sit down, and sing, and enjoy himself, but to get up, and risk reputation, life, and everything for Jesus Christ's sake. Dear friend, aspire to serve your Lord; it is a more honourable thing even than being with him.

It is also *better for the people*. Christ is going away from the Gadarenes; they have asked him to go, and he is going; but he seems to say to this man, "I am going because they have asked me to go. My leaving them looks like a judgment upon them for their rejection of me; but yet I am not going away altogether. I am going to stop with you; I will put my Spirit upon you, and so will continue with you. They will hear you though they will not hear me." Christ, as it were, resigns the pastorate of that district; but he puts another in his place, not so good as himself, but one whom they will like better; not so powerful and useful as himself, but one better adapted to them. When Christ was gone, this man would be there, and the people would come to him to hear about those swine, and how they ran down into the sea; and if they did not come to him, he would go and tell them all about it; and so there would be a permanent curate left there to discharge the sacred ministry, now that the great Bishop had gone. I like that thought. Christ has gone to heaven, for he is wanted there, and so he has left you here, dear brother, to carry on his work. You are not equal to him in any respect; but yet remember what he said to his disciples, "He that believeth on me, the works that I do shall he do also; and greater works than these shall he do; because I go unto my Father." That is why Christ does not suffer you to be with him at present. You must stop for the sake of the people among whom you live, as "he that had been possessed with the devil" had to remain for the sake of the Gadarenes, to whom he might testify concerning Christ.

His remaining, also, was *better for his family;* and do you not think that, oftentimes, a man of God is kept out of heaven for the sake of his family? You must not go yet, father; those boys still need your example and your influence. Christian mother, you must not go yet; I know that your children are grown up, and they are grieving you very much; but still, if there is any check upon them, it is their poor old mother, and you must stop till you have prayed them to God; and you will do so yet. Be of good courage. I believe that there are many here who might be in heaven, but that God has some whom he intends to bring in by them, so they must stay here a little longer. Though infirm in body, shattered in nerve, and often racked with acute pain, perhaps with a deadly disease upon you, and wishing to be gone, you must not go till your work is done.

"Howbeit Jesus suffered him not." This demoniac must go home, and tell his wife and his children what great things the Lord had done for him. Many eminent preachers have pictured the scene of his going home, so I will not try to do it. You may only fancy what it would be if it were your case; and you had been shut up in an asylum, or had been almost too bad even for that. How glad your friends were to have you taken away, and then how much more glad to find you come back perfectly well! I can imagine how the man's wife would look through the window when she heard his voice. Has he come back in a mad fit? How the children would be filled with terror at the sound of their father's voice until they were assured that there was indeed a change in him! Ah, poor sinner, you have come here to-night! Perhaps you forget that your children often have to hide away under the bed when father comes home. I know that there are such persons about, and they may even find their way into the Tabernacle. The Lord have mercy upon the drunkard, and turn his cups bottom upwards, and make a new man of him! Then, when he goes home, to tell of free grace and dying love, and of the wonderful change that God has wrought in him, he will be a blessing to his family and to all about him. It may be, dear friend, that you have to stop here till you have undone some of the mischief of your early life. You have to bring to God some of those whom you tempted, and led astray, and helped to ruin.

So, you see, dear friends, there is something better even than being with Christ; that is, working for Christ.

V. But, lastly, CONSIDER THAT THERE IS YET A CASE WHICH IS BEST OF ALL. We must always have three degrees of comparison. What is the best state of all? To be with Christ is good; to be sent by Christ on a holy errand, is better; but here is something that is best of all, namely, to work for him, and to be with him at the same time. I want every Christian to aspire to that position. Is it possible to sit with Mary at the Master's feet, and yet to run about like Martha, and get the dinner ready? It is; and then Martha will never be cumbered with much serving if she does that, and she will never find fault with her sister Mary. "But, sir, we cannot sit and stir at the same time." No, not as to your bodies; but you can as to your souls. You can be sitting at Jesus' feet, or leaning on his breast, and yet be fighting the Lord's battles, and doing his work.

In order to do this, *cultivate the inner as well as the outer life.* Endeavour not only to do much for Christ, but to be much with Christ, and to live wholly upon Christ. Do not, for instance, on the Sabbath-day, go to a class, and teach others three times, as some whom I know do; but come once and hear the Master's message, and get your soul fed; and when you have had a spiritual feast in the morning, give the rest of the day to holy service. Let the two things run together. To be always eating, and never working, will bring on repletion, and spiritual dyspepsia; but to be always working, and never eating,—well, I am afraid that you will not bear that trial so well as the gentleman who yesterday ate his first meal after forty days' fasting. Do not try to imitate him. It is not a right or wise thing to do; but very dangerous. Get spiritual food as well as do spiritual work.

Let me say to you, again, *grieve very much if there is the least cloud between you and Christ.* Do not wait until it is as thick as a November fog; be full of sorrow if it is only like a tiny, fleecy cloud. George Müller's observation was a very wise one, "Never come out of your chamber in the morning until everything is right between you and God." Keep up perpetual fellowship with Jesus; and thus you can be with him, and yet be serving him at the same time.

And mind this, *before you begin Christ's service, always seek his presence and help.* Do not enter upon any work for the Lord without having first seen the face of the King in his beauty; and in the work often recall your mind from what you are doing, to him for whom you are doing it, and by whom you are doing it; and when the work is completed, do not throw up your cap, and say, "Well done, self!" Another will say to you, by-and-by, "Well done!" if you deserve it. Do not take the words out of his mouth. Self-praise is no recommendation. Solomon said, "Let another man praise thee, and not thine own mouth; a stranger, and not thine own lips." When we have done all, we are still unprofitable servants; we have only done that which it was our duty to do. So, if you are as humble as you are active, as lowly as you are energetic, you may keep with Christ, and yet go about his errands to the ends of the earth; and I reckon this to be the happiest experience that any one of us can reach this side of the gates of pearl. The Lord bless you, and bring you there, for Christ's sake! Amen.

Exposition by C. H. Spurgeon.

MARK V. 1—20.

1, 2. *And they came over unto the other side of the sea, into the country of the Gadarenes. And when he was come out of the ship, immediately there met him out of the tombs a man with an unclean spirit,*

Our Lord crossed the Sea of Galilee on purpose to rescue this poor man from the power of the unclean spirit that possessed him. He knew that there were many who needed him on the Galilean side of the lake, and he could foresee the storm that would threaten to sink the little ship; yet he calmly said to his disciples (see chapter iv. verse 35), "Let us pass over unto the other side." As soon as the great Physician landed, a dreadful apparition appeared. "Out of the tombs", an uncanny place, rushed a man, howling and yelling like some wild beast; or worse still, under the influence of Satan, who had taken possession of him.

3, 4. *Who had his dwelling among the tombs; and no man could bind him, no, not with chains: because that he had been often bound with fetters and chains, and the chains had been plucked asunder by him, and the fetters broken in pieces: neither could any man tame him.*

See how the world deals with furiously guilty men. It tries to fetter them, or else to tame them; to keep them in check by fear of punishment, or else to subdue them to a gentleness of morality: poor work this! Christ neither binds nor tames; he changes and renews. Oh, that everywhere his aid were sought, and not so much reliance placed on the fetters of law, or the power of morals!

5. *And always, night and day, he was in the mountains, and in the tombs, crying, and cutting himself with stones.*

It must have been dreadful for travellers to pass that way at night, or to meet with this terrible madman at any hour of the day. But how terrible must have been the poor creature's own condition! We get just a glimpse of it from the words, "always in the mountains, and in the tombs, crying, and cutting himself with stones." See what Satan does with those who are in his power.

6. *But when he saw Jesus afar off, he ran and worshipped him,*

The devil does not like doing it; but if it will serve his purpose, he will pretend to be a worshipper of Christ. He comes here sometimes; he goes to all sorts of places of worship, and makes men turn worshippers who have no worship in their hearts; for there is no end to the depth of his cunning, and many are they that have served the devil best when they have pretended to worship Christ.

7. *And cried with a loud voice, and said, What have I to do with thee, Jesus, thou Son of the most high God? I adjure thee by God, that thou torment me not.*

Using the lips of this poor man, Satan spoke in him and through him. He is afraid of Christ. This dog of hell knows his Master, and crouches at his feet. He beseeches the "Son of the Most High God" not to torment him before his time.

8. *For he said unto him, Come out of the man, thou unclean spirit.*

Christ never wastes words over the devil. He speaks to him very shortly and very sharply. It would be well sometimes if we could be more laconic when we are dealing with evil. It does not deserve our words as it did not deserve Christ's words. Jesus said to the devil, "Come out of the man, thou unclean spirit."

9, 10. *And he asked him, What is thy name? And he answered, saying, My name is Legion: for we are many. And he besought him much that he would not send them away out of the country.*

The devil can pray; he did so in this case. It is not because a man is fluent in prayer that we are sure of his salvation. It is not because a man prays with such fervour that his knees knock together, that we may conclude that he is a saint. It may be that he is trembling through fear of God's judgment. Satan besought Christ much.

11, 12. *Now there was there nigh unto the mountains a great herd of swine feeding. And all the devils besought him, saying, Send us into the swine, that we may enter into them.*

Satan would rather vex swine than do no mischief at all. He is so fond of evil that he would work it upon animals if he cannot work it upon men. What unanimity there is amongst the evil spirits! "All the devils besought him, saying, Send us into the swine, that we may enter into them."

13. *And forthwith Jesus gave them leave.*

The devil cannot enter even a pig without Christ's leave. So he cannot tempt you, my friend, without our Lord's permission. You may rest assured that even this great monster of evil is under Christ's control. He cannot molest you till Jesus gives him leave. There is a chain around the roaring lion, and he can only go just as far as the Lord allows him.

13, 14. *And the unclean spirits went out, and entered into the swine: and the herd ran violently down a steep place into the sea, (they were about two thousand;) and were choked in the sea. And they that fed the swine fled,*

At which we do not at all wonder. Who would not flee when they thus saw the power of Christ?

14, 15. *And told it in the city, and in the country. And they went out to see what it was that was done. And they come to Jesus, and see him that was possessed with the devil, and had the legion, sitting, and clothed, and in his right mind: and they were afraid.*

You would have thought that it would have been said, "They marvelled, and they praised Christ for this great and wonderful deed." No, "They were afraid." If you see another converted, do not be afraid; but rather have hope that you may be saved yourself. What a beautiful sight these people saw: "they come to Jesus, and see him that was possessed with the devil, and had the legion, sitting, and clothed, and in his right mind"! That ought to have made them rejoice instead of being afraid. There are still people who are afraid of what will happen when they see those whom Christ has blessed spiritually as he had healed this man.

16, 17. *And they that saw it told them how it befell to him that was possessed with the devil, and also concerning the swine. And they began to pray him to depart out of their coasts.*

If Jesus should come to you to-night, do not ask him to go away. Open wide the door of your heart, and entreat the Lord to come in, and dwell there for ever and ever. This narrative teaches us that the Lord Jesus Christ will go away if he is asked to do so; he will not remain where his room is preferred to his company.

18—20. *And when he was come into the ship, he that had been possessed with the devil prayed him that he might be with him. Howbeit Jesus suffered him not, but saith unto him, Go home to thy friends, and tell them how great things the Lord hath done for thee, and hath had compassion on thee. And he departed, and began to publish in Decapolis how great things Jesus had done for him: and all men did marvel.*

He was told to publish what great things *the Lord* had done for him. He went and published what great things *Jesus* had done for him. Did he make any mistake? Oh, no! It is but another name for the same Person; for Jesus is the Lord; and when you speak of him as divine, and talk of him in terms fit only for God, you do but speak rightly; for so he deserveth to be praised. "And all men did marvel." So our Lord left them all wondering. Leaving this one messenger to bear testimony to him, he went his way elsewhere, to carry blessings to many others on the other side of the sea. The man appears to have gone through the wide district that bore the name of Decapolis, and his testimony to the power of Christ was so convincing that, when the Saviour revisited that part of the country, he had a very different reception from that which he received on this occasion (see chapters vii. 31—37, viii. 1—10).

HYMNS FROM "OUR OWN HYMN BOOK"—797, 847, 806.

"THE SWORD AND THE TROWEL."

CONTENTS OF SECOND CONFERENCE NUMBER, JULY, 1892.

The Great Shield of Faith. Address delivered by the late beloved President, C. H. SPURGEON, at the opening of the Fourth Annual Conference of the Pastors' College Evangelical Association, at Upton Chapel, Lambeth, April 20th, 1891.

The Gospel for the Times. Paper read by Principal David Gracey, at the Conference, May 4th, 1892.

The Cure for a Fainting Heart. Conference Sermon on Jonah ii. 7, preached by W. Y. Fullerton, May 6th.

Memorials to our late President. His "armour-bearer's" paper, read at the Conference Memorial Service, May 5th.

The Influence of the dear President's death. By Pastor John Horne, Springburn, Glasgow.

Mr. Spurgeon's Early and Later Ministry. By R. Shindler.

Sketch of Principal David Gracey.

Fifth Annual Report of the Pastors' College Students' Visitation Society.

Notices of Books.

Notes. (Mrs. Spurgeon and her Book Fund. Mr. and Mrs. Thomas Spurgeon and Pastor Charles Spurgeon. Dr. Pierson and the Tabernacle. *In Memoriam* notice of Mrs. John Jewell Penstone. Metropolitan Tabernacle Sunday-school Home and Foreign Missionary Society. College. College Missionary Association. Evangelists. Orphanage. Colportage. Personal Notes—Mr. Spurgeon's sermons in Russia, Scotland, and various parts of England.)

Lists of contributions—Pastors' College, College Missionary Association, Stockwell Orphanage, Colportage Association, Society of Evangelists, For the General Work of the Lord as most required, and C. H. Spurgeon Memorial Fund.

Twenty-fifth Annual Report of the Metropolitan Tabernacle Colportage Association.

72 pages. Price 3d. Post-free, 4d.

LONDON: PASSMORE & ALABASTER, PATERNOSTER BUILDINGS; and all Booksellers.

Metropolitan Tabernacle Pulpit.

CHRIST'S PLEA FOR IGNORANT SINNERS.

A Sermon

INTENDED FOR READING ON LORD'S-DAY, JULY 3RD, 1892,

DELIVERED BY

C. H. SPURGEON,

AT THE METROPOLITAN TABERNACLE, NEWINGTON,

On Lord's-day Evening, October 5th, 1890.

"Then said Jesus, Father, forgive them; for they know not what they do."—Luke xxiii. 34.

WHAT tenderness we have here; what self-forgetfulness; what almighty love! Jesus did not say to those who crucified him, "Begone!" One such word, and they must have all fled. When they came to take him in the garden, they went backward, and fell to the ground, when he spoke but a short sentence; and now that he is on the cross, a single syllable would have made the whole company fall to the ground, or flee away in fright.

Jesus says not a word in his own defence. When he prayed to his Father, he might justly have said, "Father, note what they do to thy beloved Son. Judge them for the wrong they do to him who loves them, and who has done all he can for them." But there is no prayer against them in the words that Jesus utters. It was written of old, by the prophet Isaiah, "He made intercession for the transgressors;" and here it is fulfilled. He pleads for his murderers, "Father, forgive them."

He does not utter a single word of upbraiding. He does not say, "Why do ye this? Why pierce the hands that fed you? Why nail the feet that followed after you in mercy? Why mock the Man who loved to bless you?" No; not a word even of gentle upbraiding, much less of anything like a curse. "Father, forgive them." You notice, Jesus does not say, "I forgive them," but you may read that between the lines. He says that all the more because he does not say it in words. But he has laid aside his majesty, and is fastened to the cross; and therefore he takes the humble position of a suppliant, rather than the more lofty place of one who had power to forgive. How often, when men say, "I forgive you," is there a kind of selfishness about it! At any rate, self is asserted in the very act of forgiving. Jesus takes the place of a pleader, a pleader for those who were committing murder upon himself. Blessed be his name!

No. 2,263.

This word of the cross we shall use to-night, and we shall see if we cannot gather something from it for our instruction; for, though we were not there, and we did not actually put Jesus to death, yet we really caused his death, and we, too, crucified the Lord of glory; and his prayer for us was, "Father, forgive them; for they know not what they do."

I am not going to handle this text so much by way of exposition, as by way of experience. I believe there are many here, to whom these words will be very appropriate. This will be our line of thought. First, *we were in measure ignorant;* secondly, *we confess that this ignorance is no excuse;* thirdly, *we bless our Lord for pleading for us;* and fourthly, *we now rejoice in the pardon we have obtained.* May the Holy Spirit graciously help us in our meditation!

I. Looking back upon our past experience, let me say, first, that WE WERE IN MEASURE IGNORANT. We who have been forgiven, we who have been washed in the blood of the Lamb, we once sinned, in a great measure, through ignorance. Jesus says, "They know not what they do." Now, I shall appeal to you, brothers and sisters, when you lived under the dominion of Satan, and served yourselves and sin, was there not a measure of ignorance in it? You can truly say, as we said in the hymn we sang just now,—

"Alas! I knew not what I did."

It is true, first, that we were ignorant of *the awful meaning of sin.* We began to sin as children; we knew that it was wrong, but we did not know all that sin meant. We went on to sin as young men; peradventure we plunged into much wickedness. We knew it was wrong; but we did not see the end from the beginning. It did not appear to us as rebellion against God. We did not think that we were presumptuously defying God, setting at naught his wisdom, defying his power, deriding his love, spurning his holiness; yet we were doing all that. There is an abysmal depth in sin. You cannot see to the bottom of it. When we rolled sin under our tongue as a sweet morsel, we did not know all the terrible ingredients compounded in that deadly bittersweet. We were in a measure ignorant of the tremendous crime we committed when we dared to live in rebellion against God. So far, I think, you go with me.

We did not know, at that time, *God's great love to us.* I did not know that he had chosen me from before the foundation of the world; I never dreamed of that. I did not know that Christ stood for me as my Substitute, to redeem me from among men. I did not know that he had espoused me unto himself in righteousness and in faithfulness, to be one with him for ever. You, dear friends, who now know the love of Christ, did not understand it then. You did not know that you were sinning against eternal love, against infinite compassion, against a distinguishing love such as God had fixed on you from eternity. So far, we knew not what we did.

I think, too, that we did not know all that we were doing in *our rejection of Christ, and putting him to grief.* He came to us in our youth; and impressed by a sermon we began to tremble, and to seek his face; but we were decoyed back to the world, and we refused Christ. Our mother's tears, our father's prayers, our teacher's admonitions, often moved us; but we were very stubborn, and we rejected Christ. We did not know that, in that rejection, we were virtually putting him away and crucifying him. We were denying his Godhead, or else we should have worshipped him. We were denying his love, or else we should have yielded to him. We were practically, in every act of sin, taking the hammer and the nails, and fastening Christ to the cross; but we did not know it. Perhaps, if we had known it, we should not have crucified the Lord of glory. We did know we were doing wrong; but we did not know all the wrong that we were doing.

Nor did we know fully *the meaning of our delays.* We hesitated; we were on the verge of conversion; we went back, and turned again to our old follies. We were hardened, Christless, prayerless still; and each one of us said, "Oh, I am only waiting a little while till I have fulfilled my present engagements, till I am a little older, till I have seen a little more of the world!" The fact is, we were refusing Christ, and choosing the pleasures of sin instead of him; and every hour of delay was an hour of crucifying Christ, grieving his Spirit, and choosing this harlot world in the place of the lovely and ever-blessed Christ. We did not know that.

I think we may add one thing more. *We did not know the meaning of our self-righteousness.* We used to think, some of us, that we had a righteousness of our own. We had been to church regularly, or we had been to the meeting-house whenever it was open. We were christened; we were confirmed; or, peradventure, we rejoiced that we never had either of those things done to us. Thus, we put our confidence in ceremonies, or the absence of ceremonies. We said our prayers; we read a chapter in the Bible night and morning; we did —oh, I do not know what we did not do! But there we rested; we were righteous in our own esteem. We had not any particular sin to confess, nor any reason to lie in the dust before the throne of God's majesty. We were about as good as we could be; and we did not know that we were even then perpetrating the highest insult upon Christ; for, if we were not sinners, why did Christ die; and, if we had a righteousness of our own which was good enough, why did Christ come here to work out a righteousness for us? We made out Christ to be a superfluity, by considering that we were good enough without resting in his atoning sacrifice. Ah, we did not think we were doing that! We thought we were pleasing God by our religiousness, by our outward performances, by our ecclesiastical correctness; but all the while we were setting up anti-Christ in the place of Christ. We were making out that Christ was not wanted; we were robbing him of his office and glory! Alas! Christ could say of us, with regard to all these things, "They know not what they do." I want you to look quietly at the time past wherein you served sin, and just see whether there was not a darkness upon your mind, a blindness in your spirit, so that you did not know what you did.

II. Well now, secondly, WE CONFESS THAT THIS IGNORANCE IS NO EXCUSE. Our Lord might urge it as a plea; but we never could. We did not know what we did, and so we were not guilty to the fullest possible extent; but we were guilty enough, therefore let us own it.

For first, remember, *the law never allows this as a plea.* In our own English law, a man is supposed to know what the law is. If he breaks it, it is no excuse to plead that he did not know it. It may be regarded by a judge as some extenuation; but the law allows nothing of the kind. God gives us the law, and we are bound to keep it. If I erred through not knowing the law, still it was a sin. Under the Mosaic law, there were sins of ignorance, and for these there were special offerings. The ignorance did not blot out the sin. That is clear in my text; for, if ignorance rendered an action no longer sinful, then why should Christ say, "Father, forgive them"? But he does; he asks for mercy for what is sin, even though the ignorance in some measure be supposed to mitigate the criminality of it.

But, dear friends, *we might have known.* If we did not know, it was because we would not know. There was the preaching of the Word; but we did not care to hear it. There was this blessed Book; but we did not care to read it. If you and I had sat down, and looked at our conduct by the light of Holy Scripture, we might have known much more of the evil of sin, and much more of the love of Christ, and much more of the ingratitude which is possible in refusing Christ, and not coming to him.

In addition to that, *we did not think.* "Oh, but," you say, "young people never do think!" But young people should think. If there is anybody who need not think, it is the old man, whose day is nearly over. If he does think, he has but a very short time in which to improve; but the young have all their life before them. If I were a carpenter, and had to make a box, I should not think about it after I had made the box; I should think, before I began to cut my timber, what sort of box it was to be. In every action, a man thinks before he begins, or else he is a fool. A young man ought to think more than anybody else, for now he is, as it were, making his box. He is beginning his life-plan; he should be the most thoughtful of all men. Many of us, who are now Christ's people, would have known much more about our Lord if we had given him more careful consideration in our earlier days. A man will consider about taking a wife, he will consider about taking a business, he will consider about buying a horse or a cow; but he will not consider about the claims of Christ, and the claims of the Most High God; and this renders his ignorance wilful, and inexcusable.

Beside that, dear friends, although we have confessed to ignorance, *in many sins we did know a great deal.* Come, let me quicken your memories. There were times when you knew that such an action was wrong, when you started back from it. You looked at the gain it would bring you, and you sold your soul for that price, and deliberately did what you were well aware was wrong. Are there not some here, saved by Christ, who must confess that, at times, they did violence to their conscience? They did despite to the Spirit of God, quenched the light of heaven, drove the Spirit away from them, distinctly knowing what they were doing. Let us bow before God in the silence of our hearts, and own to all this. We hear the Master say, "Father, forgive them; for they know not what they do." Let us add our own tears as we say, "And forgive us, also, because in some things we did know; in all things we might have known; but we were ignorant for want of thought, which thought was a solemn duty which we ought to have rendered to God."

One thing more I will say on this head. When a man is ignorant, and does not know what he ought to do, what should he do? Well, he should do nothing till he does know. But here is the mischief of it, that *when we did not know, yet we chose to do the wrong thing.* If we did not know, why did we not choose the right thing? But, being in the dark, we never turned to the right; but always blundered to the left, from sin to sin. Does not this show us how depraved our hearts are? Though we are seeking to be right, when we are let alone, we go wrong of ourselves. Leave a child alone; leave a man alone; leave a tribe alone without teaching and instruction; what comes of it? Why, the same as when you leave a field alone. It never, by any chance, produces wheat or barley. Leave it alone, and there are rank weeds, and thorns, and briars, showing that the natural set of the soil is towards producing that which is worthless. O friends, confess the innate evil of your hearts as well as the evil of your lives, in that, when you did not know, yet, having a perverse instinct, you chose the evil, and refused the good; and, when you did not know enough of Christ, and did not think enough of him to know whether you ought to have him or not, you would not come unto him that you might have life. You needed light; but you shut your eyes to the sun. You were thirsty; but you would not drink of the living spring; and so your ignorance, though it was there, was a criminal ignorance, which you must confess before the Lord. Oh, come ye to the cross, ye who have been there before, and have lost your burden there! Come and confess your guilt over again; and clasp that cross afresh, and look to him who bled upon it, and praise his dear name that he once prayed for you, "Father, forgive them; for they know not what they do."

Now, I am going a step further. We were in a measure ignorant; but we confess that that measurable ignorance was no excuse.

III. Now, thirdly, WE BLESS OUR LORD FOR PLEADING FOR US.

Do you notice when it was that Jesus pleaded? It was, *while they were crucifying him.* They had just driven in the nails, they had lifted up the cross, and dashed it down into its socket, and dislocated all his bones, so that he could say, "I am poured out like water, and all my bones are out of joint." Ah, dear friends, it was then that, instead of a cry or a groan, this dear Son of God said, "Father, forgive them; for they know not what they do." They did not ask forgiveness for themselves; Jesus asked forgiveness for them. Their hands were imbrued in his blood; and it was then, even then, that he prayed for them. Let us think of the great love wherewith he loved us, even while we were yet sinners, when we rioted in sin, when we drank it down as the ox drinketh down water. Even then he prayed for us. "While we were yet without strength, in due time Christ died for the ungodly." Bless his name to-night. He prayed for you when you did not pray for yourself. He prayed for you when you were crucifying him.

Then think of his plea, *he pleads his Sonship.* He says, "*Father,* forgive them." He was the Son of God, and he puts his divine Sonship into the scale on our behalf. He seems to say, "Father, as I am thy Son, grant me this request, and pardon these rebels. Father, forgive them." The filial rights of Christ were very great. He was the Son of God, not as we are, by adoption, but by nature; by eternal filiation, he was the Son of the Highest, "Light of light, very God of very God", the second Person in the Divine Trinity; and he puts that Sonship here before God, and says, "Father, Father, forgive them." Oh, the power of that word from the Son's lip when he is wounded, when he is in agony, when he is dying! He says, "Father, Father, grant my one request; O Father, forgive them; for they know not what they do;" and the great Father bows his awful head, in token that the petition is granted.

Then notice, that Jesus here, silently, but really *pleads his sufferings*. The attitude of Christ when he prayed this prayer is very noteworthy. His hands were stretched upon the transverse beam; his feet were fastened to the upright tree; and there he pleaded. Silently his hands and feet were pleading, and his agonized body from every sinew and muscle pleaded with God. His sacrifice was presented there before the Father's face; not yet complete, but in his will complete; and so it is his cross that takes up the plea, "Father, forgive them." O blessed Christ! It is thus that we have been forgiven, for his Sonship and his cross have pleaded with God, and have prevailed on our behalf.

I love this prayer, also, because of the *indistinctness* of it. It is "Father, forgive them." He does not say, "Father, forgive the soldiers who have nailed me here." He includes them. Neither does he say, "Father, forgive the people who are beholding me." He means them. Neither does he say, "Father, forgive sinners in ages to come who will sin against me." But he means them. Jesus does not mention them by any accusing name: "Father, forgive my enemies. Father, forgive my murderers." No, there is no word of accusation upon those dear lips. "Father, forgive them." Now into that pronoun "them" I feel that I can crawl. Can you get in there? Oh, by a humble faith, appropriate the cross of Christ by trusting in it; and get into that big little word "them"! It seems like a chariot of mercy that has come down to earth, into which a man may step, and it shall bear him up to heaven. "Father, forgive them."

Notice, also, what it was that Jesus asked for; to omit that, would be to leave out the very essence of his prayer. *He asked for full absolution for his enemies:* "Father, forgive them. Do not punish them; forgive them. Do not remember their sin; forgive it, blot it out; throw it into the depths of the sea. Remember it not, my Father. Mention it not against them any more for ever. Father, forgive them." Oh, blessed prayer, for the forgiveness of God is broad and deep! When man forgives, he leaves the remembrance of the wrong behind; but when God pardons, he says, "I will forgive their iniquity, and I will remember their sin no more." It is this that Christ asked for you and me long before we had any repentance, or any faith; and in answer to that prayer, we were brought to feel our sin, we were brought to confess it, and to believe in him; and now, glory be to his name, we can bless him for having pleaded for us, and obtained the forgiveness of all our sins.

IV. I come now to my last remark, which is this, WE NOW REJOICE IN THE PARDON WE HAVE OBTAINED.

Have you obtained pardon? Is this your song?

"Now, oh joy! my sins are pardon'd,
Now I can, and do believe."

I have a letter, in my pocket, from a man of education and standing, who has been an agnostic; he says that he was a sarcastic agnostic, and he writes praising God, and invoking every blessing upon my head for bringing him to the Saviour's feet. He says, "I was without happiness for this life, and without hope for the next." I believe that that is a truthful description of many an unbeliever. What hope is there for the world to come apart from the cross of Christ? The best hope such a man has is that he may die the death of a dog, and there may be an end of him. What is the hope of the Romanist when he comes to die? I feel so sorry for many devout and earnest friends, for I do not know what their hope is. They do not hope to go to heaven yet, at any rate; some purgatorial pains must be endured first. Ah, this is a poor, poor faith to die on, to have such a hope as that to trouble your last thoughts. I do not know of any religion but that of Christ Jesus which tells us of sin pardoned, absolutely pardoned. Now, listen. Our teaching is not that, when you come to die, you may, perhaps, find out that it is all right, but, "Beloved, now are we the sons of God." "He that believeth on the Son hath everlasting life." He has it now, and he knows it, and he rejoices in it. So I come back to the last head of my discourse, we rejoice in the pardon Christ has obtained for us. We are pardoned. I hope that the larger portion of this audience can say, "By the grace of God, we know that we are washed in the blood of the Lamb."

Pardon has come to us through Christ's plea. Our hope lies in the plea of Christ, and specially in his death. If Jesus paid my debt, and he did if I am a believer in him, then I am out of debt. If Jesus bore the penalty of my sin, and he did if I am a believer, then there is no penalty for me to pay, for we can say to him,—

"Complete atonement thou hast made,
And to the utmost farthing paid
Whate'er thy people owed:
Nor can his wrath on me take place,
If shelter'd in thy righteousness,
And sprinkled with thy blood.

"If thou hast my discharge procured,
And freely in my room endured
The whole of wrath divine:
Payment God cannot twice demand,
First at my bleeding Surety's hand,
And then again at mine."

If Christ has borne my punishment, I shall never bear it. Oh, what joy there is in this blessed assurance! Your hope that you are pardoned lies in this, that Jesus died. Those dear wounds of his bleed life for you.

We praise him for our pardon because *we do know now what we did.* Oh, brethren, I know not how much we ought to love Christ, because we sinned against him so grievously! Now we know that sin is "exceeding sinful." Now we know that sin crucified Christ. Now we know that we stabbed our heavenly Lover to his heart. We slew, with ignominious death, our best and dearest Friend and Benefactor. We know that now; and we could almost weep tears of blood to think that we ever treated him as we did. But it is all forgiven, all gone. Oh, let us bless that dear Son of God, who has put away even such sins as ours! We feel them more now than ever before. We know they are forgiven, and our grief is because of the pain that the purchase of our forgiveness cost our Saviour. We never knew what our sins really were till we saw him in a bloody sweat. We never knew the crimson hue of our sins till we read our pardon written in crimson lines with his precious blood. Now, we see our sin, and yet we do not see it; for God has pardoned it, blotted it out, cast it behind his back for ever.

Henceforth *ignorance*, such as we have described, *shall be hateful to us.* Ignorance of Christ and eternal things shall be hateful to us. If, through ignorance, we have sinned, we will have done with that ignorance. We will be students of his Word. We will study that masterpiece of all the sciences, the knowledge of Christ crucified. We will ask the Holy Ghost to drive far from us the ignorance that gendereth sin. God grant that we may not fall into sins of ignorance any more; but may we be able to say, "I know whom I have believed; and henceforth I will seek more knowledge, till I comprehend, with all saints, what are the heights, and depths, and lengths, and breadths of the love of Christ, and know the love of God, which passeth knowledge"!

I put in a practical word here. If you rejoice that you are pardoned, *show your gratitude by your imitation of Christ.* There was never before such a plea as this, "Father, forgive them; for they know not what they do." Plead like that for others. Has anybody been injuring you? Are there persons who slander you? Pray to-night, "Father, forgive them; for they know not what they do." Let us always render good for evil, blessing for cursing; and when we are called to suffer through the wrong-doing of others, let us believe that they would not act as they do if it were not because of their ignorance. Let us pray for them; and make their very ignorance the plea for their forgiveness: "Father, forgive them; for they know not what they do."

I want you also to think of the millions of London just now. See those miles of streets, pouring out their children this evening; but look at those public-houses with the crowds streaming in and out. Go down our streets by moonlight. See what I almost blush to tell. Follow men and women, too, to their homes, and be this your prayer: "Father, forgive them; for they know not what they do." That silver bell—keep it always ringing. What did I say? That silver bell? Nay, it is the *golden* bell upon the priest's garments. Wear it on your garments, ye priests of God, and let it always ring out its golden note, "Father, forgive them; for they know not what they do." If I can set all God's saints imitating Christ with such a prayer as this, I shall not have spoken in vain.

Brethren, I see *reason for hope in the very ignorance that surrounds us.* I see hope for this poor city of ours, hope for this poor country, hope for Africa, China, and India. "They know not what they do." Here is a strong argument in their favour, for they are more ignorant than we were. They know less of the evil of sin, and less of the hope of eternal life, than we do. Send up this petition, ye people of God! Heap your prayers together with cumulative power, send up this fiery shaft of prayer, straight to the heart of God, while Jesus from his throne shall add his prevalent intercession, "Father, forgive them; for they know not what they do."

If there be any unconverted people here, and I know that there are some, we will mention them in our private devotion, as well as in the public assembly; and we will pray for them in words like these, "Father, forgive them; for they know not what they do." May God bless you all, for Jesus Christ's sake! Amen.

THE PASTOR'S TRUE MONUMENT AND MEMORIAL,

AND

THE PASTOR'S LAST TESTIMONY AND TESTAMENT.

BEING

TWO SERMONS

DELIVERED AT THE METROPOLITAN TABERNACLE,

On Sunday Morning and Evening, June 19th, 1892,

ON THE 58TH ANNIVERSARY OF THE BIRTH OF C. H. SPURGEON.

BY ARTHUR T. PIERSON, D.D.

With portrait of the preacher.

These sermons deserve a world-wide circulation. The evening sermon especially contains a truly wonderful picture of Mr. Spurgeon's ministry, and one of the most complete vindications of his action in "The Down-grade Controversy" that has yet been published.

LONDON: PASSMORE AND ALABASTER, PATERNOSTER BUILDINGS, and all Booksellers.
Price 3d. Post-free 3½d.

Exposition by C. H. Spurgeon.

LUKE XXIII. 33—46. JOHN XIX. 25—30.

We have often read the story of our Saviour's sufferings; but we cannot read it too often. Let us, therefore, once again repair to "the place which is called Calvary." As we just now sang,—

> "Come, let us stand beneath the cross;
> So may the blood from out his side
> Fall gently on us drop by drop;
> Jesus, our Lord, is crucified."

We will read, first, Luke's account of our Lord's crucifixion and death.

Luke xxiii. Verse 33. *And when they were come to the place, which is called Calvary, there they crucified him, and the malefactors, one on the right hand, and the other on the left.*

They gave Jesus the place of dishonour. Reckoning him to be the worst criminal of the three, they put him between the other two. They heaped upon him the utmost scorn which they could give to a malefactor; and in so doing they unconsciously honoured him. Jesus always deserves the chief place wherever he is. In all things he must have the pre-eminence. He is King of sufferers as well as King of saints.

34. *Then said Jesus, Father, forgive them; for they know not what they do.*

How startled they must have been to hear such words from one who was about to be put to death for a supposed crime! The men that drove the nails, the men that lifted up the tree, must have started back with amazement when they heard Jesus talk to God as his Father, and pray for them: "Father, forgive them; for they know not what they do." Did ever Roman legionary hear such words before? I should say not. They were so distinctly and diametrically opposed to the whole spirit of Rome. There it was blow for blow; only in the case of Jesus they gave blows where none had been received. The crushing cruelty of the Roman must have been startled indeed at such words as these, "Father, forgive them; for they know not what they do."

34, 35. *And they parted his raiment, and cast lots. And the people stood beholding.*

The gambling soldiers little dreamed that they were fulfilling the Scriptures while they were raffling for the raiment of the illustrious Sufferer on the cross; yet so it was. In the twenty-second Psalm, which so fully sets forth our Saviour's sufferings, and which he probably repeated while he hung on the tree, David wrote, "They part my garments among them, and cast lots upon my vesture." "And the people stood beholding," gazing, looking on at the cruel spectacle. You and I would not have done that; there is a public sentiment which has trained us to hate the sight of cruelty, especially of deadly cruelty to one of our own race; but these people thought that they did no harm when they "stood beholding." They also were thus fulfilling the Scriptures; for the seventeenth verse of the twenty-second Psalm says, "They look and stare upon me."

35. *And the rulers also with them derided him,*

Laughed at him, made him the object of coarse jests.

35, 36. *Saying, He saved others; let him save himself, if he be Christ, the chosen of God. And the soldiers also mocked him, coming to him, and offering him vinegar,*

In mockery, not giving it to him, as they did later on, in mercy; but in mockery, pretending to present him with weak wine, such as they drank.

37. *And saying, If thou be the king of the Jews, save thyself.*

I fancy the scorn that they threw into their taunt: "If thou be the king of the Jews;" that was a bit of their own. "Save thyself;" that they borrowed from the rulers. Sometimes a scoffer or a mocker cannot exhibit all the bitterness that is in his heart except by using borrowed terms, as these soldiers did.

38. *And a superscription also was written over him in letters of Greek, and Latin, and Hebrew, THIS IS THE KING OF THE JEWS.*

John tells us that Pilate wrote this title, and that the chief priests tried in vain to get him to alter it. It was written in the three current languages of the time, so that the Greek, the Roman, and the Jew might alike understand who he was who was thus put to death. Pilate did not know as much about Christ as we do, or he might have written, THIS IS THE KING OF THE JEWS, AND OF THE GENTILES, TOO.

39. *And one of the malefactors which were hanged railed on him, saying, If thou be Christ, save thyself and us.*

He, too, borrows his speech from the rulers who derided Christ, only putting the words "and us" as a bit of originality. "If thou be Christ, save thyself and us."

40, 41. *But the other answering rebuked him, saying, Dost not thou fear God, seeing thou art in the same condemnation? And we indeed justly; for we receive the due reward of our deeds: but this man hath done nothing amiss.*

A fine testimony to Christ: "This man hath done nothing amiss;" nothing unbecoming, nothing out of order, nothing criminal, certainly; but nothing even "amiss." This testimony was well spoken by this dying thief.

42—46. *And he said unto Jesus, Lord, remember me when thou comest into thy kingdom. And Jesus said unto him, Verily I say unto thee, To day shalt thou be with me in paradise. And it was about the sixth hour, and there was a darkness over all the earth until the ninth hour. And the sun was darkened, and the veil of the temple was rent in the midst. And when Jesus had cried with a loud voice, he said, Father, into thy hands I commend my spirit: and having said thus, he gave up the ghost.*

He yielded his life. He did not die, as we have to do, because our appointed time has come, but willingly the great Sacrifice parted with his life: "He gave up the ghost." He was a willing sacrifice for guilty men.

Now let us see what John says concerning these hours of agony, these hours of triumph.

John xix. Verse 25. *Now there stood by the cross of Jesus his mother, and his mother's sister, Mary the wife of Cleophas, and Mary Magdalene.*

Last at the cross, first at the sepulchre. No woman's lip betrayed her Lord; no woman's hand ever smote him; their eyes wept for him; they gazed upon him with pitying awe and love. God bless the Marys! When we see so many of them about the cross, we feel that we honour the very name of Mary.

26. *When Jesus therefore saw his mother, and the disciple standing by, whom he loved, he saith unto his mother, Woman, behold thy son!*

Sad, sad spectacle! Now was fulfilled the word of Simeon, "Yea, a sword shall pierce through thy own soul also, that the thoughts of many hearts may be revealed." Did the Saviour mean, as he gave a glance to John, "Woman, thou art losing one Son; but yonder stands another, who will be a son to thee in my absence"? "Woman, behold thy son!"

27. *Then saith he to the disciple, Behold thy mother!*

"Take her as thy mother, stand thou in my place, care for her as I have cared for her." Those who love Christ best shall have the honour of taking care of his church and of his poor. Never say of any poor relative or friend, the widow or the fatherless, "They are a great burden to me." Oh, no! Say, "They are a great honour to me; my Lord has entrusted them to my care." John thought so; let us think so. Jesus selected the disciple he loved best to take his mother under his care. He selects those whom he loves best to-day, and puts his poor people under their wing. Take them gladly, and treat them well.

27. *And from that hour that disciple took her unto his own home.*

You expected him to do it, did you not? He loved his Lord so well.

28. *After this, Jesus knowing that all things were now accomplished, that the scripture might be fulfilled, saith, I thirst.*

There was a prophecy to that effect in the Psalms, and he must needs fulfil that. Think of a dying man prayerfully going through the whole of the Scriptures, and carefully fulfilling all that is there written concerning him: "That the scripture might be fulfilled, Jesus saith, I thirst."

29, 30. *Now there was set a vessel full of vinegar: and they filled a sponge with vinegar, and put it upon hyssop, and put it to his mouth. When Jesus therefore had received the vinegar,*

For he did receive it. It was a weak kind of wine, commonly drunk by the soldiery. This is not that mixed potion which he refused, wine mingled with myrrh, which was intended to stupefy the dying in their pains: "When he had tasted thereof, he would not drink;" for he would not be stupefied. He came to suffer to the bitter end the penalty of sin; and he would not have his sorrow mitigated; but when this slight refreshment was offered to him, he received it.. Having just expressed his human weakness by saying, "I thirst," he now manifests his all-sufficient strength by crying, with a loud voice, as Matthew, Mark, and Luke all testify.

30. *He said, It is finished:*

What "it" was it that was finished? I will not attempt to expound it. It is the biggest "it" that ever was. Turn it over, and you will see that it will grow, and grow, and grow, and grow, till it fills the whole earth: "It is finished."

30. *And he bowed his head, and gave up the ghost.*

He did not give up the ghost, and then bow his head because he was dead; but he bowed his head as though in the act of worship, or as leaning it down upon his Father's bosom, and then he gave up the ghost.

Thus have we had two gospel pictures of our dying Lord. May we remember them, and learn the lessons they are intended to teach!

HYMNS FROM "OUR OWN HYMN BOOK"—561, 279, 278.

Friends who desire to have the only complete record of the proceedings at the Fifth Annual Conference of the Pastors' College Evangelical Association, should procure the June and July issues of *The Sword and the Trowel*. They can be obtained through any bookseller, at 3d. each; or Messrs. Passmore and Alabaster, Paternoster Buildings, London, will send the two numbers, post free, for 8d. They contain articles, addresses, &c., by Pastors C. H. SPURGEON, J. A. Spurgeon, Charles Spurgeon, A. Bax, T. J. Longhurst, and J. Horne; Dr. Pierson; Principal David Gracey; Messrs. W. Y. Fullerton, J. W. Harrald, and R. Shindler; with much interesting information about the various institutions connected with the Tabernacle, including the Annual Reports of the Pastors' College and the Metropolitan Tabernacle Colportage Association.

Metropolitan Tabernacle Pulpit.

SOWING IN THE WIND; REAPING UNDER CLOUDS.

A Sermon

INTENDED FOR READING ON LORD'S-DAY, JULY 10TH, 1892,

DELIVERED BY

C. H. SPURGEON,

AT THE METROPOLITAN TABERNACLE, NEWINGTON,

On Thursday Evening, July 3rd, 1890.

"He that observeth the wind shall not sow; and he that regardeth the clouds shall not reap."—Ecclesiastes xi. 4.

Sow when the time comes, whatever wind blows. Reap when the time comes, whatever clouds are in the sky. There are, however, qualifying proverbs, which must influence our actions. We are not to discard prudence in the choice of the time for our work. "To every thing there is a season, and a time to every purpose under the heaven." It is well to sow when the weather is propitious. It is wise to "make hay while the sun shines." Cut your corn when there is the probability of getting it in dry.

But Solomon here is pushing the other side of the matter. He had seen prudence turn to idleness; he had noticed some people wait for a more convenient season, which never came. He had observed sluggards making excuses, which did not hold water. So he, with a blunt word, generalizes, in order to make the truth more forcible. Not troubling about the exceptions to the rule, he states it broadly thus: "Take no notice of winds or clouds. Go on with your work whatever happens. 'He that observeth the wind shall not sow; and he that regardeth the clouds shall not reap.'"

I. The first thought that is suggested by these words is this: NATURAL DIFFICULTIES MAY BE UNDULY CONSIDERED. A man may observe the wind, and regard the clouds a great deal too much, and so neither sow nor reap.

Note here, first, that *in any work this would hinder a man*. In any labour to which we set our hand, if we take too much notice of the difficulties, we shall be hindered in it. It is very wise to know the difficulty of your calling, the sorrow which comes with it, the trial which arises out of it, the temptation connected therewith; but if you think too much of these things, there is no calling that will be carried

No. 2,264.

on with any success. Poor farmers, they have a crop of hay, and cannot get it in; they may fret themselves to death if they like, and never earn a penny for a seven years' fretting! We say of their calling that it is surrounded with constant trouble. They may lose everything just at the moment when they are about to gather it in. The seed may perish under the clods when it is first sown. It is subject to blight, and mildew, and bird, and worm, and I know not what beside; and then, at the last, when the farmer is about to reap the harvest, it may disappear before the sickle can cut it. Take the case of the sailor. If he regards winds and clouds, will he ever put to sea? Can you give him a promise that the wind will be favourable in any of his voyages, or that he will reach his desired haven without a tempest? He that observeth the winds will not sail; and he that regardeth the clouds will never cross the mighty deep. If you turn from the farmer and the sailor, and come to the trader, what tradesman will do anything if he is always worrying about competition, and about the difficulties of his trade, which is so cut up that there is no making a living by it? I have heard this, I think, about every trade, and yet our friends keep on living, and some of them get rich, when they are supposed to be losing money every year! He that regardeth the rise and fall of prices, and is timid, and will do no trading because of the changes on the market, will not reap. If you come to the working-man, it is the same as with those I have mentioned; for there is no calling or occupation that is not surrounded with difficulties. In fact, I have formed this judgment from what friends have told me, that every trade is the worst trade out; for I have found somebody in that particular line who has proved this to a demonstration. I cannot say that I am an implicit believer in all I hear about this matter. Still, if I were, this would be the conclusion that I should come to, that he that observed the circumstances of any trade or calling, would never engage in it at all; he would never sow; and he would never reap. I suppose he would go to bed, and sleep all the four-and-twenty hours of the day; and after a while, I am afraid he would find it become impossible even to do that, and he would learn that to turn, with the sluggard, like a door on its hinges, is not unalloyed pleasure after all.

Well now, dear friends, if there be these difficulties in connection with earthly callings and trades, do you expect there will be nothing of the kind with regard to heavenly things? Do you imagine that, in sowing the good seed of the kingdom, and gathering the sheaves into the garner, you will have no difficulties and disappointments? Do you dream that, when you are bound for heaven, you are to have smooth sailing and propitious winds all the voyage? Do you think that, in your heavenly trading, you will have less trials than the merchant who has only to do with earthly business? If you do, you make a great mistake. You will not be likely to enter upon the heavenly calling, if you do nothing else but unduly consider the difficulties surrounding it.

But, next, *in the work of liberality this would stay us.* This is Solomon's theme here. "Cast thy bread upon the waters:" "Give a portion to seven, and also to eight;" and so on. He means, by my text, that if anybody occupies his mind unduly with the difficulties connected with liberality, he will do nothing in that line. "He that observeth the wind shall not sow; and he that regardeth the clouds shall not reap." "How am I to know," says one, "that the person to whom I give my money is really deserving? How do I know what he will do with it? How do I know but what I may be encouraging idleness or begging? By giving to the man, I may be doing him real injury." Perhaps you are not asked to give to an individual, but to some great work. Then, if you regard the clouds, you will begin to say, "How do I know that this work will be successful, this sending of missionaries to the Hottentots? Will any good come of it? Or this sending of missionaries to a cultivated people like the Hindoos? Is it likely that they will be converted?" You will not sow, and you will not reap, if you talk like that; yet there are many who do speak in that fashion. There was never an enterprise started yet but somebody objected to it; and I do not believe that the best work that Christ himself ever did was beyond criticism; there were some people who were sure to find some fault with it. "But," says another, "I have heard that the management at headquarters is not all it ought to be; I think that there is too much money spent on the secretary, and that there is a great deal lost in this direction and in that." Well, dear friend, it goes without saying that if *you* managed things, they would be managed perfectly; but, you see, you cannot do everything, and therefore you must trust somebody. I can only say, with regard to societies, agencies, works, and missions of all kinds, "He that observeth the wind shall not sow; and he that regardeth the clouds shall not reap." If that is what you are doing, finding out imperfections and difficulties, it will end in this, you will do nothing at all.

Going a little further, as this is true of common occupations and of liberality, so is it especially true *in the work of serving God*. Now, if I were to consider in my mind nothing but the natural depravity of man, I should never preach again. To preach the gospel to sinners, is as foolish a thing as to bid dead men rise out of their graves. For that reason I do it, because it has pleased God, "by the foolishness of preaching, to save them that believe." When I look upon the alienation from God, the hardness of the human heart, I see that old Adam is too strong for me; and if I regarded that one cloud of the fall, and original sin, and the natural depravity of man, I, for one, should neither sow nor reap. I am afraid that there has been a good deal of this, however. Many preachers have contemplated the ruin of man, and they have had so clear a view of it that they dare not say, "Thus saith the Lord, Ye dry bones, live." They are unable to cry, "Dear Master, speak through us, and say, 'Lazarus, come forth!'" Some seem to say, "Go and see whether Lazarus has any kind of feeling of his condition in the grave. If so, I will call him out, because I believe he can come;" thus putting all the burden on Lazarus, and depending upon Lazarus for it. But we say, "Though he has been dead four days, and is already becoming corrupt, that has nothing to do with us. If our Master bids us call him out from his grave, we can call him out, and he will come; not because he can come by his own power, but because God can make him come, for the day now is when they that are in their graves shall hear the voice of God, and they that hear shall live.

But, dear friends, there are persons to whom we should never go to seek their salvation if we regarded the winds and the clouds, for they are peculiarly bad people. We know, from observation, that there are some persons who are much worse than others, some who are not amenable to kindness, or any other human treatment. They do not seem to be terrified by law, or affected by love. We know people who go into a horrible temper every now and then, and all the hope we had of them is blown away, like sere leaves in the autumn wind. You know such, and you "fight shy" of them. There are such boys, and there are such girls, full of mischief and levity, or full of malice and bitterness; and you say to yourself, "I cannot do anything with them. It is of no use." Just so. You are observing the winds, and regarding the clouds. You will not be one of those to whom Isaiah says, "Blessed are ye that sow beside all waters."

Some one may say, "I would not mind the moral condition of the people, but it is their surroundings that are the trouble. What is the use of trying to save a man while he lives, as he does, in such a horrible street, in one room? What is the use of seeking to raise such and such a woman while she is surrounded, as she is, with such examples? The very atmosphere seems tainted." Just so, dear friend; while you observe the winds, and regard the clouds, you will not sow, and you will not reap. You will not attempt the work, and of course you will not complete what you do not commence.

So, you know, you can go on making all kinds of excuses for doing nothing with certain people, because you feel or think that they are not those whom God is likely to bless. I know this to be a common case, even with very serious and earnest workers for Christ. Let it not be so with you, dear friends; but be you one of those who obey the poet's words,—

> "Beside all waters sow;
> The highway furrows stock;
> Drop it where thorns and thistles grow;
> Scatter it on the rock."

Let me carry this principle, however, a little further. You may unduly consider circumstances in reference to *the business of your own eternal life*. You may, in that matter, observe the winds, and never sow; you may regard the clouds, and never reap. "I feel," says one, "as if I never can be saved. There never was such a sinner as I am. My sins are so peculiarly black." Yes, and if you keep on regarding them, and do not remember the Saviour, and his infinite power to save, you will not sow in prayer and faith. "Ah, sir; but you do not know the horrible thoughts I have, the dark forebodings that cross my mind!" I know that, dear friend; I do not know them. I know what I feel myself, and I expect that your feelings are very like my own; but, be they what they may, if, instead of looking to Christ, you are always studying your own condition, your own withered hopes, your own broken resolutions, then you will still keep where you are, and you will neither sow nor reap.

Beloved Christians, you who have been believers for years, if you begin to live by your frames and feelings, you will get into the same condition. "I do not feel like praying," says one. Then is the time when you ought to pray most, for you are evidently most in need; but if you keep observing whether or not you are in a proper frame of mind for prayer, you will not pray. "I cannot grasp the promises," says another; "I should like to joy in God, and firmly believe in his Word; but I do not see anything in myself that can minister to my comfort." Suppose you do not. Are you, after all, going to build upon yourself? Are you trying to find your ground of consolation in your own heart? If so, you are on the wrong tack. Our hope is not in self, but in Christ; let us go and sow it. Our hope is in the finished work of Christ; let us go and reap it; for, if we keep on regarding the winds and the clouds, we shall neither sow nor reap. I think it is a great lesson to learn in spiritual things, to believe in Christ, and his finished salvation, quite as much when you are down as when you are up; for Christ is no more Christ on the top of the mountain than he is in the bottom of the valley, and he is no less Christ in the storm by midnight than he is in the sunshine by day. Do not begin to measure your safety by your comfort; but measure it by the eternal Word of God, which you have believed, and which you know to be true, and on which you rest; for still here, within the little world of our own bosom, "he that observeth the wind shall not sow; and he that regardeth the clouds shall not reap." We want to get out of that idea altogether.

I have said enough to prove the truth of my first observation, namely, that natural difficulties may be unduly considered.

II. My second observation is this: SUCH UNWISE CONSIDERATION INVOLVES US IN SEVERAL SINS.

If we keep on observing circumstances, instead of trusting God, we shall be guilty of *disobedience*. God bids me sow: I do not sow, because the wind would blow some of my seed away. God bids me reap: I do not reap, because there is a black cloud there, and before I can house the harvest, some of it may be spoiled. I may say what I like; but I am guilty of disobedience. I have not done what I was bidden to do. I have made an excuse out of the weather; but I have been disobedient. Dear friends, it is yours to do what God bids you do, whether the heavens fall down or not; and, if you knew that they would fall, and you could prop them up by disobedience, you have no right to do it. What may happen from our doing right, we have nothing to do with; we are to do right, and take the consequences cheerfully. Do you want obedience to be always rewarded by a spoonful of sugar? Are you such a baby that you will do nothing unless there shall be some little toy for you directly after? A man in Christ Jesus will do right, though it shall involve him in losses and crosses, slanders and rebukes; yea, even martyrdom itself. May God help you so to do! He that observeth the wind, and does not sow when he is bidden to cast his seed upon the waters, is guilty of disobedience.

Next, we are guilty also of *unbelief*, if we cannot sow because of the wind. Who manages the wind? You distrust him who is Lord of north, and south, and east, and west. If you cannot reap because of a cloud, you doubt him who makes the clouds, to whom the clouds are the dust of his feet. Where is your faith? Where is your faith? "Ah!" says one, "I can serve God when I am helped, when I am moved, when I can see a hope of success." That is poor service, service devoid of faith. May I not say of it, "Without faith it is impossible to please God"? Just in proportion to the quantity of faith that there is in what we do, in that proportion will it be acceptable with God. Observing of winds and clouds is unbelief. We may call it prudence; but unbelief is its true name.

The next sin is really *rebellion*. So you will not sow unless God chooses to make the wind blow your way; and you will not reap unless God pleases to drive the clouds away? I call that revolt, rebellion. An honest subject loves his king in all weathers. The true servant serves his master, let his master do what he wills. Oh, dear friends, we are too often aiming at God's throne! We want to get up there, and manage things,—

> "Snatch from his hand the balance and the rod,
> Rejudge his judgments, be the god of God."

Oh, if he would but alter my circumstances! What is this but tempting God, as they did in the wilderness, wishing him to do other than he does? It is wishing him to do wrong; for what he does is always right; but we must not so rebel, and vex his Holy Spirit, by complaining of what he does. Do you not see that this is trying to throw the blame of our shortcomings upon the Lord? "If we did not sow, do not blame us; God did not send the right wind. If we did not reap, pray do not censure us; how could we be expected to reap, while there were clouds in the skies?" What is this but a wicked endeavour to blame God for our own neglect and wrong-doing, and to make Divine Providence the pack-horse upon which we pile our sins? God save us from such rebellion as that!

Another sin of which we are guilty, when we are always looking at our circumstances, is this, *foolish fear*. Though we may think that there is no sin in it, there is great sin in foolish fear. God has commanded his people not to fear; then we should obey him. There is a cloud; why do you fear it? It will be gone directly; not a drop of rain may fall out of it. You are afraid of the wind; why fear it? It may never come. Even if it were some deadly wind that was approaching, it might shift about, and not come near you. We are often fearing what never happens. We feel a thousand deaths in fearing one. Many a person has been afraid of what never would occur. It is a great pity to whip yourselves with imaginary rods. Wait till the trouble comes; else I shall have to tell you the story I have often repeated of the mother whose child would cry. She told it not to cry, but it would cry. "Well," she said, "if you will cry, I will give you something to cry for." If you get fearing about nothing, the probability is that you will get something really to fear, for God does not love his people to be fools.

There are some who fall into the sin of *penuriousness*. Observe, that Solomon was here speaking of liberality. He that observeth the clouds and the winds thinks, "That is not a good object to help," and that he will do harm if he gives *here,* or if he gives *there.* It amounts to this, poor miser, you want to save your money! Oh, the ways we have of making buttons with which to secure the safety of our pockets! Some persons have a button manufactory always ready. They have always a reason for not giving to anything that is proposed to them, or to any poor person who asks their help. I pray that every child of God here may avoid that sin. "Freely ye have received, freely give." And since you are stewards of a generous Master, let it never be said that the most liberal of Lords has the stingiest of stewards.

Another sin is often that of *idleness.* The man who does not sow because of the wind, is usually too lazy to sow; and the man who does not reap because of the clouds, is the man who wants a little more sleep, and a little more slumber, and a little more folding of the hands to sleep. If we do not want to serve God, it is wonderful how many reasons we can find. According to Solomon, the sluggard said there was a lion in the streets. "There is a lion in the way," said he, "a lion is in the streets." What a lie it was, for lions are as much afraid of streets as men are of deserts! Lions do not come into streets. It was idleness that said the lion was there. You were asked to preach the other night, and you could preach, but you said, no, you could not preach. However, you attended a political meeting, did you not, and talked twice as long as you would have done if you had preached? Another friend, asked to teach in a Sunday-school, said, "I have no gifts of teaching." Somebody afterwards remarked of you that you had no gifts of teaching, and you felt very vexed, and asked what right had anyone to say that of you? I have heard persons run themselves down, when they have been invited to any Christian work, as being altogether disqualified; and when somebody has afterwards said, "That is true, you cannot do anything, I know," they have looked as if they would knock the speaker down. Oh, yes, yes, yes, we are always making these excuses about winds and clouds, and there is nothing in either of them. It is all meant to save our corn-seed, and to save us the trouble of sowing it.

Do you not see, I have made out a long list of sins wrapped up in this observing of winds and clouds? If you have been guilty of any of them, repent of your wrong-doing, and do not repeat it.

III. I will not keep you longer over this part of the subject. I will now make a third remark very briefly: LET US PROVE THAT WE HAVE NOT FALLEN INTO THIS EVIL. How can we prove it?

Let us prove it, first, *by sowing in the most unlikely places.* What says Solomon? "Cast thy bread upon the waters: for thou shalt find it after many days." Go, my brothers and sisters, and find out the most unlikely people, and begin to work for God with them. Now try, if you can, to pick out the worst street in your neighbourhood, and visit from house to house, and if there is a man or a woman more given up than another, make that person the object of your prayers and of your holy endeavours. Cast your bread upon the waters; then it will be seen that you are trusting God, not trusting the soil, nor trusting the seed.

Next, prove it *by doing good to a great many.* "Give a portion to seven, and also to eight." Talk of Christ to everybody you meet with. If God has not blessed you to one, try another; and if he has blessed you to one, try two others; and if he has blessed you to two others, try four others; and always keep on enlarging your seed-plot as your harvest comes in. If you are doing much, it will be shown that you are not regarding the winds and the clouds.

Further, prove that you are not regarding winds and clouds *by wisely learning from the clouds* another lesson than the one they seem made to teach. Learn this lesson: "If the clouds be full of rain, they empty themselves upon the earth;" and say to yourself, "If God has made me full of his grace, I will go and pour it out to others If I know the joy of being saved, if I have had fellowship with him, I will make a point of being more industrious than ever, because God has been unusually gracious to me. My fulness shall be helpful to others. I will empty myself for the good of others, even as the clouds pour down the rain upon the earth."

Then, beloved, prove it still *by not wanting to know how God will work.* There is that great mystery of birth, how the human soul comes to inhabit the body of the child, and how the child is fashioned. Thou knowest nothing about it, and thou canst not know. Therefore do not look about thee to see what thou canst not understand, and pry into what is concealed from thee. Go out and work; go out and preach; go out and instruct others. Go out and seek to win souls. Thus shalt thou prove, in very truth, that thou art not dependent upon surroundings and circumstances.

Again, dear friend, prove this *by constant diligence.* "In the morning sow thy seed, and in the evening withhold not thine hand." "Be instant in season, out of season." I had a friend, who had learned the way to put a peculiar meaning upon that passage of Scripture, "Let not thy right hand know what thy left hand doeth." He thought that the best way was to have money in both pockets; put one hand into each pocket, and then put both hands on the collection-plate. I never objected to his interpretation of the passage. Now, the way to serve Christ, is to do all you possibly can, and then as much more. "No," say you, "that cannot be." I do not know that it cannot be. I found that the best thing I ever did was a thing I could not do. What I could do well, that was my own; but what I could not do, but still did, in the name and strength of the Eternal Jehovah, was the best thing I had done. Beloved, sow in the morning, sow in the evening, sow at night, sow all day long, for you can never tell what God will bless; but by this constant sowing, you will prove to demonstration that you are not observing the winds, nor regarding the clouds.

IV. I now come to my concluding observation: LET US KEEP THIS EVIL OUT OF OUR HEARTS AS WELL AS OUT OF OUR WORK.

And, first, *let us give no heed to the winds and clouds of doctrine* that are everywhere about us now. Blow, blow, ye stormy winds; but you shall not move me. Clouds of hypotheses and inventions, come up with you, as many as you please, till you darken all the sky; but I will not fear you. Such clouds have come before, and have disappeared, and these will disappear, too. If you sit down, and think of men's inventions of error, and their novel doctrines, and how the churches have been bewitched by them; you will get into such a state of mind that you will neither sow nor reap. Just forget them. Give yourself to your holy service as if there were no winds and no clouds; and God will give you such comfort in your soul that you will rejoice before him, and be confident in his truth.

And then, next, *let us not lose hope because of doubts and temptations.* When the clouds and the winds get into your heart, when you do not feel as you used to feel, when you have not that joy and elasticity of spirit you once had, when your ardour seems a little damped, and even your faith begins to hesitate a little, go you to God all the same. Trust him still.

> "And when thine eye of faith grows dim,
> Still hold to Jesus, sink or swim;
> Still at his footstool bow the knee,
> And Israel's God thy strength shall be."

Do not go up and down like the mercury in the weather-glass; but know what you know, and believe what you believe. Hold to it, and God keep you in one mind, so that none can turn you; for, if not, if you begin to notice these things, you will neither sow nor reap.

Lastly, *let us follow the Lord's mind, come what will.* In a word, set your face, like a flint, to serve God, by the maintenance of his truth, by your holy life, by the savour of your Christian character; and, that being done, defy earth and hell. If there were a crowd of devils between you and Christ, kick a lane through them by holy faith. They will fly before you. If you have but the courage to make an advance, they cannot stop you. You shall make a clear gangway through legions of them. Only be strong, and of good courage, and do not regard even the clouds from hell, or blasts from the infernal pit; but go straight on in the path of right, and, God being with you, you shall sow and you shall reap, unto his eternal glory.

Will some poor sinner here to-night, whether he sinks or swims, trust Christ? Come, if you feel less inclined to-night to hope, than ever you did before. Have hope even now; hope against hope; believe against belief. Cast yourself on Christ, even though he may seem to stand with a drawn sword in his hand, to run you through; trust even an angry Christ. Though your sins have grieved him, come and trust him. Do not stop for winds to blow over, or clouds to burst. Just as thou art, without one trace of anything that is good about thee, come and trust Christ as thy Saviour, and thou art saved. God give you grace to do so, for Jesus' sake! Amen.

Exposition by C. H. Spurgeon.

ECCLESIASTES XI., XII.

Chapter xi. Verse 1. *Cast thy bread upon the waters: for thou shalt find it after many days.*

Hoard not thy bread; for if thou dost, it will mildew, it will be of no use to thee. Cast it on the waters; scatter it abroad; give it to unworthy men if need be. Some see here an allusion to the casting of seed into the Nile when it overflowed its banks. When the waters subsided, the corn would grow, and be gathered in "after many days."

2. *Give a portion to seven,*
And if that be a perfect number, give beyond it,
2. *And also to eight;*

Give to more than thou canst afford to give to. Help some who are doubtful, some who are outside of the perfect number, and give them a portion, a fair portion. Our Saviour went beyond Solomon; for he said, "Give to every man that asketh of thee."

2. *For thou knowest not what evil shall be upon the earth.*

Thou knowest not what need there may be of thy help; nor what need may come to thee, and how thou thyself mayest be helped by those whom thou helpest now.

3. *If the clouds be full of rain, they empty themselves upon the earth:*

Some men, the fuller they get, the harder they get; but the clouds are only full that they may empty themselves. Blessed is that steward of God who gets that he may give. "If the clouds be full of rain, they empty themselves upon the earth."

3. *And if the tree fall toward the south, or toward the north, in the place where the tree falleth, there it shall be.*

The tree falls the way it is inclined; but when it has fallen, there it must be. God grant that you and I may fall the right way when the axe of death hews us down! Which way are we inclined?

4, 5. *He that observeth the wind shall not sow; and he that regardeth the clouds shall not reap. As thou knowest not what is the way of the spirit, nor how the bones do grow in the womb of her that is with child: even so thou knowest not the works of God who maketh all.*

There are great mysteries which we can never comprehend. God alone knows how the soul comes into the body, or even how the body is fashioned. This must remain with him. We do not know how sinners are regenerated. We know not how the Spirit of God works upon the mind of man, and transforms the sinner into a saint. We do not want to know. There are some who know too much already. I have not half the desire to know that I have to believe and to love. Oh, that we loved God more, and trusted God more! We might then get to heaven if we knew even less than we do.

6. *In the morning sow thy seed, and in the evening withhold not thine hand: for thou knowest not whether shall prosper, either this or that, or whether they both shall be alike good.*

You cannot make the gospel enter into men's hearts. You cannot tell how it does enter and change them. The Spirit of God does that; but your duty is to go on telling it out. Go on spreading abroad the knowledge of Christ; in the morning, and in the evening, and all day long, scatter the good seed of the kingdom. You have nothing to do with the result of your sowing; that remains with the Lord. That which you sow in the morning may prosper, or the seed that you scatter in the evening;

possibly, God will bless both. You are to keep on sowing, whether you reap or not.

7, 8. *Truly the light is sweet, and a pleasant thing it is for the eyes to behold the sun: but if a man live many years, and rejoice in them all; yet let him remember the days of darkness; for they shall be many. All that cometh is vanity.*

Take Christ away, and this is a truthful estimate of human life. Put Christ into the question, and Solomon does not hit the mark at all. If we have Christ with us, whether the days are light or dark, we walk in the light, and our soul is happy and glad; but apart from Christ, the estimate of life which is given here is an exactly accurate one—a little brightness and long darkness, a flash and then midnight. God save you from living a merely natural life! May you rise to the supernatural! May you get out of the lower life of the mere animal into the higher life of the regenerated soul! If the life of God be in you, then you shall go from strength to strength, like the sun that shineth unto the perfect day.

9. *Rejoice, O young man, in thy youth; and let thy heart cheer thee in the days of thy youth, and walk in the ways of thine heart, and in the sight of thine eyes: but know thou, that for all these things God will bring thee into judgment.*

Young man, will you dare, then, to follow your passions, and the devices of your own heart, with this at the back, "God will bring thee into judgment"? Oh no, the advice of Solomon, apparently so evil, is answered by the warning at the end, which is also true,—

10. *Therefore remove sorrow from thy heart, and put away evil from thy flesh: for childhood and youth are vanity.*

"Remove sorrow," or rather, anger, ambition, or anything else that would cause sorrow, "from thy heart; and put away evil from thy flesh." Let not thy fleshly nature rule thee; thou art in the period when the flesh is strong towards evil, when "vanity" is the ruin of many.

Chapter xii. Verse 1. *Remember now thy Creator in the days of thy youth,*

Now we get on solid ground. There was irony in the advice, "Rejoice, O young man, in thy youth; and let thy heart cheer thee in the days of thy youth, and walk in the ways of thine heart, and in the sight of thine eyes." There is no irony here; there is solid, sound advice: "Remember now thy Creator in the days of thy youth." May every young man take this advice, and carry it out!

1—3. *While the evil days come not, nor the years draw nigh, when thou shalt say, I have no pleasure in them; while the sun, or the light, or the moon, or the stars, be not darkened, nor the clouds return after the rain: in the day when the keepers of the house shall tremble,*

These arms and hands of ours shake by reason of weakness.

3. *And the strong men shall bow themselves,*

These limbs, these legs of ours, begin to bend under the weight they have to support.

3. *And the grinders cease because they are few,*

The teeth are gone.

3. *And those that look out of the windows be darkened,*

The eyesight begins to fail.

4. *And the doors shall be shut in the streets, when the sound of the grinding is low, and he shall rise up at the voice of the bird, and all the daughters of musick shall be brought low;*

The old man sleeps very lightly; anything awakens him. He hides away from public business. The doors are shut in the streets.

5. *Also when they shall be afraid of that which is high, and fears shall be in the way,*

There is none of the courage of youth. Daring is gone; prudence, not to say cowardice, sits on the throne.

5. *And the almond tree shall flourish,*

The hair is white and grey, like the early peach or almond tree in the beginning of the year.

5. *And the grasshopper shall be a burden,*

A little trouble weighs the old man down. He has no energy now. The grasshopper is a burden.

5, 6. *And desire shall fail: because man goeth to his long home, and the mourners go about the streets: or ever the silver cord be loosed, or the golden bowl be broken,*

Before the spinal cord is broken, or the skull becomes emptied of the living inhabitant.

6. *Or the pitcher be broken at the fountain, or the wheel broken at the cistern.*

The circulation of the blood begins to fail, the heart grows weak, it will soon stop. The man's career is nearly over.

7. *Then shall the dust return to the earth as it was: and the spirit shall return unto God who gave it.*

This will happen to us all, either to return to dust or else to return to God. Whether we die, and return to dust, or live until the coming of Christ, our spirit shall return to God who gave it. May the return be a joyous one for each of us!

8—11. *Vanity of vanities, saith the preacher; all is vanity. And moreover, because the preacher was wise, he still taught the people knowledge; yea, he gave good heed, and sought out, and set in order many proverbs. The preacher sought to find out acceptable words: and that which was written was upright, even words of truth. The words of the wise are as goads,*

They prick us onward, as the goad does the bullock, when he is trying to stop instead of ploughing in the furrow.

11. *And as nails fastened by the masters of assemblies, which are given from one shepherd.*

The words of the wise are driven home, like nails, and clinched. There is one great Shepherd who, by means of his servants' words, leads his flock where he would have them go.

12, 13. *And further, by these, my son, be admonished: of making many books there is no end; and much study is a weariness of the flesh. Let us hear the conclusion of the whole matter: Fear God, and keep his commandments: for this is the whole duty of man.*

Or, "this is the whole of man." It makes a man of him when he fears God and keeps his commandments; he has that which makes him "the whole man."

14. *For God shall bring every work into judgment, with every secret thing, whether it be good, or whether it be evil.*

Depend upon it that it will be so. At the last great day, there will be a revelation of everything, whether it be good, or whether it be evil. Nor need the righteous fear that revelation, for they will only magnify in that day the amazing grace of God which has put all their iniquities away; and then shall all men know how great the grace of God was in passing by iniquity, transgression, and sin.

HYMNS FROM "OUR OWN HYMN BOOK"—748, 747, 753.

Metropolitan Tabernacle Pulpit.

HARVEST JOY.

A Sermon

INTENDED FOR READING ON LORD'S-DAY, JULY 17TH, 1892,

DELIVERED BY

C. H. SPURGEON,

AT THE METROPOLITAN TABERNACLE, NEWINGTON,

On Lord's-day Evening, July 6th, 1890.

"Thou hast multiplied the nation, and increased the joy: they joy before thee according to the joy in harvest, and as men rejoice when they divide the spoil."—Isaiah ix. 3.

NOTICE that I made a correction in the version from which I am reading. The Authorized Version has it, "Thou hast multiplied the nation, and not increased the joy." This is not consistent with the connection; and the Revised Version has very properly put it, "Thou hast multiplied the nation, thou hast increased their joy." I have not any learning to display; but I think I could show you, if this were the proper time, how the passage came to be read with a "not", and I could also prove to you that, in this instance, the Revisers were right in making their alteration.

To-night, there are about eighty-two persons, who have confessed Christ before the church, and have been baptized, who are to be received into our fellowship; and we feel very grateful for this large addition to our members; and all the more so because it is no strange thing; but month by month, all the year round, they continue to come, though not in such large numbers as at this time. God be thanked for thus blessing us! We cannot allow these occasions to pass over without joying before the Lord as men rejoice when they gather in their sheaves of corn.

To bring out your joy, think of how we should feel if we did not have an increase to the church. I know churches, and you know churches, where very few are ever added to them. The good old people seem quite content to be very few. Their notion is that the way to heaven is very narrow, as indeed it is, and that therefore they must not expect many to find that way. I remember a church where the good old deacons used to say of the converts, "Summer them and winter them. Keep them out till we have tried them for a very long time." It came to pass, after the process of "summering and wintering", that a great many of them never came forward at all.

No. 2,265.

Though they were very excellent people, they never summoned courage enough to join such a church. Did you ever hear a farmer say of his wheat, " Summer it and winter it, and then take it into the barn " ? No, farmers are not such fools. But these good men were so very wise that they became otherwise; so they said, " Keep the corn out in the field ; else you will bring in some poppies, or some corn-flowers, and we do not want them. Keep the converts out of the church till you are sure that there are no hypocrites among them." Well, dear friends, we are not at all of this mind. We try to use every caution, and great prudence; and our friends do not come into this church without experiencing an examination, some of them even think it to be an ordeal ; yet I find that the more difficult it is to get into a church, the more people want to come into it; and whenever the barriers are lowered, and you tell people that they may come without any test as to the state of their souls, nobody cares to come. Well, we have taken pains and care, and have sought only to welcome the worthy, that is, those who are trusting in Jesus, yet we have had a great number come. But suppose that we had none. Well, I hope every Christian man and woman here would be troubled about it. I should not wonder if the question arose, " Had we not better put somebody else on that platform ? " That somebody who is now here would be the first to say, " If I am doing no good, let somebody else come and try ; for it would be a sad and sickening business to be fishing for souls, and never catching anything." Last winter, at Menton, I went out in a boat, where I was assured there were shoals of fish ; and I had a line, I should think it was a hundred and fifty feet long, and, after waiting hour after hour, and never feeling the fish bite, I gave up the useless occupation. I think every minister is bound to give up the spiritual fishery in any particular place if, after many days' toil, he has caught nothing for Christ. Rachel said, " Give me children, or I die." Christ's servant says, " Give me converts, or I die." Indeed, we are dead as far as our ministry is concerned unless God blesses it.

We also feel that we ought to be glad when others are joined to the church, because we look back, with exquisite pleasure, upon our own joining it. I remember the trouble it cost me to join the church. I think I went to see the pastor some four or five days running; he was always too busy to see me, till at last I told him it did not matter, for I would go to the church-meeting, and propose myself as a member ; and then he, all of a sudden, found time to see me, and so I managed to get into the church, and confess my faith in Christ. Oh, dear friends, that was one of the best days' work I ever did, when I openly declared my faith in Christ, and united myself with his people. ! I think many here could say the same; they remember when they united with the people of God, and publicly avowed their faith. You do not regret it brethren, do you ? I am sure you feel that it was a happy day when you could say,—

> " 'Tis done ! the great transaction's done :
> I am my Lord's, and he is mine."

By the peace of mind which has come to us from joining with the people of God after believing in Christ, we feel glad to see other young soldiers stooping to take up the cross of Christ, and following him, "without the camp, bearing his reproach."

I. Looking at our text, I notice in it, first, A WORD OF DISCRIMINATION. If you look carefully at the passage, you will soon see it: "*Thou* hast multiplied the nation, and increased the joy."

Observe, first, that *conversion must be the Lord's work*. The only multiplication of the Church of God that is to be desired is that which God sends: "Thou hast multiplied the nation." If we add to our churches by becoming worldly, by taking in persons who have never been born again; if we add to our churches by accommodating the life of the Christian to the life of the worldling, our increase is worth nothing at all; it is a loss rather than a gain. If we add to our churches by excitement, by making appeals to the passions, rather than by explaining truth to the understanding; if we add to our churches otherwise than by the power of the Spirit of God making men new creatures in Christ Jesus, the increase is of no worth whatever. A man picked himself up from the gutter, and rolled up against Mr. Rowland Hill, one night as he went home, and he said, "Mr. Hill, I am pleased to see you, sir. I am one of your converts." Rowland said, "I thought it was very likely you were. You are not one of God's converts, or else you would not be drunk." There is a great lesson in that answer. My converts are no good; Rowland Hill's converts could get drunk; but the converts of the Spirit of God, those who are really renewed in the spirit of their mind, by a supernatural operation, these are a real increase to the church of God. "Thou hast multiplied the nation." Pray hard that the Lord may continue to send us converts. He never sends the wrong people. However poor they may be, however illiterate, if they are converted, as they will be if the Lord sends them, they are the very people that we want. May God send us thousands more!

The text also teaches us, with a word of discrimination, that *conversion must be such as the Lord describes* in this chapter: "The people that walked in darkness have seen a great light: they that dwell in the land of the shadow of death, upon them hath the light shined." When God brings men to the church, they are the people who have undergone a very remarkable change. They have come out of darkness, palpable, horrible, into light, marvellous and delightful. God sends no other than these. If you are not changed characters, if you are not new creatures in Christ Jesus, if you cannot say, "One thing I know, whereas I was blind, now I see," the church cannot receive you as you are, and God has not sent you. Now, who can turn us from darkness unto light but God? Who can work this great miracle within the heart? Darkness of heart is very hard to move. Who but God can make the eternal light burst through the natural darkness, and turn us from the power of Satan unto God?

Next, *conversion must have a distinct relation to Christ*. Look down the chapter, just a little way, and you come to this wonderful passage: "For unto us a child is born, unto us a son is given: and the government shall be upon his shoulder: and his name shall be called Wonderful, Counsellor, The mighty God, The everlasting Father, The Prince of Peace." We want converts who know this Christ, men and women to whom he is "Wonderful", to whom he has become the "Counsellor." We want no additions to the church of those who cannot call him "The mighty God, The everlasting Father." We want men and women to whom Christ has become "The Prince of Peace." If these are added to us, the church groweth exceedingly. If others are added, they do but increase our burden; they become our weakness; in many cases they become our disgrace. Dear hearers, you know whether you are trusting Christ or not. If you are, come and confess him. If you are not, weep in secret places, and cry to God the Holy Spirit to reveal Christ to you as the Wonderful, Counsellor, and the mighty God, and then, when you know him as your Saviour, come and join yourself to his people, and God will, in your case, have multiplied the nation.

Once more, about this discrimination, *the joy must be such as God gives*. The text says, "Thou hast multiplied the nation, and increased the joy." The joy that we ought to have to-night, the joy of any growing church, will be joy such as God gives. That is the kind of joy we desire to have. If anybody wishes to see the church grow that we may excel other churches, that is not the joy that God gives. If we like to see converts because we are glad that our opinions should be spread, God does not give that joy. If we crave converts that we may steal them from other people, God does not give that joy, if it be a joy. I do not think God *is* the lover of sheep-stealers, and there are plenty such about. We do not desire to increase our numbers by taking Christian people away from other Christian communities. No, the joy which God gives is clear, unselfish delight in Christ being glorified, in souls being saved, in truth being spread, and in error being baffled. God give us a joy over those who are added to us, which shall be pure, and Christlike, and heavenly! Oh, that he might increase such joy! I think that he *has* increased it.

Did you ever worship in a place where there were more pews than people? Did you ever go to a church or chapel where the preacher could preach upon anything except the gospel of Christ, where you might hear about anything except the precious blood of Christ? That, the minister would be sure not to mention. Then, I think I see you go grumbling down the aisle after every service, or you sit there, and look up to the pulpit, and long for what you never hear, till the Sabbath becomes more wearisome than any day of the week. Oh, dear! Few people; little to be got; very little ever given; a terrible "starvation camp", where every man looks at his fellow, and wonders who is going to die next. Well, now, we ought to thank God that it is not so with us. Look on this company gathered here to-night. Think of the congregation we had this morning; remember the deep attention, and think in how many cases God has blessed the Word to the hearers. I never, personally, felt so weak, or felt so great a burden in preaching; yet I never had so large a blessing; there are more converts than ever. Glory be to God, this is the kind of joy that comes from him, a joy in him, in his Word, in his power, that out of weakness makes his servant strong.

So much by way of discrimination.

II. Now, secondly, notice A WORD OF DESCRIPTION, which is the main part of the text. The joy of the church in receiving converts may be compared to the joy in harvest. In all nations, the time of reaping the corn, and gathering it into the garner, has been regarded as a festival. What is the joy of harvest?

Well, it is *a joy which we ought to expect.* The husbandman expects a harvest. He says, "It is so many weeks to harvest." He sows his seed with a view to harvest. He turns in a man to clear out the weeds with a view to harvest. He has a barn, and he has a threshing-machine, all with a view to harvest. Well, now, every church should be looking out for a spiritual harvest. One said to me, once, "I have preached for several years, and I believe God has blessed the word; but nobody ever comes forward to tell me so." I said to him, "Next Lord's-day, say to the people, 'I shall be in the vestry, when the sermon is finished, to see friends who have been converted.'" To his surprise, ten or twelve came in; and he was taken quite aback; but, of course, quite delighted. He had not looked for a harvest, so of course he did not get it. You know the story I tell of my first student, Mr. Medhurst. He went out to preach on Tower Hill, Sunday after Sunday. He was not then my student; but one of the young men in the church. He came to me, and said, "I have been out preaching now for several months on Tower Hill, and I have not seen one conversion." I said to him, rather sharply, "Do you expect God is going to bless you every time you choose to open your mouth?" He answered, "Oh! no, sir; I do not expect him to do that." "Then," I replied, "that is why you do not get a blessing." We ought to expect a blessing. God has said, "My Word shall not return unto me void;" and it will not. We ought to look for a harvest. He who preaches the gospel with his whole heart, ought to be surprised if he does not hear of conversions; and he ought to begin to say in his heart, "I will know the reason why," and never stop till he has found it out. The joy of harvest is what we have a right to expect.

The joy of harvest, next, is *a joy which has respect to former toil.* He is bound to rejoice in a harvest who has sorrowed in ploughing, and in the sowing of the seed, and in watching his crop when it was in the ear, and when frost, and blight, and mildew threatened to destroy it. Brothers and sisters, many of us here can rejoice with the joy of harvest, because, in those converted to Christ, we see the fruit of our soul's travail. I thank God first, and I thank many of you next, that when I sit to see enquirers, I find that I am very generally the spiritual grandfather of those who come, rather than their father in the faith; for I find that you, whom God gave me in years past are, many of you, diligent in seeking the souls of others. In the case of many who join the church, their conversion is due to this sister and to that, to this brother and to that, rather than distinctly to my ministry. I am very glad to have it so. During the last two days I have spoken to two friends, both of whom said to me, "I am your spiritual grandchild." One from America said so this morning. I asked, "How is that?" The answer was, "Mr. So-and-So, whom you brought to Christ, came out to America, and he brought me to Christ." You who have had any part in the conversion of these eighty-two, who are to be received to-night, will rejoice; in proportion as you have sighed, and prayed, and been beaten, and foiled, and disappointed, in that very proportion you will rejoice with the joy of harvest.

But, next, it is *a joy which has solid ground to go upon.* I do not know of a more joyful occasion than when young men and women, and, for the matter of that, old men and women, too, are brought to confess Christ, and to unite with his people. It is a very joyful thing to attend a wedding; but it is always a speculation as to how it will turn out; but when you come to see a soul yield itself to Christ, there is no speculation about that; you have a blessed certainty. Oh, methinks the angels sing more sweetly than ever as they hear a man, or woman, or child say, "I trust in Jesus; I confess his name." When we know and believe that true faith in Christ means present salvation, there is a great joy about that. I heard, the other day, of some preachers who say that there is no such thing as a present salvation; and though they constantly preach, they tell the people, every now and then, that they may be saved when they come to die; but there is no such thing as being saved now. I should like to present those brethren with a little "Catechism for the Young and Ignorant", which Mr. Cruden was wont to give away; for, if they are not "young", they certainly must be "ignorant" of the first principles of the faith. You are saved, my dear hearer, if you have believed in Christ Jesus. You are saved even now. If you were not, I do not see any reason why we should rejoice over you with the joy of harvest.

Moreover, we believe that, if you have trusted Christ, you will be saved eternally. Angels do not rejoice prematurely over repentant sinners. They never have to say to one another, "Gabriel, Michael, you made a very terrible mistake the other day. You rejoiced in the presence of God over that man who, after all, has gone down to hell. You rang the bells too soon." Angels do not do that. Jesus gives to his sheep eternal life, and they shall never perish, neither shall any man pluck them out of his hand. Therefore, we feel that the confession of Christ is, in itself, a thing to rejoice over; and the immediate salvation that goes with it, and the eternal salvation that is included in it, warrant us in rejoicing with the joy of harvest.

Moreover, this is *a joy which looks to the future.* Men rejoice in harvest because they remember that, all through the winter, they will feed upon the food which they are now gathering. The poorest man in London has reason to be thankful for a good harvest; for it will help to make food cheaper. We are to enjoy in days to come what we gather in the harvest-time. There are sixteen girls coming from the Orphanage to join the church, and I am rejoicing in my heart over sixteen women who will, I trust, during a long life glorify Christ; sixteen matrons in the church, who shall be Deborahs, Dorcases, and Phœbes, or whoever else you may like to think of among holy women. The boys also who come, however young they may be, and however little they may appear in some men's eyes, we cannot tell to what they will grow. I may be receiving to-night a Livingstone, or a Moffat, or a Williams, or a Whitefield, or a Wesley, or some other servant of God, who, in some sphere or other, will serve him right nobly.

Beloved, some of us will soon be gone. There are some here who are older than I am, who, in the natural course of things, will soon sleep in the cemetery. Are you not glad to see others coming forward? They will "hold the fort" when you can no longer stand upon its walls; and, on account of this hope of the future, I rejoice with the joy of harvest.

This is *a joy in which many may join;* for, in the harvest, anybody who likes may rejoice. There is the proprietor of the field; he rejoices. How greatly Christ rejoices! There are the labourers; they may shout as they bring home the loads; they know what that field of wheat has cost. Let us, who are working for Jesus here, have the joy of harvest. The on-lookers, too, as they go by, and see the harvest gathered in, will stop, and even give a shout over the hedge. If you are not yourself saved, you might be glad that other people are. Even if you are not yourself going to heaven, rejoice that others are choosing the blessed road. I invite even you to come, and share with us the joy of harvest. The gleaner, Ruth, over yonder, says, "I have stooped many times. I have almost broken my back over the work; and I have only picked up this little handful." I know you, sister; and I am pleased that you snould bring even one to Christ. I know you, my brother; and I rejoice with you that you should bring even one child to the Saviour. Though you be but a gleaner, join heartily with us to-night in the joy of harvest.

Then something happens in our harvest that cannot happen in the common harvest; for the harvested ones rejoice. Sheaves cannot sing, ears of wheat cannot lift up their voices; but in our harvest the happiest of all are those who are called by divine grace. And, while they are happy, and we are happy, and all are happy, the angels hovering over the assembly to-night will mark this first Sabbath in July, and it shall be a red-letter day even to them, so many shall to-night, for the first time, come to the table of their Lord, and here confess his name.

I have a great deal more to say, but our time is nearly gone. I can only say that this is *a joy which has its moderating tone.* "Why!" say you, "what is that?" The farmer says, "I have got that load in very well; but I wonder how it will thresh out." I often think of you who are added to the church, and I think that you are first-rate people, and that I never saw better; but I wonder how you will turn out when you get inside the church. There are members of the church whom I never hear of as doing anything for Christ; they may be working away quietly, but I am afraid that some are not. I know that there are some in this church who are no better than they should be; indeed, that is true of us all; but there are some who are not what they ought to be, as to practical service for Christ. We get many passengers to ride on the coach, but not so many to pull it; plenty of people to eat the fruit, but not so many to plant fresh trees. Yet I say not even this very heavily, or with any great emphasis, for the bulk of the members of this church are earnestly engaged in the service of God, for which I bless his name. Still that is the question concerning the harvest, "How will it thresh out?"

There is another question: How much of it will be found to be real wheat in the last great day? Ah, we may judge our very best, and examine most carefully; but there always will be goats with the sheep, and tares with the wheat; and that is the dash of bitterness in our cup of rejoicing. God grant that we may not have many added to us who will deteriorate instead of growing better! How will they stand at the last great day? "Well," says one, "I am glad that you make that remark; I have always been opposed to revivals, because they bring in so many, and so many of the converts fall away." Dear friends, do you remember Mr. Fullerton's answer to that? I thought it was as good and as complete as it was humorous. He said that when persons say that they do not like revivals because certain of the converts afterwards turn back, they are like his countryman, who picked up a sovereign; but when he went with it to the bank, it turned out to be a light sovereign, and he only got eighteen shillings for it. Mark you, he found it, so the eighteen shillings were clear gain. Some time after, he saw another sovereign lying in the road, and he would not pick it up; "for," said he, "I lost two shillings by the one I picked up the other day; I shall not take you up; very likely I should only get eighteen shillings for you." So he passed on, and left it where it was. I cannot imagine an Irishman being so unwise; certainly, no Scotchman would have been; and I think no Englishman. However, that is the style of unwisdom of a man who says that, at a revival, so many come in, and then so many turn out to be bad. Well, but those who remain are a clear gain, and you ought to desire to have a like gain again and again; you will get rich through such losses, if God will continue to give them to you. However, I hope that I shall not have any light sovereigns to-night. Yet, if these converts do not turn out to be twenty shillings in the pound, but only eighteen shillings, I will be greatly rejoiced to have the eighteen shillings, and God shall have all the glory.

I think that I will here pause, though there is another division of my discourse; and, in closing, I will ask four questions.

First, *What say we of those who never sow?* Well, they will never reap; they will never have the joy of harvest. Am I addressing, in this great assembly, any professing Christians who never sow, never speak a word for Christ, never call at a house, and try to introduce the Saviour's name, never seek to bring children to the Saviour, take no part in the Sunday-school, or other service for Christ? Do I address some lazy man here, spiritually alive only for himself? Oh, poor soul, I would not like to be you, because I doubt whether you can be spiritually alive at all! Surely, he who lives for himself is dead while he lives; and you will never know the joy of bringing souls to Christ; and when you get to heaven, if you ever do get there, you will never be able to say, "Here am I, Father, and the children thou hast given me." Thou wilt have to abide eternally alone, having brought no fruit unto God in the form of converts from sin. Shake yourselves up, brothers and sisters, from sinful sloth. "Oh!" says one, "I am not my brother's keeper." No, I will tell you your name; it is Cain. You are your brother's murderer; for every professing Christian, who is not his brother's keeper, is his brother's killer; and be you sure that it is so; for you may kill by neglect quite as surely as you may kill by the bow or by the dagger.

Next, *What say we to those who have never reaped?* Well, that depends. Perhaps you have only just begun to sow. Do not expect to reap before God's time. "In due season ye shall reap if ye faint not." There is a set season for reaping. But, if you have been a very long time sowing, and you have never reaped, may I ask the question, Where do you buy your seed? If I were to sow my garden year by year, and nothing ever came up, I should change my seedsman. Perhaps you have bad seed, my dear friend, and have not sown the gospel pure and undiluted. You have not brought it out in all its fulness. Go to the Word of God, and get "seed for the sower" of a kind that will feed your own soul, for it is "bread for the eater"; when you sow that kind of seed, it will come up.

Next, *What shall I say to those who know the Lord, but have never confessed him?* What shall I say to you? Well, I do not think that I will say what I think; but I think very seriously about persons who have been converted, and yet never tell the man who was the means of saving them that it has happened. "Well," says one, "I do not think that I shall confess Christ; the dying thief did not confess him, did he? He was not baptized." No, but he was a dying thief, recollect; and if you are not baptized, I think that you will be a living thief, for you will rob God of his glory, you will rob his servant also of the comfort which he ought to receive. Our wages are to hear that souls are saved; and, if we do not hear of it, we are robbed of our wages. You muzzle the ox that treadeth out the corn, if you allow a man to toil and labour, and you get good from his service, and yet you give him no return by way of encouragement. Come out, you who have hitherto hidden away like cowards! Men or women, if you love Christ, and have never confessed him, come out straight away, and be not ashamed to say, "I am a soldier of the cross, a follower of the Lamb." May the great Captain of our salvation force you to do this right speedily!

Once more, *What say we to those who do confess Christ, and who are going to confess him to-night?* Well, we say this: "Come in, thou blessed of the Lord; wherefore standest thou without?" Beloved, when you do come in, keep your garments unspotted from the world. Come in with a true heart, and a reverent spirit, with this prayer upon your lips, "Hold thou me up, and I shall be safe." May none of you who are to-night gathered into the barn turn out to be mere weeds dried in the sun! The Lord save you, and keep you; and may you remember that the vows of the Lord are upon you; and may you never, in any way, dishonour that great name by which you are henceforth to be named!

God bless every one of this great mass of people! "Believe in the Lord Jesus Christ, and thou shalt be saved," for "he that believeth and is baptized shall be saved; but he that believeth not shall be damned." God save all of us from that fearful doom, for Christ's sake! Amen.

Exposition by C. H. Spurgeon.

ISAIAH XLIX. 13—26.

Verse 13. *Sing, O heavens; and be joyful, O earth; and break forth into singing, O mountains: for the LORD hath comforted his people, and will have mercy upon his afflicted.*

When God blesses his Church, he blesses the world through her. Hence, heaven and earth are invited to be glad in the gladness of the Church of God. Oh, that God would visit this church; nay, he has already done so, and I feel inclined to cry out, as the text does, "Sing, O heavens; and be joyful, O earth; and break forth into singing, O mountains: for the LORD hath comforted his people."

14. *But Zion said, the LORD hath forsaken me, and my Lord hath forgotten me.*

We often judge contrary to the truth; and when God is blessing us, we dream that he has forgotten us. Oh, wicked unbelief; cruel unbelief! It robs God of glory; it robs us of comfort. It snatches the song out of our mouth, and fills our soul with groaning: "Zion said, the LORD hath forsaken me, and my Lord hath forgotten me."

15. *Can a woman forget her sucking child, that she should not have compassion on the son of her womb? yea, they may forget, yet will I not forget thee.*

The child is in a condition in which it reminds the mother of itself; her sucking child, her own child. Can she forget it? It is not according to nature,—

"'Yet,' saith the Lord, 'should nature change,
And mothers monsters prove,
Sion still dwells upon the heart
Of everlasting love.'"

What is true of God's Church as a whole, is true of every member of it. If any of you think that God has passed over you, one of his believing children, you think what is untrue. He cannot do it. It would be contrary to his nature. As long as he is God, he must remember his people.

16. *Behold, I have graven thee upon the palms of my hands;*

How appropriately Christ can say this when he looks on the nail-prints, "I have graven thee upon the palms of my hands"! As I said this morning, Jesus can give nothing, he can take nothing, he can do nothing, he can hold nothing, without remembering his people: "I have graven thee upon the palms of my hands." How I love that verse of Toplady's hymn that speaks of this blessed truth!—

"My name from the palms of his hands
Eternity will not erase;
Impress'd on his heart it remains
In marks of indelible grace:
Yes, I to the end shall endure,
As sure as the earnest is given;
More happy, but not more secure,
The glorified spirits in heaven."

16, 17. *Thy walls are continually before me. Thy children shall make haste;*

There shall be many of them. Converts shall be added to the church in great numbers. They shall hurry up; they shall not be long in coming. Very often they delay too long. The promise is, "Thy children shall make haste."

17. *Thy destroyers and they that made thee waste shall go forth of thee.*

I wish this were carried out. If it were, many of the churches of Christ, which are plagued with false doctrine and worldly habits, which are laying them waste, would be delivered from those curses. The enemies outside the walls, however malicious they are, will never be so mischievous as the traitors inside the fortress. Save Troy from the wooden horse, and save Zion from the traitors in her midst, that seek to do her harm.

18. *Lift up thine eyes round about, and behold: all these gather themselves together, and come to thee.*

There is a great company coming. The church is going to be increased. Have faith in God. We are not going to receive them now by ones and twos; we thank God we receive them by tens and scores. They are coming by hundreds and by thousands; let us expect them. By faith, let us see them even now coming.*

18. *As I live, saith the LORD, thou shalt surely clothe thee with them all, as with an ornament, and bind them on thee, as a bride doeth.*

What an ornament to a church her converts are! These are our jewels. We care nothing for gorgeous architecture or grand music in the worship of God. Our true building is composed of our converts; our best music is their confession of faith. May God give us more of it!

19—21. *For thy waste and thy desolate places, and the land of thy destruction, shall even now be too narrow by reason of the inhabitants, and they that swallowed thee up shall be far away. The children which thou shalt have, after thou hast lost the other, shall say again in thine ears, The place is too strait for me: give place to me that I may dwell. Then shalt thou say in thine heart, Who hath begotten me these, seeing I have lost my children, and am desolate, a captive, and removing to and fro? and who hath brought up these? Behold, I was left alone; these, where had they been?*

Sometimes a church is brought very low; there are no additions, there is no unity, everything is breaking up, and going to pieces. When God visits that church, what a change is seen! Then people come flocking to it, and the church wonders whence the converts came. May the Lord make us wonder in that fashion! It will take a great deal to astonish us, after all these years of mercy; yet the Lord can do it. It may be he will make these latter days to be better than the former. Though we have had nearly forty years of blessing together, he may yet increase it, and give us to rejoice yet more and more.

22. *Thus saith the Lord GOD, Behold, I will lift up mine hand to the Gentiles, and set up my standard to the people: and they shall bring thy sons in their arms, and thy daughters shall be carried upon their shoulders.*

We do not mind how they are brought if they do but come; some in the arms, and some after the Oriental method of putting the child on the shoulder. When God lifts up his hand, great wonders of mercy and grace are wrought.

23. *And kings shall be thy nursing fathers, and their queens thy nursing mothers:*

It will take a long time before they learn that art, for kings and queens

---

* It is remarkable that this sermon and exposition, which were selected long ago for publication this month, should be issued just as the Tabernacle church is again having a large ingathering of converts. Those who have read the sermons regularly, have been struck with the singular appropriateness of several of them, either to the condition of the Tabernacle church, or the general state of the churches of our land. A notable instance of this fact is described in the "Personal Notes" of *The Sword and the Trowel* for July. Many can see the overruling hand of the Lord even in the order in which the sermons have been published.

have generally been destroyers of the Church of Christ. Those will be grand days when kings shall be nourishers of the Church, and queens her nursing mothers.

23. *They shall bow down to thee with their face toward the earth, and lick up the dust of thy feet;*

I have heard the first part of this verse quoted as an argument for the union of Church and State: " Kings shall be thy nursing fathers, and queens thy nursing mothers." I have not the slightest objection, if they will bow down to the Church "with their face toward the earth, and lick up the dust of her feet." What is proposed to us is that the Church should bow down to the State, with her face toward the earth, and lick up the dust of the feet of the State, by becoming obedient to rules and regulations made by princes and parliaments. This is not according to the mind of God, nor according to the heart of his people.

23. *And thou shalt know that I am the* LORD *: for they shall not be ashamed that wait for me.*

If we wait for Christ, for his coming, for the help which he brings, for the salvation that is wrought by him, we shall not be ashamed.

24—26. *Shall the prey be taken from the mighty, or the lawful captive delivered? But thus saith the* LORD, *Even the captives of the mighty shall be taken away, and the prey of the terrible shall be delivered: for I will contend with him that contendeth with thee, and I will save thy children. And I will feed them that oppress thee with their own flesh; and they shall be drunken with their own blood, as with sweet wine: and all flesh shall know that I the* LORD *am thy Saviour and thy Redeemer, the mighty One of Jacob.*

The mighty may hold their prey with a strong hand; but there is a stronger hand that will deliver the captives. It is Jehovah, the Saviour, the Redeemer, the mighty One of Jacob, who says, "I will contend with him that contendeth with thee, and I will save thy children." Here is a divine promise for every parent to plead: "I will save thy children." May the Lord give you grace to claim this promise, even now, for Jesus Christ's sake! Amen.

HYMNS FROM "OUR OWN HYMN BOOK"—423, 1,004.

Just Published. Stiff Covers, 1s. *Cloth, Gilt Edges*, 2s.

THE ESSEX LAD

WHO BECAME

ENGLAND'S GREATEST PREACHER.

THE LIFE OF CHARLES HADDON SPURGEON FOR YOUNG PEOPLE.

BY J. MANTON SMITH.

With Thirty-five Illustrations, and Introduction by Rev. JOHN SPURGEON.

PASSMORE & ALABASTER, PATERNOSTER BUILDINGS, LONDON; and all Booksellers.

Metropolitan Tabernacle Pulpit.

BLESSING FOR BLESSING.

A Sermon

Intended for Reading on Lord's-day, July 24th, 1892,

DELIVERED BY

C. H. SPURGEON,

AT THE METROPOLITAN TABERNACLE, NEWINGTON,

On Lord's-day Evening, October 26th, 1890.

"Blessed be the God and Father of our Lord Jesus Christ, who hath blessed us with all spiritual blessings in heavenly places in Christ: according as he hath chosen us in him before the foundation of the world, that we should be holy and without blame before him in love."—Ephesians i. 3, 4.

God blesses us; let us bless him. I pray that every heart here may take its own part in this service of praise.

"O thou, my soul, bless God the Lord,
And all that in me is,
Be stirrèd up his holy name
To magnify and bless!"

Sit in your seats, and keep on blessing God from the first word of the sermon to the last; and then go on blessing God till the last hour of life, and enter into heaven, into the eternal glory, still blessing God. It should be our life to bless him who gave us our life. It should be our delight to bless him who gives us all our delights. So says the text, and so let us do: "Blessed be the God and Father of our Lord Jesus Christ."

I. Our first occupation, at this time, will be that of BLESSING GOD. But how can we bless God? Without doubt the less is blessed of the Greater. Can the Greater be blessed by the less? Yes, but it must be in a modified sense. God blesses us with all spiritual blessings; but we cannot give him any blessings. He needs nothing at our hand; and if he did, we could not give it. "If I were hungry," saith the Lord, "I would not tell thee: for the world is mine, and the fulness thereof." God has an all-sufficiency within himself, and can never be thought of as dependent upon his creatures, or as receiving anything from his creatures which he needs to receive. He is infinitely blessed already; we cannot add to his blessedness. When he blesses us, he gives us a blessedness that we never had before; but when we bless him, we cannot by one iota increase his absolutely infinite perfectness. David said to the Lord, "My goodness extendeth not to

No. 2,266.

thee." This was as if he had said, Let me be as holy, as devout, and as earnest as I may, I can do nothing for thee; thou art too high, too holy, too great for me to be really able to bless thee in the sense in which thou dost bless me.

How, then, do we bless God? Well, I should say, first, that this language is *the expression of gratitude.* We say with David, "Bless the Lord, O my soul," and we say with Paul, "Blessed be the God and Father of our Lord Jesus Christ." We can bless God by praising him, extolling him, desiring all honour for him, ascribing all good to him, magnifying and lauding his holy name. Well, we will do that. Sit still, if you will, and let your heart be silent unto God; for no language can ever express the gratitude that, I trust, we feel to him who has blessed us with all spiritual blessings in Christ Jesus. Praise him also in your speech. Break the silence; speak to his glory. Invite others to cry with you, "Hallelujah!" or "Hallels unto Jah!" "Praise unto Jehovah!" Ascribe ye greatness unto our God. Oh, that all flesh would magnify the Lord with us!

This language is also *the utterance of assent* to all the blessedness that is ascribed to the Lord. After hearing how great he is, how glorious he is, how happy he is, we bless him by saying, "Amen; so let it be! So would we have it. He is none too great for us, none too glorious for us, none too blessed for us. Let him be great, glorious, and blessed, beyond all conception." I think that we bless God when we say concerning the whole of his character, "Amen. This God is our God for ever and ever." Let him be just what the Bible says he is; we accept him as such. Sternly just, he will not spare the guilty. Amen, blessed be his name! Infinitely gracious, ready to forgive. Amen, so let it be! Everywhere present, always omniscient. Amen, so again do we wish him to be! Everlastingly the same, unchanging in his truth, his promise, his nature. We again say that we are glad of it, and we bless him. He is just such a God as we love. He is indeed God to us, because he is really God, and we can see that he is so, and every attribute ascribed to him is a fresh proof to us that Jehovah is the Lord. Thus, we bless him by adoration.

We also bless God in *the spreading of his kingdom.* We can win hearts to him through his mighty grace blessing our service. We can fight against evil; we can set up a standard for the truth. We can be willing to suffer in repute, and every way else, for his name's sake. We can by his grace do all this, and thus we are blessing God. Surely, dear friends, if it is well-pleasing in God's sight that sinners should repent, if it makes heaven the gladder, and makes joy in the presence of the angels that men should repent, we are in the best and most practical way blessing God when we labour to bring men to repentance through faith in Christ Jesus.

There is also another way of blessing God which, I trust, we shall all endeavour to practise; and that is by *the doing good to his children.* When they are sick, visit them. When they are downcast, comfort them. When they are poor, relieve them. When they are hard pressed by outward adversaries, stand at their side, and help them. You cannot bless the Head, but you can bless the feet; and when you have refreshed the feet, you have refreshed the Head. He will say,

"Inasmuch as ye have done it unto one of the least of these my brethren, ye have done it unto me." If they be naked, and you clothe them; if they be sick, and you visit them; if they be hungry, and you feed them; you do in this respect bless God. David not only said, "Thou art my Lord: my goodness extendeth not to thee;" but he added, "but to the saints that are in the earth, and to the excellent in whom is all my delight." You can be good to them, and in that respect you may be blessing God. He has done so much for us, that we would fain do something for him; and when we have reached the limit of our possibilities, we long to do more. We wish that we had more money to give, more talent to use, more time that we could devote to his cause, we wish that we had more heart and more brain; sometimes we wish that we had more tongue, and we sing,—

> "Oh, for a thousand tongues to sing
> My great Redeemer's praise!"

This word "blessed" is an attempt to break the narrow circle of our capacity. It is an earnest endeavour of a burning heart to lay at God's feet crowns of glory which it cannot find: "Blessed be the God and Father of our Lord Jesus Christ."

II. But now, secondly, we shall spend a little time in VIEWING GOD in the light in which Paul sets him before us: "Blessed be the God and Father of our Lord Jesus Christ."

We bless the God of nature. What beauties he has strewn around us! We bless the God of providence. How bountifully doth he send us harvests and fruitful seasons! We bless the God of grace who hath redeemed us, and adopted us as his children. But here is a peculiar aspect of God, which should call forth our highest praises; for he is called "the God and Father of our Lord Jesus Christ."

When we see God *in connection with Christ,* when we see God through Christ, when we see God in Christ, then our hearts are all aflame, and we burst out with, "Blessed be the God and Father of our Lord Jesus Christ." God apart from Christ—that is a great and glorious theme; but the human mind fails to grasp it. The infinite Jehovah, who can conceive him? "Our God is a consuming fire." Who can draw near to him? But in the Mediator, in the Person of the God, the Man, in whom we find blended human sympathy and divine glory, we can draw nigh to God. There it is that we get our hands upon the golden harp-strings, and resolve that every string shall be struck to the praise of God in Christ Jesus.

But note carefully that God is described here as *the God of our Lord Jesus Christ*. When Jesus knelt in prayer, he prayed to our God. When Jesus leaned in faith upon the promises, he trusted in God that he would deliver him. When our Saviour sang on that passover night, the song was unto God. When he prayed in Gethsemane, with bloody sweat, the prayer was unto our God. Jesus said to Mary at the sepulchre, "Go to my brethren, and say unto them, I ascend unto my Father, and your Father; and to my God, and your God." How we ought to bless God when we think that he is the God whom our Redeemer blesses! This is the God who said of Christ, "This is my beloved Son, in whom I am well pleased." Delightful thought!

When I approach Jehovah, I approach the God of our Lord Jesus Christ. Surely, when I see his blood-stained footprints there on the ground before me, though I put my shoe from off my foot, for the place is holy ground, yet I follow with confidence where my Friend, my Saviour, my Husband, my Head has been before me; and I rejoice as I worship the God of our Lord Jesus Christ.

He is also called *the Father of our Lord Jesus Christ.* This is a great mystery. Think not that we shall ever understand the high relationship between the first and second Persons of the blessed Trinity, the Father and the Son. We speak of eternal filiation, which is a term that does not convey to us any great meaning; it simply covers up our ignorance. How God is the Father of our Lord Jesus Christ as God, we do not know; and perhaps to wish to gaze into this tremendous mystery were as great a folly as to look at the sun, and blind ourselves with its brilliance. It is so; that ought to be enough for us. God the Father is the Father of Jesus Christ as to his divine nature: "Thou art my Son; this day have I begotten thee." He is also his Father as to the human side of his nature. He was begotten of the Holy Ghost. That body of his, that human life, came of God; not of Joseph, not of man. Born of a woman, God sent forth his Son; but he was his Son then. It was God's Son that was born at Bethlehem. Gabriel said to the Virgin Mary, "That holy thing which shall be born of thee shall be called the Son of God." Now take the two natures in their wondrous blending in the person of the Lord Jesus Christ, and you see how the great God is the God and Father of our Lord Jesus Christ. Yet, sweet thought, he is my Father, too; my Father is Christ's Father. Jesus Christ's Father is our Father, and he teaches us to call him, "Our Father, which art in heaven." Often in prayer he said, "Father"; and he bids us say the same, putting the plural pronoun before it, "Our Father." Now will you not bless the Lord, who is the God and Father of our Lord Jesus Christ? Do you not feel a glowing in your hearts, as you think of the near and dear relationship into which you are brought through Jesus Christ? The God of Jesus Christ, the Father of Jesus Christ, is my God, my Father, too. Blessed, blessed, blessed, for ever blessed be that dear name!

III. Our third occupation, at this time, is that of RECOUNTING HIS GREAT MERCIES. I will read the rest of the third verse: "Blessed be the God and Father of our Lord Jesus Christ, who hath blessed us with all spiritual blessings in heavenly places in Christ."

This recapitulation of mercies is written with *full assurance;* and you will not bless God unless you have a touch of that same experience. Paul does not say, "Who has, we hope and trust, blessed us," but he writes, "Who hath blessed us." Ah, beloved, if you have a full assurance that God has blessed you in Christ, and that now his smile rests upon you, and all the benisons of the covenant are stored there for you, I think that you cannot help saying, "Blessed, blessed be the name of the Most High!" That doubt, that trembling, this it is that empties out the marrow from the bone of our blessedness. If you have suspicions about the truth of this precious Book, if you have questions about the truth of the doctrines of grace, if you have doubts about your own interest in those things, I do not wonder that you do not praise God, for a blessing which is only mine by peradventure, well, peradventure I shall be grateful for it; but peradventure I shall not. But if I know whom I have believed, if I have a firm grip of spiritual mercies, if all heavenly things are mine in Christ my Lord, I can sing, "Wake up, my glory; awake psaltery and harp; I myself will awake right early." "Blessed be the God and Father of our Lord Jesus Christ, who hath blessed us with all spiritual blessings."

With this full assurance should come *intense delight:* "Who hath blessed us." God has blessed us. Come, brethren, he has not done some trifle for us, which we can afford to ignore. He has not merely given us some absolutely necessary boons, which we must have, for we could not live without them; but he has in grace dealt still more abundantly with us. He has gone beyond workhouse fare, and made us feast with saints and princes. He has given us more than homespun garments; he has put upon us robes of beauty and of glory, even his own spotless righteousness. He has blessed us; we are blessed; we feel that we are. Each believer can say:—

> "I feel like singing all the time,
> My tears are wiped away;
> For Jesus is a Friend of mine,
> I'll praise him every day.
> I'll praise him! praise him! praise him all the time!"

We are not sitting here, and groaning, and crying, and fretting, and worrying, and questioning our own salvation. He has blessed us; and therefore we will bless him. If you think little of what God has done for you, you will do very little for him; but if you have a great notion of his great mercy to you, you will be greatly grateful to your gracious God.

Let me also remark, next, that as assurance and delight lead to blessing God, so does a *right understanding* of his mercies. To help your understanding, notice what Paul says: "Blessed be the God and Father of our Lord Jesus Christ, who hath blessed us with all spiritual blessings." An enlightened man is grateful to God for temporal blessings; but he is much more grateful to God for spiritual blessings, for temporal blessings do not last long; they are soon gone. Temporal blessings are not definite marks of divine favour, since God gives them to the unworthy, and to the wicked, as well as to the righteous. The corn, and wine, and oil, are for Dives; and Lazarus gets even less than his share. Our thanks are due to God for all temporal blessings; they are more than we deserve. But our thanks ought to go to God in thunders of hallelujahs for spiritual blessings. A new heart is better than a new coat. To feed on Christ is better than to have the best earthly food. To be an heir of God is better than being the heir of the greatest nobleman. To have God for our portion is blessed, infinitely more blessed than to own broad acres of land. God hath blessed us with spiritual blessings. These are the rarest, the richest, the most enduring of all blessings; they are priceless in value. Wherefore, let me beg you to join in blessing the God and

Father of our Lord Jesus Christ, who hath blessed you with spiritual blessings.

But did you notice that little word "all"? I must bring that out clearly. I must turn the microscope on it. "Who hath blessed us with all spiritual blessings." Surely, Paul means that we have not a spiritual blessing which God did not give. We have never earned one; we could never create one. All spiritual blessings come from the Father; he has really given us all spiritual blessings. "I have not received them," says one. That is your own fault. He hath blessed us with all spiritual blessings in Christ. A new heart, a tender conscience, a submissive will, faith, hope, love, patience, we have all these in Christ. Regeneration, justification, adoption, sanctification, perfection are all in Christ. If we do not take them out, it is the fault of our palsied hand, that has not strength enough to grasp them; but he has given us all spiritual blessings in Christ. Whenever you read your Bible, and see a great promise, do not hesitate to claim it. He hath given us all spiritual blessings in Christ. "I am afraid," says one, "that I should be presuming if I took some of the promises." He hath given us all spiritual blessings in Christ. You are in your Father's house; you cannot steal; for your Father says, " Help yourself to what you like." He has made over his whole estate of spiritual wealth to every believing child of his; wherefore take freely, and you will, by so doing, glorify God. He hath blessed us with all spiritual blessings in Christ.

This he has done in the "heavenly places." What does that mean, "Who hath blessed us with all spiritual blessings in heavenly places"? Does it not mean that he is working upon us all spiritual blessings out of the heaven where he dwells? Or does it mean much more, that he is sending us all these spiritual blessings to bring us to the heaven where he dwells, and where he would have us dwell?

I want to stir up your heart by reminding you that all the spiritual blessings we receive are the richer and the rarer because they are given to us "in Christ." Here are the blessings; and Christ is the golden casket that holds them all. When the City of London makes a man a freeman of the city, the document giving him his liberty is usually presented to him enclosed in a golden casket. Christ is that golden casket, in which we find the charter of our eternal liberty. He hath blessed us with all spiritual blessings in Christ. If they came to us any other way, we might lose them; or we might not be sure that they were genuine; but when they come to us in Christ, they come to stay, and we know that they are real. If Christ is mine, all blessings in heavenly places are mine.

I seem, to myself, to be talking very drily of things that ought to be swimming in a sea of joy and delight. Beloved, do not let my faint words rob my Lord of any of his glory. He has done such great things for you; bless his name. We cannot stand up, and ask for instruments of music with which to sound his praise; but we can sit still, and each one say, "Blessed be his name! It is all true; he has blessed me; I know that he has. He has blessed me, with a liberal hand, with all spiritual blessings. He has blessed me just where I wanted blessing, where I was poorest in spiritual things. I could make my way in business, but I could not make my way in grace; so he has blessed me with all spiritual blessings; and he has made the garments all the dearer because of the wardrobe in which he has hung them. He has given me these royal things in Christ; and as I look to my dear Lord, and see what there is for me stored up in him, I prize each thing the more because it is in him. Come, Holy Spirit, set our hearts on fire with blessing and praise to God for all the great things that he has done for us!"

IV. I shall close with this fourth remark: Let us bless God, BEHOLDING THE MANNER OF HIS GIFTS. That is described in the fourth verse: "According as he hath chosen us in him before the foundation of the world, that we should be holy and without blame before him in love."

Now, brethren, we are to praise God because all spiritual blessings have come to us in the same way as our election came, "according as he hath chosen us in him." How did that come? Well, it came of *his free, sovereign grace.* He loved us because he would love us. He chose us because he chose us. "Ye have not chosen me; but I have chosen you." If there be any virtue, if there be any praise in us now, he put it there. To the bottomless abyss of his own infinite goodness we must trace the election of his grace. Well, now, every blessing comes to us in the same way. God hath not blessed thee, my brother, with usefulness because thou didst deserve it; but because of his grace. He did not redeem thee, or regenerate thee, or sanctify thee, or uphold thee, because of anything in thee. Again and again, by the prophet Ezekiel, did the Lord remind his ancient people that the blessings he bestowed upon them were all gifts of his grace. "Therefore say unto the house of Israel, Thus saith the Lord God, I do not this for your sakes, O house of Israel, but for mine holy name's sake." And again, "Not for your sakes do I this, saith the Lord God, be it known unto you: be ashamed and confounded for your own ways, O house of Israel." Every blessing comes to us with the hall-mark of sovereign grace upon it. As the Lord distributes the gifts of his grace, he says, "May I not do as I will with my own?" He does so, and we bless, and praise, and adore the sovereign grace of God, which, having chosen us, continues to bless us according as he hath chosen us in Christ.

Next, we have to bless God that all his gifts come to us *in Christ.* Notice Paul's words, "according as he hath chosen us in him." God called us in Christ. He justified us in Christ. He sanctified us in Christ. He will perfect us in Christ. He will glorify us in Christ. We have everything in Christ, and we have nothing apart from Christ. Let us praise and bless the name of the Lord that this sacred channel of his grace is as glorious as the grace itself. There is as much grace in the gift of Christ to save us as there is in the salvation which Christ has wrought out for us. "Blessed be the God and Father of our Lord Jesus Christ."

Again, all our blessings come from *the divine purpose.* Listen: "Who hath blessed us with all spiritual blessings in heavenly places in Christ: according as he hath chosen us in him." No spiritual blessing comes to any man by chance. No man gets a boon from God through his "good luck"; it all comes according to the eternal purpose of God, which he purposed or ever the earth was.

> "Long e'er the sun's refulgent ray
> Primeval shades of darkness drove,
> They on his sacred bosom lay,
> Loved with an everlasting love."

"Before the foundation of the world", says the text, there was a purpose in the heart of God, and in that purpose we were chosen, and by that same purpose God continues to bless us. Look, beloved, God never gives his people either a gift or a grace without his purpose. Has God given you a brain clear, quick, capacious? Think for him. Has God given you a tongue fluent, eloquent? Speak for him. He does not give you these gifts without a purpose. Has God given you influence among your fellow-men? Use it for him. Your election came according to his purpose; and so have all your gifts, and much more, all your graces. Have you strong, bright-eyed faith? Have you burning zeal? Have you vehement love? Have you any of the gifts of the covenant? Use them for a purpose. God has given them for a purpose; find out what that purpose is, and glorify God thereby.

Lastly, the text tells us that God blesses us with all spiritual blessings in heavenly places in Christ: according as he hath chosen us in him before the foundation of the world, "that we should be holy and without blame before him in love." God's choice of us was not because we were holy, but *to make us holy*; and God's purpose will not be fulfilled unless we are made holy. Some people, when they talk about salvation, mean escaping from hell, and getting into heaven by the skin of their teeth. We never mean any such thing. We mean deliverance from evil, deliverance from sin. I often wonder why some people grumble because God has chosen to deliver others from sin when they themselves do not want to be delivered from sin. Like a dog in the manger, they cannot eat the hay themselves, and they growl at those who can. If you wish to be safe from sin, ask God for that great blessing, and he will give it to you; but if you do not want it, do not complain if God says, "I shall give it to such and such a person, and you that do not even ask for it shall be left without it." If you do not care to be holy, you shall not be holy. If you did care for it, and wish for it, you might have it, for God denies it to none who seek it at his hands. But if you neither wish for it, nor value it, why do you lift your puny fist against the God of heaven because he hath chosen others, that they should be holy and without blame before him in love?

The object of our election is our holiness, and the object of every spiritual blessing is our holiness. God is aiming at making us holy. Are you not glad of that? May I not say, "Blessed be the God and Father of our Lord Jesus Christ, because his aim in every gift is to make us holy"? Brothers and sisters, would we not sacrifice everything that we have, and count it no sacrifice, if we might be perfectly holy? I said to a young girl, who came to join the church, "Mary, are you perfect?" She looked at me, and said, "No, sir." I said, "Would you like to be?" "Oh, that I would! I long for it; I cry for it." Surely, the God who makes us long to be perfect, has already wrought a great work in us; and if we can say that, to be perfect, would be heaven to us, then we are already on the road to heaven, and God is working out in us his eternal purpose, which is, "that we should be holy."

There is one thing more: "That we should be holy and *without blame before him in love.*" Does that mean that we are to be loving, full of love, and without blame in that matter? Well, I am afraid that there are not very many Christians who are without blame on the score of love. I know a man, a noble man intellectually, and, in some respects, spiritually. I believe that he would die at the stake for the grand old Calvinistic faith; but he is as hard as iron; you cannot feel any kind of love to him, for he does not seem to feel any kind of love to anybody else. That man is not without blame before God in love. I have known others; wonderful Christians they appear to be, they could pray for a week; but if you are poor, and ask them for a little help, your asking will be all in vain. I do not think that they are without blame before God in love. O brothers, God has chosen us to be loving, he has ordained us to be loving; and all the innumerable blessings which he has given to us, he sends to win us to a loving spirit, that we may be without blame in that matter. Our dear friend, Mr. William Olney, whom we remember here still, and never can forget, was, I think, without blame in that matter of love. I sometimes thought that he used to shed his love on some who might have been the better for a hard word; for they were deceivers; but he could not bring his mind to think that anybody could be a deceiver; and if anybody was in want of help, no matter though their own misconduct had brought them into poverty, his hand was in his pocket, and out again, very quickly with help for them. He never failed in love; and I pray that you and I, with prudence and wisdom mixed with it, may be without blame before God in the matter of love. Love your fellow-Christians. Love poor sinners to Christ. Love those that despitefully use you. Love those round about you who are strangers to the love of God. It may be that they will see in your love some little image of the love of God, as in a drop of water you may sometimes see the sun and the heavens reflected. God make us to be reflections of the love of God! His purpose is that we may be holy and without blame before him in love.

Now, I have set before you a rare treasury. Does this treasury belong to you? My dear hearers, is Christ yours? Are you trusting him? If not, there is nothing yours. Without Christ, you can do nothing, and you are nothing, and you have nothing. Come to Jesus as you are, and put your trust in him, and then all things are yours. If Christ be yours, beloved, then I charge you bless the Lord, ay, bless the Lord again and again, for you will never bless him as much as he deserves to be blessed. Let us finish this service as we closed our worship this morning, by singing the doxology,—

"Praise God from whom all blessings flow."

Exposition by C. H. Spurgeon.
EPHESIANS I.

The Epistle to the Ephesians is a complete Body of Divinity. In the first chapter you have the doctrines of the gospel; in the next, you have the experience of the Christian; and before the Epistle is finished you have the precepts of the Christian faith. Whosoever would see Christianity in one treatise, let him "read, mark, learn, and inwardly digest" the Epistle to the Ephesians.

1, 2. *Paul, an apostle of Jesus Christ by the will of God, to the saints which are at Ephesus, and to the faithful in Christ Jesus: grace be to you, and peace, from God our Father, and from the Lord Jesus Christ.*

All down the ages this benediction comes to us, even to as many of us as are "the faithful in Christ Jesus." "Grace be to you," brethren and sisters, grace in every form of it, the free favour of God, all that active force of grace which comes of his unmerited love. May you have a fresh draught of it at this time! "And peace." May you feel a deep peace with God, with your own conscience, and with all the world! Oh, that you might find an atmosphere of quiet calm about your mind at this very moment! The double blessing of "grace" and "peace" comes "from God our Father, and from the Lord Jesus Christ."

3, 4. *Blessed be the God and Father of our Lord Jesus Christ, who hath blessed us with all spiritual blessings in heavenly places in Christ: according as he hath chosen us in him before the foundation of the world,*

One of the first doctrines of our holy faith is that of the union of all believing souls with Christ. We are blessed with all spiritual blessings in Christ. Apart from Christ we are nothing; in Christ we have "all spiritual blessings." We are rich as Christ is rich, when we are united to him by the living bond of faith. Another great doctrine of Holy Scripture is that of election. We are blessed in Christ according as the Father " hath chosen us in him before the foundation of the world." Why did God choose any unto eternal life? Was it because of any holiness in them then existing, or foreseen to exist? No, by no means; for we read thus: "According as he hath chosen us in him before the foundation of the world,"

4. *That we should be holy and without blame before him in love:*

We are chosen, not because we are holy, but that we may be made holy. The election precedes the character, and is indeed the moving cause in producing the character. Before the foundation of the world, God chose us in Christ, "that we should be holy and without blame before him in love." You see, then, beloved brethren and sisters, the end for which the Lord chose you by his grace.

5. *Having predestinated us*

Having destined us before we were born,

5. *Unto the adoption of children by Jesus Christ to himself, according to the good pleasure of his will,*

The chosen ones are adopted; they become the children of God. The universal Fatherhood of God, except in a very special sense, is a doctrine totally unknown to Scripture. God is the Father of those whom he adopts into his family, who are born again into his family, and no man hath any right to believe God to be his Father except through the new birth, and through adoption. And why God thus elects or adopts is declared here: "According to the good pleasure of his will." He does as he pleases. That old word of God is still true: "I will have mercy on whom I will have mercy, and I will have compassion on whom I will have compassion." Men do not like that doctrine; it galls them terribly; but it is the truth of

God for all that. He is Master and King, and he will sit on the throne, and none shall drag him thence.

6. *To the praise of the glory of his grace, wherein he hath made us accepted in the beloved.*
There is another precious doctrine, the acceptance of those who are adopted. We are beloved of God; he has a complacency toward us; he takes a delight in us; we are acceptable in his sight. Oh, what a blessing this is! But remember that it is all in Christ: "Accepted in the beloved." Because Christ is accepted, therefore those who are in him are accepted.

7, 8. *In whom we have redemption through his blood, the forgiveness of sins, according to the riches of his grace; wherein he hath abounded toward us in all wisdom and prudence;*
In the working out of the economy of grace, God has been lavish with his love; but yet there have been wisdom and prudence in it. He did not suffer the full light of the gospel to break in upon our eyes at first, lest we should have been blinded by it. Jesus had many things to say unto his disciples; but they could not bear them all at once; so by little and little he has led us on, and led us up, abounding always in his grace, and only limiting the display of it by our capacity to receive it.

9, 10. *Having made known unto us the mystery of his will, according to his good pleasure which he hath purposed in himself: that in the dispensation of the fulness of times he might gather together in one all things in Christ, both which are in heaven, and which are on earth; even in him:*
Everything that is in Christ shall be gathered in; all his chosen, all that the Father gave him, all that he hath redeemed by blood, all that he hath effectually brought into union with himself, shall be gathered together in one. There shall be one flock under one Shepherd.

11. *In whom also we have obtained an inheritance,*
Not only shall we have it, but we have it now. We have heaven in the price of it, in the principles of it, in the promise of it, in the foretaste of it.

11, 12. *Being predestinated according to the purpose of him who worketh all things after the counsel of his own will: that we should be to the praise of his glory, who first trusted in Christ.*
The enmity of men's hearts to this doctrine of predestination was seen in the House of Commons, not a fortnight ago, when one who ought to have known better talked about "the gloomy tenets of Calvin." I know nothing of Calvin's gloomy tenets; but I do know that I read here of predestination, and I read here that God hath his own way, and his own will, and that he reigns and rules, and so he will until the world's end; and all who are loyal subjects wish God to rule. He is a traitor who would not have God to be King; for who is infinitely good and kind as God is? Let him have his divine will. Who wishes to restrain him? Whether we wish it or not, however, the Lord reigneth; let the earth rejoice, and let his adversaries tremble. Our predestination is "according to the purpose of him who worketh all things after the counsel of his own will."

13, 14. *In whom ye also trusted, after that ye heard the word of truth, the gospel of your salvation: in whom also after that ye believed, ye were sealed with that holy Spirit of promise, which is the earnest of our inheritance until the redemption of the purchased possession, unto the praise of his glory.*
Those who believe in Christ have the Holy Spirit dwelling in them: the Holy Spirit is a part of heaven, "the earnest of our inheritance"; and wherever he dwells, it is not possible that the heart should lose the inheritance. It is entailed upon those in whom the Spirit dwells. Judge, therefore, dear brethren, whether the Spirit of God dwells in you or no.

15—23. *Wherefore I also, after I heard of your faith in the Lord Jesus, and love unto all the saints, cease not to give thanks for you, making mention of you in my prayers; that the God of our Lord Jesus Christ, the Father of glory, may give unto you the spirit of wisdom and revelation in the knowledge of him: the eyes of your understanding being enlightened; that ye may know what is the hope of his calling, and what the riches of the glory of his inheritance in the saints, and what is the exceeding greatness of his power to us-ward who believe; according to the working of his mighty power, which he wrought in Christ, when he raised him from the dead, and set him at his own right hand in the heavenly places, far above all principality, and power, and might, and dominion, and every name that is named, not only in this world, but also in that which is to come: and hath put all things under his feet, and gave him to be the head over all things to the church, which is his body, the fulness of him that filleth all in all.*

How Paul glows as he writes on this great theme! He waxes warm, and rises to an enthusiasm of eloquence. We could not stop to explain his words; that were to spoil their mystic poetry. Oh, to have a heart that can glorify Christ as Paul did! Truly, if we know ourselves to be one with Christ, and know the privileges which come to us through that blessed gate, we may indeed extol him with all our heart and soul.

HYMNS FROM "OUR OWN HYMN BOOK"—232; Ps. ciii., Version I.; 219; and the Doxology.

"THE SWORD AND THE TROWEL."

TABLE OF CONTENTS, AUGUST, 1892.

The Complex Character of Mr. Spurgeon. By Dr. A. T. Pierson.
Mr. Spurgeon's "Sword." Copy of the Inscriptions written by Mr. Spurgeon in his study Bible.
A Message from Over the Sea. By Mrs. C. H. Spurgeon. (Containing a letter written by her dear husband at Menton, December, 1891.)
The Nightingale Psalm. Poetic Version of Psalm xxiii. By Thomas Spurgeon.
The Centre of Education. By J. R. Miller, D.D.
Mr. Spurgeon's Last Drives at Menton. By Joseph W. Harrald. (With several illustrations.)
Mushroom Anchors. By J. W. H.
Mr. Spurgeon's R. T. S. Pocket-book. Outlines of sermons made at Menton, 1891-2.
Lady Hymn-Writers. By W. Y. Fullerton.
Veni, Domine Jesu! Poetry. By E. A. Tydeman.
Reminiscences of the late beloved President. By Pastor W. Julyan, Exeter.
A Preacher's Dog. (Extract from Dr. Stacey's biography.)
"After Many Days." The story of an orphan boy. By V. J. Charlesworth. (With two illustrations.)
In Memoriam—Robert Ryman, of Great Tew, Oxfordshire. By Pastor F. E. Blackaby, Stow-on-the-Wold.
Portrait and Sketch of Professor Fergusson, of the Pastors' College.
Notices of Books.
Notes.
Lists of contributions.
Annual Report of the Stockwell Orphanage.

80 pages. Price 3d. Post-free, 4½d.

LONDON: PASSMORE AND ALABASTER, PATERNOSTER BUILDINGS, and all Booksellers.

Metropolitan Tabernacle Pulpit.

LIFE FROM THE DEAD.

A Sermon

Intended for Reading on Lord's-day, July 31st, 1892,

DELIVERED BY

C. H. SPURGEON,

AT THE METROPOLITAN TABERNACLE, NEWINGTON,

On Thursday Evening, March 13th, 1890.

"And you hath he quickened, who were dead in trespasses and sins."—Ephesians ii. 1.

Our translators, as you observe, have put in the words "hath he quickened", because Paul had thrown the sense a little farther on, and it was possible for the reader not to catch it. They have but anticipated the statement of the fourth and fifth verses: "God, who is rich in mercy, for his great love wherewith he loved us, even when we were dead in sins, hath quickened us together with Christ."

Here is the point. God has quickened us, who were dead in trespasses and sins, spiritually dead. We were full of vigour towards everything which was contrary to the law or the holiness of God, we walked according to the course of this world; but as for anything spiritual, we were not only somewhat incapable, and somewhat weakened; but we were actually and absolutely dead. We had no sense with which to comprehend spiritual things. We had neither the eye that could see, nor the ear that could hear, nor the power that could feel.

We were dead, all of us; and yet we were not all like one another. Death may be universal over a certain number of bodies, and yet those bodies may look very different. The dead that lie on the battle-field, torn of dogs or kites, rotting, corrupting in the sun, what a horrible sight! Your lately-departed one, lying in the coffin, how beautiful! The corpse looks like life still; yet is your beloved one in the coffin as dead as the mangled bodies on the battle-field. Corruption has not yet done its work, and tender care has guarded the body as yet from what will surely come to it; yet is there death, sure, complete death, in the one case as well as in the other.

So we have many who are lovely, amiable, morally admirable, like him whom the Saviour looked upon and loved; yet they are dead for all that. We have others who are drunken, profane, unchaste; they

No. 2,267.

are dead, not more dead than the others; but their death has left its terrible traces more plainly visible. Sin brings forth death, and death brings forth corruption. Whether we were corrupt or not, is not a question that I need raise here; let every one judge concerning himself. But dead we were, most certainly. Even though trained by godly parents, though well instructed in the gospel scheme, though saturated with the piety that surrounded us, we were dead, as dead as the harlot of the street, as dead as the thief in the jail.

Now, the text tells us that, though we were dead, yet Christ has come, and by his Spirit he has raised us out of the grave. This text brings us Easter tidings; it sings of resurrection; it sounds in our ear the trumpet of a new life, and introduces us into a world of joy and gladness. We were dead; but we are quickened by the Spirit of God. I cannot help stopping a minute to know whether it is so with you, my dear hearers, and praying that what I may have to say may act as a kind of sieve, separating between the really living and those who only think that they are alive, so that, if you have not been quickened, if you are only "a child of nature, finely dressed," but not spiritually alive, you may be made aware of it. If you have been quickened, even though your life be feeble, you may cry to the living God with the "Abba, Father," which never comes from any lip but that which has been touched and quickened by the Holy Spirit.

I. First, let us talk a little about OUR QUICKENING. You who have been quickened will understand what I say. To those who have not, I daresay it will seem as an idle tale.

Well, dear friends, if we have been quickened, we have been *quickened from above.* "You hath HE quickened." God himself has had dealings with us. He has raised us from the dead. He made us at the first; he has new-made us. He gave us life when we were born; but he has given us now a higher life, which could not be found anywhere else. He must always give it. No man ever made himself to live. No preacher, however earnest, can make one hearer to live. No parent, however prayerful, no teacher, however tearful, can make a child to live unto God. "You hath HE quickened," is true of all who are quickened. It is a divine spark, a light from the great central Sun of light, the great Father of lights. Is it so with us? Have we had a divine touch, a superhuman energy, a something which all the learning and all the wisdom and all the godliness of man could never work in us? Have we been quickened from above? If so, I daresay that we remember something of it. We cannot describe it; no man can describe his first birth; it remains a mystery. Neither can he describe his new birth; that is a still greater mystery, for it is a secret inward work of the Holy Ghost, of which we feel the effect, but we cannot tell how it is wrought.

I think that, usually, when the divine life comes, the first consciousness that we get of quickening is *a sense of pain.* I have heard that when a man is nearly drowned, while he lies under the power of death, he feels little or nothing, perhaps has even pleasurable dreams; but when, in the process of restoring him, they have rubbed him till the blood begins to flow, and the life begins to revive a little, he is conscious of pricking and great pain. One of the tokens that life is coming back to him is, that he wakes up out of a pleasant sleep, and feels pain. Whether it be so or not with every person restored from drowning, I do not know; but I think that it is so with every person restored from drowning in the river of sin. When the life begins to come to him, he feels as he never felt before; sin that was pleasant becomes a horror to him. That which was easy to him becomes a bed of thorns. Thank God, dear hearer, if you have living pangs. It is an awful thing to have your conscience hardened, as in the very fires of hell, till it becomes like steel. To have consciousness is a great mercy, even if it be only painful consciousness, and if every movement of the life within seems to harrow up your soul. This divine life usually begins with pain.

Then, *everything surprises you.* If a person had never lived before, and had come into life a full-grown man, everything would be as strange to him as it is to a little child; and everything is strange to a new-born man in the spiritual realm into which he is born. He is startled a hundred times. Sin appears as sin; he cannot understand it. He had looked at sin before, but had never seen it to be sin. And Christ appears now so glorious to him; he had heard of Christ before, and had some apprehension of him; but now he is surprised to find that the One who he said had no form nor comeliness is, after all, altogether lovely. To the new-born soul everything is a surprise. He makes no end of blunders; he makes many miscalculations because everything is new to him. He that sitteth upon the throne saith, "Behold, I make all things new;" and the renewed man says, "My Lord, it is even so." One said to me, when joining the church, "Either I am a new creature, or else the world is altogether altered from what it was. There is a change somewhere;" and that change is from death to life, from darkness into God's marvellous light.

Now, as life comes thus with strange surprises, and mingled with pain, so, dear friends, it comes often *with many questions.* The child has a thousand things to ask; it has to learn everything. We little think of the experiments that children have to go through before they arrive even at the use of their eyes. They do not know that things are at a distance; they have to learn that fact by looking many times. So long as the object falls upon the retina, the child is not aware of whether it is a distant or a near object till some time after. What you think that you and I knew from our birth, we did not so know; we had to learn it. And when a man is born into the kingdom of God, he has to learn everything; and consequently, if he is wise, he questions older and wiser believers about this and about that. I pray you that are instructed, and have become fathers, never to laugh at babes in grace, if they ask you the most absurd questions. Encourage them to do so; let them tell you their difficulties. You, by God's grace are a man; this little one is but a new-born babe; hear what he has to say. You mothers, do this with your little children. You are interested, you are pleased, you are amused, with what they say. Thus ought instructed saints to deal with those who have been newly quickened. They come to us, and ask, "What is this? What is that? What is the other?" It is a time of asking, a time of enquiring. It is well, also, if it is a time of sitting at Jesus' feet, for there is no other place so safe to a new-born believer as the feet of Jesus. If he gets to the feet of anybody else, he is apt to get ill-instructed at a time when everything warps his judgment, when he is exceedingly impressionable, and not likely to forget the mistakes that he has made, if he has borrowed them from others. So you see what the divine life does when it comes into the soul. It comes to us with pain; it gives us many surprises; and it suggests a large number of questions.

We begin then to *make a great many attempts* at things which we never attempted before. The new-born child of God is just like the new-born child of man in some things; and after a time that child begins to walk. No, it does not; it begins to crawl; it does not walk at first. It creeps along, pleased to make any kind of progress; and when it gets upon its little feet, it moves from one chair to another, trembling at every step it takes, and presently down it goes. But it gets up again, and so it learns to walk. Do you remember when the new life came into you? I do. I remember the first week of that new life, and how, on the second Sabbath, I went to the place where I had heard the gospel to my soul's salvation, thinking that I would attend there. But, during that week, I had made many experiments, and tumbled down a great many times, and the preacher took for his text, "O wretched man that I am! who shall deliver me from the body of this death?" I thought, "Yes; I know all about that; that is my case." When the preacher said that Paul was not a Christian when he wrote those words, though I was only seven days old in divine things, I knew better than that, so I never went there any more. I knew that no man but a Christian ever could or would cry out against sin with that bitter wail; and that, if the grace of God was not with him, he would rest satisfied and contented; but that, if he felt that sin was a horrible thing, and he was a wretched man because of it, and must be delivered from it, then he surely must be a child of God, especially if he could add, "Thanks be to God, which giveth us the victory through our Lord Jesus Christ."

Beloved, we make many mistakes, and we shall continue to do so. At the same time, we learn by our experiments. You remember when you began to pray; would you like to have your first prayer printed? I believe that God liked it better than many of the collects. You might not like it so well; it would not look well in print. You remember when you first began to confess Christ to a friend. Oh, you did stutter and stammer over it! There were more tears than words; it was not a "dry" discourse; you wetted it well with tears of grief and anxiety. That was the new life putting forth powers with which it was not itself acquainted; and I believe that there are some of God's children who have powers that they will never find unless they try to use them. I should like some of you young men who do not pray at the prayer-meeting to make a start. And some of you older men, perhaps, have never preached yet; but you might if you tried; I wish you would. "I should break down," says one. I wish you would. A break-down sermon, that breaks the preacher down, might break the people down, too. There might be many advantages about that kind of discourse.

This, then, was the way in which the new life, spiritual life, came into us. We did not know what it was when it came; we had never felt like that before; we could not think that we really had passed from death to life; and yet, in looking back, we are persuaded that the throes within, the anguish of heart, the longing, and the pleading, and the wrestling, and the crying, would never have been in a dead heart, but were the sure marks that God had quickened us, and we had passed into newness of life.

II. Now, secondly, let us think of OUR PRESENT LIFE. "You hath he quickened." Well, then, we have a new life. What is the effect of this life upon us? I speak to you who are quickened by grace.

Well, first, we have become now *sentient towards God.* The unconverted man lives in God's world, sees God's works, hears God's Word, goes up to God's house on God's day, and yet he does not know that there is any God. Perhaps he believes that there is, because he was brought up to believe it; but he is not cognizant of God; God has not entered into him; he has not come into contact with God. Beloved brethren and sisters in Christ, I think that you and I can say, that to us the surest fact in all the world is that there is a God. No God? I live in him. Tell the fish in the sea that there is no water. No God? I live by him. Tell a man who is breathing that there is no air. No God? I dare not come downstairs without speaking to him. No God? I would not think of closing my eyes in sleep unless I had some sense of his love shed abroad in my heart by the Holy Ghost. "Oh!" says one, "I have lived fifty years, and I have never felt anything of God." Say that you have been dead fifty years; that is nearer the mark. But if you had been quickened of the Holy Spirit fifty minutes, this would have been the first fact in the front rank of all facts, God is, and he is my Father, and I am his child. Now you become sentient to his frown, his smile, his threat, or his promise. You feel him; his presence is photographed upon your spirit; your very heart trembles with awe of him, and you say with Jacob, "Surely God is in this place." That is one result of spiritual life.

Now you have become also *sympathetic with similar life in others.* You have a wide range, for the life of God, his life in his new-born child, is the same life that is in every Christian. It is the same life in the new-born believer as in yonder bright spirits that stand before the throne of God. The life of Christ, the life of God, is infused into us in that moment when we are quickened from our death in sin. What a wonderful thing it is to have become sympathetic with God! What he desires, we desire. His glory is the first object of our being. He loves his Son, and we love his Son. We desire to see his kingdom come as he does, and we pray for his will to be done on earth, even as it is done in heaven. We wish that death did not remain, the old nature hampering us; but, in proportion as the new life is really in us, we now run parallel with God. The holiness which he delights in we aspire after. Not with equal footsteps, but with tottering gait, we follow in that selfsame path that God has marked out for himself. "My soul followeth hard after thee; thy right hand upholdeth me."

The new life that made us sympathetic with God, and holy angels, and holy men, and with everything that is from above, has also made us *capable of great pleasure.* Life is usually capable of pleasure, but the new life is capable of the highest conceivable pleasure. I am certain that no ungodly man has any conception of the joy which often fills the believer's spirit. If worldlings could only know the bliss of living near to God, and of basking in the light of his countenance, they would throw their wealth into the sea, and ten thousand times as much, if they might but get a glimpse of this joy that can never be bought, but which God gives to all who trust his dear Son. We are not always alike. Alas! we are very changeable; but when God is with us, when the days are spiritually bright and long, and we have come into the midsummer of our heavenly bliss, we would not change places with the angels, knowing that by-and-by we shall be nearer to the throne than they are; and, while they are God's honoured servants, yet they are not beloved sons as we are. Oh, the thrill of joy that has sometimes gone through our spirits! We could almost have died with delight at times when we have realized the glorious things that God has prepared for them that love him. This joy we never knew till we received the new life.

But I must add that we are also *capable of acute pain* to which we were strangers once. God has made our conscience quick as the apple of the eye; he has made our soul as sensitive as a raw wound, so that the very shadow of sin falling on the believer's heart will cause him great pain; and, if he does go into actual sin, then, like David, he talks about his bones being broken, and it is not too strong a figure of the sorrow that comes upon the believing heart when sin has been committed, and God has been grieved. The heart itself, then, is broken, and bleeds at ten thousand wounds. Yet this is one of the results of our possessing the new life; and I will say this, the sharpest pang of spiritual life is better than the highest joy of carnal life. When the believer is at his worst, he is better than the unbeliever at his best; his reasons for happiness are always transcendently above all the reasons for joy that worldlings can ever know.

Now, dear friends, if we have received spiritual life, you see what a range of being we have, how we can rise up to the seventh heaven or sink down into the abyss. This new life makes us *capable of walking with God;* that is a grand thing. We speak of Enoch walking with God, and we look at the holiness of his life; but did anybody ever think of the majesty of his life? How does God walk? It needs a Milton to conceive of the walk of God; but he that hath the divine life walks with God; and sometimes he seems to step from Alp to Alp, over sea and ocean, accomplishing what, unaided, he would never even attempt. He that has the divine life is lifted up into the infinities; he gets to hear that which cannot be heard, and to see that which cannot be seen, for "Eye hath not seen, nor ear heard, neither have entered into the heart of man, the things which God hath prepared for them that love him. But God hath revealed them unto us by his Spirit," when he has given us the new life.

One effect of this divine life is to *put life into everything that we do.* They tell me that "creeds are dead." Yes, yes! It is a pleasant thing to hear an honest confession; they are dead to dead men. To me, that which I believe is not dead; it is a part of myself. I hold nothing as a truth that I can put away on the shelf, and leave there,

My creed is a part of my being. I believe it to be true; and, believing it to be true, I feel its living force upon my nature every day. When a man tells you that his creed is a dead thing, do not deny it for a minute; there is no doubt of the fact. He knows about himself better than you do. Oh, dear friends, let *us* never have a dead creed! That which you believe, you must believe up to the hilt; believe it livingly, believe it really, for that is not believed at all which is only believed in the letter, but is not felt in the power of it.

If you have been quickened by the Spirit of God, your prayers are living prayers. Oh, the many dead prayers that are heard at the bedside; so many good words rushed through at a canter! He that is alive unto God asks for what he wants, and he believes that he shall have it, and he gets it. That is living prayer. Beware of dead prayers; they are a mockery to the Most High. I do not think that a living man can always pray by clockwork, at such a time and such a time. It would be something like the minister's sermon which he "got up" beforehand, and upon which he wrote in the margin "weep here," "here you must show great emotion." Of course that was all rubbish; it cannot be done to order. You cannot resolve to "groan at one o'clock, and weep at three o'clock." Life will not be bound like that. I love to have an appointed season for prayer, and woe unto the man who does not have his time for prayer! But, at the same time, our living prayer bursts out hours before the appointed time, or sometimes it will not come at the time. You have to wait till another season, and then your soul is like a hind let loose. Why, sometimes we can pray, and prevail, and come off conquerors; and at another time, we can only bow at the throne, and groan out, "Lord, help me; I cannot pray; the springs seem to be all sealed." That is the result of life. Living things change. There are some personages in St. Paul's Cathedral; I have not seen them lately, but I have seen them. When I lived in the country, I came up to look at the notabilities in St. Paul's Cathedral. I have heard that they have never had a headache during the last hundred years, and no rheumatic pains, nor have they ever been troubled with the gout. The reason is that they are cut in marble, and they are dead; but a living man feels the fogs and the winds; he knows whether it is an east wind or a west wind that is blowing. Before he gets up in the morning, he begins to feel sometimes lively and sometimes dull; he does not understand himself. Sometimes he feels merry, and can sing hymns; at another time, he can do nothing else but sigh and cry, though he scarcely knows wherefore. Yes, life is a strange thing; and if you have the life of God in your soul, you will undergo many changes, and not always be what you want to be.

If we are alive unto God, every part of our worship should be living. What a deal of dead worship there is! If we go on with our services in regular routine, a large number of our friends find it difficult to keep awake. I fear that some people go to a place of worship because they get a better sleep there than they do anywhere else. That is not worship which consists in doing as Hodge did, when he said, "I like Sunday, for then I can go to church, and put my legs up, and think of nothing at all." That is all the worship a great many render to God, just getting to a place of worship, and there sitting still, and thinking of nothing at all. But if you are a living child of God, you cannot do that. If, sometimes, through the infirmity of the flesh, you fall into that state of slumber, you loathe yourselves for it, but you rouse yourself up, and say, "I must worship my God; I must sing, I must praise God. I must draw near to him in prayer."

III. I must come to my third point; for our time flies. Notice what OUR PRESENT POSITION is, if God has quickened us.

Our present position is this, first, that *we are raised from the dead.* "He hath quickened us together with Christ, and hath raised us up together." We cannot live where we used to live. We cannot wear what we used to wear. There is nobody here who would like to go and live in a grave. If you had been raised from the dead, after you had been buried in Norwood Cemetery, I will warrant you that you would not go there to-night to sleep. So the man, who has once been raised by the quickening power of the Holy Spirit, quits the dead; his old company does not suit him. If you had been raised from the dead, and had come out of your tomb, you would not go about London streets with your shroud on. You are a living man. How is it that I find some who say that they are the people of God; but yet are rather fond of wearing their grave-clothes? I mean, that they like the amusements of the world; they like to put on their shroud sometimes just for a treat. Oh, do not so! If God has made you to live, come away from the dead; come away from their habits, and manners, and customs. Life sees no charms in death. The living child of God likes to get as far as ever he can away from the death that once held him bound. "Come out from among them, and be ye separate, saith the Lord, and touch not the unclean thing; and I will receive you, and will be a Father unto you, and ye shall be my sons and daughters, saith the Lord Almighty." That is the first part of our position, that we have come to live a separated life now, and have quitted the path we trod before.

Next to that, we are *one with Christ.* He hath "quickened us together with Christ, and hath raised us up together." I told you just now that the life which the Holy Spirit gives us when we are born again, is the life of God. We are made partakers of the divine nature, of course, in a modified sense, but still in a true sense. The life everlasting, the life that can never die, is put into us then, even as Christ said, "The water that I shall give him shall be in him a well of water springing up into everlasting life." The believer's life is the life of Christ in the believer. "Because I live, ye shall live also." What a mystic union there is between the believer and his Lord! Realize that; believe in it; rejoice in it; triumph in it. Christ and you are one now, and you are made to live together with him. God grant you to know the joy of that condition!

Once more, we are told, "He hath raised us up together, and made us sit together in heavenly places in Christ Jesus." That is very wonderful. We have not only left the dead, and become joined to Christ, but we are made to *sit in heaven with Christ.* A man is where his head is, is he not? and every believer is where his Head is; and if we are members of Christ's body, we are in heaven. It is a very blessed experience to be able to walk on earth, and look up to heaven; but it is a higher experience to live in heaven, and look down on the earth; and this is what the believer may do. He may sit in the heavenlies; Christ is there as his Representative. The believer may take possession of what his Representative is holding on his behalf. Oh, to live in heaven, to dwell there, to let the heart be caught up from this poor life into the life that is above! This is where we should be, where we may be if we are quickened by the divine life.

One thing more, and I have done. We are in this position, that God is now working in us, through this divine life, to make us *the most wonderful reflectors of his grace* that he has yet formed. He has raised us up together, and made us sit together in heavenly places in Christ Jesus, "that in the ages to come he might shew the exceeding riches of his grace in his kindness toward us through Christ Jesus." The ages to come will have for their wonder the quickened children of God. When God made the world, it was a wonder, and the angels came from afar to see his handiwork. But when Christ makes the new creation, they will say no more that God made the heaven and the earth, but they will say in higher strains, "He made these new-born men and women. He made for them, and in them, new heavens and a new earth."

Ah! beloved, "It doth not yet appear what we shall be." God has given us a life that is more precious than the Koh-i-noor, a life that will outlast the sun and moon. When all the things that are shall be like old ocean's foam, which dissolves into the wave that bears it, and is gone for ever; we shall still live, and we shall live in Christ, and with Christ, glorified for ever. When the moon has become black as sackcloth of hair, the life that is within us shall be as bright as when God first gave it to us. Thou hast the dew of thy youth, O child of God; and thou shalt have yet more of it, and be like thy Lord, when he shall take thee away from every trace of death, and the corrupt atmosphere of this poor world, and thou shalt dwell with the living God in the land of the living for ever and for ever!

The practical outcome of all this is, that some of you do not know anything at all about it. If you do not, let that fact impress you. If there be a divine life to which you are a stranger, how long will you be a stranger to it? If there be a spiritual death, and you are dead, be startled; for within a little while God will say, "Bury my dead out of my sight." And what will happen to you when the word of God is, "Depart, depart, depart, depart," and unto the graveyard of souls, to the fire that never shall be quenched, you and the rest of the dead are taken away? "God is not the God of the dead, but of the living," and, unless we are made alive unto him, he cannot be our God either here or hereafter. The Lord impress this solemn truth on all your hearts by his own Spirit; for Jesus Christ's sake! **Amen.**

Exposition by C. H. Spurgeon.
EPHESIANS II.

Verse 1. *And you hath he quickened,*
Is it so? Could the apostle say that to you, and to me?

1. *Who were dead in trespasses and sins;*
Look back to what you used to be, to the hole of the pit whence ye were digged: "You hath he quickened, who were dead in trespasses and sins."

2. *Wherein in time past ye walked*
With a terrible activity of spiritual death;

2. *According to the course of this world, according to the prince of the power of the air, the spirit that now worketh in the children of disobedience:*
He makes them to be his forge. There he blows his coals, there he fabricates his instruments. Do you not hear the noise of the infernal bellows when "the children of disobedience" swear, and use unclean language? Ah, such were some of us; but we are cleansed! The evil spirit has been driven out, and he no more works in us.

3. *Among whom also we all had our conversation in times past in the lusts of ur flesh, fulfilling the desires of the flesh and of the mind; and were by nature the children of wrath, even as others.*
You that now commune with God at the mercy-seat, you that are now his favoured children, and have received power to become the sons of God, you were once heirs of wrath: "By nature the children of wrath, even as others." Holy Scripture is not complimentary to unrenewed human nature. You may search it through and through to find a single flattering word to unregenerate men; but you will search in vain. This style of speech is left to those who scout divine inspiration. They draw their inspiration from another fount, from a desire to walk according to the course of this world, according to the prince of the power of the air. They can use flattering speeches in addressing the ungodly; but the Holy Ghost never does.

4, 5. *But God, who is rich in mercy, for his great love wherewith he loved us, even when we were dead in sins,*
God loved us even when we were dead in sins. His love does not depend upon what we are; it flows from his own heart. It is not love of something good in us; it is love of us because of everything good in him. Here you see the greatness of his grace, in that "he loved us, even when we were dead in sins."

5. *Hath quickened us together with Christ,*
Ah! that accounts for everything: "together with Christ." When we get "together with Christ", then are we made alive, then are we saved. Are *you*, my dear hearers, "quickened together with Christ"?

5—7. *(By grace ye are saved;) and hath raised us up together, and made us sit together in heavenly places in Christ Jesus: that in the ages to come he might shew the exceeding riches of his grace in his kindness toward us through Christ Jesus.*
See how Paul's language grows and swells and rises as he proceeds! Just now, we read of "God, who is rich in mercy"; now the apostle speaks of "the exceeding riches of his grace", exceeding expression, exceeding comprehension, exceeding even sin itself, though that is all but infinite. "The exceeding riches of his grace" are infinity itself; but they all come to us "through Christ Jesus." Paul will speak of nothing good except that which comes "through Christ Jesus." This is the one conduit-pipe

through which the streams of living water flow to the dead in sin; God's grace comes to us "through Christ Jesus", and through him alone.

8. *For by grace are ye saved through faith;*
We have this expression, "by grace are ye saved," twice over in this chapter. Paul knew that he needed to repeat himself, or people would forget what he taught. At bottom, all the wanderings from the faith at the present day amount to this, salvation by works instead of salvation by grace. The battle of the Reformation has to be fought over again. Men are justified by grace through faith in Jesus Christ. All the enmity of natural men is against that truth. They want to be saved by their own morality, and all sorts of things that they put instead of salvation by grace through faith in our Lord Jesus Christ.

8, 9. *And that not of yourselves: it is the gift of God: not of works, lest any man should boast.*
"Oh!" said one to me just now, "the man who is saved by his own righteousness cannot do much in the line of praising." "No, my dear brother," I replied, "except he praises himself, and he can generally do that pretty well." Your self-made man usually worships his creator very earnestly; and your self-saved man glorifies him that saved him.

10. *For we are his workmanship, created in Christ Jesus*
Nothing without Christ Jesus, you see. The mark of the pierced hand is on everything: "We are his workmanship, created in Christ Jesus."

10. *Unto good works, which God hath before ordained that we should walk in them.*
God has decreed that he will have a holy people. This is his purpose, his ordinance, to which he will always stand. He will make it good. He will make sinful people holy, and disobedient people obedient to the faith.

11. *Wherefore remember, that ye being in time past Gentiles in the flesh, who are called Uncircumcision by that which is called the Circumcision in the flesh made by hands;*
Remember what you were. You were not the chosen Israelites, you have not the covenant mark in your flesh.

12. *That at that time ye were without Christ,*
Which is the worst state of all, far worse than being without circumcision.

12. *Being aliens from the commonwealth of Israel,*
Outsiders, rank outsiders, far away from any rights, or any participation in the rights of God's children.

12. *And strangers from the covenants of promise,*
Utter strangers to the covenants made with Abraham, Isaac, and Jacob.

12. *Having no hope, and without God in the world:*
It is an awful description, but a truthful description, of what we were.

13. *But now*
The apostle has turned over a new leaf in the book of our history: "but now." Oh, what a change from the past to the present! "But now"—

13. *In Christ Jesus*
See how Paul keeps harping on that one string. Note how he links us with Christ Jesus. There is nothing for us without Christ and his cross.

13. *Ye who sometimes were far off are made nigh by the blood of Christ.*
Paul can never have too much of Christ. It is Christ, Christ, Christ, Christ; like the harp of Anacreon. He wished to sing of Cadmus; but his harp resounded love alone; and so the harp of Paul resounds with Christ alone, Christ alone. He always comes back to that theme. It was said of

one eminent commentator that he could not find Christ in the Scripture where he was; but it was said of Cocceius that he found Christ where he was not. I would rather find Christ where he is not, than not find him where he is. There are plenty who err in that second direction nowadays.

14. *For he is our peace,*

Paul cannot do without Christ, you see. He will bring him in everywhere.

14. *Who hath made both one, and hath broken down the middle wall of partition between us;*

There was to be no longer the division between Jews and Gentiles.

15. *Having abolished in his flesh*

See, it is always Christ, his flesh, his blood, his life. There must always be something about him: "Having abolished in his flesh."

15, 16. *The enmity, even the law of commandments contained in ordinances; for to make in himself of twain one new man, so making peace; and that he*

I cannot help reminding you, that you must not overlook the fact that Paul will not go a hair's breadth away from Christ.

16—18. *Might reconcile both unto God in one body by the cross, having slain the enmity thereby: and came and preached peace to you which were afar off, and to them that were nigh. For through him we both have access by one Spirit unto the Father.*

There is the whole Trinity in that verse, Christ, the Spirit, the Father. It needs the Trinity to make a Christian, and when you have got a Christian, it needs the Trinity to make a prayer. You cannot pray a single prayer aright without Father, Son, and Holy Ghost.

19. *Now therefore*

Another of Paul's blessed "nows." It was "but now" a little while ago; now he has another "now." "Now therefore"—

19. *Ye are no more strangers and foreigners, but fellow-citizens with the saints, and of the household of God;*

You are not only in the kingdom, but you are in the royal household, which is better still. You are princes of the blood imperial. You are peers of the court of heaven: "and of the household of God."

20. *And are built*

You are not loose stones; you are built—

20, 21. *Upon the foundation of the apostles and prophets, Jesus Christ himself being the chief corner stone; in whom*

You see, it is always that, in him, in Christ: "in whom"—

21. *All the building fitly framed together groweth unto an holy temple in the Lord:*

There is no church without Christ, no temple without him as its cornerstone, its priest, its glory.

22. *In whom ye also are builded together for an habitation of God through the Spirit.*

And all this hangs upon that first sentence, "You hath he quickened." Is it so, beloved? If you are spiritually dead, nothing here belongs to you; but if he hath quickened you, you may take every single sentence of the chapter, and say, "That is mine, and glory be to the grace of God!"

HYMNS FROM "OUR OWN HYMN BOOK"—463, 476, 461.

Metropolitan Tabernacle Pulpit.

A QUESTION FOR COMMUNICANTS.

A Sermon

Intended for Reading on Lord's-day, August 7th, 1892,

DELIVERED BY

C. H. SPURGEON,

AT THE METROPOLITAN TABERNACLE, NEWINGTON,

On Lord's-day Evening, June 1st, 1890.

"What mean ye by this service?"—Exodus xii. 26.

In a spiritual religion, everything must be understood. That which is not spiritual, but ritualistic, contents itself with the outward form. Under the Jewish dispensation, there was a very strong tendency in that direction; but it was kept to some extent in check. Under the Christian faith, this tendency must not be tolerated at all. We must know the meaning of what we do; otherwise we are not profited. We do not believe in the faith of the man who was asked what he believed, and who replied that he believed what the church believed. "But what does the church believe?" "The church believes what I believe." "Well, but what do you and the church believe?" "We both of us believe the same thing." He could not be got to explain himself any further. We look upon such expressions as the talk of ignorance, and not the language of faith. Faith knows what she believes, and can give a reason for the hope that is in her with meekness and fear.

Concerning the Passover, the young people among the Jews were encouraged to ask their parents this question, "What mean ye by this service?" Children should be encouraged now to ask such gracious questions. I am afraid they are not prompted to do so as they used to be in Puritan times. After the sermon always came the catechizing of the children when they were at home; and every father was bound to be attentive, because he had to ask the boys and girls in the evening what they had heard; and they were more attentive then than now, because they had to be prepared to answer, and to ask any questions of their parents in return. Cultivate in your children a desire to understand everything connected with our holy faith.

In this chapter, from which I have culled my text, the parents are taught how to answer their children. If the parent be ignorant, a question from his child is inconvenient. He finds his ignorance

No. 2,268.

exposed, and he perhaps is vexed with the child who has been the innocent means of unveiling him to himself. Be ready to tell your children what the ordinances of the gospel mean. Explain baptism to them, explain the Lord's supper to them; and above all, explain the gospel; and let them know as far as words can make it plain, what is that great mystery whereby we are saved, whereby sin is forgiven, and we are made the children of God.

I thought it would be profitable, if God gave me strength for the exercise, very briefly to answer the question supposed to be put by an intelligent youth, "What mean ye by this service?"—this service that is called by some people "Holy Communion"; which is sometimes called the "Eucharist"; and among us is called "the Lord's supper", or "the breaking of bread." What does it mean?

It means many things; but chiefly five, of which I will speak now.

I. This supper is, first of all, A MEMORIAL.

If you want to keep something in mind from generation to generation, you may attempt it in many ways. You may erect a bronze column, or you may engrave a record of it upon brass in the church. The column will get sold for old bronze, and somebody will steal the brasses from the church; and the memorial will disappear. You may write it upon marble if you please; but in our climate, at any rate, the inscription is very apt to be obliterated; and the old stones, though they last long, may after a time be as dumb as the treasures of Nineveh and of Egypt were for centuries. Those monuments did preserve the records, but they were hidden under the sand, or buried beneath the ruins of cities; and though they have a tongue now, and are speaking very forcibly, yet whatever had been entrusted to them would have been forgotten while they were lying under the sand of the desert, or in the *débris* of the palaces of Koyunjik. There are other ways of preserving memorials, such as writing in books; but books can be lost. Many valuable works of the ancients have entirely ceased, and no copies of them can be found. Some of the books mentioned in the Old Testament, which were not inspired books, but still were books which we should greatly value now, have quite passed out of existence.

It is found that, upon the whole, one of the best ways of remembering a fact is to have some ceremony connected with it, which shall be frequently performed, so as to keep the fact in memory. I suppose that Absalom will never be forgotten. He built himself a pillar in the king's dale; he knew his own infamous history, and he thought that it might be forgotten. No one would care to remember it, so he built himself a monument; and there it stands, or what is reputed to be that monument, to this day, and every Arab who passes by the spot throws a stone at it. Absalom will be better remembered by the ceremony of throwing stones at his tomb than by any record in marble.

To turn your thoughts to something infinitely higher, I cannot conceive of a surer and better method of keeping the death of Christ in mind than that of meeting together, as we shall do to-night, for the breaking of bread, and the pouring out of the juice of the vine in memory of his death. Other facts may be forgotten; this one never can be. To-night, and every first day of the week, in ten thousand places of worship, believers meet together for the breaking of bread in remembrance of Christ's cross and passion, his precious death and burial. Those great facts can never pass out of mind. Jesus said to his disciples, "This do in remembrance of me." In obeying his command you are doing what is most effectual in keeping your Lord in remembrance. As I preach to-night, having no sort of reliance upon my own words, I want you to practise them as I go along; then you will be like the woman who said that, when she heard a sermon about light weights and short measures, though she forgot what the preacher said, when she got home, she recollected to burn her bushel, which was too short. So, if you can just practice the sermon as you hear it, it will be well.

Recollect, then, that you come to this table to-night to *remember an absent Friend.* Jesus has gone away. He who loved us better than any other ever loved us, has left us for a while. We sometimes take little parting gifts from friends, and they say to us—

> "When this you see,
> Remember me."

Probably, almost everybody here has, at some time or other, had certain tokens of remembrance by which they might be reminded of some dear one who is far away across the seas; out of sight, but not out of mind. You come to the communion-table, then, to remember your absent Friend.

You come, also, chiefly to *remember his great deed of love.* This supper is a memorial of what Jesus did for you when he was on the earth. "Greater love hath no man than this, that a man lay down his life for his friends." He laid down his life for you; remember that to-night. "He loved me, and gave himself for me;" dwell on that fact. Let these words wake the echoes in your hearts, "Gethsemane!" "Gabbatha!" "Golgotha!" Can you forget all that Jesus suffered there on your behalf? If you have let these things slip in any degree from your heart's affections, come and write them down again. Come to the table, and here celebrate the memorial of his love, and wounds, and agonies, and death for you.

> "In memory of the Saviour's love,
>   We keep the sacred feast,
> Where every humble contrite heart
>   Is made a welcome guest.
>
> "By faith we take the bread of life,
>   With which our souls are fed;
> And cup, in token of his blood
>   That was for sinners shed."

You are also called upon to *remember a dear Friend who,* although he has gone away, *has gone about your business.* It was expedient for you that he should go away. He is doing you more good where he has gone than he could have done if he had stayed here. He is pressing on your suit to-night. Your business would miscarry were it not for him; but within the veil that hides him from you, he is pleading for you. His power, his dignity, his merit, are all freely being employed for you. He is pleading the causes of your soul. Can you, will you, forget him? Will you not now forget everything else, and indulge the sweet memory of your faithful Lover, your dear Husband, who is married to you in ties of everlasting wedlock? Come, I pray you, keep the memorial feast of this dear Friend.

And you have to *remember a Friend who will return very soon.* He only tells you to do this till he comes. He is coming back to us. His own words are, "Behold, I come quickly!" That is not quite the meaning of what he said; it was, "Behold, *I am coming* quickly!" He is on his way, his chariot is hurrying towards us, the axles of the wheels are hot with speed. He is coming as fast as he can. The long-suffering of God delays him, till sinners are brought in, till the full number of his elect shall be accomplished; but he is not delaying; he is not lingering; he is not slack, as some men count slackness; he is coming quickly. Will you not remember him? Soon will his hand be on the door; soon for you, at any rate, he may cry, "Arise, my love, my dove, my fair one, and come away;" and soon he may be here among us, and then we shall reign with him for ever and ever.

I charge my own heart to remember my dear Lord to-night; and I pray you, brothers and sisters, let not the feebleness of my reminder deprive you now of the happiness of thinking much of Christ your Lord. Sit you still, and let all other thoughts be gone, and think only of him who loved you and died for you. Let your thoughts go back to Calvary, as you sing, in mournful accents,—

> " O sacred head, once wounded,
>   With grief and pain weigh'd down,
> How scornfully surrounded
>   With thorns, thine only crown!
> How pale art thou with anguish,
>   With sore abuse and scorn!
> How does that visage languish,
>   Which once was bright as morn!"

Oh, eyes once full of tears! Oh, shoulders once beaten with the gory lash! Oh, hands once nailed to the cruel tree! Oh, feet once fastened to the bitter cross! Soon shall we behold the Christ who loved us, and died for us. Wherefore let us observe this sacred feast in remembrance of him.

II. But I must be briefer on my second point. The second meaning of the Lord's supper is that it is AN EXHIBITION. "As often as ye eat this bread, and drink this cup, ye do shew the Lord's death till he come." We are helped to remember it by the type, the emblem, the metaphor which is supplied to us by this supper. How is that? Is there any likeness to the death of Christ in this supper? I answer, there is a great likeness.

There is *his broken body*, represented by the bread which is broken, and intended for use. His dear body was broken, marred, sadly marred, given over to the hands of death, laid in the sepulchre, wrapped about with fine linen, left there, as his enemies thought, never to rise again. In that broken bread, broken that even believing children may eat their morsel, you see Christ's body given up for his people's sake.

But there stands a cup. It is full of the red juice of the grape. What means it? He himself shall explain it: "This cup is the new testament in my blood, which is shed for you." Now, *the shedding of blood* is the great token of death. One would not long talk of killing without speaking of blood-shedding; in fact, bloodshed usually means dying by a violent death; and so did he die. They pierced his hands and his feet; the soldier thrust the lance into his side, and forthwith came there out blood and water. That stream of blood was the token that he really was dead. He hath poured out from his veins his precious life to purchase his redeemed. The broken bread, the cluster pressed into the cup, and leaving nothing but its blood-red juice, these two things symbolize Christ's death.

But, most of all, this is an exhibition of *the two things separate*, the bread and the cup. We have heard of some mixing the bread with the wine; that is not the Lord's supper. We have heard of others partaking of the wafer, as they call it, and leaving the cup; this is not taking the Lord's supper. They must be both there; the bread here, the wine-cup there; because the separation of the blood from the flesh is the surest token of death. "The blood is the life thereof;" and if the blood be drained away, there is death. Therefore the blood is represented by the cup, and the flesh is represented by the bread; these two separated are the great token and emblem of Christ's death.

We show, display, exhibit, symbolize, the death of our Lord at this table in this fashion; we partake of both symbols, eating of the bread, drinking of the cup, *the whole ministering to the support of our life*. At this table we say to all of you who do not know Christ, Christ's death is our life, and the remembrance of Christ's death is the food of our life. If any of you are spectators of the ordinance, this is the meaning of our little acted sermon, Christ has died. Christ's death is the support of our faith, the food of our souls; in token whereof we take this bread and this cup, and eat and drink. So this supper is a showing forth of Christ's death. How many here can say that Christ's death is their life? How many of you can say that you feed upon him? Dear friends, you must not come to the table unless you can say it; but if you can, come and welcome; and if you cannot, oh! may the Lord teach you the lesson that is so needful, the lesson that is so blessed, when it is once learnt, that Christ on the cross is the one hope of eternal glory.

You have thus had two meanings of the Lord's supper; first, it is a memorial; and next, an exhibition.

III. The Lord's supper is, next, A COMMUNION.

We must have this brought out prominently, or we shall miss a great deal. *We are at the Lord's table;* we eat of his bread, we drink out of his cup. This betokens friendship. When, in the East, a man has eaten of an Arab's salt, he is henceforth under his protecting care; and he who has spiritually eaten of Christ's bread, has come under Christ's protection; Christ will take care of him. All feuds are ended; an eternal peace is established between the two. It was a tender parable in which Nathan spoke of a man who had one little ewe lamb, which did eat of his own meat, and drank of his own cup, and lay in his bosom. This is your privilege, to lie in Christ's bosom, to drink out of his cup, and to eat of his bread. This is a very sweet fellowship; enjoy it to-night to the full.

We go further than that, for we not only eat of his bread, but symbolically *we feast upon him.* His flesh is meat indeed; and his blood is drink indeed. Can I really feed upon Christ? Really, yes. Carnally, no. There is no such thing as the carnal eating of his flesh and drinking of his blood; that were a horrible thing; that were to make a man a cannibal; but the spiritual feeding upon the Incarnate God, this is what we mean. He gives us his flesh to eat, and we thus enter into a fellowship of the most intense and mysterious kind; not merely eating with him, but eating him; not merely receiving from him, but receiving him himself to be the life of our hearts. May you get to that point to-night! I believe in the real presence of Christ; I do not believe in the carnal presence of the Romanist. I believe in the real presence to the believer; but that reality is none the less real because it is spiritual; and only spiritual men can discern it.

Now, beloved, if we really come in the right spirit to this table, when we have eaten the bread, it becomes part of us; when the wine is sipped, the juice of the grape enters into our constitution; we cannot separate it from ourselves. Such is our fellowship with Christ. *He is one with us, and we are one with him.* " *Quis separabit?* " "Who shall separate us from the love of God?" We are one with Christ; partners with him; all that he has is ours; all that we have is his. He gives himself to us; we yield ourselves to him. It is Christ and Co., only the little "Co." drops its name to be swallowed up in him who is all in all. There is the meaning of the bread and the cup. We take Christ into ourselves, as he has taken us up into his greater self.

But communion also means that *we are one with each other.* I wish that you would all catch that thought. I am afraid there are some members of the church here, who have never realized their union with all the rest of the members. "We, being many, are one body in Christ, and every one members one of another." One is our Master, even Christ, and all we are brethren. There should be an intimate feeling of fellowship, a readiness to help and love one another. Rejoice with them that rejoice, and weep with them that weep.

I cannot shake off from myself the idea that this makes up a large part of the meaning of the Lord's supper, the communion of saints with each other as well as the communion of the saints with Christ. May we enjoy it to-night! For my part, I like to feel, when I come to the table, that I am going to have communion, not only with this church, large as it is, not merely with the members of one denomination (I wish there were no denominations), not merely with the company of one body of Christians—would to God there were but one body of Christians throughout the whole world!—but freely inviting all who belong to any part of the visible church; I delight to think that at this table to-night I shall have fellowship with the brethren on the Congo, with the brethren in India, with the brethren in the United States, of all names, and sorts, and ages, and ranks. There cannot be two churches of Christ. There is but one Church, one Head, and one body. Though there are some very naughty children in the Lord's family, they must not be kept without their supper; there is some other way of chastening them; and as long as there is true living communion between one Christian and another, where God has given the thing signified, I dare not keep back the sign. If he gives them to have fellowship with Christ, who am I that I shall say, "Thou shalt have no fellowship with me"? I dare not say it.

The meaning of this supper, then, is communion.

IV. But a fourth meaning of the Lord's supper is A COVENANTING. Our Lord said to his disciples, "This cup is the new testament, or covenant, in my blood." We do well to sing,—

> "Thy body, broken for my sake,
> My bread from heaven shall be;
> Thy testamental cup I take,
> And thus remember thee."

When we come to the Lord's table, we must be careful that we there *take Christ to be our God in covenant.* We take the one living God to be our God for ever and ever. He gives himself to us, and we take him, and we declare, "This God is our God for ever and ever; he shall be our Guide even unto death." Do you understand that covenant relationship, every one of you? Do you know what you are doing when you take the piece of bread, and eat it, and take the cup, and drink of it? If you are truly a believer in Christ, God is in covenant with you through the body and the blood of Christ, and you recognize that blessed truth, and take him to be your God.

Now, the covenant runs thus, "They shall be my people, and I will be their God." When, therefore, we come to this covenanting table, we *agree that we will be the Lord's people;* henceforth, not the devil's, not the world's, not our own; but the Lord's. When the Lord's people are chastened, we expect to be chastened with them. When the Lord's people are persecuted, we expect to be persecuted with them. We must take them for better or worse, to have and to hold, and death itself must not part us from the Lord's people. That is the meaning of coming to this table, recognizing that, between you and God there is an agreement made that must not be broken, a covenant ordered in all things and sure, by which God becomes yours and you become his, so that you are for ever to be one of those that belong wholly to him.

Here, at the communion-table, God, the covenant God, *seals his love to us.* "Come hither, my child," saith the Lord, "I love thee, and I gave myself for thee, in token whereof put this bread into thy mouth, to remind thee of how I gave myself for thee. I love thee, so that thou art mine. I have called thee by my name, in token whereof I remind thee that I bought thee with my precious blood. Therefore, let that sip of the juice of the vine go into thy body, to remind thee that by my precious blood, which was shed for many, I have redeemed thee from going down into the pit." There are seals at that table, new seals of the covenant, new tokens, new love gifts from the Lord, to remind you of what he has done for you.

And you are to come here to-night *to testify anew your love to God.*

Here you say, "My Master, let me eat with thee! My Lord, tarry with me! Let me sit at the table with thee." If any of you have lost your first love, and have grown spiritually cold, the Saviour stands at the door, and knocks, and he says, "Open to me," and he also says that if we open to him, he will come in, and sup with us, and we with him. He said that to the angel of the church of the Laodiceans, the church which was neither cold nor hot, which he threatened to spue out of his mouth. If thou art only fit to make Christ sick, yet if thou wilt open the door to him, he will come and feast with thee to-night, and all shall be well with thee. He testifies his love to you. Come and testify yours to him to-night. That is the meaning of this bread and this cup. Your covenant with death is broken, your agreement with hell is disannulled; and now you are in covenant with God, and he is in covenant with you, even in an everlasting covenant, which shall never be broken.

V. Lastly, and very briefly, this supper signifies A THANKSGIVING. It is often called, by friends who love hard words, the "Eucharist." We have some friends who always carry a gold pencil, on purpose to put down every word that nobody understands, that they may use it next Sunday in their sermon. Such people call the Lord's supper the "Eucharist", which signifies "the giving of thanks." This is the thanksgiving service of the Church of God. It ought to be celebrated every Lord's-day. Every Sabbath should be a thanksgiving Sunday, for Jesus rose from the dead on the first day of the week, and we ought to give thanks every time we celebrate his resurrection. Certainly we should do so when we celebrate his death. What are we going to do to-night by way of thanksgiving?

Well, we are coming to a festival, not to a funeral. The choice festival of the Jewish faith was the Passover. The Lord's supper takes its place with higher joys; we come to this feast to *testify our joy in Christ*. There is bread, but there is also wine upon the table. This is to show that it is a festival for joy and delight, and you cannot praise Christ better, and give thanks to him better than by rejoicing in him. Praise him by your grateful joy. I think that we should always come to the Lord's table with a feeling of deep reverence; but that reverence should never tend to bondage. We want you not to come here quivering and shaking, as if you were slaves that came to eat a morsel of your master's bread, under fear of the lash. No, no; come, ye children; come, ye beloved ones of the Lord! Come, ye table companions of Christ, and sit at the festival he has prepared, and let your joy be full of thanksgiving!

We come to the table, next, actually to *praise the Lord for giving Christ to us*. When our Lord broke the bread, he gave thanks; when he passed the cup, he gave thanks. Again and again he gave thanks; so shall we to-night. Come ye, beloved, thankfully to praise the Father for the gift of Christ; and as you take the bread into your mouth, say in your heart, "Bless the Lord!" and as you drink of the cup, say in your spirit, "Blessed be his holy name! Blessed be the Father, for his eternal love to us; blessed be Jesus, for his love which has saved us from death; and blessed be the Holy Spirit, who has taught us to know all these precious things!"

One way in which we show our thanks to Christ is that *we receive with gratitude the emblems of his death.* Each one who communes with us will receive of the bread, and eat it, and take of the cup, and drink it. We do not hold it up, and look at it; we do not kneel down, and pay it homage; we receive it. We have done so now these many years. How long is it since we began this holy feast? Well, with some of us, it is over forty years since our first communion, and we do not want any better food. We desire to keep in memory the same Christ, to feed upon the same doctrine of the incarnation and atoning sacrifice; and if we should be spared, beloved, another forty years, which is far from likely, we shall have a sweeter tooth for Christ even than we have now. He will be more dear to us, more precious, more delightsome, even than he is to-night. So we come to the table to show our gratitude by receiving and receiving again.

Let me whisper in your ear, when this communion is over, and you shall leave this table, "Pray, beloved, that you may *go away in the same spirit as your Lord and Master did,* when, after rising from supper, he went out to the garden, not there to have a sweet hour of lonely communion with God, but there to sweat, as it were, great drops of blood falling to the ground. He went there to be arrested, to be hurried off to the bar of Annas, and Caiaphas, and Pilate, and Herod, and the rest of them. He went there, in fact, to die; but he went away singing." So I want you to go away from this communion, singing praises to God. As my dear brother said in prayer, you must have your Gethsemanes, your Golgothas; but I want you to go away from this table singing. Whatever comes, high or low, bright or dark, heaven or another age in this dark wilderness, brethren, let us sing. We often say, "Let us pray;" but to-night, at the table, I say, "Let us sing." Let us sing unto the Lord because of his great gift to us, which we to-night remember, and set forth, and commune with, and covenant with. Let us sing unto the Lord as long as we live; for we can never sufficiently praise him for all that he has done for us.

> "We'll praise our risen Lord,
> While at his feast we sit,
> His griefs a hallow'd theme afford
> For sweetest music fit."

Thus, I have explained all about the Lord's supper; do you know anything about it? Some of you are going away. You are going away! Yes, and the day shall come when you will not have anywhere to go to! When the great marriage supper is spread, and the feast of the gracious shall be held, and the whole universe shall be gathered, oh! where will you go? You will not be allowed to linger at the door, neither will you go home to wait till others shall return from the festival. You must be driven from God's presence if you come not by faith in Christ to that great feast. The fiery swords of the angel-guards shall be unsheathed, and they shall pursue you through the blackness of eternal darkness, down to infinite despair! The Lord have mercy upon you to-night, that he may have mercy upon you in that day, for Jesus' sake! Amen.

Exposition by C. H. Spurgeon.

MATTHEW XXVI. 26—30; AND 1 CORINTHIANS XI. 20—34.

We will read, first, Matthew's account of the institution of the Lord's supper.

Matthew xxvi. 26. *And as they were eating,*

In the middle of the Paschal Feast our Lord instituted the sacred festival which was ever afterwards to be known as "the Lord's supper." The one ordinance was made to melt gradually into the other: "as they were eating."

26. *Jesus took bread, and blessed it, and brake it, and gave it to the disciples, and said, Take eat; this is my body.*

"This represents my body." He could not possibly have meant that the bread was his body; for there was his body sitting at the table, whole and entire. They would have been astonished beyond measure if they had understood him literally; but they did not do so, any more than when Christ said, "I am the door," or "I am the Good Shepherd."

27. *And he took the cup, and gave thanks, and gave it to them, saying, Drink ye all of it;*

"Every one of you." Was this the Lord's supper? Yes. What say the Romanists about it? Why, that the people may not drink of the cup! Yet our Saviour says to his disciples, "Drink ye all of it."

28. *For this is my blood of the new testament, which is shed for many for the remission of sins.*

They had had sin brought to their minds; they had had a personal reminder of their own liability to sin; now they were to have a perpetual pledge of the pardon of sin, in the cup, which was the emblem of Christ's blood, "shed for many for the remission of sins."

29. *But I say unto you, I will not drink henceforth of this fruit of the vine, until that day when I drink it new with you in my Father's kingdom.*

Jesus took the Nazarite vow to drink no more, to partake no more of the fruit of the vine, till he should meet us again in his Father's kingdom. He has pledged us once for all in that cup, and now he abstains until he meets us again. Thus he looks forward to a glorious meeting; but he bids us take of the cup, and thus remember him until he comes.

30. *And when they had sung an hymn, they went out into the mount of Olives.*

To his last great battle the Champion goes singing, attended by feeble followers, who could not protect him; but who could sing with him. I think he must have led the tune; his disciples were too sorrowful to sing until his clear voice started the Hallelujah Psalms; but they joined him in the holy exercise, for "they" as well as their Lord sang the hymn. When you are about to face a trial, offer a prayer; but, if you can, also sing a hymn. It will show great faith if, before you enter into the burning fiery furnace, you can sing psalms unto the Lord who redeemeth his people.

Now let us read Paul's version of this same matter.

1 Corinthians xi. 20, 21. *When ye come together therefore into one place, this is not to eat the Lord's supper. For in eating every one taketh before other his own supper: and one is hungry, and another is drunken.*

These Corinthians had fallen into a very queer state. I do not think that any Baptist Church that I have ever known of has acted in this fashion; but when churches have no ministers, when there is an open ministry where everybody talketh and nobody listeneth, they fall into a queer condition, especially into divisions and heart-breaking strifes. It was so in the case of this church at Corinth. Here everybody brought his own provision, and some ate to the full, and others had not enough; and they thought that they were observing "the Lord's supper."

22. *What? have ye not houses to eat and to drink in?*
There is your proper place if you want a meal. Go home, and eat and drink; do not come to the sanctuary for such a purpose: "Have ye not houses to eat and to drink in?"

22, 23. *Or despise ye the church of God, and shame them that have not? What shall I say to you? shall I praise you in this? I praise you not. For I have received of the Lord that which also I delivered unto you,*
He had received it by a special revelation. Poor Paul was brought in late, he was like one born out of due time. He had not been present in the upper room with Christ at the first famous breaking of bread; so the Lord came and gave him a special revelation concerning this sacred feast, so that, whenever he spoke or wrote to any of the churches about the Lord's supper, he could say, "I have received of the Lord that which also I delivered unto you."

23, 24. *That the Lord Jesus the same night in which he was betrayed took bread: and when he had given thanks, he brake it, and said, Take, eat: this is my body, which is broken for you: this do in remembrance of me.*
The Lord's supper is a simple service of remembrance. Nothing is said about an altar, or a priest, or a sacrifice. Our Lord took bread, gave thanks for it, brake it, and gave it to his disciples, saying, "Take, eat: this is my body which is broken for you: this do in remembrance of me." Mark that "*this* do"; it will not be right to do something else instead of this; and we must not do this for any other purpose than the one he mentions, "This do in remembrance of me." This command raises a previous question, "Do we know him?" We cannot remember Christ if we do not know him.

25, 26. *After the same manner also he took the cup, when he had supped, saying, This cup is the new testament in my blood: this do ye, as oft as ye drink it, in remembrance of me. For as often as ye eat this bread, and drink this cup, ye do shew the Lord's death till he come.*

> "By Christ redeemed, in Christ restored,
> We keep the memory adored,
> And show the death of our dear Lord,
> Until he come!

> "And thus that dark betrayal-night,
> With the last advent we unite;
> By one blest chain of loving rite
> Until he come!"

27. *Wherefore whosoever shall eat this bread, and drink this cup of the Lord, unworthily, shall be guilty of the body and blood of the Lord.*
If such a man has treated "this bread" and "this cup" with contempt, he has treated "the body and blood of the Lord" with contempt; it shall be so reckoned to him. Many have been troubled by this verse. They have said, "We are unworthy." You are; that is quite true; but the text does not say anything about your being unworthy. Paul uses an adverb, not an adjective. His words are, "Whosoever shall eat this bread, and drink this cup of the Lord, unworthily," that is, in an unfit way, to gain something by it, as men used to take what they called "the sacrament" to get into certain offices, or as some come to the communion-table for the sake of charitable gifts that are for the poor of the church; this is to eat and drink "unworthily." To come carelessly, to come contemptuously, to say, "I do

not care whether I am a Christian, or not; but I shall come to the communion," this is to eat and drink "unworthily." Notice the *ly ;* we are all unworthy of this sacred feast, and if unworthiness could shut us out, who would dare to be here ?

28. *But let a man examine himself,*

Let him look himself up and down, as a lawyer cross-questions a witness, as a man examines money to see whether it has the true ring of gold about it, or not : " Let a man examine himself."

28. *And so let him eat of that bread, and drink of that cup.*

Let him come as a true believer, as sincere ; if not perfect, yet true ; if not all he ought to be, yet in Christ ; if not all he wants to be, yet still on the way to it, by being in Christ, who is " the way, the truth, and the life."

29. *For he that eateth and drinketh unworthily, eateth and drinketh damnation to himself, not discerning the Lord's body.*

He does not see the meaning of the emblems of Christ's death. He degrades the symbol by making it take the place of the thing signified. He sees the bread, but not the body ; and he damnifies himself, condemns himself, by such eating. He is a loser rather than a gainer by eating and drinking unworthily.

30. *For this cause many are weak and sickly among you, and many sleep.*

Persons coming to the Lord's table in an improper spirit are very apt to come under God's discipline; some will be taken ill; and some will die. This discipline is being carried on in every true church of God. God's providence will work in this way if many treat the table of the Lord as the Corinthians did, acting as if it were a common place for eating and drinking. Many of them were weak and sickly, and many died.

31. *For if we would judge ourselves, we should not be judged.*

If we are God's people, we shall be judged by him here for our wrongdoing. We shall not be like the world that is left to the day of judgment ; but we shall be judged now. God will visit with temporal judgments those of his children who sin against him.

32. *But when we are judged, we are chastened of the Lord, that we should not be condemned with the world.*

You know that a man will see a great deal that is wrong in children in the street, and say nothing about it ; but if it is his own boy who is up to mischief, he will give him a sweet taste of the rod. So, if you belong to God, you cannot sin deeply without having a present judgment, a present discipline ; and you ought to be thankful for it, painful though it may seem to be for the time, for " when we are judged, we are chastened of the Lord, that we should not be condemned with the world."

33. *Wherefore, my brethren, when ye come together to eat, tarry one for another.*

How gently Paul talks to these Corinthians ! They deserve to be scolded ; but he is very tender with them. He says, " If you must come together in this way, at least have the good manners to stop for one another ; and if you do come to the communion of the Lord, treat it with that respect and reverence which it deserves.

34. *And if any man hunger, let him eat at home ; that ye come not together unto condemnation. And the rest will I set in order when I come.*

May we to-night keep this feast in due order under the power of the Holy Spirit, and may we find a blessing in it to God's praise ! Amen.

HYMNS FROM "OUR OWN HYMN BOOK"—938, 947.

Metropolitan Tabernacle Pulpit.

IMPOTENCE AND OMNIPOTENCE.

A Sermon

INTENDED FOR READING ON LORD'S-DAY, AUGUST 14TH, 1892,

DELIVERED BY

C. H. SPURGEON,

AT THE METROPOLITAN TABERNACLE, NEWINGTON,

On Lord's-day Evening, February 16*th*, 1890.

"And a certain man was there, which had an infirmity thirty and eight years. When Jesus saw him lie, and knew that he had been now a long time in that case, he saith unto him, Wilt thou be made whole? The impotent man answered him, Sir, I have no man, when the water is troubled, to put me into the pool: but while I am coming, another steppeth down before me. Jesus saith unto him, Rise, take up thy bed, and walk. And immediately the man was made whole, and took up his bed, and walked."
—John v. 5—9.

This man had been lying, with many others, round the pool, hoping that it would be stirred by the angel, and that he might be put into the water first, and so might be healed. There he waited long, and waited in vain. Why did he wait? Because Jesus was not there. Where Jesus is not, you must wait. If it is only an angel and a pool, you must wait; and one may get a blessing, and many may get no blessing. But when Jesus came, there was no waiting. He walked in among the crowd of sick folk, spied out this man, bade him take up his mattress and walk home, and he was healed at once.

Now, I commend this man for waiting; I admire him for his patience and his perseverance; but I beg you not to make his case your own. He waited, for Jesus was not there. You may not wait, you must not wait; for Jesus is here. There was necessity for him to wait. As I have told you, there was an angel and a pool, and nothing more; but where Christ is, there should be no waiting. Any soul that believes in Christ to-night will be saved to-night. Any soul that looks to Christ to-night shall be saved, even though he looks from the ends of the earth. Thou mayest look now; nay, thou art commanded so to do. "Behold, now is the accepted time; behold, now is the day of salvation." "Harden not your hearts, as in the provocation." There, in that pew, or in yonder aisles, if you turn your eye by faith to Jesus, the Living One on the throne of the Highest, you shall obtain immediate cure. Waiting is all very well at the pool of Bethesda; but waiting at the pool of ordinances, as I have heard some say, is not according to the Scriptures. I read nothing about waiting there; but

No. 2,269.

I do read this, "Believe on the Lord Jesus Christ, and thou shalt be saved."

However, for the help of some who have waited till they are weary, who have persevered in the use of the means till they are becoming desponding and disappointed, let us look at this case of the impotent man at Bethesda.

I. We notice about it, first, that THE SAVIOUR KNEW THE CASE.

I only mention that, in order to say that the Saviour knows your case. *Jesus saw him lie there.* There were a great many objects for the Saviour's eye to rest upon; but he fixed his gaze upon this man, long bed-ridden, thirty-eight years impotent. Even so, Jesus knows all about your case. He sees you lie just where you are to-night, impotent, without hope, without light, without faith. He sees you; I want you to feel this to be true. He singles you out amidst this throng, wherever you sit, and his eye is scanning you from head to foot; nay, he looks within as well as without, and reads all that is in your heart.

Concerning the man at the pool, *Jesus knew that he had been a long time in that case.* He knows the years that you have been waiting. You remember being carried to the house of God by your mother. You recollect, as a boy, listening to sermons that seemed to startle you; and you went home to your little bedroom, and cried to God for mercy; but you forgot your impressions. They were like the morning mist, that vanishes in the rising sun. You came to London; you grew up to be a man; you became careless about divine things; you shook off all your early impressions. Still, you went to hear the Word preached, and oftentimes you half hoped that you might get a blessing. You heard the Word; but faith was not mixed with what you heard, so you missed the blessing. Yet still, you always had a wish that it should come to you. You never could despise godly people, or the things of Christ. You could not get them for yourself; at least, you thought you could not; but you always had some lingering wish that you were numbered with the people of God. Now, the Lord Jesus knows all about that, and the many years in which you have been waiting as a hearer; but a hearer only, and not a doer of the Word; impressed at times, but doing violence to your better feelings, and going back to a careless life. My Lord knows all about you. I cannot pick you out in this congregation; but remember, while I am preaching to-night, miracles will be wrought; processes which will change the very nature of men are going on within this house; for Christ is being preached, and his gospel is being set forth, and this is not done, with prayerful earnestness, in vain. God will bless it; he is going to bless somebody to-night. Who that somebody may be, or how many hundred somebodies there will be, I cannot guess; but he will bless his own Word, and why should he not bless you? He sees just who you are, and where you are, and what you are.

In addition to this, *our Lord knew all this poor man's disappointments.* Many times, when he had striven to get first to the water's edge, and did think that he should be able to take the happy plunge, in went some one else before him, and his hopes were gone. Another came up out of the water healed; and then, with a heavy sigh, he fell back upon his couch, and felt that it might be a long time before the angel stirred the water again, and even then he might be disappointed again. He recollected the many times when he had lost all hope; and there he lay almost in despair. Now I think I hear some one here to-night saying, "My brother found the Lord. My friend, who came with me here, found the Lord. I have lived to see my mother die in sure and certain hope of glory. I have friends who have come to Christ, but I am still living without him. When there were special services, I hoped that I might have been specially blessed. I have been to prayer-meetings, I have read my Bible in secret, and I have sometimes hoped—it was but a little hope, but still I hoped—'May be, one of these days, I may be healed.'" Yes, dear friend, and my Lord knows all about that, and he sympathizes in all the grief you feel to-night, and he hears those unspoken wishes of yours, and he knows your longing that you may be healed.

II. Now, secondly, THE SAVIOUR AROUSED THE MAN'S DESIRES. He said to him, "Wilt thou be made whole?" There he lay. I am not going to explain that lying at the pool, but just to apply it to you who are here in a similar condition.

Beware of forgetting why you are here. Beware of coming to the house of God, and not knowing why you come. I have said that, years ago, you went to places of worship in the hope of finding salvation. Well, you have kept on coming, and you have not found it; but do you now look for it? Have you not fallen into the habit of sitting and listening to sermons, and prayers, and so on, without feeling that you came for anything special for yourself? You come and you go, merely that you may attend a place of worship; that is all. The Saviour would not let the impotent man lie there satisfied because he was by the pool. No, no. He said to him, "Why are you here? Have you not some desire? Do you not want to be made whole?" My dear hearer, I wish that you were able to say "Yes" to this question. Have you come here to-night that your sin may be forgiven, that your soul may be renewed by divine grace, that you may meet with Christ? If so, I want to keep you to that point, and not to let you come, and take a sitting here, and come, and come, and come, and come, and be just like the door on its hinges out there, which turns in and turns out again, and is not a bit the better for it. Oh, do not get into mere religious habits! Ritualistic habits they will be to you, simple as the ritual will be. You come, and you go, and you are satisfied. This will never do. Christ arouses your desire as he says, "Wilt thou be made whole?"

Also, *avoid a despairing indifference.* I remember two brothers and a sister, who heard me preach for a considerable time, and they were in great distress of soul; but, at the same time, they had a notion that they could not believe in Christ, and that they must wait, I hardly know what for; and they did wait till they grew quite old. I did not know better people morally, or better hearers so far as interest in what they heard was concerned; but they never seemed to get any farther. At last they got into this state; they seemed to feel as though, if it was to be, it would be; and if it was not to be, it would not be; and that all that they could do was just to sit still, and be quiet and patient.

Patient under the apprehension of being lost for ever? Why, I do not expect the man in the condemned cell to be happy and patient when he hears them putting up his gallows! He must be concerned; he must be uneasy. I did my best to make these friends uneasy; but I confess that I fear my efforts were attended with very small results. The Saviour said to this man, "Wilt thou be made whole? You seem to be in such a state of indifference that you do not care whether you are made whole or not." No worse condition than that can be found; it is so hard to deal with. God save you from a sullen indifference, in which you leave yourselves to drift to destruction at the will of some unknown fate!

I pray you to *remember that it is yours to will,* for Christ said to this man, "Wilt thou be made whole? Thou canst not make thyself whole, but thou canst will and wish to be made whole." God's Holy Spirit has given to many of you to will and to do according to his good pleasure. You will never be saved against your will; God drags nobody to heaven by the ears. There must be in you a willing mind consenting to the work of his sovereign grace; and if it be there, I want you to exercise it to-night, as Christ wished this man to exercise it: "Wilt thou be made whole? Hast thou any wish that way, any desire or longing for healing?" I want to stir this fire, and make it burn; and if there be only a spark of desire, I would breathe upon it, and pray the Holy Spirit to breathe upon it to make it into a great flame. Paul said, "To will is present with me; but how to perform that which is good, I find not." I believe that there are some here who have the will to be saved; God be thanked for that!

"Wilt thou be made whole?" I think that the Saviour put this question for another reason, which I will turn into an exhortation. *Forego all prescribing as to how you are to be saved.* The question is not, "Wilt thou be put into that pool?" but, "Wilt thou be made whole?" The question is not, "Wilt thou take this medicine? Wilt thou that I should do this or that to thee?" but, "Wilt thou be made whole?" Have you come to this, that you are willing to be saved in God's way, in Christ's way? One says, "I want to have a dream." Dear soul, do not want any dreams; they are only dreams. Another says, "I want to see a vision." My dear friend, there is nothing in the plan of salvation about seeing visions. "I want to hear a voice," says one. Well, hear my voice, then, and may God the Holy Ghost make you to hear the voice of his Word through me! "But I want"—oh! yes, you want, you know not what you want, like many a silly child that has its fads, and fancies, and whims, and wishes. Oh, that all were willing to be saved by the simple plan of believe and live! If this is God's way, who art thou that he should make a new way for thee? When I had put the way of salvation before a friend, some time ago, she turned to me, and said, "Oh, sir, do pray for me!" "No," I said, "I will not pray for you." "Oh! but," said she, "how can you say that?" I replied, "I set before you Christ crucified, and I beg you to believe in him. If you will not believe in him, you will be lost; and I shall not pray God to make any different way of salvation for you. You deserve to be lost if you will not believe in Christ." I put it just so to her, and when she afterwards said,

" Oh, I see it now! I do look to Christ, and trust him," I said, " Now I will pray for you; now we can pray together, and sing together, if need be." But, dear friends, do not set up your own notion about how you ought to be converted. Can you find any two people who were converted in the same way? God does not make converts as men make steel pens, a gross in a box all alike. Nay, nay; but in each case there is a living man created, and every living man, every living animal, every living plant, is somewhat different from every other of its kind; and you must not look for uniformity in the work of regeneration. "Wilt thou be made whole?" Come, dost thou desire the pardon of sin? Dost thou long for a new heart and a right spirit? If so, leave off disputing as to how thou art to get them, and do what Christ tells thee to do.

"Wilt thou be made whole?" It is as if the Saviour said, "*Be more than ever in earnest now.* I know that you will to be made whole; well, now, will it more to-night than you have ever willed it before." Let the will which you have be exercised; put it forth. You are in earnest to be saved; be more in earnest to-night. You do desire to find Christ; well, desire to find Christ more to-night than ever you did in your life. You have come to an important crisis of your life; you may be at the point of death; who knows? How many have been suddenly struck down of late! If you would be made whole, I would that you might be made whole to-night. I pray that you may feel something pressing you, something that makes you end your long delay, something that makes you feel, "I have no more time to waste; I cannot afford to loiter; I must be saved to-night; I must hear the distinct ticking of God's great clock, that stands in the hall of grace, and always says, '*Now; now; now; now; now;*' and never utters any other sound." Oh, may the Lord make it to be so, by his own free grace!

Thus, you see, the Saviour aroused the desires of the man at the pool. First, he knew his case; and next, he aroused his desires.

III. Now, thirdly, THE SAVIOUR HEARD THE MAN'S PLAINT. This is what he said, " Sir, I have no man, when the water is troubled, to put me into the pool: but while I am coming, another steppeth down before me."

Some of these people had kind friends, who took turns at watching day and night, and the moment that the water was stirred, they took up their patient, and plunged him in. This man had lost all his friends; thirty-eight years of illness had worn them all out; and he said, " I have no man to put me into the pool; how can I get into the water?" So there are many in this case; they want help. While I have been at Menton, I have had the joy of leading a number of friends to Christ. When I had to leave them, and come back to London, one and another of them said to me, "What can we do without you, sir? We shall have nobody to lead us in the right way now; no one to instruct us, no one to meet our objections, nobody to solve our doubts, nobody to whom we can tell the anxieties of our hearts."

No doubt some of you would talk in the same fashion, and I must admit that *the lack of a helper is serious.* It is a great deprivation to have no man to help you in these things. Sometimes, if a friend will come up after the sermon, and just say a kindly word, it will do more good than the sermon itself. Many a poor troubled one, who has been a long time in prison, might have been sooner released if only some kind friend had reminded the brother of a divine promise which, like a key, would have opened the prison door. I agree with you that there is a great help in having an earnest Christian friend to lift you over a difficulty; to bear you down to the water's edge to which you cannot go by yourself, and to put you into the pool. It is a great loss, certainly, if you have no such friend; and I am very sorry for you. You live in a village where there is nobody to speak to you about spiritual matters, or you attend a ministry that does not feed you. You have nobody to comfort you. There are not many, after all, who can really help sinners in coming to Christ. Some who try to do so are a great deal too wise, and others are too hard-hearted. It wants special training in the school of grace if anyone is to learn to sympathize with others so as to be able really to help them. I can suppose that one here is saying, "I have no mother to speak to; I have no Christian friend in the family; I have no one to whom I can go for help; and that is why I stick fast where I am."

Well, a helper is very valuable; but I want to say that *a helper may not be so valuable as you think.* I have known some who have had plenty of Christian helpers while they were seeking the Lord; but none of them were able really to help them. If you trust in earthly helpers, and think them essential, God will not bless their efforts, and they will be of no use to you. I am afraid that many a seeker has had to say, even to good and earnest Christians, what Job said to his friends, "Miserable comforters are ye all." After all, how can a man help you much in your soul's affairs? No man can give you faith, or give you pardon; no man can give you spiritual life, or even spiritual light. Though you have no man to help you, remember that you can make too much of men, and you can trust too much in Christian helpers. I beg you to recollect that. I am afraid that there are some professors who have been helped a little too much. They heard a sermon, and were really impressed by it, and somebody was foolish enough to say to them, "That is conversion." It never was conversion at all. The friend further said, "Now, come forward, and make a profession." So they came forward, and made a profession of what they never had. Then the friend said, "Now, come to such a meeting; come and join the church. Come on;" and thus they were led, and led, and led, never having any real internal life, or spiritual energy given them from on high. They are just like children in go-carts, who are unable to walk alone. God save you from a religion that depends upon other people! There are some who have a kind of lean-to religion, resting on somebody else; when the support is taken away, what becomes of the lean-to? The good old lady who helped you for so many years dies; where is your religion then? The minister used to keep you going; you were like a whipping-top, and he like the whip that kept you spinning; when he is gone, where are you? Do not have a religion of that kind, I entreat you. Though a helper is very useful, remember that, under certain conditions, even a Christian helper may be a hinderer.

Now, my dear hearer, this is the point I have come to; you have to deal with Jesus to-night, and *dealing with Jesus, you need "no man."* You have not to deal with pools and angels; you have to deal with the Lord Jesus himself. Suppose that there is no man to help you, do you want any man when Jesus is here? The man was wanted to put you into the pool; he is not wanted to introduce you to Christ; you may speak to him yourself; you may sue out mercy for yourself; you may confess your sin yourself. You want no priest; you want a Mediator between your soul and God; but you do not want any mediator between your soul and Jesus. You may come to him where you are, and as you are. Come to him now; tell him your case; plead with him for mercy. He does not want my help; he does not want the help of the Archbishop of Canterbury; he does not want the help of anybody. He alone can meet your case. Just put your case into his hand; and then, if you have no man to be your helper, you need not lie down and fret about it; for he is able to save them to the uttermost that come unto God by him.

Now this is all very plain talk; but we want plain talk nowadays. I feel as if I had not preached on Sunday, unless I had tried to bring men to Christ. There are many high and sublime doctrines that I would like to speak of, and many deep and rapturous experiences that I would like to describe; yet I feel that I must often leave these things, and keep to the much more commonplace, but much more useful matter of persuading men, in Christ's stead, that they look away from man, and away from ordinances, and away from self, and deal with Jesus himself distinctly and directly; for then there will be no need of man, and certainly there will be no need of delay.

IV. This is my closing point. THE SAVIOUR MET THE MAN'S CASE ENTIRELY.

This impotent man has no man to help him; Christ can help him without any man. This man cannot move except with great pain. He has to crawl to the water's edge; but he need not crawl there, he need not move an inch. *The power to heal that man was in the Christ who stood there*, commissioned of God to save sinners, and to help the helpless. Please to recollect that the power that saves, and all of it, is not in the saved man, but in the Christ who saves. I take leave to contradict those who say that salvation is an evolution. All that ever can be evolved out of the sinful heart of man is sin, and nothing else. Salvation is the free gift of God, by Jesus Christ, and the work of it is supernatural. It is done by the Lord himself, and he has power to do it, however weak, nay, however dead in sin, the sinner may be. As a living child of God, I can say to-night, that,—

"On a life I did not live,
On a death I did not die,
I stake my whole eternity."

You who would be saved must do the same; you must look right out of self to him whom God has exalted to be a Prince and a Saviour to the sons of men. The Christ met that man's case, for he was able to do anything for him that he required. He meets your case, my dear hearer, for he can do anything for you that is wanted. Between here and heaven's gate, there shall never be anything required which he cannot give, or any help needed which he is not prepared to render, for he has all power in heaven and in earth.

Next, *the Lord can do more for you than you ask of him.* This poor man never asked anything of Christ, except by his looks, and by his lying there at the pool. If you feel to-night as if you could not pray, if you have needs that you cannot describe, if there is something wanted, and you do not know what it is, Christ can give it to you. You shall know what it is that you want when you get it; but perhaps now, in his mercy, he does not let you know all your needs. But here is the point, he "is able to do exceeding abundantly above all that we ask or think." May he do it in you to-night! Take comfort from the cure of the impotent man, cherish hope, and say, "Why should he not also heal me?"

Now the way in which Christ worked was very singular. *He worked by a command.* It is not a way that you and I would have selected; nor a way of which some nominal Christians approve. He said to this man, "Rise." He could not rise. "Take up thy bed." He could not take up his bed; he had been thirty-eight years unable to get off his bed. "Take up thy bed, and walk." Walk? He could not walk. I have heard some objectors say, "That preacher says to people, 'Believe.' They cannot believe. He bids them 'Repent.' They cannot repent." Ah! well, our Lord is our example; and he said to this man, who could not rise, and could not take up his bed, and could not walk, "Rise, take up thy bed, and walk." That was his way of exercising his divine power; and that is the way in which Christ saves men to-day. He gives us faith enough to say, "Ye dry bones, hear the Word of the Lord!" They cannot hear. "Thus saith the Lord, Ye dry bones, live!" They cannot live; but they do hear, and they do live; and while we are acting by faith, delivering a command which looks, upon the surface of it, to be absurd and unreasonable, the work of Christ is done by that command. Did he not say of old in the darkness, "Let there be light"? To what spake the Lord that word of power? To darkness, and to nothingness. "And there was light." Now, he speaks to the sinner, and he says, "Believe, and live." He believes, and he lives. God wants those of his messengers, who have the faith to give his command, to let the sinner know that he has not the strength to obey, that he is morally lost and ruined, and yet to say, in the name of the eternal God, "Thus saith the Lord, Rise, take up thy bed, and walk. Believe, repent, be converted, and be baptized, every one of you, in the name of the Lord Jesus Christ." This is the way in which Christ's power goes forth to the sons of men. He said to the man with the withered hand, "Stretch forth thine hand," and he did so; and he says to the dead, "Come forth," and they do come forth. His commandings are attended with enablings; and where his commands are faithfully preached, his power goes with them, and men are saved.

I close with this observation. *In obedience, power was given.* The man did not stop and wrangle with Christ, and say, "Rise? What dost thou mean? Thou lookest like a friend; but dost thou come here to make sport of me? Rise? Thirty and eight years have I been lying here, and thou sayest, 'Rise.' Dost thou think that there has ever been a minute in those eight and thirty years in which I would not have gladly risen if I could have done so, and yet thou sayest, 'Rise,' and thou sayest, 'Take up thy bed. Shoulder the rug on which thou liest.' How can I do so? It is thirty and eight years since I could lift a pound weight, and thou bidst me shoulder this mat on which I lie. Dost thou make me a theme of jest? And walk? Thou sayest, 'Walk.' Walk? Hear me, ye sick ones around me, he tells me to walk! I can scarcely lift even a finger, yet he bids me walk!" Thus he might have argued the matter out, and it would have been a very logical piece of argument, and the Saviour would have stood convicted of having spoken empty words.

Instead of speaking thus, no sooner did Christ say to him, "Rise," than he willed to rise; and as he willed to rise, he moved to rise, and rise he did, to his own astonishment. He rose, and stooping down, rolled up his mattress, all the while filled with wonder, every part of his body singing as he rolled it up, and put it on his shoulder with alacrity. To his surprise, he found that the joints of his feet and legs could move, and he walked right away with his mattress on his shoulder; and the miracle was complete. Stop, man, stop! Come here! Now, had you the strength to do this of yourself? "No, not I. I lay there eight and thirty years; I had no strength till that word 'Rise,' came to me." "But did you do it?" "Oh! yes, you see that I did it. I rose; I folded up the mattress; and I walked away." "But you were under some kind of compulsion, that made you move your legs and your hands, were you not?" "Oh! no; I did it freely, cheerfully, gladly. Compel me to do it? My dear sir, I clap my hands for joy to think that I could do it. I do not want to go back to that old mat, and lie there again; not I." "Then what did you do?" "Well, I scarcely know what I did. I believed him, and I did what he told me; and a strange, mysterious power came over me; that is the whole story." "Now explain it; tell these people all about it." "Oh! no," says the man, "I know that it is so; but I cannot explain it. One thing I know, whereas I was a cripple, now I can walk; whereas I was impotent, now I can carry my bed; whereas I was lying there, now I can stand upright."

I cannot explain salvation to you to-night, or how it takes place; but I remember when I sat in the pew as despairing a sinner as ever lived. I heard the preacher say, "Look unto Christ, and live." He seemed to say to me, "Look! Look! Look! Look!" and I did look, and I lived. That moment, the burden of my sin was gone; I was crippled with unbelief no longer; I went home a sinner saved by grace, to live to praise the Lord; and—

"E'er since by faith I saw the stream
His flowing wounds supply,
Redeeming love has been my theme,
And shall be till I die."

I am impressed that I am going to have ever so many to-night who will just obey the gospel command, "Believe, and live. Believe in the Lord Jesus Christ, and thou shalt be saved." Oh, do it! Do it now; and unto God be glory, and to thyself be peace and happiness for ever! Amen and Amen.

Exposition by C. H. Spurgeon.

JOHN V. 1—23.

Verse 1. *After this there was a feast of the Jews; and Jesus went up to Jerusalem.*

For he had respect to the Law. As long as the Law lasted, Christ observed it. Oh, that we were as careful to obey the rules of the Gospel as our Lord was to observe the ritual of the Law! Moreover, he went up to Jerusalem because he had an opportunity of addressing great numbers of people there. While I have been resting at Menton, I have been very glad to be of service to a few friends who were either seeking the Saviour, or needing some guidance in their spiritual life; but I cannot tell you how happy I am to be once more in the Tabernacle, preaching to the great congregation. Fishermen like to cast their nets where there are plenty of fish; and fishers of men delight to be where there are many men who may be enclosed in the gospel net. "After this there was a feast of the Jews; and Jesus went up to Jerusalem."

2. *Now there is at Jerusalem by the sheep market a pool, which is called in the Hebrew tongue Bethesda, having five porches.*

This pool of Bethesda was rightly called "the house of mercy"; but it might have been just as truly named "the house of misery"; for its "five porches" were the abode of many who were in misery, and who needed mercy.

3. *In these lay a great multitude of impotent folk,*

Invalid persons, diseased, and scarcely able to move.

3. *Of blind, halt, withered, waiting for the moving of the water.*

What a sight for the Great Physician to look upon! The whole world must have been to him like one huge hospital, full of "impotent folk, blind, halt, withered." Wherever he went, he was surrounded by the sick, and sad, and suffering, those who were afflicted physically, mentally, and spiritually. But there was a special reason for the gathering together of so many sufferers at the pool of Bethesda.

4. *For an angel went down at a certain season into the pool, and troubled the water: whosoever then first after the troubling of the water stepped in was made whole of whatsoever disease he had.*

It was the last remnant of miracle. Such things were common enough in Judea in her better days; but now the times of the prophets had ceased, and the day of miracles was almost over. Here, at Bethesda, were just a few relics and remnants of the good old days. Only one was cured, he that stepped into the pool first after the angel had troubled the water. It was but a scanty power that was left to the troubled water; but it was quite enough, if only one in a thousand was healed, to bring a crowd of people to wait around the pool. If only one person in a year were saved, I should not wonder if you thronged the place to hear the gospel that saved him; but your privilege is much greater. Here all who come, if they will hear and believe, shall find healing. It is not the first only, but even unto the last who shall step into the pool, that shall be healed.

5. *And a certain man was there, which had an infirmity thirty and eight years.*

That was a great proportion of the man's life. If he was a full-grown man when he was attacked with the infirmity, he had now become old and grey. What a long time to be afflicted, thirty and eight years! Have we not with us at this time some who have been afflicted with the soul-sickness of sin more than thirty and eight years?

6. *When Jesus saw him lie,*

The Great Physician fixed his eye on him, for his was an extraordinary case. Probably he was known and talked of as the man who had been paralyzed eight and thirty years. Note that it does not say, "When the man saw Jesus," but "when Jesus saw him." He did not know Jesus; possibly he had not even heard of his healing power and compassionate love. He was not seeking Jesus; but Jesus was seeking him. It was so with many of us; and therefore we sing,—

> "Jesus sought me when a stranger,
> Wandering from the fold of God;
> He, to rescue me from danger,
> Interposed his precious blood."

When Jesus saw the impotent man,—

6. *And knew that he had been now a long time in that case,*

And a long time in that place, too,—

6. *He saith unto him, Wilt thou be made whole?*

That must have seemed a strange question. What was he there for, if not to be made whole? But I will show you, by-and-by, that there was wisdom in the question of Jesus. It was no idle curiosity that moved him to enquire of the man whether he was willing to be made whole.

7. *The impotent man answered him, Sir, I have no man, when the water is troubled, to put me into the pool: but while I am coming,*

Shuffling along, as best I may, to the water's edge,—

7. *Another steppeth down before me.*

Then, of course, the curative miracle is wrought, and the curative power of the water is gone until another season, when the angel troubles it again.

8, 9. *Jesus saith unto him, Rise, take up thy bed, and walk. And immediately the man was made whole, and took up his bed and walked: and on the same day was the sabbath.*

This is our Sabbath. Oh, that we might have the same miracle wrought here to-night, upon many spiritually impotent folk!

10, 11. *The Jews therefore said unto him that was cured, It is the sabbath day: it is not lawful for thee to carry thy bed. He answered them,*

And he *did* answer them, too. It was a crushing answer.

11. *He that made me whole, the same said unto me, Take up thy bed, and walk.*

That was his warrant. None but God could have made him whole. God can set aside any of his laws if he pleases; at any rate, whatever he commands, must be right.

12. *Then asked they him, What man is that which said unto thee, Take up thy bed, and walk?*

They asked, "What *man*" had given this command. Why, if it had been a mere man who had said it, the impotent man could not either have taken up his bed, or have walked!

13. *And he that was healed wist not who it was: for Jesus had conveyed himself away, a multitude being in that place.*

He never sought notoriety; but avoided popular demonstrations in his favour. The man who had been healed had exercised faith in Jesus, but he knew very little about him. A certain something in the air and mien of Christ had won his faith; but he did not know his name, or who he was. How small may be your knowledge, and yet you may be saved by true faith!

14. *Afterward Jesus findeth him in the temple, and said unto him, Behold, thou art made whole: sin no more, lest a worse thing come unto thee.*

Probably, this man's illness had been caused by sin. Christ bids him henceforth keep clear of sin, lest a worse calamity should come upon him.

15. *The man departed, and told the Jews that it was Jesus, which had made him whole.*

Full of joy, full of delight, he must tell out the name of him who had cured him, as grateful patients like to sound the praises of their physician when he has been the means of healing them.

16. *And therefore did the Jews persecute Jesus, and sought to slay him, because he had done these things on the sabbath day.*

This was a mere pretence, an idle excuse for their enmity. They not only hated Christ; but they must besmear him with their calumnies, and make him out to be an evil-doer although he was goodness itself.

17. *But Jesus answered them, My Father worketh hitherto, and I work.*

The whole work of nature is continued on Sabbath-days as well as other days. Stars shine through the Sabbath-night, and the sun rises and sets on the Lord's-day as on all the days of the week. God's work continues. "My Father worketh," saith Christ, "and I work." "My work is my Father's work, and that goes on whatever the day may be."

18. *Therefore the Jews sought the more to kill him, because he not only had broken the sabbath, but said also that God was his Father, making himself equal with God.*

They did not understand him to preach Unitarianism; they understood him to proclaim his own true and proper Godhead, and he never contradicted them, for he was God.

19. *Then answered Jesus and said unto them, Verily, verily, I say unto you, The Son can do nothing of himself, but what he seeth the Father do: for what things soever he doeth, these also doeth the Son likewise.*

Christ's work runs parallel with that of the Father. The Father and the Son ever work in perfect harmony with one another.

20—22. *For the Father loveth the Son, and sheweth him all things that himself doeth: and he will shew him greater works than these, that ye may marvel. For as the Father raiseth up the dead, and quickeneth them; even so the Son quickeneth whom he will. For the Father judgeth no man, but hath committed all judgment unto the Son:*

The Son, as well as the Father, is the Quickener of the dead. The Son is also the Judge of all men.

23. *That all men should honour the Son, even as they honour the Father. He that honoureth not the Son honoureth not the Father which hath sent him.*

As the universal Judge, the Lord Jesus is to be honoured by all men, "even as they honour the Father." Whatever others may do, or not do, we will honour the Father, we will honour the Son, and we will honour the Holy Spirit, three in one and one in three, the one God of Israel, for ever and ever.

Hymns from "Our Own Hymn Book"—552, 556, 557.

Metropolitan Tabernacle Pulpit.

TWO "I WILLS" IN ISAIAH XLI.

A Sermon

INTENDED FOR READING ON LORD'S-DAY, AUGUST 21ST, 1892,

DELIVERED BY

C. H. SPURGEON,

AT THE METROPOLITAN TABERNACLE, NEWINGTON,

On Lord's-day Evening, March 16th, 1890.

"I will open rivers in high places, and fountains in the midst of the valleys: I will make the wilderness a pool of water, and the dry land springs of water."—Isaiah xli. 18.

You notice that, in this verse, the Lord twice says, "I will"; and in that respect this verse is in harmony with the rest of the chapter. Will the children, when they are at home, find out how many times in this chapter God says, "I will," or "Thou shalt," which is to much the same effect?

How greatly I prize a portion of Scripture which is filled with God's shalls and wills! Everything he says is precious; but his "I wills" are peculiarly precious. There are the "I wills" of the Psalms, a long list of them; and the "I wills" of Christ, a goodly company. When we come to the "I wills" of God, then we get among the precious things, the deep things, the things which minister comfort and strength to the people of God.

We sometimes say "I will"; but it is in a feeble fashion compared with the way in which God says it. People say, "'Must' is for the king." So, "I will," is for the King of kings. It is his prerogative to will. It is his sovereign right to say, "I will." When we get a chapter like the one that we have been reading, which is full of the "I wills" of God, it is worth while to pause for a few moments, and just think of what Jehovah's "I will," must mean.

It is an "I will," *uttered with deliberation.* James said, "Known unto God are all his works from the beginning of the world." We say, "I will," in a hurry; and then we take time to repent of it. We are under excitement, persuasion, or compulsion, and we say, "I will," and we are very sorry afterwards, and perhaps we are so unfaithful as not to keep our word; but God never speaks under compulsion; he is almighty. God never speaks in a hurry; he has infinite leisure. God never speaks under excitement or persuasion; that were

No. 2,270.

not like a God. His purpose is of old, and his decree is from everlasting; and the "I will," which is the mouth of the decree, is a word that is spoken with wisdom and prudence. Now, when a man speaks a thing prudently and wisely, you believe that he will carry it out, if he can. You may have much more confidence with regard to what the Lord says, for he has not spoken without due deliberation; therefore, whenever God says, "I will," you may be sure that he will perform it.

Next, when God says, "I will," his resolution is *supported by omnipotence*. You say, "I will," but you cannot do what you have promised. Your will is good enough; but you fail because of lack of the means. You say, "I will, yes, I will;" but afterwards you have meekly to say, "I pray thee, take the will for the deed; for I find that I have overshot the mark. I have promised what I am unable to perform." Now, that can never happen with God. Hath he said, and shall he not do it? Is anything too hard for the Lord, especially anything which he has promised to perform? Come, then, dear friends, if God be omnipotent, and we know that he is, when he says, "I will," we dare not doubt it; for eternal power goes forth with the word of his wisdom; and it must, yea, it shall be done. Whatever doubts we might have had, if it were not God's "I will," vanish when we come to remember that all things are possible with him.

Furthermore, when God says, "I will," we should remember that it is *sealed with immutability*. We change, we are always changing. Made of dust and ashes, we are made of material that continues to change. Hence, we say to-day, "I will," and we mean it; but to-morrow we wish that we had never said, "I will," and the next day we say, "I will not." Ah! me, the suicides that have come through resting on the word of a man who was false, and proved a traitor to his friend. But God never changes; he is the same yesterday, to-day, and for ever. The thing that has gone out of his mouth shall never be reversed. When he once says, "I will," depend on this, he still says, "I will"; and till heaven and earth shall pass away, it will still be, "I will." He is too perfect to change; for being perfect, he cannot change. A changeable being either changes from a worse to a better, in which case he was not perfect before; or else he changes from a better to a worse, in which case he will not be perfect afterwards; but God being always perfect, is always the same, never withdrawing his word, or altering his purpose. Will you not, therefore, believe the unfailing word of an unchanging God? Can you not hang upon it; and when he says, "I will," depend on it that it shall be even so?

Once more, when God says, "I will," it will be *carried out in faithfulness*. He has fulfilled his threatenings. He never idly vapours, and utters words of terror without intending to carry them out; and when it comes to promises, rest you sure that God never flatters the ear, and then deceives the man. If he did not mean to do it, he would not say, "I will." Eternal faithfulness performs what eternal wisdom declares. Shall God lie? Is he a man as thou art? Will he deceive? Will he falsely promise, and then run from his word? That be far from him, and let it be far from us thus to blaspheme his name by such a thought. Come, then, child of God, thou who knowest him, if he has said, "I will help thee," he will help thee. If he says, "I will strengthen thee," he will strengthen thee. Believe God, without the trace of doubt; and "be of good courage, and he shall strengthen your heart, all ye that hope in the Lord."

Now, all this is meant to introduce my text, with its two glorious "I wills." Let us try and get something out of them. The Lord says, "I will open rivers in high places, and fountains in the midst of the valleys: I will make the wilderness a pool of water, and the dry land springs of water."

I. I propose to apply the text as a sort of general promise to many things; and, first, to apply it to THE TRIALS OF SAINTS.

Consider, first, *their temporal trials.* God's people may be hungry and thirsty; and their anxiety may be great. Your cupboard may be bare; the flocks may be cut off from the fold, and there may be no herd in the stall; but God can feed you. Though you seek water, and there is none, he can open rivers in high places, and fountains in the midst of the valleys. Do not distrust the God of providence. Many of his children have been brought to their last loaf, and yet they have not been starved. Remember her who had nothing left but a little meal and a little oil, when the prophet came to her, and yet the barrel of meal wasted not, neither did the cruse of oil fail. Remember him who sat by the brook Cherith, and the ravens brought him bread and meat in the morning, and bread and meat in the evening. Perhaps no miracle will be wrought for you; possibly God will feed you without a miracle; and so long as it is done, you will equally praise him, whether the supply be providential or miraculous. Plead these promises: "Trust in the Lord, and do good; so shalt thou dwell in the land, and verily thou shalt be fed." "He shall dwell on high: his place of defence shall be the munitions of rocks: bread shall be given him; his waters shall be sure." What though there is nothing at present, perhaps by to-morrow morning the Lord may have opened rivers in high places, and fountains in the midst of the valleys.

Certainly my text is true in *the spiritual experience of believers.* Do you know what it is, sometimes, when spiritual things are at a very low ebb, when you cannot find any joy, and scarcely any hope, when you look into your own heart, and all seems as dry as the earth is after a long autumn drought? You have no power, no strength, scarcely any desire. You sit down, and say, "I am afraid that I am no child of God; I am given up; I am spiritually dead." Yet have you never known, within an hour, the great water-floods to be let loose, and your soul to be full of feeling, full of faith, hope, joy, love? The chariot-wheels were taken off, and the chariot dragged very heavily; but now, or ever you are aware, your soul has made you like the chariots of Amminadib. You are leaping, you are laughing, for very joy. The Lord has turned your captivity; and filled your mouth with laughter, and your tongue with singing; and done it all of a sudden, too. God can do strange things for his people, even wonderful things which they looked not for.

I was noticing that there are in our text four words relating to water. Everything had been dry before, and there was no water for the thirsty to drink. Now, here you have rivers, fountains, a pool, and springs of water. There is a difference in the four words. The first is, " rivers." "I will open rivers in high places." There shall come directly from God a rush of mighty grace, like the streams of flowing rivers. Your poor, dead, dry heart shall suddenly feel that the waters of life have come directly from the throne of God to you. There shall be " waters to swim in." You shall have abundance where before you had nothing.

The next word is "fountains", which may be rendered " wells." Now, wells are places to which people regularly go for water. They represent the means of grace. " With joy shall ye draw water out of the wells of salvation." Well, now, perhaps you have been to the means of grace, and yet obtained no comfort. You have not blamed the preacher; but you have blamed yourself very much. But, on a sudden, God appears, and opens wells in the midst of the valley. Now the service is all full of refreshment. Now are you glad, and you no more go home saying, "I thirsted, but I went to the house of the Lord in vain; for I received no comfort." See what God can do; he can make rivers of grace flow direct from his throne, and he can open wells in the customary use of the means of grace.

But then there is a third word, "I will make the wilderness a pool of water." Here you have the idea of overflowing abundance. God can give you so much joy that you will not know how to hold it all; you will have to let it be like a pool that overflows its banks. God can give you so much earnestness that you can hardly employ it all in the work that you have to do. He can give you so much nearness to himself, that your heart shall scarcely be able to contain your delight. God promises to make the wilderness "a pool of water." He does not give us just a drop of grace now and then; but he fills up the dry places till they become standing pools.

The fourth word is " springs." It seems to indicate a perpetual freshness. Where there was a long-continued drought, there shall come perpetual freshness; always something new—new thoughts of Christ, new delights in holy service, new prospects of the world to come, new communion with God. He can make the dry land " springs of water." He has promised to do so; trust his gracious word, and it shall be fulfilled in your experience even now.

I want God's people to use the text in this way, as God's promise for your temporals and for your spirituals. Oh! you that are in the wilderness, and find the sand dry and waterless, go you to God, and plead his promise. He has said, "I will," and he has said it twice over. Lay hold of an " I will," with each one of your hands; and come not away from the throne of grace till you have received an answer of peace to your petition, " Lord, do as thou hast said!"

II. Now, secondly, I am going to use the text in another way, not for God's people who are passing through trials, but as it may be applied to THE EXPERIENCE OF CONVERTS. God will for you, my dear hearers, who have been lately converted, open rivers in high places, and fountains in the midst of the valleys. He will make your wilderness a pool of water, and the dry land springs of water.

Who were these people to whom the Lord spoke? Well, they were *people who were poor and needy.* "When the poor and needy seek water." God will not do much for spiritually rich people; I mean you who say that you are rich in yourselves, and increased in goods, and have need of nothing; you who have all the grace that you want of your own making; you who trust in your own arm, and sacrifice to your own goodness. There is nothing for you in God. His grace is for the poor and needy. I think that I have some of them here to-night. They feel as if they had no right to be here; they almost wish that they could get under the seat, and hide away, they feel so very low, so broken down. It is for you, dear friends, that God will make rivers and open fountains.

When will he do it? When *they begin to seek him.* "When the poor and needy seek water." Can you expect God to bless you if you do not seek him? Your desires must be wide awake; you must be longing after God; you must cry in your heart, "I will return unto my God; I will seek mercy at his hands; I will plead with him that I may be his child." Then will the Lord begin to open fountains and rivers for you.

But the time is noted further still. It is not only when they begin to seek, but when *they begin silently to plead.* Notice the words, "When their tongue faileth for thirst, I the Lord will hear them." But they were not speaking. Yet the Lord says, " I will hear them." But they could not speak; their tongue failed them because of their suffering from thirst. Yet says the Lord, " I will hear them." A glib tongue is bad at praying. When a man prays in his heart, he is often like Moses, slow of speech. A sinner under a sense of sin is scarcely able to speak a word. Frost of the mouth, but thaw of the soul, this is what we want. Their tongue failed them; but their heart was speaking. We know that it was; for God says, "I the Lord will hear them." "I cannot pray," says one. I am glad that you cannot. God will hear you now that your tongue fails you. You used to go upstairs, and pray for a quarter of an hour, perhaps, such prayer as it was; but now, when you kneel at your bedside, there is nothing but a broken groan or two, and a tear. God will hear you now. When your tongue fails, your heart begins to pray, and God hears you. "The sacrifices of God are a broken spirit: a broken and a contrite heart, O God, thou wilt not despise."

But the time mentioned is more sorrowful still; *these people were in abject distress.* It is added, "When the poor and needy seek water, and there is none." "My day of grace is past," says one. I wonder whoever told you that lie. As long as you live, your day of grace is not past; do not believe any such thing, for—

> "While the lamp holds out to burn,
> The vilest sinner may return."

"Ah, well!" says one, "I have gone to look for mercy, and there is none." So you think. Now is *the time for divine interposition.* When you seek water, and find none, God will open rivers for you. You remember how Elijah's servant went up to the top of Carmel, and looked toward the sea, and he came back to the prophet, and said,

"There is nothing." But Elijah said, "Go again seven times." "And it came to pass at the seventh time, that he said, Behold, there ariseth a little cloud out of the sea, like a man's hand." When man says, "There is nothing," God comes in, and soon there is everything. He made the world out of nothing, and he makes new creatures out of nothing. When you get back to nothing, God has come to everything. The end of the creature is the beginning of the Creator. I may seem to be speaking these words very calmly to you to-night; but I have within myself the deep persuasion that I am picturing some here who have reached the lowest point in their experience. They are despairing; they feel the sentence of death in their members. Now is the time for God to interpose; for notice how my text breaks in: "When they seek water, and there is none," then God says, "I will. They cannot do anything; but I will open rivers in high places; I will make the wilderness a pool of water." What you want is a divine interposition. You want God to rend the heavens, and come down, and save you; and he has come down in the person of his Son. Jesus Christ is that great interposition of God, and he has come to open the rivers of grace, and to dig the wells of salvation.

The promise in the text also relates to *those who are in various positions*. There are some of you who are in very high places. You run up to the very tops of the mountains, and you fancy that God cannot reach you there; but he says, "I will open rivers in high places." A river on the top of a mountain is a wonderful thing; but God can make it so. However high you have gone, he can reach you. Others of you are ordinary sinners down in the valleys. "Well," says the Lord, "I will open fountains in the midst of the valleys." You shall find water where you are on the hill-top; you shall not have to come down to the valley for it; and if you are in the valley, you shall not have to go up to the mountain for it, it will come just where you are. I do like that thought. There are some people who seem to think that we have to go a long way to find Christ; but, indeed, Christ has come to us just where we are. To use an old illustration of mine, our railway companies generally make the station from half a mile to two or three miles from the town, so that you must have a cab or an omnibus in order to get to it; but our Lord Jesus Christ has made a station just were the sinner is. Step into the train now; the first-class carriage is right before you. You need not run for half an hour to try to get a ticket, for on this line there is "nothing to pay." "Whosoever will, let him take the water of life freely," for it flows at his feet, whether he is on the mountains or in the valleys.

Yes, and to vary the promise still more, the Lord says, "I will make the wilderness a pool of water." Have you ever seen a wilderness, a large extent of flat country covered with sand and stones? I have crossed such a wilderness on a small scale, where there was no herbage, nothing green, just a wild waste, without anything growing upon it. As for a stream of water, there was nothing of the kind, not a drop anywhere. God pictures you as being like that barren, dried-up land, and he says that he will turn you into a pool of water. Whatever you are, however barren, however worthless, God can transform you by his grace into the very opposite; and "the dry land", long dry, and always likely to be dry, shall be "springs of water." God can make springs of grace in you, which shall begin to rise and bubble up at once, and shall never cease to flow till you reach the throne of glory.

In a word, no condition can be so bad but God can change it. No sin can be so great but God can forgive it. No garment of our life can be so stained but Christ can make it white. How I love to tell you these things! How much more happy should I be if every sinner here believed them, and came to Jesus just as he is, and trusted Christ to be everything to him! I cannot stay longer to-night on that point, precious as it is, because I want to stir up the people of God by one other observation.

III. Beloved friends, this text is true with reference to THE LABOURS OF WORKERS FOR GOD. God can soon change the condition of the plot of ground on which you are at work.

I may be speaking to one here who says, "Mine is a very bad place to work in, for I cannot get the people to come and hear the gospel; there seems to be *no spirit of hearing.*" That is largely true at the present time. Somehow, the people come here, and always have come here; but look at many of our churches and chapels. Why, in many of them there are more pews than people, more spiders than immortal souls! It is a wretched business. One says to me, "You know, sir, we have had addresses to working-men." Another says, "We have had Pleasant Sunday Afternoons." Another has had a batch of fiddlers to play; but the people do not come for all that. Some who like cheap music and Sunday concerts may be attracted by such means; but people will not be drawn thus to worship God. Of course not; can they not do their own fiddling if they want that kind of music? There is nothing in that style of thing to get people to come to a place of worship. There is just now a kind of hardening come over our population; the people do not care to go to a place of worship. But do not give up preaching, my friend; do not give up working, you who long for souls to be saved, for God can suddenly give a love for his house, and an eagerness to hear the gospel. He can make the dry land springs of water, and open rivers in high places. Only let all ministers preach the old gospel, preach it earnestly, and preach it simply, and the people will come back again. God will bring them to hear; he has always done so, and why should he not do so again?

Another says, "I get the people to hear, but *there is no feeling.*" Well, I too know what it is to have preached in places that have been like ice-wells. When I have talked to the people, they have looked like so many images; there has been no stirring them, no moving them. Regular hearers are all too apt to turn into stone, and to be unmoved; but oh! you who are trying to do good, never cease from it because the people seem to be turned to stone; go on with your work all the same. If the gospel hammer does not break the rock to-day, hammer away until it does. When the old St. Paul's Cathedral had to be taken down for the present one to be built, Sir Christopher Wren had to remove some massive walls that had stood for hundreds of years; so he had a battering-ram, with a great mass of people, working away to break down the walls. I think that for four-and-twenty hours they kept right on, and there seemed to be no sign of giving way, the walls were so well built, very different from our modern walls. The structure was like a rock, it could not be stirred; but the battering-ram kept on and on and on, blow after blow, stroke after stroke, and at last the whole mass began to quiver, like a jelly, and by-and-by over went the massive walls. You have only to keep on long enough, and the same thing will happen in your work. The first blows upon the wall were not wasted; they were preparing for the others; and getting the whole structure into a condition of disintegration; and when that was done, down it came, and great was the fall thereof. Work away, brothers, work away, feeling sure that God will open rivers in high places, and fountains in the midst of the valleys. He will make the wilderness a pool of water, and the dry land springs of water.

"Well," says one, "what we want in our place is for *the ministry itself to be supplied*." Yes, that is what we want everywhere. If the minister himself is dry, what is to be done? Find fault with him, and leave him? No, dear friend, if he is a man of God, pray for him, and never rest till the Lord makes the dry land springs of water. We poor mortals, whom God has called to be preachers, are desperately dependent upon our congregations. I do not say that we rest on you first, for our chief dependence must be upon God; but a praying, loving, earnest, wakeful people will keep the minister awake; and when the people decline, and there is no life in them, it sometimes happens that the minister gets dry, too. I remember that, when Mr. Matthew Wilks was comparing preachers to pens, he said that some of them spluttered, and others did not make any mark at all. "What is to be done with them?" said he, and then he answered his own question, "Pray the Lord to dip them in the ink." I think that we must pray for all the pens that God would dip them in the ink again. Oh, for another baptism of the Holy Spirit, to put more divine power upon them! Then, when we begin to speak, God will open rivers in high places, and make the wilderness a pool of water.

But what is wanted, too, is *the same blessing upon the helpers*. What is the preacher to do, what is the church to do, if the workers are half asleep? Sunday-school teachers going through their duty with great regularity and no spirituality; people going about with their tracts when they might almost as well go about with Sunday newspapers, for they have no love to the souls of the people! What is the result if we have deacons and church-officers going about without any life or spiritual power? Well do I remember preaching in a certain place, where I was told that there was great spiritual dearth. I preached my best; and when I went down from the pulpit afterwards, there were two deacons standing against the door of the vestry, with their arms folded, and leaning back in a most comfortable attitude. I asked them if they were the deacons, and they said, "Yes." Then I said, "There is no good doing here, I suppose?" They said, "No, none." I said, "I think I know the cause of it." "Do you know the cause of it?" they asked. "Yes," I replied, "I look to the right, and I look to the left, and I see it." I do not think that the brethren liked my remark; but, at the same time, I know that it was an arrow that went home to their hearts, for they became very different men afterwards, and woke up, and God blessed the place. One sleepy Christian in a church may do much mischief. In some businesses, the whole thing is so arranged that, if one person goes to sleep, all the machinery goes wrong; and I believe that it is very much so in the church of God. You have seen a number of men, standing in a long line, and pitching bricks to one another. Suppose that one of them goes to sleep. There will be a great accumulation of bricks around him; but none of them will get to the other end of the line. Sometimes we get a member of the church asleep. I would like to hurl half a brick at him; but I suppose that I must not do that, although he makes the whole work stop. No good is done because he is asleep. One says, "I know that brother." Who is he? Would you mind just giving him a jog? Put your arm this way, and nudge him so [describing a man striking himself], and you will hit the right man, I should not wonder. If you awake, perhaps it might be the waking up of one of the most sleepy people in the church. At any rate, it is always better to take these things to ourselves than to pass them on to anybody else. It is never well to listen for other people; the Scriptural injunction is, "Take heed unto thyself."

I pray that all the members of this church, if they have any of them been like dry land, may become springs of water. Then we may look for *a change throughout the whole congregation.* Men and women will cry out, "What must we do to be saved?" There will be plenty of people to be talked to about their souls. We shall have no difficulty in increasing the church, month by month, with such as shall be saved; and then *all the neighbourhood will be transformed.* A living church, in which God has made living springs of grace to rise, will soon turn the desert in which it is situated into quite a different region. There is need for gracious work in all the neighbourhoods in which any of us live; and great need of it round about this place. How are we cursed with dens of infamy and vice all round this region, where once it was very much the reverse! And what part of London is there that might not make a Christian weep tears of blood? Can you pass through this great city without being distressed and alarmed by reason of its ever-increasing sin, and its decreasing fear of God? O friends, these things cannot go on as they are! Something bad will come of it if something good and great is not soon done by the great God of mercy. Let us cry to him in private and in public. Let us entreat the stretching out of his arm of grace, and with our prayers let us put forth earnest efforts, each one trying to bring another to Christ, and never resting—

> "Till all the chosen race
> Shall meet around the throne,
> To bless the conduct of his grace
> And make his glories known."

God bless you all, for Christ's sake! Amen.

Exposition by C. H. Spurgeon.

ISAIAH XLI. 1—20.

Verse 1. *Keep silence before me, O islands; and let the people renew their strength: let them come near; then let them speak: let us come near together to judgment.*

God invites the people to argue with him. He bids them first " listen " to him, and then " speak" to him. They had been worshipping idols; so the Lord shows them that the idols are nothing, and that all worship paid to them is a lie. He begins by asking a question:—

2, 3. *Who raised up the righteous man from the east, called him to his foot, gave the nations before him, and made him rule over kings? he gave them as the dust to his sword, and as driven stubble to his bow. He pursued them, and passed safely; even by the way that he had not gone with his feet.*

These words are supposed to allude to Cyrus, who came " from the east", and conquered "the nations", and then did good to the house of Israel. It was God who spoke of Cyrus long before he was born. What idol god has been able to utter any prophecy? Only the Most High who lives in heaven can foretell things to come. One of the best proofs of our holy religion is to be found in the prophecies which have been fulfilled to the letter in various countries, and at different periods. Now, when they dig up old stones, that have been hidden for hundreds of years from the eyes of men, they see the proofs of how God saw into the future, and bade his prophets foretell the things that should be hereafter.

4—7. *Who hath wrought and done it, calling the generations from the beginning? I the LORD, the first, and with the last; I am he. The isles saw it, and feared; the ends of the earth were afraid, drew near, and came. They helped every one his neighbour; and every one said to his brother, Be of good courage. So the carpenter encouraged the goldsmith, and he that smootheth with the hammer him that smote the anvil, saying, It is ready for the sodering: and he fastened it with nails, that it should not be moved.*

A very graphic picture of the making of an idol. The people were afraid of Cyrus, so they began to appeal to their gods. A pretty god it must have been that had to be made by a carpenter! Then the wood had to be covered over with gold plates by the goldsmith, and the god would not be complete without the help of a man smoothing with a hammer and a smith smiting upon an anvil. When it was made, they had to solder it to keep it together; and then they had to get nails to fasten it in its place lest, like Dagon, it should fall down and be broken. This is nothing but literal truth; yet what a sarcasm it is upon idolatry! What good can come of idols that are made by men, idols that cannot move, and must be fixed in their places with soldering irons?

8. *But thou, Israel, art my servant,*

You do not worship idols; you worship Jehovah, the living and true God.

8. *Jacob whom I have chosen, the seed of Abraham my friend.*

What a title for God to give to a man, " Abraham my friend"! Could not we also endeavour to get into God's friendship, where Abraham was; to trust and love God much; to talk with him much, and enjoy high and holy fellowship with him?

9. *Thou whom I have taken from the ends of the earth, and called thee from the chief men thereof, and said unto thee, Thou art my servant; I have chosen thee, and not cast thee away.*

To many here this verse will come home very sweetly. God is your God, and you are God's servants. He has chosen you; he will never repent of his choice; his election is never changed. "I have chosen thee, and not cast thee away;" and you have chosen him, and you will not cast him away. By his grace, you will never leave your God, nor forsake the ways of Christ. May his mercy keep you faithful, even to the end!

10. *Fear thou not; for I am with thee: be not dismayed; for I am thy God:*
Where God is, there is no cause for fear: "Fear thou not; for I am with thee." That is a grand argument, "Be not dismayed; for I am thy God." Everything we need lies within the compass of those words.

10. *I will strengthen thee; yea, I will help thee; yea, I will uphold thee with the right hand of my righteousness.*
Beloved believer, are you weak to-night? Claim this precious promise, "I will strengthen thee." Have you something to do that is quite beyond your strength? Take hold of this comforting word, "I will help thee." Are you ready to slip? Do you feel as if you must fall? Lean on this gracious message, "I will uphold thee with the right hand of my righteousness." Do not let these precious pearls lie at your feet to be trodden on; pick them up, and wear them, and beautify the neck of your faith with them.

11. *Behold, all they that were incensed against thee shall be ashamed and confounded: they shall be as nothing; and they that strive with thee shall perish.*
Your sins, your temptations, everything that would keep you out of heaven, and drive you away from God, the Lord will overcome all these enemies of yours, and will deliver you.

12, 13. *Thou shalt seek them, and shalt not find them, even them that contended with thee: they that war against thee shall be as nothing, and as a thing of nought. For I the LORD thy God will hold thy right hand, saying unto thee, Fear not; I will help thee.*
That is the second time that we have had that precious promise to forbid our fear; first in verse 10, and now in verse 13, "I will help thee."

14. *Fear not, thou worm Jacob,*
You are earthly, grovelling, weak, like a worm; yet even you need not fear: "Fear not, thou worm Jacob."

14. *And ye men of Israel; I will help thee,*
That is the third time that we have had that promise, "I will help thee." "Ring that silver bell again," says the Holy Spirit to Isaiah, "let it comfort my tried ones." "I will help thee."

14. *Saith the LORD, and thy redeemer, the Holy One of Israel.*
I was wonderstruck, as I looked at this verse, to find it put "Thou worm Jacob, I will help thee, saith the Lord, and thy Goel," that is the Hebrew word which is translated "Redeemer", "Thy next of kin." Is the next of kin to a worm the Almighty God? Does he undertake to be our Brother, to pay the redemption price for us, because he is our near Kinsman? So the text says. Let us drink in the comfort of it: "Thy Redeemer, the Holy One of Israel." In order to become our Redeemer, the Holy One of Israel himself became "a worm, and no man."

15. *Behold, I will make thee a new sharp threshing instrument having teeth: thou shalt thresh the mountains, and beat them small, and shalt make the hills as chaff.*
The Easterns drag a wooden machine over the corn to fetch out the grain from the ear. This is called a corn-drag, and they put teeth in it, similar to the teeth of a harrow. God said that he would turn his Church, his people, into a new corn-drag, with teeth sharp and tearing, and that they should go against their difficulties, which were like mountains, and against their trials, which were like hills, and they should thresh them small, and make them to be like chaff.

16. *Thou shalt fan them, and the wind shall carry them away, and the whirlwind shall scatter them: and thou shalt rejoice in the* L ORD, *and shalt glory in the Holy One of Israel.*

All difficulty is gone, torn to pieces small as chaff, and then winnowed away, as the chaff is blown from among the heap on the threshing-floor. What a promise this is! You who fear God, believe it, go and practise it, and see if God does not make your greatest difficulties utterly to disappear.

Now come two sweet verses:—

17, 18. *When the poor and needy seek water, and there is none, and their tongue faileth for thirst, I the* L ORD *will hear them, I the God of Israel will not forsake them. I will open rivers in high places, and fountains in the midst of the valleys: I will make the wilderness a pool of water, and the dry land springs of water.*

See what God can do. Men are thirsty, they have no water; and lo! on a sudden, behold rivers, fountains, springs, pools, floods; for God does nothing by halves. He is an all-sufficient, overflowing God. When he gives, he gives like a king. He does not measure his gifts of water by the pint and by the gallon; but here you have pools, and springs, and rivers. When he has given waters, he will give trees to grow by the waters. When God gives blessing, he makes other blessings to spring out of it.

19. *I will plant in the wilderness the cedar, the shittah tree, and the myrtle, and the oil tree; I will set in the desert the fir tree, and the pine, and the box tree together:*

Making a paradise of streams of water and lovely trees, evergreen trees of the most comely aspect, and of great variety. See what God can do. Where there was a wilderness, where there were hills and valleys, and all was dry and parched, he makes woods and forests, rivers and fountains. He can do all things. Oh, that we had faith in him! But we forget him; we turn not to him; we look everywhere but to God; we try every method except that of trusting in the living God. Have we a God? If so, why do we act as we sometimes do? Martin Luther was a very cheerful man, as a rule; but he had terrible fits of depression. He was at one time so depressed that his friends recommended him to go away for a change of air, to see if he could get relief. He went away; but he came home as miserable as ever; and when he went into the sitting-room, his wise wife Kate,—Catherine von Bora,—was sitting there, dressed in black, and her children round about her, all in black. "Oh, oh!" said Luther, "who is dead?" "Why," said she, "doctor, have you not heard that God is dead? My husband, Martin Luther, would never be in such a state of mind if he had a living God to trust to." Then he burst into a hearty laugh, and said, "Kate, thou art a wise woman. I have been acting as if God were dead, and I will do so no more. Go and take off thy black." If God be alive, why are we discouraged? If we have a God to look to, why are we cast down? Let us rejoice and be glad together; for God will do all that he has promised, for this reason:—

20. *That they may see, and know, and consider, and understand together, that the hand of the* L ORD *hath done this, and the Holy One of Israel hath created it.*

God wants you to know that he is at work on your behalf. He wants you so to trust him as to see how his promises can be applied to your case, and what his right hand can accomplish even for you. Let us trust him to-night with all our hearts.

HYMNS FROM "OUR OWN HYMN BOOK"---30, 992, 488.

Metropolitan Tabernacle Pulpit.

ALONE, YET *NOT* ALONE.

A Sermon

INTENDED FOR READING ON LORD'S-DAY, AUGUST 28TH, 1892,

DELIVERED BY

C. H. SPURGEON,

AT THE METROPOLITAN TABERNACLE, NEWINGTON,

On Lord's-day Evening, March 2nd, 1890.

"Jesus answered them, Do ye now believe? Behold, the hour cometh, yea, is now come, that ye shall be scattered, every man to his own, and shall leave me alone: and yet I am not alone, because the Father is with me."—John xvi. 31, 32.

OUR Lord looks for faith as the result of his teaching; and I think that I hear him say, at the end of every service, "Do ye now believe? You have listened; you have made remarks upon the speaker; do ye now believe? You have been made to feel, you have brushed the tear away; but do ye now believe? For anything short of believing leaves you short of salvation." I would like to put the question of my text to every hearer in this great house to-night. You have listened now to years of sermons; "Do ye now believe?" You are getting grey now, the gospel is very familiar to your ear; you have heard it preached for many, many years; but "do ye now believe?" This is the crucial point. According to your answer, truthfully given to this question, you may decide as to your condition before God, "Do ye now believe?"

Christ loves faith wherever he sees it; it is to him a precious thing. To you that believe, he is precious, he is an honour; and upon him you who believe confer all the honour it is possible for you to confer. Your trust adorns him with jewels, your confidence in him puts the crown on his head. But our Lord is very discriminating; he distinguishes between faith and presumption, and between faith and our idea of faith. These disciples said now that they were sure: "Now are we sure that thou knowest all things, and needest not that any man should ask thee." "Yes! Yes!" the Saviour seemed to say, "That is your measure of your own faith; but I do not measure it in the same way that you do." If there be any here who say, "As to the matter of faith, I need no caution, I scarcely need admonition, I believe, oh! you cannot tell how firmly." No, my dear friend, and perhaps you cannot tell how weakly you believe. At any rate, do not

No. 2,271.

mistake your belief in your own faith for faith in Christ; for belief in your own faith may be only self-conceit; but faith in Christ gives glory to God, and brings salvation to the believer.

To take the disciples down a notch, the Saviour reminds them that, whatever faith they had, they were a long while coming to it. "Do ye now believe? Three years have I been teaching you; three years have I wrought miracles in your midst; three years have you seen me, and you might in me have seen the Father, but after all this time have you at last come to a little faith?" Oh! friends, we have never any reason to boast of our faith; for we have been very long coming to it. We do trust Christ now; I hope that many of us can sincerely say that we lean all our weight on him. We believe in God, we believe also in his Son, Jesus Christ; but it took months to drive us out of our self-confidence; it took years to lift us out of despair; it has taken all this time for the Lord, in the power of his own Spirit, to work out what little faith we have.

Then our Lord reminded them of another thing more humbling still, that as their faith was long in coming, it might be very quick in going. "Do ye now believe?" saith he, "Behold, the hour cometh, yea, is now come, that ye shall be scattered, every man to his own, and shall leave me alone." O beloved, a little trouble arises, an unforeseen difficulty occurs, and where is your faith? A little persecution, the idle banter of an unbeliever, the sarcasm of an agnostic, and where is your faith? Is it not so with many, that while in good company, they can almost brag of their faith; but if the company is changed, they certainly have no faith to brag of? The men who were so glib of tongue are quiet now; and though, before, they wore their helmets bedight with plumes, they would hide them away, and hide their heads, too, if they could. They are ashamed of him, now, in whom, once, they gloried. O friends, let him that glorieth, glory only in the Lord. Let the believer never vaunt his believing, lest he be reminded how long he was in coming to it, and how soon he may be parted from it.

Our Lord's disciples did not very readily take this caution. I do not suppose any of them took it; certainly Peter did not, and the rest of them were very much like him. When Peter said to Jesus, "Though all men shall be offended because of thee, yet will I never be offended;" and "Though I should die with thee, yet will I not deny thee;" we read, "Likewise also said all the disciples." We may say to-night, "There is no man among us who will ever be a traitor to Christ; there is no woman here who will ever grow cold of heart." That is our self-flattery. What others have done, however base and mean, we too are capable of doing. If we think we are not, it is our pride, and our pride alone, that makes us think so. Our Saviour, therefore, to call the particular attention of his disciples to their danger, said, not merely "the hour cometh," but, "Behold, the hour cometh." He puts in a "Behold!" an "*Ecce!*" As the old writers used to put a hand in the margin, or an N.B., *nota bene*, to call attention to something special, so the Saviour puts here a "Behold!" "Look here!" "See this." You who have just put on your armour think that you have won the victory. "Behold, the hour cometh, yea, is now come, that ye shall be scattered, every man to his own, and shall leave me alone."

I pray you, therefore, brethren, and I speak to myself as well as to you, let us learn the lesson of our frailty; and though we are honestly trusting in Christ to-night, let each one cry, "Hold thou me up, and I shall be safe." Let the prayer go up from all of you who are in these galleries, and from all who are sitting downstairs in those pews, from the most experienced and best established of you, as well as from those who have but recently been brought to know the Lord, and let each one cry, "Lord, keep me, for I cannot keep myself!" Alas! alas! we have seen even the standard-bearers fall; and when that is the case, how sadly do the common soldiers mourn! They who stood like rocks have been made to totter. God keep us! Christ of God, keep us by thy eternal Spirit! Amen.

Now I am going to take you away from that prefatory consideration, keeping still, however, much in the same vein. Let us learn to-night from our Lord, first, *his trial:* "Ye shall be scattered every man to his own, and shall leave me alone;" secondly, *his confidence:* "And yet I am not alone, because the Father is with me;" and then, thirdly, *his example:* for in all this, we are to follow his steps. May we, if we have our Lord's trial, also have his confidence because we imitate his example!

I. First, then, notice OUR LORD'S TRIAL, for the like of it may happen to you.

He was left alone. Why, these eleven apostles that are round him, and to whom he is talking, surely they will not leave their Lord! They are so sure that they will stand any fire that may be directed against them; and yet not one of them will stand firm. They will all forsake him and flee. In the garden, the three who are his body-guard will fall asleep, and the rest of the disciples will do the same; and when he stands before Pilate and Herod, none of them will be there to defend him; not a solitary voice will be lifted up for him.

The sure ones left him whom they so certainly believed; and they were honest men, too, when they spoke so confidently. There was no hypocrisy about what they said, they meant it all; they did each one verily believe that he could go to prison and to death, and that he would do so rather than deny his Lord. In their own esteem, they were not boasting; they were only saying what they really intended to do. Here is the bitterness of your trial, when, in your hour of need, your good, honest friends are gone, your real friends fainting and weary. They cannot go your pace; they cannot confront the storm that you are called upon to face, and they are gone. Alas, for our dear Lord, what grief it was to him! They who were so confident, and they who were really true, yet, nevertheless, were scattered, and he was left alone.

They also really loved Christ. I am sure that Peter's was not a new love when he said, "Thou knowest all things; thou knowest that I love thee." He did love his Master. Even when he denied his Lord, there was love in his heart towards him. So was it with the other disciples, they all loved their Lord, yet all of them left him, and poor weak things that they were, they turned their backs in the day of battle. It is a grief to our hearts to be forsaken of good friends and loving friends. I do not know; but if you were sure that they had been hypocrites, you might almost be glad that they were gone; but your very knowledge that they were true at heart, as true as such poor things could be, increases the bitterness that they should leave you. You need not think, when this occurs in your experience, that any strange thing has happened to you, for Christ was thus left alone.

Notice, that *he was left by every man.* "Ye shall be scattered, every man to his own," "every man." When the trial comes, does not John remain? Does not he remember that dear breast on which he leaned his head? Is John gone? Yes, "every man." Christ looked, and there was none to stand by him. He must confront his accusers without a single witness in his favour; every man was gone. Ah, this was a trial, indeed! But one true friend, a Damon or a Pythias, to be faithful to one another even unto death, and the trial is not so overwhelming. But, no; every man is gone to his own, and Christ is left alone; of the people there is none with him, not even one of those who had been his most intimate friends.

What were they all at? Well, *every man was looking to his own safety:* "Ye shall be scattered, every man to his own." Is not that the very essence of selfishness and of meanness, "Every man to his own"? This is all that Christ received from the best of his followers; they left him, and went every man to his own, to his own house, to see to his own security, to screen his own character, to preserve his own life. "Every man to his own." Are these thy friends, O Jesu? Lover of men, are these thy lovers? Do you wonder if, sometimes, you find that your friends would take care of you only that they must take care of themselves? They would keep you, but then you cost too much; you are too "dear" a friend! The expense of your friendship has to be looked at, and their income will not bear it. "Every man to his own." This also the Saviour had to feel.

And, remember, this happened *when Christ's special hour was come.* "The hour cometh," Christ's hour, the hour of the power of darkness. It was then that they left him. When he did not need their friendship, they were his very good friends. When they could do nothing for him if they tried, they were his faithful followers. But the pinch has come; now might they watch with him one hour, now might they go with him amid the rabble throng, and interpose at least the vote of the minority against the masses; but they are gone. Like your swallows, they have disappeared or e'er the first frost has covered the brook. Like the green leaves of summer, where are they now in this wintry time? Alas, alas, for friendship, when it fails when most it is needed! And it did fail the Saviour then.

He was left, also, *in violation of every bond.* These men who left him were pledged to stand by him. They had given him a promise to die with him. These were his choice companions; he had called them from the fishing-smacks of Galilee, and made them his disciples. These were his apostles, the chief men in his new kingdom. They were to sit upon thrones, judging the twelve tribes of Israel. These, he had redeemed unto himself; these were to be partakers of his glory in the day of his appearing. Never were men bound to man as they were bound to Christ; and yet they left him alone. Dear friend, do not expect gratitude from your fellow-creatures; it is a very scarce thing in this world. The more you do for men, the less will be their return. I speak not now like one who thinks ill of my fellows; but I know that it is so, alas! in many instances; and if it be not your lot, you may thank God that it is not, and wonder why you are an exception to the rule. If, by-and-by, you shall come down in the world, and need the help of those you helped in days gone by, they will, as a rule, be the last to help you, and the first to tread you down. Certainly, with our Lord Jesus Christ, those who were nearest and who owed him most fled from him, and he derived from them no succour. It was "every man to his own"; and they left him alone, to be bound and beaten by his unfeeling adversaries, and to be taken away to prison and to death.

There is the first division of our subject, our Lord's trial. I say again, that a like trial may happen to some here. It has happened often to bold defenders of the faith, to find themselves left to hold the bridge alone; but it is a sharp, stern trial to the man who is called to endure it.

II. More cheery talk shall we have on our second head, which is OUR LORD'S CONFIDENCE. He says, "Ye shall leave me alone: and yet I am not alone, because the Father is with me."

Observe, then, that Christ's confidence was confidence that the Father was with him, and this confidence *kept him to his purpose.* See, the disciples flee; they are all scattered, every man to his own. Has Christ gone? Not he. John, Peter, James, Thomas, and all the rest, are gone; has Christ gone? Not he. There he stands. They have left him alone; but there he is, still standing to his purpose. He has come to save, and he will save. He has come to redeem, and he will redeem. He has come to overcome the world, and he will overcome it. They have left him alone; they have not taken him away with them. He is no coward. From his purpose he doth never fly, blessed be his name! He stood fast in that dread hour when all forsook him and fled. This was because his confidence was in God.

Next, observe, that this confidence in God not only kept him to his purpose, but it *sustained him in the prospect of the trial.* Notice how it runs: "Ye shall leave me alone: and yet I am not alone." Christ does not say, "I shall not be alone." That was true; but he said, "I *am not* alone." I love to read the experience of the child of God in the present tense, the gifts, and graces, and promises of God in the present tense: "I am not alone." "The Lord *is* my Shepherd," as well as "I *shall not* want." "He *maketh* me to lie down in green pastures; he *leadeth* me beside the still waters." He is doing everything for me now. The blessed Christ says that the prospect of God's being with him all through the trouble, and the presence of God with him now, is his comfort in the prospect of it. You who were here this morning know what a sad discourse we had from the text, "My God, my God, why hast thou forsaken me?"* I took this text for my evening discourse because it is the counterpart of the one we

---

* See *Metropolitan Tabernacle Pulpit,* No. 2,133. "Lama Sabachthani?"

considered this morning; for our Lord could truly say to his disciples, "And yet I am not alone, because the Father is with me."

Our Lord's declaration *was contradicted by appearances.* Did he not have to say to God: "Why hast thou forsaken me?" How, then, could he say, "The Father is with me"? It was true; and in a part of my morning sermon I tried to show that, while God forsook him in his official capacity as the Lawgiver and the Executive of the law, yet in his personal relation to him he did not and could not forsake him. The Father was with him. Oh, is it not blessed on the part of Christ to stand to this? He knows that his Father is with him, even when he feels in another sense that the Father has forsaken him. Beloved, if everybody leaves you, and God seems to leave you, still hold to your confidence in God. Do not believe that God can forsake his own; do not even dream it; it cannot be. He never did forsake his own; he never can; and he never will. The Father is with Jesus Christ, even when he knows that he will have to say, "Why hast thou forsaken me?"

Yet, *it was assuredly true* that the Father was with Christ when he was left alone. How was the Father with him, then? Beloved, even when the Father did not look on Christ, or give him one smile, or one word of comfort, he was still with him. How so? Well, he was with him as to his eternal purposes and covenant. They had entered into covenant together for the redemption of men, for the salvation of the elect, and they had crossed hands, and pledged each other to carry out the divine purpose and the everlasting covenant. I remember that passage about Abraham going with Isaac to mount Moriah, where Isaac was to be offered up. It is written, "So they went both of them together." So did the Eternal Father and his Well-beloved Son when God was about to give up his own Son to death. There was no divided purpose; they went both of them together. All the work of Christ was the work of the Father, and the Father supported him in it to the very full.

In the design and method of the atonement, the Father and the Son were together. "God so loved the world that he gave his Only-begotten Son;" but Jesus so loved the world that he gave himself. The atonement was the gift of the Father; but it was the work of the Son. In all that he suffered he could say, "The Father is with me in it. I am doing that which will glorify him, and content him." He went not alone to prison and to death. In all things he did that which pleased the Father, and the Father was with him in it all.

All the decrees of God were at the back of Christ. It is written in the sealed book, but who shall read it except the Christ? Whatever is written there is written in support of Christ. There is not a decree in the book of destiny but works out for Christ's glory, and according to Christ's mind. It is not merely twelve legions of angels that are behind the cross, but the God of the angels is there, too. It is not merely the forces of Providence that shall work together to achieve the purpose of the Creator, but the God of Providence, the infinite Jehovah, is in league with Jesus; and he can say it, as he goes out to die, "I am not alone: because the Father is with me." Is not this a glorious truth, that our Lord Christ was not alone?

So far as earthly companions were concerned, the words written by Isaiah could be literally uttered by Christ, " I have trodden the winepress alone." Every man was gone, but God was always with him.

Since then, *it has been made manifest* that God was with Christ. He proved it by raising him from the dead. Did not the Father also prove that he was with the Son by sending the Holy Ghost at Pentecost with divers signs and wonders? Jesus is not alone. All the work of the Holy Spirit since, in convincing men of sin, and leading them to Jesus, is a proof that he is not alone. Beloved, all the history of Providence, since the day when Christ was taken up into heaven, proves that he is not alone. Alone? The Christ alone? Why, the beasts of the field are in league with him; the stars in their courses fight for him. Every event of history, give it but time and space, will make his kingdom come. Every turn of yonder enormous wheels of Providence shall make his chariot of triumph come nearer and nearer over the necks of his foes. Even now, by faith, "we see Jesus, who was made a little lower than the angels for the suffering of death, crowned with glory and honour."

> " Look, ye saints, the sight is glorious,
> See the " Man of Sorrows " now ;
> From the fight return'd victorious,
> Every knee to him shall bow :
> Crown him, crown him ;
> Crowns become the Victor's brow."

Jesus is the focus of all power and wisdom. God is with him; and the day comes when he shall appear in his glory. In his millennial reign among the sons of God it shall be seen that he is not alone; and when he shall come in the glory of the Father, and all his holy angels with him, then shall he be able to say with even greater emphasis, " I am not alone : because the Father is with me." And when he sits upon the great white throne, and divides mankind, his friends to the right, his foes to the left, and pronounces eternal wrath upon rebels, and opens heaven to believers, then shall all worlds know that the Man of Nazareth is not alone. Alone? I seem as if I must laugh at the very thought. All heaven and earth, things present and things to come, time and eternity, life and death, are all with him. Men may forsake him, but he is not alone.

III. Now, I want, in the third place, to teach the lessons of OUR LORD'S EXAMPLE. As my time has nearly gone, I must very briefly speak of these lessons.

First, *learn fidelity when others fail.* Are you a Christian ? Do you trust Christ ? Do you love him ? Then, never desert him. " Oh ! but," says one, " the current runs the other way now." Brother, let it run; it will leave off when it has run away. I believe in him who rose again from the dead, whose righteousness doth justify me, whose blood doth wash me whiter than snow. " But the philosophers tell us that this is not scientific." I am unscientific, then, and I delight to be unscientific. " Oh, but the deep thinkers say this is inconsistent with progress ! " Well, let it be inconsistent with progress. " Oh, but all the world denies it ! " So much the worse for the world. Let it deny the truth if it will. That was a grand spirit of Athanasius when he said, "*Athanasius contra mundum*"; that is, "Athanasius against the whole world." And every Christian may be of this spirit, and ought to be of this spirit. Is this Book true? What matters it though every Tom Fool says that it is a lie! Let Tom Fools say that if they will; but it is true, and hold you to it. If God the Holy Ghost has taught you to trust in Christ, trust you in Christ, whatever other people do. What? Do you live on the breath of other men's nostrils? Do you count heads, and then jump with the larger number? Is that your way? Why, surely such a man as that is hardly worth saving. Is he a man, or is he not a cat that must look before he jumps? Nay, if thou art a man, and thou believest in Christ, stand up for Christ.

> "Stand up! Stand up for Jesus!
>   Ye soldiers of the cross!
> Lift high his royal banner;
>   It must not suffer loss:
> From victory unto victory
>   His army shall he lead,
> Till every foe is vanquish'd,
>   And Christ is Lord indeed.
>
> "Stand up! Stand up for Jesus!
>   The trumpet-call obey;
> Forth to the mighty conflict,
>   In this his glorious day;
> Ye that are men, now serve him,
>   Against unnumber'd foes;
> Your courage rise with danger,
>   And strength to strength oppose."

And when the many turn aside, stand you the more boldly and the more confidently, for your confidence and boldness are all the more needed at such a time. Your Lord did not forsake his grand errand when all men forsook him. Do not renounce your lifework and your faith, even though all others should renounce theirs.

Next, with your Master, *believe that God is all-sufficient*. Read this: "Ye shall be scattered, every man to his own, and shall leave me alone: and yet I am not alone, because"—what? "Because there will be half-a-dozen of you faithful"? No. "Because three of you will cling to me"? No. "Because the Father is with me." Oh, we do not count as we should. There is a million against you. Is God for you? Well, then, you are in the majority. What is a million, after all, but one and so many ciphers? Trust thou in God, and let the millions go their way. God is enough. When he that spoke in the academy found everybody leaving him in his speaking except Plato, he still kept on; and one said, "Speaker, thou hast no audience but Plato." "No audience but Plato?" says he; "Plato is enough for fifty orators." So, truly, if thou hast no other helper but God, stand thou where thou art; for God is not only enough for thee, but for all the faithful, weak as they may be.

Next, learn another lesson. *Rest in God, despite appearances.* Art thou very poor? Art thou weak? Art thou slandered? Art thou scourged with God's heaviest rod? Yet kick not thou at him, any more than thy Lord did. He said, "The Father is with me," even though he had to cry, "Why hast thou forsaken me?" Believe him when thou canst not see him; believe him when he smiles not; believe him when he frowns; believe him when he smites; believe him when he slays, for that is the climax of it all, to say like Job, "Though he slay me, yet will I trust in him." It is his to do what he likes; it is mine to trust him, let him do as he will. I throw my arms about my God, and say, "My God, my God," even when no sensible joys are felt, and I am obliged to walk by faith.

Lastly, struggling child of God, standing firm for the truth and the right, *expect that thy trouble will not last long.* Did you notice how Christ puts it, "Behold, the *hour* cometh"? Only an hour. "Behold, the hour cometh." It is not a year, brother, it is not a year; it is not a month; it is not a day; it is but an hour. "The hour cometh." To Christ it was a long hour certainly, when he hung upon the cross; but he calls the whole period from the bloody sweat to the death of the cross, "the hour." It is the part of faith to shorten days to hours. It is your part, to-night, to recollect that, if you have to suffer, and to stand alone for Christ, it is but for an hour. How willingly have we waited when it has been but for an hour! How cheerfully have we gone on in the dark when we have known that it was only for an hour! Our trial is but for an hour. Literally, before another hour strikes, some of us may be with God; but whether it is so with us, or not, we may still sing,—

"Let doubt, then, and danger my progress oppose,
They only make heaven more sweet at the close:
Come joy or come sorrow, whate'er may befall,
An hour with my God will make up for them all."

But if not literally only an hour, yet certainly the longest reign of persecution is but short. It is soon over when we once get home. I think that it will help to make a merry holiday in the land that flows with milk and honey, to sit one of these days by one of those rippling streams, and say, "I remember when So-and-so forsook me, and I stood fast by the truth as I knew it and believed it. They all forsook me, and it did seem hard to bear at the time; but my loneliness did not last long, it was soon over; and when the Lord said, 'Well done, good and faithful servant,' it did not seem then that it had been an hour, but only the winking of an eye, or as when, in the night, the candle is blown out, and lighted again by its own smoke, so short was the time of darkness." So it shall seem in heaven as if we never had suffered anything for Christ. The martyr shall go in the red-hot chariot from the stake; and when he gets to heaven, he shall have forgotten that he burned to death, in the exceeding joy of beholding his Master. It is but an hour, and we shall meet before the golden throne, and stand upon the sea of glass, and sing for ever, "Unto him that loved us, and washed us from our sins in his own blood, and hath made us kings and priests unto God and his Father; to him be glory and dominion for ever and ever. Amen."

Exposition by C. H. Spurgeon.

JOHN XVI. 16—33.

Verse 16. *A little while, and ye shall not see me: and again, a little while, and ye shall see me, because I go to the Father.*

Remember that the disciples were on the verge of great trouble. Their Leader and Friend was about to be taken away from them by a cruel death. They were to be tried as they had never been tried before. The Saviour therefore prepared their minds for the trial. I have often noticed that, before a great trouble comes, the Spirit of God secretly comforts in a very remarkable manner those who are to be tried. Perhaps, to-night, without knowing it, we may be near some great affliction or sorrow. If so, may the Lord store us with comfort and strength for the coming hour of need !

17, 18. *Then said some of his disciples among themselves, What is this that he saith unto us, A little while, and ye shall not see me: and again, a little while, and ye shall see me: and, Because I go to the Father? They said therefore, What is this that he saith, A little while? we cannot tell what he saith.*

It was only too plain. We often do not understand our Master because we imagine that there is some deep significance in his words when their meaning lies upon the very surface. If you would understand the gospel as you understand the common talk of life, it would be wise. If we could but bring men to believe God as a child believes its mother, practically and really, then their salvation would be a very simple and speedy matter.

19, 20. *Now Jesus knew that they were desirous to ask him, and said unto them, Do ye enquire among yourselves of that I said, A little while, and ye shall not see me: and again, a little while, and ye shall see me? Verily, verily, I say unto you, That ye shall weep and lament, but the world shall rejoice:*

Sometimes the world appears to have the best of it. Its mouth is full of laughter while the child of God cannot speak for sorrow. Ah! well, there is time enough for a change. We may very well let those laugh to-day who will have to gnash their teeth for ever. Judge not God by your present circumstances. Take the rough with the smooth. Be willing to go to heaven up the bleak side of the hill.

20. *And ye shall be sorrowful, but your sorrow shall be turned into joy.*

So, the more of it the better. If your sorrow is to be turned into joy, then the more sorrow, the more joy. Happy is he who endureth trial, since his trial is to be turned into happiness.

21, 22. *A woman when she is in travail hath sorrow, because her hour is come: but as soon as she is delivered of the child, she remembereth no more the anguish, for joy that a man is born into the world. And ye now therefore have sorrow:*

But your sorrow is the pang of life.

22. *But I will see you again, and your heart shall rejoice, and your joy no man taketh from you.*

The joy that comes by sorrow in connection with Christ is the joy of which we shall never be bereaved. Let us thank God that there is a joy which no man can take away. Happy are they who have it.

23. *And in that day ye shall ask me nothing. Verily, verily, I say unto you, Whatsoever ye shall ask the Father in my name, he will give it you.*

This is a grand promise. If we dare ask in the name of Christ, and it is not everything that we could ask for in his name—if our petition is such that we honestly judge that we may put Christ's name to it, if it is a thing that Christ would have asked, if it is a thing that Christ could have asked, let us ask in Christ's name, and the Father will give it.

24. *Hitherto have ye asked nothing in my name*:
You have not been bold enough. You have asked a few petty things, but you have never fully made use of Christ's name. How many Christians have never learned to pray in the name of Christ! They say at the end of their petition, "For Christ's sake." That is good as far as it goes. I may ask a man to give me such and such a thing for the sake of another; that is good pleading so far as it goes. But if I dare to use the authority that my friend gives me to put his name at the bottom of my request, that is another and a higher thing. To ask in the name of Christ, to plead under his authority, this is to pray indeed.

24. *Ask, and ye shall receive, that your joy may be full.*
"That your joy may be full," a ripe joy, a joy that fills your being, that sparkles in your eye, dances in your feet, leaps in your heart, an unutterable, inexpressible joy: "That your joy may be full."

25, 26. *These things have I spoken unto you in proverbs: but the time cometh, when I shall no more speak unto you in proverbs, but I shall shew you plainly of the Father. At that day ye shall ask in my name: and I say not unto you, that I will pray the Father for you:*
Though that be true,

27. *For the Father himself loveth you,*
What a delightful little sentence! "The Father himself loveth you."

27. *Because ye have loved me, and have believed that I came out from God.*
God's first love to us is from himself alone. Then there is another love that grows in his heart because of our love to his Son. You love your child. The reason lies in your own heart. After a while, that dear, loving, affectionate child has won a farther place in your affection, and you love him because of his choice and special love to you. Remember that Psalm, "Because he hath set his love upon me, therefore will I deliver him: I will set him on high, because he hath known my name." Our love of God wins from him another love, of a different sort, although it comes from the same fountain as the first: "For the Father himself loveth you, because ye have loved me, and have believed that I came out from God."

28—30. *I came forth from the Father, and am come into the world: again, I leave the world, and go to the Father. His disciples said unto him, Lo, now speakest thou plainly, and speakest no proverb. Now are we sure that thou knowest all things, and needest not that any man should ask thee: by this we believe that thou camest forth from God.*
One does not see any reason why they should have been made so strong in faith just then. But we were not there to hear Christ's words. There is many a message which depends upon the tone and manner of the speaker for its influence over the people who hear it. When you read the story afterwards, without the earnest manner and the living tone of the speaker, you do not see why it had such a strange effect upon his hearers. So we do not quite see here, by the calm reading of this narrative, why the disciples leaped all of a sudden into such confidence.

31. *Jesus answered them, Do ye now believe?*
He did not feel so sure of their faith as they did. We often think we have great heaps of the gold of faith; and it glitters very brightly, but it is not the precious metal after all. So Jesus said, "Do ye now believe?"

32. *Behold, the hour cometh, yea, is now come, that ye shall be scattered, every man to his own, and shall leave me alone: and yet I am not alone, because the Father is with me.*
These poor creatures, who were so bold and so oversure, would all be runaways. If persecution were to arise in our day, I wonder how many of

us would be found true men. Ah! you think you are true blue; but you would run at the first touch of water, not to mention fire. Are there not many of us who are but poor believers? If our faith were sharply tried, would it stand the test?

33. *These things I have spoken unto you, that in me ye might have peace. In the world ye shall have tribulation: but be of good cheer; I have overcome the world.*

Christ wants his disciples to have peace. Are you fretting to-night? Are you afraid of Monday? Are you fearful about the trials of the week? Christ wants you to be at peace. Be quiet. Be quiet. Let all lie still within your heart, and wait your Father's will. "In the world ye shall have tribulation:" on God's threshing-floor the flail will be kept going. If you are a child of God, you will have to suffer. The Captain of our salvation was made perfect through sufferings; and good soldiers of Jesus Christ must expect to pass through the same experience. As long as you are here, you will be tried: "In the world ye shall have tribulation: but be of good cheer; I have overcome the world." Think of that; the Christ who is about to sweat great drops of blood, and to die on the cross of Calvary, says, "I have overcome." It is not Julius Cæsar's "*Veni, vidi, vici;*" but it is Christ's "*Veni, vidi, vici;*"—"I came, I saw, I conquered:" "I have overcome." And as he has overcome, so shall you, if you be his true follower.

HYMNS FROM "OUR OWN HYMN BOOK"—685, 739.

"THE SWORD AND THE TROWEL."

TABLE OF CONTENTS, SEPTEMBER, 1892.

"I Will Give You Rest." A Communion Address at Menton. By C. H. SPURGEON. (Revised by himself for the Magazine.)
Letter from MRS. SPURGEON, to the Teachers and Scholars of the Metropolitan Tabernacle Sunday-school, concerning the Book Fund distribution of sermons to foreign missionaries.
The Relations of the Minister of Christ to the Holy Spirit. A Fundamental Question. By Arthur T. Pierson, D.D.
Mr. Spurgeon's R. T. S. Pocket-book. Outlines of sermons made at Menton, 1891-2.
Mr. Spurgeon's Last Drives at Menton. By Joseph W. Harrald. (With three illustrations.)
"That's my Sermon, Sir." By Elder George Goldston.
The Dying Moor. By N. Hardingham Patrick, of Tangier.
The Martyrs of Blantyre. (Illustrated Review.)
Mr. Spurgeon's Visit to Rothesay in 1878. By Pastor A. G. Short, Sandown, Isle of Wight.
"Remember Me." (Poetry.) By Pastor E. A. Tydeman, Sidcup.
Garments as a Gift. By J. Manton Smith.
The Sick Lamb. (Poetry.) By Thomas Spurgeon.
"Another Gem in the Saviour's Crown." *In Memoriam* notice of the late Mr. William Gibson, of Tasmania. By Thomas Spurgeon.
Notices of Books.
Notes. (Portrait and sketch of Elder M. Romang. Mrs. Spurgeon. Thomas and Charles Spurgeon at the Tabernacle. Poor Ministers' Clothing Society. Tabernacle Evangelists' Association. Tabernacle Prayer-meetings. Tabernacle Sunday-school Missionary Society. Tabernacle Gospel Temperance Society. College. Evangelists. Colportage. Baptisms at Metropolitan Tabernacle.)
Lists of contributions.

Price 3d. Post-free, 4d.

LONDON: PASSMORE AND ALABASTER, PATERNOSTER BUILDINGS, and all Booksellers.

Metropolitan Tabernacle Pulpit.

LONGING TO FIND GOD.

A Sermon

Intended for Reading on Lord's-day, September 4th, 1892,

DELIVERED BY

C. H. SPURGEON,

AT THE METROPOLITAN TABERNACLE, NEWINGTON,

On Lord's-day Evening, September 14th, 1890.

"Oh that I knew where I might find him!"—Job xxiii. 3.

"Oh, that I knew where I might find *him!*" Observe that Job is so taken up with his one great desire, that he forgets that everybody else is not thinking in the same way; and he uses a pronoun, though he has not before uttered the name of God. The man is carried away with his desire. He does not say, "Oh, that I knew where I might find God!" but, "where I might find *him.*" An overwhelming passion will often speak like that. See how the Song of Songs, that sweet canticle of love, begins, "Let him kiss me with the kisses of his mouth: for thy love is better than wine." There is no mention of any person's name. We forget many things when we are taken up with one thing. We forget that, as Madame Guyon wrote,—

"All hearts are cold, in every place;"

and when our heart grows warm, we fancy that all other hearts are warm, too. Remember how Mary Magdalene, when she met our Lord on the resurrection morning, and, "supposing him to be the gardener," said to him, "Sir, if thou have borne *him* hence, tell me where thou hast laid *him*, and I will take *him* away." Nay, but Mary, thou hast not mentioned the name of the person. Thou beginnest, "If thou have borne *him* hence." How should another know of whom thou speakest? This is the way of a concentrated individuality. When it is set, desperately set, upon some one object, it forgets to whom it speaks; it only remembers the beloved one upon whom its affections are fixed.

Now, this is one reason why the man who is earnestly seeking after God is often misunderstood. He does not speak as one would speak who was cool and calm. His heart is hot within him, and his words are fire-flakes; so that those about him say, "The man is mad. He is not sober, as he used to be; he is going out of his mind." I would to God that many were so mad that they cried in the depths of their soul, "Oh, that I knew where I might find him!" for, if God knows whom you are seeking, it is of small consequence whether your

No. 2,272.

fellow-creatures know, or do not know. If he accepts you, do not be cast down if men misunderstand you.

Thus, you see, Job's longing was all-absorbing; it was also personal, he longed personally to find God. I know many people who have great longings; but they are for things that are trivial compared with the longing of Job. Job does not sigh to comprehend the incomprehensible. He does not wish to find out the divine decree. He does not trouble about where free agency and predestination meet. He does not desire to know, out of mere curiosity, or for the attainment of barren knowledge; but his cry is, "Oh, that I knew where *I* might find him! Oh, that I could get at God! Oh, that I could have dealings with the Most High! Oh, that I could feel at perfect peace with him, and rest in him, and be happy in the light of his countenance!" Now, some of you, perhaps, in years gone by, were very curious and anxious about various theological questions; the time was when you would have disputed with almost anyone who came along; but you have given all that up; and now you want to find God, and to be reconciled to him. You want to know from God's own lips that there is peace between you, and that he loves you, and will never cease to love you. You have been, perhaps, for weeks trying to find a way of access to God; and, though there is such a way, and it is close to you, you have not yet perceived it. This one thing occupies your mind, not that you may know about God, or split hairs about doctrinal theories concerning him, but that you may find HIM. I would to God it were the case with everyone in this congregation, that you either had him or were sighing and crying after him. This is not a point upon which any man can afford to be neutral. We must find God; for if we do not, we are ourselves lost.

On further reading the text, I feel still more pleased with Job's determination about getting to God. He says, "Oh, that I knew *where* I might find him!" He does not make any condition as to where he might find God. If it were in heaven, he would try to scale its heights. If it were in the abyss, he would hopefully plunge into the deep. If God be far away, at the uttermost ends of the earth, Job is willing to go there. If God is to be found in his temple, or, for the matter of that, in the lowest dungeon, Job only wants to know where he may find him; and if he may find him, he will not make any conditions as to where it may be. We noticed in our reading that Job said, "Oh, that I knew where I might find him! That I might come even to his *seat!*" He was willing to come even to God's judgment-seat if he could not find him anywhere else.

It will be a great mercy for you if you are so anxious to find God that you will not set any bounds as to where you shall find him. You would be glad to find him at your usual place of worship; but you would be just as glad to find him in the midst of quite another people. You would be thankful to find him in your own chamber when you bow your knee in prayer; but you would be quite as pleased to find him in the midst of your business. You would rejoice to find him whether it was in the heat of noontide, or in the cool of midnight. Your cry is, "Only let me find him, and time and place shall be of no consequence to me."

With regard to instrumentalities, also, you would be pleased to be converted to God by a learned and eloquent minister; but you would be quite as willing to find Christ by means of the most illiterate. You will be quite content with the man against whom you have been prejudiced, if God will but bless him to you. Ay, though it were your own servant girl, or some boy in the street, if they could but tell you the way of salvation so that you could find God, you would be perfectly satisfied! I know you would, for you put in no "ifs" or "buts" or conditions. Your one cry is, "Oh, that I knew where I might find him!" You are absorbed with that one desire; your whole soul is possessed by that one earnest longing to find God. This desire is intensely personal and practical, and it inspires you with the full determination that, at all costs and all hazards, if you can but find out where God is, you will come to him.

Now, I am going to talk about this desire to find God. I have had it from one or two here present who are deeply anxious, that this is the cry of their spirit day and night, "Oh, that I knew where I might find him!" In trying to meet their case, our first enquiry will be, *What sort of desire is this?*—the desire that makes a man, or a woman, or a child, cry out, "Oh, that I knew where I might find him!" And, secondly, *What is the answer to it?* How can they find God? And, thirdly, *Why are some so long in finding God?*

I. Our first question, concerning this longing to find God, is, WHAT SORT OF DESIRE IS THIS?

I answer, first, that *it takes many forms*, according to the circumstances of the person who has the desire. In Job's case, it was a somewhat hazardous desire to come before the court of God to have his righteousness established. I have no doubt that, in bitterness of soul, many a sincere man, when maligned and lampooned, has wished that he could turn to God, and have the matter judged by him. "Thou knowest," says he, "that I am not wicked; I have not been false; I have not been treacherous. Let the case against me be tried by the great Judge of all, who is righteous and impartial. Oh, that I knew where I might find him!"

But the desire is better and more usual on the part of children of God when they have lost the light of his countenance. Beloved, the model Christian is the man who always walks in the light, as God is in the light. But how few there are of these comparatively! Many, I half fear the most of us, are at times in the dark. We wander; we lose our first love; we grow lukewarm; and then God hides his face. Many and many a true child of God has sighed out of the depth of his spirit, "Oh, that I knew where I might find him!" Are any of you less happy than you used to be? Are you less holy than you used to be? Are you less in prayer than in former years? Have you less tenderness of conscience? Have you less joy in the Lord? Are you doing less for Jesus, and are you more content with the little that you do? Are you going back? Well, then, if God has not hidden his face from you, in all probability he will; and then, when you are in a dry and thirsty land where no water is, you will be like the fainting hart that panteth for the water-brooks, and you will cry out after God. If you do not, it will be a damning mark. If you can live without your God, you who profess to be a child of God, it will look as if you never were his child. God has spoiled some of us for the world. It is never a matter of self-denial to us to give up its pleasures; for we have no taste for them. If we do not find joy in God, we are of all men most miserable. The brooks and cisterns are dry; and if the smitten rock does not yield us water, we thirst, we faint, we die.

But, beloved, I want to dwell mainly upon this cry as coming from the convicted sinner who has not yet rejoiced in God. He has a burden pressing heavily upon him, and he knows that he can never get rid of it except through the grace of God in Jesus Christ; and he wants to get rid of it. So it has come to this, that day and night he says, " Oh, that I knew where I might find him! " I like this form of the desire best of all; and I would willingly spend and be spent, that I might encourage and help any who are thus seeking God as their Saviour.

Let me say this to any such who are here. *This desire is quite contrary to the desire of nature.* You feel yourself lost, and yet this cry comes to your tongue, " Oh, that I knew where I might find him! " My dear friend, this is not a natural desire. When you were satisfied with the world, you never had this desire. Time was when it never crossed your soul for a moment. When Adam and Eve sinned, they did not want to find God; they hid themselves among the trees of the garden. And you, while you love sin, do not want to find God. You are like Jonah, you would willingly take ship, and flee from God's presence, even to Tarshish. No, the natural man, without the Holy Spirit, never said, " Oh, that I knew where I might find him! " I should like you to get just a ray of light, not more, out of that remark. That ray of light might cheer you while we proceed.

I think that *this desire never comes except by grace.* It never takes full possession of any man unless it is wrought in him by the grace of God. There may be a transient desire, but it is no more a sign of spiritual health than is the hectic flush of consumption a proof that the poor patient possesses vigorous physical strength. In the excitement of a revival meeting, you may say, " I wish I was a Christian," but to carry this desire about with you, to have it always within you as a deep ground-swell of your soul, " Oh, that I knew where I might find him! " this is the work of the Holy Ghost. I trust that we have many here who feel these first pangs of the new birth; for where God begins with us by working in us this desire, he will, in due time, gratify it. If he gives us hunger, he gives us bread to satisfy its cravings. If he gives us a desire for himself, he gives us himself to satisfy that desire.

Then it is sweet to think that *this desire is met by the seeking of the Saviour.* The desire of a man after God is paralleled by Christ's desire after him. " The Son of man is come to seek and to save that which was lost." Now, when a sheep begins to seek its shepherd, and at the same time the shepherd is seeking it, it cannot be long before the two meet. I read to you, last Thursday night, a letter from a poor soul, a harlot, who had come in here on the Sabbath morning, and God had met with her. You know how easy it is to make up such a letter with the idea of asking charity; but there was no name to this note, and it contained no request for charity. It was a true letter. There was one part of it that I commend to you. The writer said, "Before you receive this letter, I shall be home at my father's house, from which I wickedly ran away." Ah, there is the point, that going home, that getting back to the father! Now, I have no doubt that the father had sought his girl, but when the girl began to seek him, there would be a meeting very soon. If there is a soul here that wants Christ, Christ wants you. If you were sitting now upon Samaria's well, he would come and sit by you, and he would say to you, "Give me to drink," for you alone can assuage the Saviour's thirst, the thirst to save, the thirst to forgive, the thirst to bring wanderers home to the great Father's house. Oh, friend, if this cry be your cry, "Oh, that I knew where I might find him!" I can see much to comfort you in the thought that, while you are seeking the Lord, he is also seeking you.

But let me add that *it will be well if this desire never gets satisfied except by God;* for there are so many who do not seek till they find him. A friend, writing to me, says, "You have taken away from me all my comfort; you have destroyed my self-righteousness; you have left me in a dreadful condition through the Word of God which you have preached to me. I used to go to early celebrations. I was at church three times a day. I thought that I took the very body and blood of Christ in the holy Eucharist. I have rested in my works; and now the whole structure is gone. I can rest in none of those things any more. My one cry is (and please to sing to-night that hymn that ends),—

'Give me Christ, or else I die!'"

My dear friend, your letter gave me great delight. I was glad to give out that hymn; but I pray you do not get content till you do find God, for you can come here, you know, and you may even succeed in deceiving us so that you may be baptized, and join the church, and take the communion, and you may rest in all that without saving faith in Christ, and you will not be an inch nearer to God than you were when you rested in the ceremonies of your former church. It is only God who can save you, only God in Christ who can give true rest to your soul. Men may change their churches, and only change their refuge of lies; but if they come to Christ, whatever church they are in, if they have found him, and are trusting in him, and in him alone, their peace will be like a river, and their righteousness as the waves of the sea. God bless any here who are opening their mouths, and panting with this strong desire; but do be sure that you are never comforted till Jesus comforts you! Never be fed except with the bread of heaven. Never rest until you find rest in him whom God has appointed to be our rest, or else you will make a blunder, a fatal blunder, after all.

II. Our second question, concerning this desire, "Oh, that I knew where I might find him!" is, WHAT IS THE ANSWER TO IT?

Well, in the first place, there is something in the desire itself that gives you comfort; for *God is near you now.* If you want God, he is everywhere, he is here, he is nearer to you than your hands and feet, nearer to you than your eye or your nerve. He is within you, and round about you. You might ask, with the Psalmist, "Whither shall I flee from thy presence?" and find that task to be impossible; but if you really wish to find God, you may readily do so. He is here; you have not to pray at Jerusalem, nor yet at Mount Gerizim.

"Where'er we seek him, he is found,
And every place is hallowed ground."

Believe it, and speak to him now; show him your heart now; appeal to him now, for he is truly near you at this moment.

But you wish to lay hold upon him. Then remember that *God is apprehended only by faith.* Eyes are of no use in this case; you cannot see a Spirit. Ears are of no use in this case; you cannot hear a Spirit. Your senses may be put aside now; the new sense, the new eye, the new ear, is faith. If thou believest, thou shalt see, and thou shalt hear. Come, deal with God, who is near thee now, by faith. Believe that he is near thee; speak to him; gladly trust him. Faith will apprehend all of God that can be apprehended; and out of faith shall come many other blessed things that will make thee still more familiar with thy God. But now, even now, put out the arms of an inward faith, and say, "I believe thee." Faith comprehends the Incomprehensible, and takes the Infinite within itself.

But still, if what you mean is, "Oh, that I knew where I might find him, in the sense of calling him my own, and having a joyful belief in his love!" well, then, I would say to you, *if you want to find him, search his Word.* If you will read the Bible with the steady resolve to find God in Christ within its pages, I am morally certain that you will not have to read it long. There is here a holy magnetism, which, if a man comes in contact with these sacred words, shall begin to operate upon him. If you will take the Book, and search it through to learn how God is to be found, you will find him.

Then, in connection with the Word written, *go and hear the Word spoken,* for there are minds that are more affected by speech than by what they read. If you will only hear attentively a faithful gospel minister, it will not be long before you find God. If you go to hear a man merely because he is clever, or one who will tell you stories and interest you, you may never get any good out of him. But if you go saying, "I want to find Christ during this service; I want to lay hold on God to my soul's eternal salvation;" I do not think that you will long frequent some places of worship that I could mention without saying, "I have found God."

Next to that, if you do not seem to profit by the reading and hearing of the Word, *seek the Lord in prayer.* Get thee to thy chamber; there cry unto thy God, and cease not thy cry; for if thou wilt seek for him as for silver, and search for him as for hidden treasure, thou shalt surely find him. Prayer has a wonderful effect on God. He turns at the cry that comes from the heart. He is sure to look to the man who cries to him for mercy.

And at the same time that you are in prayer, or in connection with it, *meditate on divine things.* Especially meditate on the person of Christ, God and Man; on the work of Christ, especially his atoning sacrifice. Meditate on the promises; meditate on God's wonders of grace recorded in this delightful Book. Think and pray, and then think and pray again; and my impression is that you will not long have to say, "Oh, that I knew where I might find him!"

Yet is there one more word for you. If you would find God, *he is to be found in Christ Jesus*, "reconciling the world unto himself, not imputing their trespasses unto them." Do you know the Man Christ Jesus? Can you by faith see him? Fall at his feet; accept him as your Saviour; trust him as the Giver and Forgiver, as saving from death and imparting life. Come and take Christ, and you have found God. No man believes in Christ and remains without the favour of God. Oh, that thou wouldst believe in Christ now! This morning I preached about his incarnation, Immanuel, God with us. Think much on this. "The Word was made flesh, and dwelt among us." God came here among men, and took the form of a mortal creature, and here lived and died. Think of that, and believe in him who is God and Man. Then think much of his life, of the many that he healed, the sick ones that he relieved, the sinful that came to hear him, to whom he spoke only words of love. Look through the life of Christ, and I am persuaded that, if thou art willing to do so, thou wilt find amongst those who came to him a case parallel to thy own, and wilt find him dealing with it in love and mercy; and, whilst thou art perusing that wondrous life of love, thou wilt find God. But if it be not so, go a little further.

"Go to dark Gethsemane,
Ye that feel the tempter's power."

Stand amid the shade of the olives; hear the Son of God groaning out his very soul, his sweat, as it were great drops of blood, falling to the ground. He pleaded there for sinners, for the guilty. Follow him to Pilate's hall, see him scourged and spat upon; and go, at length, to Calvary, and sit down there in meditation, and mark the wounds in his blessed body, those sacred founts of blood. See his emaciated frame exposed before the sun to the gaze of cruel men. Watch him till you hear him cry, "It is finished." Then see the soldier set his heart abroach; for, even after death, his heart for us its tribute poured; and then, as thou dost remember that he made the heavens and the earth, and yet did hang upon that tree for the guilty, believe thou, and trust him.

"Oh!" says one, "I cannot believe." Now, it is a curious thing that, when I have met with persons who find it difficult to believe, I have often been obliged to say to them, "Well, now, there is a strange difference between you and me; for you cannot believe, and I cannot disbelieve." That is to say, when I see Christ, the Son of God, dying for guilty men, I cannot make myself disbelieve. It seems to me to flash its own evidence upon my soul; and I am convinced by the sight I see. How is it that you cannot believe when the Almighty God is one with his sinful creatures, and dies to save them from eternal death? "Who his own self bare our sins in his own body on the tree." When you see that marvel of marvels, how can you disbelieve? I charge you, by the living God, look to Jesus on the cross, as Israel in the wilderness, bitten by the serpents, looked to the brazen serpent, and by that look lived.

I think this is the way to find God, that is, to come to Christ; for, remember that he is not dead. He is risen. Where is the Christ now? He is at the right hand of God. He maketh intercession for us; yea, for the rebellious also, that the Lord God may dwell among them. Dost thou believe that Christ makes intercession for sinners? Then trust thyself with him, first as thy Redeemer, and now as thy Intercessor; and so, by a simple trust, thou shalt find thy God, and no more say, "Oh, that I knew where I might find him!"

III. I have finished my discourse when I have very briefly answered the third question: WHY ARE SOME SO LONG IN FINDING GOD?

I answer, partly because *they are not clear as to what they are seeking*. If you want to find God, well, here he is. You yourself know that he is everywhere, so that you have found him. But what I fear some of you want, is some kind of mark, some sign, some feeling. Now, that is not seeking God; you are seeking something in addition to God. I am sure that, in the hour of trial, nothing will stand a man in good stead but simple faith in God by Jesus Christ. "Oh!" says one, "I read of a man, the other day, who was under most wonderful conviction, and of another who had a very remarkable dream, and of another who heard a voice speaking to him." Yes, yes, and all these pretty things are very well when you have faith in Christ. But if you do not trust yourself to Christ, these things are not worth a penny, for some day you will say to yourself, "How do I know that I did hear that voice? Might I not have been deceived? How can I be sure that that dream meant anything? May I not have eaten something for supper that made me dream it? And that joy that I felt may have been all a delusion." But if you want God without any of these things, you want exactly what you do need, and I pray you to come and take it by faith in Jesus. Here am I, a guilty sinner; that I know and confess. Jesus Christ came into the world to save sinners; that I know by the witness of this Book. I am told that, if I trust him, I am saved. I do trust him, I will not ask for a dream, or a vision, or a voice, or anything. Why should I? Beggars must not be choosers. If God gives me his salvation as he gives it to anybody else, I am perfectly happy, even though I have no striking story to tell, and shall never point a moral or adorn a tale with any anecdote about myself. I am afraid, however, that many are not wanting God so much as wanting the odds and ends that sometimes go with him.

Again, there are some who are crying after God, who are *hankering after their own idols*. Ah, me! you would like to keep some of your self-righteousness, or some of your sins. One of our friends, coming up from the Norfolk Broads, told me that when the time came to row home, he began pulling away at the oars, and he thought that it was a very long way, and that the scenery was very monotonous, with the same old willow-tree and everything the same as when he started; and someone going by said, "I suppose you know, old fellow, that you have got your anchor down." That is exactly what he had forgotten, and he was rowing with his anchor still down. You will not find God that way if you have an anchor still down. I do not know what your anchor is; perhaps it is the wine-cup, you still take that drop too much. Perhaps it is an evil woman. Perhaps it is some trick in trade that you have been used to. Perhaps it is some secret sin that cannot be told. You cannot find God while you keep that. Achan, how can God come to thy tent, unless it is for judgment, while the Babylonish garment is hidden in the ground? Away with the idols, and then shall you find the true God.

And yet again, there are some who are *waiting to feel their need more;* and they think that they cannot come to Christ till they feel more than they do at present. Now, again I must get you to alter your cry. I thought that your cry was, "Oh, that I knew where I might find him!" But now your cry is, "Oh, that I knew that I really needed him!" Have you not had enough of that experience? Time was with me when I thought too much of it. I believe a deep ploughing does us good; but, if a man is always ploughing, and never sows anything, he will never have a harvest. Some of you are looking too much to your sense of need. You are not saved by your sense of need; you are saved by the supply of that need. Come as you are. "I have not a broken heart," says one. Come to Christ for a broken heart. "I have not a tender conscience," says another. Come to Christ for a tender conscience. You are not to get half the work done yourself, and then to come to Christ to have it finished. Come as you are, just as you are, hard heart and all. Come along with you, and trust yourself to Jesus, and you shall find your God.

I am afraid that there are a great many also who are *clouded in their minds by the great sorrow through which they have passed,* for you can be so distressed and distracted that you do not judge clearly. You remember Hagar when the water in her bottle was spent, and her boy was dying of thirst. Just there, close behind her, was a well of water. The angel said to her, "What aileth thee, Hagar?" And we read, "God opened her eyes, and she saw a well of water." Some of you have salvation at your finger-tips, and you do not know it. You have it in your mouth, as Paul says, and you do not know it, or else you would swallow it down, and live by it at once. Salvation is not up there in the heights, or down here in the deeps. The apostle puts it thus, "If thou shalt confess with thy mouth the Lord Jesus, and shalt believe in thine heart that God hath raised him from the dead, thou shalt be saved. For with the heart man believeth unto righteousness; and with the mouth confession is made unto salvation." "He that believeth and is baptized shall be saved." So runs the gospel. Look for no other way. Believe. I said not, "Feel," but "Believe." Dream not, dote not, imagine not, but believe; say with thine heart, "I believe that Jesus Christ came into the world to save sinners; and I trust him to save me."

> '' 'Tis done, the great transaction's done;
> I am my Lord's, and he is mine.' "

Now thou shalt begin a new life of obedience and holiness, wrought in thee as the result of thy having believed in Jesus Christ, whom God has set forth to be the propitiation for sin. Will you have Christ or not, sinner? If you will not have him, you must perish; if you will have him, he gives himself freely to you; and nothing is freer than a gift. Take him, and go your way happy as the angels. God bless you! Amen.

Exposition by C. H. Spurgeon.

JOB XXIII.

Job is in great physical pain through the sore boils that cover him from head to foot; he is still smarting under all the bereavements and losses he has sustained; and he is somewhat irritated by the hard speeches of his friends. We read, in the second chapter of this book, that "they had made an appointment together to come to mourn with him and to comfort him." "Job's comforters", even to this day, are regarded as those whose room is preferred to their company. As the result of all the trials through which Job was called to pass, there is, in this chapter, somewhat of bitterness. We need not wonder at it; the wonder is that there is not more. You ought, in estimating a man's actions or words, to judge of his circumstances at the time. Do not take Job's words by themselves; but consider in what condition he was; think what you would have done if you had been in his place, and you will not censure him, as you might otherwise have done.

Verses 1, 2. *Then Job answered and said, Even to day is my complaint bitter: my stroke is heavier than my groaning.*

He could not express all his pain. He felt that he did not complain too much. His stroke was heavier than his groaning. His words had bitterness in them; but he thought that they were justified by his affliction.

3. *Oh that I knew where I might find him!*

Job longed to find his God; he wanted to come to him. He had been slandered by men; so he turns from the court of injustice below to the divine Court of King's Bench above, where he is sure of a righteous verdict: "Oh that I knew where I might find him!"

3. *That I might come even to his seat!*

To his mercy-seat, and even to his judgment-seat. Job was willing to appear even there.

4. *I would order my cause before him, and fill my mouth with arguments.*

He felt that he dared plead before God. He was not guilty of the things laid to his charge; so he would be bold to speak even before God's judgment-seat. If Job had known a little more of God, as he did before his life ended, he might not have talked so glibly about ordering his cause before him, and filling his mouth with arguments. We remember how he afterwards spoke to the Lord, "I have heard of thee by the hearing of the ear: but now mine eye seeth thee. Wherefore I abhor myself, and repent in dust and ashes." Who among us would desire to come and argue our case with God without our heavenly Advocate?

5. *I would know the words which he would answer me, and understand what he would say unto me.*

He was willing to hear God's side of the argument, patient and anxious to understand the mind of God with whom he desired to plead. So far so good. There are some who do not wish to know what God would say unto them; so long as they may express their own passionate desires, they have no ear and heart waiting to hear the voice of God. Very beautiful is the next verse:—

6. *Will he plead against me with his great power? No; but he would put strength in me.*

He has confidence in the Lord that, if he could have an audience with him, God would not use his power against him; but, on the contrary, would strengthen him in order that he might state his case. Do I speak to a troubled heart here? Come to God with your burden. He will not use his power against you; but he will help you to plead with him. Trembler, come and bow at his feet! He will not spurn thee, he will lift thee up. Despairing one, look to the Lord! He will not turn his wrath upon thee; but he will help thee to plead with him. "Will he plead against me with his great power? No; but he would put strength in me."

7—9. *There the righteous might dispute with him; so should I be delivered for ever from my judge. Behold, I go forward, but he is not there; and backward, but I cannot perceive him: On the left hand, where he doth work, but I cannot behold him: he hideth himself on the right hand, that I cannot see him:*

Job had done his best to find his God. Forward, backward, to the right, and to the left, he had gone in all directions after him; but he could not find him. I know there are persons here to-night who are in that condition; and you will never rest, I hope, until you do find the Lord. He is not far from you. I trust that with many of you, to-night is the happy hour in which your long searching shall end in a delightful finding.

10. *But he knoweth the way that I take:*

If I do not know his way, he knows mine. If I cannot find him, he can find me. Here is my comfort: "He knoweth the way that I take."

10. *When he hath tried me, I shall come forth as gold.*

Here the true Job comes to the front. You get the gracious man once more on his feet. He staggered a little; but he stands firm now: "When he hath tried me, I shall come forth as gold." So will you, my tried sister, my afflicted brother. The trial of your faith is but for a time; there will come an end to this furnace-work; and when God has tried you, tested you, and taken away your dross, he will bring you forth, and you will be pure gold, meet for the Master's use.

> "In the furnace God may prove thee,
> Thence to bring thee forth more bright;
> But can never cease to love thee:
> Thou art precious in his sight:
> God is with thee,
> God thine everlasting light."

11. *My foot hath held his steps, his way have I kept, and not declined.*

Happy Job, to be able to say that, and to speak the truth; but there is a touch of self about it which we cannot quite commend. Be holy; but do not claim to be holy. Be thou steadfast before God, firm in thine obedience to him; but do not mention it; for thy hope lies somewhere else. Yet we cannot condemn Job for declaring that he had kept God's way. His friends were pleading against him, so he felt that he must defend himself.

12. *Neither have I gone back from the commandment of his lips; I have esteemed the words of his mouth more than my necessary food.*

Job was a happy man to be able to say that. I hope that many of you could say the same. If you were tried with great bodily pain and depression of spirit, you could say, through divine grace, "I have not turned away from God." These are days when we want men of principle; men who can put their foot down, and keep it down, men who cannot be turned aside. They call this firmness, "bigotry." It is, however, only another name for Christian manliness. If you dare to do right, and face a frowning world, you shall have God's commendation, "Well done, good and faithful servant."

13. *But he is in one mind, and who can turn him?*

God has one mind, and he will carry out what he wills. It is vain for any man to think of turning him from his eternal purpose.

13, 14. *And what his soul desireth, even that he doeth. For he performeth the thing that is appointed for me: and many such things are with him.*

You will find that men who are much tried fall back upon the granite foundation of the divine decree. God has ordained it, so they yield to it; they acquiesce in it because it is according to the eternal purpose of the Most High. Though we say little about it now, there may come a time when some of you will have to say, as Job does, "For he performeth the thing that is appointed for me: and many such things are with him."

15. *Therefore am I troubled at his presence: when I consider, I am afraid of him.*

It is a bad sign when a man of God becomes afraid of God. Yet is there a holy awe which may degenerate into a servile fear which hath bondage; but even this may be the foundation of a holy confidence which will keep us in obedience to the Lord.

16. *For God maketh my heart soft,—and the Almighty troubleth me:*

Are you saying that to-night? If so, I am glad you are here. I have, for many years, been compassed about with a large number of persons who come from the ends of England and Scotland, and from longer distances, too, in despair of soul, and seeking comfort; but I think that never in my life have I had more than I have had this week, persons unknown to me before, who are under conviction of sin, and feeling the hand of God heavy upon them. Hard tugs have I had to bring them out of Giant Despair's Castle. The Holy Ghost alone can do this work; but he sometimes makes use of a sympathetic brotherly word to give light to those who are in the dark. I am praying that he may do so to-night; for there may be some here who say with Job, "God maketh my heart soft, and the Almighty troubleth me."

17. *Because I was not cut off before the darkness, neither hath he covered the darkness from my face.*

He wished he had died before he came to such trouble, or that by some means such trouble had been turned away from him. May the Lord, if he sends you Job's trouble, send you Job's consolation! May he glorify himself by your patient endurance, if he lays upon you his heavy hand!

HYMNS FROM "OUR OWN HYMN BOOK"—607, 594, 606.

"THE SWORD AND THE TROWEL"

FOR SEPTEMBER, 1892, CONTAINS:—

"I Will Give You Rest." A Communion Address at Menton. By C. H. SPURGEON. (Revised by himself for the Magazine.)
Letter from MRS. SPURGEON, to the Teachers and Scholars of the Metropolitan Tabernacle Sunday-school.
The Relations of the Minister of Christ to the Holy Spirit. By Arthur T. Pierson, D.D.
Mr. Spurgeon's R. T. S. Pocket-book. Outlines of Sermons made at Menton, 1891-2.
Mr. Spurgeon's Last Drives at Menton. By Joseph W. Harrald. (With three illustrations.)

"That's my Sermon, Sir." By Elder George Goldston.
The Dying Moor. By N. Hardingham Patrick, of Tangier.
The Martyrs of Blantyre. (Illustrated Review.)
Mr. Spurgeon's Visit to Rothesay in 1878. By Pastor A. G. Short.
"Remember Me." (Poetry.) By Pastor E. A. Tydeman, Sidcup.
Garments as a Gift. By J. Manton Smith.
The Sick Lamb. (Poetry.) By Thos. Spurgeon.
"Another Gem in the Saviour's Crown." By Thomas Spurgeon.
Notices of Books, Notes, Accounts, &c.

Price 3d. Post-free, 4d.

LONDON: PASSMORE AND ALABASTER, PATERNOSTER BUILDINGS, and all Booksellers.

Metropolitan Tabernacle Pulpit.

FICKLE FOLLOWERS.

A Sermon

Intended for Reading on Lord's-day, September 11th, 1892.

DELIVERED BY

C. H. SPURGEON,

AT THE METROPOLITAN TABERNACLE, NEWINGTON,

On Thursday Evening, March 27th, 1890.

"And it came to pass, that, as they went in the way, a certain man said unto him, Lord, I will follow thee whithersoever thou goest. And Jesus said unto him, Foxes have holes, and birds of the air have nests; but the Son of man hath not where to lay his head. And he said unto another, Follow me. But he said, Lord, suffer me first to go and bury my father. Jesus said unto him, Let the dead bury their dead: but go thou and preach the kingdom of God. And another also said, Lord, I will follow thee; but let me first go bid them farewell, which are at home at my house. And Jesus said unto him, No man, having put his hand to the plough, and looking back, is fit for the kingdom of God."—Luke ix. 57—62.

Sometimes nobody appeared to come to Christ. He preached, but no followers appeared as the result of his preaching. At another time, we see that many came, and desired to be numbered with his disciples; but they were not all of the right kind. Luke has collected here three instances, which I think are typical of many more of those who seemed to be true followers of Jesus, who, nevertheless, did not continue with him, and were not really converts. I think that these three are put together here for the comfort of those of us who preach the gospel; that when we are disappointed, we may perceive that we are not worse off than our Master was; and that, when we think that we have brought men to conversion, and find, after all, that they are not converted, we may not give up the work or be discouraged, but may say to ourselves, "It was always so; it was so with the Prince of preachers. May we not reasonably expect that it will be so with us also?"

Our Saviour never refused anybody who came to him, and who ought to have been accepted by him. His own words were, "Him that cometh to me, I will in no wise cast out." That is a true description of his dealing with men at all times. If they do but come sincerely and truly, he always welcomes them. On the other hand, he did not shovel them in indiscriminately; he did not gather them to himself wholesale. He did not go about, as it were, soliciting their

No. 2,273.

patronage, willing to take in anybody so long as he could swell the number of his followers. Oh, no! we have good evidence here that he knew how to shut the door as well as to open it. He knew as well how to warn the pretentious as to accept the penitent. He was ready for the sincere with open heart and open hand; but he was faithful to those who were self-deceived, or those who, through ignorance, professed what was not really true. Now, we ought to be the same, dear friends. We should always be anxious to receive all who will come to Christ. At the same time, we must exercise judgment, and not put down everybody as converted simply because he says that he is; but we must judge, and watch, and try, and test, lest we help self-deception, and come to be the servants of Satan by bolstering up the delusions of mistaken men and women.

One thing I do not like about these three people of whom I am going to speak to you to-night, and that is, that in the case of no one of them does there appear to be any sense of sin. There is nothing said about repentance, or about their feeling their deep need of a Saviour. They are like many we know. With no tear in the eye, strangers to a broken heart, they become religious mainly of themselves, and they become irreligious of themselves. What they gained themselves they lost themselves. But, where there is really a deep ploughing work done, when the seed comes up, it lives. Where the foundation is digged deep, when the house is built, it stands. When there is stripping, there is afterwards real clothing. When there is a probing of the wound, the healing is a true healing, and not a pretence. I regret, therefore, that there should be so many persons, outside of my text, who have not any repentance. They seem to jump into their religion as men do into their morning bath, and then jump out again just as quickly, converted by the dozen, and unconverted one by one till the dozen has melted away; not really converted, otherwise they would never be unconverted again. I believe that we are going to have a great many converts. We are praying over them, and praying for them; and we want to know what sort of men and women they ought to be. We want to know how to deal wisely with them in the name of our loving, tender, but faithful Saviour. We shall learn from his treatment of those who came to him how we should deal with those that come to us.

Now, first, *there are some would-be followers of Christ who do not consider*, as in the first case. Secondly, *there are some would-be followers of Christ who do not put Christ first*, as in the second case. And, thirdly, *there are some would-be followers of Christ who still hanker after the world*, and want to have Christ and the world, too. Neither of these three sets of followers will ever prove a comfort to us or a glory to God.

I. First, THERE ARE SOME WOULD-BE FOLLOWERS OF CHRIST WHO DO NOT CONSIDER. The first man, and he was a scribe, too, said, "Lord, I will follow thee whithersoever thou goest." What that might mean, what that might involve, he did not ask, and therefore did not know. He was sincere as far as he knew; but then he did not know much. Had he known more, he would have said less.

Like our Lord, we meet with *many persons who are great at resolving*. "I will; that I will. Solemnly, I declare that I will." They are willing to make that declaration as publicly as you like; and stand up, or fall down, or do anything else to declare that they have resolved. I frequently hear persons exhorted to give their hearts to Christ, which is a very proper exhortation; but that is not the gospel. Salvation comes from something that Christ gives you, not something that you give to Christ. The giving of your heart to Christ follows after the receiving from Christ of eternal life by faith. It is easy to work our friends up so that they say, "We will give our hearts to Christ," but they may never do so, after all. If, with broken heart and contrite sigh, they had confessed their guilt, and had penitently cried, " God be merciful to me a sinner," they might not have looked quite so well, but there would have been more hope of them. We cannot come to Christ unless Christ comes to us, and gives us a broken heart and a contrite spirit. If there be no repentance, depend upon it that that faith which we think we have is not the faith that will save us. Give me faith with tears in her eyes; I know her to be the true child of God. The faith that makes me feel my ruin, confess my sin, and lay hold of eternal life, because otherwise my merits will bring me to eternal death, this is the faith which saves. But some people are very great at resolving rather than repenting and believing.

These people show, generally, *very great confidence in themselves.* This man said, " Lord, I will follow thee whithersoever thou goest." There is no prayer, "Lord, help me to follow thee," " Hold thou me up, and I shall be safe," " Leave me not, or I shall wander from thee," but it is just this, "I have made up my mind to this, and I am a strong-minded person, and able to carry out what I determine. Lord, I will follow thee whithersoever thou goest." That is our duty; but that duty we shall never attain apart from divine help. " He that trusteth in his own heart is "—what? A convert? No, " a fool", and " a fool" is another name for a sinner. Go, write on water, and return to-morrow to read the phrase thou hast inscribed; and when thou hast done that, trust thine own determinations. Go, and say that thou wilt pluck the moon out of her orbit, or stay the sun in his blaze at mid-day; and when thou hast done these things, then canst thou so control thyself as to be ever faithful to thy Lord without his help. I would have you deal far more in confession than in resolving, much more in believing than in bearing testimony to anything you have done yourself, or hope to do yourself, or resolve to do yourself. This first man is very big; he talks great swelling words, and he feels that he can do what he says, and in the simplicity of his ignorant heart, he says, " Lord, I will follow thee whithersoever thou goest."

Do you not think that, perhaps, there was at the back of that declaration, *some secret idea that he would be a gainer by it temporally?* May not this man have thought that Jesus Christ had come to set up a temporal kingdom, and that, by following him, he would get a high place in that new kingdom? If even Christ's apostles began to contend which should be the greatest, and two of them wished to sit, the one on his right hand and the other on his left, I cannot wonder if this half-disciple had some idea that he was going to be a great deal better off as to carnal things for being a follower of Christ. Now, it may be that some here imagine that the Christian life is all pleasure and joy, that there will be no persecution to endure, no affliction to bear. It may be that you have imagined that the way to heaven is by a grass path, rolled every inch of it; and that when you say, "Lord, I will follow thee whithersoever thou goest," you mean that you will follow him through Jerusalem when everybody waves the palm-branch, and casts his garment in the way. Do you know anything about Gethsemane, and the bloody sweat, about Gabbatha, and the cry, "Crucify him!" and about Golgotha, that scene of deadly woe? Will you follow him there when the many turn aside? Will you witness there that he alone hath the living word? You think it shall be all king's weather with you if you go with Christ. Know ye not that Christ leads us where the fiercest winds do blow, and where the stormy blast pitilessly hurls the sleet into our faces, and where we must perish if we live on earthly comforts? The people of God are a tried people; but many fancy that it cannot be so, and so they say, "Lord, I will follow thee whithersoever thou goest."

Now, notice that *Christ undeceived this man in a very wonderful way*, by telling him, "Foxes have holes, and the birds of the air have nests; but the Son of man hath not where to lay his head." He told that scribe that, if he became his follower, he must share with him, for the disciple is not above his Lord, nor the servant above his Master. What will you have to share if you follow Christ? You will have to follow a friendless Man without a home, and often with no one to understand him. If you take him to be your Leader, you will have to travel over a rough road. Oh, may none of you ever profess Christianity for the sake of what you can get! I can assure you that, in these days, those who follow Christ for loaves and fishes will find the loaves very small and the fishes very full of bone.

The Saviour meant this scribe to know also that, if he followed him, not only would he gain no wealth by it, but he would get very little kindness as the result of it, for our Saviour had no home of his own. There were kind friends, like those at Bethany, who often entertained him, yet there were nights when the fox went to his lair, and the crow went to the wood, but the Saviour had to tarry till his head was wet with dew, and his locks with the drops of the night, for no man gave him shelter. Christ says to this scribe, "You will be treated like that; you will lose many of your friends; those who are of your own household will become your enemies; those who now admire you will then abhor you; and those who now call you a fine fellow, and are pleased to entertain you, will then shut the door in your face. That is what you have to expect." When this man heard that, his enthusiasm, I suppose, cooled down. He was like Mr. Pliable, when he tumbled into the Slough of Despond. He said the Celestial City might be a very fine place; but, if the way to it was so bad as that, anybody might have that city for him; he should not go plodding through miry ways in order to get to it. Many a man, when he has found that there is a cross as well as a crown, has foregone the crown because he could not bear the cross.

Does any one here say, "That was rather a hard method of our Lord, to tell this hopeful person that, and so discourage him"? Ah! dear friend, *it was a very safe and proper method*. Our Lord wants not to gather to his army those who cannot be soldiers. If we cannot endure what lies before us, it is better for us honestly to turn back than to pretend to go forward. If we enlist a man who is not sincere at the first, we are doing him a serious injury; we are doing ourselves an injury; we are doing the whole cause of Christ a solemn injury before the eyes of men; for all they that go back, like dogs to their vomit, bring disgrace upon the good cause. All those who say that they are Christ's, and then go and live ungodly lives, stain the name of Christ. They do more injury through having made a profession, than they would have been capable of doing if they had never made that profession. Now, as the church hastily counts up her numbers, and says, "So many were converted," the world has another register, and counts up the apostates, the backsliders, the wanderers; and it is a serious blow struck at the crown and the glory of Christ when the world can say, "Such and such a man bore Christ's name, but he acted like a servant of the devil." Hence our Lord was wise, as the great heart-searching Saviour, to let this man know the worst side of religion; that, if he did take up with it, he might know what the cost of it would be. So would I say to everyone here, that we want you to come, we want you to join the army of Christ, we want you to be followers of the Redeemer, but not unless you will count the cost first. We beg you not to take the name of Christ upon you, unless you are truly his in your very soul. Do not dare to be added to the Church of God, unless heart, soul, and spirit, your whole nature goes with your profession, and you become truly and really a follower of Christ. The enthusiastic often comfort a preacher, but they as often delude him. Let him be on his guard, and try well, with searching truth and with the untiring preaching of the whole gospel, those who come to him, lest the great heap on the threshing-floor should suddenly prove to be nothing but chaff, when God's great fan comes to blow upon it. We must keep the fan of the gospel going, that the chaff may be divided from the wheat, for God would have us separate between the precious and the vile, and then shall we be as his mouth.

II. Now, secondly, THERE ARE SOME WOULD-BE FOLLOWERS OF CHRIST WHO DO NOT PUT CHRIST FIRST.

The second case mentioned in this chapter is different from the first: "And he said unto another, Follow me." This man was not a volunteer. The first man was, and he broke down in his preliminary examination. This man was, so to speak, a pressed man, impressed by the command of Christ, "Follow me," and he broke down, too. Every true volunteer into the army of Christ is a pressed man. The grace of God has pressed him in; but every one who is impressed into the army of Christ is also a volunteer, for he is made willing in the day of God's power; so that, in the kingdom of Christ, the pressed man and the volunteer are the same.

Still, there is a difference in this case. *This man had a distinct command from the Lord:* "Follow me." That is a very solemn thing, to have a command from the Lord coming to the heart, and then to repel it. I would have you very cautious when you hear the Word of God preached, or when you read it. If, at any time, it comes to you with unusual power, if it seems to arrest you, to lay an iron hand upon your shoulder, if you feel it difficult to get away from it, I pray you do not try to get away from it; for, if you do, you will add very greatly to your guilt. When Jesus himself seems to say to you, "Follow me," be not deaf to the divine message, close not your ear to the heavenly command. Have not some of you sat in these seats sometimes, and felt that, if you could but get home, if you could but be spared to get to your little chamber to bow your knee in prayer, you would be very different from what you had ever been, for a voice which seemed more than human was calling to you, and you could not but hear it? I beseech you, never trifle with such a message as that. O my hearers, never trifle with truth at all; but especially with truth that has a voice which you are compelled to hear; for, if you do, it will go hard with you. This man was called by Christ, who said to him, "Follow me."

The excuse which he made seemed very natural. "He said, Lord, suffer me first to go and bury my father." To bury his father might be a duty of nature; but to put that first—"Suffer me first"—indicated where his heart was. He was willing to be a Christian; that is to say, a Christian *and something else;* but the something else must be written in large capitals, and then, at the bottom, in very small type, "and a Christian." Do you not know a great many people of that sort? Philosophical and Christian, but the Christian is quite a secondary consideration. They are like the man whose child was asked, "Is your father a Christian?" and who replied, "He is a Christian, I think; but he has not worked much at it lately." There are many Christians of that sort nowadays. They work at their own business, and they do a little now and then, between whiles, in Christianity. You are no Christian unless you put Christ first. He will not come into your heart to sit in the worst chair in the house. He will not come into your soul to be lodged in the garret. He must have the best room, and the best seat in the room; he must be first, and not even father and mother may come before the Lord Jesus Christ. A young man says, "Yes, I must first become a journeyman or a master; I must first be married; I must see to the main chance." Oh, the world is your main chance, is it? Then you are no follower of Christ. If Christ be not first with thee, Christ is nothing to thee. You cannot have him to play with; you must surrender your whole life to him, and make him the first and last object of your life's ambition, if you have him at all.

But with regard to what this man said about burying his father, if there was some force in it to our ear, the Saviour who knew everything saw that *there was no force in it;* for he said, "There are other people to bury your father; but I have called upon you now to come and follow me. Nobody else can do that for you; but the burial of your father can be done by others whom I have never called, and who know nothing about the divine life. Let the dead bury their dead." You would be surprised if I were to read you the letters which I receive about different things which the writers say I ought to do and could do. Of course, I ought to take a side in politics, and appear at the next political meeting. Of course, I shall not, because there are plenty of dead people to bury dead politics, and they may go and do it. My business is to preach the gospel. Someone then says, "You should take up social questions." There are plenty of dead people to handle social questions; let them handle them if they like the work; my business is to preach the gospel of Jesus Christ. Then it is said, "You ought to provide amusements for the people." Ought I? There are plenty of fools to do that without my going into competition with them; my business is to preach the gospel. When a man is once called by Christ, he may say of a great many things, "Well, they are very proper; very proper, indeed, for others to attend to. Dead people want burying, and ought to be buried. It is a pity that there should be any difficulty about their being buried; but there are enough dead people to bury them. There are not enough living ones to preach the gospel; there are not enough to follow Christ." "Follow me," said Christ, "I must be first; and as for these other things, there are other people who can properly attend to them. It is more in their line. The dead know where the graves are; the dead know all about funerals. Follow me, and let the dead bury their dead."

After all, if he had gone home to bury his father, *it would have involved so much loss of time to him.* As a follower of Christ, during that time he would not have been attending to his work. If he could have gone home to the funeral, and preached Christ to the mourners, it would have been all in his day's work; but as he would not have done so, and did not think of doing so, he was only going simply to pay his debt of courtesy. He was losing so much time that ought to be given to his Master.

And here was the worst result of this request: *it produced unsound discipleship.* Oh, what a mass we have of very questionable discipleship towards Christ, where somebody or something is put before Christ! If you judge the man's life as it really is, you will find there is something that has a higher place in it than love to Christ. Judge him by his conversation: is Christ first there? There is a deeper emotion in his heart caused by politics, it may be, than by religion. I know some of our brethren, most respectable people I have no doubt they are, but if there is a meeting upon some political question, they are all excitement. They shout "Hurrah!" They nearly rave, and act as if they ought to have a strait waistcoat on. But go to the prayer-meeting, and you will find they are as dull as death there. When there is anything to be done for Christ, you cannot stir them; they seem to have gone into a soporific condition. May God save us from that state of heart and life! If Christ is not first, he ought to be; and if we do not make him first, above all other things put together, we do not know him at all. You are no Christian if you are not altogether a Christian. If every part of you be not consecrated to Christ, I fear that no part of you is consecrated to him; at all events, this faulty discipleship will never produce much fruit, or bring much glory to God. With this second class of would-be disciples our Master was troubled, and so are we.

III. Now, thirdly, THERE ARE SOME WOULD-BE FOLLOWERS OF CHRIST WHO STILL HANKER AFTER THE WORLD. "And another also said, Lord, I will follow thee." He is another volunteer; "but let me *first*." Something must be done first by him, too. There would have been no hurt in what he said if he had not put in that word "first." "Let me first go bid them farewell, which are at home at my house." Well, now, the objection to this was that he did not intend to come right straight out from the world. He did not mean to come out there and then for Christ; but he must go home, and bid them farewell first.

We know, first, that *this was a very dangerous procedure*, because the probability was that, when he went home to bid them farewell, they would get crying over him, so that it would take a month to say farewell, and then he would have to say farewell again, and perhaps keep on saying it all the rest of his life. No man leaves sin little by little. No, there is nothing that will do as an escape from sin but total abstinence from it, to have done with it, and cut the connection altogether by God's grace, and that without taking a farewell of it. O young man, when you are thinking of leaving the world, be afraid of those farewells! They have been the ruin of hundreds of hopeful people. They have been almost persuaded; but they have gone to their old companions just to give them the last kiss, and the last shake of the hand, and we have not seen anything more of them. It is a dangerous operation, this trying to part with the world by degrees; gently, in a courteous way, little by little. You will never do it. No man becomes a follower of Christ in that mode. No; like Paul on the way to Damascus, turn at once from being an enemy into a friend of Christ, and cry directly, "Who art thou, Lord?" and "What wilt thou have me to do?" for this is true conversion.

Next, I do not know that this young man was wrong in his proposition to go home; but, *he was going for the wrong purpose.* You notice that his object was to "bid farewell" to all his friends. Suppose he had said, "Master, I will follow thee, and to prove how I will follow thee, I will go home, and fetch my wife; I will go home, and bring my children; I will go home, and talk to my brother; I will go home, and in thy name and by thy power, I will bring to thee my cousin." But, no; he says that he is going to bid them "good-bye"; so he is not going with the heroic motive of winning them to Christ, like Matthew, when he called his old companions together, and Christ sat at the table, and preached the gospel to them. That was a grand bidding "good-bye" to the world; but this young man is simply going to bid them all farewell. Beloved, if you go to your old companions, go and tell them what the Lord has done for you.

It was a manifestation of indecision. He would follow Christ, but—well, that home of his, all those dear faces at home. Our Lord would not have forbidden his seeing them again at another time; but now, first, he asks to go and see them; first, as if they would not be there another week, or another month, he must go there first. So we find plenty of people who are thus undecided; they would like to go to heaven by that broad road along which the multitude of men are going down to hell. "Yes, write my name in the church-book; but I shall keep it on the books of the club where I go and do a little bit of gambling; at any rate, just for a time. I must keep to my old companions for a while. I will be a Christian one of these days; but just now I have—well, the fact is, I have an engagement; I promised, and I must keep my promise." Oh, there is no hope of men while they are like this, swinging between the two states. They must take the grand decisive step, and say, "Now I have cut the cable that bound me to the world; I have done with these dangerous shores; I have put out to the broad deep sea of consecration to God, never to come back to these rocks again."

This man's request *showed a want of appreciation of Christ*. Do you not think so? Why, if Jesus said to any one of us who are in our right minds, "Follow me," should we not think it our highest honour, our greatest delight, to be his followers? Ay, let him lead us over the ground where we see his blood-bedabbled footprints, and we will glory in following him whithersoever he goeth! Oh, when we start back, and must have a little more sin, and a little more of the pleasures of worldly company, and a little more going out with others where we ought not to go, it shows that the root of the matter is not in us, and we are not really brought to the Lord!

And, finally, *it showed great unfitness for the holy work*, for the Master said, "No man, having put his hand to the plough, and looking back, is fit for the kingdom of God." When the ploughman starts with his plough, he keeps his eye right in front, looking straight ahead. If his heart is not in his work, every now and then, when he ought to be driving one way, he looks the other, and so he makes his plough boggle, and get out of the rut. On he goes a little way, and then looks back. He ploughs another bit, and again looks back. He is a fine ploughman! He will never win the gold medal in a ploughing contest, I am sure. He is not fit to follow the plough at all; he is not up to his work. The ploughman who is always looking here and there and everywhere, instead of looking straight ahead, is a most faulty ploughman. Now, we want for Christ to-night, and every day and every night, men and women who will say, "I am for Christ, for him to live, for him to labour, for him to suffer, for him, if need be, to die. Straight ahead, turning neither to the right hand for this that I may gain, nor to the left hand for fear of what I may lose, but straight ahead, by that divine grace which has come into my soul, and made me feel that Christ is all my salvation, and all my desire, straight ahead I plough towards the end of the field." God grant us to have many such converts! They only come by a simple faith in Christ, by having done with self, by having laid aside self-righteousness and sin, and coming straight away to him who alone can make sinful men to be his true disciples.

If there is anything in this discourse that belongs to any of you, will you kindly take it home? If you do not like it, take it home all the more; and if you even get angry at the truth that I have proclaimed, and think that it is very personal, then hug it closely to you, because it must be meant for you. That truth which pleases us is often stolen; but that truth which grieves us is our own property. We had better keep it until it has grieved out of us the sin which makes us grieved at it. I do not ask you to put on any cap that does not fit you; but, if there is one that does fit, wear it, and go with it before the throne of grace, and cry to God to set the wrong right.

May God bless these words of mine to the warning of many, for Jesus Christ's sake! Amen.

Exposition by C. H. Spurgeon.

LUKE IX. 37—62.

Our Lord had been on the mountain, and had been transfigured; and when he came down, the first person that he met was the devil, with whom he had to come in contact. Whenever you or I get up on the mountain-top, and have a very happy and delightful experience, we may expect to be in a battle before long. Our joy is, however, a preparation for the conflict; it nerves our spirit, and makes us strong to meet the great enemy of our souls.

Verses 37—40. *And it came to pass, that on the next day, when they were come down from the hill, much people met him. And, behold, a man of the company cried out, saying, Master, I beseech thee, look upon my son: for he is mine only child. And, lo, a spirit taketh him, and he suddenly crieth out; and it teareth him that he foameth again, and bruising him hardly departeth from him. And I besought thy disciples to cast him out; and they could not.*

There they were, all baffled and defeated; and their enemies were looking at them with many a grin of contempt and scorn. Now comes the conquering Captain. He will turn the tide of battle when his troops are flying before the enemy. He comes, and with a word he gathers them together again.

41. *And Jesus answering said, O faithless and perverse generation, how long shall I be with you, and suffer you? Bring thy son hither.*

If you have been praying for some dear one, and the devil is not cast out, but the one for whom you have pleaded seems to be worse rather than better, notwithstanding all your prayers and all your efforts, hear the Master himself saying to you to-night, as he said to the father of this child, "Bring thy son hither."

42. *And as he was yet a coming, the devil threw him down, and tare him.*

This is Satan's usual way. Whenever he is about to be cast out of anyone, he grows angry; and if he cannot destroy, he will worry, just as a bad tenant will do injury to the house if he cannot any longer keep possession of it. "As he was yet a coming, the devil threw him down, and tare him." Perhaps I speak to some to-night who are coming to Christ, and yet have worse fears than ever. They are more troubled than ever they were before. Well, you are like this poor child: "As he was yet a coming, the devil threw him down, and tare him." It was, however, the devil's last throw.

42. *And Jesus rebuked the unclean spirit, and healed the child, and delivered him again to his father.*

How well it is done, how perfectly it is done, how easily it is done, how quickly it is done when Christ comes on the scene! Let us pray distinctly to-night for those who have been our failures hitherto. They will not be Christ's failures if in prayer and by faith we bring them to him.

43. *And they were all amazed at the mighty power of God.*

But while they were amazed, many of them did not believe. It is one thing to be astonished, it is another thing to be humbled, and to be led to simple faith in Christ. Never be content with any emotion but that which leads you to believe in Jesus for yourself.

43, 44. *But while they wondered every one at all things which Jesus did, he said unto his disciples, Let these sayings sink down into your ears: for the Son of man shall be delivered into the hands of men.*

Just after the transfiguration, just after he had cast out the devil, he tells his disciples that "the Son of man shall be delivered into the hands of men." The shadow of the cross fell upon Christ long before the substance of the cross was on his shoulder. He never forgot that the day would come when he must lay down his life as a ransom for many, and he never started back from it, either.

> "This was compassion like a God,
> That when the Saviour knew
> The price of pardon was his blood,
> His pity ne'er withdrew."

45. *But they understood not this saying, and it was hid from them, that they perceived it not: and they feared to ask him of that saying.*

They were not as yet spiritual enough to spy out his meaning; and when they had even a faint glimmering of it, it made them feel so sad, so cast down, that they did not dare to go and ask him fully to explain it. Do not you think that you and I may have, to-night, something pressing upon us that would all vanish if we but took it to Jesus? And yet we fear to ask him of that saying. Let us drive away that fear, and be familiar with our Lord, and tell him everything that vexes our spirit.

46. *Then there arose a reasoning among them, which of them should be greatest.*

Sad, sad, sad, a hundred times sad! When he was talking of his death, and of his being delivered into the hands of wicked men, his disciples were disputing as to who should be the greatest. Ah, brethren, but we may be guilty of quite as great an inconsistency. If, after Christ's death for us on the cross, and after he has given up everything for us, and has washed us in his heart's blood, if we begin to want to be great and famous in the eyes of men, what wretches we are! May God deliver us from all ambition, from every kind of self-seeking, and from any measure of pride! Otherwise, we are inconsistent in pretending to follow such a Master as the Lord Jesus.

47, 48. *And Jesus, perceiving the thought of their heart, took a child, and set him by him, and said unto them, Whosoever shall receive this child in my name receiveth me: and whosoever shall receive me receiveth him that sent me: for he that is least among you all, the same shall be great.*

The way to rise in the ranks of Christ, is to go down. Be willing to do the meanest thing, and you are growing in Christ's esteem. When you are great, you are little. When you are nothing, then are you great. The Lord take away from us the black drops of pride that make us stand up on our dignity, and think we must be somebody! Somebody? God will not use you as long as you are somebody; but when you are nobody, then will God greatly magnify you, and use you in his Church.

49. *And John answered and said, Master, we saw one casting out devils in thy name; and we forbad him, because he followeth not with us.*

This man who was casting out demons was a dissenter, he was not with the regular church. He was doing good; but still, what right had he to do it? John said, "He followeth not with us." He was outside the pale; and even John, with all his loving disposition, felt that he must blow that candle out. He had no right to shine in anything but the regular, orthodox candlestick. "We forbad him, because he followeth not with us."

50. *And Jesus said unto him, Forbid him not: for he that is not against us is for us.*

Jesus also said that no man could do a miracle in his name, and then lightly go and speak evil of him; so that it was for the good of the cause to let the irregular practitioner go on with this business. Besides, if anybody can cast a devil out, by all means let him do it; for there is none too much of the power of casting out devils; and, remember, that these gentlemen who found fault, could not cast the devil out themselves. They had been beaten in this very task; and yet, when somebody else did it in the power of God, they began to complain, and forbid them. That is surely being like the dog in the manger. God save us from falling into that spirit!

51. *And it came to pass, when the time was come that he should be received up,*

Is not that a wonderful expression? Christ is to die, and to be buried. Ah! but this word comprehends everything, "that he should be received up." Think not of the gloom of death, specially concerning your dear friends who have lately fallen asleep. Think of their being received up. They did seem to go down; they went as low as the grave; but they could not go any lower. Thank God for his abounding mercy in receiving them up.

51. *He stedfastly set his face to go to Jerusalem,*

To go where he must be scourged, and spit upon, and crucified: "He stedfastly set his face to go to Jerusalem."

52, 53. *And sent messengers before his face: and they went, and entered into a village of the Samaritans, to make ready for him. And they did not receive him, because his face was as though he would go to Jerusalem.*

He used to be welcomed in Samaria; but now the evil spirit has come to the front again: "They did not receive him, because his face was as though he would go to Jerusalem," and they wished nobody to go up to the feast at Jerusalem, but desired all to stop and worship God with them on Mount Gerizim. So they would not receive him.

54, 55. *And when his disciples James and John saw this, they said, Lord, wilt thou that we command fire to come down from heaven, and consume them, even as Elias did? But he turned, and rebuked them, and said, Ye know not what manner of spirit ye are of.*

When you read the Old Testament, you will remember that the spirit of the Old Testament was in accordance with the law of Moses; but you are not under the law but under grace, and the spirit of Christ is another spirit, not the spirit of judgment, bringing down fire from heaven, but the spirit of mercy, bringing life and blessing from above.

56. *For the Son of man is not come to destroy men's lives, but to save them. And they went to another village.*

That was all Christ did by way of punishment of these Samaritans: he "went to another village." Yet, gentle as was this treatment, it was really a very severe punishment, such a punishment as will fall on all of you who reject Christ. If you will not receive him, he will go to somebody else. If you will not hear him, somebody else will; and if, when you hear him, you will not accept him, it may be that you will not hear him many times more, the word may never again be spoken with any power to you, but Christ will go to somebody else.

57—62. *And it came to pass, that, as they went in the way, a certain man said unto him, Lord, I will follow thee whithersoever thou goest. And Jesus said unto him, Foxes have holes, and birds of the air have nests; but the Son of man hath not where to lay his head. And he said unto another, Follow me. But he said, Lord, suffer me first to go and bury my father. Jesus said unto him, Let the dead bury their dead: but go thou and preach the kingdom of God. And another also said, Lord, I will follow thee; but let me first go bid them farewell, which are at home at my house. And Jesus said unto him, No man, having put his hand to the plough, and looking back, is fit for the kingdom of God.*

HYMNS FROM "OUR OWN HYMN BOOK"—45, 636, 667.

Metropolitan Tabernacle Pulpit.

GOD'S PEOPLE MELTED AND TRIED.

A Sermon
Intended for Reading on Lord's-day, September 18th, 1892,

DELIVERED BY

C. H. SPURGEON,

AT THE METROPOLITAN TABERNACLE, NEWINGTON,

On Thursday Evening, February 19th, 1891.

"Therefore thus saith the Lord of hosts, Behold, I will melt them, and try them; for how shall I do for the daughter of my people?"—Jeremiah ix. 7.

Observe, here, that God represents himself as greatly concerned to know what to do with his people. Of course, he speaks after the manner of men; for, as the infinitely wise God, knowing all things from the beginning, Jehovah knew what he would do. But yet, in order that we may understand something of the workings of the divine mind, he represents himself as brought to a non-plus, and saying, in the words of our text, "How shall I do for the daughter of my people?" There are some men and women in the world who seem to greatly perplex those who love them, and who desire their welfare. They are a great perplexity to those with whom they live, and who labour for their good, and it seems as if God himself regarded it as a matter of perplexity when he said, "How shall I do for the daughter of my people?"

But notice, next, the Lord is so resolved to save his people, that he will use the sternest possible means rather than lose any of those whom he loves. He says here, "I will melt them, and try them; I will cast them into the furnace, and put them into the melting-pot. I will make the fire so hot that their iron hearts shall melt; and, though they be like hell-hardened steel, devoid of feeling, I will make it so hot for them that they shall be melted. As men assay metal, pouring out the molten mass in a red-hot or white state, I will melt them, and try them." Sinners, that God may save you, he will do the roughest things with you. He will not spare you any kind of sorrow here, or any sort of loss, or any measure of despair of spirit, so that he may bring you to himself. He asks the question, as though he were very anxious to avoid using his rough ways, "How shall I do for the daughter of my people?" But he answers the question with all the severity of almighty love, "Behold, I will melt them, and try them."

No. 2,274.

There is nothing else to be done with them, so I will do that by which alone they can be saved."

Observe, once more, in our preface, that God's concern about his people, and his resolve to use strange ways with them, springs out of his relationship to them; for he says, "How shall I do for the daughter of *my* people?" "*My* people." They were his, though they were so far away from him through their evil ways. Though they had gone from evil to evil, though their lives provoked him to the highest degree, yet he did not disown them. He remembered the covenant that he made for them with Abraham, and with Isaac, and with Jacob; and because of that covenant, he thought upon them for good, and resolved to save them somehow. When God has chosen a man from before the foundation of the world, and when he has given that man over to Christ to be a part of the reward of his soul's travail, he will adopt strange means to accomplish his sacred purpose, and he will carry out that purpose, let it cost him what it may.

We are going to apply these principles in three ways: first, to *the matter of conversion;* secondly, to *the matter of Christian life;* and thirdly, to *the Church of God in its corporate capacity.*

I. First, these principles may be applied to THE MATTER OF CONVERSION. There is a very simple way of being saved; it should be, I hope it is, the common way. It is *the simple way of following the call of grace*. This should be your way; I hope it is. The gospel is preached, you believe it; Christ is set before you, you accept him, you trust him, you are saved. Without any violence, your heart is opened, as with the picklock of grace. God puts the latch-key into the door, and steps into your heart without a word. "Whose heart the Lord opened," we read of Lydia. Even if you have known nothing of the terror of the Lord, if you have had no strange convulsion of feeling, no earthquake, and tempest, and thunder, God is in the still small voice; and you are saved by his grace as much as those who have had a deeper experience.

This is the way of salvation, but *there are some who will not come this way*. There is the Wicket Gate. They have but to knock, and it will be opened; but they prefer to go round about through the Slough of Despond, or to get under the care of Mr. Worldly Wiseman, who leads them round by the house of Mr. Legality, who dwells in the village of Morality, and there they go with their burdens on their backs, which they need not carry even for a single hour, for they would roll off directly if they would but look to Jesus, and believe in him. But they will not do this. There are some of whom God has to say, "How shall I do for the daughter of my people?" Why is this?

Well, some of them have a crooked sort of mind, they never can believe anything straight; they must go round about. I know a friend, whose conversation is always of this kind; if he were in King William Street, and I were in the Borough, he could not come across London Bridge to me, he would find it necessary to go at least as far as Hammersmith before he crossed the river, and then he would come round to me; that is how he always talks. I sometimes get a little tired of that style; and I wish he would come to the point at once. There are some minds of that sort. You say to some people, "Believe and live." Then they begin scratching their heads a bit, and saying, "What is it to believe, and what is it to live? And how can a man live by believing, and does he believe first, or does he live first? And if he lives before he believes, then how does believing make him live?" I could puzzle away like that all night if I liked; any fool can put stools in the way for people to tumble over. There are some minds that seem to be made with what I may call a circumbendibus, that cannot take the truth as God puts it, believing him as a child believes his father; they must somehow twist it about, wrest it, distort it, contort it. Oh, that the Lord would give them another mind! "Except ye be converted, and become as little children, ye shall not enter into the kingdom of heaven." O you wise people, you deep and subtle people, you very thoughtful folk who cannot think that God means what he says, and that a sinner has only to look to Christ and live; but imagine that there must be some particular kind of spectacles to be worn through which you are to look, or that you are to get to some point of the compass from which to look, or that you are to do something else beside look, oh, that you would lay aside all this, for you are making the work of your salvation needlessly difficult! It is of such as you that God saith, "How shall I do for the daughter of my people?"

But some others are obstinate in sin. They are not happy in it; but they will not give it up. They have had some very serious talks with their conscience, and they know that they are wrong, yet they persist in continuing to be wrong. They mean to be right some day, but not yet. They wish somehow that they had overcome the difficulty, but they cannot face it; they cannot give up their evil habits. They still cling to them; and, though often persuaded, and threatened, and moved, they still stand where they always stood, obstinately continuing in sin, while God repeats the enquiry, "How shall I do for the daughter of my people?"

Some others are unwilling to confess sin at all. They think themselves wrong; but they try to make excuses. They are wrong, but not so very wrong. They are such poor, frail creatures, and so greatly tempted; it cannot be very wrong for them to sin. The mind is so easily led astray; surely that is the fault of heredity, or the fault of environment, or the fault of—well, they really make it out that it is the fault of God; so they say in their thoughts, if they do not dare to put it into words. But as for confessing that they are sinners, they will not come to that. Before they will cry, "Father, I have sinned," they will have to be melted, I expect. Before they will ever come to confess their iniquity, they will have to pass through the melting-pot.

Then there are some people who are not saved, but who are outwardly very religious. They have never omitted going to church, or, perhaps, to the meeting-house, whichever they think the better of the two; and they have been brought up carefully, and they have said their prayers regularly, and they have had family prayer, too. They have a Bible; they do not read it much, but still they have one. They are very nice people, everybody thinks that they are Christians; yet all this religion of theirs is not worth a single farthing, for there is no heart-work in it, no repentance of sin, no love to God, no faith in Christ. The robe of their self-righteousness clings to them, and prevents their coming to rest in Jesus. Sinful self is bad enough to get rid of, but righteous self is even worse. Self-righteousness is a kind of mud that will not be brushed off. The man who is bespattered with it does not let it get dry; he renews it every day. The self-righteous man thinks he is too good to go to heaven by the way a sinner goes, and so he never goes at all.

Some, who have no forms of religion, are, nevertheless, wonderfully self-righteous. They are not Christians; but in their own opinion they are quite as good as Christians; in fact, they think they are a great deal better. Yet their conscience must tell them that this is a lie. Still, they flatter themselves in their own conceit, and hide away in a refuge of lies, till God himself says, "How shall I do for the daughter of my people?" And we cannot answer the question except it be in the words of the text, where the Lord says, "Therefore I will melt them, and try them." They will have to go into the fire, and be melted down before they will be meet for the Master's use.

There are some others who will not come to Christ because they are so full of levity and fickleness. They are all froth, all fun. They live like butterflies; they suck in the juices from the flowers, and only flit from one to the other. They are easily impressed one way and another; but there is no heart in them. "Ephraim is a silly dove without heart." They have no stability, they are fickle; they are like the morning cloud, that is soon blown away: as the early dew, that melts in the beams of the rising sun, so is their goodness soon departed from them. How are they to be saved? Some of you have been aroused fifty times already; and if you had been at some places of worship, you would say that you had been converted a dozen times; but we shall never flatter you into that delusion, I hope. I have heard some people say that they have been converted ever so many times. How can a person be born again more than once? I have heard of being born again, and I know that it is possible; but to be born again, and again, and again, must be impossible; that cannot be. Yet people of this sort are good, bad, or indifferent, just as the fit takes them, for they are fickle, changeable; one does not know where to find them.

And withal, there is another class of persons that are insincere. There is no depth of earth about them. They do not really feel what they think they feel; and when they say that they believe, they do not really believe in their heart. They promise, too, when they are ill, what saints they will be if the Lord will but raise them up; but when they get well again, they are not saints. How many have promised and vowed that if they but escaped in such an accident, or their lives were spared in such a disease, they would seek the Lord; yet they have done nothing of the kind! So again, to-night, the question has to be asked about them by God, "How shall I do for the daughter of my people?"

Now, having brought before you these characters, or held up the looking-glass of God's Word so that they might see themselves in it, I want you to notice how God does deal with such people very often. According to my text, *they will have to feel the furnace.*

I have noticed, during a considerable period of time, some of the self-righteous and the outwardly-religious put into the fire and melted, by being permitted to fall into some gross and open sin. I knew a young man, an excellent and worthy young fellow he was to all appearance; but he was wrapped up in his own righteousness entirely, and there was no getting at him. Under the stress of a sudden temptation in the workshop, he distinctly told a falsehood. It was a very sorrowful business. Nobody but himself knew that he had done so; it was never found out; but he knew that he had told a falsehood distinctly and wilfully; and he felt so ashamed of himself that all his pretty buildings of self-righteousness vanished away in a moment, and instead of being great and grand, as he had been aforetime, he had to come to Christ with the publican's prayer, "God be merciful to me a sinner." He had such a sense of right and wrong, that he condemned himself outright. He came to me in an awful state of mind. There were thousands of men who would have done what he had done, and never thought the worse of themselves for it; but he had a conscience, and a truthful spirit, and he felt mean as dirt for having told his master a falsehood. God blessed that experience to him. He was melted right down; and, in the bitterness of his spirit, he cried, for weeks, for mercy, and glad enough he was to find it at the Saviour's feet. I pray God that none of you self-righteous people may be left to go into an open sin; but it may be that the Lord may leave you to yourselves, to let you see what you really are, for you probably have no idea what you are. I, as the servant of God, might flood my face with tears, and weep over you if I could prophesy what you will yet do if restraint be taken from you, for in your heart there are the eggs of all manner of sins, and it only needs favourable circumstances for these to be hatched out into a very cage of unclean birds. That is one way in which I have seen men melted.

Some, again, have been melted down by temporal calamities. I have seen a very great man, with his diamond ring flashing on his finger—I was almost going to say, "and with bells on his toes," for he would almost have liked to wear them there if he could, to call attention to his superior position and his eminent rank. He was a gentleman, he felt that he was; and as to preaching to him as a poor sinner, he was offended at the idea. He had good health and strength, too, and he was not going to die. He counted it one of the wisest things to "drive dull care away." He was merry-hearted, full of spirits, and the gospel had no power over him. "Take it to the dying," said he; "take it to the poor people down in the slums; it is the right thing for them; but I—I do not require it." Yes, but when his fortune melted, he began to melt a little; and when his health went, and he found himself on a sick-bed, and those who once did him reverence forgot him, and he was almost without a friend, he wanted to come round to God by the back door somehow, and cry, "God be merciful to me a sinner." Oh, yes, there are some who cannot be saved as long as they have a silver spoon in their mouths; but when they are brought to poverty, it is the nearest way round to the Father's house, round by the far country where they would fain fill their bellies with the husks that the swine eat. Some years ago, a young gentleman, whose father was a godly man, told me that he was keeping race-horses, and betting. I said to him, "That is right, bet all your money away, and when you have nothing left, you will come to your father's God. Maybe that is the way home for you, an empty pocket, a ragged coat, and a sick body. Then, perhaps, you will turn to God." The Lord has often done so with men. Am I speaking to any who are passing through such a trial as that? God grant that your poverty shall lead you to the best riches, and your sickness conduct you to eternal health!

At other times, without any overt sin, without any temporal trouble, God has ways of taking men apart from their fellows, and whipping them behind the door. It has been my lot to meet with, not merely hundreds, but I think I may say, thousands of souls in this condition; and wherever I go, I feel an intense happiness in meeting with miserable, broken-hearted souls, because I believe they are on the way to the possession of a new heart and a right spirit. God is dealing with them in a way of love, though his way seems to them to be very rough. I have tried to cheer them. I have prayed with and for them. They have told me that their sin haunts them day and night; they cannot hope for mercy; they cannot think that God will ever blot out their transgressions. Their Bible seems to thunder at them, as they read it. Their heart is heavy, their friends think them melancholy, and talk about putting them in an asylum, and I do not know what besides. They are ground down, and brought low. This is all meant to work for their good; they would not come to God any other way. It is by such an experience that God is fulfilling his word, "I will melt them, and try them."

In all this God has one great object. It is just this, first, to hide pride from men. God will not save us, and have us proud. He will not let any one of us throw up his cap, and glorify himself for his own salvation. Grace must have the glory of it from first to last.

Beside that, God means to take us out of our sin, and to do that he makes it to be a bitter and an evil thing to us. All that he is doing is to make our sin too heavy for us to carry, and to make us sick of sin, and fond of Christ, and earnest after holiness. Blessed is the blow that almost crushes you if it breaks off the connection between you and sin.

The drift of all this experience is to bring us to Christ, to the great sacrifice; and none ever will come to Christ but those who have nowhere else to go. No man ever puts into this port except under stress of foul weather. Souls try to go anywhere except to Christ; but when they cannot go anywhere else, and they are done for, and ruined, and lost, then it is that they fly to him, and take him to be their all in all. Why, it takes a long time to get even a child of God fully to understand the way of salvation by sacrifice. I went to see my venerable friend, George Rogers, yesterday. He is close upon ninety-two, and cannot leave his bed. He has to lie there, and can do nothing for himself; but his mental faculties are as bright as ever. I was not long with him before he said to me, "They do not seem to savour now the sacrifice of Christ; and," he added, "you know that Peter believed in the deity of our Lord, and he made such a delightful confession of the deity of Christ that the Master said, 'Blessed art thou, Simon Bar-jona: for flesh and blood hath not revealed it unto thee, but my Father which is in heaven.' But," said Mr. Rogers, "although Peter knew the deity of Christ, and knew it well, he did not know Christ's sacrifice, for no sooner did his Master begin to tell him that he was to be crucified, and so on, than 'Peter took him, and began to rebuke him, saying, Be it far from thee, Lord; this shall not be unto thee.' He could not believe it; he could not see the sacrifice; and his Lord had to call him 'adversary', and to say to him, 'Get thee behind me: thou art an offence unto me: for thou savourest not the things that be of God, but those that be of men.'" My dear old friend said, "Until we can see the sacrifice of Christ, we have not seen things as they really are in God's sight; and any gospel, even if it appears to glorify Christ, and has his deity in it, savours of the things of men, and not of the things of God, if it leaves out Christ's sacrifice." Mr. Rogers was right; there must be the sacrifice of Christ; it is that savour which we are to make known in every place. That is a sweet savour unto God which we are never to cease to give forth as long as we can speak. But, oh, it takes such a time with some to bring them to smell that blessed savour of the sacrifice of the Son of God! When they do perceive it, they get peace, and light, and love, and liberty; but, until then, God himself seems to say concerning them, "How shall I do for the daughter of my people?"

I have dwelt so long upon the matter of conversion that my time is largely gone. I beg you who can pray to join me in asking God to bless the word I have spoken.

II. But, in the second place, I want to say something to Christians; for, IN THE MATTER OF CHRISTIAN LIFE, God seems to say, "What shall I do for the daughter of my people? I will melt them, and try them."

Some Christians go from joy to joy. Their path, like that of the light, shineth more and more unto the perfect day. Why should not you and I be like that? Why should not we simply believe, and keep on believing, and go on rejoicing, serving God with all our heart, and resting in the precious blood of Jesus?

There are *other Christians who appear to make much progress in divine things, but it is not true progress.* Some appear to have a great deal of knowledge. They talk as if they knew everything; but when you come to examine them closely, you find that they do not know hardly anything that they ought to know. Some, too, get a very wonderful experience. You see them swagger about, you hear them brag of it, until you are disgusted with them. That experience which a man boasts of is an experience he ought to be ashamed of. Some, too, seem to have great ability. To hear them talk of what they can do, you would imagine that they could drive the church before them, and drag the world behind them, and I do not know what besides. Paul said, "When I am weak, then am I strong;" but these people are so strong that they never know what weakness means. As for the progress that some professors make in sanctification, why, just look at some of them, and listen to their tall talk! They have not sinned for years! The very principle of sin seems to have died out of them! Poor deluded souls! This is what they say, mark you, not what I believe. As for their graces, they have all things and abound. They are as patient as martyrs. They believe as strongly as John Knox or Martin Luther. You ordinary Christians cannot attain to their stature. If they were to stand bolt upright, they would strike the stars from their places; they are so great and tall. And yet—and yet, there is nothing in their boasting after all. I do not say that they know that much of their wonderful religion is false. No; but they have wrong ideas, confused notions, addled brains, and so they do not know their own real state. Whereas they say that they are rich, and increased in goods, and have need of nothing, they are all the while naked, and blind, and poor, and miserable.

The worst thing about their condition is that some of them do not want to know their real state. They half suspect that it is not what they say it is; but they do not like to be told so; in fact, they get very cross when anyone even hints at the truth. No one is so imperfect in temper as the perfect man; he soon shows his imperfection. He is just the brother who must not be touched. You must stand a long way off, and look at him with reverence, or else he is soon sorely grieved at you. Some do not want to know their real condition. They have an idea that, perhaps, they are not what they seem to be; but they would not have their dream roughly broken. Instruction is not desired by them. Why are they to be instructed? They know a great deal more than anybody else can teach them, and they like the man who will speak flatteringly to them, and who will make them believe that what they say is all gospel. Now, there are such people in all our congregations, of whom God might well say, "How shall I do for the daughter of my people?"

This is what he will do with a great many who are now inflated with a false kind of grace: "I will melt them, and try them," says the Lord of hosts. *He will put them to a test.* Here is a man who has a quantity of plate, and he does not know the value of it, so he takes it to a goldsmith, and asks him what it is worth. "Well," says he, "I cannot exactly tell you; but if you give me a little time, I will melt it all down, and then I will let you know its value." Thus does the Lord deal with many of his people. They have become very good, and very great, as they fancy, and he says, "I will melt them."

This is a natural test for silver and gold, the very best kind of test for precious metal. But in the process of melting, if it is with you, my brethren, as it is with me, the bulk is very much reduced. When God begins to melt us by letting fierce corruptions burn within us, or by allowing our spirits to be depressed and our minds to be darkened, oh, what a shrinkage there seems to be almost immediately in that melting-pot! What fear takes hold upon us then, lest we should shrink to nothing, and disappear altogether!

Then, also, the fashion of the precious metal is marred; its beauty soon departs. That silver vase was beautifully fashioned; but when it is melted, nothing of the chaste design remains. All that is of human fashioning is lost in the melting-pot. Were you ever in the melting-pot, dear friends? I have been there, and my sermons with me, and my frames and feelings, and all my good works. They seemed to quite fill the pot till the fire burned up, and then I looked to see what there was unconsumed; and if it had not been that I had a simple faith in my Lord Jesus Christ, I am afraid I should not have found anything left. This is what God will do with all his people unless they walk very humbly with him. "He that is down needs fear no fall." He that is pure gold will lose nothing in the melting; but he that is somebody in his own opinion, will have to come down a peg or two before long. It is well that it is so; for if it were not, we should soon grow proud, and worldly, and careless, and even licentious; for it is strange, but it is true, that the next thing to a boast of perfect holiness has almost always, throughout history, been intense licentiousness. How it comes to be so, perhaps they who study metaphysics can tell; but so it has constantly been in the history of mankind. When you fancy that you are out of gunshot, there is an enemy close at hand. When you dream that the road is safe, there is a pitfall just before you. When you say, "I am perfectly holy," the very pride that makes you say so is an indication of a deadly cancer of self-righteousness that is eating into your very soul.

Now, beloved, *the result of melting is truth and humility.* The result of melting is that we arrive at a true valuation of things. The result of melting is that we are poured out into a new and better fashion. And, oh, we may almost wish for the melting-pot if we may but get rid of the dross, if we may but be pure, if we may but be fashioned more completely like unto our Lord!

If any of you who have been converted are undergoing a melting just now, do not be staggered at it. It is no strange thing that has happened unto you, and it is no evil thing. You have, no doubt, needed it. You were growing too gross, too careless, and it was necessary for you that you should be melted. Now God has given you the highest proof of his love in this melting, this scourging, this suffering, this down-breaking, this annihilating of carnal confidence, this hanging up of Mr. Presumption by the neck that he may die, that self may fall, and that Jesus may be all in all. God grant that it may be so!

III. I was going to speak about this principle in THE MATTER OF THE CHURCH OF GOD IN ITS CORPORATE CAPACITY; but I will speak of that at another time, if the Lord permit. This you may take for granted, that, if God has chosen us, but we are not willing to go in his way, and humbly trust in Jesus, and have him to be our all in all, the Lord will not give us up, but he will melt us, and try us, till we are fit to run in any mould that he likes to use.

God bless you, and save you, and comfort you, for Jesus Christ's sake! Amen.

Exposition by C. H. Spurgeon.
JEREMIAH IX.

Verse 1. *Oh that my head were waters, and mine eyes a fountain of tears, that I might weep day and night for the slain of the daughter of my people!*

Jeremiah foresaw that the Chaldeans would come up, and so many would be slain that the nation would be almost destroyed.

2. *Oh that I had in the wilderness a lodging place of wayfaring men; that I might leave my people, and go from them! for they be all adulterers, an assembly of treacherous men.*

He mourned because of the doom that awaited them; but he equally mourned because of the sin that would bring that doom upon them. He wished that he could get away into one of those refuges which were provided in lonely places, where travellers might lodge for a night.

3. *And they bend their tongues like their bow for lies:*

They made use of the tongue, as if it were a bow, to shoot out falsehood. It is a very graphic description of the men of Jeremiah's day. He dips his pen in his heart's blood as he writes about them.

3. *But they are not valiant for the truth upon the earth;*

Oh, no! No one stood up for the truth in those days; no man was willing to suffer for it, to argue for it, or even to own it.

3. *For they proceed from evil to evil, and they know not me, saith the* LORD.

They grew worse and worse. It is the way of wicked men to ripen into greater sin. They proceeded from evil to evil; and Jeremiah had Jehovah's testimony for it that, though they knew a great many things, they did not know the LORD: "They know not me, saith the LORD."

4. *Take ye heed every one of his neighbour, and trust ye not in any brother: for every brother will utterly supplant, and every neighbour will walk with slanders.*

It was an evil time indeed when, even in the domestic circle, there could be no brotherly confidence. "Every brother will utterly supplant." Jacob's name, you remember, was supplanter; and all these men were Jacobs, each one ready to supplant his brother, to throw him on one side that he might occupy his place. As to neighbourly conduct, there was none; the neighbours were all gossips and slanderers of one another.

5. *And they will deceive every one his neighbour, and will not speak the truth: they have taught their tongue to speak lies, and weary themselves to commit iniquity.*

What a sad state they were in! Their tongues spoke lies without any teaching; but they schooled them till they were masters of the art of lying. They were D.D.s, doctors of dissembling; they understood the art thoroughly. They had taught their tongue to speak lies, and they had committed so much evil that they even tired themselves in the doing of it.

6. *Thine habitation is in the midst of deceit; through deceit they refuse to know me, saith the* LORD.

Putting forth all their critical ingenuity to get rid of God, his Word, inspiration, and the divine sacrifice, doing all they could that they might not know God.

7, 8. *Therefore thus saith the* LORD *of hosts, Behold, I will melt them, and try them; for how shall I do for the daughter of my people? Their tongue is as an arrow shot out; it speaketh deceit: one speaketh peaceably to his neighbour with his mouth, but in heart he layeth his wait.*

Do you wonder that Jeremiah wept? With so true a spirit, so tender and sympathetic, he could not bear it when man had become man's worst enemy, and no man could be relied upon, for all practised and spoke deceit.

9. *Shall I not visit them for these things? saith the* LORD: *shall not my soul be avenged on such a nation as this?*

Divine justice sets the fire of indignation burning. Nothing excites God's wrath more than continued falsehood and deceit, unkindness, unbrotherly conduct, and unholiness of life. Put all these evils together, and you have more than enough God-provoking sins calling for an avenging visitation.

10. *For the mountains will I take up a weeping and wailing, and for the habitations of the wilderness a lamentation, because they are burned up, so that none can pass through them; neither can men hear the voice of the cattle; both the fowl of the heavens and the beast are fled; they are gone.*

The prophet pictures what the Chaldeans would do. They would not only destroy the cities, but they would even rob the hills of their cattle, and sweep the fields till there would be nothing left that men could gather.

11. *And I will make Jerusalem heaps, and a den of dragons; and I will make the cities of Judah desolate, without an inhabitant.*

Jeremiah had to live to see all this. The thought of it pulled up the sluices of his tears, and made him wish that all the clouds and seas and rains would come, and dwell in his eyes, for his grief had need of all the watery things that nature could produce. George Herbert sings, and I quote his lines to illustrate the depth of Jeremiah's griefs:—

> "Let every vein
> Suck up a river to supply mine eyes,
> My weary, weeping eyes, too dry for me,
> Unless they get new conduits, new supplies,
> To bear them out, and with my state agree."

12. *Who is the wise man, that may understand this? and who is he to whom the mouth of the* LORD *hath spoken, that he may declare it, for what the land perisheth and is burned up like a wilderness, that none passeth through?*

The land would never have been desolate if it had not been for the wickedness of the people. Sin—sin it is that does the mischief. There are some who cavil at the punishment that God puts upon sin; they would do better if they found fault with the sin which brings its own punishment with it. There is nothing arbitrary in God's justice; he allows sin itself to ripen, and when it is finished, it bringeth forth death eternal.

13, 14. *And the* LORD *saith, Because they have forsaken my law which I set before them, and have not obeyed my voice, neither walked therein; but have walked after the imagination of their own heart, and after Baalim,*

After many Baals, is the meaning; many are the gods that men make for themselves when they turn away from Jehovah.

14, 15. *Which their fathers taught them: therefore thus saith the* LORD *of hosts, the God of Israel; Behold, I will feed them, even this people, with wormwood, and give them water of gall to drink.*

You cannot sin without suffering. If you will not drink of the waters of obedience, but will drink of the waters of rebellion, they shall be bitter.

16. *I will scatter them also among the heathen, whom neither they nor their fathers have known: and I will send a sword after them, till I have consumed them.*

A patriot for man, a prophet for God, do you marvel that he wept?

17. *Thus saith the* LORD *of hosts, Consider ye, and call for the mourning women, that they may come; and send for cunning women, that they may come:*

These were the hired mourners, the women who were paid to go to funerals, and simulate grief. "Send for your weepers now;" said the LORD of hosts, "for if you ever needed mourners, you need them now."

18, 19. *And let them make haste, and take up a wailing for us, that our eyes may run down with tears, and our eyelids gush out with waters. For a voice of wailing is heard out of Zion,*

These were no mock mourners; but real weepers, who had cause to mourn.

19. *How are we spoiled! we are greatly confounded,*

Why did they not say, "How have we sinned"? No; men will think of the punishment they suffer; but they will overlook the sin they commit.

19. *Because we have forsaken the land, because our dwellings have cast us out.*

Why did not they say, "Because we have forsaken the LORD, because we have cast off the worship of Jehovah"? You cannot bring men to that point. They quarrel with the rod rather than with the hand that holds it. They mourn over the result of sin; but to the sin itself they still cling.

20, 21. *Yet hear the word of the LORD, O ye women, and let your ear receive the word of his mouth, and teach your daughters wailing, and every one her neighbour lamentation. For death is come up into our windows,*

It did not wait to come in by the door. In time of war or pestilence, death comes how it will through every casement, closed or open.

21. *And is entered into our palaces, to cut off the children from without, and the young men from the streets.*

Generally, in war, they spare the children; and they carry the young men away as captives. The Chaldeans were cruel; they killed the little ones, and they slew the young men.

22. *Speak, Thus saith the LORD, Even the carcases of men shall fall as dung upon the open field, and as the handful after the harvestman, and none shall gather them.*

So dreadful was the devastation that was wrought by these Chaldeans on account of the people's sin, that dead bodies lay like heaps of dung that the husbandman strews upon the field.

23, 24. *Thus saith the LORD, Let not the wise man glory in his wisdom, neither let the mighty man glory in his might, let not the rich man glory in his riches: but let him that glorieth glory in this, that he understandeth and knoweth me, that I am the LORD which exercise lovingkindness, judgment, and righteousness, in the earth: for in these things I delight, saith the LORD.*

This was the God who turned again to his rebellious people, and who would have been glad if they had but known him. He would have made them richer than the rich, and wiser than the wise, and mightier than the mighty; but they would not have the things in which Jehovah delighted.

25. *Behold, the days come, saith the LORD, that I will punish all them which are circumcised with the uncircumcised;*

If they sin like others, they shall die like others, circumcised or uncircumcised, baptized or unbaptized.

26. *Egypt, and Judah, and Edom,*

You see that Judah is sandwiched in between Egypt and Edom. Those who were the people of God are put in the same category with the accursed nation, because they had forsaken him, and mixed up with them.

26. *And the children of Ammon, and Moab, and all that are in the utmost corners, that dwell in the wilderness: for all these nations are uncircumcised, and all the house of Israel are uncircumcised in the heart.*

If the heart be not right with God, vain are all external rites.

HYMNS FROM "OUR OWN HYMN BOOK."—552, 544, 586.

Metropolitan Tabernacle Pulpit.

BELIEF, BAPTISM, BLESSING.

A Sermon

Intended for Reading on Lord's-day, September 25th, 1892,

DELIVERED BY

C. H. SPURGEON,

AT THE METROPOLITAN TABERNACLE, NEWINGTON,

On Lord's-day Evening, February 9th, 1890.

"And he took them the same hour of the night, and washed their stripes; and was baptized, he and all his, straightway. And when he had brought them into his house, he set meat before them, and rejoiced, believing in God with all his house."—Acts xvi. 33, 34.

The gospel, attended by the Spirit of God, is always victorious; but it is very pleasant to make notes of its victories. The gospel came to Lydia, a devout woman, who was one given to prayer, and who worshipped God, although she did not know the Lord Jesus Christ. She was a woman of tender heart, and she was soon won. The Lord gently knocked at the door of her heart, and it was opened. She heard Paul's plain preaching, she received the truth, was baptized, and became the corner-stone of the church at Philippi. "Well," says one, "that is an instance of what the gospel does with delicate, tender, gentle natures." Now, here is an old soldier; he has been in the wars, he has earned distinction, and has been appointed to the office of jailor at Philippi, an office of some importance under the Roman Emperor. He is a man who knows the sight of blood; he is of a coarse, though apparently honest, disposition. He keeps prisoners, and that is not an office that brings much gentleness with it; and he is under very stern law. He himself carries out strict discipline in the prison. He is as hard as a bit of the lower millstone. What will the gospel do with him? Brethren, it triumphed as much in the jailor at Philippi as it did in the lady from Thyatira; and while it won its way into the heart of the dealer in purple, it also worked its way into the heart of the dealer in crimson, who had often shed precious blood. The victory over the rough Philippian jailor was as illustrious as the victory over the gentle and devout Lydia.

I want specially to call your attention to this point; the Philippian jailor stands before us as one who was converted, and baptized, and who brought forth useful fruit all in the compass of an hour or so. "Straightway," says my text. It also says, "The same hour of the night." This man was brought from darkness into marvellous light on a sudden; so ·distinctly brought, that he avowed his conversion there and then, and went on to prove its reality there and then, in his own house, by entertaining the men whom, a few hours before, he had thrust into the inner prison, and whose feet he had made fast in the stocks.

In a great many cases, conversion may be said to be a slow work. I do not think that it really is so; but it appears to be so. There is the early training, there is the awakening of conscience, there is the seeking to find Christ, the struggling, the little light, the dim hope, the faith like a grain of mustard seed, by-and-by a little confidence, afterwards faith more clear, and then, after a long time, comes the public avowal of the joy and peace received through believing. We have a great many people round us who are very slow. Why it is, I do not know; for this is not a slow age. People are fast enough about the things of this world. We cannot travel fast enough. Everything must be done at express speed; but in the things of God there are numbers of persons who are as slow as snails. I have often wondered how the snail got into the ark; he must have started very early to get in. I am thankful that he did get in, however, as certainly as the hare or the gazelle; and many of our crawling friends, I trust, will be found in heaven, and will be really saved, although they are a long while in coming to Christ. It takes a long time to get some of them even a small distance on the road towards a comfortable assurance of salvation.

I have no doubt that the work of grace is very gradual in some people; it is like the sunrise in this country. I am sure that you cannot tell, on foggy mornings, when the sun does rise. I have sometimes questioned whether he ever does rise in England; at all events, I have seen very little of him for the last few days. I believe that the sun has been seen in England; I take it as a matter of trust that that ruddy wafer that I saw the other day really was the sun; although it is a great contrast to the king of day who rules in the sunny South. Who can tell when he begins to shine upon the earth? There is a little grey light, by-and-by a little more, and a little more, and at last you can say that the sun has fairly risen. So it is with some Christians. There is a tiny gleam of light, and then a little more light, and then a further ray of light; but it is only after a considerable time that you can say that the full light has really come into their souls. Yet, mark you, there is a moment when the sun's disc first appears above the horizon. There is a moment when the circle of the sun is really first visible, just an instant, the smallest portion of time; and, in conversion, there must be a time in which death has gone, and life has come; and that must be as sharp a division as the razor's edge could make. There really cannot be anything between life and death. The man is either dead or alive; and there must be some point at which he ceases to be dead, and becomes living. A man cannot be somewhere between condemnation and justification; there is no land in between. The man is either condemned on account of sin, or he is justified through the righteousness of Christ; he cannot be between those two states; so that, after all, in its essence, salvation must be an instantaneous thing. It may be, it will be, surrounded by a good deal that seems to lead up to it, and makes it appear to be gradual; but, in reality, if you get to the root of the matter, there is a turning-point, well-defined and sharp, and if not clear to you, it is clear to the Great Worker, who has wrought in the heart that is changed from death to life, and from condemnation through sin to justification through Jesus Christ.

I. In this Philippian jailor's case, everything is sharp, clear, distinct. In considering it, I will first call your attention to the fact that HERE IS A PERSON CONVERTED AT ONCE.

This man's conversion was wrought at once. *There was no previous thought.* There is nothing that I can imagine in his previous life that led up to it. He had not been plied with sermons, instructions, invitations, entreaties. Probably, up to that night, he had never even heard the name of Jesus Christ; and what he did hear was that these two men, who had come to Philippi preaching Christ, were to be treated with severity, and kept safely. Therefore, he thrust them into the inner dungeon, and made their feet fast in the stocks. All his previous education was un-Christian, if not anti-Christian. All his former life, whatever may have been his Roman virtues, was quite clear of anything like Christian virtue. He knew nothing about that. Nothing could be a greater contrast than the ethics of Rome and the teachings of Christ. This jailor was a good Roman, but he was nothing of a Christian when he thrust the apostles into prison; and yet, before the sun again rose, there was not a better Christian anywhere than that man was. He had passed from death unto life; he was resting on the Christian foundation; he was the possessor of Christian graces. Hear that, ye who have never thought of Christ; and let any man, who came in here to-night a total stranger to true religion, pray that the like may be the case with him, that ere the midnight bell shall toll, he, too, may find the Saviour.

What do you think impressed this man? I think, in part, it may have been *the behaviour of Paul and Silas.* They had no curses on their lips when he made their feet fast in the stocks. They used no ribald language when he thrust them into the innermost cell. They let fall words, I do not doubt, the like of which he had never heard; and their patience, their cheerfulness, their dauntless courage, their holy joy, must all have struck him. They belonged to a different order of prisoners from any he had ever seen before. The jail at Philippi had never held the like of these before, and the jailor could not make them out. He went to bed that night with many thoughts of a new character. Who were these men? Who was this Jesus of whom they spoke?

Then, in the middle of the night, *a singular miracle was wrought.* The prison is shaken by an earthquake. The keeper rises. The prisoners must have gone; for the doors are open. He had not carelessly left them unbolted; he had fastened them before he went to bed; but they are all open, and the prisoners are without chains; they will get away, and he will have to suffer for it. He puts the sword to his own breast; he is about to kill himself, when, just at that moment, he hears a loud voice crying, " Do thyself no harm:

for we are all here." What a surprise for him! What a revulsion of feeling those words caused! "We are all here." He thinks to himself, "Truly there is a God; it must be the God of Paul and Silas who has wrought this miracle." He begins to tremble; he has lived without knowing this God; he has ill-treated the messengers of this God. He brings them out; he respectfully addresses them, "Sirs," he earnestly cries to them, "What must I do to be saved?" The idea of being lost has come over him. It is not that he is afraid to die, for he was about to put himself to death; but he is afraid of what is to follow after death. He is a lost man, and therefore he asks, "What must I do to be saved?"

Now it is that *he is plainly told the way of salvation*. It was put with great brevity, "Believe on the Lord Jesus Christ, and thou shalt be saved, and thy house." Probably he did not understand it when he heard it; and so "they spake unto him the word of the Lord, and to all that were in his house." His wife, his children, his servants, whoever made up his household, all gathered round the two preachers; and they explained the way of salvation, salvation by faith on Christ, salvation by the atoning sacrifice of Christ, salvation by faith in the precious blood of Christ. Paul and Silas doubtless told the company that whosoever believed in Jesus should not perish, but have everlasting life. The jailor believed it, believed every word of it; and he was therefore saved, and saved at once. If you have never heard the gospel before, and you hear it to-night, and believe in Christ, you will be saved at once. If you have been hitherto a total stranger to all good things, yet, if you now receive the blessed tidings of mercy through the Son of God, pardon through his shed blood, you shall go out of this house justified, saved, saved in an instant, saved by the simple act of faith. It is a happy circumstance that the gospel is so simple. There are certain preachers who seem as if they must mystify it, like the negro, who said, "Brethren, I have read you a chapter, and now I will confound it." No doubt there are many who are always making out the gospel to be a very difficult thing to understand; philosophical, deep, and so on; but it was meant for the common people, it was given not merely for the élite, the learned, the instructed, but, "the poor have the gospel preached to them," and the gospel is suitable to be preached to the poor. This is the gospel, "Believe on the Lord Jesus Christ, and thou shalt be saved, and thy house." Trust Christ; and if thou dost, thou shalt be saved.

II. Secondly, HERE IS A PERSON CONFESSING HIS FAITH AT ONCE. "He was baptized, he and all his, straightway."

Should a person be baptized as soon as he believes? As a rule, yes; but there may be good reasons why he should not be. There was no good reason for delay in this man's case, for, in the first place, *his conversion was clear as noonday*. Paul had no question about it. The man was really converted. Silas felt sure of it, too; and they did not hesitate to baptize him and all his household, for they all believed in God. Remember how it was with Philip and the eunuch. That Ethiopian nobleman said, "See, here is water: what doth hinder me to be baptized?" Philip replied, "If thou believest with all thine heart, thou mayest." That being so, they went down both into the water, both Philip and the eunuch, and he baptized him there and then. If the baptizer believes that the professor of faith in Christ is sincere, then he may not hesitate. If he has any doubt about that, if he is afraid that the confession is made in ignorance, or made without due thought, then it may be incumbent upon him to wait a while; but otherwise, he must do as Ananias did to Saul of Tarsus, he must baptize him upon profession of his faith, as soon as he applies. The jailor's conversion, then, was clear.

In his case, also, *there was no other reason for delay*. In the case of many young persons, there are reasons for delay. I remember, in my own case, my parents not believing in the baptism of believers, and I, being between fifteen and sixteen years of age, thought it my duty to consult my father and mother, and ask their counsel and advice. I think I did right; I did not expect them to see with me, but I did expect them to give me their loving concurrence, which they did; and I waited until I had obtained it. Sometimes it will be right on the part of other young people to do the same. There may be reasons, and practical reasons for delay, physical, moral, spiritual; I cannot go into them all at this time. A man may be excusable who, though a believer, is not immediately baptized, seeing that he intends to be as soon as it would be fitting and right and decorous, and, in connection with other duties, a right thing. But there was no reason for delay in the jailor's case. The man was his own master, and his children and his servants had no difficulty in gaining his consent to their baptism, seeing that he himself was about to lead the way in confessing Christ in the Scriptural fashion.

In this man's case, note also, that *he was not hindered by selfish considerations*. Had the jailor been like some people that I know of, he would have found plenty of reasons for delaying his baptism. First, he would have said, "Well, it is the middle of the night. Would you have me baptized at this hour?" He would have said that he did not know that there were conveniences for baptism, for it is so easy to find it inconvenient when you do not like it. He might also have said, "I do not know how the magistrates will like it." He did not care about the magistrates. Perhaps he would lose his situation. He did not take his situation into consideration. Then, what would the soldiers in the Philippian colony say when they heard that the jailor had been baptized into the name of Christ? Oh, the guffaws of the guard-room, the jokes that there would be all over Philippi! This brave man did not take those things into consideration; or if he did, he dismissed them in a moment. It was right for him, now that he believed in Christ, to confess his faith in Christ; and he would do it, and he would do it "straightway." Ah, dear friends, there are some of you here who have never come out as Christians! You are what I call the rats behind the wainscot, or the black beetles that come out at night, when there is nobody about, to get a bit of food, and then go back again. You never say what you are; you never come out on Christ's side. I am not going to condemn you; I wish that you would condemn yourselves, however, for I think that you ought to judge that you are acting a very mean part. The promise of eternal life is not made to a faith which is never avowed.

Allow me to say that over again. The promise of salvation is not made to a faith which is never avowed. "He that believeth and is baptized, shall be saved." "With the heart man believeth unto righteousness; and with the mouth confession is made unto salvation." Our Lord's own words are, "Whosoever therefore shall confess me before men, him will I confess also before my Father which is in heaven;" and he also said, in connection with this confession, "but whosoever shall deny me" (which must mean, whosoever does not confess me) "before men, him will I also deny before my Father which is in heaven." If you have not faith enough in Christ to say that you believe in him, I do not think that you have faith enough in Christ to take you to heaven, for it is written concerning the place of doom, "the fearful", that is, the cowardly, "and unbelieving, shall have their part in the lake which burneth with fire and brimstone."

The fact was, *this man was in downright earnest*, and therefore he would not delay his baptism. He had enlisted in the army of Christ, and he would wear Christ's regimentals straightway. I wish that some who profess conversion, or who profess to desire to be converted, were as much in earnest as this jailor was. "Well," says one, "do not be too severe upon us; I hope that I am a Christian, although I have never confessed Christ yet." Why do you not confess Christ, if you belong to him? I spoke like this to a man who had been, according to his own confession, twenty years a Christian. He had never joined the church; he had never made any open profession of religion; and when I spoke to him, what do you think he said to me? He said, "He that believeth shall not make haste." "Well," I replied, "if you were to be baptized, and to join the church to-morrow morning, I do not think that there would be much haste in it as you have been a believer twenty years; but a much more suitable text for you would be this word of the Psalmist, 'I made haste, and delayed not—to keep thy commandments.'"

"Well," says another, "I have put it off a little while, and———." "A little while!" Is that what you allow your boy to say to you? You say to him, "John, go up into the city for me on an errand." In about an hour afterwards, you see him still at home, and you ask why he has not done your bidding, and he says, "Father, I have put it off a little while." I think it is likely that you would make him recollect that excuse, and not repeat it. But if you were to see him still about the house, hour after hour, and he said to you that he was not disobedient, but he had some little things of his own that he wanted to see to first, I fancy you would teach him what a son's duty is. A servant of that kind would probably have to find a new master very quickly; and do you call yourself a servant of Christ when you have been putting off confessing him by being baptized, putting it off, and putting it off, until, as far as I can see, you are as far off obedience to your Lord's command as ever you were? This jailor, "the same hour of the night" made confession of his faith, "and was baptized, he and all his, straightway," and soon they were all sitting down with Paul and Silas at a love-feast, enjoying happy fellowship with the people of God. Dear friend, if you are converted, do not stand back from confessing Christ. You rob your minister of his wages; for it is his reward to hear that God has blessed your soul. You are also robbing the church. If you have a right to stand out, and not confess Christ, everybody else has the same right; and where would there be any confession of Christ, or any visible church, or any ordinances, or any minister? If you have a right not to come to baptism, and the Lord's Supper, every other Christian has a right to neglect these things also. Then, why were these ordinances instituted at all? What is Christ in his own house? Is he Master, or are you the master; and do you take liberty to do or not do just what you please? Come along, and let my text be true of all of you who believe, "He was baptized, he and all his, straightway."

III. Now, thirdly, HERE IS A PERSON USEFUL AT ONCE. Useful? What could he do?

Well, he did all he could. First, *he performed an act of mercy :* "He took them the same hour of the night, and washed their stripes." Dear, good men, they were covered all over with the marks of the Roman rods. They had been beaten black and blue, and the blood had flowed freely. I think I see how tenderly the jailor washed their stripes. It was before he was baptized that he brought forth fruits meet for repentance. The ill-used ministers needed washing; how could their wounds be healed unless they were properly washed? With all the dust and dirt of the street and the grit of the prison-house in the weals and the wounds, how could they heal? "He washed their stripes." I like to read these words. I am sure Paul and Silas must have enjoyed to have their stripes washed by one who, a little while ago, had been so rough with them. I do not know that he could have done anything better to show his sincere repentance.

He washed their stripes; and when he had done that, and had been baptized, we read that he brought them into his house, and set meat before them. Thus, *he exercised hospitality.* He used his hands and his bath in washing the disciples; now he uses his table, his larder, and his dining-room to entertain them. What more could he do? Seeing that it was the middle of the night, I cannot think of anything more that he could do. So now, if you love the Lord, if you have only just believed in him, begin to do something for him at once. It is a pity that we have so many Christian people, so-called, who do nothing for Christ, literally nothing. They have paid their pew-rent, perhaps; and that is all Christ is to have out of them! He dies for them, redeems them with his precious blood, and they have done nothing for him in return. "I do not know what I could do," says one. I know you could do something. This jailor, within the boundaries of his prison, can do the most needful thing for Paul and Silas; and you, within the boundaries of this house, can do something for Jesus Christ. I would ask you, if you have only to-night believed in Christ, do something for him to-night. By speaking to your wife, or children, or servants, or neighbours, do something for Christ to-night. There is probably no minister shut up in prison in any part of your house, and needing to have his stripes washed. If not, there may be some poor soul somewhere near you that wants a little help. Do an act of charity for Christ's sake. Or there may be some child of God whose heart you could cheer to-night. Do an act of hospitality for some needy saint, and so show your gratitude for what the Lord has done for you. You must do something for Christ if you are a real Christian.

We want to have a church in which all the members do something, in which all do all they can, in which all are always doing all they can, for this is what our Lord deserves to have from a living, loving people bought with his precious blood. If he has saved me, I will serve him for ever and ever; and whatever lies in my power to do for his glory, that it shall be my delight to do, and to do at once. Oh, if some of you get saved to-night, when you get home, there will be a difference in your house! Ah, and within a day or two, even your cat will know that there is a change in you! Everybody in the house will know that you are different from what you were. When a man who has been a drinker gets saved, or one who has been accustomed to use bad language, or one who has given way to passion, or a Sabbath-breaker, or a godless, Christless wretch,—when he gets converted, it is as if hell were turned into heaven, and the devil transformed into an angel. God make it so with any such who are here, by the working of sovereign grace!

I seem, at this moment, to recollect that morning when I found the Saviour. It was a cold snowy morning; and I remember standing before the fire, leaning on the mantel-shelf, after I got home, and my mother spoke to me, and I heard her say outside the door, "There is a change come over Charles." She had not had half-a-dozen words with me; but she saw that I was not what I had been. I had been dull, melancholy, sorrowful, depressed; and when I had looked to Christ, the appearance of my face was changed; I had a smile, a cheerful, happy, contented look at once, and she could see it; and a few words let her know that her melancholy boy had risen out of his despondency, and had become bright and cheerful. May some such change as that pass over you!

IV. Here is one thing more to finish with. Fourthly, HERE IS A PERSON PERFECTLY HAPPY AT ONCE. When the jailor had brought Paul and Silas into his house, "he set meat before them, and rejoiced, believing in God with all his house."

Oh, that was a happy, happy time! "He rejoiced, believing in God with all his house." *He rejoiced that he was saved.* His heart kept beating "Hallelujah! hallelujah! hallelujah!" As he sat at that table with his two strange guests, he had indeed cause for joy. His sin was forgiven; his nature was changed; he had found a Saviour; he had given up his idol gods, and he rejoiced, believing in God. He had been told to believe on the Lord Jesus Christ. He was no Unitarian. He believed Jesus Christ to be God; and he rejoiced, believing in God with all his heart.

And then *he rejoiced that all his household were saved.* What a delight it was to see all his household converted! There was his wife. If she had not been converted, it would have been a very awkward thing for him to have asked Paul and Silas in to that midnight meal. She would have said, "I do not want prisoners coming into my best parlour, and eating up all the cold meat." She would not have liked it; as a prudent housewife, she would have objected to it. But there was Mrs. Jailor waiting on them all with a holy happiness, a new kind of cheerfulness. I do not know whether they had any boys or girls. It may be, or may not be; but however many there were in his household, children or servants, they all believed, "believing in God with all his house." They were all baptized, too, the sons and daughters, and the servants also, for they were included in the household. I do not like it when you count up your household, and leave out Mary Ann, the little servant girl, the last you have had in. You treat her as a drudge; but if she has come into your family, reckon her to be a part of your household; and pray God that they may all be converted—Jane and Mary, your own children, and the other people's children who have come into your houses to do necessary domestic work for you.

The jailor's rejoicing was also *a seal of the Spirit upon his fidelity*. Would it not be delightful for him to sit down with the two preachers of the Word in the middle of the night? Those two men must have had good appetites. They had probably had nothing to eat for many hours, and they had been lying in their dreadful dungeon with their feet in the stocks, after having been cruelly beaten; so they were prepared to eat, whether it was the middle of the night or the middle of the day. And the rest of the family came, and sat down at the table with them, and all rejoiced. Such a night in a prison had never been known before. The jailor "rejoiced, believing in God with all his house."

I think that I heard a friend over there fetch a deep sigh as I quoted those last words of my text. I know what it meant; it meant that he has not all his house converted. Ah, dear brother, I cannot sympathize with you by experience; for I thank God that I have had all my house brought to Christ; but it must be a great sorrow to have that biggest boy of yours acting as he does, or to have that dear girl, of whom you had such bright hopes, turning aside to crooked ways! Let me ask you a question—Have you had faith about your house? Remember that Paul said to the jailor, "Believe on the Lord Jesus Christ, and thou shalt be saved, *and thy house*." May God give you faith about your house! You have had faith about yourself, and you are saved; exercise faith about your children; cry to God to give you faith about them. Pray believingly that they may be led to have faith for themselves, and so may be saved.

Oh, that all in this great assembly may meet in heaven! You who have heard the Word these many years, may you to-night believe in Christ, and live! You who have never listened to it before, may you also come to Christ, and believe in him, as the jailor did; and like him, you shall be saved! The Lord shall have all the praise and the glory; but oh, that he would work this miracle of mercy to-night! Let us pray for it. Amen.

Exposition by C. H. Spurgeon.

ACTS XVI. 9—34.

Verse 9. *And a vision appeared to Paul in the night; There stood a man of Macedonia, and prayed him, saying, Come over into Macedonia, and help us.*

Our dreams often follow the leading thoughts of the day; or, if not of the day, yet the chief thoughts that are upon the mind. Paul dreams about mission work, for his heart is in it. I should not wonder if some before me, who are deeply engaged in earnest Christian work, have often dreamt about their Sunday-school, or their mission-station. Where the mind goes when we are awake, it often goes when we are asleep. This vision that appeared to Paul was supernatural; and was an indication of what God wanted him to do.

10. *And after he had seen the vision, immediately we endeavoured to go into Macedonia, assuredly gathering that the Lord had called us for to preach the gospel unto them.*

In the vision, the man prayed, "Come over into Macedonia, and help us." The best help that Paul could render to the Macedonians was "to preach the gospel unto them." The best help you can give men socially is to help them religiously; and the best religious help is to preach the gospel to them.

11, 12. *Therefore loosing from Troas, we came with a straight course to Samothracia, and the next day to Neapolis; and from thence to Philippi, which is the chief city of that part of Macedonia, and a colony: and we were in that city abiding certain days.*

Waiting to know what they were to do. In God's work, we are not to go on in blundering haste. Sometimes, a little waiting may be good for us; and by waiting, we may find out the true path of success.

13. *And on the sabbath we went out of the city by a river side, where prayer was wont to be made;*

Some quiet corner, where good people were wont to gather by the brook to pray.

13. *And we sat down, and spake unto the women which resorted thither.*

This was probably the first religious meeting of Christians that was ever held in Europe. It is remarkable that it was a prayer-meeting, a prayer-meeting attended by women, a prayer-meeting to which two ministers came, and preached the gospel to the women who resorted thither. To be able to be present at a prayer-meeting ought always to be reckoned a great privilege to all of us who are Christians. In this way the gospel first came to us; in this way the gospel will be best preserved to us; and in this way we may best obtain guidance from God as to how we may carry the gospel to others.

14, 15. *And a certain woman named Lydia, a seller of purple, of the city of Thyatira, which worshipped God, heard us: whose heart the Lord opened, that she attended unto the things which were spoken of Paul. And when she was baptized,*

She seems to have become a believer in Christ, and to have been baptized at once.

15. *And her household, she besought us, saying, If ye have judged me to be faithful to the Lord, come into my house, and abide there. And she constrained us.*

Lydia was evidently a woman of some property. The purple which she sold was an expensive article. She seems to have been engaged in business on her own account; and when Paul met with her, she was far off from her workshop and her home. She had a house, therefore, in the place to which she had come to sell her purple; and she "constrained" the men of God to make use of her house, and to tarry there. Thus was Christianity brought into Europe, for which we praise the name of the Lord.

16. *And it came to pass, as we went to prayer, a certain damsel possessed with a spirit of divination met us, which brought her masters much gain by soothsaying:*

She professed to tell fortunes, and to speak under inspiration. She was really "possessed" by an evil spirit.

17, 18. *The same followed Paul and us, and cried, saying, These men are the servants of the most high God, which shew unto us the way of salvation. And this did she many days. But Paul, being grieved, turned and said to the spirit, I command thee in the name of Jesus Christ to come out of her. And he came out the same hour.*

Here was an evil spirit bearing witness to the truth of God, and it grieved Paul. When you hear a bad man ridiculing religion, do not be surprised; what else could you expect from him? But if you heard the devil recommending Christ, then you ought to be grieved, for the Lord Jesus does not want patronage or praise from Satan. Men would begin to suspect that Christ was in league with Satan, if Satan began to speak well of Christ. Dread to be spoken well of by ungodly men; for there is great danger in such praise. There may be a motive at the bottom of the flattery which may be full of mischief. Paul, being grieved, silenced the demon, and cast him out of the damsel. Like his Lord, he would not allow the devil to testify concerning himself and his mission.

19, 20. *And when her masters saw that the hope of their gains was gone, they caught Paul and Silas, and drew them into the market-place unto the rulers, and brought them to the magistrates,*

They dragged them into the Forum, the place where the courts usually sat, and brought them before the magistrates, "saying"—what? "These men have cured a demoniac, they have performed a miracle, and cast a devil out of a young woman"? Oh! no; there would have been no wrong in that, so they must invent a charge. What do they say?

20, 21. *Saying, These men, being Jews, do exceedingly trouble our city, and teach customs, which are not lawful for us to receive, neither to observe, being Romans.*

They did not know that Paul himself was a Roman citizen, or they surely would not have brought such a charge as that against him.

22. *And the multitude rose up together against them: and the magistrates rent off their clothes, and commanded to beat them.*

They beat them first, and tried them afterwards. That is often the rule with those who persecute God's people: let them be hanged out of the way, and then we will enquire what they teach.

23—25. *And when they had laid many stripes upon them, they cast them into prison, charging the jailor to keep them safely: who, having received such a charge, thrust them into the inner prison, and made their feet fast in the stocks. And at midnight Paul and Silas prayed, and sang praises unto God:*

Another prayer-meeting, and a praise-meeting, too. There were only two persons at it; but they "prayed, and sang praises unto God."

25. *And the prisoners heard them.*

Paul and Silas were in the lower prison. The sound of their prayer and praise rose up through the different tiers of cells where other prisoners were confined.

26. *And suddenly there was a great earthquake, so that the foundations of the prison were shaken: and immediately all the doors were opened, and every one's bands were loosed.*

This was no common earthquake. An ordinary earthquake might have brought the prison down about their ears; but it would not have loosed the bands of the prisoners.

27. *And the keeper of the prison awaking out of his sleep, and seeing the prison doors open, he drew out his sword, and would have killed himself, supposing that the prisoners had been fled.*

For the law was that, if a jailor lost a prisoner, he was to suffer whatever penalty the prisoner would have suffered. He therefore knew that, in all probability, his own life would be taken; and, strange to say, to save his life he would kill himself. Suicide is ever absurd and unreasonable. The worst that could happen to him would be to die by the sword of justice; and to escape from that, he tries to die by the sword of a suicide.

28. *But Paul cried with a loud voice, saying, Do thyself no harm: for we are all here.*

Every prisoner was loosed from his bands, but not one had escaped; nor had any even attempted to escape, which was another miracle; for men who see their bands broken, and the prison doors open, are pretty sure to run away. These men did not, for a heavenly charm was upon them. They kept in their cells, so that Paul could cry out to the jailor, "Do thyself no harm: for we are all here."

29. *Then he called for a light, and sprang in, and came trembling,*

Conscious of the supernatural, compelled to feel the hand which he had never perceived before, he hastened into the inner prison, where he had thrust the servants of Christ;

29. *And fell down before Paul and Silas,*

Whom he had handled so roughly just now;

30. *And brought them out, and said, Sirs,*

What a word to address to those who were still in his charge as prisoners!

30—34. *What must I do to be saved? And they said, Believe on the Lord Jesus Christ, and thou shalt be saved, and thy house. And they spake unto him the word of the Lord, and to all that were in his house. And he took them the same hour of the night, and washed their stripes; and was baptized, he and all his, straightway. And when he had brought them into his house, he set meat before them, and rejoiced, believing in God with all his house.*

May God give to many of us to know the happy experience of that believing, baptized, and blessed household!

Hymns from "Our Own Hymn Book"—660, 670, 674.

The C. H. Spurgeon Memorial Fund.—The donations already received amount to about £8,400. This is a very good commencement; but it is hoped that the amount will be so greatly increased that the many important institutions founded by Mr. Spurgeon will receive substantial and permanent aid. All donations should be addressed:—Treasurer, Memorial Fund, Metropolitan Tabernacle, Newington, London, S.E.

Metropolitan Tabernacle Pulpit.

FORGIVENESS, FREEDOM, FAVOUR.

A Sermon

INTENDED FOR READING ON LORD'S-DAY, OCTOBER 2ND, 1892,

DELIVERED BY

C. H. SPURGEON,

AT THE METROPOLITAN TABERNACLE, NEWINGTON,

On Thursday Evening, April 10*th,* 1890.

"And this is the manner of the release: Every creditor that lendeth ought unto his neighbour shall release it; he shall not exact it of his neighbour, or of his brother; because it is called the LORD'S release."—Deuteronomy xv. 2.

THIS wonderful transaction of "the Lord's release" came at the end of every seven years. It was according to the gracious law of God for Israel that there should be, first of all, a rest one day in seven. Next, there were feast days one month in seven; and then there came, every seventh year, a year of rest for the land, in which they did not till it, but left it to lie fallow. Then, after the seven sevens were complete, there came on the fiftieth year, an extraordinary year of rest, in addition to the usual one; this was called the year of Jubilee.

I believe that there is a spiritual meaning in this succession of rests; but I have not time to enter upon the explanation of it now, except to say that, doubtless, that last seven of sevens represents the restitution of all things, when the Lord Jesus shall have gathered his people in to rest for ever and ever with himself in his glory. Till then, we go from seven to seven every week; our Sabbaths are so many staves of the golden ladder by which we climb up to the eternal Sabbath. We bless God that we still retain, at least, that vestige of the seven; for blessed are our eyes that they see, and our hearts that they enjoy, the one day of rest every week. What should we do without it?

Once, then, in seven years, there was a year of perfect rest; and I cannot help remarking again, as I did in the reading, what happy people the chosen people would have been, if they had but hearkened to God's commands! Only imagine a country where, for a whole year, there would be nothing to do. The land would bring forth her own fruit, and everybody might eat of it, sitting under his own vine and fig-tree, having no tillage of the field or pruning of the vine, but having an opportunity given to him of spending the whole year in the service and worship of the Most High. When the people afterwards

No. 2,276.

revolted from the Lord, and desired a king to reign over them, he told them, by the mouth of the prophet Samuel, the manner of the king whom they would choose, so that they might know the difference between the Lord's rule and their king's. The earthly monarchs ground them down, and oppressed them, and brought them into all manner of bondage; but the Lord's yoke was only this, that they should rest and serve him here, and enjoy him for ever hereafter.

These high privileges were attended, in the case of the people of Israel, with high spiritual commands. The laws given to Israel were not intended for Moabites, and Edomites, and Egyptians. They could not have understood them; they would probably even have laughed at them; but the spiritually-minded among God's chosen people, and there were some such, would delight in these commands, and obey them. Look at the command in the present chapter, that any Israelite, who had sold his liberty to a brother Hebrew, should go free at the end of six years. It was a strange command, a blessedly generous one; but it was added that he should not go out empty, but that he should be furnished with abundant help from the flock, from the threshing-floor, and from the wine-press, and that he who gave him this fresh start in life should not do it grudgingly. The Hebrew has it, "Loading him, he shall be loaded; thou shalt adorn his neck with thy gifts." He was to have an abundance given to him; and this was to be done cheerfully, not grudgingly. A delight was to be felt in thus setting free a brother of the chosen race, and starting him once more on the journey of life. It is a grand command.

Do you not think that it should always be so, that they who receive much should have much required of them; and that they who serve a generous God should be themselves generous? Is there not reason in that precept of the Saviour, " Freely ye have received, freely give " ? May not the Lord expect of us much more than he does of others? If you are chosen out of mankind, redeemed from among men, called out from the fallen mass, quickened with a life which they do not know, and privileged with access to God and communion with heaven to which they are strangers, should not the law of God's house be a higher and a nobler one than a law that could be given to those who are strangers to him, and aliens from the commonwealth of Israel? Do not, therefore, if you are Christians, measure yourselves with others, and say, "If I do as much as my neighbour does, it suffices." You who are of the blood royal of heaven, princes in God's kingdom, will you behave yourselves like paupers? You who have been redeemed with blood, whose every fetter has been struck off, will you act like slaves? Let it not be so. Rise to your true dignity. Act worthy of your privileges, and accept with joy of your Father and your King a law which others cannot understand, and which they would think unreasonable and impracticable. It was so with the laws which were given to these people. It is true that, on one side of them, they were somewhat toned down in certain respects to suit their weaknesses; but in other respects, they were heightened and elevated above what any human legislature would ever have thought of enacting.

However, that is not my subject to-night. I want to speak to you about the Lord's release.

It seems to me that this passage, first of all, teaches us concerning *the release which the Lord desired his people to give;* but, secondly, and typically, it speaks to us of *the release which the Lord himself gives to us.* He does not command us to do what he will not much more abundantly do himself. "Be ye perfect, even as your Father which is in heaven is perfect." Your Lawgiver is himself an example of the fulfilment of every gracious and noble precept in his own law.

I. First, then, let us consider THE RELEASE WHICH THE LORD DESIRED HIS PEOPLE TO GIVE.

First, *they were to forgive their debtors.* They were, at the end of every seven years, to release every man his debtor from the debt which he had accumulated. I suppose that, as soon as the year began, there was a release given. A man might pay if he could, and he should do so. A man might, at some future time, if his circumstances altered, discharge the debt which had been remitted; but as far as the creditor was concerned, it was remitted. It is the opinion of some commentators that it only signifies that the man was to be let alone during that year; but that the debt still remained. I do not think that such an interpretation would have occurred to anybody who read the chapter by itself. You can take the idea to the chapter, and foist it upon it, if you like; but it certainly is not there in the natural run of the words. All the Jewish interpreters, albeit that they often twisted their law, are agreed upon this, that it was an absolute forgiveness of the debt incurred which was intended here; and I will not give our Jewish brethren any blame for being too lenient in money matters. I think, perhaps, that they may be a little inclined the other way; and if their Rabbis all teach that this was an absolute wiping out of the debt, I think that, for once, I must agree with their Rabbis, and accept their interpretation, as it evidently is the plain meaning of the passage. I am no learned man, and therefore I read the passage as it stands. I think that the Lord would have the creditor at the end of six years absolutely wipe out the debt; and I am more certain of it because he anticipates the objection that many would begin to say, "The year of release is at hand," and would therefore refuse to lend. Many of them, who were what is called prudent, and who were inclined towards hardheartedness, would naturally say, "No, we are not going to make a loan when it is so near the time when it will have to be forgiven, and the loan will become a gift." Hence the Lord says, "Beware that there be not a thought in thy wicked heart, saying, The seventh year, the year of release, is at hand; and thine eye be evil against thy poor brother, and thou givest him nought." Oh, what a relief it must have been to the debtors! And when it was really done, what a comfort and lightness of heart it must have brought to the creditors, too, when they saw their poor brethren able to enjoy life again, and no longer having their days darkened with the shadow of a heavy debt!

The next thing was, that *they were never to exact that debt again.* Observe in the text, "He shall not exact it of his neighbour, or of his brother." After that year, he was to have no further claim; or if he thought that he had a claim, he was never to use any legal means, or any kind of physical force, or any threats, to obtain what was due. It was to be regarded as done with, as far as any legal claim was concerned. The moral claim might remain; and the honest, upright-minded Israelite might take care that his brother Israelite should not lose anything through him; but, still, according to the divine command, there was to be no exacting of it. My dear brother Williams, in his prayer, spoke of the generosity of God as seen in these commands; and, depend upon it, none but a generous Lawgiver would have made such a law as this. It is noble-hearted, full of loving-kindness; and we could expect that none but a people in whose midst there was the daily sacrifice, in the midst of whom moved the high priest of God, would be obedient to such a precept.

Observe next, that *they were to do this for the Lord's sake:* "because it is called the Lord's release." They were to do it with an eye to a blessing from God: "For the Lord shall greatly bless thee in the land which the Lord thy God giveth thee for an inheritance to possess it: only if thou carefully hearken unto the voice of the Lord thy God." It is not enough to do the correct thing, it must be done in a right spirit, and with a pure motive. A good action is not wholly good unless it be done for the glory of God, and because of the greatness and goodness of his holy name. It would ennoble an Israelite to give a release to one's debtor, and say, "It is called the Lord's release," to act, as it were, as lieutenant of the great King of kings. It will ennoble you to give a discharge, not in your own name, but in Christ's name, and for his sake, because you love him. The most powerful motive that a Christian can have is this, "For Jesus' sake." You could not forgive the debt, perhaps, for your brother's sake; there may be something about him that would harden your heart; but can you not do it for Jesus' sake? This is true charity, that holy love which is the choicest of the graces. That text in John's first Epistle is not only, "We love him because he first loved us," but many versions read it, "We love because he first loved us." Even our love towards men, when it flows out in acts of mercy and deeds of kindness, should spring from the fact that Christ first loved us.

And then, like the Israelites, we may look believingly to the gracious reward that God gives. We do not serve God for wages; but still we have respect unto the recompense of the reward, even as Moses had. We do not run like hirelings; but yet we have our eye upon the prize of our high calling in Christ Jesus. A Christian should often perform acts of kindness, for which he may only meet ingratitude, acts of kindness to the unthankful and to the evil, in the full belief that there will come a day when Christ will accept such things as done unto himself, and will say, "Come, ye blessed of my Father, inherit the kingdom prepared for you from the foundation of the world: for I was an hungered, and ye gave me meat: I was thirsty, and ye gave me drink." This law, given to Israel, is a law given to us so far as the motive for keeping it is concerned. Let us do good unto all men, for God's glory, for Christ's sake, and let us have an eye to that day when every holy action done unto the Lord shall receive reward from him.

Next, notice, as you read down the chapter, that they were not only to perform this kindness once, but *they were to be ready to do it again.*

The creditor, who had absolved his debtor once, must not begin to say to himself, "I shall not lend any more; this business of the seven years, this statute of limitations, makes a dead loss of it." No, if he does think so, the ninth verse tells him that it is a thought in his wicked heart: "Beware that there be not a thought in thy wicked heart,"—"in thy heart of Belial,"—so the Hebrew runs, as if such a thought brought him down from Israel to Belial, and made the man of God to be a loose man, a man who feared not Jehovah at all. Beloved, it is the part of Christians not to be weary in well doing; and if they get no reward for what they have done from those to whom it is done, still to do the same again. Remember how gracious God is, and how he giveth to the unthankful and the evil, and maketh his rain to fall upon the field of the churl as well as upon the field of the most generous. He is good to all, and his tender mercies are over all his works. We may carry the idea of only helping the worthy a great deal too far, till we cease to be imitators of Christ, and rather become dispensers of justice than of love; and this is not the work for a Christian man to do.

Next, observe, that while they were to forgive and remit, on this seventh year, the loans which remained unpaid, *they were also to let the bondman go*. He was a Hebrew; but he was so poor that he had sold his land, and now at last he had been obliged to sell himself into slavery. "Take me," said he, "and I will be your servant, if you give me bread to eat, and raiment to put on;" and the law allowed it, and so there were some few Hebrews who had their fellow Hebrews in servitude to them. That servitude was of an exceedingly light kind, for if ever one of these so-called slaves ran away, it was contrary to law to return him to his master; he might break the servitude when he pleased. At the end of the sixth year, when the Hebrew servant might go free, it often happened that he had been treated so well in his servitude that he had no desire to go, but he was willing to have the awl thrust through the lobe of his ear, that he might be fastened to the door-post of his master to abide in servitude as long as he lived. But at the end of the six years, the Hebrew servant was free to go if so it pleased him.

Now, according to the law, *the bondman was to be sent away freely*. It was not to be thought a hardship to part with a servant man or woman. However useful they might have been in the house or field, however much they were felt to be necessary to domestic comfort or farm service, they were to be allowed to go; and, what was more, they were *not to go empty handed*, but they were to receive a portion out of every department of the master's wealth, from his flock, his threshing-floor, and his wine-press. They were to go away well loaded, even as Israel went out of Egypt, as we read, "He brought them forth also with silver and gold." This was a grand law; and does it not teach God's people how kind they ought to be? A miserable, miserly, hard, close-fisted Christian—is there such a thing? It is not for me to be a judge. One who would take his brother's labour without payment, and at the end of the term would offer him no kind of remuneration, but leave him to starve—is he a child of God? How dwelleth the love of God in him? God would have his people not only do what is righteous, but what is generous; and act, not only justly, but kindly to all with whom they come in contact. Further, *this setting free of their brother at the specified time was to be done for a certain reason:* "Thou shalt remember that thou wast a bondman in the land of Egypt, and the Lord thy God redeemed thee." How can you hold another a bondman when God has set you free? How can you treat another with unkindness when the Lord has dealt so generously with you? Down at Olney, when Mr. Newton was the rector of the parish, he put up in his study this text where he could always see it when he lifted his eyes from his text while preparing his sermon, "Remember that thou wast a bondman in the land of Egypt, and the Lord thy God redeemed thee." Would it not do many Christians good if they had that text often before their eyes? Would it not excite gratitude to their Redeemer, and tenderness towards those who happened to be in subjection to them, tenderness to every sinner that is a bondslave under the law, tenderness to the myriads that swarm these streets, slaves to sin and self, and who are perishing in their iniquity? This was to be the reason why Israel should act generously towards bondservants. Let it stand as a reason why we should act kindly towards all about us.

As far as most of us are concerned, it may be that we are not creditors to anybody, and we are not likely to crush anybody by exacting their debts. If we do not happen to be in that position, yet the law is spiritual, and it has its own teaching, and surely it means just this—*Let us readily forgive.* I know not how true it is, but I have heard that if that venerable and godly man, Mr. Rowland Hill, had any kind of fault, it was that, sometimes, when he thought that persons had acted very wrongly to him, he could not very readily forgive them. One of his hearers said he remembered that, one Sabbath-day, Mr. Hill had spoken very severely about a certain person, not more severely than was just, but perhaps more severely than was generous, and when he was offering the prayer, "Forgive us our trespasses," the hearer noticed that the good man hesitated at the words, "As we—as we—forgive them that trespass against us." He had evidently a little struggle with himself, and he was so sincere and transparent a man that he showed it even in the public service. Do not some of you, at times, find it rather difficult to forgive those that trespass against you? Possibly you have been very angry with your boy this afternoon; it would have been as well to have given him a kiss before you left home. It may be that your dear girl has in some way offended you; it would have been as well to have told her that you had forgiven her. You had good reasons, perhaps, for not doing so; I will not go into them. However, may I ask you to forgive her as soon as you get home? It may be that you will be doing no good to your child by doing what is hardly justifiable as from yourself. Be ready to forgive your children. There is reason to make that remark; for I have known persons sitting here, who have excluded a son or daughter from their house because of some marriage that the parents did not like, or for some other reason. You said, "She shall never darken my door again." And you are a Christian man! I would say to you, if I knew you were here, "I wish that you would never darken the communion-table again until that kind of feeling was gone from you once for all." How can you say, " Our Father, which art in heaven," while there is still towards your own child, whether young or old, something which you say you cannot forgive? Make up your mind never to go to heaven if you cannot forgive people; for you cannot enter the pearly gates while you cherish an unforgiving spirit.

Or is it some friend of yours with whom you have quarrelled? You two have parted; you were dear friends once; but now, like a great cliff that has been split in the middle, there you stand frowning upon one another. Let it be so no longer. If there is any personal pique or ill-will, let it be cast into the depths of the sea. Whatever may be the story, I do not want to hear it. Surely, the time has come when all that should be wiped out once for all. "Let not the sun go down upon your wrath," is a good precept. I have heard of two friends who had differed greatly, and spoken very bitterly; and the sun was just going down, so one of them said, "I must not let the sun go down on my wrath; I will go, and try to be reconciled to my friend, and half way to his friend's house he met his friend coming to him, on the same errand, and they met joyfully to forgive each other. May it be so with all true Christians!

Once again, dear friends, I think the spirit of this release of the Lord is this, *Never be hard on anybody.* It is true that the man made the bargain, and he ought to keep to it; but he is losing money, and he cannot afford it; he is being ruined, and you are being fattened by his mistake. Do not hold him to it. If you have made a losing bargain, you should stand to it; for the Christian man "sweareth to his own hurt, and changeth not;" but if the loss is on the other side, cancel the bond as speedily as may be, and let not the poor man have to go with his tears before Almighty God, and blame you for your cruelty. No Christian man can be a sweater of workers; no Christian man can be a grinder of the poor; no man, who would be accepted before God, can think that his heart is right with him when he treats others ungenerously, not to say unjustly.

That, I think, is the spirit of the first part of my subject, the release which the Lord desired his people to give, that which is called, "the Lord's release."

II. But now, secondly, and as briefly as I can, let us consider THE RELEASE WHICH THE LORD GIVES TO US.

Let me proclaim to every sinner here, who owns his indebtedness to God, and feels that he can never discharge it, that if you will come, and put your trust in Christ, the Lord promises *oblivion to all your debt,* forgiveness of the whole of your sins. I need not repeat the long black list, for conscience has made you read it up and down, and down and up, and you have become familiar with the roll of your iniquities. The Lord is prepared to wipe them all out; he will do what he bids his people do: "it is called the Lord's release." He will release thee from thy sin if thou believest in Jesus Christ.

This release shall be followed up by *a non-exacting of the penalty for ever.* If thou art pardoned of God, he will never exact of thee any punishment because of thine iniquities or transgressions; nay, neither in this life, nor in that which is to come, will he require it at thy hands. He will give thee a full discharge, one that can be pleaded in the High Court of Heaven above. "Who shall lay anything to the charge of God's elect? It is God that justifieth. Who is he that condemneth? It is Christ that died, yea, rather, that is risen again." If thou wilt come to thy God, acknowledging thy debt, and confessing thine inability to pay it, he will so wipe it out that thou shalt never hear of it again for ever; and if thy sins be searched for, they shall not be found.

Notice, next, that God will do all this for thee *on the ground of thy poverty*. See the fourth verse: "Save when there shall be no poor among you." They should not remit a debt if ever there should come a time when there should be no poor among them; but, as long as there was a man who was poor, they were to remit the debt. You noticed how we sang,—

> " 'Tis perfect poverty alone
> That sets the soul at large."

When you cannot pay half a farthing in the pound of all your great debt of sin, when you are absolutely bankrupt, then may you believe that Jesus Christ is your Saviour. When you are absolutely helpless and hopeless, only believe that Jesus is the Christ, and put your trust in him, and God will remit and discharge all your liabilities, and you shall go away clear before him.

I may be addressing a soul here that says, "I like that thought, I wish I could catch hold of it; but I feel myself to be such a slave that I cannot grasp it." Well, *the Lord may allow a soul to be in bondage for a time;* indeed, it may be needful that he should. The Hebrew might be in bondage six years, and yet he went free when the seventh year came. There are reasons why the Spirit of God is to some men a Spirit of bondage for a long time. Hard hearts must be melted, proud stomachs must be brought down. Some men's wills are like an iron sinew; some men's self-righteousness is hard to slay, even though it be shot through the heart seven times. There are many who would be rebellious against God very soon, if they found forgiveness too soon; so he brings down their heart with labour; they fall, and there is none to help. I may be speaking to one here who has been a long time in bondage. I passed through that state myself, and many a time have I gripped the hand of a poor man or woman in abject distress and despair, almost ready to go into an asylum, and I have said, "I know all about that experience; I know that the Lord does, for a while, suffer the heart to be ploughed, and torn, and rent, to make it ready for the good seed." Have you ever seen God's ten black horses come out, I mean the ten commandments, have you heard the ploughman crack the whip, have you seen that awful plough that is just behind those horses, and how they have dragged that plough up the soul and back again, and up the soul and back again, till the field of the soul has been ploughed from end to end? Then, when you thought that the work was all done, the horses have been turned sideways, and there has been cross-ploughing back and back again, tearing up the whole nature, and breaking every clod to powder.

God has his scarifiers at work upon some men; yet for all that it is not because he hates them, but because he loves them, and means to get out of them a heavy harvest of joy and thankfulness in the years to come.

Once more, *the man was set free at the end of the sixth year,* paying nothing for his liberation. Though not free-born, nor yet buying his liberty with a great sum, yet he was set free. O Lord, set some soul free to-night! Oh, that every slave here, who was in bondage, may get his liberty to-night, to the praise of the glory of God's grace!

And when the Lord sets poor souls at liberty, *he always sends them away full-handed.* He gives something from the flock, and from the threshing-floor, and from the wine-press. Some of us were rich, indeed, the first day we came to Jesus. We know more now than we knew then; but we do not possess more than we had then; for we had Christ then, and he is all; and we cannot get more than all. God gave us heaven within us then. Oh, how we laughed for joy that day! We shall never forget it. We were not to be beggars or paupers any more; all the riches of heaven were bestowed upon us.

There is one thing which may be said here. *This act never seems hard to the Lord.* He says to the Hebrew, in the eighteenth verse, "It shall not seem hard unto thee, when thou sendest him away free." It never seems hard to Christ when he sets a sinner free. Why, some of you pray as if you thought that Christ was hard-hearted! It is you who are hard-hearted. You pray as if you thought God had to be moved to mercy. It is you who need to be moved to accept the mercy. God is generous enough; he will set you free, and load you daily with his benefits, and delight to do it, if you trust his dear Son. In fact, to make worlds, is nothing to him compared with saving souls. He takes the big hammer of his omnipotence, and brings it down on the anvil of his wisdom, and worlds fly like sparks all over the sky when he is at that work; and he thinks nothing of it. But he rests in his love, and rejoices over his people with singing when he is at work for their salvation. This is the very joy of his heart; it is never hard for him to set free those who have been in bondage.

One thing I feel sure of, and that is, *if the Lord sets us free, we shall want to remain his servants for ever.* We will go straight away to the door-post, and ask him to use the awl; for, though we are glad to be free, we do not want to be free from him. No, no! "O Lord, truly I am thy servant; I am thy servant. . . . . Thou hast loosed my bonds." Once set free, then I wish to be bound to the Lord for ever. Come, dear heart, if you find Christ to-night, if you believe in him, and are at liberty, come and have your ear bored. You do not like baptism; come and have your ear bored. You do not like to join the church, and confess Christ. Well, I know that it may be a "bore" to you; but for all that, come and have your ear bored. Come and say, "I will go no more out for ever. Since the Lord has set me free, I will serve him all my days."

The Lord bless these words to many, for Jesus' sake! Amen.

Exposition by C. H. Spurgeon.

LEVITICUS XXV. 1—7, 17—22, AND DEUTERONOMY XV. 1—18.

Leviticus xxv. Verses 1, 2. *And the* LORD *spake unto Moses in mount Sinai, saying, Speak unto the children of Israel, and say unto them, When ye come into the land which I give you, then shall the land keep a sabbath unto the* LORD.

The Jews had much rest provided for them. If they had had faith enough to obey God's commands, they might have been the most favoured of people; but they were not a spiritual people, and the Lord often had to lament their disobedience as in the words recorded by Isaiah, "O that thou hadst hearkened to my commandments! then had thy peace been as a river, and thy righteousness as the waves of the sea."

3, 4. *Six years thou shalt sow thy field, and six years thou shalt prune thy vineyard, and gather in the fruit thereof; but in the seventh year shall be a sabbath of rest unto the land, a sabbath for the* LORD:

Think of a Sabbath a year long, in which nothing was to be done but to worship God, and so to rest!

4, 5. *Thou shalt neither sow thy field, nor prune thy vineyard. That which groweth of its own accord of thy harvest thou shalt not reap, neither gather the grapes of thy vine undressed: for it is a year of rest unto the land.*

A restful period in a restful land; all land to have rest, and yet to have fruitfulness in that rest; the rest of a garden, not the rest of a task. Thus is it oftentimes with God's people, when they rest most, they work best; and while they are resting, they are bearing fruit unto God.

6, 7. *And the sabbath of the land shall be meat for you; for thee, and for thy servant, and for thy maid, and for thy hired servant, and for thy stranger that sojourneth with thee, and for thy cattle, and for the beast that are in thy land, shall all the increase thereof be meat.*

There was to be no private property in the spontaneous produce of that year. It was free to everybody; free even to the cattle, which might go and eat what they would, and where they would.

17—21. *Ye shall not therefore oppress one another; but thou shalt fear thy God: for I am the* LORD *your God. Wherefore ye shall do my statutes, and keep my judgments, and do them; and ye shall dwell in the land in safety. And the land shall yield her fruit, and ye shall eat your fill, and dwell therein in safety. And if ye shall say, What shall we eat the seventh year? behold, we shall not sow, nor gather in our increase: then I will command my blessing upon you in the sixth year, and it shall bring forth fruit for three years.*

Not merely for the one year of rest, but fruit for three years.

22. *And ye shall sow the eighth year, and eat yet of old fruit until the ninth year; until her fruits come in ye shall eat of the old store.*

They were to have enough for the year of rest, and for the next year in which the harvest was growing, and still to have something over for the ninth year. They scarcely could want as much as that; but God would give them more than they actually needed, exceeding abundantly above what they asked or even thought.

That Sabbatical year had other blessings connected with it. Let us read about them in the Book of Deuteronomy, chapter fifteen.

Deuteronomy xv. Verses 1, 2. *At the end of every seven years thou shalt make a release. And this is the manner of the release: Every creditor that lendeth ought unto his neighbour shall release it; he shall not exact it of his neighbour, or of his brother; because it is called the* LORD's *release.*

What a wonderful title for it, "the LORD's release"!

3. *Of a foreigner thou mayest exact it again : but that which is thine with thy brother thine hand shall release ;*

How was a man to pay when he did not sow or reap during the Sabbatical year ? The foreigner did not observe the year of rest; consequently he was bound to pay, and it was only fair that he should do so; but for the Israelite, who carried out the divine law, there was provision made if he was in debt.

4. *Save when there shall be no poor among you;*

If there were no poor, then there would be no need for this law.

4—6. *For the LORD shall greatly bless thee in the land which the LORD thy God giveth thee for an inheritance to possess it : only if thou carefully hearken unto the voice of the LORD thy God, to observe to do all these commandments which I command thee this day. For the LORD thy God blesseth thee, as he promised thee :*

That little clause, "as he promised thee," is worth noticing. This is the rule of God; he deals with us "according to promise."

6. *And thou shalt lend unto many nations, but thou shalt not borrow ; and thou shalt reign over many nations, but they shall not reign over thee.*

If God's people had done his will, they would have been like their language; it is observed of the Hebrew by some, that it borrows nothing from other tongues, but lends many words to various languages.

7—9. *If there be among you a poor man of one of thy brethren within any of thy gates in thy land which the LORD thy God giveth thee, thou shalt not harden thine heart, nor shut thine hand from thy poor brother : but thou shalt open thine hand wide unto him, and shalt surely lend him sufficient for his need, in that which he wanteth. Beware that there be not a thought in thy wicked heart, saying, The seventh year, the year of release, is at hand; and thine eye be evil against thy poor brother, and thou givest him nought; and he cry unto the LORD against thee, and it be sin unto thee.*

Moses, moved by the Spirit of God, anticipates what would very naturally occur to many : "Then I shall not lend anywhere near the seventh year; if I do, I shall lose it, for I must release my debtor then." The hard-hearted would be sure to make this their evil excuse for lending nothing. But here the Hebrew is warned against such wicked thoughts, lest, refusing to lend to his poor brother for this cause, the needy one should cry to God, and it should be accounted sin on the part of the merciless refuser.

10, 11. *Thou shalt surely give him, and thine heart shall not be grieved when thou givest unto him : because that for this thing the LORD thy God shall bless thee in all thy works, and in all that thou puttest thine hand unto. For the poor shall never cease out of the land :*

They would have done so, they might have done so, if the rule of God had been kept; but inasmuch as he foresaw that it never would be kept, he also declared, "the poor shall never cease out of the land."

11. *Therefore I command thee, saying, Thou shalt open thine hand wide unto thy brother, to thy poor, and to thy needy, in thy land.*

See how God calls them, not "the poor", but "thy poor" and "thy needy." The Church of God should feel a peculiar property in the poor and needy, as if they were handed over, in the love of Christ to his people, that they might care for them.

12. *And if thy brother, an Hebrew man, or an Hebrew woman, be sold unto thee, and serve thee six years; then in the seventh year thou shalt let him go free from thee.*

He might be under an apprenticeship of servitude for six years; but the seventh year was to be a year of rest to him, as it was a year of release to debtors, and of rest to the land.

13. *And when thou sendest him out free from thee, thou shalt not let him go away empty:*
To begin life again with nothing at all in his pocket.

14. *Thou shalt furnish him liberally out of thy flock, and out of thy floor, and out of thy winepress: of that wherewith the LORD thy God hath blessed thee thou shalt give unto him.*
Who would think of finding such a law as that on the statute-book? Where is there such a law under any governor but God? The Theocracy would have made a grand government for Israel if Israel had but been able to walk before God in faith and obedience.

15. *And thou shalt remember that thou wast a bondman in the land of Egypt, and the LORD thy God redeemed thee: therefore I command thee this thing to day.*
The remembrance of their own deliverance out of Egyptian bondage was to make them merciful and kind to their own bondservants.

16—18. *And it shall be, if he say unto thee, I will not go away from thee; because he loveth thee and thine house, because he is well with thee; then thou shalt take an aul, and thrust it through his ear unto the door, and he shall be thy servant for ever. And also unto thy maidservant thou shalt do likewise. It shall not seem hard unto thee, when thou sendest him away free from thee; for he hath been worth a double hired servant to thee, in serving thee six years;*
He has had no pay; he has been always at his work; he has been worth two ordinary hired labourers; let him go, therefore, and let him not go away empty.

18. *And the LORD thy God shall bless thee in all that thou doest.*

HYMNS FROM "OUR OWN HYMN BOOK"—551, 544, 545.

"THE SWORD AND THE TROWEL."
TABLE OF CONTENTS, OCTOBER, 1892.

Fellowship with God's Greatness. A Missionary Address. By C. H. SPURGEON.
"Our Sufficiency is of God." A Missionary's Testimony. By N. H. Patrick, of Tangier.
Prayer as the Resort of the Minister of Jesus Christ. By Arthur T. Pierson, D.D.
Mr. Spurgeon's Last Drives at Menton. By Joseph W. Harrald. (With three illustrations.)
Enlarging the Cap Factory.
Four Mottoes for Earnest Souls. By W. Y. Fullerton.
A Batch of New-comers at the Stockwell Orphanage. (With illustration.)
Dr. Nettleton as a Preacher. By R. Shindler.
Medical Mission Work in Tangier. Letter from Dr. Churcher.
Worthless Weapons. By Robert Spurgeon, Madaripore, Bengal.
A Providential Disappointment. By John Burnham.
Psalm civ. (Poetry.) By Pastor E. A. Tydeman.
Romanism as it is. (Review of "Life inside the Church of Rome", by the Nun of Kenmare.)
Fishing. By Pastor W. Higlett, Albion, Brisbane, Queensland.
The Rose of Sharon. (Poetry.) By Pastor C. A. Slack, Faversham.
Notices of Books.
Notes. (The crisis at the Tabernacle. Mr. Moody's meetings at the Tabernacle. C. H. Spurgeon Memorial Fund. C. H. Spurgeon's Sermons and Expositions. Sermons on the tomb at Norwood Cemetery. Foreign translations of Mr. Spurgeon's works. Norcott's *Baptism Discovered.* "Lady Hymn-Writers." Tabernacle prayer-meetings. Poor Ministers' Clothing Society. Tabernacle Gospel Temperance Society. College. College Missionary Association. Evangelists. Colportage. Orphanage. Personal Notes. Baptisms at the Tabernacle.) Lists of contributions.

Price 3d. Post-free, 4d.

LONDON: PASSMORE AND ALABASTER, PATERNOSTER BUILDINGS, and all Booksellers.

Metropolitan Tabernacle Pulpit.

SYCHAR'S SINNER SAVED.

A Sermon

INTENDED FOR READING ON LORD'S-DAY, OCTOBER 9TH, 1892,

DELIVERED BY

C. H. SPURGEON,

AT THE METROPOLITAN TABERNACLE, NEWINGTON,

On Lord's-day Evening, April 13*th,* 1890.

"Jesus answered and said unto her, If thou knewest the gift of God, and who it is that saith to thee, Give me to drink; thou wouldest have asked of him, and he would have given thee living water."—John iv. 10.

I could not help saying, in the reading, that the woman's answer to our Lord was, at least, somewhat brusque, if not really rude; but, with great meekness, Jesus took no notice of it so as to blame her for her tone, or for her unkind manner. He was too intent upon saving her soul to care about a little rudeness on her part. Learn a lesson from your Lord's conduct. When you are dealing with souls, do not always expect them to yield to you at once; do not expect them even to receive your expostulations with thankfulness. Be prepared to be repelled, and even to be ridiculed; and when it so happens, do not be put out of temper, or out of heart, but go straight on with your work whichever way they may go.

Our Saviour, instead of being vexed at the rudeness of the woman, said to her, "If thou knewest." "Ah, poor soul, thou dost not know to whom thou art speaking thus rudely!" "If thou knewest the gift of God, and who it is that saith to thee, Give me to drink; thou wouldest have asked of him, and he would have given thee living water." Oh, that we might have a passion for the souls of men! May we be vehement in our desire, with a love that burneth like coals of juniper! May we not be put off by any discouragements; but let us resolve that, before we have done with any poor sinner, we will do all in our power to bring him to Christ, so that, if men are lost, it shall not be our fault; and if they are saved, we will, at least, have this part in it, that we have set Christ plainly before them as their soul's only hope.

Now, our Saviour, having thus set us an example of great meekness, went on to read this woman's heart in a very singular manner; and, reading her heart, he foretold what her action would be when her

No. 2,277.

ignorance was removed. It is a difficult thing to tell what people will do under such and such circumstances; for men and women are very unaccountable creatures; but the Saviour made a prediction as to what this woman would do. That will be my first point, *Jesus foretold what her action would be when her ignorance was removed;* and then, secondly, I will show you that *the fact justified the prediction.* As soon as the woman knew who it was that spoke to her, she asked him for the living water; Jesus gave it to her, and she went on her way rejoicing.

I. First, then, JESUS FORETOLD WHAT HER ACTION WOULD BE WHEN HER IGNORANCE WAS REMOVED. He saw in her a kindly disposition towards right things; but she was hindered by her ignorance. If that hindrance could be taken away, she would at once travel in the right road.

Let me mention *the points of saving knowledge* which it was desirable for her to know.

These were, first, the nature of salvation. "If thou knewest the gift of God." Thousands of people in the world do not know what salvation means. They conceive, if they have any notion of it at all, that it means escaping from hell, and going to heaven when they die, which is a very imperfect and incorrect idea of salvation. "The gift of God is eternal life," and that is salvation. God gives to all who believe in Christ a new life, a vital principle, something to be within them always, the reigning and ruling principle of their lives. Salvation means salvation from sin. To the drunkard, it is salvation from the drink; to the swearer, it is salvation from a profane heart; to the unchaste, it is salvation from impurity. It means deliverance from the power of evil in the life, and submission to the power of that which is good and gracious, by which sin shall be cast out. You remember the meaning of the name Jesus. "Thou shalt call his name Jesus, for he shall save his people from their sins." The salvation that we have to preach produces a change of heart, a renewal of nature, a deliverance from the power of the devil, and brings the renewed man under the supreme power of the Holy Spirit of God. If some men knew this, they would begin to seek for it. Are there not many here who feel that they ought to turn over a new leaf, and they do not know how to do it? They have not the power, even though they have in a measure the will. Now, salvation brings you both will and power; it saves you not only from the wrath to come, but from the sin that is within you now. That is the nature of salvation.

This woman did not know the freeness of salvation. "If thou knewest the gift of God,"—"the *gift* of God." She thought, perhaps, that it had to be bought with money, or procured by sacrifices, or attained by good works after a long period of preparation. The Saviour assured her that salvation was the gift of God; freely given, not because it is deserved, but because God delights to bless even the unthankful and the evil; given, not because of penances, or austerities, or myriads of prayers, or floods of tears, but freely given to every soul that is willing to accept it by faith in Jesus Christ. Oh, if many knew this, they would seek to have it; but they do not know what salvation is, and they do not know that it is to be had for nothing, and to be had on the spot. "If thou knewest the gift of God."

Further, it was needful for this woman to know the person of Christ. "If thou knewest who it is that saith to thee, Give me to drink." Some do not know who the Christ is. Though he has been here, and lived, and died, and is gone to heaven, and is preached by tens of thousands of preachers, and his blessed Book is with you to this day, yet you do not know that the Saviour is God over all blessed for ever, the second Person of the sacred Trinity, the Son of God and yet Man. He took upon himself the nature of man, was born into this world, lived a suffering and obedient life, died an ignominious and painful death, and now he has risen from the dead, and he is sitting at the right hand of God, even the Father, and will shortly come to judge the quick and the dead according to our gospel. Now this is he, this God, this Man, this Mediator between God and men, who is to be trusted. He was commissioned of God, and therefore he was called the Christ, the anointed. He has come into the world on purpose to do the will of him that sent him, and to finish his work. Oh, ye sons and daughters of men, if ye would be saved, ye must come and trust yourselves with the Incarnate God, who is bone of your bone, and flesh of your flesh!

This woman also did not know the freeness of Christ, for when our Saviour said, "If thou knewest the gift of God," he really meant himself. Paul said, "Thanks be unto God for his unspeakable gift." This is he, the gift of the Father. Christ has not come into the world simply to save the rich, or the learned, or those who struggle through many examinations to obtain a high degree of human wisdom. He died also for the poor, for you who know your own ignorance, and bewail it, for you who know your sinnership, and repent of it. He came not to call the righteous, but sinners to repentance. God has given his Son Jesus Christ, freely given him. You may have him for the asking; you may have him for the taking. "Whosoever believeth in him hath everlasting life," and if you will but trust him, there is life eternal for you. It was important that this woman should know this. "If thou knewest the gift of God, and who it is that saith to thee, Give me to drink."

If you look at the text, you will now see *the conduct which follows this saving knowledge.* Christ foretold what this woman would do when her ignorance was removed. What would she do?

Well, first, she would sink the idea of giving Christ anything. He began by saying to this sinful woman, "Give me to drink," but he afterwards said, "If thou knewest the gift of God, thou wouldest have asked of him." I am continually hearing, from converts and others, the expression, "I gave my heart to Christ," as a description of conversion. Now I do not find fault with that expression, for we must give our hearts to Christ; but very seriously let me say that I am afraid that that phrase will do much mischief unless it is well guarded and looked after. The gospel is not, "Give your hearts to Christ, and you shall be saved." The gospel is, "Believe on the Lord Jesus Christ,"—that is, trust him, "and thou shalt be saved." When you do that, you will be sure to give him your heart by-and-by, if not at once. Salvation is not by your giving anything to Christ, but by Christ giving something to you. I am glad that you have given your heart to Christ; but have you learnt first this lesson, that he gave his heart for you? We do not find salvation by giving Christ anything. That is the fruit of it; but salvation comes by Christ giving us something—something, did I say? —by Christ giving us everything, by his giving us himself. I used to notice that a good deal of Sunday-school teaching to the children was, "Dear child, love Jesus." That is not the way of salvation. The way of salvation is to trust Jesus. The fruit of salvation is that the dear child does love Jesus; but that is not the way of salvation. The way of salvation is to take Christ, to trust Christ. When you are saved, the proof of it will be that you will give your heart to Christ; but do not let us turn things upside down lest, beginning with a little blunder, we should go on to some great error, and set up again the ruinous doctrine which once sank the world in darkness, the doctrine of an imaginary salvation by our own works.

Next, the text suggests the idea of asking of Christ as the first thing for us to do. How many there are, who know that salvation is a gift; but they never seek it! They know that it is all of grace; but they never ask for it. An occasional prayer, when you are half-asleep at night; now and then an expression of a wish that you were better, that is all the effort you put forth. The Lord says, "Ye shall seek me, and find me, when ye shall search for me with all your heart." Men seek after gold as if they had a thousand hearts; but they seek after grace as if their heart were cut into a thousand pieces, and only one solitary thousandth part of it went after the blessing. This woman did really ask of Christ, and asked with earnestness; and so must you. If you did but know Christ, if you did but know the value of his salvation, if you did but know the freeness of it, my hearers, you would get to your knees, and you would never rise from them again till you had found him who alone can save your souls. Let me ask you unsaved ones, do you cry to God for mercy? Are you in earnest about it? Does your very soul go up to God in prayer? If not, do not wonder that you still remain in the gall of bitterness. How can you expect God to give to you that which you do not value enough to ask for heartily?

This woman, when her ignorance was removed, would be led to put asking first, and then really to ask; and, next, receiving would graciously follow the asking. I call your attention to the words, "Thou wouldest have asked of him, and he would have given thee." Dear hearer, if you had asked, you would have had. "Ye have not because ye ask not." Sitting in that pew to-night, without God, without Christ, it is because you have not sought him, you have not cried for him. Had you sought him, you would have found him, "for everyone that asketh receiveth; and he that seeketh findeth; and to him that knocketh it shall be opened." I do not like merely to utter this truth; I wish I could press it home upon your heart, and that you would feel that, if you have not asked, it is right that you should not have received, and that if you had asked, you would not have asked in vain. "Thou wouldest have asked, and he would have given."

Then she would have received, and the preciousness of the gift would have been apparent. The result would have been that she would have been a happy woman, greatly prizing the gift of God, greatly valuing the dear Saviour, singing in her delight because she had found him who could take all her sin away, and send her back to Sychar, a renewed woman. Instead of being a destroyer of the souls of men, she would become a herald of the cross to them, and the means of their salvation.

So our Saviour pictured what she would have done. I wonder whether it is true about any of you here, that you have only kept from prayer because you have not known better; you have not found Christ because you really did not know anything about him. You have been making mistakes and blunders, and that is why you are not saved. Now we have explained the matter to you, and you can see it, I trust that not another day will begin and end without your seeking and finding Christ, and so entering into eternal life.

Now consider *the line of action which this teaching suggests to us.*

If it is, in many cases, the fact, that nothing but ignorance is keeping men out of eternal life, if it be true of many that, if they did but know, they would ask and they would receive, then if you have not found Christ, be wise enough to try and learn all about him. Do not remain in ignorance where that ignorance is not bliss, but endless woe. Wake yourself up, and say, " If I can find out what salvation is, I will find it out, even if I have to burn the midnight oil, and wear my eyes away in searching through the sacred Book. I will hear as well as read. I will know all that I can about salvation, and about this Jesus, the Son of God, the unspeakable gift of God." Well, take care that you do go where Christ is most preached. A little girl heard her mother say, " We went to the house of God to hear about Jesus." " Mother," said she, " at the place where aunty goes, they do not hear anything about Jesus, I am sure, for I went with her every time, and I never heard anything about him." Do not go to places where Christ is not preached. Let those go who have no souls to be saved, if there be such people; but you, dear hearers, are in an anxious state; you want to find salvation; and lest ignorance should hinder you, take heed what you hear, and take heed how you hear. I was but a child when I first began to seek the Saviour; but I have a distinct recollection that as soon as the sun shone into my little bedchamber, I was awake; and what was I reading? *Doddridge's "Rise and Progress of Religion in the Soul", Alleine's "Alarm to the Unconverted"*, and books of that order, I read when I was but a child, in the hope that I might somehow find Christ, and be saved. When I went to a place of worship, I took no notice of the music of the organ, or the eloquence of the preacher. I kept listening with this one thought in my mind, " Oh, that I might but find salvation! Oh, that I might but find Christ!" Whenever that is the case with anyone, depend upon it, sooner or later, the ignorance that bars the way will melt and disappear; and you will ask, and God will give, and there will be joy in heaven and joy in your own heart because you are saved.

One thing more. If you do discover the truth, then go on learning more about it that you may tell it to others. It is of the nature of the grace of God, when it gets into one heart, that it wants to flow into another. The woman of Sychar believes in Jesus. Now she must go, and tell the men of the city about the Christ. I wonder whether she went to the men with whom she had sinned. Women did not often speak openly to men in those Oriental regions; but this woman did. She had broken through the laws of decorum and of the Word of God, so away she goes, and says to the men, "Come, see a man, which told me all things that ever I did: is not this the Christ?" Go on learning about Christ, I say, that you may teach it to others; and never think a day is well spent unless you have spoken to someone about your Master, unless you have at least dropped one tiny seed somewhere to bring forth fruit to his praise. Our Saviour predicted that the woman would ask, and that she would receive, if she could but get rid of the ignorance that weighed her down.

II. My second point is, that all this came true. THE FACT JUSTIFIED THE PREDICTION. When this woman's ignorance was taken away, she did what Christ said she would do.

First, let me remind you that, *what she did know stood her in good stead.* She was not converted when she came to Christ, very far from it; but she did know something about him, for she said to him, "I know that Messias cometh, which is called Christ." It is a good beginning when you know anything. I heard, yesterday, a piece of bigotry concerning Dissenters which astonished me for the moment, and then I said, "I am rather glad to hear it, for I like to meet with men nowadays who believe anything, for the generality of people do not believe anything at all, and there is hope of a man, or a woman, who really does know and believe something." If you have one solid bit somewhere, we can get a fulcrum for our lever, and so can move you. This woman said, "I know that Messias cometh." Teachers of the children in the Sunday-schools, it may be years hence, but if you have taught a child really to know something, that knowledge may be the beginning of his salvation. It was partly by common tradition, partly by conversation, and partly by the belief of her associates that this woman came to say, "I know that Messias cometh."

Then she had got into her head another thing, that when he did come, he would tell them all things. "When he is come, he will tell us all things." In effect, the woman's belief led her to say, "When the Messiah comes, we shall all be set right. Now, we Jews and Samaritans have had a quarrel about where we ought to worship. The Samaritans say that mount Gerizim is the place where the blessing was pronounced, and that we ought to worship here. They only believe, as you know, in the Pentateuch. Those five books of Moses do not say much about Jerusalem, or about a temple. Clinging to that grand old Pentateuch, I believe in worshipping here at Gerizim; but the Jews say that we ought to worship at Jerusalem. Well, when Messias comes, he will tell us all things."

She had that idea firmly fixed in her mind. Where did she get it? I will read you the passage, in order that you may see how a single text may give a hook on which a soul may hang. One single text may be a little bit of solid rock, on which you may plant your lever, and begin to lift the heavy weight of an immortal soul. In the eighteenth chapter of Deuteronomy, beginning at the fifteenth verse, we read as follows: "The LORD thy God will raise up unto thee a Prophet from the midst of thee, of thy brethren, like unto me; unto him ye shall hearken; according to all that thou desiredst of the LORD thy God in Horeb in the day of the assembly, saying, Let me not hear again the voice of the LORD my God, neither let me see this great fire any more, that I die not. And the LORD said unto me, They have well spoken that which they have spoken." They need a Mediator; they shall have a Mediator to speak to them from me. Now, here is the special verse, "I will raise them up a Prophet from among their brethren, like unto thee, and will put my words in his mouth; and he shall speak unto them all that I shall command him." This woman pulled the text about a little; but she gathered this from it, "There is a great Prophet to come, God's anointed Prophet, the Messiah, or Christ; and when he comes, we shall know him by this, that he will tell us all things. He will more fully expound the truth of God about which we may now be in doubt." That is what she did know, and that helped her a great deal.

But, next, what our Lord told her was a still greater help to her; for *he directed her to himself*. He began first by preaching the gospel to her. He would give her living water, and if she drank it, it would remain in her for ever a well of water, springing up unto everlasting life; and he was ready to give her this living water there and then.

Next, he unveiled her life before her. He told her that she had had five husbands, and that the man with whom she then lived was not her husband. With two or three strokes he drew her portrait. She marvelled at this. It is a great thing for a man to see himself; it is a greater thing for him to see his Saviour. After you are once converted, do not study yourself; study your Lord. God has given one object for the soul's eye to rest upon, and that is Christ; keep your eye always resting upon him. But, in order to her conversion, she was made to see herself, a wretched woman, living in abominable sin; and she was astonished at the sight; but even that helped her.

Then the Saviour took her off from all outward religion. He said to her, "Woman, believe me, the hour cometh, when ye shall neither in this mountain, nor yet at Jerusalem, worship the Father." Jesus told her that the hour had come when the true worshippers would worship the Father in spirit and in truth. Notice, too, that Christ took her off from the Samaritan worship. He said, " Salvation is of the Jews." But then he took her off the Jewish worship, too, and said, "Neither in this mountain, nor yet at Jerusalem." It is all very well for you to try to convert a Roman Catholic into an English Churchman; that is converting him from a Samaritan to a Jew. It is all very well for you to turn him from a Wesleyan into an Independent, or from an Independent into a Baptist, or from an Arminian into a Calvinist. The fact is, you have to get him off everything but Christ, and you have not done your work until you have brought him to know that no profession of religion, no outward ceremonies whatever, can save the soul. "They that worship God must worship him in spirit and in truth : for the Father seeketh such to worship him."

The Saviour had done this woman great service. He had preached to her the gospel, unveiled her sin, taken her off herself, and off all external religiousness. Then came the main point of all, he revealed himself to her, unveiling the sacred majesty of his divine glory. He said to her, "I that speak unto thee am he." When she said, "I know that Messias cometh," he at once spoke that grand word, "I am he." Now, dear friend, if the Lord has given you only to know one truth, hold on to it; and may he teach you more of yourself, and more of himself, and bring you to know that Jesus Christ is the sole and only Saviour, even as he brought this woman to know it!

Well, once more, *her own experience of Christ settled her faith.* I do not know whether you see my drift. The woman had the idea in her mind that, when the Messiah came, he would tell all things. She listened to Christ, and when he drew a picture of her entire life, something began to whisper in her heart, "He is telling you all things that ever you did. Is not this the Christ?" And when Christ said to her, "I that speak unto thee am he," the work was completed; and off she went, and said to the men the first thing that she could think of. She said, "You know that the Messiah, when he comes, is to tell us all things. Moses said that in Deuteronomy; you remember the passage in the Pentateuch. Now," said she, "I have met with a Man who has told me all things that ever I did; at least, he has told everything in one particular line. Do you not think that this must be the Messiah?" In her poor, womanly way, she had argued herself into that belief, and I think that it was good, reasonable argument, too. I have known many a soul get to heaven with no better guidance than some one text of Scripture. One truth will guide a man to heaven, though fifty may feed him better than one. When a bridge is to be made across some deep chasm, what is to be done? The first thing is to shoot an arrow across, or a gunshot that will carry a thread. When you have a thread across, you can pull a string over the gulf. When you have the string across, you can pull a thicker and stronger cord across. That can pull a rope, that rope can carry a bigger rope, that one can bear a cable; and, by-and-by, when you have got your cables across, you can begin to make your iron bridge. Now, in this woman's heart, that one belief, "I know that Messias cometh, which is called Christ," was like the thread shot across the chasm. "When he is come, he will tell us all things," was like the piece of string; and when she found that she had met with One who did tell her all things, she had a cable across the chasm. This is the way in which God removes ignorance; this is the way in which God builds up faith; little by little; and I therefore pray any of you who believe even a little, to hold on to it, and not to give it up. Search the Scriptures, and hear the gospel, until you believe a great deal more; and, believing that Jesus is the Christ, sent of God to save sinners, trust him wholly, trust him alone, and so you shall enter into eternal life.

I think that I hear one ask, "Do you mean to say that that woman was saved?" Yes, I expect to meet her in heaven. Amongst the fair daughters of the New Jerusalem, the woman that was waiting at the well will surely be found. "But she was such a shocking character," says one. She was a shocking character; I hope that there is not any woman here half as bad as she was, though there may be, and there may even be some worse than she was; but she was saved, and so will you be, if you go the same way that she went. There may be men here who are steeped in vice much worse than this poor woman ever was. You generally blame the woman, and the man is allowed to go scot free. But to-night, man or woman, I do not care which you are, even if you have committed the same sin—the very same—and are guilty in the sight of God, and before your own conscience, yet listen to two things that Jesus said to that woman.

The first was, "Woman, believe me." Woman, believe Christ. Man, believe Christ. Never mind me; never mind ministers or priests. Believe Christ, the Sent One of God; for he cannot lie. He speaks the truth. Believe him, and believe in him, that is, trust him, rest upon him for salvation.

And then Jesus left her with this word ringing in her ears, the last word that he spoke, "I that speak unto thee am he." Believe that Christ is he whom God has sent to save sinners. Believe that Christ is he who took our sin, the Lamb of God that taketh away the sin of the world. Believe him as he says, "I am he," and say to him, "I, Lord, am like this woman, one of the chief of sinners; but I believe that thou art the Saviour of sinners, and I trust myself with thee. Save me, Lord, for thine own name's sake!"

Now, you see, I have brought the horses to the water; but I cannot make them drink. I have set Christ before you; but I cannot make you have him. May the Holy Spirit help you to take him to-night once for all! Do not go away till he has done so. Give not sleep to your eyes, nor slumber to your eyelids, till you have closed in with Christ, and accepted him as your Saviour; for when you fall asleep to-night, you may never wake up again on this earth. It will be a dreadful thing to wake up in the land where hope can never come, where you shall see afar off God's chosen ones; but, as for yourself, you shall be told that there is a great gulf fixed between you and them, so that they cannot come to you, and you cannot go to them. "Repent ye, and believe the gospel." May the Holy Spirit constrain you to do so even now, for Jesus' sake! Amen.

"THE SWORD AND THE TROWEL"

For October, 1892, contains:—

Fellowship with God's Greatness. A Missionary Address. By C. H. Spurgeon.
"Our Sufficiency is of God." A Missionary's Testimony. By N. H. Patrick, of Tangier.
Prayer as the Resort of the Minister of Jesus Christ. By Arthur T. Pierson, D.D.
Mr. Spurgeon's Last Drives at Menton. By Joseph W. Harrald. (With three illustrations.)
Enlarging the Cap Factory.
Four Mottoes for Earnest Souls. By W. Y. Fullerton.
A Batch of New-comers at the Stockwell Orphanage. (With illustration.)
Dr. Nettleton as a Preacher. By R. Shindler.
Medical Mission Work in Tangier. Letter from Dr. Churcher.
Worthless Weapons. By Robert Spurgeon, Madaripore, Bengal.
A Providential Disappointment. By John Burnham.
Psalm civ. (Poetry.) By Pastor E. A. Tydeman.
Romanism as it is. (Review of "Life inside the Church of Rome", by the Nun of Kenmare.)
Fishing. By Pastor W. Higlett, Albion, Brisbane, Queensland.
The Rose of Sharon. (Poetry.) By Pastor C. A. Slack, Faversham.
Notices of Books, Notes, Accounts, &c.

Price 3d. Post-free, 4d.

London: Passmore and Alabaster, Paternoster Buildings, and all Booksellers.

Exposition by C. H. Spurgeon.
JOHN IV. 1—42.

Verses. 1—3. *When therefore the Lord knew how the Pharisees had heard that Jesus made and baptized more disciples than John, (though Jesus himself baptized not, but his disciples,) he left Judæa, and departed again into Galilee.*

Our Lord knew that the Pharisees would assail him now that he was prospering, and gathering disciples. He, therefore, went away from them; as he did on other occasions. Whenever the cause of God grows, Satan is sure to be violent against it.

Notice that our Saviour did not himself baptize his followers. Now, if baptism depended upon the character or the office of the baptizer, Jesus would certainly have done it; but to show us that the person baptizing does not impart any grace to the person baptized, our Lord baptized not, but left that work to his disciples.

4. *And he must needs go through Samaria.*

Men say that, "'Must' is for the king;" but our King puts himself under an imperative "must", under a divine necessity. Though obliged to do nothing, yet he obliges himself to do deeds of mercy and grace.

5, 6. *Then cometh he to a city of Samaria, which is called Sychar, near to the parcel of ground that Jacob gave to his son Joseph. Now Jacob's well was there.*

Holy men often impart an interest to the very place which they inhabit. We should not have cared anything about Sychar, or its well, if Jacob had not been there. Where godly men have been, the ground is sacred. How much more so where the God of men comes to visit us!

6. *Jesus therefore, being wearied with his journey, sat thus on the well: and it was about the sixth hour.*

Only half a day spent on his journey, yet he is weary. See, brethren, how he was compassed with infirmity. Our Great High Priest so truly took our flesh, that he was wearied with his journey. He that rolls the stars along was weary in the middle of the day. So weary was he, that he sat in the very attitude of weariness, as best he could, on the curb of the well: "Jesus therefore, being wearied with his journey, sat *thus* on the well."

7. *There cometh a woman of Samaria to draw water: Jesus saith unto her, Give me to drink.*

Wonderful words of condescension! The Creator is asking drink of his creature. Perfect Holiness is asking of a sinner. He, without whom there were no clouds, or rain, or springs, or wells, saith to a sinful woman, "Give me to drink."

8, 9. *(For his disciples were gone away unto the city to buy meat.) Then saith the woman of Samaria unto him, How is it that thou, being a Jew, askest drink of me, which am a woman of Samaria? for the Jews have no dealings with the Samaritans.*

In effect, the woman said, "Now that you are thirsty, you can ask drink of me; but at another time, proud Jew that you are, you would not speak to a Samaritan." Surely, this was rather a brusque answer, if not really rude. If she had known who it was to whom she was speaking, she would not have answered him thus.

10. *Jesus answered and said unto her, If thou knewest the gift of God, and who it is that saith to thee, Give me to drink; thou wouldest have asked of him, and he would have given thee living water.*

Something better than the water from Jacob's well. Though thou hast denied him a simple draught of water, he would not have denied thee something infinitely better, namely, living water. She little knew what that living water was.

11, 12. *The woman saith unto him, Sir, thou hast nothing to draw with, and the well is deep: from whence then hast thou that living water? Art thou greater than our father Jacob, which gave us the well, and drank thereof himself, and his children, and his cattle?*

That last word, "cattle", lets us see wherein the water of Jacob's well could never be compared to the living water that Jesus gives. If beasts can partake of it, it is not that high and spiritual thing which immortal souls need, which Jesus came to give. Unwittingly, the woman had answered her own question, "Art thou greater than our father Jacob?"

13, 14. *Jesus answered and said unto her, Whosoever drinketh of this water shall thirst again: but whosoever drinketh of the water that I shall give him shall never thirst; but the water that I shall give him shall be in him a well of water springing up into everlasting life.*

If Christ gives you grace, it is eternal life that he gives you; it is not a life that can die; it is not a grace that you can lose. It is everlasting life; a supply of living water which turns to a spring or well, and always remains within the heart that receives it.

15. *The woman saith unto him, Sir, give me this water, that I thirst not, neither come hither to draw.*

She had caught the Lord's meaning so far as the perpetuity of the water was concerned, but still she did not know what the living water was. It was all a riddle to her, as I am afraid it is to some of you. There is many a Doctor of Divinity who cannot explain what the living water is.

16. *Jesus saith unto her,*

As she had apparently learned nothing by his instruction, he now tried another plan with her, and began to deal with her conscience.

16, 17. *Go, call thy husband, and come hither. The woman answered and said, I have no husband. Jesus said unto her, Thou hast well said, I have no husband:*

Praise people whenever you can. There was nothing good about this woman, but she had spoken the truth: "Thou hast well said, I have no husband." Our Lord purposely laid the emphasis on the last word.

18. *For thou hast had five husbands; and he whom thou now hast is not thy husband: in that saidst thou truly.*

What an exposure of the life she was living! Jesus laid bare what she and her companion in sin may have thought that no man knew: "He whom thou now hast is not thy husband: in that saidst thou truly."

19. *The woman saith unto him, Sir,*

She is getting more respectful now. When conscience begins to work, men treat the ministry with greater deference.

19, 20. *I perceive that thou art a prophet. Our fathers worshipped in this mountain:*

How pleased she was to get away from that unpleasant subject of her five husbands and the man who was not her husband! How anxious people are to salve their consciences by discussing religious matters of a general character! When you come a little too close to them, they edge off if they can; so this woman said, "Our fathers worshipped in this mountain."

20, 21. *And ye say, that in Jerusalem is the place where men ought to worship. Jesus saith unto her, Woman, believe me,*

Our Saviour gave the woman good gospel advice, "Woman, believe me."

21, 22. *The hour cometh, when ye shall neither in this mountain, nor yet at Jerusalem, worship the Father. Ye worship ye know not what: we know what we worship: for salvation is of the Jews.*

They have the oracles of God. The Saviour comes of the Jews. They are right as far as they follow the instruction they have received; and you Samaritans are wrong in keeping to the law of Moses alone, and rejecting the rest of the Scriptures.

23, 24. *But the hour cometh, and now is, when the true worshippers shall worship the Father in spirit and in truth: for the Father seeketh such to worship him. God is a Spirit: and they that worship him must worship him in spirit and in truth.*

All the true worship in the world is of God's seeking. None would ever worship him aright if he did not lead them to it. He seeks them, and then they seek him.

25, 26. *The woman saith unto him, I know that Messias cometh, which is called Christ: when he is come, he will tell us all things. Jesus saith unto her, I that speak unto thee am he.*

Now were her eyes opened. That last word had made her see.

27. *And upon this came his disciples, and marvelled that he talked with the woman:*

How big they were, how wise in their own conceit, to be astonished that Christ was talking with a woman! The followers of Christ often get much too big for their places, and too big to please their Master, too. Though "they marvelled that he was speaking with a woman," as the Revised Version translates it,—

27. *Yet no man said, What seekest thou? or, Why talkest thou with her?*

They dared not do that; they had too much awe of him. But, do you know, I have often wished that they had done so? I should like to have read what Christ would have said to them. How he would have reproved them for thinking that he had degraded himself by talking with a woman, or with anybody. Our Saviour would have vindicated woman's place in the world in a way that one might have liked to have heard.

28. *The woman then left her waterpot, and went her way into the city,*

Why should she stop any longer? The faces of the disciples did not look pleasant; but their Master had comforted her. She would not stop to lose that comfort by hard words from the disciples: she "went her way into the city."

28—32. *And saith to the men, Come, see a man, which told me all things that ever I did: is not this the Christ? Then they went out of the city, and came unto him. In the mean while his disciples prayed him, saying, Master, eat. But he said unto them, I have meat to eat that ye know not of.*

39, 40. *And many of the Samaritans of that city believed on him for the saying of the woman, which testified, He told me all that ever I did. So when the Samaritans were come unto him, they besought him that he would tarry with them: and he abode there two days.*

Two days of Christ's personal ministry—what might not come of that?

41, 42. *And many more believed because of his own word; and said unto the woman, Now we believe, not because of thy saying: for we have heard him ourselves, and know that this is indeed the Christ, the Saviour of the world.*

Would God that many might be brought to know that Christ, the Saviour, to-night! Amen.

HYMNS FROM "OUR OWN HYMN BOOK"—492, 507, 561.

Metropolitan Tabernacle Pulpit.

FEEDING ON THE WORD.

A Sermon

Intended for Reading on Lord's-day, October 16th, 1892,

DELIVERED BY

C. H. SPURGEON,

AT THE METROPOLITAN TABERNACLE, NEWINGTON,

On Thursday Evening, May 8th, 1890.

"Hearken diligently unto me, and eat ye that which is good, and let your soul delight itself in fatness."—Isaiah lv. 2.

How important it is that we should hear God, that we should have an attentive ear to his Word; and that it should, through our ears, reach our souls, and become to us, consciously, the living Word of the living God! The great gate of commerce between heaven and the town of Mansoul, is Ear-Gate. We can see but little of the things of the kingdom; but we can hear much concerning them.

We are told, not only to "hearken" to God, but to "hearken diligently." You cannot have too much hearing of the right kind of truth, nor too much of the right kind of hearing. Some people like few sermons, and those very short; but, when a soul is hungry after God and eternal life, it puts another meaning on this exhortation, "Hearken diligently." It cannot hear too much; it cannot hear too often; it cannot hear too intensely. Faith comes by hearing; and hence, Satan tries to block up that gateway of mercy. If he can persuade men not to hear, then he can keep them out of the way of grace; but the exhortation of our text sets wide open this door of salvation, at which the Lord himself stands and cries, "Hearken diligently unto me."

You, dear friends, love to hear the Word of the Lord; therefore, I need not dwell upon that exhortation; but I do pray that no one may hear in vain. "Take heed *what* ye hear," and "take heed *how* ye hear." Do not be content merely to open Ear-Gate; but rest not satisfied until the King himself comes riding through that gate right up to the very citadel of the town of Mansoul, and takes possession of the castle of your heart.

With this brief introduction, we will come to the consideration of our main text, which follows upon the exhortation. We are to "hearken diligently" to this message from the Lord's lips, "Eat ye that which is

No. 2,278.

good, and let your soul delight itself in fatness." Here are four things; first, *the food;* next, *the feeding;* then, *the welcome;* and lastly, *the delight.*

I. First, here is FOOD : " Eat ye that which is good."

I ask about this food, first, *How is it presented to us?* It is presented to us freely. The invitation is, " Come and eat." There was a word about buying; but, as I said in the reading, that was soon covered up with, " Buy without money and without price." Others are trying to get salvation by their own efforts. The rich man spends his money; the poor man spends his labour; but both of these ways come from self, and they mean self-salvation—every man his own saviour. This is not the method to which you are called; you are, indeed, put off that way. "Wherefore do ye spend money for that which is not bread? and your labour for that which satisfieth not?" You are called simply to hear, that your souls may live; and, having heard, you are bidden freely to partake of that which is good, and that which is rich, which God has provided. We need still to say that the grace of God is free. No merit is asked, nothing to fit you for its reception, nothing as a compensation to God for the gift of it. Grace is free as the air you breathe. Eternal salvation comes without a penny of cost to every hungry, needy, bankrupt soul that is willing to receive it.

Further, while it is thus presented freely as to any labour with which to procure it, it is also presented freely as to its quality, its highest quality. You are not permitted to drink freely of water, and then to purchase wine. You are not invited to come and eat freely that which is good, and then to spend your labour for that which is fat. No, the richest dainties of God's house are as free as the bread he gives to hungry souls. You think that you will be highly favoured if you are allowed to partake of the crumbs that fall under the table, and so indeed you will be; but the daintiest morsels on the table are as free to you as those crumbs. Sanctification is as much a gift of God as justification; and the highest perfection in heaven is as much the gift of grace as the first cry of, " God, be merciful to me a sinner." It is all graciously given; and you are invited to come, not only to the waters, but to drink wine and milk, to eat that which is good, and to delight yourselves in fatness.

This royal bounty is freely given; and freely given to the most undeserving. The only limitation is no limitation at all : " Ho, every one that thirsteth!" All of you who are dissatisfied, or discontented, who have not obtained what you wanted; who are longing for something, you hardly know what it is you do long for; you who have a thirst insatiable but yet indescribable, who came here to-night saying, " I wish I had it; others that I know have it; I hardly know what it is that they have; but oh, that I might have it!"—you will find out what it is when you have received it. You hardly know yet what the taste of wine and milk may be. You hardly know yet what the fat things full of marrow, that are part of Christ's great gospel feast, can possibly be. You shall know them by-and-by; but, be you who you may, come and welcome; sinner, come. If thou hast nothing, Christ is everything. Though thou art unworthy, he is infinitely worthy; and so he presents to thee food to-night on the freest possible terms; or, indeed, without any terms or conditions at all, for he puts it thus, "Eat ye that which is good, and let your soul delight itself in fatness."

I ask, next, *What is this food?* I answer, first, it is the Word of God. The soul can never feed to the satisfying of the understanding, the conscience, the heart, except upon divinely-revealed truth. Thou must know what God would have thee know. Therefore attend, and hearken diligently, that the God-breathed truth may become nutriment to thy spirit.

Better still, the food is the Incarnate Word of God; for Christ Jesus, the Son of man, the Son of God, is *the* Word. If men feed on him, they shall find that his flesh is meat indeed, and his blood is drink indeed. Remember his own words, "This is the bread which cometh down from heaven, that a man may eat thereof, and not die. I am the living bread which came down from heaven: if any man eat of this bread, he shall live for ever: and the bread that I will give is my flesh, which I will give for the life of the world." This is God's Bread given to you, his Only-begotten Son, clothed in human flesh, living and dying for the sons of men. Happy are they who feed on this heavenly manna.

What is this bread? Well, it is the grace of God. As you read this chapter through, you find that the Lord refers first to his Word, and bids you hear it. Next, he speaks of his Son, whom he has given to be a witness to his people. Further on, he magnifies his grace, and speaks of wonderful changes which that grace works in those to whom it is given. Oh, how satisfying is the grace of God! "He giveth more grace." We live upon grace; it is our daily bread, grace for every trial, grace for every duty, grace for every sin, and grace for every grace. "Of his fulness have all we received, and grace for grace." This is the food for you. Thirsty with sin, thy sin is quenched with grace. May God grant us grace to feed upon grace, to live upon his Word, and to feast upon his Son!

I ask yet another question, *What is the nature of this food?* It is good; it is good, in every sense of the word "good." It is satisfying. It is pure; no harm can ever come by eating it. This heavenly food is good, and good for you, good for you to-night, good for you at any time, good for you living, good for you dying. All other foods that men seek after are unsubstantial; they can surfeit, but they cannot satisfy; they can cloy, but they cannot content; but the food that has come down from heaven, if a man does but take it into himself, shall be the best food he ever ate.

Moreover, this food is described here as being fatness: "Let thy soul delight itself in fatness." Within the Word of God, there are certain choicer truths; in Christ, there are certain choicer joys; in grace, there are certain choicer experiences than men at first realize. It is not merely bread and food, but it is marrow and fatness. There are "tit-bits" for the Lord's children. "Let your soul delight itself in fatness." "In this mountain shall the Lord of hosts make unto all people a feast of fat things, a feast of wines on the lees, of fat things full of marrow, of wines on the lees well refined." I hope that, before we have done to-night, we shall have introduced some poor soul to the fatness, the choice, special parts of God's most holy Word. It is not lean meat that God gives you, not scrapings from a bone; but he feeds us royally, he gives us of the best he has, and plenty of it. "He daily loadeth us with benefits." He gives us meat to eat of which even angels do not know.

> "Never did angels taste above,
> Redeeming grace, and dying love."

These things are our soul's daily nourishment.

II. But now, secondly, here is FEEDING. One of the most important words in our text is that little word eat: "Eat ye: eat ye."

Food is of no use until it is eaten; and here, often, is the crucial question with seeking souls. "I see that Christ is the Bread of life that I want; but how am I to eat him?" Well, now, really, you ought not to need any instruction on this point. We take a great many orphans into the Orphanage, and some of them are very ignorant, and we have to teach them a great many things; but we have no class for teaching them to eat. They all know how to do that, and to do it pretty heartily, too. If men were hungry, they would know how to eat, if they had the bread. It is because men are not really hungry on account of sin that they come and ask us, "What do you mean by this eating?" Yet it may be that some are sincere in asking the question, so I will answer it.

To eat is, first, to *believe*. To "eat" a truth, you must believe it to be true. To "eat" Christ, you must believe him to be the Christ of God. To "eat" the grace of God, you must believe it to be "the grace of God, which bringeth salvation."

> "Artful doubts and reasonings be
> Nailed with Jesus to the tree."

I will gladly lend you a nail or two, and the use of a hammer as well, for I like not these doubts. They are in the air like midges; they fly about everywhere, and certain brethren endeavour to multiply the pests. But, oh, that you, poor sinner, would have done with doubts, and simply believe! Believe what is certainly true, for God cannot lie, and what he reveals is infallibly sure. Believe it.

Well, after you have done that, to eat is chiefly to *appropriate*. A man takes a piece of bread into his hand; but he has not eaten it till he has put it into his mouth, and swallowed it, and it has gone down into the secret parts of his very self, and has become his very own. When a thing is eaten and digested, it cannot be restored. You may take away my house; you may take away my money; but you cannot take away from me yesterday's dinner. You must take Christ in the same way that you eat your food; that is, appropriate him. Say, "He is mine; I take him to be wholly mine. This Christ, this grace, this pardon, this salvation, I believe it; and I now trust in it, rest in it, appropriate it, and take it to be my own." "Suppose that I should make a mistake in taking it," says one. Nobody ever did. If thou canst take it, God has given it to thee. If thou hast grace to grasp Christ, though thou thinkest thyself a thief in doing so, there is no roguery in it. What God sets before thee, take, and ask no questions. Oh, what a blessed thing it is when a soul is enabled to feed upon the Word of God, to feed upon the Christ of God, to feed upon the grace of God! You cannot do wrong in so doing. It is written, "Him that cometh to me, I will in no wise cast out." "Let him that is athirst come. And whosoever will, let him take the water of life freely." This is to eat,—to appropriate.

But after you have eaten, you know, the full process of eating includes digestion. How do I digest the Word of God? I know what it is to read, and mark, and learn it; but how do I inwardly digest it? When thou dost *meditate* upon it. Oh, what a blessed work is that of sacred meditation, turning the truth over and over and over in the mind, throwing it into the winepress of memory, and treading it out with the feet of thought, till the ruby juice flows out, and thou dost drink thereof, and art satisfied! Meditate upon the Word; think much of what God has done for thee. Think over his thoughts; turn over his words; and thus thy soul will grow strong.

Feeding also means *trusting yourself wholly to Christ.* The man who eats his breakfast, goes about his business trusting to the strength which that morning's meal will give him; and when noontide comes, and he feels faint, he eats again, without a doubt that what he eats will nourish him; and he goes back to his work, and uses muscle and sinew, trusting his food to supply him with power. It is just the same with Christ. Take him, and believe that he will help thee to go about thy business, to bear thy trouble, to meet thine adversary, to serve without weariness, and to run without fainting. This is to eat that which is good; it is to take freely into thine own self Christ, his grace, his Word, and to live thereon, that thou mayest grow thereby.

I should like to make this plain to all of you; but I cannot make it any plainer than this. You have Christ before you; take him. "Oh, but I am not fit," says one. A man who is very hungry might say that he is not "fit" for dinner; but, if he is a sensible man, he just falls to and eats. So let it be with you; whatever your unfitness may be, you are welcomed by the invitations of this chapter. Come along with you; enter the banquet-hall at once, and feed to the full.

III. My third head is WELCOME. What does the Lord say? "Eat ye that which is good, and let your soul delight itself in fatness."

Do you see, here is, first, *no stint?* "Eat, eat, eat, eat, and let your soul delight itself in fatness." It is not said, "Here is a pair of scales; here is a plate; here is a knife. The law allows so many ounces of meat to you, just so much, and you must not have half-an-ounce over." Nothing of the kind. You are just taken to the table, and the exhortation is, "Eat to your heart's content. Let your soul delight itself in fatness." There is no stint.

As there is no stint, so there is *no reserve.* It is not said, "Now you may eat those two things; but you must not touch that nice fat morsel over there; that is for Joseph; that is for the particular favourite, not for you." No, poor soul, when God invites you to his table, you may have anything there is on the table. No matter though it be eternal life, though it be communion with Christ, though it be immutable love, thou mayest eat it. Take it, take it; for thou art not called here to sit, as they used to have it, "below the salt", among the inferior folk; you are called to sit at the table like any of the princes, and the great King himself says, " Eat ye that which is good, and let your soul delight itself in fatness."

So, too, there is *no end* to the feast. "Eat; keep on eating. Delight yourself in fatness; keep on delighting yourself in fatness. You will never use it all up." I read of a country once, though I hardly believed the description of it; for it was said that the grass grew faster than the cows could eat it. Well, there is a country that I know of, where the grass grows faster than the sheep can eat it. You may eat all you will out of the divine Word; but you will find that there is more left than you have taken; and it seems as if there were more after you had taken it, as if the grass grew deeper as you fed more ravenously upon it. You will find it so. God puts no reserve as to time. In the morning, feed on his Word; at noontide, drink to strengthen thy life out of the Sacred Scriptures; and at night, feed thy heart, yet again, upon thy evening portion.

I want to talk to you a little about this feeding, and especially in reference to the fatness of divine truth. There are some of God's people who do not live upon the richer meats of his Word. Poor souls, some of them never get a taste of them. Perhaps they attend a ministry where the richer meat is never brought out. The "clods and stickings" of the gospel they will get; but not the prime joints, not the best parts of the gospel. Well, well, if that is all that their ministers have to give them, it is well that they should give them that; but if any man has learned by experience to feed upon the deep things of God, and the meat that sustains the soul, let him not fail to put it in due season upon the children's table. Why, some of you dare not make a good meal on the doctrine of election! If you did, you would find it to contain " fat things full of marrow." The doctrine of the perseverance of the saints, the doctrine of the immutable love of God, the doctrine of the union of the believer with Christ, the doctrine of the eternal purpose that can never fail—why, I have seen many a child of God sniff at these things! Well, well, well, we must not find fault with them. Babes, of course, do not like meat. Poor creatures, they have not teeth enough yet to bite meat, and we must give them milk. Only let not the babes kick at us who can eat meat. We must eat the strong meat, for it is the very food of our souls.

Different foods are for different growths of grace; but it is a pity that the children of God should habitually neglect the richer joints of the gospel. There are some of them who measure themselves by others. I do believe that some of God's people are afraid of being too holy, which fear need never haunt them much. Some of them are afraid of being too happy, because they know a dear soul, who is a kind of weather-glass to them, and she is not very often happy, and so they are afraid that they must not be. How many a person has set up Mr. Little-Faith to be his model, or Mr. Ready-to-Halt, with his crutches, to be a kind of pattern to him! Now, Ready-to-Halt was a very sensible man; he would not advise other people to use crutches. They were good for him; but he wished that he had never wanted them. So is it with a mournful child of God, there are some of the best who are of a sorrowful spirit; but I would not recommend *you* to be like them. If that man on the other side of the table dares not eat the marrow and fatness, that is no reason why you should not have your share if you can enjoy it.

There are some people (I will not judge them), who always want to know, when they come to God's feast, how little food will be sufficient, what is the minimum upon which a person could live. Dear, dear, I never tried that plan; and I do not recommend you to go to-night, and consult a doctor to know what is the smallest amount of food upon which a man could live. There are, I fear, a good many of you working out that problem with regard to your souls. You say, "Well, now, do you not think that one sermon on Sunday is quite enough?" Then, there is the prayer-meeting, and you say, "It is only a prayer-meeting; we shall not go to that." So you go from Sunday to Sunday, sometimes, you one-sermon-a-week people, and you say, "I feel unhappy; I have many doubts and fears." I should think you have. If you had only one meal a week, you would feel a little hollow here and there; and if you only get one spiritual meal a week, it is no wonder that you are weakly. The text says, "Eat ye that which is good, and let your soul delight itself in fatness." It does not put to you that strange proposition of trying how little spiritual food you can live upon.

There are others, who are very sincere, who always ask how much they may take. May I take a promise? Poor soul that I am, may I dare to call Jesus mine? Why, I am the very lowest of the people of God, may I dare to think about everlasting love? When you go to a feast, the question is not what *you* are, but what the host is; and, if he has spread the table, and invited you, make no "bones" about it, as men say, but eat what he sets before you. Ah, dear hearts! if we had not more than we deserved, we should not even be alive in the land of mercy. Everything that God gives is of grace, not of merit, not of desert; therefore, unworthy though thou be, take it.

"Oh! but," says one, "I am afraid of being presumptuous." Oh, yes, I know! There are a great many who are afraid of presumption, and they make a mistake about what presumption is. I think I told you, one day, of two little boys, to whom their mother said, "Now, John and Thomas, I shall take you out next Monday for a day's holiday." Well, it was Thursday or Friday, and one of them began to talk about it with all his might: "I am going out for a holiday next Monday; I know I am; I am going out for a holiday next Monday." His little brother was "afraid to presume"; so he said that he thought, perhaps, he might go out for a holiday next Monday, but he was afraid to presume. The other little fellow, when he got up on Saturday morning, said, "Mother, is it Monday yet?" and he was as happy as a lark with the idea that the Monday must come very soon. Now, which of the two was presumptuous? I do not think that the boy who believed his mother's promise was presumptuous; I think that he was a good, humble, believing child; but I think that the other boy, who argued, "Well, you see, mother cannot afford to take us out; perhaps it will be wet; and mother, perhaps, will not keep her word; she will forget it." I say, he was presumptuous, and did not deserve to go at all. You who doubt are vastly more presumptuous than you would be if you would simply believe.

Let me encourage you, dear friends, to put in practice my text, "Eat ye that which is good, and let your soul delight itself in fatness." Feed your souls on precious truth. Do not say, "Oh, that is high doctrine!" My dear friend, you have no business to call doctrine high or low. If it is in God's Word, believe it, and live upon it. "Oh, but those are deep things!" Some people even say that they are "Calvinistic." Never mind if they are; they will not hurt you. I am of the mind of the old lady who said, when she heard a certain preacher, "I like to hear that kind of minister, he is a high Calvary preacher." That was a good mistake to make; I would like to be a "high Calvary preacher"; and preach up Jesus Christ and him crucified with all my might. Do not be afraid to feed on anything that Christ is, or did, or promised. Fall to with a glorious appetite, "and eat ye that which is good, and let your soul delight itself in fatness." If there are any high enjoyments, raptures, ecstasies, delights, if you lose yourself in heaven begun below, if you can feel the Lord very near you, well, be ready to dance for joy. "Let your soul delight itself in fatness."

But as to holy exercises, such as prayer, and prayer continued, prayer strong and mighty, and such as praise, too, that is akin to the music of heaven, do not hold back from them. Go in for them with all your might. "Let your soul delight itself in fatness." Oh, our poor starveling services, our weak, impotent drawings near to God! May we be delivered from them, and may we get into the marrow and fatness of real communion with the Most High!

Above all, do not neglect to feed on what you have not yet received, but what is yours in the hand of Christ. On the glory yet to be revealed, on the glories of the Second Advent, especially, often dwell; and let your hearts take fire as you think of them, and let your spirit grow strong with an intense delight, because HE is coming. HE is coming quickly; and who knows when he may appear? Live upon the promise of his coming, and rejoice therein. "Eat ye that which is good, and let your soul delight itself in fatness."

IV. Now, my time has gone, and therefore I will not preach upon the fourth head, which was to have been DELIGHT; but I will just say these few words on this part of my theme.

There is no peril in holy joy, in delighting yourself in God's Word, and delighting yourself in Christ. You may be as happy as ever you can be, and there will be no danger in it: for "the joy of the Lord is your strength." The joy of the Lord is your safety; the joy of the Lord will be your restoration, if you have wandered away from him.

There will be no idleness, or selfishness, produced by this fat feeding. The more you feed on God's Word, the more you will work for the good of others. You will not say, "I am saved, and therefore I will let others perish." Oh, no! You will have an intense, burning desire to bring others in to feed upon "free grace and dying love." There are none who love the souls of men so much as those who love their Lord much. When they have themselves had much forgiven, and they know it, they go and seek their fellow-sinners, and try to bring them to the Saviour's feet.

Dear friends, may you get such meals upon the rich things of the Word of God that you may come to *a sacred contentment,* till you shall not say, like Esau, "I have enough," but shall say, like Jacob, "I have all things"! May you be unable to wish for anything more! May you be so complete in Christ, so fully supplied in him, that you can say, "The Lord is my Shepherd; I shall not want"!

May you also attain to *a sense of holy security;* not of carnal security, for that is dangerous; that is ruinous; but holy security, so that you can say, "I know whom I have believed, and am persuaded that he is able to keep that which I have committed unto him against that day." "Of what persuasion are you?" said one man to another. "Of what persuasion am I? I am of this persuasion, that he is able to keep that which I have committed unto him." This is a blessed persuasion. May you have it, and keep it all your days!

Then, next, may you come into *a state of perfect rest!* "Rest in the Lord, and wait patiently for him." "We that have believed do enter into rest." "There remaineth therefore a rest to the people of God." But there is a rest which they enjoy even now; may you get it!

May you also come into *a state of complete resignation to the will of God!* If we sang with our hearts that beautiful hymn (Number 691) just now, we are able to leave everything with God, and let him do what he likes with us. May you just feel that your will is what God's will would have it to be, and that God's will shall be your will! Then you will let your soul delight itself in fatness.

Lastly, may you be filled with *a happy expectancy!* May you be able to say with our poet,—

> "My heart is with him on his throne,
> And ill can brook delay;
> Each moment listening for the voice,
> 'Rise up, and come away.'"

Oh, to live in the suburbs of heaven, to get into the vestibule of God's great palace, and to stop there, and hear the singing of the seraphim inside the walls! There is such a thing as feeling, on the Hill Beulah, the breezes from the distant Celestial City. When the wind sets the right way, you may often smell the spices of the glory-land where Emmanuel is King, and his beloved lie in his bosom for ever. I pray that you may all have this. Do not say, "We cannot." Do not fear that you cannot, but rather listen to the text, and carry it out, "Eat ye that which is good, and let your soul delight itself in fatness."

Oh, that some poor soul would get his first mouthful of Christ tonight! Take him. I have seen a hungry child sent by his mother to the baker's. There is a little piece of bread put in as a "makeweight", and the poor child eats it on the way home. I give you leave to do that to-night. Carry the truth away with you, and keep it; but eat a bit as you go home. Lay hold on Christ to-night, now, before you leave the Tabernacle. May his grace enable you to do it; and then sit down, and eat, and eat, and eat for ever of this precious, inexhaustible provision of God's infinite love; and to him shall be glory for ever and ever. Amen.

Exposition by C. H. Spurgeon.

ISAIAH LV.

To-night we shall read that precious chapter of gospel invitation, the fifty-fifth of Isaiah, which, I hope, you all know by heart.

Verse 1. *Ho, every one that thirsteth,*

God would have the attention of sinners; he calls for it. Are not sinners eager for God? Oh, no! It is God who is eager for sinners; and so he calleth "Ho!" Men pass by with their ears full of the world's tumult; and God calleth, again and again, "Ho! Ho!" Be you rich or poor, learned or illiterate, if you are in need, and specially if you feel your need, "Ho, every one that thirsteth."

1. *Come ye to the waters,*

There are only in one place waters that can quench your thirst; and God calls you that way: "Come ye to the waters."

1. *And he that hath no money;*

Water is a thing that is sold, not given away, in the East; and he that needs it, must buy it. But he who buys of God, has nothing to pay: "He that hath no money."

1. *Come ye, buy, and eat; yea, come, buy wine and milk without money and without price.*

See how God's good things grow as we look at them. The first invitation was, "Come ye to the waters;" the next was, "Eat;" but this one speaks of "wine and milk." Our first idea of the gospel is very simple, it is water for our thirst. Soon we find that it is food for our hunger. Presently we discover it to be wine for our delight, and milk for our perpetual sustenance. There is everything in Christ; and you want him. Come and have him. There is no other preparation needed but that you feel your need of him.

"This he gives you;
'Tis his Spirit's rising beam."

What a cheering verse this is to begin with!

2. *Wherefore do ye spend money for that which is not bread? and your labour for that which satisfieth not?*

If you spend your money for that which is not bread, you are likely to be disappointed. "Oh, but," you say, "I have made many an effort." Yes, I know you have; but, if you labour for "that which satisfieth not", I do not wonder that you are not satisfied. Let your past defeats drive you to your God. If you have failed hitherto, so much the more reason why you should listen to the Lord's message. He says to you,—

2. *Hearken diligently unto me,*

Salvation comes through the ear, more than through the eye. Hearken; hearken; hearken diligently, with both your ears, with all your heart, hearken unto your God.

2. *And eat ye that which is good, and let your soul delight itself in fatness.*

If we will hear, and will believe, we shall be satisfied; we shall be delighted; we shall be overjoyed. The Lord can take our thirst away, and give instead a delight in fatness.

3. *Incline your ear,*

Hold it near the mouth of the gracious Speaker. Be willing to hear what God has to say. Take out that wool of prejudice that has prevented you from hearkening to God's voice: "Incline your ear."

3. *And come unto me: hear, and your soul shall live; and I will make an everlasting covenant with you, even the sure mercies of David.*

"When thus you live, I will make an everlasting covenant with you. I am not the God of the dead, but of the living; and when once, through hearing the divine Word, you have come to life, I will be your God."

4. *Behold, I have given him*

One greater than David, even the Beloved of the Lord, the Only-begotten, the Messiah Prince, the King of kings, even Jesus.

4. *For a witness to the people, a leader and commander to the people.*

God did not give us an angel to lead us, but he gave us his Son; and he did not merely give us his Son to be an example, but to die for us, to bleed to death on our behalf, to be our Substitute, dying in our place and stead. "I have given him." This is the greatest wonder that ever was. "God so loved the world that he gave his Only-begotten Son;" not, "God so loved the saintly; God so loved the earnest; God so loved the moral;" but "the world", the common-place, sinful world; he so loved those who lay dead in trespasses and sins "that he gave his Only-begotten Son, that whosoever believeth in him should not perish, but have everlasting life." And the Father, in giving his Son, gives him a promise:—

5. *Behold, thou shalt call a nation that thou knowest not, and nations that knew not thee shall run unto thee because of the LORD thy God, and for the Holy One of Israel; for he hath glorified thee.*

So, brethren, the gospel must succeed. Christ must have whole nations to come to him; they must come; they shall come; for God has glorified his Son, and he glorifies him in this among other ways, in bringing nations to his feet. The gospel is no experiment; there is not a question as to its success. There may be dark days just now, and our hearts may sink as we look around; but the Father will keep his promise to the Son, and that encourages us to look up in the darkest hour. This fact, which is more than a promise, will never be altered, "He hath glorified thee."

6. *Seek ye the LORD while he may be found, call ye upon him while he is near:*

Oh, may the Holy Spirit make every word I read to be effectual with you! God himself speaks to you to-night, out of a Book which not only *was* inspired, but *is* inspired; and he says to-night, freshly from his own lip to you that have not rest of heart, "Seek ye the LORD while he may be found." He may be found; therefore seek him. "Call ye upon him while he is near." He is near; therefore call upon him.

7. *Let the wicked forsake his way,*

Do not let him wait till he has finished this thing, or done the other, or till he has so much to bring in his hand. Let him run away from his old master, and from his old way, and from his old self at once. May God help him so to do!

7. *And the unrighteous man his thoughts: and let him return unto the LORD, and he will have mercy upon him; and to our God,*

Whom we love, and in whom we trust, and who has pardoned us: "to our God."

7. *For he will abundantly pardon.*

The marginal reading is, "He will multiply to pardon." He will pardon, and pardon, and pardon, and pardon, and pardon, and pardon, *ad infinitum.* Enormous as the sin may be, God's pardon shall suffice to put it all away. Is this message too hard for you to believe? Oh, broken heart! does this divine truth seem to you to be too good to be true? Oh, trembling one! does it seem impossible that the righteous God can cast all your sins behind his back, and drown them in the depths of the sea? Listen still to our Lord's gracious words:—

9—11. *For as the heavens are higher than the earth, so are my ways higher than your ways, and my thoughts than your thoughts. For as the rain cometh down, and the snow from heaven, and returneth not thither, but watereth the earth, and maketh it bring forth and bud, that it may give seed to the sower, and bread to the eater: so shall my word be that goeth forth out of my mouth: it shall not return unto me void, but it shall accomplish that which I please, and it shall prosper in the thing whereto I sent it.*

God's Word is not ineffectual. If thou wilt hear it, it will bless thee. When God sends snow and rain, they go not back again. The earth receives them; they sink into her pores; they refresh her secret life. Receive thou, O black heart, the Word of God, as the earth receives the snow! O thou dry heart, receive thou the Word as the dry ground receives the shower. It shall not go back again; it shall sink into thine inmost soul; it shall save thee. God can save thee. Believe it; receive his Word into thy heart, and it shall save thee. Mark who you are, who are spoken to in the first and second verses, you who are thirsty, you who have no money, you who have laboured, and are disappointed with the fruit of your toil.

12. *For ye shall go out with joy,*

You poor people who are invited to come to the waters, you who have nothing of your own, "Ye shall go out with joy."

12. *And be led forth with peace:*

To some places you can "go" by yourselves; to others you must be "led"; but in either case you shall have "joy" and "peace."

12. *The mountains and the hills shall break forth before you into singing,*

They do not look like singing, do they? They look as if their only music would be the howling of the wild winds about their brow, or the roaring of the wild beasts along their sides; but for you, for you, ye thirsty ones, they shall break forth into singing.

12. *And all the trees of the field shall clap their hands.*

Trees seem to have little sympathy with weary hearts; but when weary hearts find peace with God in Christ, as I trust some will to-night, then even the trees of the field seem to be in harmony with man, and they clap their hands in jubilant exultation.

13. *Instead of the thorn shall come up the fir tree, and instead of the brier shall come up the myrtle tree: and it shall be to the* LORD *for a name,*

Yes, it shall make God's name great when you are converted; for you will talk about what the Lord has done for your soul, and that will bring God fame: "It shall be to the LORD for a name."

13. *For an everlasting sign that shall not be cut off.*

O ye that thirst, O ye hungry, O ye unsatisfied, may the reading of this Word be blessed to you to-night! Amen.

HYMNS FROM "OUR OWN HYMN BOOK"—708, 732, 691.

Metropolitan Tabernacle Pulpit.

JOY HINDERING FAITH.

A Sermon

INTENDED FOR READING ON LORD'S-DAY, OCTOBER 23RD, 1892,

DELIVERED BY

C. H. SPURGEON,

AT THE METROPOLITAN TABERNACLE, NEWINGTON,

On Lord's-day Evening, May 25th, 1890.

"And while they yet believed not for joy, and wondered, he said unto them, Have ye here any meat? And they gave him a piece of a broiled fish, and of an honeycomb. And he took it, and did eat before them. And he said unto them, These are the words which I spake unto you, while I was yet with you, that all things must be fulfilled, which were written in the law of Moses, and in the prophets, and in the psalms, concerning me. Then opened he their understanding, that they might understand the scriptures."—Luke xxiv. 41—45.

The disciples were gathered together with the doors of the house fast closed, for they were afraid of the Jewish mob. Suddenly HE came, HE who was chief in their thoughts, the Christ whom they had seen dead upon the cross, whom some of them had helped to bury. There he stood before them, and "they were terrified and affrighted." As on a former occasion, on the Sea of Galilee, so now they said, "It is a spirit," and they cried out for fear. The Saviour did his best to disabuse their minds of their mistake. He said to them, "Handle me, and see; for a spirit hath not flesh and bones, as ye see me have. And when he had thus spoken, he showed them his hands and his feet." He went as far as he well could go to prove that he was a real man, composed of real flesh and bones.

Then they believed, for it was perfectly clear that he had risen from the dead, and was in their midst. They had hardly begun to believe that their Lord was really with them, before it seemed too good to be true. A wave of joy came rolling up, and then appeared to be sucked back again, and they seemed to be sucked back by it. They believed not for joy; they were astounded; they were full of wonder. They did believe, else they would have had no joy; but the very joy swallowed up the thing of which it was born, and they did not believe because of the excess of joy. This is an experience which has been very common; and I merely take this text to-night that I may deal with some persons who have found Christ, and are saved, but who are now troubled because it seems too good to be true.

First, then, to-night, I shall speak, if I have strength to do so,

No. 2,279.

upon *the difficulty under which they laboured:* "They yet believed not for joy." Secondly, I shall speak upon *the manner in which our Lord helped them to get over the difficulty.* He first ate a piece of fish and a portion of a honeycomb in their presence, and then opened their understanding, that they might understand the Scriptures.

I. First, then, THE DIFFICULTY UNDER WHICH THEY LABOURED. "They believed not for joy."

This is not the only instance in which joy has seemed to stop the flow of faith. *It has occurred on other occasions.* You have an early instance of it in the Book of Genesis. Will you kindly turn to Genesis xlv. 25, 26? Jacob had lost his beloved Joseph; he believed him to be dead; he had been shown a bloody coat which he knew was his son's; but now the brothers come back from Egypt with news that Joseph is yet alive, and is governor over all the land of Egypt. "And they went up out of Egypt, and came into the land of Canaan unto Jacob their father, and told him, saying, Joseph is yet alive, and he is governor over all the land of Egypt. And Jacob's heart fainted, for he believed them not." It was too good to be true, and his heart sank within him. "You must be deceiving me," he said. He knew that his sons had been liars before; indeed, if this report was true, they had been liars before, and now he cannot believe their news, it is too much for him, and the old man swoons away. So have I met with many who had been told that Christ had saved them, and they believed it; and after believing it, it seemed as if it was presumption to believe any such thing, and they were thrown back into doubt and despondency again.

Job was once in a similar condition, for he says in his Book, the ninth chapter, and the sixteenth verse, "If I had called, and he had answered me; yet would I not believe that he had hearkened unto my voice." He had such a fear of God, he saw so much of his own unworthiness, and of God's greatness, that he says that, if he had prayed, and God had heard him, he could not have believed it to be true. This is a more spiritual case than that of Jacob; but it makes a very good parallel instance as to the fact that joy itself may cause unbelief.

The same idea comes up in Psalm cxxvi. You remember the words, "When the Lord turned again the captivity of Zion, we were like them that dream." They seemed to say, "We could not believe it. We thought it was all imagination, a freak of fancy, the high play of spirits in dreamland; surely it cannot be true."

If you want another case, you have that of Peter as recorded in the twelfth chapter of the Acts of the Apostles. When Peter had been brought out of prison, the angel led him into the street, and he found that he was free; but he "wist not that it was true which was done by the angel; but thought he saw a vision." He could not believe that every barrier to his escape had been removed, and that he was really out of prison. There is a young woman mentioned in the same chapter, who was very much of the same mind as Peter. Read the thirteenth and fourteenth verses: "And as Peter knocked at the door of the gate, a damsel came to hearken, named Rhoda. And when she knew Peter's voice, she opened not the gate for gladness, but ran in, and told how Peter stood before the gate." Why did she not let him in? Ah! she was too glad to do that. As the woman at the well left her waterpot when she found Christ, so did Rhoda leave Peter standing outside the door; she was too glad to let him in. A hungry man, when he at last finds bread, may be too glad to eat. A thirsty man may come to the fountain, and for a moment be too glad to stoop down and drink of its cooling stream. Men and women are strange paradoxes. We are made up of paradoxes; we are the most curious creatures in all the world. We believe and get glad, and then we disbelieve because we are glad, for we think that it cannot be true joy, or true faith. I do not understand you, my brethren, because I do not understand myself; and I do not believe that you understand yourselves. The mercy is that you do not need to understand yourselves; you are in the hands of a great Physician who knows all about you, and who will prescribe for you where you cannot even tell what is the matter with yourself.

I have given you these instances out of the Scriptures; but *such cases are common enough in our experience.* Here is one who has heard preached the doctrine of immediate salvation by faith; he understands that—

> "The moment a sinner believes,
> And trusts in his crucified God,
> His pardon at once he receives,
> Redemption in full through his blood."

He has believed, and he has received redemption in full; and now he says to himself, "Can it be really true? What! all my sins forgiven? Am I whiter than snow? That great sin of mine, that seemed to turn all my being to crimson and scarlet, is that washed out?" It seems too good to be true; and the man's doubts come thick upon him by reason of the very greatness of the pardon which he has grasped.

Suppose, further, that it is whispered in his ear, "You are redeemed from among men by a special redemption, for Christ loved the Church, and gave himself for it; the Good Shepherd laid down his life for the sheep; and you are a part of his Church, you are one of his sheep; and therefore specially and peculiarly redeemed out of mankind." As he turns it over, he believes in a general redemption for all sinners; but he cannot believe in this special, peculiar, effective substitution; and he says to himself, "It is too wonderful to be mine. For me to have a special part in what Christ did, how can that be?" You first rejoice because you believe it, and then you begin to doubt it because you rejoice. Perhaps it is whispered in your ear still further, "You were chosen from before the foundation of the world, you are espoused to Christ, married unto him in an everlasting wedlock, you are a member of his body, of his flesh, and of his bones; and because he lives, you shall live also; you shall be with him where he is, and shall behold his glory." You feel so full of delight that you can hardly bear yourself; but you have scarcely begun to be delighted before the whisper comes, "It is too good to be true; it must be all a mistake;" and so you believe not for joy.

Suppose that you should sometimes have those high enjoyments, those love-feasts, those banquets in the hall of love with Christ;

suppose that you should come to lean your head, with holy John, upon his bosom, and not only know his love, but be caught up, as it were, into the third heaven of immediate fellowship with him. Now, you feel as if you could die for very joy, until there comes this cold, shivering doubt, "You are altogether mistaken; you are a mere fanatic; you are an enthusiast; for God could not have admitted a man, such as you are, into such close fellowship." Often have I met with persons troubled in this manner; and it is to them that I speak.

Now, let me ask, *what is the occasion of this difficulty?* Why do we get these doubts about the great mercy of God? I answer, first, because of a deep sense of unworthiness. If any man here could see himself as he is, and then could see the fulness of God's love to him, I believe that it would make every individual hair of his head stand upright with astonishment; and, next to that, it would carry him right away with a ravishment of adoring wonder. "Such a wretch, such a beast, such an almost devil as I was, and yet loved of God!" It would startle him. Hear how David puts it, "So foolish was I, and ignorant; I was as a beast before thee. Nevertheless, I am continually with thee; thou hast holden me by my right hand." The sense of our own desert makes it seem too good to be true that we should really be saved.

Next, the habitude of fear in which some of us were found, creates this difficulty. We were accustomed to think of our sin despairingly. Month after month, some of us could see no hope; nay, not a ray of light; so that, when the light did come, it was too much for our poor eyes. Have you never gone suddenly into the light, and found yourself less able to see than you were when you were in the dark?

"When God reveal'd his gracious name
And changed my mournful state,
My rapture seem'd a pleasing dream,
The grace appear'd so great,"

because of the mournful state in which I had been before.

Then, perhaps, most of all it seems hard to believe because of the intensity of our former anxiety. These disciples had been intensely thoughtful about Christ, and anxious about him, and that was why they could not in a moment believe that he was really risen from the dead. And when a man has been thinking long about his soul, when he has felt his sin like lead, when he has looked into the awful burnings of infinite justice, when he has heard, as it were, the sentence, "Depart, ye cursed," ringing in his ears, do you wonder that he wants to be quite sure that he is really forgiven? He cannot take that for granted. He looks, and looks, and looks, and looks again; and he cannot rest till he is certain that his sin is all blotted out, and that he is "accepted in the Beloved." Hence, even the very delightfulness of the idea of being justified by faith in Christ causes a doubt to enter the heart.

Further, I do not wonder that the doubt comes in when you think of the simplicity of the way of salvation. Look! I have been for years trying to save myself; I have gone to Abana and Pharpar, and washed, and washed, and washed, and I am still a leper; and then, one day, I do but believe, I do but go and wash in Jordan, and at once my leprosy is gone. I should think that, if the woman, whose issue of blood was staunched when she touched the hem of Christ's garment, felt in her body that she was healed of that plague, she must also a moment after have had the fear, "But surely it will come back again; I cannot have been cured in so simple a way. I have been to all the doctors, and have spent all my money, and I only grew worse. Am I really healed?" So, when a sinner sees himself saved by nothing but believing, by simply trusting Christ, do you wonder that an early thought with him is, "This must be too good to be true, to be saved so simply"?

Add to this the immediateness of divine grace, and you understand where the difficulty arises. If it took a month to save a man, if it took seven years to put sin away, I could understand that by degrees we should come to believe in the process, though I do not know but what we might very likely get fresh doubts out of that process; but to be saved in a moment, to pass from death to life in less than the twinkling of an eye, all sin forgiven more quickly than a watch can tick; this is the work of salvation, the giving of the new birth, the passing of the act of indemnity and oblivion, and this takes no time whatever.

"'Tis done! the great transaction's done;
I am my Lord's, and he is mine."

And then the saved soul turns round, and says, "Can it be true that I am really saved; I who just now was in the very depths of despair?"

Now, I am only going to deal with this difficulty in the following few words, to show you that *it has no solid basis.* Thou sayest, "Can this be true?" because it is so good. My answer is—You want something good, do you not? You want something greatly good. Could anything save you but a great act of grace? Tell me. Are you not of Richard Baxter's mind when he prayed, "Lord, give me great mercy, or no mercy; for little mercy will not serve my turn"? If anybody says, "It is too good to be true," say, "It is no better than I want. I want perfect pardon; I want complete renewal; I want to be made a child of God; I want to be saved." It is not too good to be true; for it is not too good to be what you want.

Do you not think, also, that great things belong to God? Do you expect God to be little in his mercy, little in his gifts, little in his grace? You make a great mistake if you do; for as the heavens are higher than the earth, so are his ways higher than man's ways. The greatness of the goodness which you receive should be to you a letter of commendation. If it were little, it might come from man. If it be too great to come from man, that proves that it comes from God. Let the greatness rather reassure you than cause you to doubt. When a doubt arises from the simple way of salvation, let me put this to you—What other way would save you? I know that I shall never get to heaven by any way but the way of faith; I have not even a fragment of confidence in anything that I have ever done, or ever designed to do.

" I'm a poor sinner, and nothing at all,
But Jesus Christ is my all in all."

O my dear hearer, you may surely be content with a way that suits you, the way of believing! "It is very easy," you say. It is not too easy for you; you could not go a harder way. To faint away into the arms of Christ, and throw your whole weight upon him, let it not seem too simple for you, for this is all that you can do; ay, and more than you ever will do unless the grace of God leads you to do it. Do not, therefore, doubt the way because it is so simple. What other way could you have?

Once more, do not say that the gift of God's grace is too good to be true, for those of us who live in the daily enjoyment of it are by nature no better than you, and yet it has come to us. Why should it not come to you? I never saw the man yet whom I would have put behind myself in the matter of salvation. If I had had to guess which man in this congregation would not be saved, I should not have guessed any man but myself. I stood in the rear rank; not that I had openly sinned worse than others, but there were certain elements of character that caused me to despair; yet I was fetched in by God's grace, and why should not you also be brought in? "Ah!" say you, "I am a very odd person." So am I; you are not odder than I am. "Oh!" says one, "but I am such a strange body." So am I; I am a lot out of all the catalogues. Whosoever you are, be you who you may, come along to Christ; he cannot cast you away, for he has said, "Him that cometh to me, I will in no wise cast out." Come to Christ, dear friend, and he will not cast you out. This truth is not too good to be true; if I have not found it too good to be true, you will not find it too good to be true. Lay hold of it, and believe it.

Thus I have tried to set before you the difficulty that the disciples were in when they believed not for joy.

II. Now, in the second place, I shall only be able to speak briefly upon THE MANNER IN WHICH OUR LORD HELPED THEM TO GET OVER THE DIFFICULTY.

Of course, their main point was that they could not believe that Jesus was risen from the dead; it seemed too good to be true.

The Lord helped them out, first, *by a fuller view of what he could do.* They had handled him; they had seen and felt that he was real substantial materialism, composed of flesh and blood, which spirits have not. He takes a piece of fish, and eats it; he takes a piece of honeycomb, dripping with honey, and eats it; and, as I think, he gave them a part of the same food. If they were not satisfied with looking at him, and handling him, they should have a further evidence that he was in the body; for he could eat and drink like any other individual.

Now, I pray the Lord to give to any here, who say, "It is too good to be true," a clearer view of himself. If you will think more of him who brings you this great salvation, you will not be less astonished, but you will be less doubtful. Think of who he was, God, in the bosom of the Father; and the Father, in giving him, gave himself. It is no trifling salvation, depend upon it, that God comes to work out. If it had been a small salvation, he might have sent Gabriel, and said to him, "Go and save those sinners"; but as God himself comes to do the work, you may depend upon it that it is a great salvation.

And when our Lord came here, he not only lived and laboured, but he suffered. He was "a Man of sorrows and acquainted with grief." He was mocked, spit upon, scourged, crucified. He died. He who only hath immortality, died. Does that cross over yonder mean a little salvation? Do the groans of Christ mean little gifts for men? Do those gory shoulders, ploughed by the lash, mean trifles for trifling sinners? Do the five wounds, and the cruel scorn, and the great passion, all mean a small salvation for sinners? Oh! no, beloved, they mean great salvation for giant sinners, the sons of Anak, a great salvation for the biggest sinners that ever lived. Think of the cross of Calvary, and Christ on it, and you will never say that the great salvation he wrought out is too good to be true.

But he is alive again, and he has gone up yonder, through the shining ranks of cherubim and seraphim, to the throne of God. And what is he doing? Pleading for sinners, making intercession for the transgressors. Is that a little thing for which the Christ prays? He might have made one of his saints to be the intercessor if it had been some trifling thing; but it is a great, priceless, infinite boon for which Christ prays before the Father.

Listen, once more. Christ has joined the glory of his name with the work of salvation. He cares more to be a Saviour than to be a King. His highest glory comes from his rescuing men from going down into the pit. Creation glorifies God. The morning stars sang together, and all the sons of God shouted for joy when the world was made; but God did not think that was a work to rejoice over; he merely said that it was good. He could have made fifty more worlds, ay, fifty million worlds, if he had pleased. But when Jesus saves men by laying down his life for his chosen, it is written, "He will rest in his love, he will joy over thee with singing." Think of Jehovah, the Triune God, bursting into song! He sings; for all his glory is wrapped up in the salvation of men. Is it then a trifle? No. I rejoice in the greatness of salvation; and believe in it the more because it is so great, and so worthy of the glory of God. I hope that neither you nor I will fall into the difficulty of the disciples when they believed not for joy.

But now our Saviour did another thing. After thus manifesting himself, *he began to open up to them the Scriptures*. Ah! that is what we all want for the removal of our doubts. The least read Book in the world, in proportion to its circulation, is the Bible. I believe that "Jack the Giant Killer" is more read than the Bible in proportion to the number of persons who have the books. It is sad that it should be so. There is the daily paper, and there is the weekly religious paper, as it is called, and these two together put on the table hide away the Bible. We need to read our Bibles more; we must read our Bibles more. If we do, what shall we read there?

Well, we shall read of a great fall that took place in the Garden of Eden. You know, they tell us now that, when Adam fell, he broke his little finger, and it was done up, and he recovered; but that is not what the Bible says. He broke his neck, and a great deal more than his neck. Oh, what a fall was there, my brethren! Then you and I and all of us fell down. It was a fall which dislocated man altogether. Well, now, for a great fall you must have a great salvation. Therefore do not be astonished when you read of a great salvation. It is involved in the meaning of the great disaster of the fall.

Then, the fall brought on great depravity. Although they make it out now that man, through the fall, has only suffered very slightly, just a little toothache, or something of that sort, yet the Scripture does not tell us so. His whole head is sick, and his whole heart faint, and from the sole of his foot to the crown of his head he is nothing but wounds, and bruises, and putrefying sores. "The heart is deceitful above all things, and desperately wicked." Now you must have a great salvation to meet this great depravity. There must be a great work of grace to turn this ship right-about, to lay a mighty hand upon the helm, and reverse its course.

Next, beloved, if you read the Bible carefully, you will find that there is such a thing as great sin. Ah! you do not need to read your Bible for that. Reading your own heart, by the light of the Bible, and remembering that every evil thought as well as every evil word, ay, and every evil imagination, is sin before God, you will see what a mass of sin one single human being is defiled with. You want a great salvation because of great sin.

Further, if you read your Bibles, you will find that there is a great hell. Everything in the Bible is according to scale. When men talk of a little hell, it is because they think they have only a little sin, and believe in a little Saviour; it is all little together. But when you get a great sense of sin, you want a great Saviour, and feel that, if you do not have him, you will fall into a great destruction, and suffer a great punishment at the hands of the great God. As you would escape a great hell, believe in a great salvation, and henceforth never be staggered because it is great.

And then there is a great heaven. Oh, what a heaven! Have any of us any idea of what it will be like? We sit and meditate upon it, and we sing about it, and we sometimes half think that we are there; but we are not by a very long way. When we once get inside the gates, we shall say, with the Queen of Sheba, "The half was not told me."

> "Then shall I see, and hear, and know
> All I desired or wish'd below;
> And every power find sweet employ
> In that eternal world of joy."

To get you there, you must have a great salvation. Therefore, do not begin to say, "It is too good to be true." Come, now, surely you are not going to be a fool, and have the world, and give up your hope of going to heaven. I am often wonderstruck at the way in which God, in his infinite love, makes some men go the way that they never thought of going. There are persons in this house to-night, with whom I have conversed lately, children of ungodly parents, brought up in the midst of worldly amusements. Suddenly, softness fell upon their hearts, and they began to think; the things that they loved they began to loathe; they could not tell why; they sought the house of prayer; they learnt the way of salvation, and laid hold on Christ. When they go home to-night, there is not one of the family that will welcome them; and they themselves strove hard to get away when

God began to work upon their heart; but the harpooner in this pulpit, by God's grace, sent a harpoon in so deep that, whales as they were, they could never get it out. They dived deep into the sea of greater sin; but that harpoon held them. The next time that they came up to breathe, they got another harpoon, and they were at last wounded to such an extent that they had to yield; and now they are yielding, with the full concurrence of their will, to the Lord who has mastered them, and led them captive, and now leads them in triumph. Glory be to God for this! You have to go to heaven, my friend, anyhow; you are bound for glory, and you must go there. There is a tug, just in front of you, that will draw you there; and you shall not be lost on the way. Wherefore, if such be your grand destiny, do not wonder that, on the voyage, you have great things from God almost too great, at times, to be believed.

I have done when I have said one thing more. If even joy sometimes hinders our believing, do not let us think much about joy, or much about sorrow. The man who always thinks about being comfortable is generally the most uncomfortable being in the world; and the man who is always thinking about being happy goes the right way to work to be always unhappy. If we are to be saved by our feelings, we shall get saved and lost every other day, for we are just like the weather-glass. They said to me yesterday, "The glass is going back." Very likely it was; but it does not rain for all that. Then another day they say, "The glass is going up," and then I find it generally does rain; so I give up the glasses, and begin to wonder whether there is any truth in them at all. Sometimes my feelings say to me, "You are no child of God," and then I begin to pray, and so I know that my feelings have deceived me. Another time they say to me, "Oh, you are a child of God, that is certain!" and then I get as proud as Lucifer, and that a child of God should never be. What is the good of looking to your feelings at all? Walk by faith. Believe the gospel. Cling to God's promises. If they fail you, all is lost; but they cannot fail you. Rest in the finished work of Christ, and as for joys and sorrows,—

> "Let them come, and let them go,
> Fickle as the winds that blow."

You need place no reliance upon them. Hold on to this, "Christ died for the ungodly." "He that believeth in him is justified from all things." "He that believeth in him is not condemned." Hold you to that, and then come what will, sink or swim, all will be well with your souls.

The Lord bring us all to that blessed condition, for Jesus Christ's sake! Amen.

Exposition by C. H. Spurgeon.

LUKE XXIV. 13—48.

Verses 13—15. *And, behold, two of them went that same day to a village called Emmaus, which was from Jerusalem about threescore furlongs. And they talked together of all these things which had happened. And it came to pass, that, while they communed together and reasoned, Jesus himself drew near, and went with them.*

When two saints are talking together, Jesus is very likely to come and make the third one in the company. Talk of him, and you will soon talk with him. I would that believers more often spoke the one to the other about the things of God. It has been said that, in the olden time, God's people spake often one to another; and now we have altered that, and God's people speak often one against another. It is an alteration; but it certainly is not an improvement. May we get together again, and, like these two disciples, talk of all the things that happened in Jerusalem eighteen centuries ago! If we have less of reasoning than they had, let us have more of communion.

16. *But their eyes were holden that they should not know him.*

Christ was there; but they did not perceive him. Our eyes may be very easily shut so that we do not see Christ even when he is close to us; we see a thousand things; but we miss the Master.

17. *And he said unto them, What manner of communications are these that ye have one to another, as ye walk, and are sad?*

Christian people, why are you sad? It should not be so. And when you talk, why do you increase each other's sadness? Is that wisdom? Surely, the Master might say to some here present, "Why are ye sad?" I hope that he will enable you to shake off the sadness, and to rejoice in him.

18—20. *And the one of them, whose name was Cleopas, answering said unto him, Art thou only a stranger in Jerusalem, and hast not known the things which are come to pass there in these days? And he said unto them, What things? And they said unto him, Concerning Jesus of Nazareth, which was a prophet mighty in deed and word before God and all the people: and how the chief priests and our rulers delivered him to be condemned to death, and have crucified him.*

These were sad things to talk about. They thought that they had lost all when they had lost Christ; and yet there is no theme in all the world that is more full of joy than talk about the crucified Christ. This is strange, is it not? If we look beneath the surface, we shall see that the darkest deed that was ever perpetrated has turned out to be the greatest blessing to mankind; and that the cruellest crime ever committed by mortal man has been made the channel of the divinest benediction of God.

21—23. *But we trusted that it had been he which should have redeemed Israel: and beside all this, to day is the third day since these things were done. Yea, and certain women also of our company made us astonished, which were early at the sepulchre; and when they found not his body, they came, saying, that they had also seen a vision of angels, which said that he was alive.*

How innocently they tell the story! How they convict themselves of stark unbelief! And the Master hears it all patiently and quietly. What a strange sensation it must have been for him to hear them talking about him in this singular way when, all the while, they did not know who the "stranger" was to whom they were speaking! Have you ever thought of what the Saviour must think of many things that we say? We think them wise; but they must be very foolish to the eye of his infinite wisdom, and very shallow to him who sees everything to the bottom.

24, 25. *And certain of them which were with us went to the sepulchre, and found it even so as the women had said: but him they saw not. Then he said unto them, O fools, and slow of heart to believe all that the prophets have spoken:*

He loved them tenderly, but he rebuked them strongly, I had almost said sternly: "O fools, and slow of heart!" I am afraid that is our name: "fools." I am afraid that it may be said of us that we are "slow of heart to believe." We want so many proofs. We very readily disbelieve, but we very slowly believe. If you had a piano in your house, and you left it for months; and when you came back, you found it all in beautiful tune, you would be sure that somebody must have been there to put it in tune; but if, on the other hand, you left it to itself, and it got out of tune, you would say that such a condition was only what was to be expected. So it is natural for us to get out of tune. Sometimes we ring out glad music on the high sounding cymbals, and we lift up the loud hallelujahs of exultant joy; but soon we are down again in the deeps, and strike a minor key. Grace alone can raise us; nature, alas! sinks if left to itself.

26, 27. *Ought not Christ to have suffered these things, and to enter into his glory? And beginning at Moses and all the prophets, he expounded unto them in all the scriptures the things concerning himself.*

The best Book, with the best Teacher, descanting upon the best of subjects. Everywhere this Book speaks about Christ; and when Christ explains it, he only brings himself more clearly before our minds.

28. *And they drew nigh unto the village, whither they went:*

They were sorry to be nearing their destination. They would have liked to walk to the ends of the earth in such company, and listening to such conversation.

28. *And he made as though he would have gone further.*

Christ intended to go further unless the two disciples constrained him to tarry with them.

29. *But they constrained him, saying, Abide with us: for it is toward evening, and the day is far spent.*

That is our prayer to the Lord Jesus to-night, "Abide with us, dear Master; we had thy blessed company this morning; and now the sun is almost down, abide with us!" Let each one of us pray the prayer that we often sing, for, morning, noon, and night, this is a suitable supplication:—

> "Abide with me from morn till eve,
> For without thee I cannot live;
> Abide with me when night is nigh,
> For without thee I dare not die."

29—31. *And he went in to tarry with them. And it came to pass, as he sat at meat with them, he took bread, and blessed it, and brake, and gave to them. And their eyes were opened, and they knew him;*

In the breaking of bread Christ is often known. It is a wonderful emblem. Even if this breaking of bread were not the observance of the Lord's Supper, it was something very like it. Christ's blessing and breaking of bread anywhere are the true token of himself.

31—33. *And he vanished out of their sight. And they said one to another, Did not our heart burn within us, while he talked with us by the way, and while he opened to us the scriptures? And they rose up the same hour, and returned to Jerusalem,*

It was getting late; but it is never too late to tell of Christ's appearing, and never too early. Such a secret ought not to be kept an hour, and therefore "they rose up the same hour, and returned to Jerusalem."

33—36. *And found the eleven gathered together, and them that were with them, saying, The Lord is risen indeed, and hath appeared to Simon. And they told what things were done in the way, and how he was known of them in breaking of bread. And as they thus spake, Jesus himself stood in the midst of them,*

You see that, while they were talking about Christ, he came, and stood in their midst. Speak of your Master, and he will appear. Oh, happy people! who have but to talk of Jesus, and lo! he comes to them.

37—40. *But they were terrified and affrighted, and supposed that they had seen a spirit. And he said unto them, Why are ye troubled? and why do thoughts arise in your hearts? Behold my hands and my feet, that it is I myself: handle me, and see; for a spirit hath not flesh and bones, as ye see me have. And when he had thus spoken, he shewed them his hands and his feet.*

They knew those signs, the marks of his crucifixion. They ought to have been convinced at once that it was even he.

41. *And while they yet believed not for joy,*

Does joy stop faith? Beloved, anything stops faith if we will let it. Faith is a divine miracle. Wherever it exists, God creates it, and God sustains it; but without God, anything can hinder it: "while they yet believed not for joy,"—

41. *And wondered, he said unto them, Have ye here any meat?*

That is, "anything eatable."

42. *And they gave him a piece of a broiled fish,*

Which, as fishermen, they were pretty sure always to have.

42. *And of an honeycomb.*

As a second course, to complete the meal.

43. *And he took it, and did eat before them.*

Some of the old versions add, "and gave the rest to them," which I think is very likely to have been the case. It would be all the more convincing to them if he really ate before them, and then that they also partook of the same food of which he had taken part.

44, 45. *And he said unto them, These are the words which I spake unto you, while I was yet with you, that all things must be fulfilled, which were written in the law of Moses, and in the prophets, and in the psalms, concerning me. Then opened he their understanding, that they might understand the scriptures,*

Good Master, do the same with us to-night!

46, 47. *And said unto them, Thus it is written, and thus it behoved Christ to suffer, and to rise from the dead the third day: and that repentance and remission of sins should be preached in his name among all nations, beginning at Jerusalem.*

This gospel message was to be proclaimed among all nations, "beginning at Jerusalem", but not ending there. It has been preached to us; let us see to it that we pass it on to those who have never heard it yet.

48. *And ye are witnesses of these things.*

We also are called to be "witnesses of these things." May the Lord make us to be faithful and true witnesses, for his name's sake! Amen.

HYMNS FROM "OUR OWN HYMN BOOK"—103 (Vers. III.), 126, 576.

Metropolitan Tabernacle Pulpit.

GOD'S HANDWRITING UPON DAVID.

A Sermon

Intended for Reading on Lord's-day, October 30th, 1892,

DELIVERED BY

C. H. SPURGEON,

AT THE METROPOLITAN TABERNACLE, NEWINGTON,

On Thursday Evening, August 7th, 1890.

"All this, said David, the LORD made me understand in writing by his hand upon me, even all the works of this pattern."—1 Chronicles xxviii. 19.

The temple was not to be built according to the designs of David, or Solomon, or any other man. It was to be built according to a pattern which God himself had formed. In the things of God, we are not left to follow our own judgments and devices; but we are to look to the law and to the testimony for our instructions. To God's Word we must always come for our orders. What God has commanded, is binding upon us in his Church; what he has not commanded, we may safely leave undone.

You will notice that David here says that he received the designs and the details of the temple from God, who wrote them, not on tables of stone, but on his servant's heart by his own hand. Now, it was very necessary that everything should be arranged and planned for the temple, and that it should be built according to a pattern; for it was to be a type, an eminent type of Christ, and also a type of his Church, which is a temple for God's own indwelling. Now, no man knew what God meant to teach by that temple; and, consequently, if the building had been left to human judgment, it would not have been a true type; for who can make a type if he knows not what it is to typify? God alone knew what he intended to teach by this building, so the temple, that it might convey divine teaching, must be arranged according to divine command.

Moreover, the temple was for God's own dwelling. Should not the Most High have a house after his own mind? If he was to be the Tenant, should it not be built to suit him? And who knows what God requires in a habitation but God himself? The best that can be built is too poor for him. Stephen said, "Solomon built him an house. Howbeit, the Most High dwelleth not in temples made with hands." Yet, if even in type it was to be the dwelling-place of God, it must be built according to God's own requirements.

No. 2,280.

Besides, the temple was to be the throne of the great King; and if the very principle on which that throne was built was the will-worship of man's own judgment, there would have been a violation of the great principle of obedience at the fountain-head. I take it that, in the Church of God, I have no right to decree anything, nor John Wesley, nor John Calvin, nor any greater than they. God is alone supreme. Christ is the one Head of his Church; and we must, in all that we do in the building of his Church, consult with him, or else we act upon lawless principles, and cast off the authority of the Church's true King and Head, and we come under some other law. This would be, at the very centre of our holy service, setting an example of lawlessness and rebellion against God. That must never be; his temple must be built according to a pattern of his own drawing; and his Church and all holy work must be carried on according to his direction if we are to expect a blessing.

The point to which I call your attention is this, that God gave the directions to David by impressing them upon his mind, upon his heart, by his own hand. He did not so much draw a plan, and hand it to David, and say to him, "Build the temple according to that design," but he made him think carefully and prayerfully over the whole matter. Perhaps, in the visions of the night, and often, as he turned the subject over in his thoughts by day, God's Spirit came, and revealed to David what he needed to know as to how this house was to be built: "All this, said David, the Lord made me understand in writing by his hand upon me, even all the works of this pattern."

I shall, to-night, first, call your attention to *the singular instructions given to David;* then, coming home to ourselves, I shall speak upon *the spiritual tuition of the saints in the truth of God*, which is very similar to this instruction given to David; and, before I close, I shall have a word or two to say as to *the duty of the transmission of what we have received.* If God has taught us, we are bound to do what David did, commit the same to faithful men, that, before we go hence, we may have started others in work for the Lord, and not ourselves retire leaving God's work undone.

I. First, then, dear friends, I call your attention to THE SINGULAR INSTRUCTIONS GIVEN TO DAVID.

David received his instructions by the writing of God upon his heart with God's own hand. Note this, *David did not receive them by consultation with others.* David did not send to Hiram, king of Tyre, to ask his judgment; nor did he call in a Bezaleel, or some other skilful man, to give him advice. God himself taught him. This reminds me of what Paul said, "I consulted not with flesh and blood." "The gospel which was preached of me is not after man. For I neither received it of man, neither was I taught it, but by the revelation of Jesus Christ." Depend upon it, if you learn anything aright, you will have to learn it of God; and, although consultation with others may often be very serviceable upon some points, yet you must not take them into consultation on the question whether you shall believe God's Word or not. That is to have supreme authority; and, albeit there are some who are deeply taught in the things of God, who may at times be helpful to you, you must not defer to what they say so as to miss the instructions that the Lord himself gives you. No man's voice is to be sovereign to you; but only the voice of God the Holy Spirit, speaking out of this Book, which contains all things that you need for life and godliness. May God the Holy Ghost give you grace to fetch all your instructions from it! David did not consult with others about building the temple; and we are not to obtain our creed by consultation with other men, but to go to God himself, and to pray him to write it upon our heart with his own hand.

Observe, also, that *David did not slavishly follow the former model.* In the wilderness, Israel had a tent covered with skins as the meeting-place between Jehovah and the people. It was a simple structure, easily moved; but now the tabernacle was to be swallowed up in the temple; and, albeit that the general shape of the temple reminds you strongly of the tabernacle, yet David had a fresh revelation, and fresh guidance in what he had done. I like to see a man keep to the old things; but even in doing so he may make a mistake, for there may be old things that can be supplanted by newer and better things. Keep your eye lifted up to God, with whom nothing is old, and nothing is new. Wait at his footstool; submit your heart, like a tablet, for him to write upon it all his instructions; and then do as he hath said.

According to the context, *God gave to David instructions about the details of the work.* I commend the reading of this chapter to you; it may at first seem to have little in it; but the more you study it, the more will it teach you. Among other things, God revealed to David "the pattern of the porch, and of the houses thereof, and of the treasuries thereof, and of the upper chambers thereof, and of the inner parlours thereof, and of the place of the mercy-seat." God will teach you, if you will wait upon him, the details of your work, the details of his gospel, the detailed explanation of your experience. "In all thy ways acknowledge him, and he shall direct thy paths." As one said to me, the other day, and I thought very wisely, "God directs his servants' steps, and also his servants' stops when they are not able to take any steps, but feel bound to stand still." God directs them in not acting as well as in acting. You may go to him for detailed guidance, and especially in the matter of his service. If you would know what is his mind, yield yourself to the teaching of the Holy Spirit, and consult this Book, for it will tell you everything about the porches, and the houses, and the treasuries, and the upper chambers, and the inner parlours, and the place of the mercy-seat, and everything else that you need to know.

Further, *the directions given were extremely minute.* You noticed, in our reading, that there was gold by weight for the lampstands, and for the lamps which stood upon them. Now, no man, unless he had made a candelabrum or lampstand of the kind before, could tell how much gold it would take; the most skilful tradesman here, though himself a dealer in such things, would not readily know exactly the weight of gold required; but if the one who needs the knowledge has never made such things, if he has been a king used to the sword, how can he know how much silver is wanted for a candlestick, how much gold is needed for a seven-branched lampstand, and how much for the lamps to stand thereon? It is a wonderful instance of what inspiration can do, how the Spirit of God could teach his servant David all the little ins and outs of this wonderful making of the vessels for the house of the Lord, even down to the basons: "for the golden basons he gave gold by weight for every bason; and likewise silver by weight for every bason of silver." All was arranged exactly. If we will follow the Word of God closely, under the guidance of the Holy Spirit, we shall find that it enters into the details of our private life, into the details of our church life, into the details of our troubles, our wants, and our joys. God will direct you in everything if you are willing to be directed. "Be ye not as the horse, or as the mule, which have no understanding: whose mouth must be held in with bit and bridle;" but be willing to be directed by God; and you shall not be without direction even in the smallest matter.

And, yet again, *the innermost things were laid bare to David.* Nobody saw the cherubim; I speak broadly, for once in a year the high priest went into the holy place, but then he scarcely saw the cherubim, for, with the smoke of the incense which went up around him before the mercy-seat, everything in that place must have become dim. They were almost unseen objects; yet David had seen them in his mind's eye. He had had a representation of them written on his heart by the hand of God, for so we read; "and gold for the pattern of the chariot of the cherubims, that spread out their wings, and covered the ark of the covenant of the Lord." There was a pattern of this printed on the understanding and heart of David. Oh! yes; the Lord will let you see everything that can be seen; there is no stint in his revelation to the man who is willing to see. There are unspeakable words; yet Paul heard them, though he could never tell them; it was not lawful for him to utter them. There are secrets of the Lord, but they are "with them that fear him; and he will show them his covenant." There are things that are within the veil so far as most men are concerned; but to the man who is in Christ, the veil is rent, and the veil which was on his own heart and mind has been taken away by the Spirit of God, and he can see the things of God, and rejoice therein, even as David did.

Now, we are told in the text, and I must come back to the very words of it, "The Lord made me understand in writing by his hand upon me." *David not only knew the details; but he understood them.* He had a clear insight into what God meant by the instructions given. Now, dear friends, the hardest thing in the world is to give a man understanding. It is our duty, in our preaching and teaching, to make things very clear to the understanding; but if people have not any understanding, we cannot give it to them; but God can. When the understanding itself is darkened, and ceases to be an understanding, God can so renew it that it shall be all clear and bright, and it shall be able to comprehend the things of God. "The Lord made me understand." Oh, what a privilege! Not merely, "made me hear", but "made me understand." And how did the Lord do it? "In writing," says David, "by his hand upon me." The writing was written on David's own mind; he had not to go upstairs to fetch it; he had not to say, "I cannot always carry it about with me;" but he did always carry it about with him wherever he went; for God had written upon David himself.

And it was *written there by the hand of God*. Now, I am coming to my chief point. "The Lord made me understand in writing by his hand upon me." God writes his law in the Bible; but we do not understand it; God writes it on our heart, and then we do understand it. There it lies in the letter, and we may be dull of understanding, and not comprehend it; but if it comes here in the spirit of it, our heart is no longer dull, but being quickened of God, it receives the things of the Spirit of God. The carnal mind cannot know spiritual things; but God gives us a spiritual mind, and then we begin to understand spiritual things. "The Lord made me understand in writing by his hand upon me." We learn much from the gifts of God's hand; but not so much as from the hand itself. Sometimes God lays his hand upon his child very heavily. You can forget his gifts; but you cannot forget the pressure of that hand. At times, he will press his hand upon us till he seems to crush us to the very heart, till we stagger, and anguish breaks our spirit. There is no writing like that which God writes with a steel pen right into the soul; and sometimes he makes very heavy down-strokes, and very sharp, cutting up-strokes, when he writes upon the fleshy tablets of the heart his mind and will, as he wrote upon the heart of David all the details about the building of the temple at Jerusalem.

II. That brings me, then, to my second point, which is this, THE SPIRITUAL TUITION OF THE SAINTS IN THE TRUTH OF GOD.

I remark, first, that *God still writes upon the heart of men*. He prefers fleshy tablets and his own Spirit to any paper and ink. Paul wrote to the Corinthians, " Ye are our epistle written in our hearts, known and read of all men: forasmuch as ye are manifestly declared to be the epistle of Christ ministered by us, written not with ink, but with the Spirit of the living God; not in tables of stone, but in fleshy tables of the heart." God makes a new heart to write upon; and when he has made a new heart, then he takes his pen, and writes there the law of his house. Have *you* ever had God's Word written on your hearts? I know that some of you have; but I am afraid that some of you have not, because I know how easy it is to hear a sermon, and to read the Bible, and say, "Oh, that is wonderful!" and then to go out into the world, and act clean contrary to what you heard from the preacher, or found written in the Word of God.

Now, let me show you a little in detail *how God writes the great truths of his Word on our hearts*. We come to this blessed Book, and we find that man is fallen, that man is ruined by sin. Did you ever feel that it was so with you? You remember a time when you knew that you were fallen, when you could see your heart to be corrupt, and felt yourself to be lost, ruined, and undone. Ah! then the Lord made you understand in writing by his hand upon you. This Book tells us that, without Christ, we can do nothing; we are dead; we are without strength. Did you never find it so? Why, when you began to seek the Lord, some of you, you found that your boasted strength had all evaporated! You could not feel aright, nor think aright, nor act aright; and, though you tried hard, yet you were like Samson when his hair was shorn, you were too feeble to accomplish any good thing. Then you learned a doctrine in this way. I may have preached it to your ears; but God laid it on your heart. You knew that it was so; for the Lord had taught it to you by his Spirit; and nobody can ever beat it out of you now. Then there came a time when you read in the Scriptures that Christ is the Saviour of his people, and that whosoever looks to him shall live. You believed that to be true as you heard it preached, and read it in the Book, and you did look; you looked to Christ, you gazed upon him as he hung upon the accursed tree for you. Now, tell me, did you not, when you looked, find immediate and glorious salvation? Did not the burden roll from your shoulders? Did not the disease depart from your heart? Can you not say to-night,—

"Happy day, happy day,
When Jesus washed my sins away"?

And then the doctrine of the atoning sacrifice, the doctrine that the blood of Jesus Christ, God's Son, cleanseth us from all sin, that also you were made to understand in writing by the hand of the Lord upon you; and no power on earth or in hell can take that doctrine from you. Since then, you have learned other doctrines, possibly the five points of Calvinism, or the fifty points of any other system; but you never learned them from merely reading them in the Scriptures, you never really knew them till the pen of God began to move up and down upon your inward nature, and your heart received the impression the Lord intended to convey to it. It may be that there are more truths to be written on your heart yet; but we shall not know them all until we get home to our Father's house. Meanwhile, let us keep on reading more of God's Word, and making more of its truths our own; but, depend upon it, this is the main thing, to get by real personal experience what we perceive to be written by the revelation of God. "The Lord made me understand in writing by his hand upon me." The Lord make it to be so with every minister of Christ here, and every Sunday-school teacher, and every Christian worker of every kind! May we know what is written in the Book by what is written on our heart!

Now I believe that *the Lord does this with regard to our great Pattern:* "even all the works of this pattern." We have one great Pattern whom we are all to imitate. You know who it is to whom we sing very often,—

"Be thou my Pattern; make me bear
More of thy gracious image here!"

May the Lord himself write upon us according to that glorious Pattern! Who but the Holy Spirit can work in us the humility of Christ, the courage of Christ, the self-denial of Christ, and full obedience to the Father's will such as he rendered? Who can give us all this but the Christ to whom we sing,—

"Cold mountains, and the midnight air
Witness'd the fervour of thy prayer;
The desert thy temptation knew,
Thy conflict and thy victory, too"?

Let none of us think that we cannot be like Christ. Let nobody say, "The Pattern is too difficult for us to copy." No, no, my brother; let us weep our eyes out that we fall so short of it, and let us strive after it according to his striving, who worketh in us mightily, and never be content till we are indeed like him. What did the Psalmist say? "I shall be satisfied when I awake with thy likeness." We shall never be satisfied till then; therefore let us sit in the light of Christ till he is photographed upon us, and we go forth as living portraits of the divine Pattern.

I want, for a minute or so, to show you how the Lord can reveal to you, his servants who love and fear him, everything you need to know about the great work of salvation. In the Word of God we have a model of salvation; and you who want to teach others had better conform all your teaching to this model. The Lord can teach you and will teach you all things that you need to know about his Church and the temple of his salvation. Read the eleventh verse of this chapter again: "Then David gave to Solomon his son *the pattern of the porch*." O you young men, who are going to be ministers, mind that you get a good clear view of the pattern of the porch! Tell the sinner to come to Christ just as he is; do not begin setting up some fine porch of feelings or preparations. Set up the pattern of the porch, the wicket gate, with the light shining through it, and these words written over it, "Knock, and it shall be opened unto you." Preach a full Christ to empty sinners, and tell them that all the fitness he requires of them is that they should feel their need of him, and tell them that he gives them even that; they are not to look within themselves for it. If they do not feel their need, they must come to him to get the feeling of their need, for from the very beginning it is all of grace, and all of Christ. So, my brethren, get a clear view of "the pattern of the porch."

"*And of the houses thereof*," the places where the priests and Levites dwelt. Get a clear view of the houses that Christ gives his people to dwell in; how they dwell in him, how they abide in him, and go no more out for ever. I cannot enlarge on this; but you can think it out for yourselves, and explain it to your hearers and scholars. Think of those mansions of present joy and future bliss which they shall have who come in by the true and living way, even by Christ Jesus, who is the one way of entrance into the temple of salvation.

"*And of the treasuries thereof*." Notice that when you preach Christ, pray to have written upon your heart, as well as in this Book, something about the treasuries of God's house. Oh, the infinite riches of the covenant of grace! Oh, the all-sufficiency of Christ Jesus, our Lord! Oh, the fulness of power that is to be found in the Holy Ghost! Oh, the heaps of blessedness which are stored away for believers in the person of their divine Lord and Master! Get in your own heart a good clear view of the treasuries of the temple of salvation, and then go and preach about them to others.

And what next? "*And of the upper chambers thereof.*" Have you ever been in those upper chambers, where you get a view of the glory yet to be revealed? Then you have been near to heaven, and near to your God. Perhaps you have not attained to that height yet. If not, may the Lord write on your heart the plan of the upper chambers!

"*And of the inner parlours thereof.*" I thought, as I read this over, and tried to look deeply into it, that I did know a little about the inner parlours thereof. Oh, there are sweet fellowships, there are communings which nobody knows but the man who has dwelt where Jesus is, and who continues to abide in him! He shall ask what he will, and it shall be given him; and he shall continually joy in God through Jesus Christ. Get a good view of the inner parlours thereof. May the pattern of them be written on your own heart, and then go and tell others about them.

And here is one thing more: "*And of the place of the mercy seat.*" You often sing,—

> "There is a place where Jesus sheds
> The oil of gladness o'er our heads!
> A place, than all beside more sweet,
> It is the blood-stain'd mercy-seat."

May you have written on your heart the pattern "of the place of the mercy seat!" It was inside the veil, you know, above the ark of the covenant, and under the wings of the cherubim, the place where God met with Moses and Aaron, and shone forth in the light of the Shekinah, making glad their willing eyes. God grant that you may know by daily experience the power of prayer, at the place of the mercy seat! Then go and tell poor sinners about it, and tell poor saints about it, too, according as the Spirit of God has written it with his own hand upon your heart.

III. But now the time has almost gone, so I must briefly finish with my third point, that is, THE DUTY OF THE TRANSMISSION TO OTHERS OF ANYTHING THAT GOD WRITES ON YOUR HEARTS. Tell others what God has told you. Our Lord said to his disciples, "What ye hear in the ear, that preach ye upon the house tops." He says the same to us. "To whom shall I go?" say you. Well, take David as your example.

First, *David told Solomon all about it.* "Ah!" you say, "My boy is no Solomon." That is all the more reason why you should teach him. Perhaps David might have been excused from teaching Solomon, as he was already so wise; but the fact that he did instruct him teaches us that the wisest child needs to be taught the things of God. If your boy is not a Solomon, you will need to teach him twice over, or many times, if need be. Teach him nineteen times over; and, if necessary, teach him twenty times over. If anybody asks, "Why do you teach him twenty times?" say that it is because you found that nineteen times did not bring him salvation, and you meant to keep on till he was saved. Tell Solomon about it. Say to him, "My son, come here, and listen to what your father has tasted and handled of the good Word of the Lord. Hear what your father has experienced of divine grace."

Well, perhaps you say, "Yes, I will talk to my boys about the Saviour; shall I speak to anyone else?" Next, dear friend, *talk about Christ to chosen companions.* I count it a high privilege if I can get a little personal conversation with a choice young man, one who has great ability, and one whom we have reason to believe God has called to do a great work for him. David knew that God had chosen Solomon to build the temple, and therefore he was very particular to give him the details that he had received from the Lord. Perhaps a Christian woman here says, "You would not have me talk to a young minister, would you?" Well, my dear sister, you know what we read about Priscilla and her husband Aquila. They were not very great people, they were simply tent-makers, but they talked to Apollos in such a way that he was for the rest of his life indebted to that humble man and woman. Some of those whom God has used, and will yet use still more, will tell you that they owe a great deal to humble people who have talked to them about Christ. The godly women, who sat spinning and darning stockings in the sunshine at Bedford, talked with one another about the things of God, and John Bunyan stopped and listened to what they said, and he profited all the rest of his days by their holy talk. If you have the opportunity, and come across any choice young minds, be sure to tell them what God has told you about his great plan of salvation.

Then, lastly, *David gathered all the people together, and told them about the temple.* In the next chapter, we read, "Furthermore David the king said unto all the congregation, Solomon my son, whom alone God hath chosen, is yet young and tender, and the work is great: for the palace is not for man, but for the Lord God." They soon began to give the gold, and the silver, and the brass, and the wood, and the precious stones for the temple. See that you tell out to all you can what God has told you. I am afraid that some here have not yet found out their life-work. We get into the habit of wanting so much "talent" in preachers. May "talent" be thrown into the bottomless pit! It has done more hurt to the Church of God than it ever did good. If plain Christian men would begin to talk about Christ wherever they have opportunity, it would usher in a golden age. Perhaps there has come in here a troubled sinner wanting to find a Saviour. Try to speak to him. "Oh!" you say, "he might be offended." So he might; but that would not kill you. Tell him about Jesus Christ, and if he gets to heaven through what you tell him, he will forgive you for not having given him a handsome card with your name on it to introduce yourself. If you get a soul to heaven, the rudeness of an impromptu address will never occur to that soul. God help us to be up and doing, telling out what he has written in our hearts, and unto his name shall be the praise!

Perhaps you have never had anything written on your heart, my dear hearer. Then, lay your heart before the Lord to-night with this simple prayer, "Lord, write on it!" And if he writes on it that one word "Jesus", it will be all that you can want. God bless you, every one, for Jesus Christ's sake! Amen.

Exposition by C. H. Spurgeon.
1 CHRONICLES XXVIII.

Verse 1. *And David assembled all the princes of Israel, the princes of the tribes, and the captains of the companies that ministered to the king by course, and the captains over the thousands, and captains over the hundreds, and the stewards over all the substance and possession of the king, and of his sons, with the officers, and with the mighty men, and with all the valiant men, unto Jerusalem.*

David, in his old age, and soon to die, summoned a great representative assembly of the notables of his kingdom.

2. *Then David the king stood up upon his feet,*

He was ill, and obliged to keep his bed; but he left his couch for this solemn occasion. He did not even remain seated, although extremely weak; but he stood up upon his feet.

2. *And said, Hear me, my brethren, and my people:*

Those who read carefully will notice the sweetness of David's style now that he is about to die. It was after the great sin of his life, and after he and his subjects had suffered because of his numbering the people, that he calls the men before him "my brethren." He had sometimes spoken of them as his servants; but now he adopts a very humble style, and putting himself on a level with them, he says to them, "Hear me, my brethren, and my people."

2, 3. *As for me, I had in mine heart to build an house of rest for the ark of the covenant of the* LORD, *and for the footstool of our God, and had made ready for the building: but God said unto me, Thou shalt not build an house for my name, because thou hast been a man of war, and hast shed blood.*

Admire the frankness of David in telling the people what God had said to him. There is no other biography in the world like the Bible, for it tells the faults and follies of those whose history it records. David was a man after God's own heart; yet, as he had been used as a sword, for the defence of God's people, and the destruction of their enemies, he could not be permitted to build the temple. He frankly tells the people all that God had said; it would not reflect any honour upon himself, but it was true, and therefore he kept nothing back. One falls in love with David for the frankness of his utterance. When a king, and an aged man, and just about to die, he tells the people all this story.

4. *Howbeit the* LORD *God of Israel chose me before all the house of my father to be king over Israel for ever: for he hath chosen Judah to be the ruler; and of the house of Judah, the house of my father; and among the sons of my father he liked me to make me king over all Israel:*

He delights to dwell upon the election of God. It was not by the right of primogeniture that he was chosen king; it was by the will and good pleasure of God. Judah was one of the younger tribes, and yet it was made the royal tribe. In Judah, the house of Jesse was of no great importance; yet God chose it as the royal family; and in the household of Jesse, David was the youngest, yet the Lord "liked" him, and chose him to be king over all Israel.

5. *And of all my sons, (for the* LORD *hath given me many sons,) he hath chosen Solomon my son to sit upon the throne of the kingdom of the* LORD *over Israel.*

David seems to harp upon this sweet string of the divine choice. I wonder that so many good people are afraid of this blessed doctrine. They fight shy of it; they seem to run away at the very sound of the word "election." Yet is it the very joy of saints. God hath chosen them, and ordained them to be his servants.

6—8. *And he said unto me, Solomon thy son, he shall build my house and my courts: for I have chosen him to be my son, and I will be his father. Moreover I will establish his kingdom for ever, if he be constant to do my commandments and my judgments, as at this day. Now therefore in the sight of all Israel the congregation of the LORD, and in the audience of our God, keep and seek for all the commandments of the LORD your God: that ye may possess this good land, and leave it for an inheritance for your children after you for ever.*

Thus he talked with the great number of the nobility and chief men of his kingdom who were gathered round him.

9. *And thou, Solomon my son, know thou the God of thy father,*

God is very dear to us; but perhaps under no aspect is he more tenderly near us than as the God of our father: "My son, know thou the God of thy father."

9. *And serve him with a perfect heart and with a willing mind: for the LORD searcheth all hearts, and understandeth all the imaginations of the thoughts: if thou seek him, he will be found of thee; but if thou forsake him, he will cast thee off for ever.*

What a covenant this was under which Solomon stood! Alas! he was not as true to God as he should have been; and though we hope he was not cast away for ever, yet under his rule Israel began to decay, and he pierced himself through with many sorrows in his latter days.

10. *Take heed now; for the Lord hath chosen thee to build an house for the sanctuary: be strong, and do it.*

It is fine to hear this old man, in his weakness, stirring up the young man. We generally expect to see the youths full of zeal, and the old men somewhat slow; but grace can turn the tables against nature. Here the old man, feeble as to his body, is vigorous as to his spirit.

11. *Then David gave to Solomon his son the pattern of the porch, and of the houses thereof, and of the treasuries thereof, and of the upper chambers thereof, and of the inner parlours thereof, and of the place of the mercy seat,*

He had it all ready in his mind; and before he died, he passed over the plans of that wonderful piece of architecture to his son Solomon.

12, 13. *And the pattern of all that he had by the spirit, of the courts of the house of the LORD, and of all the chambers round about, of the treasuries of the house of God, and of the treasuries of the dedicated things: also for the courses of the priests and the Levites, and for all the work of the service of the house of the LORD, and for all the vessels of service in the house of the LORD.*

Everything was laid down, catalogued, and arranged so that Solomon had only to follow the plans given to him by his father, and all would be right. Think of the love of David to his God. Though he might not build the temple, he would draw the plans for it; and though he might not live to see it completed, yet he would, in his own mind, arrange all the courses of the priests and the Levites, and every detail, even to the placing of the vessels of service in the courts of the Lord's house.

14, 15. *He gave of gold by weight for things of gold, for all instruments of all manner of service; silver also for all instruments of silver by weight, for all instruments of every kind of service: even the weight for the candlesticks of gold,*

Or, the candelabra.

15. *And for their lamps of gold, by weight for every candlestick, and for the lamps thereof: and for the candlesticks of silver by weight, both for the candlestick, and also for the lamps thereof, according to the use of every candlestick.*

They were not for the burning of candles, but for oil lamps. There was a lampstand, with seven lamps upon the stand; and there were ten of these in the temple. There was only one in the tabernacle; but there were ten in the temple. David arranged everything. Those seven-branched golden candlesticks stood like pastors of the church; and the little silver candlesticks were carried about like evangelists, who go from place to place that the whole house of God may be served with light. Everything was by weight. God knows what he would have in his house, and he measures out to each one according to his need.

16, 17. *And by weight he gave gold for the tables of shewbread, for every table; and likewise silver for the tables of silver: also pure gold for the flesh-hooks, and the bowls, and the cups: and for the golden basons he gave gold by weight for every bason; and likewise silver by weight for every bason of silver:*

I like to think of David planning all these little things, first receiving instruction from God, then waiting upon God for further direction, and thinking not only about the great golden candelabra, but about the silver candlesticks, and the flesh-hooks, and the bowls, and the cups, and the basons. They who love God love everything that has to do with him; they have a holy concern even for the smaller matters pertaining to the house of the Lord.

18—20. *And for the altar of incense refined gold by weight; and gold for the pattern of the chariot of the cherubims, that spread out their wings, and covered the ark of the covenant of the LORD. All this, said David, the LORD made me understand in writing by his hand upon me, even all the works of this pattern. And David said to Solomon his son, Be strong and of good courage, and do it:*

Do not talk about it; do not sit down, and dream over the plans, and think how admirable they are, and then roll them up; but, "Be strong and of good courage, and do it."

20. *Fear not, nor be dismayed: for the LORD God, even my God, will be with thee;*

What a pretty touch that is! "The LORD God, even my God, will be with thee."

20. *He will not fail thee, nor forsake thee, until thou hast finished all the work for the service of the house of the LORD.*

Therefore, be of good courage, you that are working for God, for he will not fail you, nor forsake you, until you have finished all the work for the service of the house of the Lord.

21. *And, behold, the courses of the priests and the Levites, even they shall be with thee for all the service of the house of God: and there shall be with thee for all manner of workmanship every willing skilful man, for any manner of service:*

God always finds men for his work. We sometimes see a lot of cowards run away, and we say to ourselves, "What will happen now?" Why, God will find better men than they are! And when there seems to be a paucity of really valiant men in Israel, God has them in training; and that awkward squad out there will yet become a band of brave men for the service of the house of God.

21. *Also the princes and all the people will be wholly at thy commandment.*

Thus the grand old man finished up his life by starting another to carry on the work which he was obliged to leave.

HYMNS FROM "OUR OWN HYMN BOOK"—328, 455, 488.

Metropolitan Tabernacle Pulpit.

OUR LORD IN THE VALLEY OF HUMILIATION.

A Sermon

Intended for Reading on Lord's-day, November 6th, 1892,

DELIVERED BY

C. H. SPURGEON,

AT THE METROPOLITAN TABERNACLE, NEWINGTON,

On Thursday Evening, June 5th, 1890.

"And being found in fashion as a man, he humbled himself, and became obedient unto death, even the death of the cross."—Philippians ii. 8.

PAUL wishes to unite the saints in Philippi, in the holy bands of love. To do this, he takes them to the cross. Beloved, there is a cure for every spiritual disease in the cross. There is food for every spiritual virtue in the Saviour. We never go to him too often. He is never a dry well, or a vine from which every cluster has been taken. We do not think enough of him. We are poor because we do not go to the gold country which lieth round the cross. We are often sad because we do not see the bright light that shines from the constellation of the cross. The beams from that constellation would give us instantaneous joy and rest, if we perceived them. If any lover of the souls of men would do for them the best possible service, he would constantly take them near to Christ. Paul is always doing so; and he is doing it here.

The apostle knew that, to create concord, you need first to beget lowliness of mind. Men do not quarrel when their ambitions have come to an end. When each one is willing to be least, when everyone desires to place his fellows higher than himself, there is an end to party spirit; schisms and divisions are all passed away. Now, in order to create lowliness of mind, Paul, under the teaching of the Spirit of God, spoke about the lowliness of Christ. He would have us go down, and so he takes us to see our Master going down. He leads us to those steep stairs down which the Lord of glory took his lowly way, and he bids us stop while, in the words of our text, he points us to the lowly Christ: "Being found in fashion as a man, he humbled himself, and became obedient unto death, even the death of the cross."

Before Paul thus wrote, he had indicated, in a word or two, the height from which Jesus originally came. He says of him, "Who, being in the form of God, thought it not robbery to be equal with God." You and I can have no idea of how high an honour it is to be

No. 2,281.

equal with God. How can we, therefore, measure the descent of Christ, when our highest thoughts cannot comprehend the height from which he came? The depth to which he descended is immeasurably below any point we have ever reached; and the height from which he came is inconceivably above our loftiest thought. Do not, however, forget the glory that Jesus laid aside for a while. Remember that he is very God of very God, and that he dwelt in the highest heaven with his Father; but yet, though he was thus infinitely rich, for our sakes he became poor, that we, through his poverty, might be rich.

The apostle, having mentioned what Jesus was, by another stroke of his pen reveals him in our human nature. He says concerning him that, "He made himself of no reputation, and took upon him the form of a servant, and was made in the likeness of men." A great marvel is that Incarnation, that the eternal God should take into union with himself our human nature, and should be born at Bethlehem, and live at Nazareth, and die at Calvary on our behalf.

But our text does not speak so much of the humiliation of Christ in becoming man, as of his humiliation after he took upon himself our nature. "Being found in fashion as a man, he humbled himself." He never seems to stop in his descent until he comes to the lowest point, obedience unto death, and that death the most shameful of all, "even the death of the cross." Said I not rightly, that, as you cannot reach the height from which he came, you cannot fathom the depth to which he descended? Here, in the immeasurable distance between the heaven of his glory and the shame of his death, is room for your gratitude. You may rise on wings of joy, you may dive into depths of self-denial; but in neither case will you reach the experience of your divine Lord, who thus, for you, came from heaven to earth, that he might take you up from earth to heaven.

Now, if strength be given me for the exercise, I want to guide you, first, while we *consider the facts of our Lord's humiliation;* and, secondly, when we have considered them, I want you *practically to learn from them some useful lessons.*

I. First of all, CONSIDER THE FACTS OF OUR LORD'S HUMILIATION.

Paul speaks first of *the point from which he still descends:* "Being found in fashion as a man, he humbled himself." My gracious Lord, thou hast come far enough already; dost thou not stop where thou art? In the form of God, thou wast; in the form of man, thou art. That is an unspeakable stoop. Wilt thou still humble thyself? Yes, says the text, "Being found in fashion as a man, he humbled himself." Yet, surely one would have thought that he was low enough. He was the Creator, and we see him here on earth as a creature; the Creator, who made heaven and earth, without whom was not anything made that was made, and yet he lieth in the virgin's womb; he is born; and he is cradled where the hornèd oxen feed. The Creator is also a creature. The Son of God is the Son of man. Strange combination! Could condescension go farther than for the Infinite to be joined to the infant, and the Omnipotent to the feebleness of a new-born babe?

Yet, this is not all. If the Lord of life and glory must needs be married to a creature, and the High and Mighty One must take upon himself the form of a created being, yet why does he assume the form of man? There were other creatures, brighter than the stars, noble spiritual beings, seraphim and cherubim, sons of the morning, presence-angels of the eternal throne; why did he not take their nature? If he must be in union with a creature, why not be joined to the angels? But, "He took not on him the nature of angels; but he took on him the seed of Abraham." A man is but a worm, a creature of many infirmities. On his brow death has written with his terrible finger. He is corruptible, and he must die. Will the Christ take that nature upon him, that he, too, must suffer and die? It was even so; but when he had come so far, we feel as if we must almost put ourselves in the way to stop him from going farther. Is not this stoop low enough? The text says that it was not, for, "Being found in fashion as a man, he humbled himself," even then.

What will not Christ do for us who have been given to him by his Father? There is no measure to his love; you cannot comprehend his grace. Oh, how we ought to love him, and serve him! The lower he stoops to save us, the higher we ought to lift him in our adoring reverence. Blessed be his name, he stoops, and stoops, and stoops, and, when he reaches our level, and becomes man, he still stoops, and stoops, and stoops lower and deeper yet: "Being found in fashion as a man, he humbled himself."

Now let us notice, next, *the way in which he descended after he became a man:* "He humbled himself." We must assume that he has stooped as low as our humanity; but his humanity might have been, when born, cradled daintily. He might have been among those who are born in marble halls, and clothed in purple and fine linen; but he chose not so. If it had pleased him, he might have been born a man, and not have been a child; he might have leaped over the period of gradual development from childhood to youth, and from youth to manhood; but he did not so. When you see him at home at Nazareth, the apprenticed son, obedient to his parents, doing the little errands of the house, like any other child, you say, as our text says, " He humbled himself." There he dwelt in poverty with his parents, beginning his life as a workman's boy, and, I suppose, running out to play with youthful companions. All this is very wonderful. The apocryphal gospels represent him as having done strange things while yet a child; but the true Gospels tell us very little of his early days. He veiled his Godhead behind his childhood. When he went up to Jerusalem, and listened to the doctors of the law, though he astonished them by his questions and answers, yet he went home with his parents, and was subject to them, for, " He humbled himself." He was by no means pushing and forward, like a petted and precocious child. He held himself in, for he determined that, being found in fashion as a man, he would humble himself.

He grew up, and the time of his appearing unto men arrived; but I cannot pass over the thirty years of his silence without feeling that here was a marvellous instance of how he humbled himself. I know young men who think that two or three years' education is far too long for them. They want to be preaching at once; running away, as I sometimes tell them, like chickens with the shell on their heads. They want to go forth to fight before they have buckled on their armour. But it was not so with Christ; thirty long years passed over his head, and still there was no Sermon on the Mount. When he did show himself to the world, see how he humbled himself. He did not knock at the door of the high priests, or seek out the eminent Rabbis and the learned scribes; but he took for his companions fishermen from the lake, infinitely his inferiors, even if we regarded him merely as a man. He was full of manly freshness and vigour of mind; and they were scarcely able to follow him, even though he moderated his footsteps out of pity for their weakness. He preferred to associate with lowly men, for he humbled himself.

When he went out to speak, his style was not such as aimed at the gathering of the *élite* together; he did not address a few specially cultured folk. "*Then drew near unto him all the scribes and Pharisees for to hear him.*" Am I quoting correctly? Nay, nay: "*Then drew near unto him all the publicans and sinners for to hear him.*" They made an audience with which he was at home; and when they gathered about him, and when little children stood to listen to him, then he poured out the fulness of his heart; for he humbled himself. Ah, dear friends, this was not the deepest humiliation of the Lord Jesus! He allowed the devil to tempt him. I have often wondered how his pure and holy mind, how his right royal nature could bear conflict with the prince of darkness, the foul fiend, full of lies. Christ allowed Satan to put him to the test, and spotless purity had to bear the nearness of infamous villainy. Jesus conquered; for the prince of this world came, and found nothing in him; but he humbled himself when, in the wilderness, on the pinnacle of the temple, and on the exceeding high mountain, he allowed the devil thrice to assail him.

Personally, in his body, he suffered weakness, hunger, thirst. In his mind, he suffered rebuke, contumely, falsehood. He was constantly the Man of sorrows. You know that, when the head of the apostate church is called "the man of sin", it is because it is always sinning; and when Christ is called "the Man of sorrows", it is because he was always sorrowing. How wonderful it is that he should humble himself so as to be afflicted with the common sorrows of our humanity; yet it was even so! "Being found in fashion as a man," he consented even to be belied, to be called a drunken man and a wine-bibber, to have his miracles ascribed to the help of Beelzebub, to hear men say, "He hath a devil, and is mad; why hear ye him?"

"He humbled himself." In his own heart there were, frequently, great struggles; and those struggles drove him to prayer. He even lost consciousness of God's presence, so that he cried in sore anguish, "My God, my God, why hast thou forsaken me?" All this was because still he humbled himself. I do not know how to speak to you upon this great subject; I give you words; but I pray the Holy Spirit to supply you with right thoughts about this great mystery. I have already said that it was condescension enough for Christ to be found in fashion as a man; but after that, he still continued to descend the stairway of condescending love by humbling himself yet more and more.

But notice, now, *the rule of his descent;* it is worth noticing: "He humbled himself, and became obedient." I have known persons try to humble themselves by will-worship. I have stood in the cell of a monk, when he has been out of it, and I have seen the whip with which he flagellated himself every night before he went to bed. I thought that it was quite possible that the man deserved all he suffered, and so I shed no tears over it. That was his way of humbling himself, by administering a certain number of lashes. I have known persons practise voluntary humility. They have talked in very humble language, and have decried themselves in words, though they have been as proud as Lucifer all the while. Our Lord's way of humbling himself was by obedience. He invented no method of making himself ridiculous; he put upon himself no singular garb, which would attract attention to his poverty; he simply obeyed his Father; and, mark you, there is no humility like obedience: "To obey is better than sacrifice, and to hearken than the fat of rams." To obey is better than to wear a special dress, or to clip your words in some peculiar form of supposed humility. Obedience is the best humility, laying yourself at the feet of Jesus, and making your will active only when you know what it is God's will for you to do. This is to be truly humble.

In what way, then, did the Lord Jesus Christ in his life obey? I answer,—there was always about him the spirit of obedience to his Father. He could say, "Lo, I come: in the Volume of the Book it is written of me, I delight to do thy will, O my God: yea, thy law is within my heart." He was always, while here, subservient to his Father's great purpose in sending him to earth; he came to do the will of him that sent him, and to finish his work. He learned what that will was partly from Holy Scripture. You constantly find him acting in a certain way "that the Scripture might be fulfilled." He shaped his life upon the prophecies that had been given concerning him. Thus he did the will of the Father.

Also, there was within him the Spirit of God, who led and guided him, so that he could say, "I do always those things that please the Father." Then, he waited upon God continually in prayer. Though infinitely better able to do without prayer than we are, yet he prayed much more than we do. With less need than we have, he had a greater delight in prayer than we have; and thus he learned the will of God as man, and did it, without once omitting, or once transgressing in a single point.

He did the will of God also, obediently, by following out what he knew to be the Father's great design in sending him. He was sent to save, and he went about saving, seeking and saving that which was lost. Oh, dear friends, when we get into unison with God, when we wish what he wishes, when we live for the great object that fills God's heart, when we lay aside our wishes and whims, and even our lawful desires, that we may do only the will of God, and live only for his glory, then we shall be truly humbling ourselves!

Thus, I have shown you that Jesus did descend after he became man; and I have pointed out to you the way and the rule of his descending. Now, let us look, with awe and reverence, at *the abyss into which he descended.* Where did he arrive, at length, in that dreadful descent? What was the bottom of the abyss? It was death: "He humbled himself, and became obedient unto death, even the death of the cross." Our Lord died willingly. You and I, unless the Lord should come quickly, will die, whether we are willing or not: "It is appointed unto men once to die." He needed not to die, yet he was willing to surrender his life. He said, "I have power to lay it down, and I have power to take it again. This commandment have I received of my Father." He died willingly; but, at the same time, he did not die by his own hand; he did not take his own life as a suicide; he died obediently. He waited till his hour had come, when he was able to say, "It is finished," then he bowed his head, and gave up the ghost. He humbled himself, so as willingly to die.

He proved the obedience of his death, also, by the meekness of it, as Isaiah said, "As a sheep before her shearers is dumb, so he openeth not his mouth." He never spoke a bitter word to priest or scribe, Jewish governor or Roman soldier. When the women wept and bewailed, he said to them, "Daughters of Jerusalem, weep not for me, but weep for yourselves, and for your children." He was all gentleness; he had not a hard word even for his murderers. He gave himself up to be the Sin-bearer, without murmuring at his Father's will, or at the cruelty of his adversaries. How patient he was! If he says, "I thirst," it is not the petulant cry of a sick man in his fever; there is a royal dignity about Christ's utterance of the words. Even the "Eloi, Eloi, lama sabachthani," with the unutterable gall and bitterness it contains, has not even a trace of impatience mingled with it. Oh, what a death Christ's was! He was obedient in it, obedient not only till he came to die, but obedient in that last dread act. His obedient life embraced the hour of his departure.

But, as if death were not sufficiently humbling, the apostle adds, "even the death of the cross." That was the worst kind of death. It was a violent death. Jesus fell not asleep gently, as good men often do, whose end is peace. No, he died by murderous hands. Jews and Gentiles combined, and with cruel hands took him, and crucified and slew him. It was, also, an extremely painful death of lingering agony. Those parts of the body in which the nerves were most numerous, were pierced with rough iron nails. The weight of the body was made to hang upon the tenderest part of the frame. No doubt the nails tore their cruel way through his flesh while he was hanging on the tree. A cut in the hand has often resulted in lockjaw and death; yet Christ's hands were nailed to the cross. He died in pain most exquisite of body and of soul. It was, also, a death most shameful. Thieves were crucified with him; his adversaries stood and mocked him. The death of the cross was one reserved for slaves and the basest of felons; no Roman citizen could be put to death in such a way as that, hung up between earth and heaven, as if neither would have him, rejected of men and despised of God. It was, also, a penal death. He died, not like a hero in battle, nor as one who perishes while rescuing his fellow-men from fire or flood; he died as a criminal. Upon the cross of Calvary he was hung up. It was an accursed death, too. God himself had called it so: "Cursed is every one that hangeth on a tree." He was made a curse for us. His death was penal in the highest sense. He "bare our sins in his own body on the tree."

I have not the mental, nor the physical, nor the spiritual strength to speak to you aright on such a wondrous topic as that of our Lord in the Valley of Humiliation. There have been times with me when I have only wanted a child's finger to point me to the Christ, and I have found enough in a sight of him without any words of man. I hope that it is so with you to-night. I invite you to sit down, and watch your Lord, obedient unto death, even the death of the cross. All this he did that he might complete his own humiliation, he humbled himself even to this lowest point of all, "unto death, even the death of the cross."

II. If you have this picture clearly before your eyes, I want you, in the second place, to PRACTICALLY LEARN SOME LESSONS FROM OUR LORD'S HUMILIATION.

The first is, learn to have *firmness of faith* in the atoning sacrifice. If my Lord could stoop to become man; and if, when he had come as low as that, he went still lower, and lower, and lower, until he became obedient unto death, even the death of the cross, I feel that there must be a potency about that death which is all that I can require. Jesus by dying has vindicated law and justice. Look, brethren, if God can punish sin upon his own dear Son, it means far more than the sending of us to hell. Without shedding of blood there is no remission of sin; but his blood was shed, so there is remission. His wounds let out his life blood; one great gash opened the way to his heart; before that, his whole body had become a mass of dripping gore, when, in the garden, his sweat was as it were great drops of blood falling to the ground. My Lord, when I study thy sacrifice, I see how God can be "just, and the Justifier of him which believeth in Jesus." Faith is born at the cross of Christ. We not only bring faith to the cross, but we find it there. I cannot think of my God bearing all this grief in a human body, even to the death on the cross, and then doubt. Why, doubt becomes harder than faith when the cross is visible! When Christ is set forth evidently crucified among us, each one of us should cry, "Lord, I believe, for thy death has killed my unbelief."

The next lesson I would have you learn from Christ's humiliation is this, cultivate a great *hatred of sin*. Sin killed Christ; let Christ kill sin. Sin made him go down, down, down; then pull sin down, let it have no throne in your heart. If it *will* live in your heart, make it live in holes and corners, and never rest till it is utterly driven out. Seek to put your foot upon its neck, and utterly kill it. Christ was crucified; let your lusts be crucified: and let every wrong desire be nailed up, with Christ, upon the felon's tree. If, with Paul, you can say, "God forbid that I should glory, save in the cross of our Lord Jesus Christ, by whom the world is crucified unto me, and I unto the world;" with him you will also be able to exclaim, "From henceforth let no man trouble me: for I bear in my body the marks of the Lord Jesus." Christ's branded slave is the Lord's freeman.

Learn another lesson, and that is, *obedience*. Beloved, if Christ humbled himself, and became obedient, how obedient ought you and I to be! We ought to stop at nothing when we once know that it is the Lord's will. I marvel that you and I should ever raise a question or ask a moment's delay in our obedience to Christ. If it be the

Lord's will, let it be done, and done at once. Should it rend some fond connection, should it cause a flood of tears, let it be done. He humbled himself, and became obedient. Would obedience humble me? Would it lower me in man's esteem? Would it make me the subject of ridicule? Would it bring contempt upon my honourable name? Should I be elbowed out of the society wherein I have been admired, if I were obedient to Christ? Lord, this is a question not worth the asking! I take up thy cross right joyfully, asking grace to be perfectly obedient, by the power of thy Spirit.

Learn next, another lesson, and that is, *self-denial*. Did Christ humble himself? Come, brothers and sisters, let us practise the same holy art. Have I not heard of some saying, "I have been insulted; I am not treated with proper respect. I go in and out, and I am not noticed. I have done eminent service, and there is not a paragraph in the newspaper about me." Oh, dear friend, your Master humbled himself, and it seems to me that you are trying to exalt yourself! Truly, you are on the wrong track. If Christ went down, down, down, it ill becomes us to be always seeking to go up, up, up. Wait till God exalts you, which he will do in his own good time. Meanwhile, it behoves you, while you are here, to humble yourself. If you are already in a humble position, should you not be contented with it; for he humbled himself? If you are now in a place where you are not noticed, where there is little thought of you, be quite satisfied with it. Jesus came just where you are; you may well stop where you are; where God has put you. Jesus had to bring himself down, and to make an effort to come down to where you are. Is not the Valley of Humiliation one of the sweetest spots in all the world? Does not the great geographer of the heavenly country, John Bunyan, tell us that the Valley of Humiliation is as fruitful a place as any the crow flies over, and that our Lord formerly had his country house there, and that he loved to walk those meadows, for he found the air was pleasant? Stop there, brother. "I should like to be known." says one. "I should like to have my name before the public." Well, if you ever had that lot, if you felt as I do, you would pray to be unknown, and to let your name drop out of notice; for there is no pleasure in it. The only happy way seems to me, if God would only let us choose, is to be known to nobody, but just to glide through this world as pilgrims and strangers, to the land where our true kindred dwell, and to be known there as having been followers of the Lord.

I think that we should also learn from our Lord's humiliation to have *contempt for human glory*. Suppose they come to you, and say, "We will crown you king!" you may well say, "Will you? All the crown you had for my Master was a crown of thorns; I will not accept a diadem from you." "We will praise you." "What, will you praise me, you who spat in his dear face? I want none of your praises." It is a greater honour to a Christian man to be maligned than to be applauded. Ay, I do not care where it comes from, I will say this; if he be slandered and abused for Christ's sake, no odes in his honour, no articles in his praise, can do him one-tenth the honour. This is to be a true knight of the cross, to have been wounded in the fray, to have come back adorned with scars for his dear sake. O despised one, look upon human glory as a thing that is tarnished, no longer golden; but corroded, because it came not to your Lord.

And, O beloved, I think, when we have meditated on this story of Christ's humbling himself, we ought to feel our *love to our Lord* growing very vehement! We do not half love him as we ought. When I read the sentences of Bernard, half Romanist, but altogether saint, I feel as if I had not begun to love my Lord; and when I turn over Rutherford's letters, and see the glow of his heart toward his divine Master, I could smite on my breast to think that I have such a heart of stone where there ought to be a heart of flesh. If you hear George Herbert sing his quaint, strange poetry, suffused with love for his dear Lord, you may well think that you are a tyro in the school of love. Ay, and if you ever drink in the spirit of McCheyne, you may go home, and hide your head, and say, "I am not worthy to sing,—

"'Jesu, lover of my soul,'

for I do not return his love as I ought to do." Come, seek his wounds, and let your hearts be wounded. Come, look to his heart that poured out blood and water, and give your heart up to him. Put your whole being now among the sweet spices of his all-sufficient merit, set all on fire with burning affection, and let the fragrance of it go up like incense before the Lord.

Lastly, let us be inflamed with a strong *desire to honour Christ.* If he humbled himself, let us honour him. Every time that he seems to put away the crown, let us put it on his head. Every time we hear him slandered,—and men continue to slander him still,—let us speak up for him right manfully.

> "Ye that are men, now serve him,
> Against unnumbered foes;
> Your courage rise with danger,
> And strength to strength oppose."

Do you not grow indignant, sometimes, when you see how Christ's professed Church is treating him, and his truth? They are shutting him out still, till his head is wet with dew, and his locks with the drops of the night. Proclaim him King in the face of his false friends. Proclaim him, and say that his Word is infallibly true, and that his precious blood alone can cleanse from sin. Stand out the braver because so many Judases seem to have leaped up from the bottomless pit to betray Christ again. Be you firm and steadfast, like granite walls, in the day when others turn their backs, and fly, like cravens.

The Lord help you to honour him who humbled himself, who became obedient unto death, even the death of the cross! May he accept these humble words of mine, and bless them to his people, and make them to be the means of leading some poor sinner to come and trust in him! Amen.

Exposition by C. H. Spurgeon.

PHILIPPIANS II. 1—18.

Verses 1, 2. *If there be therefore any consolation in Christ, if any comfort of love, if any fellowship of the Spirit, if any bowels and mercies, fulfil ye my joy, that ye be likeminded, having the same love, being of one accord, of one mind.*

Paul did not mean to doubt that there is "any consolation in Christ, any comfort of love, any fellowship of the Spirit, any bowels and mercies," for no one knew better than he did how those blessings abound to them that are in Christ Jesus. He put it by way of argument. If there be consolation in Christ, since there is consolation in Christ, since there is comfort of love, since there is fellowship of the Spirit, be one in Christ; be not divided; love one another: "be likeminded, having the same love, being of one accord, of one mind."

3. *Let nothing be done through strife or vainglory;*

"Nothing": never give to exceed other givers. Never preach that you may be a better preacher than anybody else; never work in the Sunday-school with the idea of being thought a very successful teacher. "Let nothing be done through strife or vainglory."

3. *But in lowliness of mind let each esteem other better than themselves.*

There is some point in which your friend excels you. Notice that rather than the point in which you excel him. Try to give him the higher seat; seek yourself to take the lowest room.

4. *Look not every man on his own things, but every man also on the things of others.*

Have a large heart, so that, though you care for yourself in spiritual things, and desire your own soul-prosperity, you may have the same desire for every other Christian man or woman.

5. *Let this mind be in you, which was also in Christ Jesus:*

What an example we have set before us in the Lord Jesus Christ! We are to have the mind of Christ; and that in the most Christly way, for here we have Christ set out to the life:—

6. *Who, being in the form of God, thought it not robbery to be equal with God:*

For he was equal with God.

7. *But made himself of no reputation,*

Emptied himself of all his honour, of all his glory, of all his majesty, and of all the reverence paid to him by the holy spirits around the throne.

7, 8. *And took upon him the form of a servant, and was made in the likeness of men: and being found in fashion as a man, he humbled himself,*

He had not descended low enough yet, though he had come down all the way from the Godhead to our manhood: "he humbled himself."

8, 9. *And became obedient unto death, even the death of the cross. Wherefore God also hath highly exalted him,*

He stooped, who can tell how low? He was raised, who shall tell how high? "Wherefore God also hath highly exalted him."

9. *And given him a name which is above every name;*

He threw away his name; he emptied himself of his reputation. How high is his reputation now! How glorious is the name that God hath given him as the reward of his redemptive work!

10, 11. *That at the name of Jesus every knee should bow, of things in heaven, and things in earth, and things under the earth; and that every tongue should confess that Jesus Christ is Lord, to the glory of God the Father.*

Now is he higher than the highest. Now every one must confess his divinity. With shame and terror, his adversaries shall bow before him; with delight and humble adoration, his friends shall own him Lord of all: "that every tongue should confess that Jesus Christ is Lord, to the glory of God the Father." See how the greatest glory of Christ is the glory of the Father. He never desired any other glory but that. The highest honour you can ever have, O child of God, is to bring honour to your Father who is in heaven. Do you not think so? I know you do.

12. *Wherefore, my beloved, as ye have always obeyed, not as in my presence only, but now much more in my absence, work out your own salvation with fear and trembling.*

Get out of self. Work out your salvation from pride, from vainglory, from disputations and strife.

13. *For it is God which worketh in you both to will and to do of his good pleasure.*

You may very well work out what God works in. If he does not work it in, you will never work it out; but while he works within your spirit both to will and to do, you may safely go on to will and to do; for your willing and your doing will produce lowliness of spirit, and unity of heart with your brethren.

14. *Do all things without murmurings and disputings:*

Do not say, "You give me too much to do; you always give me the hard work; you put me in the obscure corner." No, no; "do all things without murmurings." And do not begin fighting over a holy work; for, if you do, you spoil it in the very beginning, and how can you then hope for a blessing upon it? "Do all things without murmurings and disputings."

15. *That ye may be blameless and harmless,*

None finding fault with you, and you not finding fault with others; neither harming nor harmed: "blameless and harmless."

15. *The sons of God, without rebuke,*

So that men cannot rebuke you, and will have to invent a lie before they can do it; and even then the falsehood is too palpable to have any force in it: "without rebuke."

15. *In the midst of a crooked and perverse nation, among whom ye shine as lights in the world;*

You cannot straighten them; but you can shine. They would destroy you if they could; but all you have to do is to shine. If Christian men would give more attention to their shining, and pay less attention to the crooked and perverse generation, much more would come of it. But now we are advised to "keep abreast of the times", and to "catch the spirit of the age." If I could ever catch that spirit, I would hurl it into the bottomless abyss; for it is a spirit that is antagonistic to Christ in all respects. We are just to keep clear of all that, and "shine as lights in the world."

16. *Holding forth the word of life;*

You are to hold forth the Word of life as men hold forth a torch. Your shining is largely to consist in holding forth the Word of life.

16. *That I may rejoice in the day of Christ, that I have not run in vain, neither laboured in vain.*

God's ministers cannot bear the thought of having laboured in vain; and yet if some of us were to die, what would remain of all we have done? I charge you, brethren, to think of what your life-work has been hitherto. Will it remain? Will it abide? Will it stand the test of your own departure? Ah, if you have any fear about it, you may well go to God in prayer, and cry, "Establish thou the work of our hands upon us; yea, the work of our hands, establish thou it." Paul cared much about God's work; but he did not trouble about himself.

17. *Yea, and if I be offered upon the sacrifice and service of your faith, I joy, and rejoice with you all.*

If he might be poured forth as a drink-offering on their behalf, or offered up as a whole burnt-offering in the service of the Saviour, he would be glad. He could not bear to have lived in vain; but to spend his life for the glory of his Lord, would be ever a joy to him.

18. *For the same cause also do ye joy, and rejoice with me.*

To live and to die for Jesus Christ, with the blessing of the Father resting upon us, is a matter for us to joy in unitedly and continually. God help us so to do!

HYMNS FROM "OUR OWN HYMN BOOK"—284, 294, 819.

"THE SWORD AND THE TROWEL."

TABLE OF CONTENTS, NOVEMBER, 1892.

Cedars and Hyssops. An Early Sermon. By C. H. SPURGEON. (Illustrated.)
The Theme of Earth and Heaven. By Thomas Spurgeon.
The Preacher among his Books, and with his Themes. By Arthur T. Pierson, D.D.
"Ecce Homo!" (Poetry.) By Pastor E. A. Tydeman.
Miss Robinson's "Yarns." Incidents of Work among Soldiers at Aldershot, Portsmouth, &c. (With three illustrations.)
Tears, their Usefulness and Power. By John A. Stooke, Chefoo, China.
Mr. Spurgeon's Last Drives at Menton. By Joseph W. Harrald. (With two illustrations.)
The Rippling Rill. By Thomas Spurgeon.
"I Slept all Night, and Didn't Know it." By J. Manton Smith.
Mr. Thomas Spurgeon and the Tabernacle. (The Special Church-meeting. Farewell Address at the Tabernacle. Departure for New Zealand.)
C. H. Spurgeon Memorial Fund. Letter from Pastor T. W. Medhurst.
Notices of Books. (*John Ploughman's Sheet Almanack for* 1893. *Spurgeon's Illustrated Almanack for* 1893. *C. H. Spurgeon's* FIRST *and* LAST *Words at the Tabernacle.* &c., &c., &c.)
Notes. (Mr. Moody's Mission at the Tabernacle. Surrey Square Mission. Surrey Gardens Memorial Hall. College. Evangelists. Orphanage. Colportage. Personal Note. Baptisms at the Tabernacle.)
Lists of contributions.

Price 3d. Post-free, 4d.

LONDON: PASSMORE AND ALABASTER, PATERNOSTER BUILDINGS, and all Booksellers.

Metropolitan Tabernacle Pulpit.

DAVID'S PRAYER IN THE CAVE.

A Sermon

INTENDED FOR READING ON LORD'S-DAY, NOVEMBER 13TH, 1892,

DELIVERED BY

C. H. SPURGEON,

AT THE METROPOLITAN TABERNACLE, NEWINGTON,

On Lord's-day Evening, May 18th, 1890.

"Maschil of David; A Prayer when he was in the cave."—Title of Psalm cxlii.

"A PRAYER when he was in the cave." David did pray when he was in the cave. If he had prayed half as much when he was in the palace as he did when he was in the cave, it would have been better for him. But, alas! when he was king, we find him rising from his bed in the evening, and looking from the roof of the house, and falling into temptation. If he had been looking up to heaven, if his heart had been in communion with God, he might never have committed that great crime which has so deeply stained his whole character.

"A prayer when he was in the cave." God will hear prayer on the land, and on the sea, and even under the sea. I remember a brother, when in prayer, making use of that last expression. Somebody who was at the prayer-meeting was rather astonished at it, and asked, "How would God hear prayer under the sea?" On enquiry, we found out that the man who uttered those words was a diver, and often went down to the bottom of the sea after wrecks; and he said that he had held communion with God while he had been at work in the depths of the ocean. Our God is not the God of the hills only; but of the valleys also; he is God of both sea and land. He heard Jonah when the disobedient prophet was at the bottoms of the mountains, and the earth with her bars seemed to be about him for ever. Wherever you work, you can pray. Wherever you lie sick, you can pray. There is no place to which you can be banished where God is not near, and there is no time of day or night when his throne is inaccessible.

"A prayer when he was in the cave." The caves have heard the best prayers. Some birds sing best in cages. I have heard that some of God's people shine brightest in the dark. There is many an heir of heaven who never prays so well as when he is driven by necessity to pray. Some shall sing aloud upon their beds of sickness, whose voices were hardly heard when they were well; and some shall sing God's high praises in the fire, who did not praise him as they should

No. 2.282.

before the trial came. In the furnace of affliction the saints are often seen at their best. If any of you to-night are in dark and gloomy positions, if your souls are bowed down within you, may this become a special time for peculiarly prevalent communion and intercession, and may the prayer of the cave be the very best of your prayers!

I shall, to-night, use David's prayer in the cave to represent the prayers of godly men in trouble; but, first, I will talk of it as a picture of *the condition of a soul under a deep sense of sin*. This Psalm of the cave has a great likeness to the character of a man under a sense of sin. I shall then use it to represent *the condition of a persecuted believer;* and, thirdly, I shall speak of it as revealing *the condition of a believer who is being prepared for greater honour and wider service* than he has ever attained before.

I. First, let me try and use this Psalm as a picture of THE CONDITION OF A SOUL UNDER A DEEP SENSE OF SIN.

A little while ago, you were out in the open field of the world, sinning with a high hand, plucking the flowers which grow in those poisoned vales, and enjoying their deadly perfume. You were as happy as your sinful heart could be; for you were giddy, and careless, and thoughtless; but it has pleased God to arrest you. You have been apprehended by Christ, and you have been put in prison, and now your feet are fast in the stocks. To-night, you feel like one who has come out of the bright sunshine and balmy air into a dark, noisome cavern, where you can see but little, where there is no comfort, and where there appears to you to be no hope of escape.

Well, now, according to the Psalm before us, which is meant for you as well as for David, your first business should be to *appeal unto God*. I know your doubts; I know your fears of God; I know how frightened you are at the very mention of his name; but I charge you, if you would come out of your present gloom, go to God at once. See, the Psalm begins, "I cried unto the Lord with my voice; with my voice unto the Lord did I make my supplication." Get home, and cry to God with your voice; but if you have no place where you can use your voice, cry to God in silence; but do cry to him. Look Godward; if you look any other way, all is darkness. Look God-ward; there, and there only, is hope. "But I have sinned against God," say you. But God is ready to pardon; he has provided a great atonement, through which he can justly forgive the greatest offences. Look God-ward, and begin to pray. I have known men, who have hardly believed in God, do this; but they have had some faint desire to do so, and they have cried; it has been a poor prayer, and yet God has heard it. I have known some cry to God in very despair. When they hardly believed that there could be any use in it, still it was that or nothing; and they knew that it could not hurt them to pray, and so they took to their knees, and they cried. It is wonderful what poor prayers God will hear, and answer, too; prayers that have no legs to run with, and no hands to grasp with, and very little heart; but still, God has heard them, and he has accepted them. Get to your knees, you who feel yourselves guilty; get to your knees, if your hearts are sighing on account of sin. If the dark gloom of your iniquities is gathering about you, cry to God; and he will hear you.

The next thing to do is, *make a full confession*. David says, "I poured out my complaint before him; I shewed before him my trouble." The human heart longs to express itself; an unuttered grief will lie and smoulder in the soul, till its black smoke puts out the very eyes of the spirit. It is not a bad thing sometimes to speak to some Christian friend about the anguish of your heart. I would not encourage you to put that in the first place; far from it; but still it may be helpful to some. But, anyhow, make a full confession unto the Lord. Tell him how you have sinned; tell him how you have tried to save yourself, and broken down; tell him what a wretch you are, how changeable, how fickle, how proud, how wanton, how your ambition carries you away like an unbridled steed. Tell him all your faults, as far as you can remember them; do not attempt to hide anything from God; you cannot do so, for he knows all; therefore, hesitate not to tell him everything, the darkest secret, the sin you would not wish even to whisper to the evening's gale. Tell it all; tell it all. Confession to God is good for the soul. "Whoso confesseth and forsaketh his sins shall have mercy." I do press upon any of you who are now in the gloomy cave, that you seek a secret and quiet place, and, alone with God, pour out your heart before him. David says, "I shewed before him my trouble." Do not think that the use of pious words can be of any avail; it is not merely words that you have to utter, you have to lay all your trouble before God. As a child tells its mother its griefs, tell the Lord all your griefs, your complaints, your miseries, your fears. Tell them all out, and great relief will come to your spirit. So, first, appeal to God. Secondly, make confession to him.

Thirdly, *acknowledge to God that there is no hope for you but in his mercy*. Put it as David did, "I looked on my right hand, and beheld, but there was no man that would know me." There is but one hope for you; acknowledge that. Perhaps you have been trying to be saved by your good works. They are altogether worthless when you heap them together. Possibly you expect to be saved by your religiousness. Half of it is hypocrisy; and how can a man hope to be saved by his hypocrisy? Do you hope to be saved by your feelings? What are your feelings? As changeable as the weather; a puff of wind will change all your fine feelings into murmuring and rebellion against God. Oh, friend, you cannot keep the law of God! That is the only other way to heaven. The perfect keeping of God's commandments would save you if you had never committed a sin; but, having sinned, even that will not save you now, for future obedience will not wipe out past disobedience. Here, in Christ Jesus, whom God sets forth as a propitiation for sin, is the only hope for you; lay hold on it. In the cave of your doubts and fears, with the clinging damp of your despair about you, chilled and numbed by the dread of the wrath to come, yet venture to make God in Christ your sole confidence, and you shall yet have perfect peace.

Then, further, if you are still in the cave of doubt and sin, venture to *plead with God to set you free*. You cannot present a better prayer than this one of David in the cave, "Bring my soul out of prison, that I may praise thy name." You are in prison to-night, and you cannot get out of it by yourself. You may get a hold of those bars, and try to shake them to and fro, but they are fast in their sockets; they will not break in your hands. You may meditate, and think, and invent, and excogitate; but you cannot open that great iron gate; but there is a hand that can break gates of brass, and there is a power that can cut in sunder bars of iron. O man in the iron cage, there is a hand that can crumble up thy cage, and set thee free! Thou needest not be a prisoner; thou needest not be shut up; thou mayest walk at large through Jesus Christ the Saviour. Only trust him, and believingly pray that prayer to-night, "Bring my soul out of prison, that I may praise thy name," and he will set you free. Ah, sinners do praise God's name when they get out of prison! I recollect how, when I was set free, I felt like singing all the time, and I could quite well use the language of Dr. Watts,—

"Oh, for a thousand tongues to sing
My great Redeemer's praise!"

My old friend, Dr. Alexander Fletcher, seems to rise before me now, for I remember hearing him say to the children that, when men came out of prison, they did praise him who had set them free. He said that he was going down the Old Bailey one day, and he saw a boy standing on his head, turning Catherine wheels, dancing hornpipes, and jumping about in all manner of ways, and he said to him, "What are you at? You seem to be tremendously happy;" and the boy replied, "Ah, old gentleman, if you had been locked up six months, and had just got out, you would be happy, too!" I have no doubt that is very true. When a soul gets out of a far worse prison than there ever was at Newgate, then he must praise "free grace and dying love", and "ring those charming bells," again, and again, and again, and make his whole life musical with the praise of the emancipating Christ.

Now, that is my advice to you who are in the cave through soul-trouble. May God bless it to you! You need not notice anything else that I am going to say to-night. If you are under a sense of sin, heed well what I have been saying; and let other people have the rest of the sermon that belongs more especially to them.

II. I pass on to my second point. This Psalm may well help to set forth THE CONDITION OF A PERSECUTED BELIEVER.

A persecuted believer! Are there any such nowadays? Ah, dear friends, there are many such! When a man becomes a Christian, he straightway becomes different from the rest of his fellows. When I lived in a street, I was standing one day at the window, meditating what my sermon should be, and I could not find a text, when, all of a sudden, I saw a flight of birds. There was a canary, which had escaped from its cage, and was flying over the slates of the opposite houses, and it was being chased by some twenty sparrows, and other rough birds. Then I thought of that text, "My heritage is unto me as a speckled bird; the birds round about are against her." Why, they seemed to say to one another, "Here is a yellow fellow; we have not seen the like of him in London; he has no business here; let us pull off his bright coat, let us kill him, or make him as dark and dull as ourselves." That is just what men of the world try to do with Christians. Here is a godly man who works in a factory, or a Christian girl who is occupied in book-folding, or some other work where there is a large number employed; such persons will have a sad tale to tell of how they have been hunted about, ridiculed, and scoffed at by ungodly companions. Now you are in the cave.

It may be that you are in the condition described here; *you hardly know what to do.* You are as David was when he wrote the third verse, "When my spirit was overwhelmed within me." The persecutors have so turned against you, and it is so new a thing to you as a young believer, that you are quite perplexed, and hard put to it to know what you should do. They are so severe, they are so ferocious, they are so incessant, and they find out your tender points, and they know how to touch you just on the raw places; that you really do not know what to do. You are like a lamb in the midst of wolves; you know not which way to turn. Well, then, say to the Lord, as David did, "When my spirit was overwhelmed within me, then thou knewest my path." God knows exactly where you are, and what you have to bear. Have confidence that, when you know not what to do, he can and will direct your way if you trust him.

In addition to that, it may be that *you are greatly tempted.* David said, "They privily laid a snare for me." It is often so with young men in a warehouse, or with a number of clerks in an establishment. They find that a young fellow has become a Christian, and they try to trip him up. If they can, they will get up some scheme by which they can make him appear to have been guilty, even if he has not. Ah, you will want much wisdom! I pray God that you may never yield to temptation; but may hold your ground by divine grace. Young Christian soldiers often have a very rough time of it in the barracks; but I hope that they will prove themselves true soldiers, and not yield an inch to those who would lead them astray.

It will be very painful if, in addition to that, *your friends turn against you.* David said, "There was no man that would know me." Is it so with you? Are your father and mother against you? Is your wife or your husband against you? Do your brothers and sisters call you "a canting hypocrite"? Do they call you a "Methodist", or a "Presbyterian", not themselves knowing the meaning of the words? Do they point the finger of scorn at you when you get home? And often, when you go from the Lord's table, where you have been so happy, do you have to hear an oath the first thing when you enter the door? I know that it is so with many of you. The Church of Christ in London is like Lot in Sodom. In this particular neighbourhood, especially, it is hard for Christian people to live at all. You cannot walk down the streets anywhere without having your ears assailed with filthy language; and your children cannot be permitted to run these streets because of the abominable impurity that is on every hand round about us. Things are growing worse with us, instead of better; they who look for brighter times must be looking with their eyes shut. There is grave occasion for Christians to pray for young people who are converted in such a city as this, for their worst enemies are often those of their own household. "I should not mind so much," says one, "if I had a Christian friend to fly to. I spoke to one the other day, and he did not seem to interest himself in me at all." I will tell you what hurts a young convert. Here is one just saved; he has really, lovingly, given his heart to Christ, and the principal or manager where he works is a Christian man. He finds himself ridiculed, and he ventures to say a word to this Christian man. He snuffs him out in a moment, he has no sympathy with him. Well, there is another old professing Christian working near at the same bench; and the young convert begins to tell him a little about his trouble, and he is very grumpy and cross. I have noticed some Christian people who appear to be shut up in themselves, and they do not seem to notice the troubles of beginners in the divine life. Let it not be so among you. My dear brothers and sisters, cultivate great love to those who, having come into the army of Christ, are much beset by adversaries. They are in the cave. Do not disown them; they are trying to do their best; stand side by side with them. Say, "I, too, am a Christian. If you are honouring that young man with your ridicule, let me have my portion of it. If you are pouring contempt upon him, give me a share of it, for I also believe as he believes." Will you do that? Some of you will, I am sure. Will you stand by the man of God who vindicates the Lord's revealed truth? Some of you will; but there are plenty of fellows who want to keep a whole skin on their body, and if they can sneak away out of any fight for the right, they are glad to get home and go to bed, and there slumber till the battle is over. God help us to have more of the lion in us, and not so much of the cur! God grant us grace to stand by those who are out and out for God, and for his Christ, that we may be remembered with them in the day of his appearing!

It may be that the worst point about you is that *you feel very feeble.* You say, "I should not mind the persecution if I felt strong; but I am so feeble." Well, now, always distinguish between feeling strong and being strong. The man who feels strong is weak; the man who feels weak is the man who is strong. Paul said, "When I am weak, then am I strong." David prays, "Deliver me from my persecutors; for they are stronger than I." Just hide yourself away in the strength of God; pray much; take God for your refuge and your portion; have faith in him; and you will be stronger than your adversaries. They may seem to pull you over; but you will soon be up again. They may set before you puzzles that you cannot solve; they may come up with their scientific knowledge; and you may be at a discount: but never mind that; the God who has led you into the cave will turn the tables for you one of these days. Only hold on, and hold out, even to the end. I am rather glad that there should be some trouble in being a Christian, for it has become such a very general thing now to profess to be one. If I am right, it is going to be a very much less common thing than it is now for a man to say, "I am a Christian." There will come times when there will be sharp lines drawn. Some of us will help to draw them if we can, when men shall not wear the Christian garb, and bear the Christian name, and then act like worldlings, and love the amusements and the follies of worldlings. It is time that there was a division in the house of the

Lord, and that the "ayes" went into one lobby, and the "noes" into the other lobby. We have too long been mixed together; and I for one say, may the day soon come when every Christian will have to run the gauntlet! It will be a good thing for genuine believers. It will just blow some of the chaff away from the wheat. We shall have all the purer gold when the fire gets hot, and the crucible is put into it, for then the dross will be separated from the precious metal. Be of good courage, my brother, if thou art now in the cave, the Lord will bring thee out of it in his own good time!

III. Now, to close, I want to speak a little about THE CONDITION OF A BELIEVER WHO IS BEING PREPARED FOR GREATER HONOUR AND WIDER SERVICE.

Is it not a curious thing that, whenever God means to make a man great, he always breaks him in pieces first? There was a man whom the Lord meant to make into a prince. How did he do it? Why, he met him one night, and wrestled with him! You always hear about Jacob's wrestling. Well, I dare say he did; but it was not Jacob who was the principal wrestler: "There wrestled a man with him until the breaking of the day." God touched the hollow of Jacob's thigh, and put it out of joint, before he called him "Israel"; that is, "a prince of God." The wrestling was to take all his strength out of him; and when his strength was gone, then God called him a prince. Now, David was to be king over all Israel. What was the way to Jerusalem for David? What was the way to the throne? Well, it was round by the cave of Adullam. He must go there, and be an outlaw, and an outcast, for that was the way by which he would be made king. Have none of you ever noticed, in your own lives, that whenever God is going to give you an enlargement, and bring you out to a larger sphere of service, or a higher platform of spiritual life, you always get thrown down? That is his usual way of working; he makes you hungry before he feeds you; he strips you before he robes you; he makes nothing of you before he makes something of you. This was the way with David. He is to be king in Jerusalem; but he must go to the throne by the way of the cave. Now, are any of you here going to heaven, or going to a more heavenly state of sanctification, or going to a greater sphere of usefulness? Do not wonder if you go by the way of the cave. Why is that?

It is, first, because, if God would make you greatly useful, he must *teach you how to pray.* The man who is a great preacher, and yet cannot pray, will come to a bad end. A woman who cannot pray, and yet is noted for the conducting of Bible-classes, has already come to a bad end. If you can be great without prayer, your greatness will be your ruin. If God means to bless you greatly, he will make you pray greatly, as he does David who says in this part of his preparation for coming to his throne, "I cried unto the Lord with my voice: with my voice unto the Lord did I make my supplication."

Next, the man whom God would greatly honour must *always believe in God when he is at his wits' end.* "When my spirit was overwhelmed within me, then thou knewest my path." Are you never at your wits' end? Then God has not sent you to do business in great waters; for, if he has, you will reel to and fro, and be at your wits' end, in a great storm, before long. Oh, it is easy to trust when you can trust yourself; but when you cannot trust yourself, when you are dead beat, when your spirit sinks below zero in the chill of utter despair, then is the time to trust in God. If that is your case, you have the marks of a man who can lead God's people, and be a comforter of others.

Next, in order to greater usefulness, many a man of God must be taught *to stand quite alone.* "I looked on my right hand, and behold, but there was no man that would know me." If you want men to help you, you may make a very decent follower; but if you want no man, and can stand alone, God being your Helper, you shall be helped to be a leader. Oh, it was a grand thing when Luther stepped out from the ranks of Rome. There were many good men round him, who said, "Be quiet, Martin. You will get burnt if you do not hold your tongue. Let us keep where we are, in the Church of Rome, even if we have to swallow down great lumps of dirt. We can believe the gospel, and still remain where we are." But Luther knew that he must defy Anti-Christ, and declare the pure gospel of the blessed God; and he must stand alone for the truth, even if there were as many devils against him as there were tiles on the housetops at Worms. That is the kind of man whom God blesses. I would to God that many a young man here might have the courage to feel, in his particular position, "I can stand alone, if need be. I am glad to have my master and my fellow-workmen with me; but if nobody will go to heaven with me, I will say farewell to them, and go to heaven alone through the grace of God's dear Son."

Once more, the man whom God will bless must be the man who *delights in God alone.* David says, "I cried unto thee, O Lord: I said, thou art my refuge and my portion in the land of the living." Oh, to have God as our refuge, and to make God our portion! "You will lose your situation; you will lose your income; you will lose the approbation of your fellow-men." "Ah!" says the believer, "but I shall not lose my portion, for God is my portion. He is situation, and income, and everything to me; and I will hold by him, come what may." If thou hast learnt to "delight thyself in the Lord, he will give thee the desires of thine heart." Now thou art come into such a state that God can use thee, and make much of thee; but until thou dost make much of God, he never will make much of thee. God deliver us from having our portion in this life, for, if we have, we are not among his people at all!

He whom God would use must be taught *sympathy with God's poor people.* Hence we get these words of David, in the sixth verse, "I am brought very low." Mr. Greatheart, though he must be strong to kill Giant Grim, and any others of the giants that infest the pilgrim path, must be a man who has gone that road himself, if he is to be a leader of others. If the Lord means to bless you, my brother, and to make you very useful in his church, depend upon it he will try you. Half, perhaps nine-tenths, of the trials of God's ministers are not sent to them on their own account; but they are sent for the good of other people. Many a child of God, who goes very smoothly to heaven, does very little for others; but another of the Lord's children, who has all the ins and outs and changes of an experienced believer's life has them only that he may be the better fitted to help others; to sit down and weep with them that weep, or to stand up and rejoice with them that rejoice. So then you, dear brethren, who have got into the cave, and you, my sisters, who have deep spiritual exercises, I want to comfort you by showing you that this is God's way of making something of you. He is digging you out; you are like an old ditch, you cannot hold any more, and God is digging you out to make more room for more grace. That spade will cut sharply, and dig up sod after sod, and throw it on one side. The very thing you would like to keep shall be cast away, and you shall be hollowed out, and dug out, that the word of Elisha may be fulfilled, "Make this valley full of ditches. For thus saith the Lord, Ye shall not see wind, neither shall ye see rain; yet that valley shall be filled with water." You are to be tried, my friend, that God may be glorified in you.

Lastly, if God means to use you, you must get to be *full of praise*. Listen to what David says, "Bring my soul out of prison, that I may praise thy name: the righteous shall compass me about; for thou shalt deal bountifully with me." May God give to my brothers and sisters here, who are just about being tried for their good, and afflicted for their promotion, grace to begin to praise him! It is the singers that go before; they that can praise best shall be fit to lead others in the work. Do not set me to follow a gloomy leader. Oh, no, dear sirs, we cannot work to the tune of "The Dead March in *Saul*"! Our soldiers would never have won Waterloo if that had been the music for the day of battle. No, no; give us a *Jubilate*: "Sing unto the Lord who hath triumphed gloriously; praise his great name again and again." Then draw the sword, and strike home. If thou art of a cheerful spirit, glad in the Lord, and joyous after all thy trials and afflictions, and if thou dost but rejoice the more because thou hast been brought so low, then God is making something of thee, and he will yet use thee to lead his people to greater works of grace.

I have just talked to three kinds of people to-night. May God grant each of you grace to take what belongs to you! But if you see any of the first sort before you go out of the building, any who are in the cave of gloom under a sense of sin, if you want to go to the communion, but feel that you ought to stop and comfort them, mind that you do the latter. Put yourself second. There is a wonderful work to be done in those lobbies, and in those pews, after a service. There are some dear brethren and sisters who are always doing it; they call themselves my "dogs"; for they go and pick up the birds that I have wounded. I wish that they might be able to pick up many to-night. Oh, that some of you might always be on the alert to watch a face, and see whether there is any emotion there! Just paddle your own canoe alongside that little ship, and see whether you cannot get into communication with the poor troubled one on board, and say a word to cheer a sad heart. Always be doing this; for if you are in prison yourself, the way out of it is to help another out. God turned the captivity of Job when he prayed for his friends. When we begin to look after others, and seek to help others, God will bless us. So may it be, for his name's sake! Amen.

Exposition by C. H. Spurgeon.

PSALM LVII.

To the chief Musician, Al-taschith, Michtam of David, when he fled from Saul in the cave.

This is one of the "Destroy not" Psalms; for that is the meaning of the title, *Al-taschith*, which is used here, and in Psalms lviii., lix., and lxxv.

Michtam of David. David's golden Psalm, "when he fled from Saul in the cave." In this Psalm we see the calmness of David's heart when he was in great peril. He was a man of peace; and to be hunted cruelly, as he was by Saul, greatly pained him. Yet, with all the sensitiveness of his nature, he did not fall into unbelief; for his sensitiveness was balanced by his confidence in his God. You will see how, greatly as he was afflicted, he was greatly strengthened.

Verse 1. *Be merciful unto me, O God, be merciful unto me:*

He pleads twice; for his was an urgent case. He would have the Lord help him at once; for, perhaps, if the Lord's mercy came not to him at once, it would be too late; so he cried, "Be merciful unto me, O God, be merciful unto me."

1. *For my soul trusteth in thee:*

This is the feather on the arrow of prayer that guides it straight to the heart of God. This is the condition attached to the promise, "According to your faith be it unto thee." If you can truly plead that your soul is trusting in God, you may be assured that he will not deny you his mercy.

1. *Yea, in the shadow of thy wings will I make my refuge, until these calamities be overpast.*

What a sweet realization there is here of the power of God to protect him! Just as the little chick hides beneath the mother's wing, and knows no fear, so says David, "in the shadow of thy wings will I make my refuge." There was no refuge to be seen; but David does not ask to see; an unseen God is all that faith wants. If it be only a shadow, yet the shadow of Jehovah's wings is substantial enough for our confidence: "In the shadow of thy wings will I make my refuge, until these calamities be overpast." They will be overpast; the worst calamity will not last for ever. We shall think differently of these rough times by-and-by; we ought not to give up in despair, and cast away our confidence while we are in the thick of the fight. Until the calamities are overpast, it should be our joy to run under God's protecting wings, and hide ourselves securely there.

2. *I will cry unto God most high; unto God that performeth all things for me.*

Faith is never dumb; true faith is a crying faith. If thou hast a confidence in God of such a kind that thou dost not need to pray, get rid of it; for it is of no use to thee; it is a false confidence, it is presumption. Only a crying faith will be a prevailing faith. "I will cry unto God most high:" the very height and sublimity of God is an attraction to faith; for though he is so high, he can and will stoop. Though God is so high, he can lift me up above the storm; for he is above it himself, and he can set me above it, too. "I will cry unto God most high;" and David sweetly adds, "unto God that performeth for me." The translators have inserted the words, "all things", and very properly, too; but David leaves, as it were, a gap, so that we may fill in anything that we please. Thus do we—

"Sing the sweet promise of his grace,
And the performing God."

He is not one who gives us promises, and then puts us off without the thing promised; but he fulfils the promises he has made, he is the Faithful Promiser: "God that performeth for me."

3. *He shall send from heaven, and save me from the reproach of him that would swallow me up.*

If he cannot find any means upon earth for saving David, he will send from heaven to do it; but he will save him. God is sure to find an ark for his Noahs if the floods should cover the whole earth; and when they cannot be preserved any longer on the earth, he will catch them away to himself in heaven; but he will surely take care of his own: "He shall send from heaven, and save me." If there were only one of his people in danger, he would rend the heavens in order to save him: "He shall send from heaven and save me," not only from the danger to my life, but from danger to my character: "from the reproach of him that would swallow me up." Often, the enemies of the righteous are so fierce and cruel that they would, like some huge python, swallow up the godly man, devour him, make an end of him, make one meal of him, if they could; but God will not allow them to do so. He will send from heaven, and deliver us from the reproach of them that would swallow us up.

3. *God shall send forth his mercy and his truth.*

The Psalmist had only prayed for mercy; twice he had said, "Be merciful unto me." But God always answers us more largely than we ask in our prayers; he does exceeding abundantly above what we ask or even think. So his truth comes with his mercy, as a double guard to protect his people: "God shall send forth his mercy and his truth."

4. *My soul is among lions: and I lie even among them that are set on fire, even the sons of men, whose teeth are spears and arrows, and their tongue a sharp sword.*

Yet, notice that David says, "I lie" there, that is the emphatic word; and the force of that word conveys this idea, "I recline there; I feel at ease, notwithstanding the danger of my position; I recline, and rest, even among them that are set on fire." Oh, the calm confidence of the faith that forgets the adversary when once she has hidden herself under the shadow of Jehovah's wings! The description given of ungodly persecutors is very strong: "whose teeth are spears and arrows." Their mouth seems to contain a deadly armoury; they have no molars to grind their food, they are all canine teeth, cruel, cutting. You must know some such critical spirits, that seem to be all teeth, and whose every tooth is a spear or an arrow. But their tongue is worse than their teeth, for it is not only a sword, but "a sharp sword", a sharpened sword. Oh, how tongues will cut and wound! You may heal the cut of a sword; but who shall heal the cut of a deadly, cruel, malicious, slanderous tongue? Yet for all that, David was not dismayed, but he said, "I lie down among such men, my soul is among lions." Like Daniel among the lions, so does this man of God take his night's rest, as calmly as though he were sleeping in his own bed at home.

5. *Be thou exalted, O God, above the heavens; let thy glory be above all the earth.*

David so rises above his present circumstances that he begins to praise his God. O beloved, there is no condition in which God ought to be robbed of a song! What if I am sick? Yet my Lord must have my music, even if the harp-strings are not well tuned. What if I am poor? Yet why should I be poor towards him, and deny him my need of praise? What if I am busy? Yet I must still find time for praising him. How sweetly David seeks to exalt and glorify his God, "Be thou exalted, O God, above the heavens; let thy glory be above all the earth."

6. *They have prepared a net for my steps; my soul is bowed down: they have digged a pit before me, into the midst whereof they are fallen themselves.*

They hunted him as they spread a snare for a bird, or as they sought to entrap a wild beast by digging a pit, and covering it over that he might stumble into it. David scarcely has time to tell us of their devices before he discovers that their plans have come to nought: "they have digged a pit before me, into the midst whereof they are fallen themselves." You may go calmly on, my persecuted friend, for those who seek to do the righteous hurt, will only hurt themselves; their bows shall be broken, their arrows shall fall back into their own bosoms. Only be thou still, and let the wicked alone; let God fight for thee, and do thou hold thy peace.

7. *My heart is fixed, O God, my heart is fixed: I will sing and give praise.*

That is enough for me, I will not stop my singing for all my adversaries. Let them howl like lions, I will sing on. Let them dig their pits, I will sing on. I find this my best employment, to keep on praising my God.

> "All that remains for me
> Is but to love and sing,
> And wait until the angels come
> To bear me to the King."

8. *Awake up, my glory; awake, psaltery and harp: I myself will awake early.*

My tongue, the glory of my frame, be not thou silent! Bestir thyself! "I myself will awake early," or, "I will awake the dawning." I will call the sun up to be shining; I will bid him wake to shine to the honour of my Lord. With the earliest birds I will make one more singer in the great concert-hall of God. I will not want more rest, or a longer time to myself to consider all my troubles, I will give my best time, the first hour of the day, to the praise of my God.

9. *I will praise thee, O Lord, among the people: I will sing unto thee among the nations.*

I will make the Gentiles hear it. They that know not the Lord shall be astonished when they hear me praising him, and they shall ask, "Who is this God of whom this man makes so much?"

10, 11. *For thy mercy is great unto the heavens, and thy truth unto the clouds. Be thou exalted, O God, above the heavens: let thy glory be above all the earth.*

God give us that same calm praiseful frame of mind that David possessed if we are called to endure such trials as fell to his lot!

HYMNS FROM "OUR OWN HYMN BOOK"—138, 73 (Part II.), 30.

Just Published. Price One Penny.

JOHN PLOUGHMAN'S SHEET ALMANACK for 1893.

"As soon as the late beloved Editor was well enough, he commenced the proverbs for 1893; and before his translation, he had advanced so far with them, that it was a comparatively easy task for other hands reverently to complete the set of 365. The centre picture on the Almanack is a new view of the Menton sitting-room, in which Mr. Spurgeon wrote most of the proverbs; another illustration represents a French farm scene, which he wished his readers to see; and the third is one that he had selected for the present issue. For these reasons, we think that we may expect a very large demand for the sheet, which is now ready. Let it be hung up in every kitchen, cabin, office, and workshop. It will cheer and help many."—*Extract from notice in November "Sword and Trowel."*

PASSMORE AND ALABASTER, 4, PATERNOSTER BUILDINGS, LONDON; and all Booksellers.

Metropolitan Tabernacle Pulpit.

CHRIST'S ONE SACRIFICE FOR SIN.

A Sermon

Intended for Reading on Lord's-day, November 20th, 1892,

DELIVERED BY

C. H. SPURGEON,

AT THE METROPOLITAN TABERNACLE, NEWINGTON,

On Lord's-day Evening, June 29th, 1890.

"Now once in the end of the world hath he appeared to put away sin by the sacrifice of himself."—Hebrews ix. 26.

I NEED not read the text again, for I shall not go far away from it; but again and again shall we come back to these precious words about our Lord's one great sacrifice for sin.

What Christ meant to do on the cross, he actually did. I always take that for granted. He did not die in vain; he did not leave any part of his work undone. Whatever was his intent, by the laying down of his life, he accomplished it; for, if not, dear friends, he would come here again. If any of his work were left undone, he would return to the earth that he might finish it, for he never did leave a work incomplete, and he never will. Christ effected the redemption of his people by one stroke; coming here, and living, and dying. He put away sin; he did not merely try to do it, but he actually accomplished the stupendous work for which he left his glory-throne above.

He did not die to make men salvable; he died to save them. He did not die that their sin might be put away by some effort of their own; but he died to put it away. "Once in the end of the world hath he appeared to put away sin by the sacrifice of himself." There was one death, one sacrifice, one atonement, and all the work of man's redemption was for ever accomplished; so that we can sing,—

"Love's redeeming work is done;
Fought the fight, the battle won."

If the mission on which Christ came to this earth had not been fulfilled, I say again, he would have returned to complete the work that he had begun.

No. 2,283.

That would have meant that he should often have been offered since the foundation of the world, an idea which we cannot hold for a single moment. For Christ to die twice, would be contrary to all analogy. He is the second Adam. He, therefore, is like unto men. Read the words of Paul in the verse following our text, "It is appointed unto men *once* to die" (not twice), "but after this the judgment: so Christ was *once* offered to bear the sins of many; and unto them that look for him shall he appear the second time without sin unto salvation." For him, who is the true Adam, to die twice, would be contrary to the analogy of things.

It would be also most repugnant to all holy feeling. For Christ once to die a shameful death upon the cross on Calvary, has made an indelible mark upon our heart, as though it had been burned with a hot iron. I have sometimes half said to myself, "God forbid that his dear Son should ever have died!" The price seemed too great even for our redemption. Should he die, the Holy One and the Just, the glorious, and blessed Son of God? The answer to that question is, that he has died. Thank God, he can never die again! It were horrible to us to think that it should be possible that he should ever be called upon to bear our sins a second time.

It would be traitorous to his person, it would be dishonourable to his gospel, to suppose that his sacrifice is still incomplete, and that he might be called upon to die again because his first death had not satisfied the claims of divine justice. The simple suggestion, even for the sake of argument, is almost blasphemous. Christ either paid the ransom-price for his people, or he did not. If he did, it is paid; if he did not, will he come again, think you? That can never be. Toplady knew that truth when he taught the saints to sing to their Lord,—

> "Complete atonement thou hast made,
> And to the utmost farthing paid
> Whate'er thy people owed:
> Nor can his wrath on me take place,
> If shelter'd in thy righteousness,
> And sprinkled with thy blood."

The idea that Christ's one sacrifice for sin is not sufficient to accomplish his purpose, is also opposed to revelation. We are told that, "Christ, being raised from the dead, dieth no more, death hath no more dominion over him. For in that he died, he died unto sin once: but in that he liveth, he liveth unto God." The sinner for whom Christ died is free because of his Substitute's death; and the Substitute himself is free, for he has discharged every liability, and given to God the full satisfaction that divine justice required.

> "He bore on the tree the sentence for me,
> And now both the Surety and sinner are free."

Take a good look at Calvary; get the cross distinctly photographed upon your eyeballs; behold the five wounds and the bloody sweat. The whole gospel was hung on the cross. It was all there; the battle and the victory, the price and the purchase, the doom and the deliverance, the cross and the crown. See again, in the death of Christ on the cross, a clear idea of what he meant to do, and of what he actually did when he laid down his life for us; and be you glad that once, and only once, this great deed had to be done. Nothing more is wanted, Christ has put away the sin of those for whom the covenant was made, according to the word that we read just now, "Their sins and iniquities will I remember no more." "Now, where remission of these is, there is no more offering for sin."

That will stand as a preface. Now I want, with great earnestness,—I fear with much weakness, but still with great earnestness,—to set before you, beloved friends, a summary of the way in which Christ has saved his people. It matters not how feebly the truth is put to you; if you do but lay hold of it, and firmly grasp it by faith, your souls are saved. I shall have to speak to you briefly upon five things; first, *the gigantic evil:* "sin." Secondly, *the glorious Remover of it:* "HE." Thirdly, *the memorable event:* "Once in the end of the world hath he appeared." Fourthly, *the special sacrifice:* "the sacrifice of himself." Fifthly, and lastly, *the grand achievement:* "to put away sin by the sacrifice of himself."

I. First, notice, in considering what our text says that Christ has done, THE GIGANTIC EVIL. "Once in the end of the world hath he appeared to put away *sin*."

"Sin." It is a very little word, but it contains an awful abyss of meaning. "Sin" is transgression against God, rebellion against the King of kings; violation of the law of right; commission of all manner of wrong. Sin is in every one of us; we have all committed it, we have all been defiled with it. Christ came "to put away sin." You see, the evil is put in one word, as if wrong-doing was made into one lump, all heaped together, and called, not "*sins*", but "*sin*." Can you catch the idea? All the sinfulness, all the omissions, all the commissions, and all the tendencies to rebel that ever were in the world, are all piled together, hill upon hill, mountain upon mountain, and then called by this one name, "sin."

Now, sin is *that which makes man obnoxious to God.* Man, as a creature, God loves. Man, as a sinner, God cannot love. Sin is loathsome to God; he is so pure that he cannot bear impurity, so just that the thought of injustice is abhorrent to him. He cannot look upon iniquity without hating it; it is contrary to his divine nature. His anger burns like coals of juniper against sin. This it is that makes sin so dreadful to us, because, in consequence of it, we have become obnoxious to God.

And sin, dear friends, also *involves man in punishment.* Inasmuch as we have committed sin, we are exposed to the just and righteous wrath of God. Wherever there is sin, there must be penalty. Laws made without the sanction of reward and punishment are inoperative. God will never suffer his righteous law to be broken with impunity. His word still declares, "The soul that sinneth, it shall die." Where there is sin, there must be punishment; and although the doctrine is not preached as often as it ought to be, yet every man's conscience knows that there is a dreadful hell, there is a worm that dieth not, there is a fire that never can be quenched, and all these are reserved for unforgiven sinners. This makes sin so terrible an evil. Unless

God vacates the throne of the universe, sin must be visited with punishment, and banished from his presence.

Yet again, dear friends, *sin effectually shuts the door of hope on men.* The guilty cannot dwell with God while they are guilty. They must be cleansed from sin before they can walk with him in white. Into heaven there entereth nothing that defileth; and if you and I are not pardoned, we must be separated from God for ever. Nothing we can do, while sin remains upon us, can bring us reconciliation with God. Sin must be put away first. It lies across the road to heaven, and blocks up the door by which we come to God; and, unless it be removed, we are lost, lost, lost, and lost for ever.

Do you all know, in your consciences and hearts, what sin means? I remember that, when I learned that dread lesson, I felt that I was the most unhappy youth in all Her Majesty's dominions. Sin went to bed with me, and scared me with visions. Sin rose with me, and made the most glorious landscape dark and gloomy. I had a terrible sound of judgment to come ever ringing in my ears. I knew that I was guilty; I did not need for God to condemn me, I condemned myself; I sat in judgment upon my own heart, and I condemned myself to hell. Sin! If you really feel it, no burning-irons in the hand of the most cruel inquisitor would ever pain you as sin does. Speak of diseases, and there are some that cause intense agony, but there is no disease that pains like sin on the conscience. Sin on the conscience! It is a prison, a rack, a cross whereon all joy hangs crucified, and bleeding to death.

That is the first thing in my text, the gigantic evil. In proportion as you feel the evil of sin, you will rejoice to hear that Christ came to put away sin by the sacrifice of himself. That is my next point.

II. In the second place, having spoken of the gigantic evil that needed to be removed, let me now speak of THE GLORIOUS REMOVER OF IT. Who was it that undertook to remove this mountain of guilt? "Once in the end of the world hath HE appeared." Who is this that has appeared to put away sin?

I will not delay for a moment, but tell you at once that he that appeared was *very God of very God.* He against whom sin had been committed, he who will judge the quick and the dead; he it was who appeared to put away sin. Is there not great comfort in this fact? It is the Son of God who has undertaken this more than Herculean labour. He appeared, sinner, to save you; God appeared, to put away sin. Lost one, to find you, the great Shepherd has appeared; your case is not hopeless, for he has appeared. Had anybody else than God undertaken the task of putting away sin, it could never have been accomplished; but it can be accomplished now, for HE who appeared is one with whom nothing is impossible. Listen to that, and be comforted.

Who is it that appeared? It is HE, *the commissioned of the Father.* Christ did not come as an amateur Saviour, trying an experiment on his own account; he came as the chosen Mediator, ordained of God for this tremendous task. The Saviour that I preach to you is no invention of my own brain. He is no great one who, of his own accord alone, stepped into the gap without orders from heaven. No; but he appeared whom the Father chose for the work, and sent, commissioned to perform it. His very name, Christ, tells of his anointing for this service.

> "Thus saith God of his Anointed;
> He shall let my people go;
> 'Tis the work for him appointed,
> 'Tis the work that he shall do;
> And my city
> He shall found, and build it too."

"He appeared," he who was *pledged in covenant* to do it; for, of old, before the world was, he became the Surety of the covenant on behalf of his people. He undertook to redeem them. His Father gave him a people to be his own, and he declared that he would do the Father's will, and perfect those whom the Father had given him. "He appeared." Ah, dear friends, if the brightest angel had appeared to save us, we might have trembled lest he should be unequal to the task; but when he comes whom God has sent, whom God has qualified, and who is himself God, he came upon an errand which he is able to accomplish. Think of that, and be comforted.

III. But now, in the third place, we come to THE MEMORABLE EVENT mentioned in our text. We are told that, in order that he might save us, Christ appeared: "Once in the end of the world hath *he appeared.*" He could not sit in heaven, and do this great work. With all reverence to the blessed Son of God, we can truly say that he could not have saved us if he had kept his throne, and not left the courts of glory; but he appeared. I have not to tell you, at this time, that he will appear, although that also is true, for "unto them that look for him shall he appear the second time without sin unto salvation," but he has appeared.

He appeared, first, as *a babe at Bethlehem*, swaddled like any other child. This babe is "the Mighty God, the Everlasting Father, the Prince of peace;" and he has "appeared" on earth in human form. Made in fashion as a man, he has taken upon himself our nature, the Infinite is linked with the infant, the Eternal with the puling child. He, on whom all worlds are hanging, hangs upon a woman's breast. He must do that, or he cannot put away sin.

Thirty years rolled on; and he had toiled, in obscurity, as a carpenter at Nazareth. The Baptist comes, and proclaims the advent of the Redeemer, and he is there to the moment. Into the waters of Jordan he descends, and John with him; the servant baptizes his Lord; and, as he rises from the water-floods, the heavens are opened, the dove descends, it rests upon him, and God proclaims him to be his Son, in whom he is well pleased. Thus Christ, *anointed at Jordan,* appeared to inaugurate his public ministry, and, by his baptism, to begin working a robe of righteousness which is for ever to adorn us, poor naked sinners. "In the end of the world he appeared;" his manifestation commenced at Bethlehem, and was continued at Jordan.

Three more years rolled by, years of toil and suffering; and now the great debt was to be paid, the bill was presented; would he be there to meet it? The charge was laid; would he be there to answer to it? Where should he be but among those olives *in Gethsemane, surrendering himself?* The night is chill, the moon is shining; and he is there in prayer. But what prayer! Never did the earth hear such groans and cries. He is there wrestling; but what wrestling! He sweats, as it were, great drops of blood falling to the ground. The sinner is called for, and the sinner's Substitute has put in an appearance on his behalf in the lonely garden of Gethsemane, so rightly named, the olive-press. In a garden man's first sin was committed; in a garden man's Substitute was arrested.

But now comes the darkest hour of all. Christ appeared *on Calvary, atoning for sin.* The sun is veiled as though unable to look upon such a scene of sorrow. Hear the dread artillery of heaven; the Father thunders forth his wrath against sin. Behold the flames of fire, the forked lightnings of God's anger against all iniquity. Who is to bear them? In whose breast shall they be quenched? HE comes. On yonder tree he presents himself; he hides not his face from shame and spitting; and, at last, upon the cross, he hides not himself from divine desertion. Hear his piteous cry, "My God, my God, why hast thou forsaken me?" Then was fulfilled the prophecy given by the mouth of Zechariah, "Awake, O sword, against my shepherd, and against the man that is my fellow, saith the Lord of hosts." That sword is sheathed in Christ's heart.

> "Jehovah bade his sword awake,
> O Christ, it woke 'gainst thee;
> Thy blood the flaming blade must slake,
> Thy heart its sheath must be!
> All for my sake, my peace to make:
> Now sleeps that sword for me."

Yes, Christ appeared; he was visibly crucified among men; and observed by the gloating eyes of cruel men of hate, he appeared in that dread day of judgment and of vengeance. So it was, and only so, that he was able to put away sin.

We have come thus far, and the path has been strewn with wonders; but only he who knows the meaning of the word "sin" will see any wonder in it. If sin has made the earth tremble under your feet, if sin has scorched you like the blast of a furnace, if sin has burned into your very soul, and killed all your joy, you will hear with delight that God appeared here as man, for this purpose, to put away sin.

IV. Now, we must go a step farther, and consider THE SPECIAL SACRIFICE which Christ offered. He who appeared put away sin by a sacrifice, and that sacrifice was himself: "Once in the end of the world hath he appeared to put away sin by *the sacrifice of himself.*"

There was never any way of putting away sin except by sacrifice. The Bible never tells us of any other way; human thought or tradition has never discovered any other way. Find a people with a religion, and you are sure to find a people with a sacrifice. It is very strange; but, wherever our missionaries go, if they find God at all thought of, they find sacrifices being offered. It must be so; for man has this law written upon his very conscience.

Christ must bring a sacrifice; but observe what it was; *he offered himself.* "He appeared to put away sin by the sacrifice of himself," *his whole self.* Christ did not give to us merely a part of himself; he gave *himself*. Let me say those sweet words again, "He loved me, and gave himself for me." His blood? Yes. His hands, his feet, his side? Yes. His body, his soul? Yes; but you need not say all that; "He gave *himself*." "Who his own self bare our sins in his own body on the tree." Whatever Christ was in himself, he gave that; he offered himself as a sacrifice for sin. What a wonderful sacrifice! Ten thousand bullocks, myriads of sheep, enough to cover all the pastures of the earth, what would their blood avail? But God, God incarnate, Immanuel, God with us, offers himself. What condescension, what love, what infinite pity, that he should sacrifice himself for his enemies, for those who had broken his holy law!

Christ offered himself alone. He put away sin by the sacrifice of *himself;* not by the sacrifice of his Church, not by the sacrifice of martyrs, not by the offering of wafers and consecrated wine; but by the sacrifice of himself alone. You must not add anything to Christ's sacrifice. Christ does not put away sin through your tears, and your grief, and your merit, and your almsgiving. No, he put away sin by the sacrifice of *himself;* nothing else. You must take nothing from Christ's sacrifice, and you must add nothing to it.

That sacrifice, too, if I read the Greek aright, was *a slain sacrifice*, a bloody sacrifice. Christ gave his life. It is written, "Without shedding of blood is no remission." He shed his blood. "The blood is the life thereof," is true of Christ's sacrifice; for without bloodshedding it would have been of no avail. He poured out his soul unto death. In instituting that dear memorial feast, which you are bidden to observe in remembrance of him, he said, "This is my blood of the new testament, which is shed for many for the remission of sins." The putting away of sin was accomplished by Christ dying in the room, and place, and stead of guilty men. Christ says, "I will take the punishment of sin." He takes it; he bears it on the cross. Sinful man, hear this! Take that fact to be true, and rest your whole soul on it, and you are saved. Christ died for believers. "God so loved the world, that he gave his only begotten Son, that whosoever believeth in him should not perish, but have everlasting life." If you believe in Christ, that is, if you trust him; if you trust him now, if you trust him altogether, if you trust him alone, and say, "There I am resting, believing that Christ died for me," you are saved; for Christ has put away your sin; you shall not die. How can a man die when his sin is put away by Christ's all-sufficient sacrifice?

"If sin be pardon'd, I'm secure;
Death hath no sting beside;
The law gives sin its damning power;
But Christ, my Ransom, died."

Christ's appearing, then, was that he might, as a High Priest, present a sacrifice; he presented himself to the death on the cross; he died, and by that dying he has put away sin.

V. That brings me to my closing point, THE GRAND ACHIEVEMENT. Christ appeared "*to put away sin.*" What can that mean?

It means, first, that Christ has put away sin *as to its exclusion of men from God.* Man, by his sin, had made this world so obnoxious to Jehovah that God could not deal with its inhabitants apart from Christ's sacrifice. He is infinitely merciful, but he is also infinitely just; and the world had become so putrid a thing that he declared that he repented that he had made man upon the earth. Now this whole world of ours must have gone down into eternal ruin had not Christ come. John the Baptist cried, "Behold the Lamb of God, which taketh away the sin of the world," the whole bulk of it. It was there and then removed at one stroke, so that God could deal with man, could send an embassage of peace to this poor guilty world, and could come upon gospel terms of free grace and pardon to deal with a guilty race. That was done. You may all thank God for that.

But there is more wanted than that. When God comes to deal with men, we find, next, that Christ has for every believer taken away sin *as to its punishment.* I mean what I say. God cannot punish twice for the same offence; and to lay sin upon Christ, and then to demand its penalty of those for whom he stood as Substitute, would be to demand compensation twice and punishment twice for one offence; but this can never be.

> "Payment God cannot twice demand,
> First at my bleeding Surety's hand,
> And then again at mine."

That were a gross injustice; and the Judge of all the earth must do right. Behold, then, this fact. If thou believest in Christ Jesus, he bore the punishment of thy sin. In that short space upon the tree, the infinity of his nature enabled him to render to God's justice a vindication which is better than if all for whom he died had gone to hell. Had all been lost, God's justice would not have been vindicated so well as when his own dear Son—

> "Bore, that we might never bear,
> His Father's righteous ire."

He has made the law more honourable by his death at its hands than it could have been if all the race of men had been condemned eternally. Oh, soul, if thou believest in Jesus, the chastisement of thy peace was upon him, and with his stripes thou art healed! "He was made a curse for us, as it is written, Cursed is every one that hangeth on a tree." And was he cursed for me, and shall I be cursed, too? That would not be consistent with divine equity. The true believer may plead the justice as well as the mercy of God in the matter of his absolution. If Christ died, then all who were in Christ died with him; and when he rose, they all rose with him; and when God accepted him by raising him from the dead, he accepted all who were in him. Glory be to his holy name!

Further, Christ put away sin, *as to its condemning power.* You have felt the condemning power of sin; I have supposed you have done so. If so, listen. "There is, therefore, now no condemnation to them that are in Christ Jesus." Thou art a sinner, but thy sin is not imputed to thee, but to him who stood as thy Sponsor, thy Paymaster, thy Surety. Thy sins were numbered on the Scapegoat's head of old, even on Christ, the divinely-ordained Substitute for all his people. As David wrote, "Blessed is the man unto whom the Lord imputeth not

CHRIST'S ONE SACRIFICE FOR SIN.

iniquity, and in whose spirit there is no guile!" Thy sin doth not condemn thee; for Christ has been condemned in thy stead. "Neither do I condemn thee," saith the Lord; "Go in peace."

Yet once more, sin is put away now *as to its reigning power*; for, if sin be pardoned through the atoning blood, we come to love Christ; and loving Christ, away goes every sin. The man for whom Christ died, who knows it, who knows that Christ put away sin, must love Christ; and loving Christ, he must hate sin, for to love sin and to love Christ at the same time, would be impossible. If he bore my guilt, then I am not my own; for I am bought with a price, even with his most precious blood. He that suffered in my stead shall now my Master be. I lie at his dear feet, and bless his name.

> "Oh, how sweet to view the flowing
> Of his sin-atoning blood,
> With divine assurance knowing
> He has made my peace with God!"

When you get as far as that, then you love Christ, and serve him. I have told you before of the bricklayer who fell off a scaffold, and was taken up so injured that it was seen that he must soon die. A good clergyman, bending over him, said, "My dear man, you had better make your peace with God." The poor fellow opened his eyes, and said, "Make my peace with God, sir? Why, that was done for me more than eighteen hundred years ago by him who took my sin, and suffered in my stead." Thank God for that! I hope that many of you could say the same; you would not then talk about making your peace with God, or about doing something to reconcile you to God. The very thought of adding anything to Christ's finished work, is blasphemy. Believe that he has done all that is required, and rest in it, and be happy all your days.

With this remark I finish. Sin is put away *as to its very existence*. Where has sin gone to when a man believes in Christ? Micah says, "Thou wilt cast all their sins into the depths of the sea," where they will never be fished up again. The devil himself may fish to all eternity, but he will never fish them up again. God has cast the sins of believers into the depths of the sea. Where have they gone? "As far as the east is from the west, so far hath he removed our transgressions from us." How far is the east from the west? Will you go and measure it on the globe? Fly up to the heavens, and see how far you can go east, and how far you can go west. Is there any bound to space? So far has God removed our transgressions from us.

A more wonderful expression is this, "Thou hast cast all my sins behind thy back." Where is that? Where is God's back? Is there any place behind his back? He is everywhere present, and everywhere seen. It must be nowhere at all, then; and our sins are thrown into the nowhere. He that believes in Christ may know of a surety that his iniquities have gone into the nowhere. Listen once more: "In those days, and in that time, saith the Lord, the iniquity of Israel shall be sought for, and there shall be none; and the sins of Judah, and they shall not be found." Thus is sin annihilated for all who trust the Saviour. Listen to Daniel's description of the work of

Messiah the Prince, "to finish the transgression, and to make an end of sins." If he has made an end of them, there is an end of them. O my heart, sing hallelujah! Let every beat of my pulse be a hallelujah unto him who has put away my sin! Poor sinner, if you are black as the devil with sin, crimson to the very core with iniquity, yet wash in the fountain filled with the blood of the Lamb, and you shall be whiter than snow; for the Lord Jesus, by the sacrifice of himself, hath for ever put away the sin of all who trust him.

Dear hearers, have you laid hold of this great truth? Then I do not care to what sect you belong; and I do not care what your standing in life is; and I do not care what your opinion in politics may be. Has Christ put away your sin? If he has, be as happy as the days are long in summertime; and be as bright as the garden is gay in June. Sing like angels; you have more to sing about than angels have; for never did they taste redeeming grace and dying love. They were never lost, and therefore never found; never enslaved, and therefore never redeemed. God in human flesh has died for you. God loved you so that he would be nailed to a tree for you. You have sinned; but you are to-day as if you had never sinned. "He that is washed is clean every whit." "And ye are washed." Oh, I say again, let your heart beat hallelujah! Let your pulse seem to say, "Bless, bless, bless, bless, bless the Lord!"

"Oh!" says one, in a mournful and sorrowful tone, "I am afraid it is not so with me." Well, then, do not go to sleep to-night till it is. If thou believest in the Lord Jesus Christ, it is so. "Well, I hope that it is so," says one. Away with your hoping! What is the good of that? There are many people that go hoping, hoping, hopping, hopping. Get out of that hoping and hopping; and walk steadily on this sure ground: Christ died for all who believe in him, effectually died, not died according to that theory which teaches that he died no more for Peter than he did for Judas, and died for those who are already in hell as much as he died for those who will be in heaven. The universal theory of the atonement has precious little comfort in it; albeit that Christ's death was universal in the removal of the hindrance to God's dealing on terms of mercy with the world, yet he laid down his life for his sheep. He loved his Church, and gave himself for it. He hath redeemed us from among men, out of men. He hath taken us to be his own by the purchase of his blood; we are redeemed, washed, saved. If this is your case, go home, and be glad; let nobody beat you in holy merriment. There is a passage at the end of the parable of the prodigal that I like very much, "and they began to be merry." The parable does not tell us when they left off being merry; but I suppose they are merry still. I know that, ever since my Father put the ring on my finger, and shoes on my feet, and gave me the kiss of love, and I knew that I was forgiven, I have been merry, and I mean to be merry still, till my merriment is lost in the merriment above, where they keep perpetual holiday, and sing to the praise of the Redeemer, "Thou wast slain, and hast redeemed us to God by thy blood out of every kindred, and tongue, and people, and nation." To him be honour, and glory, and blessing, for ever and ever! Amen.

Exposition by C. H. Spurgeon.

HEBREWS IX. 24—28; AND X. 1—18.

Chapter ix., verse 24. *For Christ is not entered into the holy places made with hands,*

Christ has not entered into any earthly temple or tabernacle.

24—26. *Which are the figures of the true; but into heaven itself, now to appear in the presence of God for us: nor yet that he should offer himself often, as the high priest entereth into the holy place every year with blood of others; for then must he often have suffered since the foundation of the world: but now once—*

And only once—

26. *In the end of the world hath he appeared to put away sin by the sacrifice of himself.*

The Levitical priests continually repeated their sacrifice, for it was not effectual when offered only once; but our great High Priest has once for all presented a sacrifice which has made a full atonement for all his people's sins, and there is therefore no need for it to be repeated.

27. *And as it is appointed unto men once to die,*

Notice how the apostle continues to introduce that important little key-word "once."

27, 28. *But after this the judgment: so Christ was once offered—*
Only once—

28. *To bear the sins of many; and unto them that look for him shall he appear the second time without sin unto salvation.*

May we be amongst the privileged company that look for him!

Chapter x., verse 1. *For the law having a shadow of good things to come, and not the very image of the things, can never with those sacrifices which they offered year by year continually make the comers thereunto perfect.*

A man could go to the Levitical sacrifices twenty years running, and yet be no forwarder. He must go again and again as long as he lived. They were only figures and shadows and types; the real sacrifice is Christ.

2. *For then—*
If they had been effectual,—

2. *Would they not have ceased to be offered? because that the worshippers once purged should have had no more conscience of sins.*

Once forgiven, the sin would not have come back again. If the sacrifice had really cleansed the conscience of the offerer, he would not have had cause to present it again.

3—5. *But in those sacrifices there is a remembrance again made of sins every year. For it is not possible that the blood of bulls and of goats should take away sins. Wherefore when he cometh—*

He who is the essence of it all, "When he cometh,"—

5—7. *Into the world, he saith, Sacrifice and offering thou wouldest not, but a body hast thou prepared me: in burnt offerings and sacrifices for sin thou hast had no pleasure. Then said I, Lo, I come (in the volume of the book it is written of me,) to do thy will, O God.*

Types were no longer needed when the great Antitype had come. Christ was no longer pre-figured, for he was there in person. He put away the old shadows of the blood of bulls and goats when he brought his own real sacrifice, the true atonement for sin.

8, 9. *Above when he said, Sacrifice and offering and burnt offerings and offering for sin thou wouldest not, neither hadst pleasure therein; which are offered by the law; then said he, Lo, I come to do thy will, O God. He taketh away the first, that he may establish the second.*

The old law is gone, the first sacrifice is no longer presented, for the second is come, the real offering of Christ the Lamb of God.

10. *By the which will we are sanctified through the offering of the body of Jesus Christ once for all.*

Once, and only once. How Paul loves to recall this fact!

11, 12. *And every priest standeth daily ministering and offering oftentimes the same sacrifices, which can never take away sins: but this man,—*

Note these glorious words, "This Man,"—

12, 13. *After he had offered one sacrifice for sins for ever, sat down on the right hand of God; from henceforth expecting till his enemies be made his footstool.*

He would not have sat down if his work had not been done. He would not have ceased from his priestly service of presenting sacrifice if his one offering had not been sufficient. This Man's offering once, once, once, has done all that God demanded, and all that man required.

14. *For by one offering he hath perfected for ever them that are sanctified.*

This glorious message is for *you*, beloved, if you believe in Christ. By his one sacrifice he has done all that you need; he has perfected you for ever.

15—17. *Whereof the Holy Ghost also is a witness to us: for after that he had said before, This is the covenant that I will make with them after those days, saith the Lord, I will put my laws into their hearts, and in their minds will I write them; and their sins and iniquities will I remember no more.*

Treasure up these golden words: "Their sins and iniquities will I remember no more."

18. *Now where remission of these is, there is no more offering for sin.*

The offering for sin is in order that sin may be put away; and if it be put away, so that God himself will remember it no more, what more is wanted? What more could be desired? Wherefore, let us rest in the one great finished work of Christ, and be perfectly happy. Sin is gone, wrath is over, for those for whom Christ died; they are perfected for ever through his one great sacrifice.

HYMNS FROM "OUR OWN HYMN BOOK"—395, 280, 289.

Just Published. Price One Penny.

SPURGEON'S ILLUSTRATED ALMANACK for 1893.

"For several years, Mrs. Spurgeon has selected the texts for her dear husband's little Book Almanack; and this fact has caused many readers to speak of it as her Almanack. The one about to be issued is hers in a double sense. Not only has she chosen the passages of Scripture for daily meditation throughout the year, and written an interesting letter concerning them; but other articles from her pen appear in the book. The illustrations were almost all selected by Mr. Spurgeon, of whom an excellent portrait is given; and there are also four exquisite little articles by the late beloved Editor, for which special illustrations have been prepared. We trust that all old friends will purchase and distribute the Almanacks for 1893, and that many new friends will be induced to do so by the information we have here given."—*Notice from November "Sword and Trowel."*

PASSMORE & ALABASTER, PATERNOSTER BUILDINGS, LONDON; and all Booksellers.

Metropolitan Tabernacle Pulpit.

"CLEAR SHINING AFTER RAIN."

A Sermon

Intended for Reading on Lord's-day, November 27th, 1892,

DELIVERED BY

C. H. SPURGEON,

AT THE METROPOLITAN TABERNACLE, NEWINGTON,

On Lord's-day Evening, July 20th, 1890.

"As the tender grass springing out of the earth by clear shining after rain."—2 Samuel xxiii. 4.

What a blessing it is to the country if, at certain seasons, we have a time of clear shining after the rain! Under some circumstances, nothing but sunshine will save the crops that are ready to be reaped; and there will be great loss to the farming interest, and, indeed, to us all, unless we have the sunshine when it is needed. We must never neglect to pray to the Lord who alone can give, to the natural world, clear shining after rain.

Our text, however, has a higher meaning than this. These words occur in David's description of a fit, true, and wise ruler. All rulers have not been fit to rule; indeed, in David's day, and in most Oriental countries at the present time, the King, the Sultan, the Emperor, the Shah, all rule for themselves. Their one great business is to extort all the taxes they can from the people, and to give them as little as possible in return. To fleece the sheep, is the great business of an Oriental shepherd; to feed them, does not seem to enter into his mind. But David says that, where rulers were wise, just, and upright, their country flourished. A good ruler, especially in the East, where he had everything in his own hand when he came to the throne, was like "a morning without clouds"; and the people round him grew like the grass in times when, after heavy showers of rain, the sun looks forth with cheerful rays, and warms the earth into verdure. We may be thankful, dear friends, that we do not know what despotic rule means; for, good as it may occasionally happen to be, it may also be intolerably bad. Let other lands have what masters they will, but let us be free, and our own masters still, as we still are, thanks to the gracious providence of God that has smiled upon us.

The beautiful simile, by which David sets forth the rule of a good king, I will first take out of its connection, and look at it for other purposes; and then I will put it back into its connection, and use it

No. 2,284.

as David used it, only in a higher sense. The beautiful picture that he draws is produced by a combination, first, rain, and then, clear shining after rain; and the most flourishing condition of spirituality is produced by the same two causes; it comes as the result of a combination of rain and sunshine. We shall never rise to the highest spiritual state by having all rain and no sunshine. Although we may prefer it, we shall never attain to the fullest fruit-bearing by having all sunshine, and no rain. God puts the one over against the other, the dark day of cloud and tempest against the bright day of sunshine and calm; and when the two influences work together in the soul, as they do in the natural world, they produce the greatest degree of fertility, and the best condition of heart and life.

I intend to use the text in four ways; and first, I shall show you how the "clear shining after rain" is manifested *in the heart of the convert.* In the second place, I shall point out to you how this "clear shining after rain" often produces the best condition of things *in the soul of the believer.* Thirdly, I shall prove to you that our text makes a very happy combination *in the ministry of the Word;* and, in closing, I shall speak to you about the "clear shining after rain" *in the ages to come.*

I. I shall begin by showing you how the "clear shining after rain" is manifested IN THE HEART OF THE CONVERT.

When a man is truly converted, do you know how it is manifested? All conversions are not alike; there is a very great difference between them. Some are very definite; you can tell to a minute when the man is converted. Others are very indistinct; there is a long previous preparatory process, and you cannot say exactly when the man turned to God. If you get up to-morrow morning, and do not look at the Almanack, but look toward the east, and take a pencil and try to mark down exactly when the sun rises, I think it is highly probable that you will not manage the task correctly. On an extremely clear and bright morning, you might tell, to a second, when the rim of the sun appeared above the horizon; but we do not often have clear, bright mornings nowadays. We have not seen the sun much lately; and, probably, you would find that he was up before you had made the pencil mark, and most likely you would learn that he was up before you had discovered when he rose. So it is often in the workings of divine grace. Some men have the light of God; but they cannot tell when the light first came to them. Let none of you imagine that you are not converted because you do not know the hour when it occurred; otherwise, you would be as foolish as I should be if I said to some old lady, "How old are you?" "Well, I am somewhere about eighty." "But when was your birthday? Do you not remember your birthday?" "No, sir, I do not." Suppose I were to tell her she was not alive because she did not know her birthday, I should be very foolish; and if you say to yourself, "Soul, you were never born again because you do not know when the event happened," you will be very foolish, too. If you can say, "One thing I know, whereas I was blind, but now I see," be satisfied and grateful, even though you cannot tell when the great miracle was wrought. Conversions, then, are not all alike.

Yet, as a usual rule, *the work of grace begins in the heart with a time of gloom.* Clouds gather; there is a general dampness round about; the soul seems saturated with doubt, fear, dread. There is something coming, but the soul knows not what; it feels that it is very sinful, and deserves whatever punishment God may send. Perhaps some of you are passing through that stage of experience just now. You get sadder and yet more sad every day; and yet you do not quite know why. You used to go to the theatre, and you enjoyed it; but you went the other night, and it seemed very dreary to you, as indeed it is. You went off to some gay company, where you used to be very merry; but you seemed quite out of spirits, you could not join in their merriment, you were glad to get home. Something ails you; something ails you. Yes, the clouds are gathering over your head. That is how grace usually begins to work in the soul that God means to save and bless.

After the clouds, in the next place, *the rain falls.* The real work of the Spirit of God often follows upon an inward depression of spirit. Now you begin really to repent of sin; now are you sorry for the past; now you begin to sigh and cry for Christ. You wish you knew him; you wish you loved him. Tears begin to drop; or if they do not actually fall from your eyes, yet there are inward weepings, and your soul is getting moist now with deep contrition, hatred of sin, dread of God's anger, the fear of the wrath to come, and a wish to lay hold on eternal life. Now the rains, the blessed rains, have come, and softened your heart. If we were to water all the fields in summer-time, when the sun is shining with a scorching heat, it would be of very little use indeed. An Irish friend of mine once said, that he had carefully noticed that it did not rain when the sun was shining; but that, whenever it rained, there were always some clouds to keep the sunshine off. There is a great truth in what my friend said. Rain becomes doubly precious to the earth when all the surroundings are suitable for its reception. All the atmosphere becomes damp; whereas, if rain could fall when all is dry and warm, mischief might come of it. Well, now, God's Holy Spirit loves to come and work in man a congenial atmosphere, a holy tenderness, a devout heartbreaking; then with the clouds he brings a heavenly rain.

What comes after the rain? Then, *the sun shines:* "clear shining after rain." I am describing the conversion of a man to God, not in a cast-iron style; for, as I have already told you, experiences differ. But, as a rule, after the softening, saturating influences of the Holy Spirit have come to the man, then the clouds go, the rain ceases, and there comes clear shining. The sun shines out. The man perceives that he is a sinner, but that Christ has come to save him. He sees his own blackness; but he believes that Christ can make him whiter than the snow. He mourns his own rebellions; but he rejoices that he is made a reconciled child, and admitted into the sacred family. Now look at him; his face is full of brightness; he looks as if he would like to dance, he feels so happy. His sins are washed away, he has believed in Jesus, he has rested in Christ's finished work, and now he is as merry as the birds in May. His cheerful exclamation is, "I feel like singing all the time," for he is enjoying the clear shining after the rain. I should like to encourage any here to-night who are going through the rain time. Believe me, it will not last for ever; you shall yet say, "Lo, the winter is past; the rain is over and gone; the flowers appear on the earth; the time of the singing of birds is come." It will come all the sooner to you if you at once come to Christ. Look to him as lifted up on the cross for you; and you are now saved. God grant that you may do so at once!

Well, now, what happens after this? We have come as far as the clear shining after rain; what follows this? Why, *then everything grows*. The grass is sure to grow when we have mist and heat together; and when a soul, having felt its need of Christ, at last beholds the light of his countenance, then it begins to grow. I love to see young converts with all the freshness of their new-born faith; they have not borrowed their language from other people. I like to see them with their zeal; they are not quite so prudent as some of us older people are. You will find that they are doing this, and doing that, and doing the other good thing, and the prudent people tell them not to do too much. My dear young friend, do not listen to them! There is many an old saint who has been spokesman for the devil when he has tried to hold a young Christian back from doing more for Christ. I had a number of kind friends when I began labouring for the Lord, and especially when I began to preach; and these kind friends provided me with an unlimited quantity of blankets, and very wet blankets they were, too. They were afraid that I should get too hot in my Master's service, so they were always ready with wet blankets to damp my ardour. I do think that, sometimes, when Satan wants to repress the zeal of young converts, he finds more efficient servants among good people than he does among bad ones. Brethren, let the young converts grow; they will not grow too fast. Let them serve God zealously; they will not do too much for him. Let them burn with vehement zeal; there are plenty in the world who will try to cool it down. God grant that our young friends may be able to resist that chilling influence, and still may be full of earnest might and spiritual strength in the service of their Saviour!

That, then, is the usual method of the progress of a convert; clouds, rain, clear shining, and then growth. We pray that we may see this process perfected in very many.

II. But now, secondly, I am going to use the text in another way. This "clear shining after rain" often produces the very best condition of things IN THE SOUL OF THE BELIEVER.

You will see this state of things manifested in *trial followed by deliverance*. Were you ever nearer to God, my dear tried friend, than after a very heavy affliction, when God appeared for you, and brought you out of it? I can only speak for myself; but I must say this, in times of prosperity I have not always felt so much the nearness of God as in moments of great sorrow and tribulation, when I have sobbed myself to sleep upon the breast of my dear Lord; and when I have awaked, and have found that he has done for me what my helplessness could not do, and has set me free from my foes, and made me to rejoice in his name, then have I seen him; then have I known him, when he has delivered my soul from death, mine eyes from tears, and my feet from falling. See, then, dear souls, you who love the Lord, you may expect to have trials, and you may expect to have deliverances, too, for your very best state of growth comes of the two together; rain, and then the clear shining after the rain; trial followed by deliverance.

Next, this experience is realized in *humiliation of self followed by joy in the Lord.* It is a very healthy thing for a man to be made to know himself; and if he is made to know himself, he will have no cause for boasting. There is not a corner in our nature in which we may sit down, and say, "I have something which is good within me which I have myself wrought out." If there be anything good in us, it is the gift of God alone. The Lord often takes us down into our own natural hearts; and there conducts us from chamber to chamber, that we may see our own filthiness and vileness. I suppose that nobody here knows quite how bad he is by nature. If we could know it fully, our reason might reel. We might never be able to hope again, if we fully knew all the depravity of our hearts. Now, for a man to have plenty of rain to make him feel how evil he is, and then to have coupled with that a full conviction of the greatness and blessedness of Christ, and of his own interest in Christ; to see sin, and then to see the one great Sacrifice for sin; to see our death, and then to see Christ our life; this is the very best condition for any of us to be in. I would not have you glory in Christ, I do not think you can rightly glory in Christ, unless you also sorrow because of your own distance from him, and your own natural depravity. It is for our good to have this twofold experience. We might get presumptuous if we were allowed always to enjoy the clear shining; we might think that there was no reason to watch, no further cause to carry the shield of faith, or to wield the sword of the Spirit. To preserve us from this evil, we often get taken down a notch or two. We are made to see our necessity, that we may value, all the more, the riches of God in Christ Jesus. Put those two together, deep self-humiliation and highly prizing our precious Christ, and you have a condition of things in which a child of God can grow.

Next, I think there is another happy combination of rain and clear shining, namely, *tenderness mixed with assurance.* I like to meet with that man, whom Mr. Bunyan speaks of in his "Pilgrim's Progress", who was, above many, tender of sin. He was not afraid of lions; but he was dreadfully afraid of sins. He was not afraid of Vanity Fair; it had no charms for him; but he had some doubts about his interest in the celestial country. I love to see a child of God who, like Mr. Fearing, is very tender of sin. I know some who hardly dare put one foot before the other, for fear they should do wrong. I do not like this tenderness to become morbid; for then it causes unnecessary grief; but yet holy tenderness is a very beautiful characteristic of a child of God when it has mingled with it the clear shining of a full assurance that enables the man to say, "I know whom I have believed; I know I am God's child; I know that none shall pluck me from his hand."

"More blessed, but not more secure,
Are the glorified spirits in heaven."

These two things, tenderness and assurance, operating together, will produce a high state of spiritual fertility. It is a dreadful thing to see the full assurance of some men! I heard of one man, in a public-house, saying, as he drank I do not know how many glasses of beer, "I may take what I like, for I am a child of God." O wretched blasphemer! What worse blasphemy could there be than such talk as thine? He who is a true child of God says to himself, "I do not ask how far I may go without crossing the line of safety; but I do ask that I may be kept from temptation and sin; and if there are some things that I might do, if they expose me to temptation, or expose others to it, I will have nothing to do with them." Give me, then, a man of tender heart, who, at the same time, mixes full assurance with his tenderness. He is the man who will bring forth fruit unto holiness, and the end everlasting life.

Once again, our text suggests to us the blending of *experience and knowledge*. Read the Westminster Assembly's Confession of Faith; by all manner of means get a clear view of the doctrines of grace, so that you can state them to others, and know why you hold them firmly yourself; but, remember, if you do not experience them in your own heart, if you do not know the power of them in your own life, you know nothing at all about them. Dry doctrine, without the damping of the Spirit of God, may only make fuel for your eternal destruction. When a man accommodates his religion up in the garret of his head, and never takes it down into the parlour of his heart, that man's religion is vain. We must experience the power of the gospel in our own souls if it is to be of real service to us.

"True religion's more than notion,
Something must be known and felt."

It is very nice to talk about Christ; but do you trust him as your Saviour? It may be very easy to speak about the new birth; but have you felt it? When you get these two things together, first the rain of gracious experience, and then the clear shining of intellectual knowledge of Scripture, then will you bring forth fruit unto God.

I must not linger longer over this very interesting point of the clear shining after rain as illustrated in the soul of the believer.

III. But now, in the third place, I think, dear friends, our text makes a very happy combination IN THE MINISTRY OF THE WORD.

You know that, nowadays, people will listen to anybody, provided that he is a clever preacher. I am often astonished at congregations that had a grand old man for preacher, who always preached them good sound doctrine, and I thought their church was a very tower of orthodoxy; but when he dies, they pick on somebody who preaches no one knows what; but, then, he does it cleverly, and so they have him, to their eternal disgrace, and to the injury of the Church of God.

What is a good sermon? Well, I am very much of the opinion of old King George the Third, in his latter days. The old man knew the truth, and loved it; and when he used to hear his fine court chaplains, he would often go out of the chapel, and say, "It will not do; nothing to feed a soul on." Old George had not too much brains; but all the things he did know, he clung to. Another time, as he went out of the chapel, he would say, "That will do; that will do; a soul can feed on that." That was his way of judging a sermon: "Can a soul feed on it?" And if a soul could not feed on it, it did not suit George the Third. I hope that it will not suit you either, unless it stands this test, Can a soul feed on it? You may have the best china dinner-service, and the silver plate, and the damask table-cloth; but if, on the table, there is nothing but dry bones, I should not recommend you to go there to dinner. We want something to eat both for our bodies and our souls if they are to be kept healthy.

He who would have a fruitful ministry must have clear shining after the rain, by which I mean, *first, law, and then, gospel*. We must preach plainly against sin. In our ministry there must be rain, we must have the clouds and darkness, and divine justice bearing heavily upon the sinner's conscience. Then comes in Christ crucified, full atonement, simple faith, and clear shining of comfort to the believing sinner. But there must be the rain first. He who preaches all sweetness and all love, and has nothing to do with warning men of the consequences of sin, may be thought to be very loving; but, in truth, he is altogether unfaithful to the souls of men. I do not suppose that any of you women can sew without needles. Yet your object is not simply to get the needle into the stuff, is it? No; you want to get in a bit of cotton, or thread, or silk. Well, now, try whether you can sew with a piece of silk alone. You cannot do so. You must put in the needle first, must you not? And he who would do any work for God, must have a sharp needle, as he deals plainly with the sin of man, and he must then draw after it the silken thread of the gospel of Christ. There must be rain first, and clear shining afterwards.

But, dear friends, when we come to deal with you, we have to tell you that what we want to see in you is, *first, repentance, and then zeal:* rain, and then clear shining. I am always sorry if my ministry produces men and women who, on a sudden, seem to become Christians directly, without any sense of sin, without any softening, without any fear of divine wrath, for I am afraid that those clear shinings without any rain will parch the ground, and make it dry, but never cause it to bring forth true fruit unto God. In our ministry, dear friends, it must not be so; and here I speak to my fellow-Christians as well as to myself. Your ministry may be in the Sunday-school, or in street-preaching, or sick-visiting, but all true ministry must have rain about it as well as sunshine.

If your service is to be successful, bringing glory to God, there must be in it, *first, prayer, and then, blessing*. You must go forth with prayer, you must go forth weeping, bearing precious seed, and afterwards there will come the clear shining, when you return rejoicing, bringing your sheaves with you. God will bless and prosper your work if you go to it in the spirit of your Saviour; but there must be deep anxiety in your soul, and great longings and anguish before God, if you expect to have the Lord's blessing resting upon your efforts to serve him.

I think my text also means *grace softening, and then shining*. I wish that the Lord would visit all his Church with a heavy shower of rain; I mean, by way of softening the Church, making the Church loving in spirit, and anxious for souls. Then what would happen? The Lord would soon visit it with clear shining, and we should see conversions as numerous as the blades of grass which spring up in the fields. Oh, come, come, divine dew, and rest on this assembly now, and on this church all the days of the week! Then shine, O Sun of righteousness, with glorious warmth and power, and we shall soon see a plentiful harvest, to the praise and glory of our God!

This is, I think, the meaning of the expression, " clear shining after rain", as applied to the ministry of the Word.

IV. I have done when I have said just this much with regard to the clear shining after rain IN THE AGES TO COME.

I am no prophet, nor the son of a prophet. Every now and then I see the walls of our city placarded with an intimation that something very wonderful is going to happen in such and such a year. Now, believe me, brethren, it may be, but then it may not be. Whenever I find a brother quite sure about what will happen on April the 1st, in such and such a year, I begin to wonder whether he knows anything at all about the subject; I suspect that all those who prophesy in these days, apart from the sacred Word, are as much to be respected as the Norwood gipsy, and no more. And yet I am now going to turn prophet, taking my prophecy out of the Word of God.

And, first, *times of gloom are to be expected.* There has been held, in this city of London, a conference with regard to the establishment of peace. I heartily sympathize with the grand object of that conference. Oh, that wars might cease unto the ends of the earth! War is the sum of all villanies. There is nothing to be said for it. It is a monstrous thing that men should murder one another wholesale. But there will be no end of war from anything that you and I can do apart from preaching the gospel of Christ. When the King comes, when Jesus comes, when the King shall reign in righteousness, there will be an end to war; but till then there will be wars and rumours of wars; and when you hear of them, do not be disturbed as though everything was going to pieces. There will be clear shinings after the rain. Ay, though it be a reign of blood, afterwards he shall shine out who is our peace, and who will set up an unsuffering kingdom which shall know no end. In religious matters, do not expect that the world will go on getting better and better. I think the belief that it is already much improved has a very slight foundation of fact. We have learned the art of hiding sin behind the vestments of hypocrisy, but we are not much better after all. We have changed the fashion of sin, but the sin is there. Now, do not expect to see the churches always sound, and religion always spreading. You may see, somebody will see, a falling away before the coming of Christ, and a departure from the faith. "The love of many shall wax cold." It shall come to pass that, if you ask for faith, you will scarcely find it, for, " When the Son of man cometh, shall he find faith on the earth ?" Scarcely. It will be a very rare commodity; but be not distressed, even though all men are turned aside from the Christ of God, for there will be "clear shinings after the rain."

Although times of gloom are to be expected, *an age of light will follow.* There will come a day when Christ shall reign amongst his ancients gloriously; when the ungodly shall hide themselves in obscure places, and the meek shall have dominion in the earth, and the sons of God in that morning shall be owned as the noblest of men. There is to come yet "a thousand years" (whatever that period may mean) of a reign of righteousness, wherein the whole of the earth shall be filled with the glory of God, and become the vestibule of heaven. Have comfort about that glorious truth.

Now, dear friend, with regard to yourself, it may be that, unless the Lord shall soon come to his temple, you will grow old, and as you grow old, the clouds will return after the rain. You will get into times of infirmity when there will be rain, and rain, and rain, and rain, and, perhaps, little sunshine; yet expect that, before you die, you will come to the clear shining after the rain. There is a place called the land of Beulah. It lieth on the verge of the Jordan; but it also lieth, with that little stream before it, on the verge of the heavenly Canaan. That land is full of light and flowers, and I have heard that, if the wind blows in the right direction, you may hear the music of heaven in that land, and from a hill in that land you may see the Celestial City. I have known some old men and women who have reached the land of Beulah. It has been a great delight to me to sit and talk with them in their last days. They have had clear shinings after the rain. They have told me all about the rain, about the children dying, about the wife who was buried long ago, about the poverty they passed through, about the persecution they endured, and so on, and so on. All that is rain; but they have never been able to tell me all about the clear shinings; but they have said that they felt as happy as they could be out of heaven, and they had no particular wish about whether they should stay or whether they should go. I saw, the other day, an old man, who had passed his ninety-first year; and though he looked like little more than a skeleton, it was grand to hear him speak of the faithfulness of God, and the doctrines of the gospel. He was as clear on those points as ever he was; and, perhaps, even firmer. It was a great treat to listen to him. I pray that all of us may, in due time, get to the land Beulah, where all is bright and happy; and there may we dwell till the post comes from the King to say that we must pass the stream to joyfully behold our Lord; and, oh, what clear shining after rain will there be when we once get home, when we behold his face, and when we, like himself, have risen from the dead, and stand perfect and complete in our flesh to behold our God! Oh, the glory and the bliss of being—

"For ever with the Lord,"

after the rain is over and gone! Go through it. Never be afraid of all the drenchings you may get on your way to glory. Get home as quickly as you can along the good old road; for, after the rain, comes the clear shining. Be this the motto of each one of you from this sweet Sabbath evening hour, "Clear shining after rain." God bless you all! Amen.

Exposition by C. H. Spurgeon.

PSALM XXXII.

A Psalm of David,

You can see David all through this Psalm; here we have David's sin, David's confession of sin, David's pardon. It is a Psalm of David. Oh, that we might each one make it our own! It is entitled—

Maschil.

This is an instructive Psalm. The experience of one man is instructive to another. We learn the way in which we should walk, and sometimes the way in which we should not walk, by observing the footsteps of the flock. The Psalm begins with blessing.

Verse 1. *Blessed is he whose transgression is forgiven, whose sin is covered.*

I think I hear a sort of sigh of relief, as if the man had been burdened with a load of guilt, and now at last his sin is put away; and his sigh has more solemn joy in it than if it had been a song: "Blessed is he whose transgression is forgiven, whose sin is covered." Beloved, you must know the bitterness of sin before you can know the blessedness of forgiveness; and you must have such a sight of sin as shall break your heart before you can understand the blessedness of the divine covering, that sacred coverlet which hides sin effectually, blots it out, and even makes it cease to be. "Blessed is he whose transgression is forgiven, whose sin is covered." Would you not think so, dear burdened heart, if it ever came to your lot? I hope that it will be so to-night. Do not we think so, who remember the day when almighty mercy forgave us our transgression, and covered our sin? Indeed we do. This is one of the greatest blessednesses out of heaven. Perhaps, for a sort of still soft melody with much of the minor in it, this is the sweetest music in the whole Book, "Blessed is he whose transgression is forgiven, whose sin is covered."

Now David must put the same truth in another form. He loves to reduplicate, to repeat again and again a truth which is very precious to him.

2. *Blessed is the man unto whom the LORD imputeth not iniquity, and in whose spirit there is no guile.*

Here are two reasons for the man's blessedness: sin is not laid to his charge, and he is no longer deceitful; he no longer tries to palliate and to excuse his sin; he makes a clean breast of it; and God, in a higher sense, gives him a clean breast. He acknowledges the justice of God, and God displays his infinite mercy to him.

Now David tells us how he learned this sacred blessedness; what were the ways by which he went, which ended at last in this divine sweetness.

3, 4. *When I kept silence, my bones waxed old through my roaring all the day long. For day and night thy hand was heavy upon me: my moisture is turned into the drought of summer. Selah.*

I understand this to have been the feeling of David after his great sin, before he confessed it. He tried to excuse it to his conscience. It has been thought by some that David was, for at least nine months, in a very insensible state; but he does not appear to have been so. All the time until his sin was confessed and acknowledged, he was miserable. Because there was divine grace in his heart, sin could not dwell there with comfort. As he would not own his sin before the bar of God, pleading guilty, and waiting for judgment, as he kept silence, it preyed upon him so, that he seemed to grow prematurely old, and that, not only in his skin and his flesh, but his very bones were affected: "My bones waxed old." Those solid pillars of the house of manhood trembled and were shaken under his awful sense of sin. You cannot be a child of God and sin, and then be happy.

EXPOSITION.

Other men may sin cheaply, but you cannot. If you are a man after God's own heart, and you venture into uncleanness, it will sting you as does a viper; it will burn within your bones like coals of juniper

"When I kept silence, my bones waxed old through my roaring all the day long." David did pray, but he did not dare to call it prayer. It was like the moaning and groaning of a beast that is wounded, and faint, and near to die; and this terrible pain was upon him always: "For day and night thy hand was heavy upon me." God has a heavy hand for his sinful children. Other fathers may spoil their children with indulgence; but the Lord will not spoil his children. If we sin, we shall feel the weight of God's hand. We ought to thank him for this; for though it brings great sorrow, yet it brings great safety to us. The worst thing that can happen to a man is to be allowed to sin, and yet to be happy in it. One of the best things for an erring believer is a taste of his Father's rod.

"Thy hand was heavy upon me: my moisture is turned into the drought of summer." All David's joy was squeezed out, pressed out, by the heavy hand of God. His flowers ceased to bloom; his fruit was withered; his experience was nothing but a hard drought, without a drop of moisture.

When David had gone so far, and had played only on the bass strings so long, he said, "Selah," that is, "Screw up the harp strings, let us put them in tune again. We are going up to something better now."

5. *I acknowledged my sin unto thee, and mine iniquity have I not hid. I said, I will confess my transgressions unto the LORD; and thou forgavest the iniquity of my sin. Selah.*

Oh, how swift is the divine compassion! Quick upon the heels of confession came that word from Nathan, "The Lord also hath put away thy sin; thou shalt not die." I can fancy David standing there, with the hot tears in his eyes, never so broken down as when his sin was all forgiven. Before he knew that he was pardoned, he stood tremblingly fearful, brokenhearted before God; but when Nathan had said (I will repeat those gracious words), "The Lord also hath put away thy sin; thou shalt not die," oh, what gratitude he felt, and what tenderness, and what hatred of sin! Dear hearer, if you are burdened under a sense of sin, go and make confession to God straight away. If you feel very heavy to-night at the recollection of some great and grievous offence, if some scarlet spot is on your hand, and you cannot get rid of it, go and show it to God. With penitential honesty confess the sin, and it shall be forgiven you.

"Selah." Now David puts the harp strings right again. They still seem to suffer from the previous strain; and so he says "Selah" once more. "Sursum corda." Lift up the heart; let the whole soul go up to God.

6, 7. *For this shall every one that is godly pray unto thee in a time when thou mayest be found: surely in the floods of great waters they shall not come nigh unto him. Thou art my hiding place;*

He had talked, in the first verse, of his sin being covered. Now he not only hides his sin beneath the divine covering, but he hides himself beneath the divine shelter: "Thou art my hiding place." Thus does the believer sing—

> "Rock of Ages, cleft for me,
> Let me hide myself in thee."

7. *Thou shalt preserve me from trouble;*

Lord, if thou hast taken away the greatest of all troubles, that is, guilt on the conscience, if thou hast really forgiven me, what trouble have I to be afraid of? "Thou shalt preserve me from trouble."

7. *Thou shalt compass me about with songs of deliverance. Selah.*

If thou hast pardoned me, there is the making of all manner of music in the fact of my pardon. He that is washed by the precious blood of Jesus is the man to sing. Has not God made a chorister of him? John tells us, in the Revelation, that one of the elders said to him, concerning the white-robed throng, "These are they which came out of great tribulation, and have washed their robes, and made them white in the blood of the Lamb. Therefore are they before the throne of God, and serve him day and night in his temple."

"Selah." David must screw up the strings of his harp again, for now he wishes to exult in God, and to magnify his holy name, as he listens to his Lord's gracious words.

8. *I will instruct thee and teach thee in the way which thou shalt go: I will guide thee with mine eye.*

Here is another blessing. The God who has forgiven the errings of the past, will preserve us from erring again. God's flowers always bloom double. He gives us justification; but he adds sanctification. He pardons our sins; but he also makes disciples and scholars of us, and teaches us the art of holiness, which is the noblest art that man can learn: "I will instruct thee and teach thee in the way which thou shalt go: I will guide thee with mine eye." When we are willing to be guided, we hardly need a word from God; a look is enough, just a glance of his eye: "I will guide thee with mine eye."

9. *Be ye not as the horse, or as the mule, which have no understanding: whose mouth must be held in with bit and bridle, lest they come near unto thee.*

Do you want bits and bridles? If you want them, you shall have them. If you will be a horse or a mule, you shall be treated as horses and mules are. There are some Christians that need to be driven with a very sharp snaffle; and they need to have their mouth made very tender, for now they are hard-mouthed; and, sometimes, they take the bit between their teeth, and try to run away instead of doing God's bidding. Usually, the rods with which God scourges us are made of reeds grown in our own gardens. When God hides his face from his people, it is almost always behind clouds of dust which they have themselves made. You will have sorrow enough in the ordinary way to heaven; do not make an extra rod for your own back.

10. *Many sorrows shall be to the wicked:*

This refers to you who are outside the family of God, who do not come under his rod, you are not in his love and favour, for you have no faith in his dear Son. Do not think that you will escape punishment. If the Lord "scourgeth every son whom he receiveth", what will he do with his enemies? "Many sorrows shall be to the wicked."

10. *But he that trusteth in the LORD, mercy shall compass him about.*

He always wants mercy; for he is a sinner still. He shall always have mercy; for his Saviour lives still. "Mercy shall compass him about."

11. *Be glad in the LORD, and rejoice, ye righteous: and shout for joy, all ye that are upright in heart.*

Be demonstrative; let men see that you are happy: "Shout for joy, all ye that are upright in heart." The Psalm is a joyful one, after all. David's experience has taken him through a deep sense of his own sin; but it has brought him out into an elevated sense of God's mercy; so he closes the Psalm with the jubilant exhortation, "Shout for joy, all ye that are upright in heart." So let us do this night, and for ever. Amen.

HYMNS FROM "OUR OWN HYMN BOOK"—686, 716, 749.

Metropolitan Tabernacle Pulpit.

PAUL THE READY.

A Sermon

INTENDED FOR READING ON LORD'S-DAY, DECEMBER 4TH, 1892,

DELIVERED BY

C. H. SPURGEON,

AT THE METROPOLITAN TABERNACLE, NEWINGTON,

On Thursday Evening, May 22nd, 1890.

"I am ready."—Romans i. 15.

I THINK Paul might have used these words as his motto. We had once a Saxon king called Ethelred the Unready; here we have an apostle who might be called Paul the Ready. The Lord Jesus no sooner called to him out of heaven, "Saul, Saul, why persecutest thou me?" than he answered, "Who art thou, Lord?" Almost directly after, his question was, "Lord, what wilt thou have me to do?" He was no sooner converted, than he was ready for holy service; and "straightway he preached Christ" in the synagogues at Damascus. All through his life, whatever happened to him, he was always ready. If he had to speak to crowds in the street, he had the fitting word; or if to the *élite* upon Mars' hill, he was ready for the philosophers. If he talked to the Pharisees, he knew how to address them; and when he was brought before the Sanhedrim, and perceived the Pharisaic and Sadducean elements in it, he knew how to avail himself of their mutual jealousies to help his own escape. See him before Felix, before Festus, before Agrippa, he is always ready; and when he came to stand before Nero, God was with him, and delivered him out of the mouth of the lion. If you find him on board ship, he is ready to comfort men in the storm; and when he gets on shore, a shipwrecked prisoner, he is ready to gather sticks, to help to make the fires. At all points he is an all-round man, and an all-ready man; always ready to go wherever his Master sends him, and to do whatever his Lord appoints him.

In talking at this time about Paul's readiness, I shall, first, dwell for a little while upon *the state of Paul's mind*, as indicated by his declaration, "I am ready." Secondly, I shall show that *this state of mind arose from excellent principles;* and, thirdly, I shall point out that *this readiness produces admirable results* wherever it is to be found.

I. First, let us consider THE STATE OF PAUL'S MIND, which enables him to say, "I am ready."

No. 2,285.

I shall refer you to four passages where he expresses his readiness. The first is our text. Here we have *Paul's readiness to work*. "So, as much as in me is, I am ready to preach the gospel to you that are at Rome also." He had preached the gospel throughout a great part of Asia, he had crossed over into Europe, he had proclaimed the Word through Greece; and if ever an opportunity should occur for him to get to the capital of the world, whatever might be the danger to which he would be exposed, he was prepared to go. He was ready to go anywhere for Jesus, anywhere to preach the gospel, anywhere to win a soul, anywhere to comfort the people of God. "I am ready." There is no place to which Paul was not ready to go. He was ready to make a journey into Spain; and if he did not come to this island of ours, which is a matter of question, undoubtedly he was ready to have gone to the utmost isles of the sea, and to lands and rivers unknown, to carry his Master's mighty Word. Are we as ready as Paul was to go anywhere for Jesus, or do we feel that we could only work for Christ at home, and that we should not dare to go to the United States, or to Australia, or into some heathen land? Oh, may God keep us always on tiptoe, ready to move if the cloud moves, and equally ready to stay where we are if the cloud moveth not!

If Paul went to Rome, he would be going into the lion's mouth; but he was ready for that, for lions had no kind of terror for him. He had fought with beasts at Ephesus. In spirit he had died in the mouth of the lion many a time, counting not his life dear unto him. I wish we were ready for all danger, all slander, all contumely, all poverty, all or anything that it might cost us to preach Christ where he is not known. The apostle was ready to go anywhere with the gospel, but he was not ready to preach another gospel; no one could make him ready to do that. He was not ready to hide the gospel, he was not ready to tone it down, he was not ready to abridge it or to extend it. He said, "I am not ashamed of the gospel of Christ: for it is the power of God unto salvation to everyone that believeth; to the Jew first, and also to the Greek." As to the matter of preaching the gospel, Paul was always ready for that; he kept not back any one of its truths, nor any part of its teaching. Even if it should bring upon him ridicule and contempt, though it should be to the Jews a stumbling block, and to the Greeks foolishness, Paul would say, "As much as in me is, I am ready to preach the gospel" to them all. He did not always feel alike fit for the work; he did not always find the same openings, or the same freedom in speech; but he was always ready to preach wherever the Lord gave him the opportunity.

If you will kindly turn to Acts xxi. 13, you will read, in the second place, of *Paul's readiness to suffer*. He says, "I am ready not to be bound only, but also to die at Jerusalem for the name of the Lord Jesus." This is perhaps a greater thing than the former one; to be ready to suffer is more than to be ready to serve. To some of us it has become a habit to be ready to preach the gospel; but here was a man who was ready to suffer for the name of the Lord Jesus; so ready that he could not be dissuaded from it. He might preach the gospel; but why must he go to Jerusalem? All the world was before him; why must he go to that persecuting city? Everybody told him that he would have bonds and imprisonment, and perhaps death; but he cared nothing about all that; he said, "I am ready, I am ready."

Beloved friends, are we ready to be scoffed at, to be thought idiots, to be put down amongst old-fashioned fossils? Perhaps so. Are we ready, if we should be required to do so, to lose friends for Christ's sake, to have the cold shoulder for Christ's sake? Perhaps so. Are we also ready, if it be the Lord's will, to go home, to be carried upstairs, and to lie there for the next three months? Are we as ready as that poor woman, who said, "The Lord said to me, 'Betty, mind the house, look after the children,' and I did it. By-and-by, he said, 'Betty, go upstairs, and cough twelve months.' Shall I not do that also, and not complain, for it is all that I can do?" "I am ready." You remember what is on the seal of the American Baptist Missionary Society, an ox with a plough on one side and a halter on the other, ready for either, ready to serve, or ready to suffer. You have not come to the highest style of readiness till you are ready for whatever the will of God may appoint for you. Unreadiness from this point of view is very common; but it shows unsubdued human nature. It is a relic of rebellion; for when we are fully sanctified, when every thought is brought into subjection to the mind of God, then the cry is not, "As I will," but "As thou wilt."

Ah! dear friends, while I am talking very feebly to you, I should not wonder but what you are saying to yourselves, "This is above us as yet; we shall need much more teaching of the Holy Spirit before we are ready for unknown sufferings, for lonely sufferings, for suffering that seemeth to have no good in it, useless suffering, for being put on the shelf, for being laid aside from the holy services of God's house, and from the little works that once we were able to do for Christ. Are you ready? Can you answer, "Ready, aye, ready"? So it should be with you if you belong to Christ; and so it was with Paul.

The third passage I must now quote is not exactly the same in words; but it means the same as the others. It tells us of *Paul's readiness to do unpleasant work.* I am afraid many of God's servants fall short here. The passage is in 2 Cor. x. 6: "And having in a readiness to revenge all disobedience, when your obedience is fulfilled." The church at Corinth had sunk into a very sad condition. It was a church that did not have any minister; it had an open ministry, and nobody knows what mischief comes of that kind of thing. Paul recommended them to try what a minister could do for them; for he said, "I beseech you, brethren, (ye know the house of Stephanas, that it is the firstfruits of Achaia, and that they have addicted themselves to the ministry of the saints,) that you submit yourselves unto such." They were too gifted for that, and everybody wanted to speak. When a church is all mouth, what becomes of the body? If it were all mouth, it would simply become a vacuum, nothing more; and the church in Corinth became very much that. It was nobody's business to administer discipline, for it was everybody's business; and what is everybody's business is nobody's business, as we well know; so no discipline was administered, and the church became what we call "all sixes and sevens." It stands in the Scriptures for ever as a warning against that method of church government, or, rather, of no church government at all.

Paul, when he went among these people, determined to administer discipline, and to try to put things right. He was not going to Corinth with a sword, or with any carnal weapon, or with anything of unkindness or hasty temper; but he was going with the Word of God. He wrote, "The weapons of our warfare are not carnal, but mighty through God to the pulling down of strongholds;" and he meant to go among the Corinthian professors, and pull down the stronghold of heathen vice that had entered the church to such an extent, that even at the Lord's table some of them were drunken. Paul meant to deal honestly with all who were dishonouring the name of Christ. Now, dear friends, I speak especially to brethren whom God has put into the ministry, or put into office in the church, are you ready for this unpleasant duty? Oh, it costs some of us a great deal to say a strong thing! Perhaps we cannot say it at all without getting into a temper; and then we had better not say it at all. It is not easy to have firmness in the language combined with sweetness in the manner of uttering it. It is easy to congratulate friends, it is not difficult to condemn them in the gross; but it is another think to speak personally and faithfully to each erring one, and to be assured in our own souls that, as far as we have any responsibility in the matter, we will not tolerate an Achan in the camp, and will not have evil done knowingly in the house of God. It should be our endeavour, as God has made us overseers, not to overlook things that are evil, but really to oversee everything that is committed to our charge, and to try to set right whatever is wrong.

Is it not the case with you who are private members of churches, do you not sometimes find it difficult to rebuke sin? Even profane swearing will come under the notice of many Christian people without a word of rebuke from them. They say they thought it best to hold their tongue; you mean you thought it easiest for yourselves. Sometimes known wickedness comes before the eyes of Christians, and they excuse themselves, and say, "We did not like to interfere." "Perhaps they were too gentle," you say; I suggest that they were too lazy, too much inclined to save their own precious skins, too anxious to have the soft side of this life, and not willing to endure hardness as good soldiers of Jesus Christ. Are you ready, as Paul was, to exhibit a holy indignation against sin, and lovingly and tenderly, yet firmly, in the name of the Lord to see that evil does not go unrebuked? If any man has come to this, I will not say that I envy him; but that I desire to be found in that position, so that, when the Lord cometh, none of the evil of this generation may lie at my door. When he shall come, and find his church lukewarm, faithless, adulterated by worldliness and all manner of heresies, I pray that he may not have to point his finger at unfaithful pastors, and say of any one of us, "Thou art the man who art responsible for this sad state of affairs." Oh, may God make us ready for whatever is laid upon us; however unpleasant and contrary to our mind and feeling the task may be, may we be ready to do the Lord's work, faithful even to the end!

Now, once more, will you kindly turn to 2 Timothy iv. 6, where you have a verse well known to you all, "For I am now ready to be offered, and the time of my departure is at hand." *Paul was ready to die;* he was ready to loose his cable from earth, and to sail away to the haven of the blessed; and well he might be, for he could add, "I have fought a good fight, I have finished my course, I have kept the faith: henceforth there is laid up for me a crown of righteousness, which the Lord, the righteous Judge, shall give me at that day; and not to me only, but unto all them also that love his appearing." Beloved friends, we cannot be ready to die unless we have been taught how to live. We who are active, and have talents to use, and health and strength with which to use those talents, must go on with "the greatest fight in the world" till we can say, "I have fought a good fight." We must go on running the Christian race till we can say, "I have finished my course." We must go on guarding the Word of God, and holding fast the truth of God, till we can say, "I have kept the faith." It will be hard work to lie dying if we have been unfaithful. God's infinite mercy may come in, and forgive and help us; and we may be "saved; yet so as by fire;" but if we would look forward to death with perfect readiness, having no dread or fear about it, but being as ready to die as we are to go to our beds to-night, then we must be kept faithful to God by his almighty grace. The faith must keep us, and we must keep the faith.

Thus, you see, Paul was ready for service, ready for suffering, ready for unpleasant duty, and ready to die. If I were to go round this Tabernacle, and ask of everyone, "My friend, are you ready in these four ways?" how many of you would be able to answer, "We are ready"? I am afraid many would have to shake their heads, and say, "I do not know what to say; I am doing my best in some style, but I cannot say that I have the readiness which the apostle claimed."

II. Let me show you now that PAUL'S READINESS AROSE FROM EXCELLENT PRINCIPLES. That is our second point.

As for Paul's *readiness to preach*, I should trace that to his solemn conviction of the truth of the gospel. If a man only *thinks* it is true, he will not care whether he preaches it, or does not preach it; but if he *knows* it is true, then he must preach it. I do not think we need find much fault with people nowadays for being too positive and dogmatic about the truth of God; the present current runs in quite another direction. A feeble faith, which might almost be mistaken for unbelief, is the common thing; and hence there is no great readiness to speak. Paul wrote to the Corinthians, "As it is written, I believed, and therefore have I spoken; we also believe, and therefore speak." If I get a grip of a thing and know it is true, then I must tell it to others. The backbone of the preaching of Christ is a conviction of the truth of Christ.

Paul also had a dauntless courage in this matter. He said, "Woe is unto me if I preach not the gospel!" Whatever happened to him if he did preach it, he had counted the cost, and he was quite ready for all the consequences of his action. He had a holy self-denial; so that he put himself out of the question. "I am ready for anything; I am ready to preach this gospel, if I am stoned, if I am thrown out of the city as dead, if I am imprisoned, if I am sent into the den of Cæsar at Rome." Paul was ready, because his courage had been given him of God.

Paul was ready to preach the gospel at Rome because he had freed himself from all entanglement. You know how he put it, in writing to his son Timothy, "No man that warreth entangleth himself with the affairs of this life; that he may please him who hath chosen him to be a soldier." There are some of us who get so tied up, and entangled, that we are not ready to do God's service because we are all in knots through too much worldly business. Try, dear friends, you who are the servants of Christ, to keep yourselves as clear as you can of all entanglements. You have your living to earn; but serve God while you are earning it. If you see an opportunity of getting rich, but in order to do so you will have to deny yourself from Christ's work, you will have to give up week-night services, and so on, do not thus entangle yourself; keep yourself as clear as you can. Her Majesty does not expect one of her soldiers to take to farming, and then to send word that he cannot go to battle because he has to get in his hay harvest, or he has his wheat to cut. He must come whenever he is called; and blessed is that good soldier of Jesus Christ who can come when he is wanted by his King and Captain. Sir Colin Campbell, when told that he was wanted to go to India, was asked, "How long will you take to get ready, Sir Colin?" He replied, "Twenty-four hours"; and in twenty-four hours he was ready to go. A Moravian was about to be sent by Zinzendorf to preach in Greenland. He had never heard of it before; but his leader called him, and said, "Brother, will you go to Greenland?" He answered, "Yes, sir." "When will you go?" "When my boots come home from the cobbler;" and he did go as soon as his boots came home. He wanted nothing else but just that pair of boots, and he was ready to go. Paul, not even waiting for his boots to come home from the cobbler, says, "I am ready." Oh, it is grand to find a man so little entangled that he can go where God would have him go, and can go at once.

Paul had, besides, such love for men, whether they were Jews, or Romans, or any other people, that he was ready to go anywhere to save them. He had also such zeal for God that it was a happiness to him to think of going to the furthest region if he might but preach Christ where He was not known; not building on another man's foundation, but laying the first stone of the edifice himself. This, then, accounted for his readiness to preach; a holy conviction of the truth of what he had to preach, and of the need of preaching it.

But what helped Paul to be *ready to suffer?* Some here will have to suffer for Jesus Christ's sake, though they may never be called to preach. Well, I should say, dear friends, first, that Paul was completely consecrated to the Lord. He was not his own, he was bought with a price; and that led him to feel that his Master might do whatever he liked with him. He belonged to Christ, he was Jesus Christ's branded slave, and he was absolutely at Christ's disposal. Moreover, he had such trust in his Lord that he felt, "whatever he does with me, it will be good and kind, and therefore I will make no condition, I will have no reserve from him; it is the Lord, let him do what seemeth him good." He had resolved to serve his Lord; and, therefore, if he had to be bound, or to die, he would not shrink back. He could have sung, as we sometimes sing, but he could carry it out better than we do,—

"Through floods and flames, if Jesus lead,
I'll follow where he goes."

A whole-hearted consecration, a child-like confidence, a deep-toned submission, these will make us ready for suffering, whatever it may be.

But however did Paul screw himself up to be *ready to exercise discipline?* That is, to me, the ugliest point of all. How could he bring himself to be able to do that? I think it was because he had not received his gospel of men, nor by men; and he had learned not to depend upon men, nor to look for their approval as the support of his life. He was able to lean on the Saviour, and to walk alone with his Lord. So long as he had Christ with him, he wanted nobody else. Paul had learned the fear of God, which casteth out the fear of man. "Who art thou, that thou shouldest be afraid of a man that shall die, and of the son of man which shall be made as grass; and forgettest the Lord thy Maker?" Remembering man leads to the forgetting of God. If we learn to speak very plainly, yet very lovingly, habitually cultivating frankness towards all Christian people, and even towards the ungodly, and do not know what it is to ask of any man leave to speak the truth, how much better it will be all round! May the Holy Spirit deepen in us the fear of God, and so take away from us the fear of man! Then, with Paul, each of us will be ready to say, even concerning the most unpleasant duty, "I am ready."

But how came he to be able to say that he was *ready to die?* I will not dwell upon that. I have already told you that he felt ready to die because he could say that, as far as he had gone, he had finished the work God gave him to do, and he had kept the faith. Ah, dear friends, it is nothing but keeping faithful to God that will enable you to treat death as a friend! One dereliction of duty will be sufficient to rob you of comfort. When a traveller is walking, a very small stone in his shoe will lame him; and a very small offence against the integrity that God requires of his servants may do us great mischief. Did you ever notice, in Gideon's life, that he had seventy sons, his own legitimate sons, and that he had one son who was the child of a harlot, and that one, Abimelech, killed his father's seventy sons? So it may be that a good man has seventy virtues, but if he tolerates one wrong thing, it will be enough to rob him of the comfort of all the good things of this life, so that, when he comes to die, he may go limping and lame. Ay, and all his life long, he may go, like David did, halting even to the grave. May the Lord in mercy and love keep us right! If he teaches us how to live, we shall know how to die.

It is not dying that is the great difficulty; it is living. If we are but helped to fight the good fight of faith, to finish our course, and to keep the faith, we shall die right enough. As Mr. Wesley said when the good woman asked him, "Do you not sometimes feel an awe at the thought of dying?" "No," he replied, "If I knew for certain that I was going to die to-morrow night, I should do just exactly what I am going to do. I am going to preach (I think it was) at Gloucester this afternoon, and this evening; and I shall go to lodge with friend So-and-so. I shall stay up with him till ten o'clock, and then I shall go to bed; and I shall be up at five, and ride over to Tewkesbury; and I shall preach there, and shall go to friend So-and-so's for the night; and I shall go to bed at ten o'clock, and whether I live or not, it does not matter at all to me, for if I die, I shall wake up in glory. That is what I am going to do, whether I live or die." It was said of Mr. Whitefield, that he never went to bed at night, leaving even a pair of gloves out of its place; he used to say that he would like to have everything ready in case he might be taken away. I think I see that good man standing, with a bedroom candle in his hand, at the top of the staircase, preaching Christ the last night of his life to the people sitting on the stairs; and then going inside the room, and commending himself to God; and going straight away to heaven. That is the way to die; but if you do not live like Wesley and Whitefield lived, you cannot die like Wesley and Whitefield died. May God grant us grace that we may be perfectly ready to die when the time for our departure is at hand!

III. Now I finish by saying that THIS READINESS PRODUCES ADMIRABLE RESULTS.

First, *it prevents surprise.* It is always bad to be taken by surprise. He who lives unto the Lord shall not fear evil tidings, for his heart is fixed, trusting in the Lord. If you are perfectly submissive to God's will, and, as you crossed your threshold to-night, you heard that your child was dead, or that your dearest friend was smitten with sore sickness, you would say, "Well, I stoop to the surrender; when I had my children, I did not think they were immortal; I knew they would die, and I have stood ready for anything that might happen to them." Oh, brethren, it is because we are not submissive, not sanctified, not fully resigned to God's will, that we get tripped up every now and then, and do not quite know where we are! May the Lord give us the grace to be prepared for every emergency!

Again, when a man is ready, *it prevents loss of time and opportunity.* Many a sportsman has lost his bird because he was not ready to take aim; many a fisherman has lost his fish because he has not been ready to grasp his rod, and put the line into the stream. Many a preacher has, no doubt, missed the mark because, when he might have said a word for Christ, he was not ready to say it. Have you not often gone home, and said to yourself, "Now I recollect what I ought to have said. That man made an observation, and I could not tell at the moment what to reply to it; I know now what I should have said"? It is a fine thing to be wise when it is too late; but it would be much better if we waited upon God, and asked him to make us ready, ever ready, to speak for him in every place, and at any time, whenever an opportunity occurs.

Readiness also helps us *to make good use of every occasion.* He who is ready as each occasion comes, not only snatches the first part of it, but all the rest of it; he is prepared to deal with the whole thing as it proceeds. He who is always doing his Master's work learns how to do it well, but he who only does it occasionally is like a bad workman who half forgets his craft because he is so much engaged in doing something else. God keep us all ready! May you be ready to-night to say a good word to somebody on your way home, and to serve God in your family when you get home!

To be ready *puts a bloom on obedience,* and presents it to God at its best. Some Sunday-school children were once asked what was the meaning of doing the will of God on earth as it is done in heaven; and they gave some very pretty answers. One said, "In heaven they do God's will always;" another said, "They do God's will cheerfully;" but one said, "Please, Sir, they do God's will directly." That is the thing; that is how it is done in heaven, directly. May we be in such a state of heart that we are ready to do the Lord's will directly!

In this readiness, our *obedience is multiplied;* I mean, that any one act is multiplied, for the man who is ready to do the right thing has already done it in the sight of God. The Lord accepts it as done; and then, if the man still remains ready, he does, as it were, do the thing again, and when it is actually done he is still ready to do it again. If the act is only one, yet to God's eye it hath a teeming multitude of obedient actions swarming around it.

To be ready, especially to be ready to die, *removes all fear of death.* I wish we could all sing as she did, who died in her sleep, and left this verse written on a piece of paper by her bedside,—

> "Since Jesus is mine, I'll not fear undressing,
> But gladly put off these garments of clay;
> To die in the Lord, is a covenant blessing,
> Since Jesus to glory through death led the way."

If we are ready as Paul was, all fear of death will be gone from us.

And I think it *takes away a thousand ills* if we are ready for service, ready for suffering, ready to die. I will tell you one thing, dear sister over yonder, you would not be so ready to halt as you are if you were ready for the Lord's work and the Lord's will. And you who are ready to perish, would get out of that sad kind of readiness if you came and trusted Christ, and became ready to suffer, or to do the Master's will. The Lord is ready to pardon; may we be ready to believe, and may we come at once to Him, accept salvation through Jesus Christ, and then all through the rest of our lives say to the great Captain of our salvation what good sailors reply to their captain's call, "Ready, aye ready! Ready for storms and ready for calms; ready for whatever Thou dost command, ready for whatever Thou dost ordain!" The Lord bless you, dear friends, and give all of you this readiness, for Christ's sake! Amen.

Exposition by C. H. Spurgeon.

ISAIAH LXIII.

Some of you will remember that chapter lxii. ends with the announcement of the Saviour's coming: "Say ye to the daughter of Zion, behold, thy salvation cometh; behold, his reward is with him, and his work before him." The present chapter describes his coming.

Verse 1. *Who is this that cometh from Edom, with dyed garments from Bozrah?*

Who can HE be, this mysterious personage, this friend of God's people, this destroyer of their enemies? Who can HE be?

> "Who is this that comes from Edom,
> All his raiment stain'd with blood;
> To the slave proclaiming freedom;
> Bringing and bestowing good:
> Glorious in the garb he wears,
> Glorious in the spoils he bears?"

1. *This that is glorious in his apparel, travelling in the greatness of his strength? I that speak in righteousness, mighty to save.*

He that has come to save us is majestic in his person, but he is also mighty in his power to save. When we ask, "Who is this?" the answer comes to us, "I that speak in righteousness, mighty to save." Listen to this, you who feel that you are great sinners, you who know that you need a mighty Saviour. Here is one able to do for you all that you need. He comes from the field of battle, from the place of conquest, where he has fought the fight on your behalf, and won for you the victory over sin, and death, and hell. Who is he?

> "'Tis the Saviour, now victorious,
> Travelling onward in his might;
> 'Tis the Saviour, oh, how glorious
> To his people is the sight!
> Jesus now is strong to save;
> Mighty to redeem the slave."

2, 3. *Wherefore art thou red in thine apparel, and thy garments like him that treadeth in the winefat? I have trodden the winepress alone; and of the people there was none with me:*

In all Christ's redeeming work he was alone. None could help him to redeem his people. He must alone pay the ransom price. None could help him in his last great battle, when he stood forth as the sole Champion of all whom his Father had given to him.

> "Death and hell will he dethrone,
> By his single arm alone."

3, 4. *For I will tread them in mine anger, and trample them in my fury; and their blood shall be sprinkled upon my garments, and I will stain all my raiment. For the day of vengeance is in mine heart, and the year of my redeemed is come.*

It was the day of vengeance on the enemies of God, vengeance on sin, and death, and hell; and it was the year of redemption for the great host of believers in Christ, for whom his garments were dyed in his own most precious blood. Notice how the great Redeemer speaks of his chosen people: "My redeemed."

5, 6. *And I looked, and there was none to help; and I wondered that there was none to uphold: therefore mine own arm brought salvation unto me; and my fury, it upheld me. And I will tread down the people in mine anger, and make them drunk in my fury, and I will bring down their strength to the earth.*

Dear friends, I will not go into a full explanation of these verses just now; I have often explained them to you; but this is the one lesson that they teach, there is a Saviour "mighty to save." Nothing can destroy those who put their trust in him; he will overthrow every enemy of our souls if we take him to be our Saviour.

Now the prophet speaks again:—

7. *I will mention the lovingkindnesses of the LORD, and the praises of the LORD, according to all that the LORD hath bestowed on us, and the great goodness toward the house of Israel, which he hath bestowed on them according to his mercies, and according to the multitude of his lovingkindnesses.*

It is well to talk of God's love and God's mercy, for, if we afterwards speak of our own sin and unfaithfulness, it tends to set our sin in a clearer light, and we are the more ready to confess it, and to mourn over it. God has dealt well with us; and, therefore, that we have dealt ill with him, is the more shameful. See what he did for his ancient people, and behold in his action a picture of what he has done for his spiritual Israel.

8. *For he said, Surely they are my people, children that will not lie: so he was their Saviour.*

He thought well of them, he said, "They will be true to me." He loved them; he chose them; he put them in a place of trust and honour; he entered into fellowship and sympathy with them.

9. *In all their affliction he was afflicted, and the angel of his presence saved them: in his love and in his pity he redeemed them; and he bare them, and carried them all the days of old.*

This is what he did for them in Egypt, what he did for them in the desert. He was very near them, one with them, very tender to them.

10. *But they rebelled, and vexed his holy Spirit; therefore he was turned to be their enemy, and he fought against them.*

Hear ye this, ye people of God! This is what God will do to you if you rebel against him, and vex his Holy Spirit; he will turn to be your enemy, and will fight against you. If God's people will not yield to his love and his pity, they must suffer from his hand and his rod.

11. *Then he remembered the days of old, Moses, and his people, saying, Where is he that brought them up out of the sea with the shepherd of his flock? where is he that put his holy Spirit within him?*

God begins to think of the past, and of what he did for his people in the days of old.

12—14. *That led them by the right hand of Moses with his glorious arm, dividing the water before them, to make himself an everlasting name? That led them through the deep, as an horse in the wilderness, that they should not stumble? As a beast goeth down into the valley, the Spirit of the LORD caused him to rest: so didst thou lead thy people, to make thyself a glorious name.*

See what God did for his people in his tenderness and lovingkindness. Is it not strange that, after that, they rebelled against him?

15. *Look down from heaven, and behold from the habitation of thy holiness and of thy glory: where is thy zeal and thy strength, the sounding of thy bowels and of thy mercies toward me? are they restrained?*

If you are in trouble to-night, if you have lost the light of God's countenance, here are words for you to use in prayer to God.

16. *Doubtless thou art our father, though Abraham be ignorant of us, and*

Israel acknowledge us not: thou, O LORD, art our father, our redeemer; thy name is from everlasting.

Get a hold of this great truth, believer. Say, "God is my Father. He is my Father still; and though he smite me, though he frown upon me, I will not quit my hold on him; I will still plead his dear Son's name, and wait for his mercy, trusting in his grace."

17—19. *O LORD, why hast thou made us to err from thy ways, and hardened our heart from thy fear? Return for thy servants' sake, the tribes of thine inheritance. The people of thy holiness have possessed it but a little while: our adversaries have trodden down thy sanctuary. We are thine: thou never barest rule over them; they were not called by thy name.*

I pointed out to you, at the beginning of our reading, that this chapter appropriately follows the preceding one. It is itself most suitably followed by chapter lxiv.; indeed, the first verse of that chapter belongs to this one, and should not have been separated from it. God's people, in their low estate, recognized that deliverance must come from the Lord alone, so they prayed, "Oh that thou wouldest rend the heavens, that thou wouldest come down, that the mountains might flow down at thy presence, as when the melting fire burneth, the fire causeth the waters to boil, to make thy name known to thine adversaries, that the nations may tremble at thy presence!" God bless the reading of his Word, and give us his presence during the whole of the service, for Christ's sake. Amen!

HYMNS FROM "OUR OWN HYMN BOOK"—639, 694, 658.

"THE SWORD AND THE TROWEL."

TABLE OF CONTENTS, DECEMBER, 1892.

Beaten Oil for the Light. An Address to the Students of the Pastors' College. By C. H. SPURGEON.
Nature, God's Handiwork. By James Crowther.
The Preacher among his People. By Arthur T. Pierson, D.D.
Different Styles of Preaching. By C. H. SPURGEON.
Mr. Thomas Spurgeon's Volume of Poems. (A Review, with Extracts, from *Scarlet Threads and Bits of Blue*, just published by Messrs. Passmore and Alabaster, price 1s., and 1s. 6d.)
Lessons from the Loom. By Pastor J. Peden, Foxton, Leicestershire.
Mr. Spurgeon's Last Drives at Menton. By Joseph W. Harrald. (With two illustrations.)
"Ecce Rex!" (Poetry.) By Pastor E. A. Tydeman.
"It is Finished." By C. H. SPURGEON. (Copied from a young lady's album.)
"John Ploughman's" Last Messages.
A Tiny Teacher from the Orphanage.
Joy from the Word of God. By Thomas Boston.
The Old Hermit. By Pastor Albert Priter, Shipley, Yorkshire.
Another Trophy of the Hop-pickers' Mission. By John Burnham.
A Promising Work in Leicester. A Statement and an Appeal by W. Y. Fullerton. (Illustrated.)
Notices of Books.
Notes. (Pastor Charles Spurgeon. Mr. Thomas Spurgeon. Dr. Pierson. Deaths of Mr. John T. Olney, Mr. W. C. Murrell, and Mr. J. Alabaster. Tabernacle Maternal Society. Home Counties' Baptist Association. Tabernacle Loan Tract Association. Surrey Gardens Memorial Hall. Tabernacle Sunday-school Teachers' Soirée. Mr. Dunn's Bible-class. College. College Missionary Association. Evangelists. Orphanage. Colportage. Personal Notes by Mrs. C. H. Spurgeon.)
Lists of Contributions.
Preface and Index to Volume XXVIII.
Index of Texts of Sermons, &c., by C. H. SPURGEON in Volumes I. to XXVIII.

Price 3d. Post-free, 4½d.

LONDON: PASSMORE AND ALABASTER, PATERNOSTER BUILDINGS, and all Booksellers.

Metropolitan Tabernacle Pulpit.

AN ANCIENT QUESTION MODERNIZED.

A Sermon

INTENDED FOR READING ON LORD'S-DAY, DECEMBER 11TH, 1892,

DELIVERED BY

C. H. SPURGEON,

AT THE METROPOLITAN TABERNACLE, NEWINGTON,

On Lord's-day Evening, May 4th, 1890.

"And the people said unto me, Wilt thou not tell us what these things are to us, that thou doest so?"—Ezekiel xxiv. 19.

EZEKIEL'S wife died. His heart was bleeding; but he received orders from his divine Master that he should not mourn, nor weep, nor make any sign of mourning whatever. It was a strange command, but he obeyed it. The people understood that Ezekiel was a prophet to them in all that he did; his actions did not concern himself alone. He was a teacher, not only by his words, but by his acts; so the people gathered round him, and said to him, "What is the meaning of this? It has some bearing upon our conduct; tell us what it has to do with us." He soon explained to them that, before long, they also would lose by sword, and pestilence, and famine, the dearest that they had, and they would not be able to have any mourning for the dead. They would be themselves in such a state of distress that the dead would die unlamented, the living having enough to do to mourn over their own personal sorrows. It was a terrible lesson, and it was terribly taught.

Now, dear friends, just as Ezekiel, at his Lord's command, did many strange things entirely with a view to other people, we must remember that many things that we do have some relation to others. As long as we are here, we can never so isolate ourselves as to become absolutely independent of our surroundings; and it is often well, when we note the behaviour of other people, to say to somebody, if not to them, as the people did to Ezekiel, "Wilt thou not tell us what these things are to us?"

I am going to use the text at this time thus. First, *this should be your question to the Lord Jesus Christ, our divine Prophet.* When we see him taken forth to die without the camp, may we not solemnly say to him, "Wilt thou not tell us what these things are to us, that thou doest so?" When I have spoken a little upon that, I shall then say to the people who will see us gathering at the table of our Lord

No. 2,286.

to-night, *this may be your question to the church,* "Wilt thou not tell us what these things are to us, that thou doest so?" After I have explained that matter, I shall want to speak to our friends who are not coming to the communion-table with us, but are going home, or going to sit in the upper gallery, and I shall say to them, *this is our question to you,* "Wilt thou not tell us what these things are to us, that thou doest so?"

I. First, then, THIS SHOULD BE YOUR QUESTION TO THE LORD JESUS. Very reverently, though, as far as I am concerned, very feebly, let us approach our divine Master, and looking at him in his wondrous passion, let us earnestly ask him, "Wilt thou not tell us what these things are to us, that thou doest so?" Do you see him? There he is, amid the dark shadow of the olives, bending low, and pleading with God. He pleads, and pleads, and pleads again till he is covered with sweat. Sweat, did I say? 'Tis blood, and it is so plenteous that it falleth to the earth, "*great drops of blood falling down to the ground.*" Man sweats for bread, which is the staff of life; but it needs a bloody sweat to win life itself, and Jesus pours it out. Dear Master, while that bitter cup is at thy lip, canst thou stay a minute to tell us what these things are to us that thou doest so? His answer is, "Sin is an exceedingly bitter thing; and to remove it, costs me the agony of my soul. It is not easy to bear the wrath of God; I have cried, 'If it be possible, let this cup pass from me;' but if I would save you, it is not possible." Hear that, my brethren, listen, and learn it well. Never trifle with sin; never make a spot which will need a bloody sweat to wash it away. Never laugh at that over which Christ had to agonize; and never count redemption a trifle when to him it was a pouring out of his soul unto death.

But do you see through the trees the lanterns twinkling? Men are coming, evil men, with rough voices, with torches, and lanterns, and staves to take the blessed pleading One. He rises to meet them; he speaks a word, and down they fall. He can release himself, there is no need for him to be captured; but *he yields himself up without a struggle;* and they take him to do unto him according to their wicked will. Dear Master, while the traitor's kiss is still wet upon thee, and thou art being led away bound to Caiaphas, tell me, I pray thee, what meanest thou by all this? What has this to do with us? He answers, "I go willingly; I must be bound, for sin has bound you; sin has bound your hands, sin has hampered and crippled you, and made you prisoners. You are the bond-slaves of Satan, and I must be bound to set you free." O beloved, learn the lesson well. Sin always enslaves you. Free thought, free love, free living, in the highest sense, are to be found alone in the service of God; sin brings no freedom, it binds. As Christ was bound and delivered up to die, so does sin bind man, and lead him forth to the second death. This is what Jesus Christ's resignation to his captors means to us.

But now they have taken him before his judges. He stands before Annas, and Caiaphas, and Pilate. His enemies accuse him violently; but *he answers them not a word.* Pilate says to him "Answerest thou me nothing?" Blessed Sufferer, like a lamb in the midst of wolves, tell us, if thou wilt speak a word, why this silence? And he whispers into the hearts of his beloved, "I was silent, for there was nothing to say;· willing to be your Advocate, what could I say? You had sinned, though I had not. I might have pleaded for myself; but I stood there for you, in your room, and place, and stead; and what could I say, what excuse, what apology, what extenuation could I urge?" All that could be said was, "Guilty, Lord, guilty." That is all that you may dare to say to God, for you have nothing to plead when you stand upon the ground of your own merits; and so the silent Christ was eloquent in the condemnation of sin; and we thank him that he answered not a word, when wicked men clamoured against him.

But now, do you see, they are scourging him, they are crowning him with thorns, they are mocking him, blindfolding him, and then smiting him with the palms of their hands? *What scorn, what shame, they poured on him!* Blessed One, blessed One, wilt thou not tell us what these things are to us? I think I hear him speak from that sacred head, once wounded, and he says, "I must be put to shame, for sin is a shameful thing. No scorn is too great for sin, it deserves to be loathed, to be treated with contempt, to be dashed over the walls of the universe as a thing unclean, mean, despicable." Christ, in that great shame of his, teaches us to hate sin, to treat it with contempt, to turn away from it with loathing, for it is a mean thing for a creature to rebel against his Creator, for a man to be an enemy of his God.

But now, you see, they take him out through the streets of Jerusalem; along the *Via Dolorosa* he pursues his weary walk, blood-drops falling on the pavement, himself staggering beneath the load of the cross. Why do they not let him rest? Those weeping women could have found him shelter. No, he must not rest, Jerusalem cannot hold him, there is not a house that can retain him, there is not one who can give him shelter, for *he is going out to die.* He must go without the city gate. I do not know whether there was, or was not, "a green hill far away"; but I know that it was "without the city wall." My Master, my Master, why goest thou without the city wall? Tell me, Jesus, why goest thou out there, to the place of public execution, the Old Bailey, the Tyburn of Jerusalem? Why art thou here? And he answers, "I suffer without the gate because God will not tolerate sin in his city. Sin is an unclean thing; and I, though not myself unclean, yet standing in the stead of the unclean, must die outside the city gates." And so I see him, as they throw him on his back, and nail his hands and feet to the cross, and then lift him up as a gazingstock for guilty men. Oh! why, oh! why, thou Son of God, art thou lifted up like the brazen serpent of Moses? Why are thou lifted up between earth and heaven? And he answers, "That I may draw all men unto me. Earth refuses me, and heaven denies me shelter, I hang here, the Just for the unjust, that I may bring men to God." How I wish that I could speak this explanation of my crucified Master in more piercing and penetrating, and yet more tender tones! My hearers, you must understand this sublime mystery, or you cannot be saved. Jesus dies, that we may not die. He is made a curse, that we may have the blessing. He is treated as a felon, that we may be treated as the children of God. Blessed be his name, thus has he told us what these things are to us that he does so!

They take him down from the cross, for he is dead; but before they take him down, they pierce his heart, and even after death that heart for us its tribute pours. Somewhere, amongst the matter of the globe, is the very blood and water that flowed from his side; and though perhaps nobody thinks with me, yet I set it over against the fact that, somewhere on the earth, are the pieces of the two tables of stone which Moses broke beneath the mount. Better still, Christ's wondrous atonement is always here, always operating, always reconciling men to God, always opening a way of access for guilty men to the righteous Lord. Again I say, blessed be his holy name!

But they have buried him, and he lies in his cell alone through the long, dark night of death; but *the third morning sees him rise.* Or ever the sun is up, the Sun of Righteousness has arisen, with healing in his wings. Jesus has quitted the tomb, and I invite all sinners to say to the risen Redeemer, " Wilt thou not tell us what these things are to us, that thou doest so?" This is what I understand that his resurrection means to us, he is able to save to the uttermost them that come unto God by him, seeing he ever liveth to make intercession for them.

He not only rises from the dead; but *he ascends to his Father.* He has gone home now; the cloud received him out of the sight of his followers. With the sound of the great trumpets of glory he has returned to his kingdom, and to his throne. Ask him what he means by that, and he will tell you that he has led captivity captive, and "received gifts for men, yea, for the rebellious also." What a word is that to every heart that is conscious of rebellion! Christ has received gifts for you. Learn that lesson, I pray you. Believe on him, and live. Cast yourself at his feet, and be forgiven. Yield yourself up to him, and be his servant henceforth and for ever.

This is a wide theme; but my strength will not enable me to say more upon this part of it, namely, our question to the Lord Jesus.

II. Now, dear friends, in a few minutes we shall lift the damask covering from the communion-table, and you will find upon it a supply of bread and wine. We are coming to that table to think of our Lord, and I think that I hear some of you ask, " Wilt thou not tell us what these things are to us, that thou doest so?" THIS MAY BE YOUR QUESTION TO THE CHURCH. That will be our second point.

We are coming here, to-night, *to keep Christ's death in remembrance.* I love to see our dear friends come to the Lord's table as often as they can. I am very sorry if I cannot be here every week; for, if there be a time appointed for the breaking of bread, it is the first day of the week. Every first day of the week, if you can, come to the table as a part of your Sabbath worship. This service is intended to be a memorial of Christ's death. The best memorial of an event is not to rear a column, or erect a statue, or engrave a record on brass. All these things are frail and pass away. The tooth of time eats up the brass; the foot of the ages dashes down the statue or the column. The best memorial of any event is to associate with it the observance of some rite, or some ceremony frequently repeated; this will cause it to be a perpetual memorial. Now, as long as half-a-dozen Christians meet together for the breaking of bread, Christ's death can never be forgotten. However poor you may be, or however illiterate, when you come to the breaking of bread, you are helping to record, as in eternal brass, the greatest fact in all human history, the fact that Jesus Christ died for our sins according to the Scriptures. If this were all, it would be no little thing. It means to you who do not come just this, that some of us mean to keep this memorial before our eyes. You may forget it; but to you our action is so far significant, that, whatever you may do, we mean to perpetuate as long as we live, and we trust that our children after us will perpetuate this which we esteem to be a priceless fact, that the Son of God died for guilty men, the Sinless One for the sinful, to bring them to God. That is what this memorial has to do with you.

We are not, however, coming to the table merely to look at the bread and the wine. We are coming there *to eat and to drink, to show our personal benefit by Jesus Christ's death.* We wish all who see us to know that we enjoy the result of Christ's death. We have a life that feeds upon his sacrifice; we have a hope that makes Christ to be its very meat and drink. There is a something about Christ who died that is indeed life-giving and that is sustaining and strengthening to our new-born spirit. If you are up in the gallery, as spectators of the ordinance, you say to us by your actions, "Tell us what these things are to us." Well, we have to say this to you, that if you will not have these emblems of Jesus Christ's death to be your meat and drink, at any rate, we will. What we say further to you is, if you do not feed on Christ, why do you not feed on him? Have you any better bread? Have you any firmer faith than the faith we have in his atoning sacrifice? Have you a deeper peace than Jesus gives to us? Have you a surer hope of heaven than faith in Christ gives? Have you a brighter hope? We know you have not; and, therefore, while to us his flesh is meat indeed, and his blood is drink indeed, we say that these things are to you a rebuke, a question, a suggestion concerning something lacking in you.

But, beloved friends, we not only come to the table to eat and to drink, but there is this point about the communion, that *we come together to declare our unity in Jesus Christ.* If I went home, and broke bread, and drank of the juice of the vine by myself alone, it would not be the observance of the Lord's Supper. It is a united participation. It is a festival. It is a token and display of brotherhood. Those who will come to the table to-night will say practically, "We are one, 'We, being many, are one body of Jesus Christ, and everyone members one of another.'" I think that I hear you say, "Wilt thou not tell us what these things are to us, that thou doest so!" Well, they are to you this, if you do not believe in Christ, you are not of the brotherhood. If you do not feed upon Christ, you are not one with him, you are not one of his people. There is another brotherhood; and if you do not belong to the brotherhood of Christ, you belong to the other fraternity. They who are not with Isaac are with Ishmael; they who are not with Jacob are with Esau; they who are not the seed of the woman are the seed of the serpent. To-night, as with a drawn sword, Christ divides this congregation into two parts. If you believe in him, you are his; but if you believe not in him, there is a present condemnation resting upon you. It is well that you should know this fact, when God's people come together for the communion, it incidentally means that they leave the rest of the congregation behind.

Once more, when this communion is over, if we live, we shall meet again next Lord's-day, and when that is over, if we are spared, we shall meet again the following Lord's-day. *We meet continually, to show our belief in Jesus Christ's coming again.* More than fifty-two times in the year is this table spread in our midst; for, frequently, in different parts of the Tabernacle, the elders and deacons and other friends meet, and commune with the Lord, doing this often in remembrance of him. Here is the point to which I call your attention, we are to do this "until he come." Every celebration of the Lord's supper speaks, not with the voice of a trumpet, but still with a clear sound, and it says, "The Lord is coming. He is on the way back. This is one of the tokens that he is coming again." As for himself, before he went away, he took the great Nazarite vow. He said that he would drink no more of the fruit of the vine till he should drink it new with his disciples in his Father's kingdom; and he remained the great Abstainer, who had sworn never to drink of the cup till he should pledge them again in the new wine of his Father's kingdom; but he bids us go on drinking of it until he shall come again to receive us unto himself, that where he is there we may be also.

Perhaps you still enquire, "Wilt thou not tell us what these things are to us, that thou doest so?" Well, they are this to you, that, whether you remember Jesus Christ's coming or not, he is coming; he is coming quickly. When you read, "Behold, I come quickly," it does not mean, "I shall be here soon;" but it means, "I am coming quickly." A man may be coming quickly from New York to-night, and yet he may not be here to-morrow, he may not be here for another week, but he is coming quickly all the same. Christ is coming as quickly as he can; long leagues of distance lie between him and us, and he is covering them with the utmost speed. The glowing wheels of his chariot, whose axles are hot with the haste of his journey, are hurrying over the weary way; he is coming quickly. I should not be surprised, certainly I should not be distressed, if he came before I have finished this sermon. Could you all say as much as that? Oh, how some of us would stand up, and welcome him with gladdest acclaim if he should make his blessed presence manifest upon this platform before this evening's service is over! I know no reason why he should not come to-night. The times and seasons are all unknown to us. We venture upon no prophecy; but as often as we come to the communion-table, we say to you, "He will come." When he comes, the day of the Lord will be darkness, and not light, to every unbeliever. When he comes, woe unto his adversaries! How will they face their Judge? Now Judas, come and kiss him! Now Pilate, ask him "what is truth?" Now, ye Jews, come and spit in his face! Now, impenitent thief, come and cast bitter sayings in his teeth! What are they at? See how they try to slink away; they have not a word to say. Nay, I hear them burst into agonizing shrieks, crying to the mountains and rocks, "Fall on us, and hide us from the face of him that sitteth on the throne, and from the wrath of the Lamb: for the great day of his wrath is come;

and who shall be able to stand?" Ah! you, who used to brag and boast, sing another tune now that Christ has come! You who despised him, you who would have nought to do with him, what would you not give if he were now your Friend? Make him to be your Friend to-night by putting your trust in him, and then you will be ready for his coming. Let him come when he may, his coming will be full of love and joy to all who have trusted him.

Thus I have answered two sets of questions, first for my Master, and then for my brethren in the church.

III. Now, in closing, THIS IS OUR QUESTION TO YOU, "Wilt thou not tell us what these things are to us, that thou doest so?"

First, there are some of you who are here to-night who do not often go to a place of worship; I know you. Shall I tell you what you do on Sunday morning? Well, I do not know that it would do anybody any good if I did, so I will not. Shall I tell you how you generally spend the afternoon and evening of the Lord's-day? You know as well as I do, perhaps better; so I will not tell you. But here you are now, for once in a while. *By seldom coming to the Lord's house, you teach us your utter indifference.* Your carelessness seems to say to me, "God is nobody, put him in a corner. Get on in business; mind the main chance. God and eternity are only for fools. Gospel? Salvation? Oh, they are trifles, not worth anybody's consideration!" What about the Sabbath, which God appoints to be his own? "Well, he has given us six days out of seven, so we will steal from him the other one. We will not give him even an hour, if we can help it, for who is the Lord that we should obey his voice?" You seem to say, "What is heaven, and what is hell?" O sirs, this is the pratical teaching of your lives! If you are living in indifference, you are teaching your children this, you are teaching your neighbours this, you are teaching me this, as far as I am willing to learn it; but I am not willing to learn it, for I cannot believe that hell is a thing to be trifled with. You can trifle yourself into it; but you cannot trifle yourself out of it. There is no opening of the iron gate when once it has closed upon you. And heaven is not a thing to be trifled with. How many have I seen die with the light of heaven on their faces! How have I heard them talk of beginning already its endless joys while yet they were here! Have we not often rejoiced at the deathbeds of believers, who have died with glory flowing into their souls? I have seen too much of this to think heaven a trifle. I expect to go there myself before long; and I mind not how soon it may be. I read, the other day, that one called on my old grandfather, and said to him, "Mr. Spurgeon, you are getting old." He replied, "Yes, I am; I am eighty-seven, and I should like to go home next week; but I should like better to go home to-day, for I have been here as long as I want to be, and I am not as equal to preaching as I used to be. I should like to go home, and do some of the singing up above." Well I cannot trifle with that heaven where my grandfather has gone, I have too many friends there to run any risk of not going there myself. Perhaps you think in your own mind, "I do not want to be lost." Then, I pray you, cease your indifference; give God your Sabbaths; go and hear the gospel preached, and when you hear it, think over it, read your Bibles, begin to pray, and talk to your children about God and Jesus Christ and heaven. Why do so many of you forget your God? How can you live without him? How can you live without a Saviour? These things are grievous to me, and they ought to be very grievous to you; and you ought to have done with this indifference at once. God help you to have done with it even now!

There are others of you who are not indifferent; you come to the services, and you are attentive listeners; but just observe what you are going to do to-night. We shall want all the ground-floor and the greater part of this first gallery for communicants; but *you are going home, and so telling us that you have no part in the communion.* Yes, the Lord's table is spread, Christ is to be remembered, fellowship is to be had with him, and you are going home! I know, my friend over yonder, that you do not quite like it, because you have to leave your wife behind you. My dear boy up in the gallery, you do not quite like it, for your mother will stay behind, and you will stop about somewhere, I daresay, to walk home with her. I do not like your departing from God's people, for it makes me think of a hymn that I used to hear sung years ago,—

> " Oh, there will be weeping
> At the judgment seat of Christ!"

When the last parting comes, when mother is caught up to dwell with Christ, and her boy, whom she loved so well, is driven away into outer darkness, there will be weeping, and wailing, and gnashing of teeth. A dividing day must come. You may grow with the wheat, but the time will come when the tares must be separated from it, when the Lord will say to his reapers, "Gather ye together first the tares, and bind them in bundles to burn them: but gather the wheat into my barn." I hope that you will not go home many Sundays, leaving dear ones at the communion-table; but that, having trusted Christ as your Saviour, you will remain with them to show forth his death in his own appointed way.

I hear another say, "I am not going home; *I shall remain at the ordinance as a spectator.*" I always like to see you look on. I like to see the birds come where the chickens are being fed; they always will do so, you know. If you feed your chickens well, there will be sure to be sparrows in the trees near, waiting while the chickens are feeding; and afterwards the sparrows will come, and have their portion. So I expect it will be with you; when you have been looking on for a little while, you will drop down from the gallery, and you will get in among the birds Christ came to feed. You are getting into a place of happy danger. Get where the shots fly, and one of them may make a target of you. Oh, that it might be so!

But to-night you are going to be only a spectator. Will you tell me what that means, *only a spectator ?*

> " There is a fountain filled with blood,
> Drawn from Immanuel's veins;
> And sinners plunged beneath that flood
> Lose all their guilty stains;"

but you are only a spectator! There is my Father's house, and prodigals returning are clasped in his arms, the ring is on their finger, and the shoes are on their feet, but you are only a spectator! In Paris, during the siege, when it was straitly shut up, there were meals given at certain times in appointed places; but what would you have thought, if you had been there, and had been allowed to come to the window, and see the feeding, and yourself remain only a spectator? I pity the poor shoeless urchins, on a cold winter's night, who stand against a London cook-shop, flattening their noses against the great plate of glass, and looking in, and seeing all the steaming joints, while they are only spectators. Do not be so, I pray you; there is room for you at the gospel feast, and a hearty welcome, too.

Do not be merely spectators; but if you mean to be so, then I say this to you, *there will be no spectators in heaven.* They will all partake of the feast above, or they will not be there. And, I grieve to add, *there will be no spectators in hell.* You will have to participate in the award of vengeance, or else in the gift of mercy. Therefore have done with being spectators.

"Come guilty souls, and flee away,
Like doves, to Jesu's wounds."

Come and put your trust in him who died for the ungodly. He that believeth in him is not condemned. Would to God that you would believe in him to-night! I feel that God has helped me to speak to you. It has been no small task to me in my weakness; and now I want the Lord to give me some souls to-night. I expect to be paid for this service. When one preaches with joy and comfort, and is full of health and strength, there is a great delight in the work; but now, to-night, when it is heavy work to get a thought, and to utter it, I expect my wages in another form; and I shall go home to my Master, and say, "Lord, give me my wages!" If he asks me what I want, I shall say to him, "Lord, I should like the soul of that young man who sits in the aisle there, and of that old man in the top gallery who has been so interested while he has been listening; and I should like half a dozen of those young women over there." I believe that, when I once began to plead with my Lord, I should ask for every one of you. At any rate, why should I leave anyone out? Which one should I leave out? When I was preaching once in the great plough-shed of Mr. Howard, of Bedford (they had cleared out all the ploughs to make room for a large congregation), his dear old father was sitting on the platform with me, and in the afternoon I prayed that the Lord would give us some souls, I asked that a few might be converted. After the service, the good old saint said, "I enjoyed your preaching; but I did not enjoy your praying. I did not say 'Amen' when you asked the Lord to give us a few souls. My dear brother," he said, "I would not be content unless he gave us hundreds. Go in for it to-night," he added, "pray for hundreds to be converted." I thought, what a good thing it was to have a brother with larger faith than one's own! Now may the Lord make some of you, who have great faith, like good old Mr. Howard, to pray the Lord to save the whole ship's company here to-night! Why should they not all be brought in, to the praise of the glory of his grace? God grant it, for Jesus Christ's sake! Amen.

Exposition by C. H. Spurgeon.

EZEKIEL XXXIII. 1—20; 30—33.

Verses 1—4. Again the word of the LORD *came unto me, saying,* Son *of man, speak to the children of thy people, and say unto them,* When *I bring the sword upon a land, if the people of the land take a man of their coasts, and set him for their watchman: if when he seeth the sword come upon the land, he blow the trumpet, and warn the people; then whosoever heareth the sound of the trumpet, and taketh not warning; if the sword come, and take him away, his blood shall be upon his own head.*

In that case the watchman is quite clear; he has done his duty, he has sounded an alarm, and a fitting alarm, upon the trumpet; he has sounded it immediately, without loitering or delaying. He has not been afraid of giving uneasiness to men; he has done his duty, fearless of remark, and he is clear. Happy also is he in knowing that, by heeding the trumpet's warning blast, many have escaped the threatened danger.

Still, even then it seems that there are some who hear the trumpet, and will not take the warning. That is the sad part of our service; it makes the most successful ministry to be fringed with black. It cannot be all joy for him who wins the most souls for God; for at times he can sympathize with his brethren the prophets in their sorrowful enquiry, "Who hath believed our report? And to whom is the arm of the Lord revealed?" Listen to this, you who hear the gospel, and yet do not repent. If you heed not the warning, your blood will be upon your own head.

5, 6. He heard the sound of the trumpet, and took not warning; his blood shall be upon him. But he that taketh warning shall deliver his soul. But if the watchman see the sword come, and blow not the trumpet, and the people be not warned; if the sword come, and take any person from among them, he is taken away in his iniquity; but his blood will I require at the watchman's hand.

This is a very solemn truth. It not only concerns me, and the many ministers of Christ who are here, but it is for all of you who know the Lord, for you also are set as watchmen to your families, to your neighbours, to the class which you teach, or which you should teach, in the Sunday-school. May God grant that we may, each one of us, be delivered from other men's sins, for we may become partakers with them in their iniquity unless we bear our testimony against them, and give them warning of the consequences of their evil-doing!

7. So thou, O son of man, I have set thee a watchman unto the house of Israel;

It is not merely the people who took a man of their coasts, and set him for their watchman; but, "I have set thee." Oh, the solemn ordination of a true servant of Christ! It is not by laying on of hands of man, nor by a pretended descent from the apostles; it is a call from God.

7. Therefore thou shalt hear the word at my mouth, and warn them from me.

That is the way to preach, to get the sermon from the mouth of God, and then to speak it as the mouth of God. Dear teachers, wait upon God for that which you are to teach; take it warm with love out of the very mouth of God, and then speak it for God out of your own mouth. Good will surely come of such teaching as that.

8. When I say unto the wicked, O wicked man, thou shalt surely die; if thou dost not speak to warn the wicked from his way, that wicked man shall die in his iniquity; but his blood will I require at thine hand.

Even as God required Abel's blood at the hand of Cain, and pronounced him cursed because he was guilty of that blood, so will he require the blood of perishing men at the hands of those set over them, and a curse shall come upon them if they be found negligent.

9, 10. Nevertheless, if thou warn the wicked of his way to turn from it; if he do not turn from his way, he shall die in his iniquity; but thou hast delivered thy soul. Therefore, O thou son of man, speak unto the house of Israel; Thus ye speak, saying, If our transgressions and our sins be upon us, and we pine away in them, how should we then live?

This is as much as to say, "We cannot get away from our sins; there is no hope of our living." When men get into the iron cage called "Despair", there really seems to be no hope that they will turn from their sin. There is no hope in themselves; their only hope is in the Lord.

11, 12. Say unto them, As I live, saith the Lord GOD, I have no pleasure in the death of the wicked; but that the wicked turn from his way and live: turn ye, turn ye from your evil ways; for why will ye die, O house of Israel? Therefore, thou son of man,

Notice how often God calls Ezekiel the son of man. He had many wonderful visions; but he was to be kept humble by being constantly reminded that he was nothing more than a son of man. He was to be kept sympathetic with the people; they were men, and he was one of them: a "son of man." It seems hard that any mother's son of ours should die and perish; the thought that he will perish for ever, is terrible indeed to one who recognizes his union with the race as a "son of man."

12. Say unto the children of thy people, The righteousness of the righteous shall not deliver him in the day of his transgression: as for the wickedness of the wicked, he shall not fall thereby in the day that he turneth from his wickedness; neither shall the righteous be able to live for his righteousness in the day that he sinneth.

It is not merely what we have been, but what we are, and what we shall be, that will have to be taken into account. If we have been righteous in our own esteem, what of that if we turn from it? If we have been sinful, yet if, by God's grace, we turn from it, the past shall be blotted out.

13. When I shall say to the righteous, that he shall surely live; if he trust to his own righteousness, and commit iniquity, all his righteousnesses shall not be remembered; but for his iniquity that he hath committed, he shall die for it.

There is no salvation for any man without final perseverance, and if that final perseverance were not secured to us in the covenant of grace, there would be no salvation even for the brightest believer, or the most sparkling professor. What are our lights in themselves? Will they not soon burn dim unless the secret oil of God's grace shall keep them bright? Whatever point any of you have reached, do not begin to put your confidence in that. If you had seemed to be righteous through a lifetime of seventy years, yet, unless the grace of God kept you even to the end, you must perish. The mercy is that we have many precious promises concerning the eternal safety of all who are in Christ, and God will not fail to fulfil every one of them.

14—17. Again, when I say unto the wicked, Thou shalt surely die; if he turn from his sin, and do that which is lawful and right; if the wicked restore the pledge, give again that he had robbed, walk in the statutes of life, without committing iniquity; he shall surely live, he shall not die. None of his sins that he hath committed shall be mentioned unto him: he hath done that which is lawful and right; he shall surely live. Yet the children of thy people say, The way of the Lord is not equal: but as for them, their way is not equal.

Sinners are very fast in judging God. Oh, that they would judge themselves! It is not the Lord who is unjust; it is the balances and weights of men that are unjust. Oh, that they did but know it!

18—20. *When the righteous turneth from his righteousness, and committeth iniquity, he shall even die thereby. But if the wicked turn from his wickedness, and do that which is lawful and right, he shall live thereby.*

Now let us read at the thirtieth verse.

30, 31. *Also, thou son of man, the children of thy people still are talking against thee by the walls and in the doors of the houses, and speak one to another, every one to his brother, saying, Come, I pray you, and hear what is the word that cometh forth from the* LORD. *And they come unto thee as the people cometh, and they sit before thee as my people, and they hear thy words, but they will not do them: for with their mouth they shew much love, but their heart goeth after their covetousness.*

This is another of the great sorrows of the prophetic calling, that however accurately we report the Lord's message, however earnestly we try to drive it home to the consciences of our hearers, it must often be said, "They sit before thee as my people, and they hear thy words, but they will not do them; for with their mouth they show much love, but their heart goeth after their covetousness."

32. *And, lo, thou art unto them as a very lovely song of one that hath a pleasant voice, and can play well on an instrument: for they hear thy words, but they do them not.*

Preaching seems to such people to be only a song, or a piece of acting for their amusement; but it is not so. They that can find sport in the things of God, will find it dull sport in hell when they shall be for ever driven away from the presence of God, and from the glory of his power.

33. *And when this cometh to pass, (lo, it will come,) then shall they know that a prophet hath been among them.*

But then it will be too late for them to know it; for they will have missed their opportunity of profiting by the message that the prophet delivered to them. God grant that it may not be so with any one of us, for his abounding mercy's sake! Amen.

HYMNS FROM "OUR OWN HYMN BOOK"—560, 898, 938.

INTERESTING MEMENTOS OF C. H. SPURGEON.

Suitable for Distribution at Christmas and New Year.

BREAKING THE LONG SILENCE. Mr. Spurgeon's last two Addresses, delivered at Menton, on New Year's Eve, and New Year's Morning, 1892, in a tastefully-printed booklet. Price 6d. Many sermon-readers will be glad to possess and distribute this charming *souvenir* of Mr. Spurgeon's last sojourn in the sunny South.

PEACE! PERFECT PEACE! A touching Address by Mr. Spurgeon, delivered at Menton, on the Bishop of Exeter's well-known Hymn. Uniform with the above. Price 6d.

PASSMORE & ALABASTER, PATERNOSTER BUILDINGS, LONDON; and all Booksellers.

Metropolitan Tabernacle Pulpit.

"IF THERE BE NO RESURRECTION,——."

A Sermon

INTENDED FOR READING ON LORD'S-DAY, DECEMBER 18TH, 1892,

DELIVERED BY

C. H. SPURGEON,

AT THE METROPOLITAN TABERNACLE, NEWINGTON,

On Thursday Evening, February 20th, 1890.

"Now if Christ be preached that he rose from the dead, how say some among you that there is no resurrection of the dead? But if there be no resurrection of the dead, then is Christ not risen: and if Christ be not risen, then is our preaching vain, and your faith is also vain. Yea, and we are found false witnesses of God; because we have testified of God that he raised up Christ: whom he raised not up, if so be that the dead rise not. For if the dead rise not, then is not Christ raised: and if Christ be not raised, your faith is vain; ye are yet in your sins. Then they also which are fallen asleep in Christ are perished. If in this life only we have hope in Christ, we are of all men most miserable."—1 Corinthians xv. 12—19.

Our religion is not based upon opinions, but upon facts. We hear persons sometimes saying, "Those are your views, and these are ours." Whatever your "views" may be, is a small matter; what are the facts of the case? We must, after all, if we want a firm foundation, come down to matters of fact. Now, the great facts of the gospel are that God was incarnate in Christ Jesus, that he lived here a life of holiness and love, that he died upon the cross for our sins, that he was buried in the tomb of Joseph, that the third day he rose again from the dead, that after a while he ascended to his Father's throne where he now sitteth, and that he shall come by-and-by, to be our Judge, and in that day the dead in Christ shall rise by virtue of their union with him.

Now, very soon, within the Church of God, there rose up persons who began to dispute about the fundamental and cardinal principles of the faith, and it is so even now. When those outside the Church deny that Christ is the Son of God, deny his atoning sacrifice, and deny his resurrection, we are not at all astonished; they are unbelievers, and they are acting out their own profession. But when men, inside the Church of God, call themselves Christians, and yet deny the resurrection of the dead, then is our soul stirred within us, for it is a most solemn and serious evil to doubt those holy truths. They know not what they do, they cannot see all the result of their unbelief; if they could, one would think that they would start back with horror, and replace the truth, and let it stand where it ought to stand, where God has put it.

No. 2,287.

The resurrection of the dead has been assailed, and is assailed still, by those who are called Christians, even by those who are called Christian ministers, but who, nevertheless, spirit away the very idea of the resurrection of the dead, so that we are to-day in the same condition, to some extent, as the Corinthian church was when, in its very midst, there rose up men, professing to be followers of Christ, who said that there was no resurrection of the dead. The apostle Paul, having borne his witness, and recapitulated the testimony about the resurrection of Christ, goes on to show the horrible consequences which must follow if there be no resurrection of the dead, and if Christ be not risen. He showed this to be a foundation truth; and if it was taken away, much more was gone than they supposed; indeed, everything was gone, as Paul went on to prove.

Beloved friends, let us never tamper with the truth of God. I find it as much as I can do to enjoy the comfort of the truth, and to learn the spiritual lessons of God's Word, without setting up to be a critic upon it; and I find it immeasurably more profitable to my own soul believingly to adore, than unbelievingly to invent objections, or even industriously to try to meet them. The meeting of objections is an endless work. When you have killed one regiment of them, there is another regiment coming on; and when you have put to the sword whole legions of doubts, doubters still swarm upon you like the frogs of Egypt. It is a poor business, it answers no practical end; it is better far firmly to believe what you profess to believe, and to follow out to all the blessed consequences every one of the truths which, in your own heart and soul, you have received of the Lord.

One of the truths most surely believed among us is that there will be a resurrection of all those who sleep in Christ. There will be a resurrection of the ungodly as well as of the godly. Our Lord Jesus said to the Jews, "Verily, verily, I say unto you, The hour is coming, and now is, when the dead shall hear the voice of the Son of God: and they that hear shall live. For as the Father hath life in himself; so hath he given to the Son to have life in himself; and hath given him authority to execute judgment also, because he is the Son of man. Marvel not at this: for the hour is coming, in the which all that are in the graves shall hear his voice, and shall come forth; they that have done good, unto the resurrection of life; and they that have done evil, unto the resurrection of damnation." Paul declared before Felix the doctrine of the "resurrection of the dead, both of the just and unjust;" but his argument with the Corinthians specially referred to believers, who will rise from the dead, and stand with Christ in the day of his appearing, quickened with the life that quickened him, and raised up to share the glory which the Father has given to him.

I. Paul's argument begins here, and this will be our first head, IF THERE BE NO RESURRECTION, CHRIST IS NOT RISEN.

If the resurrection of the dead is impossible, Christ cannot have risen from the dead. Now, *the apostles bore witness that Christ had risen.* They had met him, they had been with him, they had seen him eat a piece of a broiled fish and of a honeycomb on one occasion. They had seen him perform acts which could not be performed by a spirit, but which needed that he should be flesh and bones. Indeed, he said, "A spirit hath not flesh and bones, as ye see me have." One of them put his finger into the print of the nails, and was invited to thrust his hand into Christ's side. He was known by two of them in the breaking of bread, a familiar token by which they recognized him better than by anything else. They heard him speak, they knew the tones of his voice; they were not deceived. On one occasion, five hundred of them saw him at once; or, if there was any possibility of a mistake when they were all together, they were not deceived when they saw him one by one, and entered into very close personal communion with him, each one after a different sort. "Now," says Paul, "if there be no resurrection of the dead, if that is impossible, then, of course, Christ did not rise; and yet we all assure you that we saw him, and that we were with him, and you have to believe that we are all liars, and that the Christian religion is a lie, or else you must believe that there is a resurrection of the dead."

"But," says one, "Christ might rise, and yet not his people." Not so, according to our faith and firm belief, *Christ is one with his people*. When Adam sinned, the whole human race fell in him, for they were one with him; in Adam all died. Even those that have not sinned after the similitude of Adam's transgression have, nevertheless, died. Even upon infants the death-sentence has taken effect, because they were one with Adam. There is no separating Adam from his posterity. Now, Christ is the second Adam, and he has a posterity. All believers are one with him, and none can separate them from him. If they do not live, then he did not live; and if he did not rise, then they will not rise. But whatever happened unto him must also happen unto them. They are so welded together, the Head and the members, that there is no dividing them. If he had slept an eternal sleep, then every righteous soul would have done the same, too. If he rose again, they must rise again, for he has taken them unto himself to be part and parcel of his very being. He died that they might live. Because he lives they shall live also, and in his eternal life they must for ever be partakers.

This is Paul's first argument, then, for the resurrection of the righteous, that, inasmuch as Christ rose, they must rise, for they are identified with him.

II. But now he proceeds with his subject, not so much arguing upon the resurrection of others as upon the resurrection of Christ; and his next argument is, that, IF THERE BE NO RESURRECTION, APOSTOLIC PREACHING FALLS: "If Christ be not risen, then is our preaching vain" (see the fourteenth verse). "Yea, and we are found false witnesses of God; because we have testified of God that he raised up Christ: whom he raised not up, if so be that the dead rise not."

If Christ was not raised, the apostles were false witnesses. When a man bears false witness, he usually has a motive for doing so. What motive had these men, what did they gain by bearing false witness to Christ's resurrection? It was all loss and no profit to them if he had not risen. They declared in Jerusalem that he had risen from the dead, and straightway men began to hale them to prison, and to put them to death. Those of them who survived bore the same testimony. They were so full of the conviction of it, that they went into distant countries to tell the story of Jesus and his resurrection from the dead. Some went to Rome, some to Spain; probably some came even to this remote island of Britain. Wherever they went, they testified that Christ had risen from the dead, and that they had seen him alive, and that he was the Saviour of all who trusted in him. Thus they always preached, and what became of them? I may say, with Paul, that "they were stoned, they were sawn asunder, were tempted, were slain with the sword: they wandered about in sheepskins and goatskins; being destitute, afflicted, tormented." They were brought before the Roman Emperor again and again, and before the pro-consuls, and threatened with the most painful of deaths; but not one of them ever withdrew his testimony concerning Christ's resurrection. They still stood to it, that they had known him in life, many of them had been near him in death, and they had all communed with him after his resurrection. They declared that Jesus of Nazareth was the Son of God, that he died and was buried, that he rose again, and that there was salvation for all who believed in him.

Were these men false witnesses? If so, they were the most extraordinary false witnesses who ever lived. What were their morals? What kind of men were they? Were they drunkards? Were they adulterers? Were they thieves? Nay; they were the purest and best of mankind; their adversaries could bring no charge against their moral conduct. They were eminently honest, and they spoke with the accent of conviction. As I have already said, they suffered for their testimony. Now, under the law, the witness of two men was to be received; but what shall we say of the witness of five hundred men? If it was true when they first declared that Jesus Christ rose from the dead, it is equally true now. It does not matter though the event happened nearly nineteen hundred years ago; it is just as true now. The apostles bore witness which could not be gainsaid, and so it still stands. We cannot assume that all these apostolic men were false witnesses of God.

If we even suppose that they were mistaken about this matter, *we must suspect their witness about everything else;* and the only logical result is to give up the New Testament altogether. If they were mistaken as to Christ having risen from the dead, they are not credible witnesses upon anything else; and if they are discredited, the whole of our religion falls with them; the Christian faith, and especially all that the apostles built on the resurrection, must be turned out of doors as altogether a delusion. They taught that Christ's rising from the dead was the evidence that his sacrifice was accepted, that he rose again for our justification, that his rising again was the hope of believers in this life, and the assurance of the resurrection of their bodies in the life to come. You must give up all your hope of salvation the moment you doubt the Lord's rising from the dead.

As for Paul, who puts himself with the rest of the apostles, and says, "If Christ be not risen, we are found false witnesses of God," I venture to bring him forward as a solitary witness of the most convincing kind. I need not remind you how he was at first opposed to Christ. He was a Pharisee of the Pharisees, one of the most intolerant members of the sect that hated the very name of Christ. He had a righteousness that surpassed that of the men of his times. He was a religious leader and persecutor; and yet he was so convinced of the appearance of Christ to him on the way to Damascus, that from that time he was completely turned round, and he preached with burning zeal the faith which once be blasphemed. There is an honesty about Paul which convinces at once; and if he had not seen the Saviour risen from the dead, he would not have been the man to say that he did. Dear brethren, you may rest assured that Jesus Christ did rise from the dead. You cannot put down these good men as impostors; you cannot reckon the apostle Paul among those readily deceived, or among the deceivers of others; so you may be sure that Jesus Christ did rise from the dead, according to the Scriptures.

III. Once more, Paul's argument is that, IF THERE BE NO RESURRECTION, FAITH BECOMES DELUSION.

As we have to give up the apostles and all their teaching, *if Christ did not rise from the dead*, so we must conclude that *their hearers believed a lie:* "your faith is also vain." Beloved, I speak to you who have believed in the Lord Jesus Christ, and who are resting in him with great comfort and peace of mind, yea, who have experienced a great change of heart, and a great change in your lives through faith in Christ. Now, if he did not rise from the dead, you are believing a lie. Take this home to yourselves: if he did not literally rise from the dead on the third day, this faith of yours, that gives you comfort, this faith which has renewed you in heart and life, this faith which you believe is leading you home to heaven, must be abandoned as a sheer delusion; your faith is fixed on a falsehood. Oh, dreadful inference! But the inference is clearly true if Christ is not risen; you are risking your soul on a falsehood if Christ did not rise from the dead. This is a solemn statement. I said last Sabbath, and I repeat it,—

"Upon a life I did not live,
Upon a death I did not die,
I risk my whole eternity."

It is so. If Jesus Christ did not die for me, and did not rise again for me, I am lost; I have not a ray of comfort from any other direction; I have no dependence on anything else but Jesus crucified and risen; and if that sheet-anchor fails, everything fails with it, in my case; and so it must in yours.

"Your faith is also vain," wrote Paul to the Corinthians, for, *if Christ is not risen, the trial will be too great for faith to endure*, since it has for the very keystone of the arch the resurrection of Christ from the dead. If he did not rise, your faith rests on what never happened, and is not true; and certainly your faith will not bear that, or any other trial. There comes to the believer, every now and then, a time of great testing. Did you ever lie, as I have done several times, upon the brink of eternity, full of pain, almost over the border of this world, fronting eternity, looking into the dread abyss? There, unless you are sure about the foundation of your faith, you are in an evil case indeed. Unless you have a solid rock beneath you then, your hope will shrink away to nothing, and your confidence will depart.

When you are sure that "the Lord is risen, indeed," then you feel that there is something beneath your foot that does not stir. If

Jesus died for you, and Jesus rose for you, then, my dear brother, you are not afraid even of that tremendous day when the earth shall be burned up, and the elements shall melt with fervent heat. You feel a confidence that will bear even that test. If Christ did not rise from the dead, and you are resting your soul on the belief that he did rise, what a failure it will be for you in another world, what disappointment when you do not wake up in his likeness, what dismay if there should be no pardon of sin, no salvation through the precious blood! If Christ is not risen, your faith is vain. If it is vain, give it up; do not hold on to a thing that is not true. I would sooner plunge into the water, and swim or wade through the river, than I would trust myself to a rotten bridge that would break down in the middle. If Christ did not rise, do not trust him, for such faith is vain; but, if you believe that he did die for you, and did rise again for you, then believe in him, joyously confident that such a fact as this affords a solid basis for your belief.

IV. Now I am going to advance a little further. Paul says next that, IF THERE BE NO RESURRECTION, THEY REMAINED IN THEIR SINS: "If Christ be not raised, your faith is vain; ye are yet in your sins."

Ah! can ye bear that thought, my beloved in Christ, that ye are yet in your sins? I think that the bare suggestion takes hold upon you, terrifies you, and chills your blood. A little while ago, you were in your sins, dead in them, covered with them as with a crimson robe, you were condemned, lost. But now, you believe that Christ has brought you out of your sins, and washed you and made you white in his precious blood; ay, and has so changed you that sin shall not have dominion over you, for now you are by grace a child of God. Well, but, if Christ did not rise again, you are yet in your sins.

Observe that; for *then there is no atonement made;* at least, no satisfactory atonement. If the atonement of Christ for sin had been unsatisfactory, he would have remained in the grave. He went there on our behalf, a hostage for us; and if what he did upon the tree had not satisfied the justice of God, then he would never have come out of the grave again. Think for a minute what our position would be, if I stood here to preach only a dead and buried Christ! He died nearly nineteen hundred years ago; but suppose he had never been heard of since. If he had not risen from the dead, could you have confidence in him? You would say, "How do we know that his sacrifice was accepted?" We sing right truly,—

"If Jesus ne'er had paid the debt,
He ne'er had been at freedom set."

The Surety would have been under bonds unless he had discharged all his liability; but he has done so, and he has risen from the dead,—

"And now both the Surety and sinner are free."

Understand clearly what I am saying. The Lord Jesus Christ, the Son of God, took upon himself the sum total of the guilt of all his people. "The Lord hath made to meet upon him the iniquity of us all." He died, and by his death obtained the full discharge of all our obligations. But his rising again was, so to speak, the receipt in full, the token that he had discharged the whole of the dread liabilities which he had taken upon himself; and now, since Christ is risen, you who believe in him are not in your sins. But, if he had not risen, then it would have been true, "Ye are yet in your sins."

It would have been true, also, in another sense. The life by which true believers live is the resurrection-life of him who said, "Because I live, ye shall live also." But *if Christ is not risen, there is no life for those who are in him.* If he were still slumbering in the grave, where would have been the life that now makes us joyful, and makes us aspire after heavenly things? There would have been no life for you if there had not first been life for him. "Now is Christ risen from the dead," and in him you rise into newness of life; but, if he did not rise, you are still dead, still under sin, still without the divine life, still without the life immortal and eternal that is to be your life in heaven throughout eternity.

So, you see, once more, the consequences that follow: "If Christ be not raised, your faith is vain; ye are yet in your sins."

V. Now follows, if possible, a still more terrible consequence. IF THERE BE NO RESURRECTION, ALL THE PIOUS DEAD HAVE PERISHED: "Then they also which are fallen asleep in Christ are perished." "Perished", by which is not meant "annihilated"; they are in a worse condition than that.

One phrase must be explained by the other which went before it; *if Jesus Christ is not risen, they are yet in their sins.* They died, and they told us that they were blood-washed and forgiven; and that they hoped to see the face of God with joy; but if Christ rose not from the dead, there is no sinner who has gone to heaven, there is no saint who ever died, who has had any real hope; he has died under a delusion, and he has perished.

If Jesus Christ be not raised, the godly dead are yet in their sins, and *they can never rise;* for, if Christ did not rise from the dead, they cannot rise from the dead. Only through his resurrection is there resurrection for the saints. The ungodly shall rise to shame and everlasting contempt; but believers shall rise into eternal life and felicity because of their oneness with Christ; but, if he did not rise, they cannot rise. If he is dead, they must be dead, for they must share with him. They are, they ever must be, one with him; and all the saints who ever died, died under a mistake if Christ did not rise. We cast away the thought with abhorrence. Many of us have had beloved parents and friends who have died in the Lord, and we know that the full assurance of their faith was no mistake. We have seen dear children die in sure and certain hope of a glorious resurrection; and we know that it was no error on their part. I have stood by many death-beds of believers, many triumphant, and many more peaceful and calm as a sweet summer evening. They were not mistaken. No, dear sirs, believing in Christ, who lived, and died, and rose again, they had confidence in the midst of pain, and joy in the hour of their departure. We cannot believe that they were mistaken; therefore we are confident that Jesus Christ did rise from the dead.

VI. Once more, IF THERE BE NO RESURRECTION, OUR SOURCE OF JOY IS GONE. If Jesus did not rise from the dead, we, who believe that he did, are of all men the most miserable: "If in this life only we have hope in Christ," and we certainly have no hope of any other life, apart from Christ, "we are of all men most miserable."

What does Paul mean? That Christian men are more miserable than others, if they are mistaken? No, he does not mean that; for even the mistake, if it be a mistake, gives them joy; the error, if it be an error, yields them a present confidence and peace. But supposing they are sure that they are under an error, that they have made a mistake, their comfort is gone, and they are of all men the most miserable.

Believers have given up sensuous joys; they have sedulously given them up; they find no comfort in them. There are a thousand things in which worldlings find a kind of joy, all of which the Christian loathes. Well, if you have given up the brown bread, and cannot eat the white, then are you starved indeed. If we consider the mirth of the worldling to be no better than the husks of swine, and there be no bread for us, in the fact that Christ rose from the dead, then we are hungry indeed.

And, more than that, *we have now learned superior things.* We have learned to love holiness, and we seek after it. We have learned to love communion with God, and it has become our heaven to talk with our Father and our Saviour. We now look after things which are spiritual; and we try to handle the things that are carnal as they should be handled, as things to be used, but not abused. Now if, after having tasted these superior joys, they all turn out to be nothing, and they must turn out to be nothing if Jesus did not rise from the dead, then we are indeed of all men the most miserable.

More than that, *we have had high hopes,* hopes that have made our hearts leap for joy. We have been ready sometimes to go straight away out of the body, with high delights and raptures, in the expectation of being "with Christ, which is far better." We have said, "Though after my skin worms destroy this body, yet in my flesh shall I see God: whom I shall see for myself, and mine eyes shall behold, and not another." We have been transported with the full conviction that our eyes "shall see the King in his beauty: they shall behold the land that is very far off;" and if that be not sure, if it can be proved that our hopes are vain, then are we of all men the most miserable.

You will wonder why I have been so long in bringing out these points, and what I am driving at. Well, what I am driving at is this. After all, everything hinges upon a fact, an ancient fact, and if that fact is not a fact, it is all up with us. If Jesus Christ did not rise from the dead, then his gospel is all exploded. What I want you to notice is this, that there must be a basis of fact in our religion; these things must be facts, or else nothing can give us consolation.

Our eternal hopes do not depend upon our moral condition; for, observe, these men in Corinth would not have been better or worse if Christ had not risen from the dead. Their character was just the same. It had been fashioned, it is true, by a belief that he did rise from the dead; but whether he did or did not, they were just the same men, so that their hope did not depend upon their good moral condition. The apostle does not say, "If you are or are not in such and such a moral condition," but, "If Christ be not raised, your faith is vain; ye are yet in your sins." So, my beloved, the reason of your being safe will be that Christ died for you, and that he rose again; it is not the result of what you are, but of what he did. The hinge of it all is not in you: it is in him, and you are to place your reliance, not upon what you are, or hope to be, but wholly and entirely upon a great fact which transpired nearly nineteen hundred years ago. If he did not rise from the dead, you are in your sins still, be you as good as you may; but if he did rise from the dead, and you are one with him, you are not in your sins; they are all put away, and you are "accepted in the Beloved."

Now I go a step further. The great hope you have does not hinge even upon your spiritual state. You must be born again; you must have a new heart and a right spirit, or else you cannot lay hold of Christ, and he is not yours; but still, your ultimate hope is not in what you are spiritually, but in what he is. When darkness comes over your soul, and you say, "I am afraid I am not converted," still believe in him who rose from the dead; and when, after you have had a sight of yourself, you are drifting away to dark despair, still cling to him who loved you, and gave himself for you, and rose again from the dead for you. If thou believest that Christ is risen from the dead, and if this be the foundation of thy hope of heaven, that hope stands just as sure, whether thou art bright or whether thou art dull, whether thou canst sing or whether thou art forced to sigh, whether though canst run or whether thou art a broken-legged cripple, only able to lie at Christ's feet. If he died for thee, and rose again for thee, there is the groundwork of thy confidence, and I pray thee keep to it. Do you see how Paul insists upon this? "If Christ be not raised, your faith is vain; ye are yet in your sins." The inference is that, if Christ be raised, and you have faith in him, your faith is not vain, and you are not in your sins, you are saved. Your hope must not be here, in what your hands can do, but there, on yonder cross, in what he did, and there, on yonder throne, in him who has risen again for your justification.

The hardest thing in the world seems to be to keep people to this truth, for I have noticed that much of the modern-thought doctrine is nothing but old self-righteousness tricked out again. It is bidding men still to trust in themselves, to trust in their moral character, to trust in their spiritual aspirations, or something or other. I stand here to-night to say to you that the basis of your hope is not even your own faith, much less your own good works; but it is what Christ has done once for all, for "ye are complete in him," and you can never be complete in any other way.

Here, again, I would have you notice that Paul does not say that your being forgiven and saved depends upon your sincerity and your earnestness. You must be sincere and earnest; Christ is not yours if you are not; but still, you may be very sincere, and very earnest, and yet be wrong all the while; and the more sincere and earnest you are in a wrong way, the further you will go astray. The self-righteous man may be very sincere as he goes about to establish a righteousness of his own; but the more he does it, the more he ruins himself. But here is the mark for you to aim at, not at your sincerity, though there must be that; but if Christ was raised, and that is where you are resting your hopes, then you are not in your sins, but you are accepted in Christ, and justified in him.

This is where I stand, and I pray every believer to keep here. There are many new discoveries made in science; we are pleased to hear it. I hope that we shall be able to travel more quickly, and pay less for it. I hope that we shall have better light, and that it will not be so expensive. The more true science, the better; but when science comes in to tell me that it has discovered anything about the way to heaven, then I have a deaf ear to it. "If Christ be not risen, then is our preaching vain, and your faith is also vain; ye are yet in your sins." But if Christ be risen, then I know where I am. If it be really so, that he is God in human flesh; if he took my sin, and bore the consequences of it, and made a clear sweep of it from before the judgment-seat of the Most High; and if his rising again is God's testimony that the work is done, and that Christ, who stood as Substitute for me, is accepted for me, oh, hallelujah, hallelujah! What more do I need, but to praise and bless the name of him who has saved me with an effectual salvation? Now will I work for him. Now will I spend and be spent in his service. Now will I hate every false way, and every sin, and seek after purity and holiness; but not, in any sense, as the groundwork of my confidence. My one hope for time and eternity is Jesus, only Jesus; Jesus crucified and risen from the dead.

I do not know any passage of Scripture which, more thoroughly than this one, throws the stress where the stress must be, not on man, but on Christ alone: "If there be no resurrection of the dead, then is Christ not risen: and if Christ be not risen, then is our preaching vain, and your faith is also vain." O dear hearer, if thou wouldst be saved, thy salvation does not lie with thyself, but with him who left his Father's bosom, and came down to earth a babe at Bethlehem, and hung upon a woman's breast; upon him who lived here, for thirty-three years, a life of suffering and of toil, and who then took all the sin of his people upon himself, carried it up to the tree, and there bore all the consequences of it in his own body,—

"Bore all that Almighty God could bear,
With strength enough, but none to spare."

Jesus Christ bore that which has made God's pardon an act of justice, and vindicated his forgiveness of sin so that none can say that he is unjust when he passes by transgression. Christ did all that; and then, dying, was laid in the tomb, but, the third day, his Father raised him from the dead in token that he spoke the truth when he said, on the cross, "It is finished." The debt is paid now; then, O sinner, leave thy prison, for thy debt is paid! Art thou shut up in despair on account of thy debt of sin? It is all discharged if thou hast believed in him who was raised from the dead. He has taken all thy sin, and thou art free. That handwriting of ordinances that was against thee is nailed to his cross. Go thy way, and sing, "The Lord is risen indeed," and be as happy as all the birds in the air, till thou art, by and by, as happy as the angels in heaven, through Jesus Christ our Lord. Amen.

Exposition by C. H. Spurgeon.

I CORINTHIANS XV. 1—20.

Verse 1, 2. *Moreover, brethren, I declare unto you the gospel which I preached unto you, which also ye have received, and wherein ye stand; by which also ye are saved, if ye keep in memory what I preached unto you, unless ye have believed in vain.*

Paul preached the gospel, his hearers received it, and also stood in it: "wherein ye stand." It is essential to salvation to hear the gospel, to receive it, and then to stand in it.

Now, what was this gospel? Paul is going to tell us; and instead of making a list of doctrines, he mentions a set of facts.

3. *For I delivered unto you first of all that which I also received,*

Notice that the preacher does not make the gospel. If he makes it, it is not worth your having. Originality in preaching, if it be originality in the statement of doctrine, is falsehood. We are not makers and inventors; we are repeaters, we tell the message we have received.

3. *How that Christ died for our sins according to the scriptures;*

This, then, is the gospel, that Jesus "died for our sins", taking our sins upon himself. He bore the death penalty for us, "according to the Scriptures." There are plenty of Scriptures, Old Testament Scriptures, which teach this great truth by way of prophecy.

4. *And that he was buried,*

This was necessary as a proof of his death, and as the ground work of his rising again.

4. *And that he rose again the third day according to the scriptures:*

This is the gospel, Christ dead, buried, risen again, ever living. We must dwell upon these points, for they are the essentials of the gospel.

5, 6. *And that he was seen of Cephas, then of the twelve: after that, he was seen of above five hundred brethren at once; of whom the greater part remain unto this present,*

When Paul wrote,—

6, 7. *But some are fallen asleep. After that, he was seen of James; then of all the apostles.*

In different places, and at different hours; sometimes by one, sometimes by eleven, once by five hundred brethren at once, Jesus was seen after he had risen from the dead. As I have often said, there is no historical fact that is so well authenticated as that Jesus Christ rose from the dead.

8. *And last of all he was seen of me also, as of one born out of due time.*

Paul calls himself an abortion, and speaks of himself as one hardly worth mentioning; yet he had seen the Lord after his resurrection from the dead. He was not a man to be deceived, for he had persecuted the Church of Christ. He was exceedingly mad against the Messiah; so that if he said that he had seen Jesus of Nazareth, and that he was converted by the sight, we may be quite sure that it was so. Paul was not a man to undergo all the sacrifices he had to endure, for the sake of a mere dream.

9, 10. *For I am the least of the apostles, that am not meet to be called an apostle, because I persecuted the church of God. But by the grace of God I am what I am: and his grace which was bestowed upon me was not in vain; but I laboured more abundantly than they all: yet not I, but the grace of God which was with me.*

No man could be more thoroughly with Christ, heart and soul, than that Paul who, aforetime, had been the blood thirsty Saul of Tarsus. His witness may well be believed ; and, in connection with all that went before it, it proves beyond all doubt that he who was crucified and was laid in the tomb, did certainly rise again, and was seen in life after death.

11. *Therefore whether it were I or they, so we preach, and so ye believed.*

There was not a doubt about that. All the apostles, all the early Christians preached the resurrection of Christ; and the Corinthians, when they became Christians, believed it.

12. *Now if Christ be preached that he rose from the dead, how say some among you that there is no resurrection of the dead?*

What! had they got so far as that, to call themselves Christians, and yet they doubted the truth of the resurrection of the dead? Yes, they spirited it away, they made it into a kind of myth or fable; and yet they called themselves Christians. That the heathen should not believe it, was not wonderful; but that those who professed to believe that Christ had risen from the dead, yet doubted the resurrection of his people, was indeed a strange thing. Paul argues with them about this matter.

13, 14. *But if there be no resurrection of the dead, then is Christ not risen: and if Christ be not risen, then is our preaching vain, and your faith is also vain.*

If Jesus Christ did not rise from the dead, we are preaching a falsehood. If he did not rise from the dead, you are believing a falsehood, and our preaching and your believing are nothing but vanity.

15—17. *Yea, and we are found false witnesses of God; because we have testified of God that he raised up Christ: whom he raised not up, if so be that the dead rise not. For if the dead rise not, then is not Christ raised: and if Christ be not raised, your faith is vain; ye are yet in your sins.*

If Jesus Christ is not risen, he has done nothing for you; you are not saved, you are not pardoned, you are not renewed. It is all a myth, all a piece of deceit. If that fact be given up, that Christ rose from the dead, everything connected with salvation is also given up.

18. *Then they also which are fallen asleep in Christ are perished.*

All the godly saints died resting in the risen Christ; and if he is not risen, they died under a delusion, and they have perished.

19. *If in this life only we have hope in Christ, we are of all men most miserable.*

Those who are believers in Christ, says Paul, are miserable dupes if he has not risen from the dead. They are believing and resting all their hopes upon a lie. It makes them happy, truly; but if you can take away from them that hope, by persuading them that what it is grounded upon is not true, you have made them miserable indeed.

20. *But now is Christ risen from the dead, and become the firstfruits of them that slept.*

Paul has been arguing on every supposition, and now he comes back with his own positive witness that Christ is risen. You remember that Jesus died at the time of the Passover, as the one great Paschal Lamb; but he rose again on the first day of the week, and that was the feast of firstfruits with the Jews. They brought handfuls of wheat from the fields to show their gratitude to God, and in order that a blessing might rest on all the crop; and Paul uses Christ's rising on that particular day as a figure: "Now is Christ risen from the dead, and become the firstfruits of them that slept." He lives. He is the firstfruits, and the full harvest will follow. All who are in him will rise from the dead; for he is one with them, and none can separate them from him, nor sever him from them. They died in him, and they live because he liveth, blessed be his name!

HYMNS FROM "OUR OWN HYMN BOOK"—289, 309, 609.

Metropolitan Tabernacle Pulpit.

THE EMPTY PLACE: A CHRISTMAS DAY SERMON.

A Sermon

Intended for Reading on Lord's-day, December 25th, 1892,

DELIVERED BY

C. H. SPURGEON,

AT THE METROPOLITAN TABERNACLE, NEWINGTON,

On a Christmas Day Evening.

"And David's place was empty."—1 Samuel xx. 25.

There may be much to learn from an empty place. The world thinks much of the places which have been emptied through the home-going of its celebrated men. Those who have served the world are remembered by it; those who have served the Church are remembered, too; and empty chairs in the world, in the Church, and in the family, awaken a great many recollections.

I do not intend to keep to one subject to-night; I think I have, in these words about David's place, a roving commission; and keeping to my text, I shall be able to consider a great many subjects, and to speak briefly upon each.

I. First, then, let us think of THE EMPTY PLACE IN THE PERSECUTOR'S HOUSE: "David's place was empty."

David had good reason for vacating his place at Saul's table, for the passionate king was so malicious, and so embittered against him, that he sought his life. Saul had, on several occasions, in his fits of mad anger, hurled javelins at the man to whom he owed so much, and the envious king determined to put his rival to death at the first convenient opportunity. David, therefore, very properly left a place in which his life was continually in peril.

Oh, how happy are we, in these days, that we are not subjected to the fierce sufferings, and the cruel persecutions, which the early Christians, and even our own forefathers had to endure! How often, in a Jewish family, as soon as a young man had become a follower of Christ, from that moment none of his household would acknowledge him. He was a follower of the hated Nazarene! "A curse be upon him," said his father; and even a mother's tenderness seemed to be dried up, so that she could not think of him without bitterness and gall. A like thing happened also in the old Roman

No. 2,288.

families. The child of a Roman noble had stepped into some little place where humble and unlettered people met to hear the gospel preached, to sing songs in the name of Jesus, and to keep holy one day in the week; and there that youthful heart had learnt the story of the cross, and by the grace of God had been brought to love the Saviour. As soon as the fact was made known, the officers of justice would take away the child from the father's house, and hale the young believer off to prison, and so another seat was empty. When persecution grew very hot in the old Roman times, you know how the good, and the great, and the true, the strong and the old, the young man and the maiden, had alike to flee for their lives. If they remained, it was only to be dragged before the Roman prætor, and short work was made of them at the stake or in the arena. After a little while, nothing was left of them but a heap of ashes from the martyr fire, or a few bones that the wild beasts did not care to eat. Thus another "David's place was empty."

Horrible work was wrought, too, when the Church of Rome had its full power, and the officers of the Inquisition, at dead of night, knocked at the door of some Christian man, and demanded either himself, or his wife, or son, or daughter. They had to surrender themselves without a word, that they might be immured in the damp, dark vaults of that hellish institution, never to be seen again, except, on some dreadful day, when they were marched out, in derision, to be burnt alive because they would not bow before images of ivory and wood, and call those idols the Christ to whom homage and reverence should be paid. You know how it was in our own land, how many a seat was empty during the persecutions of Queen Mary; and after that, when our noble sires would not conform to the established Church of this land, and, therefore, were hunted into the dens and caves of the earth, as though they had been wild beasts, instead of men of whom the world was not worthy. Many of the bravest and best of England's sons and daughters fled away to America, and found another and a safer home there, in New England, where the wild rocks were less flinty than the hearts of men here in England.

Often and often, when persecution has arisen for the truth's sake, David's seat has been empty. If martyr days should come back again, could we vacate our places? Could the husband let his wife and children go for Christ's sake? Could the child again give up the father's love? Could you wrench yourselves away from all your dear ones, to prove that you were truly Christ's, and that you loved him better than father or mother, husband or wife, or any of your kin? God grant that the true martyr spirit may not die out of our heart, even if, in God's gracious providence, it be not called into terrible exercise as among the brave peasants of Switzerland, or the noble covenanters of Scotland, or the old Nonconformists of this country! At any rate, whatever we are called to endure, may we be true and loyal to the gospel for which our fathers bled and died; and if the times of persecution should ever come again, and come they may, may we be ready again to vacate the place of comfort, luxury, and peace for our Lord Jesus Christ's sake!

II. There is another place which sometimes becomes empty, that is, THE PLACE OF SINFUL PLEASURES. This empty place is the result of the working of God's grace in the heart.

I know that, concerning some here, it may be said, with very great thankfulness, that David's place is empty. Ah, dear friend, where was your place, seven years ago, on such a night as this in our so-called Christian land? Ah, well, we do not want you to tell where it was, you had better be silent about that; but, with a holy blush, and then with devout thankfulness to God, rejoice that, so far as you are concerned, David's place in the seat of the scornful is empty now. You know that the ale-bench would not suit you now, nor the place where the lascivious song awakens enthusiastic applause from the ribald throng; you would be out of place in the company of the flippant, the foolish, the blasphemous, and those who find their pleasures in forgetting their God, and think it no sin to break through his laws. No, thank God, that place is empty now!

Grace makes a wonderful change in a man. It is not so much that he dares not go where he used to find delight; he would not go if he were paid for it, nay, if he were even flogged to make him go. Old pleasures are not given up by us simply because we think them wrong; we know they are evil, and that would be one reason for abandoning them; but we give them up also because they are no longer pleasures to us. We have no delight whatever in them now, nor would we have them if we were free to choose them for ourselves. Were the law of God suspended, and we were permitted to take as much of the pleasure of sin as we liked, we would decline to take any, since it is not pleasure to us. Oh, be thankful, dear friend, that grace has made such a change in you, and resolve in your heart that, as grace has done this for you, you will use your utmost endeavours to get the same gracious work done for your friends, that others may be captured from Satan's ranks. Oh, what a gap God sometimes makes in the devil's army, when he takes one of his most active soldiers, and enlists him in the army of Jesus Christ, and then makes a recruiting-sergeant of him to enlist others for his new Captain! There are no servants of God like those who have been valiant soldiers of Satan. Saul of Tarsus, when once made into an apostle, was not only not a whit behind the very chief, but we may venture to say that he was the very foremost of all the apostles, and did more for Christ than any of them. Oh, may many a David's place, among those who are seeking sinful pleasures, be speedily emptied by God's almighty grace! And if the devil should fill it up with another of his foolish votaries, may God be pleased to empty that place again and again! May many, like Moses, choose rather to suffer affliction with the people of God, than to enjoy the pleasures of sin for a season.

III. Now I shall speak of other empty places which are better than those I have mentioned. During the past year, it has happened several times, to some of us, that David's place has been empty. I mean that, for a time, THE PLACE OF OUR OCCUPATION HAS BEEN EMPTY.

Perhaps some of you have not had a single hour's sickness during the past year; I will remind you of your mercies that you may be very grateful to God for them. Some of us have had days, some have had weeks, and some have had even months, when David's place was empty. Not long at a time, perhaps, but usually some time or other during the year, this pulpit has had to be empty, so far as the regular preacher was concerned. Infirmities lay aside the preacher, for a while, at any rate; and with many here there comes, every now and then, a season when they have to be away from the chapel, and from the business, and from the family circle, and there is extra watchfulness in the household, and there is special care, and it may be that, sometimes, there is cause for anxiety and fear. Perhaps, in some of your cases, there has been much of needful concern. Remember those nights when the fever was about to turn, those hours when there were anxious whisperings by the loved ones around your bed, "Will he get over it? Can he survive?" You remember those trying experiences; I want you to remember them, in order that you may bless the Lord, who has spared your life, and raised you up again to health and strength. If David's place has not been often empty, be grateful for the health that God has given you; if it has been empty for a while, but you are still in the land of the living, be grateful for the restoration which the Lord has granted to you.

But brethren and sisters, I want to ask you, and myself also, are we rendering unto God due recompense for all that he has given to us? He has favoured us with prolonged life; is that life being spent for him? It may be that, on that sick-bed, we turned our face to the wall, and prayed in the bitterness of our spirit, and we then vowed what we would do if the Lord would spare our lives; or, if we did not put it absolutely into the form of a vow, we resolved that if we were raised up again, we would be more fervent and more diligent in the Master's cause than we had been aforetime. Have we redeemed those promises? Do I awaken any memories of shame? Methinks I should; I do in my own heart, and I should not wonder if I do in yours also. If so, then let the prayer go up from each heart, "My Lord, thou hast redeemed me with thy precious blood, and made me thine; thy vows are upon me, and I bring myself again to thee on this last Sabbath night of another year, and I say, bind the sacrifice with cords, even with cords to the horns of the altar!

'My life, which thou has made thy care,
Lord, I devote to thee!'

Show me what thou wouldest have me to do; give me strength and wisdom to do it; keep me diligently in thy service, steadfast in thy fear, until David's place be empty here below for the last time, and thou dost take me up to fill another place which thou hast prepared for me at thy right hand!"

I thought it might be well to awaken these thoughts in the minds of those of you who are specially concerned in this part of my subject.

IV. During the past year, many of you now present have had A PLACE IN THE ASSEMBLY OF GOD'S PEOPLE.

I do not quite like to put the question about how often David's place in the congregation of the righteous has been empty. I have very little need ever to say anything to you, dear friends, about any want of regular attendance upon the means of grace. I think no people I have ever heard of are more commonly found listening to the preaching of the Word, or joining in religious service. Yet there may be some of you who have absented yourselves when you should have been present; or there may be members of other congregations who have fallen into lax and loose habits with regard to forsaking the assembling of themselves together, "as the manner of some is," even as it was in Paul's day. Let any such who may be with us check those habits as soon as they begin. They are very detrimental to all spiritual growth. I do not think you will find a man in good health if he takes his meals at all sorts of irregular hours. As a rule, the body needs its regular periods of receiving nourishment and sustenance; and it is the same with the soul. You will scarcely find a Christian to be in sound health if he neglects the appointed time for being fed with spiritual meat.

You who are unconverted should take special notice of this part of my theme. I think that I need not say very much to the Christian about attending the Lord's house, for he loves the place where God's honour dwelleth. He can say,—

"I have been there, and still would go,
'Tis like a little heaven below."

But as for you who are not converted, I delight to see you in the house of God, willing and even anxious to listen to his Word; for who can tell, who can tell, but what God may bless it to you? "Faith cometh by hearing, and hearing by the Word of God." When you are away from the sound of the preacher's voice, there seems less probability that grace will meet you, to awaken your conscience, and turn you to Christ. While you are gathered with the Lord's people, I would fain hope that God will bless to your soul's salvation the truth that is preached. Be often, then, in that place of worship where Jesus Christ is lifted up; and seek to obtain a personal interest in his great salvation.

I love to see you hovering round the Word, listening to the preaching of the gospel; but do not, I pray you, let it always be true that you are hearers only; for, if you are hearers only, and not doers of the Word, you are simply destroying your own souls. Do you know what is your great danger, you who are hearers only, and who are not always hearers? You are running a fearful risk of losing your souls.

What I fear concerning some of you is, that you will postpone your decision, and wait, and wait, and wait, and wait, till you will not feel as much interest as you now do in listening to the gospel, and gradually you will come to the house of prayer less often, and David's place will be more often empty; and, by-and-by, the gospel will grow so stale to you, and this poor voice of mine will sound with so dull a tone, and my message will seem so commonplace, that your seat will be found always empty. When this comes to pass, I fear that you will be found wandering further and further from the paths of right, and truth, and hope, and that you will be utterly and hopelessly lost. May God decide you for Christ Jesus ere this year of grace has passed away! May it be, even now, the year of our Lord to your soul, the year in which the Lord himself shall come into your spirit, and take possession of your entire nature! Then I know that David's seat in the assembly of God's people will not be often empty.

V. I have now to say just a few words specially to the members of the church about THEIR PLACE AT THE PRAYER-MEETING. "David's place was empty." What was being done then? "Well, it was *only a prayer-meeting!*" Yes, but, but, but, but, but, but, that is saying a great deal. Did any member of the church give that answer? I do not think even one would do so; but I would like to enquire of all the members of this church, "How many times have you been to the prayer-meeting this year?" There are some of you who are never away unless something absolutely prevents you from coming. I am glad even to see some of you come in late on Monday nights. If you cannot come at seven, come at half-past seven, or come at eight; come at any time that you can, so that you may but throw in your portion of supplication with the rest of the brethren and sisters. But I am ashamed of some of our members. They will say, "Whom do you mean?" Last Sunday week, a little boy came to this Tabernacle for the first time; so, when I stood up and began to preach, the little fellow said to his nurse, "Nurse, is Mr. Spurgeon talking to me?" I wish you would all say that, if my words apply to you; for I am talking to some of the members of the church when I say that I am ashamed of you who never come to the prayer-meetings. I do not mean this rebuke for you who live at a very great distance, or who are fully occupied with your families or business cares; for you would be wrong to come. God forbid that I should ask you to present to him one duty stained with the blood of another duty! But there are some who might be here, and ought to be here at our prayer-meetings; and they are spiritually suffering positive mischief in their own souls through their absence, besides the loss that they are causing to the treasury of the church; for the wealth of the church lies in the power of intercession. The measure of the church's influence will be found to be in exact proportion to the amount of prayer presented by the members; for if there is not much prayer, there cannot be much power. "But we can pray at home," says one. Yes, I know you can; but, as a rule, I think the people who pray at home are those who pray at prayer-meetings, too. The assembling of ourselves together for prayer, is very generally (special circumstances being taken into consideration) the exponent of our private prayer. Do let me stir up any of you whose places at the prayer-meetings have been empty, and let it not be so again.

My beloved in the Lord, my fellow-soldiers in Christ, what has been the source and secret of our strength, as a church, up till this time? It has been our prayer. How well do I remember what prayer-meetings we had in Park Street! When we began, we were so very few and feeble that, in most of the prayer-meetings we had, we met in a little vestry; but we soon had to burst open our doors, and get into the chapel, and we have never gone back into the vestry since then. And oh, the power that the Lord graciously gave us in prayer! I felt there, and many of you felt, that we seemed by our supplications to bring down the blessing of God upon us; and then our numbers were speedily increased, souls were converted, and God was glorified. If we slacken prayer, we shall condemn ourselves. We have proved, not by hearsay, but by personal experience, that prayer is power; and if we relax our prayer even to a small extent, or even for a little while, we shall deserve to have this place made a by-word and a hissing, and all our prosperity taken from us, and Ichabod written upon our walls. May God grant that this voice may be silent in death ere this people shall ever cease to be a praying people! Rather may our prayerfulness be quickened, and our intercessions multiplied; and let it not be said of any men or women here who fear the Lord, that their place is empty when God's people assemble together for prayer.

VI. There is another David's place that is sometimes empty, and that ought not to be so, it is THE PLACE OF CHRISTIAN SERVICE.

My dear brethren and sisters, our gifts are various; God has been pleased to place us in different positions, and to give us different talents; but every saved man or woman has some work to do for Christ. Are we doing that work? There is our Sunday-school; it troubles me if I ever know that teachers are wanted there. There are many other schools where members of this church are occupied as teachers. We are supplying, I might say without any exaggeration, half the Sunday-school teachers of half the denominations in the district; for I have always said to you, "Go anywhere that you can find an opportunity of doing good; never mind where it is. If you have ability to teach, go and teach in anybody's school where your services are needed." Yet there are some among us who hide their talents in a napkin, and do not use them; and, as a consequence, there is some David's place empty.

You are not all called to the same work for Christ. I like to miss to-night some of those I saw here this morning; and I should not mind missing some of you for the same reason. Why? Because they are gone to teach in the Ragged-schools, or to speak at the mission-stations, or in the lodging-houses. When a Christian man says to me, "There are workers needed at such and such a Ragged-school, or mission-hall; I should like to be hearing a sermon, but I would rather be doing good than getting good," I say to him, "Right, my brother, while London is what it is, you must be content to get one sermon a-day, and feed your soul on that, and then go and do all you can for your Lord the rest of the Sabbath." It would be well for the younger members of our churches to be for a time in constant attendance on the means of grace, because they need to be instructed in divine things; but every instructed Christian is bound to be a worker for Christ among the perishing masses all around us.

Seek to serve your Saviour wherever he opens a door of usefulness. You need not go to-night into the street to preach, the weather is not suitable for open-air services just now; but when the summer comes, let every corner of the street have its evangelist, and let every man, woman, and child, who love the Lord, do the work he desires them to do; and let it not be said of any one of us that "David's place was empty." Oh, the joy of doing good! Brethren, next to heaven, the greatest joy that can be found is the joy of doing good to others. Did you ever meet some poor man, who said to you, "Bless your heart, you led me to the Saviour"? Did you ever see a woman look you in the face with unspeakable love, and say to you, "You are my father in Christ Jesus; you brought me to the Saviour's feet"? If you once knew this joy, you would always be hungering after more of it; you would never be fully satisfied with what you have done, and would be ever wanting to do yet more and more. I have tasted of this sweetness, and I have found it so refreshing to my spirit that I would have every member of this church taste of it, too. When our Lord reads the roll of those who are doing all the good they can in Sunday-school, and Ragged-school, and in preaching, teaching, visiting, tract-distributing, or what not, I hope you all will be able to answer, humbly but firmly, "Here am I, my Master, doing thy work as thou dost enable me."

I believe that many of you will be doing Christ's work best at home. You need not teach in the Sunday-school, you can have one in your own house. Many a daughter is better occupied in seeing after the younger ones of her own family than anywhere else. Yet with such exceptions as these, I beg you to take the general run of what I have said; I speak unto wise men, judge ye what I say, and believe me that there is something to be done by each one who loves the Lord. You are not accountable to me, or to the elders of the church; but you are accountable to the Crown Prince, the Prince Imperial of heaven, Christ Jesus, our Lord. He has bought you with his precious blood; you are his. Then, serve him; and let not your place of service ever be vacant through your neglect or indolence.

VII. Again, "David's place was empty." I hope that OUR PLACE AT THE LORD'S TABLE will not be empty at any time when it is possible for us to occupy it.

There are not any in this church, known to me, who absent themselves from the Lord's table very grossly; but still there is room for improvement in this matter in the case of some of us. I like to go to that table every week; and my own solemn conviction is, that that is none too often. If there be any rule about it in Scripture, there certainly is no rule for going once a month, much less for once a quarter; if there be any rule, it is that, on the first day of the week, when we meet together, we should break bread in memory of our Saviour's dying love. I commend it to our brethren and sisters to consider whether they keep the feast as often as they should, remembering our Master's wondrous passion and death. It may be that they lose much spiritual benefit because their place at the Lord's table is empty, when it should be filled.

VIII. But I must hasten on towards the conclusion. Brethren, to-morrow, when you will be keeping the Christmas feast, there will be many family gatherings, and in those family gatherings there will be SOME HOUSEHOLDS WHERE DAVID'S PLACE WILL BE EMPTY.

As I came here, I was thinking of what inroads death has made in this congregation this year. There have been many vacancies made, and there will be many more next year. I miss from one seat, a sister whom I saw upon her dying bed; and, from another part of the building, a brother whose cheering words in his last moments did my soul good. I miss here one and there another; I could run my finger along these pews in the area, and I could come up on this platform, and I could truly say, concerning one who has been called

THE EMPTY PLACE: A CHRISTMAS DAY SERMON.

home this year, "David's place is empty." We can hardly say that literally, because his son fills it, and long may he fill it, and have God's blessing resting upon him! But here and there, and everywhere in this Tabernacle, I miss some who have gone home. Our family gathering is gradually breaking up; thank God, it is being reformed up yonder, where there will be no death and no parting.

When you get to your family gathering, perhaps you will have to remember that your mother has died this year, or it may be that your father has gone home, or perhaps it was the eldest son, or that sweet curly-headed child. Perhaps, to-morrow, you will be merry; and I do not say to you, "Be not so," but let these memories come over you, let them direct your thoughts upward, let them remind you that family gatherings are only for a time, and that the great gathering is above. There the immortals meet, there the feast never ends. Look away from earth with all its joys. Let them that have wives be as those that have none, let them that have children look on their children as dying ones. Let kinships, and friendships, and all these things, be regarded as they are, as evanescent, as things that perish in the using. Hear the trumpet sound, "Up and away," and let your hearts be where Jesus is, and let your treasure be there also. Those dear ones who are in heaven beckon us to follow them, and we signal to tell them that we are on the way. Surely, they must look upon us with amazement if they see us hugging the things of earth as though we were to stay here for ever. Let our conversation be in heaven, and let our affection be set on things above, and not on things on the earth.

IX. My last reflection is this: THERE WILL BE NO EMPTY PLACE IN HEAVEN. In that great family gathering up above, they will not be able to say, "David's place is empty."

Beloved, if you are a believer in Christ, if you are the poorest saint, and the least worthy of consideration in the whole household, yet you shall have your place in heaven; you *must* have it, for God will not have one empty seat there, and nobody but yourself can fill your place. Our Lord Jesus Christ says,—mark his words,—"*I go to prepare a place.*" That is something; but note the next words, "I go to prepare a place *for you*," for you, not for somebody else, but for *you*. If you are a believer in Jesus Christ, you *must* have the place which Jesus Christ has gone to prepare for you. There is a crown in heaven which can fit no other head but mine; and there is a harp in heaven out of which no other fingers but mine can bring music. There is a mansion in the skies which nobody but you can ever occupy; and there are joys for you only, and a place in the complete circle of God's elect that must be filled, and must be filled by you. Oh, what joy is this! Press onward, my brother, go on bravely; if the darkness thickens, and the dangers multiply, Christ is your life, and you cannot die. The everlasting wings shall cover you, and the everlasting arms shall be underneath you. You shall meet us in the place where all the family shall be present, and the great Father and the elder Brother shall welcome them all, and no "David's place" shall be empty. May I be there, may we all be there; and God shall have the praise! Amen and amen.

Exposition by C. H. Spurgeon.

PSALM CIII.

Let us read, dear friends, the one hundred and third Psalm, not because we do not know it, but because I trust that we know it by heart, and feel that it is a fit expression for our heart's thankfulness on this last Sabbath evening of another year.

Verse 1. *Bless the LORD, O my soul:*

He has been blessing thee; now begin thou to bless him. If, during the week, thou hast been busy about the things of the world now leave these unimportant matters, and come to the grandest exercise in which an intelligent spirit can be engaged. "Bless the Lord, O my soul." Let there be no sleeping now, no coldness, no indifference; let it be real soul-work. His blessings have been real, let thy praises be real, too.

1. *And all that is within me, bless his holy name.*

Bless the whole of his name, and especially the holiness of it; be glad that thou hast a holy God. There was a time when this was a terror to thee, for thou wast unholy, and unable to delight in God's holiness; but he has cleansed and washed thee, and now thou canst rejoice in the whole of his character, in the *whole*ness, or the *holi*ness, of his blessed name.

2. *Bless the LORD, O my soul,*

Do it again. If thou hast praised him now in thy heart, lift up thy heart yet higher. Let the praise come up from a greater depth, from the very bottom of thy heart, and let it rise to a loftier height, even to the highest heaven. "Bless the Lord, O my soul."

2. *And forget not all his benefits:*

Thou hast a bad memory for good things; but now try to make thy memory awake, forget not any of God's benefits. If thou canst not remember all, yet do not wilfully forget any of them: "Forget not all his benefits." Here is a list to help thy memory:—

3. *Who forgiveth all thine iniquities;*

Canst thou not praise the Lord for this? One of those iniquities, like a millstone about thy neck, would be sufficient to sink thee into hell; but God forgives them all. He does it now as much as ever he did. He still forgives, for the forgiveness of God to his people is a continuous act. Do thou, then, continually praise him, and rejoice in him.

3. *Who healeth all thy diseases;*

None can set the human frame in order but he who made it. Medicines and physicians are of little service unless God blesses the doctor's skill. Especially does the Lord heal soul sicknesses; and they are very many and very terrible. Bless his name that he continues still to heal. As fresh complaints break out in thy poor flesh or spirit, and thy soul mourns over them, he comes, and gives the healing balm.

4. *Who redeemeth thy life from destruction;*

Keeping thee from the gates of the grave; and, better still, delivering thee from the jaws of hell.

4. *Who crowneth thee with lovingkindness and tender mercies;*

The Lord has made a king of thee; and what an empire is thine! And what a crown is this which thou dost wear! Other crowns make the head lie uneasy; but this is the softest, the best, the richest coronet that ever crowned head did wear. Thou mayest be content to keep it though all the Cæsars should offer all their pomp to thee in exchange for thy crown: "He crowneth thee with lovingkindness and tender mercies."

EXPOSITION. 623

5. *Who satisfieth thy mouth with good things; so that thy youth is renewed like the eagle's.*

The mouth of man is very hard to fill. There are some men's mouths that never will be filled until the sexton gives them a shovelful of earth; for they are covetous and greedy, and always hungry after more; but God has filled thy mouth, not with earth, nor with earth's treasure, but "with good things", the very best things. The best of the best he has given thee, all that thy heart desireth, in giving thee himself; so that thy youth, when thou growest old, and feeble in thy spirit, returns to thee once more. Bless the Lord, then, for all these mercies.

6. *The LORD executeth righteousness and judgment for all that are oppressed.*

He lets the oppressor go on for a while; but sooner or later, there comes a terrible retribution. There is nothing of oppression in this world that can live long; for God is abroad, and oftentimes even the horrors of war make an end to the equal horrors of oppression. God interposes in dreadful judgments to execute vengeance on those that oppress the poor.

7. *He made known his ways unto Moses, his acts unto the children of Israel.*

Bless him for this. Bless him for the Old Testament Scriptures. Bless him that he did not hide himself of old; but did speak to his people, and reveal himself by his prophets, and by the types and symbols of the law. Bless his name, and study much the revelation of his ways and acts, and get all the good out of it that thou canst.

8. *The LORD is merciful and gracious,*

Bless him, O my soul! Bless him for this, for where wouldst thou have been if he had not been merciful? Where wouldst thou be if he were not gracious, giving grace to keep thee what thou art, and to make thee better?

8. *Slow to anger, and plenteous in mercy.*

Blessed words! Any who are under a sense of sin will suck honey out of these choice expressions. "Slow to anger." God does get angry at last when grace has had her day; but he is "plenteous in mercy."

9. *He will not always chide:*

He will chide sometimes. He would not be a kind Father if he did not. That is a cruel father to his children who never chides them. This was Eli's sin, and you know how it brought destruction upon him and his house. Our Father takes care to chide us when we need it; but "he will not always chide."

9, 10. *Neither will he keep his anger for ever. He hath not dealt with us after our sins; nor rewarded us according to our iniquities.*

Brothers and sisters, bless his name for this. Let every verse, as we read it, awaken fresh gratitude; and let us keep up the music of our souls in harmony with the language of the Psalm.

11, 12. *For as the heaven is high above the earth, so great is his mercy toward them that fear him. As far as the east is from the west, so far hath he removed our transgressions from us.*

They are gone. There is a chasm between us and our sins which will never be bridged. To an infinite distance has the great Scapegoat carried away all the sins of his people; they shall never return to us.

13. *Like as a father pitieth his children, so the LORD pitieth them that fear him.*

The best of them need pity. There is something to pity in them; and because the Lord pities them, he will not lay too heavy a burden upon them, he will not demand too much of them. He will not give them over to their enemies. He deals tenderly with them because they are so weak.

14. *For he knoweth our frame; he remembereth that we are dust.*

Sometimes we do not remember that ourselves; we think that we are iron, and we fancy that we shall last for ever; but the Lord "remembereth that we are dust."

15, 16. *As for man, his days are as grass: as a flower of the field, so he flourisheth. For the wind passeth over it, and it is gone; and the place thereof shall know it no more.*

Before even the mower's scythe comes, the hot eastern wind has dried up the grass, and it is gone. How little a thing carries us away! It seems as if it did not need death to come with a sharp scythe to cut down such frail creatures as we are; he does but breathe upon the field, and all the flowers are withered at once. Oh, that we might all be prepared for such a speedy end of our lives, and not look upon this world as a place for a long stay; but only as the meadow in which we, in common with other feeble flowers, are blooming out our little hour!

17. *But the mercy of the LORD is from everlasting to everlasting upon them that fear him,*

Blessed be his name that mercy had no beginning, and shall never have an end. You and I are of yesterday, and therefore we pass away to-morrow; but God is ever the same, and of his years there is no end, because he is without beginning; and such is his love to his people, eternal, and unchangeable. Bless his name for this, dear friends. Do not forget what is to be the accompaniment to the reading of the Psalm; but constantly bless the Lord, praise him, and magnify his holy name.

17, 18. *And his righteousness unto children's children; to such as keep his covenant, and to those that remember his commandments to do them.*

Bless him for his goodness to our children. Some of us have seen the covenant of the Lord kept to our children as well as to ourselves. May we all have that blessing in the case of all that spring of us!

19. *The LORD hath prepared his throne in the heavens; and his kingdom ruleth over all.*

Bless him for his sovereignty. A God who did not reign would be no God to us; but "the Lord reigneth, let the earth rejoice;" and let his people be glad because he "hath prepared his throne in the heavens," beyond the reach of all man's attacks or assaults. Beyond all time and change, the Lord reigneth on for ever and ever, "and his kingdom ruleth over all." It extends over all things that are on the earth, and above it, and beneath it; angels and men and devils are all subject to his sway.

20—22. *Bless the LORD, ye his angels, that excel in strength, that do his commandments, hearkening unto the voice of his word. Bless ye the LORD, all ye his hosts; ye ministers of his, that do his pleasure. Bless the LORD, all his works in all places of his dominion: bless the LORD, O my soul.*

I think, before we pray, we must bless and magnify the Lord by singing Milton's version of Psalm 136:—

> "Let us with a gladsome mind,
> Praise the Lord, for he is kind:
> For his mercies shall endure,
> Ever faithful, ever sure."

HYMNS FROM "OUR OWN HYMN BOOK"—103 (Version II.), 136 (Song I.), 821.

END OF VOLUME XXXVIII.